ESSEX PAUPER LETTERS
1731–1837

RECORDS OF SOCIAL AND ECONOMIC HISTORY
NEW SERIES 30

ESSEX PAUPER LETTERS 1731–1837

EDITED BY
THOMAS SOKOLL

Published for THE BRITISH ACADEMY
by OXFORD UNIVERSITY PRESS

Oxford University Press, Great Clarendon Street, Oxford OX2 6DP

Oxford New York

*Athens Auckland Bangkok Bogotá Buenos Aires Calcutta
Cape Town Chennai Dar es Salaam Delhi Florence Hong Kong Istanbul
Karachi Kuala Lumpur Madrid Melbourne Mexico City Mumbai
Nairobi Paris São Paulo Shanghai Singapore Taipei Tokyo Toronto Warsaw*

*and associated companies in
Berlin Ibadan*

*Published in the United States by
Oxford University Press Inc., New York*

*British Library Cataloguing in Publication Data
Data available*

ISBN 0-19-726242-2

*Typeset by the editor
Printed in Great Britain
on acid-free paper by
Antony Rowe Limited
Chippenham, Wiltshire*

To Cornelia

Foreword

This 30th volume in the new series of *Records of Social and Economic History* illustrates the contribution which the publication of a body of records can make to 'history from below', as well as consolidating the entry of the series into the nineteenth century. 'Pauper letters' are a class of records which have been noted, rather in passing, by several social historians and historians of the poor law, but which await the serious study which publication of this volume will do much to make possible. They are letters written by, or on behalf of, men and women who in the majority of cases had moved away and were seeking relief from the overseers of the poor of their parish of settlement. A few were written by educated or professional scribes, but the great majority were written by the claimants themselves or some semi-literate friend or neighbour from the same social class, in a direct rendering in idiomatic language and phonetic spelling of ordinary forms of speech, so that these letters are an invaluable record of the ways in which ordinary folk expressed their views of their own lives, their various setbacks and disasters, and their expectations of support from the poor law. The collection printed here contains all the known surviving pauper letters in Essex archives from the period of the Old Poor Law: the earliest dates from 1731, but surviving letters are very thin on the ground before 1800 (although many others may have been written without being preserved), and more than 80 per cent of the collection comes from the period 1817-35. Similar letters are known to have been written under the new administrative structure of the New Poor Law, and lie in the PRO awaiting investigation. Meanwhile, in this excellently edited volume Dr Sokoll, with a searching scrutiny of the provenance, reliability, and the limitations as well as the potential of the documents, has made available to scholars a rich source bearing on the lives of the poor as seen by themselves, on the nature of the early forms of popular literacy, and on the detailed workings of the Old Poor Law where, in practice, relief was routinely granted to out-residents who fell on hard times and removal to parishes of settlement was frequently not enforced. There is material here which will carry forward the fundamental revisions, which have been under way for the last 20 years, in the way in which the poor and the poor law are seen.

February 2001

F. M. L. Thompson
Chairman, Records of Social and
Economic History Committee

Contents

ESSEX PAUPER LETTERS

Acknowledgements

The preparation of this volume has taken nearly ten years, and it is a pleasure to name at least some of the many people who have helped me. First of all, I wish to thank Richard Smith, Peter Mathias and their fellow members on the Editorial Committee of the British Academy's 'Records of Social and Economic History' for inviting me to prepare the pauper letters from Essex for their series. For generous financial support, I am grateful to the Research Commission of the FernUniversität Hagen, the Wellcome Unit for the History of Medicine at the University of Oxford, the Cambridge Group for the History of Population and Social Structure and the Friends of Historic Essex. At the British Academy, James Rivington and Janet English were very good to me. Thanks are also due to the Essex Record Office for allowing me to consult and reproduce the material in their custody. The staff of that fabulous institution were helpful in every way, and I should like to record my particular thanks to Janet Smith.

I hope that my two foremost scholarly mentors and friends, Ludolf Kuchenbuch and Peter Laslett, will accept the book as an intellectual tribute. It was not least their inspiration and example that have given me the necessary stamina. Peter, with his own editorial work on one of the geniuses of political theory, set a high standard of what it means to constitute a critical text. He kept encouraging me and never failed to cheer me up with teasing remarks about his great former expertise in 'fussing about Locke's commas'. For fifteen years, Ludolf and I have been engaged in researching and teaching the social history of literacy in pre-modern European society from a broad comparative perspective, on the basis of a radical notion of source criticism. This approach, which we have come to refer to as 'scriptual materialism', rests on the programmatic assumption that the historian is not just concerned with texts, but also with the investigation of the production process of these texts, which includes the careful study of the physical features of the surviving records. As far as the textual documentation in the present edition is concerned, Ludolf also expressed the underlying idea better than I could ever do. He said it seemed to him (he is a medievalist) that I had treated 'my' pauper letters in the same way as the nineteenth-century pioneers in the field of critical historical editions had treated 'their' papal bulls and royal charters.

Throughout my work, Stefan Hanemann was a model research assistant. He solved all the complex technical tasks involved in the project, processed the microfilms, transcribed the material into computer files and did the typesetting of the entire volume. He also shared with me in the final checking of the edited text against the original papers at the Essex Record Office. In the last year, Ulrike Vordermark joined me in the endless toil of preparing the indexes. So did two of my children, Jacob and Charlotte Sokoll, and my friends Penny Ormerod, Peter King and Richard Wall, who answered all sorts of major and minor queries. Penny also did the proof reading of the apparatus. My sister-in-law, Lillian Camphausen, stepped in when I got into panic about the subject index. For expert secretarial support with the appendix and the indexes, I also have to thank Tamar Klais.

Numerous friends read parts of the edition and various drafts of the introduction. I should like to name in particular Peter King, Peter Laslett, Penny Ormerod, Richard Smith, Simon Szreter and Richard Wall in England; my companions of the Bochum *Habilkränzl*, Christian Jansen, Thomas Mergel, Maria Osietzki, Susanne Rouette, Willibald Steinmetz and Benjamin Ziemann; and Uta Kleine, Ludolf Kuchenbuch and Eckhard Meyer-Zwiffelhoffer the Historical Institute at Hagen, who were always there when I felt desperate for immediate advice. None of all these people, however, should be held responsible for any of the mistakes that remain.

The final and deepest thanks go to my family. For years, my children had to put up with a father who tended to be absent even when he was at home. My dear wife never lost her confidence that one day this book would be finished. It is to her patience, understanding and partnership that I owe most.

Historisches Institut
FernUniverität Hagen
St Valentine's day, 2001   Thomas Sokoll

Figures and maps

Tables

Plates

(*between page 278 and page 279*)

Plate I: *Simple standard*. ERO D/P 94/18/42 Pauper letter from Arthur Tabrum in [the parish of Christchurch in] London to James Read, vestry clerk of Chelmsford, 5 January 1826 (**179**)

Plate II: *Deficient pieces*. ERO D/P 95/18/3 Anomymous pauper letter surviving from Little Dunmow (**590**); ERO D/P 238/18/1 Pauper letter from Mary Keeling in Maldon [Essex] to [John] Sewell [overseer of] Mundon (**629**); ERO D/P 203/18/1 Pauper letter from [Mary] Mitchel in Ipswich [to the parish of St Botolph, Colchester] 30 September 1818 (**300**); D/P 138/18/11 Pauper letter from Lucy Bayley [in the parish of St James in Colchester] (**410**)

Plates III-IV: *High standard*. ERO 178/18/23 Pauper letter from William James in Chelmsford to Robert Alden [overseer of the parish of St Peter] in Colchester, 25 September 1821 (**445**)

Plates V-VII: *Older hand*. ERO 178/18/23 Pauper letter from William James in Chelmsford to Robert Alden [overseer of the parish of St Peter] in Colchester, 28 September 1828 (**550**)

Plate VIII: *Oral writing*. ERO D/P 203/18/1 Pauper letter from [Benjamin] Brooker [in Ipswich to the parish of St Botolph in Colchester, 10 July 1828] (**377**); ERO 178/18/23 [Pauper letter from Benjamin Brooker in Ipswich to Robert Alden, overseer of the parish of St Peter in Colchester, before 2 December 1825] (**510**)

Plates IX-XII: *Letter turned into file*. ERO D/P 264/18/42 Pauper letter from George Smee in Norwich to [Jeremiah] Wing [overseer of] Braintree in Braintree, 9 May 1826 (**14**)

Plates XIII-XIV: *Formal petition*. ERO D/P 94/18/42 Pauper letter from Ann Marsh [in Shoreditch] in London to the churchwardens [and overseers] of Chelmsford [11 October 1824] (**133**)

Plates XV-XVI: *Return of post*. ERO D/P 94/18/42 Pauper letter from Susan[nah] Halls in Ipswich to James Read, overseer of Chelmsford [15 May 1825] (**156**)

Plates XVII-XVIII: *Private letter*. ERO D/P 264/18/42 Pauper letter from John Barnes in Billericay [Essex] to [his mother] Mrs Digby in Braintree, 24 July 1827 (**17**)

Plates XIX-XX: *An early piece*. ERO D/P 203/18/1 Pauper letter from Jane Cross in Canterbury to Austin Vailant, churchwarden of the parish of St Botolph in Colchester, 24 April 1755 (**281**)

Abbreviations

ERO Essex Record Office, Chelmsford (and branches at Colchester
and Southend)
PP Parliamentary Papers
PRO Public Record Office, London

Within the apparatus of the edition, two published papers dealing with
some of the Essex Pauper Letters in detail have also been given with
short titles: Sharpe, 'Bowels of compation' and Sokoll; 'Old age in poverty'. The full titles are to be found in the bibliography.

List of Essex Pauper Letters, 1731-1837, by place of receipt

No.	Date	Sender	Place of sender	Addressee
	Aveley			
1	31 May 1825	Sarah Taylor	Deptford [Surrey]	[J.W.] Clover
2	5 Sep [1831]	James Smith	Woolwich, Kent	Overseer
3	8 Feb 1832	James Smith	Woolwich [Kent]	Mr Sewell
4	6 Sep 1832	James Smith	Woolwich, Kent	Overseers
5	[25 Sep 1832]	James Smith	Woolwich [Kent]	Overseers
6	13 Dec 1832	Mary Wood	Mile End New Town, London	Mr Sewell
7	18 Feb 1833	Elizabeth Sheepard	Lambeth, London	Mr Sewell
8	21 Mar 1833	James Smith	Woolwich [Kent]	Mr Sewell
9	[no date]	E. Feild	[no place]	[no addressee]
	Great Bardfield			
10	26 Jan 1835	John Smith	Sutton, Surrey	Samuel Dodd, overseer
11	3 May 1836	John Dennison	Debden [Essex]	Overseers
12	[no date]	Jacob Brown	Laindon[-cum-Basildon Essex]	Mr Smith
	Braintree			
13	22 Dec 1823	Ann Hitchcock	Feering [Essex]	Churchwardens and overseers
14	9 May 1826	George Smee	Norwich	[Jeremiah] Wing
15	22 May 1826	Thomas Elsegood	Norwich	Overseer
16	29 Jan 1827	Thomas Cleare	Braintree	[no addressee]
17	24 July 1827	John Barnes	Billericay [Essex]	Mrs Digby
18	16 Jan 1828	Samuel Spooner	Norwich	[Jeremiah] Wing, overseer
19	26 Feb 1828	George Smee	Norwich	[no addressee]
20	18 June 1828	John Gibson	Little Baddow [Essex]	Overseer
21	14 July 1828	Phillis Webb	Ipswich	James Joscelyne
22	13 Sep 1828	Phillis Webb	Ipswich	James Joscelyne
23	20 Sep 1828	Samuel Spooner	Norwich	[Jeremiah] Wing
24	Oct [1828]	Samuel Spooner	[Norwich]	Overseer
25	17 Nov 1828	Samuel Spooner		Overseers
26	20 Nov 1828	William King	Bethnal Green, London	[Robert] Medcalf
27	27 Nov 1828	James Tidman	Farningham, Kent	Churchwardens and overseers
28	30 Nov [1828]	James Smith	[St Pancras] London	Overseer

No.	Date	Sender	Place of sender	Addressee

Braintree (contd.)

No.	Date	Sender	Place of sender	Addressee
29	2 Dec 1828	Hannah Porter	Chelmsford	Eliza Green
30	16 Dec 1828	Maria Cousins	[Braintree]	Overseers
31	18 Dec 1828	Phillis Webb	Ipswich	Mr Rebel
32	30 Apr 1829	[William King]	[Bethnal Green] London	[Robert] Medcalf
33	7 July 1829	William Webb	Ipswich	Mrs Fish
34	25 July 1829	Mary Smith	[St Pancras] London	Overseer
35	5 Aug 1829	William King	London	[Robert] Medcalf
36	11 Feb 1830	Elizabeth Watty	Chester-le-Street [Durham]	Overseers
37	25 Feb 1830	William King	London	[Robert] Medcalf
38	12 Mar 1830	William King	London	Overseer
39	4 June [1830]	Adam Turthing	Chelmondiston, Suffolk	[no addressee]
40	[27 Sep 1830]	Stephen Linzell	[Cheshunt, Herts.]	Overseers
41	12 Nov 1830	Sarah Smee	Colchester	Overseers
42	9 Apr 1831	William King	London	Overseer
43	15 Apr 1831	Joseph Brand	Brentwood [Essex]	[no addressee]
44	[18 Apr 1831]	Stephen Linzell	Cheshunt [Herts.]	Overseer
45	3 June 1831	George Whitaker	Cambridge	[William] Boulton, overseer
46	11 June 1831	James Gray	[Shoreditch] London	[William] Boulton
47	1 July 1831	William Goodwin	[Norwich]	[Samuel] Shave
48	2 July 1831	James Gray	[Shoreditch] London	Phoebe Gray
49	18 July 1831	Joseph Brand	Brentwood [Essex]	Mrs Boullin
50	24 Nov 1831	S[tephen] Linzell	[Cheshunt, Herts.]	William Coote, overseer
51	16 Dec 1831	William King	London	[no addressee]
52	[22 May 1832]	James Smee	[Norwich]	Mr Browne
53	18 July 1832	William King	London	Overseer
54	18 Oct 1832	William King	London	Overseer
55	[23] Oct 1832	Maria Godfry	[St Pancras] London	Overseers
56	2 Nov 1832	Abraham Stuck	Upminster [Essex]	Churchwardens and overseers
57	25 Nov 1832	John Spearman	[Whitechapel] London	Mr Taylor
58	[3 Dec] 1832	Edward Orwell	Leeds	James Joscelyn
59	8 Dec 1832	John Spearman	[Whitechapel] London	Overseers
60	5 Apr 1833	John Spearman	[Whitechapel] London	Overseer
61	8 May 1833	John Spearman	[Whitechapel] London	Overseer
62	11 May 1833	William King	[Bethnal Green] London	Overseer
63	19 May 1833	John Smoothy	Wethersfield [Essex]	[no addressee]
64	8 June 1833	John Spearman	[London]	[John] Goodale
65	[18 June 1833]	Maria Godfry	[St Pancras, London]	Robert Joscelyne
66	21 June 1833	Susan Spooner	Norwich	[John] Goodale
67	17 July 1833	William King	[London]	Overseer
68	22 Sep 1833	William Marsh	Devonport [Devon]	Overseer
69	[23 Sep 1833]	Maria Godfry	[St Pancras] London	[John] Goodale, overseer

No.	Date	Sender	Place of sender	Addressee
Braintree (contd.)				
70	25 Sep 1833	Maria Godfry	[St Pancras] London	[John] Goodale, overseer
71	8 Feb 1834	John Spearman	London	Overseers
72	4 Mar 1834	William King	London	Overseer
73	[21 Apr 1834]	M[aria] Godfry	[St Pancras] London	Overseers
74	31 July [1834]	William King	London	Overseer
75	Sep 1834	[William King]	London	[no addressee]
76	2 Oct 1834	William King	London	Overseers
77	[1834]	Henry Spearman	[St Botolph without Bishopsgate] London	Overseer
78	29 June 1835	John Cardinal	[Great] Dunmow [Essex]	[no addressee]
79	[no date]	Thomas Cleare	[Braintree]	[no addressee]
80	[no date]	Robert Sewell	[Braintree]	[no addressee]
Steeple Bumpstead				
81	6 Dec 1816	Joseph Wright	Braintree	Mr Jackson
82	11 Jan 1817	Thomas Turner	Newmarket [Suffolk]	Mr Jackson
83	24 Feb 1817	William Trudget	Ingatestone [Essex]	[no addressee]
84	28 July 1817	G. Allam	London	Mr Jackson
85	[27 Sep 1825]	Mary Ann Page	[St Giles-in-the-Fields, London]	John French, vestry clerk
86	5 Jan 1827	Hannah Mansfield	Wickham [St Pauls, Essex]	[no addressee]
87	23 Oct 1831	Ann Trudgett	[St Marylebone, London]	Mr Howes
88	19 Mar 1833	Joseph Derham	Brighton	Mr Fitch
89	9 Nov 1833	Thomas Albion	Cambridge	Overseers
90	22 Dec 1835	Mary Pannel	Hertford	Charles Pannel
91	1 Jan [1837]	Edward Roads	Sheffield	Mr Beans
92	12 Jan 1837	Edward Roads	[Sheffield]	Mr Baines
93	26 Mar 1837	Thomas Albion	Cambridge	Mr Brooks
Great Burstead				
94	31 Oct 1833	James Willson	Springfield Goal [Chelmsford]	Sarah Willson
95	7 June 1834	George and Mary Pateman	Gibraltar	[no addressee]
96	[no date]	William Catt	[no place]	[no addressee]
97	[no date]	William Pryor	Spitalfields [London]	[no addressee]
Canewdon				
98	[21 Sep 1825]	Sarah Albon	Horringer, Suffolk	Mr Lodwick Esq.
Chelmsford				
99	15 Oct [1820]	William Ardley	Kelvedon [Essex]	Overseer
100	17 Jan [1823]	William Ardley	Romford [Essex]	Overseer
101	29 July 1823	William Holden	Hampstead	John Stokes

No.	Date	Sender	Place of sender	Addressee

Chelmsford (contd.)

No.	Date	Sender	Place of sender	Addressee
102	9 Nov 1823	Mary Munrow	Lambeth [London]	Joseph Wiffen, overseer
103	15 Nov 1823	William Holden	Hampstead	Mr Goymer, overseer
104	5 Dec 1823	David Rivenall	St George in the East, London	Joseph Wiffen, overseer
105	7 Dec 1823	William Day	Thorpe[-le-Soken, Essex]	James Read
106	18 Dec 1823	Mary Munrow	[Lambeth, London]	Joseph Wiffen
107	29 Jan [1824]	[Mary] Munrow	[Lambeth, London]	[no addressee]
108	1 Feb 1824	Davey Rising	Halstead [Essex]	Governor of the poorhouse
109	1 Feb 1824	[Susannah] Halls	Ipswich	Overseer
110	5 Feb 1824	Samuel Hearsum	St Marylebone [London]	Mr Goymer
111	[after 5 Feb 1824]	Susannah Halls	Ipswich	Mr Goymer, overseer
112	15 Feb 1824	Davey and Susannah Rising	Halstead [Essex]	Overseer
113	10 Mar 1824	Mary Hearsom	[St George] London	[Thomas] Archer
114	[28 Apr 1824]	John Argent	Bethnal Green, London	Overseer
115	4 May 1824	David Rivenall	[St George in the East] London	Overseer
116	29 May 1824	David Rivenall	House of Correction [Clerkenwell] London	Overseer
117	4 June 1824	M[ary] Munrow	Lambeth [London]	Overseer
118	10 June 1824	Isaac Harridge	[Newington] London	Overseer
119	11 June [1824]	S[arah] Manning	Stratford [Essex]	[James] Read, overseer
120	11 June 1824	Arthur Tabrum	[St Saviour] London	Overseer
121	12 June 1824	R[ody] Jolliff	Hertford	[no addressee]
122	16 June [1824]	Lucy Nevill	[St Botolph] Colchester	[no addressee]
123	21 June 1824	Susannah Halls	Ipswich	Overseer
124	[29 June 1824]	Jane Hills	[St John, Westminster, London]	Overseers
125	[7 July 1824]	Jane Hills	[London]	Overseer
126	[8 July 1824]	Hannah Death	London Hospital [Whitechapel, London]	Dr Prichard
127	26 July 1824	Rachel Brown	[Clerkenwell] London	Thomas Archer
128	26 July 1824	Ann Marsh	London	Robert Marsh
129	1 Aug 1824	Davey and Susannah Rising	Halstead [Essex]	Mr Gimore, overseer
130	2 Aug 1824	David Rivenall	St George in the East, London	[John] Shepee
131	27 Sep 1824	Susannah Rising	Halstead [Essexc]	Governor of the poorhouse
132	[11 Oct 1824]	Phebea Joice	Ingatestone [Essex]	James Read
133	[11 Oct 1824]	Ann Marsh	[Shoreditch] London	[no addressee]
134	[4 Nov 1824]	[Susannah] Halls	Ipswich	Overseer

No.	Date	Sender	Place of sender	Addressee
Chelmsford (contd.)				
135	[Nov 1824]	Susannah Halls	Ipswich	Mr Andrews, overseer
136	18 Dec 1824	Sarah Baynes	Thaxted [Essex]	Mr Marrion, churchwarden
137	21 Dec 1824	Thomas Carritt	[Newington] London	Overseer
138	10 Jan 1825	Thomas Cooper	Woolwich, Kent	Overseer
139	12 Jan 1825	David Rivenall	St George in the East, London	Mr Shepping
140	15 Jan 1825	Lucy Nevill	[St Botolph, Colchester]	[no addressee]
141	22 Jan 1825	Ann Cooper	Woolwich [Kent]	Overseer
142	27 Jan 1825	Susannah and Davey Rising	Halstead [Essex]	Governor of the poorhouse
143	28 Jan [1825]	Thomas and Ann Cooper	Woolwich [Kent]	Overseer
144	2 Feb 1825	Sarah Baynes	Thaxted [Essex]	Mr Marrion, churchwarden
145	11 Feb 1825	Ann Cooper	Woolwich [Kent]	[James] Read, overseer
146	22 Feb 1825	David Rivenall	St George in the East, London	Overseer
147	25 Feb 1825	Ann Cooper	Woolwich [Kent]	[James] Read, overseer
148	3 Mar 1825	A[nn] Cooper	Woolwich [Kent]	Overseer
149	[12 Mar 1825]	A[nn] Cooper	[Woolwich, Kent]	Overseer
150	[27 Mar 1825]	A[nn] Cooper	Woolwich [Kent]	[no addressee]
151	18 Apr 1825	Rachel Brown	[Clerkenwell] London	[Thomas] Archer
152	18 Apr 1825	Mary Hearsom	London	Thomas Archer, Esq.
153	24 Apr 1825	Susannah and Davey Rising	[Halstead, Essex]	Overseer
154	7 May 1825	Thomas Carritt	[Newington] London	Overseer
155	8 May [1825]	Daniel Rust		Charles Rust
156	[15 May 1825]	Susan[nah] Halls	Ipswich	James Read, overseer
157	17 May 1825	Arthur Tabrum	[Christchurch] London	James Read, vestry clerk
158	19 May 1825	Susan Bright	Mildenhall [Suffolk]	James Read, vestry clerk
159	25 May [1825]	Daniel Rust	[no place]	Sarah Rust
160	26 May 1825	Sarah Manning	Stratford [Essex]	James Read, vestry clerk
161	29 May [1825]	S[usan] Bright	Mildenhall [Suffolk]	J[ames] Read
162	1 June 1825	Ann Herbert	[Bermondsey] London	[no addressee]
163	20 June 1825	Thomas and Ann Cooper	Woolwich [Kent]	Overseer
164	20 June 1825	Samuel White	Halstead [Essex]	Mr Joselyne
165	[27 June 1825]	Jane Hills	[London]	Overseers
166	1 July 1825	Ann Cooper	Woolwich [Kent]	Overseer
167	[14 July 1825]	Jane Hills	[St Sepulchre, City of] London	[no addressee]

No. Date	Sender	Place of sender	Addressee
Chelmsford (contd.)			
168 1 Oct 1825	Jane Hills	[London]	Overseers
169 4 Oct 1825	Susan[nah] and Davey Rising	Halstead [Essex]	Overseer
170 5 Oct 1825	Jane Hills	[London]	Overseers
171 16 Oct 1825	Arthur Tabrum	[Christchurch] London	James Read, overseer
172 [*before* 8 Nov 1825]	Susannah Halls	Ipswich	Overseer
173 13 Nov 1825	Arthur Tabrum	[Christchurch] London	James Read, vestry clerk
174 [15 Nov 1825]	S[usan] Alexander	Ipswich	James Read
175 15 Nov 1825	David and Sarah Rivenall	[St George in the East] London	Overseer
176 27 Dec 1825	Rachel Brown	[Clerkenwell] London	[James] Read, overseer
177 29 Dec 1825	Jane Hills	Westminster, London	Overseer
178 [2] Jan 1826	Rody Jolliff	Hertford	James Read
179 5 Jan 1826	Arthur Tabrum	[Christchurch] London	James Read, vestry clerk
180 26 Jan 1826	Samuel White	Halstead [Essex]	James Read, overseer
181 30 Jan 1826	David and Sarah Rivenall	[St George in the East] London	[Thomas] Archer, churchwarden
182 25 Feb 1826	Samuel White	Halstead [Essex]	James Read, overseer
183 27 Feb 1826	David and Sarah Rivenall	[St George in the East] London	James Read, vestry clerk
184 27 Feb 1826	Samuel White	Halstead [Essex]	James Read, vestry clerk
185 1 Mar 1826	Susannah Rising	Halstead [Essex]	James Read, vestry clerk
186 13 Mar 1826	David Rivenall	[St George in the East] London	Overseer
187 28 Mar 1826	Jane Hills	Westminster, London	Overseer
188 28 Mar 1826	Sarah and David Rivenall	[St George in the East] London	James Read, vestry clerk
189 29 Mar 1826	Arthur Tabrum	[Christchurch] London	J[ames] Read, assistant overseer
190 26 Apr 1826	David and Sarah Rivenall	[St George in the East] London	[James] Read
191 10 May 1826	David and Sarah Rivenall	[St George in the East] London	Churchwardens or vestry clerk
192 [May 1826]	David Rivenall	[St George in the East, London]	Overseer
193 16 June 1826	Samuel White	Halstead [Essex]	James Read
194 18 July 1826	David Rivenall	[St George in the East] London	Overseer
195 26 July 1826	Sarah Manning	Stratford [Essex]	James Read, vestry clerk
196 29 July 1826	David Rivenall	[St George in the East] London	Overseer
197 3 Aug 1826	Samuel White	Halstead [Essex]	James Read, overseer

No.	Date	Sender	Place of sender	Addressee
	Chelmsford (contd.)			
198	15 Aug 1826	Rody Jolliff	Hertford	James Read
199	27 Aug 1826	Eliza Jackson	[Kensington] London	Overseer
200	3 Sep 1826	Arthur Tabrum	Christchurch, London	James Read, vestry clerk
201	27 Sep 1826	David Rivenall	[St George in the East, London]	Overseer
202	4 Oct 1826	Susannah and Davey Rising	Halstead [Essex]	Governor of the poorhouse
203	[12 Oct 1826]	David Rivenall	[St George in the East, London]	Overseer
204	11 Dec 1826	Arthur Tabrum	[Christchurch] London	James Read, vestry clerk
205	[15 Dec 1826]	David Rivenall	St George in the East, London	Overseer
206	15 Jan 1827	Rachel Brown	[Clerkenwell] London	James Read
207	22 Jan 1827	Samuel White	Halstead [Essex]	James Read
208	24 Jan 1827	Davey and Susan-[nah] Rising	Halstead [Essex]	Governor of the poorhouse
209	25 Jan [1827]	David Rivenall	[St George in the East, London]	Overseer
210	2 Feb 1827	R[ody] Jolliff	Hertford	James Read
211	12 Feb 1827	Mercy Pool	[St George, Hanover Square] London	[James] Read, overseer
212	18 Feb 1827	Arthur Tabrum	Christchurch, London	J[ames] Read, vestry clerk
213	19 Feb 1827	Sarah Manning	Stratford [Essex]	James Read
214	19 Mar 1827	Isaac Harridge	Newington, London	Mr Swardley, overseer
215	28 Mar 1827	Jane Hills	London	Overseer
216	18 Apr 1827	Arthur Tabrum	Christchurch, London	James Read, assistant overseer
217	30 Apr 1827	Mercy Pool	[London]	[James] Read, overseer
218	[15 May 1827]	David Rivenall	[St George in the East, London]	Overseer
219	17 May 1827	Isaac Betts	Mitcham, Surrey	Overseer
220	18 May 1827	Mercy Pool	London	[James] Read, overseer
221	[18 May 1827]	David Rivenall	[St George in the East, London]	Overseer
222	25 May 1827	Robert Griffith	Dedham [Essex]	Overseer
223	26 May 1827	Arthur Tabrum	Christchurch, London	James Read, assistant overseer
224	31 July 1827	Isaac Wright	St Alfege [City of] London	Overseer
225	24 Aug [18]27	David Rivenall	Cold Bath Fields Prison [Clerkenwell] London	Overseer
226	28 Aug 1827	Sarah Manning	Stratford [Essex]	James Read
227	24 Sep 1827	P[hilip] Noon	Colchester	Overseers

No.	Date	Sender	Place of sender	Addressee
Chelmsford (contd.)				
228	1 Oct 1827	William Holden	St Marylebone, London	James Read
229	4 Oct 1827	Arthur Tabrum	[Christchurch] London	James Read
230	22 Oct 1827	William Holden	[St Marylebone] London	James Read
231	25 Oct 1827	David Rivenall	[St George in the East] London	[no addressee]
232	31 Oct [1827]	David Rivenall	[St George in the East, London]	Overseer
233	23 Nov 1827	Hugh Constable	Halstead [Essex]	James Read
234	28 Nov 1827	Arthur Tabrum	Christchurch, London	James Read
235	2 Dec 1827	Hugh Constable	Halstead [Essex]	Governor of the poorhouse
236	10 Dec 1827	Isaac Wright	[St Alfege, City of] London	Overseer
237	[30 Dec 1827]	Robert Tapple	Ipswich	Overseer
238	31 Mar 1828	Arthur Tabrum	Christchurch, London	James Read, assistant overseer
239	4 Apr 1828	David Rivenall	[St George in the East] London	Overseer
240	14 May 1828	Mr Manning	Stratford [Essex]	[James] Read, vestry clerk
241	21 May 1828	Samuel White	Halstead [Essex]	James Read, vestry clerk
242	30 May 1828	Samuel White	Halstead [Essex]	James Read
243	2 June 1828	William Holden	Middlesex Hospital [St Marylebone, London]	Overseer
244	3 July [1828]	Sarah Rivenall	[St George in the East] London	Overseer
245	10 July 1828	Arthur Tabrum	Christchurch, London	James Read, assistant overseer
246	[11] July 1828	Samuel Hearsum	St Marylebone, London	Overseers and parish officers
247	18 Aug 1828	John Wybrow	Lambeth, London	[James] Read
248	[3 Sep 1828]	Isabella Weeden	[St George in the East] London	James Read
249	12 Sep 1828	David Rivenall	[St George in the East, London]	Overseer
250	13 Sep 1828	Thomas Carritt	[London]	James Read
251	20 Sep [1828]	David Rivenall	London Hospital [Whitechapel] London	Overseer
252	3 Oct 1828	S[amuel] White	Halstead [Essex]	James Read, vestry clerk
253	14 Oct 1828	Thomas Carritt	Cambridge	James Read
254	26 Oct 1828	Thomas Carritt	Cambridge	James Read
255	27 Oct 1828	Sarah Manning	Stratford [Essex]	[James] Read, vestry clerk
256	21 Nov 1828	Mary Mason	[Stepney] London	Overseer
257	22 Nov 1828	David Rivenall	St George in the East, London	Overseer

No.	Date	Sender	Place of sender	Addressee

Chelmsford (contd.)

No.	Date	Sender	Place of sender	Addressee
258	30 Nov 1828	William and Mary Mason	[Stepney] London	Overseer
259	4 Dec 1828	Sarah Manning	Stratford [Essex]	[James] Read, vestry clerk
260	23 Dec 1828	Arthur Tabrum	Christchurch, London	James Read, overseer
261	31 Dec 1828	Harriet Twin	Glemsford, Suffolk	[James] Read, overseer
262	12 Jan 1829	David Rivenall	[St George in the East] London	Overseer
263	[10 Feb 1829]	William Holden	Western Hospital [St Marylebone, London]	[James] Read, overseer
264	19 Feb 1829	Samuel White	Halstead [Essex]	[no addressee]
265	25 Feb 1829	Sarah Rivenall	St George in the East, London	Overseer
266	29 Mar 1829	Harriet Twin	[St Botolph] Colchester	[James] Read
267	29 Mar 1829	Jane Wall	[Mile End Old Town] London	Overseers
268	[13 Apr 1829]	Sarah Manning	Stratford, Essex	[James] Read, vestry clerk
269	[14 Apr 1829]	Elizabeth Philbrick	Wivenhoe [Essex]	Overseers
270	16 Apr 1829	Sarah Albra	[St Andrew Holborn] London	Mr Crimer
271	20 Apr 1829	William and Sarah Duke	Kentish Town [St Pancras] London	Overseers
272	6 May 1829	Arthur Tabrum	[Christchurch] London	James Read, overseer
273	13 May 1829	Harriet Twin	[St Botolph] Colchester	[James] Read, overseer
274	18 May 1829	Thomas Carritt	Cheapside [City of] London	Overseer
275	19 May 1829	David Rivenall	St George in the East, London	[Joseph] Wiffen
276	21 May [1829]	Sarah Manning	[Stratford, Essex]	[James] Read, vestry clerk
277	[May 1829]	Sarah Rivenall	[St George in the East, London]	Overseers
278	10 June 1829	Henrietta Carritt	Cheapside, London	Mr Creamer

Great Chishall

No.	Date	Sender	Place of sender	Addressee
279	12 Mar 1788	Thomas Bray	Edmonton [Mdx.]	Churchwardens and overseers

Great Coggeshall

No.	Date	Sender	Place of sender	Addressee
280	12 Mar 1750	Thomas Morse	[Great] Coggeshall [Essex]	Churchwardens and overseers of St John Baptist, Hereford

St Botolph, Colchester

No.	Date	Sender	Place of sender	Addressee
281	24 Apr 1755	Jane Cross	Canterbury	Austin Vailant, churchwarden

No.	Date	Sender	Place of sender	Addressee
St Botolph, Colchester (contd.)				
282	24 Apr 1813	George Watson	Shoreditch, London	Mr Bugg
283	[8 Dec] 1814	John Hall	[Chelmsford]	Overseer
284	2 Oct [1815]	Sarah Withnell	Bethnal Green, London	[James] Cole
285	18 Oct 1815	John Seowen	[City of] London	[William] Mason
286	11 Dec [1815]	Sarah Withnell	Bethnal Green, London	[James] Cole
287	19 Dec 1815	Sarah Withnell	[Bethnal Green] London	[William] Mason
288	14 Jan 1816	Samuel Balls	Hull	[James] Cole
289	16 Mar 1816	Mary Rabey	[St John, Westminster] London	[William] Mason
290	6 May 1816	John Hall	Chelmsford	[William] Mason
291	4 Mar 1817	Sarah Hall	Chelmsford	[no addressee]
292	19 Mar 1817	John Hall	Chelmsford	[William] Mason
293	31 Mar 1817	Sarah Hall	Chelmsford	Overseer
294	24 Apr 1817	Sarah Hall	Chelmsford	Mr Arthur, overseer
295	20 May 1817	Sarah Hall	Chelmsford	John Rudkin
296	5 June 1817	John Hall	[Chelmsford]	[John] Rudkin
297	26 Aug 1818	John Hall	Chelmsford	John Rudkin
298	9 Sep 1818	John Hall	Chelmsford	[no addressee]
299	24 Sep 1818	John Hall	Chelmsford	[no addressee]
300	30 Sep 1818	[Mary] Mitchel	Ipswich	[no addressee]
301	10 Dec 1818	James Haxell	Colchester	Overseer
302	11 Dec 1818	John Hall	Chelmsford	[no addressee]
303	21 Dec 1818	John Hall	Chelmsford	[no addressee]
304	29 Dec 1818	Sarah Mitchel	Ipswich	[John] Rudkin
305	[1818]	Elizabeth Hines	[St Anne] Soho, London	[no addressee]
306	[1818]	[Elizabeth] Hines	[St Anne Soho] London	Mr Dodd
307	4 Jan 1819	Sarah Mitchel	Ipswich	[John] Rudkin
308	25 Jan 1819	Sarah Davis	Whitechapel, London	Mr Dodd
309	5 Feb [1819]	John Hall	Chelmsford	[no addressee]
310	11 Feb 1819	John Hall	Chelmsford	[no addressee]
311	30 Mar 1819	Sarah Mitchel	Ipswich	[John] Rudkin
312	9 May 1819	Elizabeth Hines	[St Anne] Soho, London	Mr Dodd
313	21 June [1819]	Sarah Hall	Chelmsford	[no addressee]
314	29 June 1819	S[arah] Mitchel	Ipswich	[no addressee]
315	2 July 1819	Sarah Hall	Chelmsford	[no addressee]
316	9 July 1819	James Clark	[St George in the East] London	Overseers
317	30 Aug 1819	William and Ann Lester	Sudbury [Suffolk]	[no addressee]
318	6 Sep 1819	John Hall	Chelmsford	[no addressee]
319	12 Nov 1819	John Hall	Chelmsford	[no addressee]
320	21 Feb 1820	George Watson	[Shoreditch] London	Mr Osborn
321	15 Mar 1820	Sarah Hall	Chelmsford	[no addressee]
322	9 May [1821]	Mary Taylor	Hadleigh [Suffolk]	[James] Cole
323	29 Mar 1826	Anonymous	Woolwich, Kent	James Upshire
324	7 June 1826	S[amuel] and J[ames] Moore	[St Martin-in-the-Fields] London	[no addressee]
325	[26] July 1826	George Little	Rayleigh [Essex]	Gentlemen of the parish

No.	Date	Sender	Place of sender	Addressee

St Botolph, Colchester (contd.)

No.	Date	Sender	Place of sender	Addressee
326	1 Aug 1826	Sarah Challis	Chelmsford	[William] Chisolm, overseer
327	7 Aug 1826	Rachel Clark	London	Overseers
328	19 Aug 1826	George John Tye	[St Anne Soho] London	Revd Hoblen
329	24 Aug 1826	S[amuel] and J[ames] Moore	[St Martin-in-the-Fields] London	[William] Chisolm, overseer
330	3 Sep 1826	John Hall	Chelmsford	[no addressee]
331	4 Sep 1826	S[amuel] and J[ames] Moore	[St Martin-in-the-Fields, London]	[William] Chisolm
332	[5 Sep 1826]	Rachel Clark	[London]	Overseer
333	[5 Sep 1826]	Rachel Clark	London	Overseer
334	7 Sep 1826	George John Tye	[St Anne Soho, London]	William Chisolm
335	11 Sep 1826	George John Tye	[St Anne Soho] London	William Chisolm, overseer
336	12 Sep 1826	S[amuel] and J[ames] Moore	[St Martin-in-the-Fields] London	[William] Chisolm
337	19 Oct 1826	S[amuel] and J[ames] Moore	[St Martin-in-the-Fields] London	[William] Chisolm
338	[12] Dec [1826]	Elizabeth Lane	St Luke Old Street, London	[no addressee]
339	20 Dec 1826	Thomas Hall	[Bermondsey] London	[William] Chisolm
340	4 Jan 1827	Thomas Hall	[Bermondsey, London]	[William] Chisolm
341	11 Jan 1827	John Hall	Chelmsford	[William] Chisolm
342	11 Jan 1827	Thomas Hall	Bermondsey, London	[William] Chisolm
343	13 Jan 1827	Edmund Cross	London	Edmund Cross
344	18 Jan 1827	Thomas Hall	[Bermondsey] London	[William] Chisolm
345	[25 Jan 1827]	Thomas Hall	Bermondsey, London	[William] Chisolm
346	28 Jan 1827	T[homas] Hall	[Bermondsey] London	[William] Chisolm
347	[5] Feb 1827	Thomas Hall	Bermondsey, London	[William] Chisolm, overseer
348	7 Feb 1827	Elizabeth Lane	[St Luke Old Street] London	[William] Chisolm, overseer
349	20 Feb [1827]	Edmund Cross	London	[William] Chisolm
350	20 Feb 1827	Thomas Strutt	Chelmsford Prison [Chelmsford]	Mr Harris Esq.
351	[Mar 1827]	[Mrs] D. Springet	[Romford, Essex]	[William] Chisolm
352	[22 May 1827]	George Watson	[London]	Mr Chisnall, overseer
353	[27 July 1827]	E[lizabeth] Hines	[Ipswich]	Overseer
354	20 Aug 1827	Elizabeth Lane	[St Luke Old Street, London]	Overseer
355	23 Aug 1827	Elizabeth Lane	[St Luke Old Street] London	[William] Chisolm, overseer
356	27 Sep 1827	E[lizabeth] Hines	Ipswich	[William] Chisolm, overseer
357	12 Nov 1827	R. Springet	Romford [Essex]	[William] Chisolm
358	13 Nov 1827	Ann Lester	Sudbury [Suffolk]	Overseer
359	20 Nov 1827	George Watson	London	[no addressee]
360	18 Dec 1827	G[eorge] and Hannah Watson	London	William Chisolm

No.	Date	Sender	Place of sender	Addressee

St Botolph, Colchester (contd.)

No.	Date	Sender	Place of sender	Addressee
361	1 Jan 1828	[Elizabeth] Hines	St Anne Soho, London	[William] Chisolm, overseer
362	17 Jan [1828]	Hannah Steward	Hadleigh, Suffolk	Mr Orford
363	[9 Feb 1828]	Thomas Goody	[Colchester, St Botolph]	[William] Chisolm, overseer
364	11 Feb 1828	George John Tye	Colchester	Mr Harris
365	18 Feb 1828	R. Springet	Romford [Essex]	[William] Chisolm
366	18 Feb 1828	George John Tye	[no place]	[William] Chisolm
367	25 Feb 1828	George John Tye	[no place]	William Chisolm
368	10 Mar [1828]	George Watson	London	[no addressee]
369	25 Mar 1828	John Balls	Maldon [Essex]	Mr Bugg
370	1 Apr 1828	Ann Lester	Sudbury [Suffolk]	[William] Chisolm, overseer
371	7 Apr 1828	John Balls	Maldon [Essex]	[no addressee]
372	22 Apr 1828	George Watson	London	[William] Chisolm
373	[Apr 1828]	George Watson	[London]	[no addressee]
374	7 May 1828	R. Springet	Romford [Essex]	[William] Chisolm
375	[18 June 1828]	Elizabeth Hines	St Anne Soho, London	Overseers
376	1 July 1828	George Watson	[London]	[William] Chisolm
377	[10 July 1828]	[Benjamin] Brooker	[Ipswich]	[no addressee]
378	22 July [1828]	George Watson	[London]	[William] Chisolm
379	26 Aug 1828	Robert Ray	[Setchey, Norfolk]	William Chisolm, assistant overseer
380	[15 Sep 1828]	[Elizabeth Baker]	[St Botolph, Colchester]	[no addressee]
381	19 Sep 1828	Ann Bacon	Sudbury [Suffolk]	[William] Chisolm
382	6 Oct 1828	Susan Pitt	[St Giles] Colchester	[William] Chisolm, overseer
383	8 Oct 1828	George Little	Thundersley [Essex]	Overseer
384	3 Apr [1829]	George John Tye	[no place]	Mr Bugg
385	4 Apr 1829	George John Tye	[no place]	Mr Theobald
386	Oct 1829	Francis Fowler	[Bermondsey] London	[no addressee]
387	8 Dec 1829	James Anderson	Whitechapel London	Overseer
388	18 Aug 1830	John Harvey	[Shoreditch] London	Mr Bugg, overseer
389	1 Dec 1830	James Anderson	Whitechapel London	Overseer
390	15 Dec 1830	Elizabeth Anderson	[Whitechapel] London	John Hall
391	16 Apr [1833]	Mary Balls	[St Mary] Maldon [Essex]	Mr Bugg
392	15 Nov 1834	Marian Nevill	Mersea [Essex]	Mr Pretty
393	5 Aug 1835	James Bottom	[St Saviour] London	Mr Pretty, overseer
394	1 Jan [1836]	Sarah Finch	Chatham [Kent]	[no addressee]
395		Isaac Bugg	[no place]	Overseer
396	17 Aug	Mary Taylor	Hadleigh [Suffolk]	[William] Chisolm, overseer

St James, Colchester

No.	Date	Sender	Place of sender	Addressee
397	15 Oct 1810	Rachel Shoreg	[Bethnal Green] London	[no addressee]
398	30 Sep 1811	Mary Mayden	[St Leonard, Colchester]	[no addressee]
399	9 Dec 1811	J. and C. Wire	Stratford, Essex	Mr Brett, overseer

No.	Date	Sender	Place of sender	Addressee

St James, Colchester (contd.)

No.	Date	Sender	Place of sender	Addressee
400	17 Dec [1811]	J. and C. Wire	Stratford [Essex]	[*no addressee*]
401	2 July 1813	J. Harden	St Marylebone, London	Mr Wetherley
402	13 Jan 1814	Sarah Finch	[St George] London	[*no addressee*]
403	[24 Jan 1814]	Sarah Finch	[St George, London]	Mr Beat
404	21 Mar [1814]	William and Mary Mann	[Bethnal Green] London	Mr Wetherley
405	17 Jan 1817	John Enos	Sheerness, Kent	William Harden
406	6 Apr 1833	James Russell	[Newington] London	Parochial authorities
407	8 Apr 1833	Charlotte Game	Mendlesham, Suffolk	Mr Jackson, overseer
408	13 May 1833	James Russell	[Newington] London	Parochial authorities
409	16 June 1833	Mary Cooper	Chelmsford	[*no addressee*]
410	[*no date*]	Lucy Baley	[Colchester, St James]	[*no addressee*]
411	[*no date*]	Mary Sumner	[*no place*]	Mr Breets

St Peter, Colchester

No.	Date	Sender	Place of sender	Addressee
412	21 Nov 181[7]	George Rowe	Bocking [Essex]	Mr Cod, overseer
413	[1817]	James Blatch	[*no place*]	Mr Banister
414	15 Feb 1818	George Rowe	[Great] Coggeshall [Essex]	Mr Banister, overseer
415	16 Feb 1818	James Howell	Ely	Churchwardens and overseers
416	8 May 1818	Widow Shepperd	Romford, Essex	Overseer
417	19 July 1818	J. Berry	London	Elizabeth Berry
418	20 July 1818	William James	Chelmsford	S. P. Carr
419	7 Aug 1818	William James	Chelmsford	[James] Allen, overseer
420	13 Sep 1818	James Howell	Ely	Overseers
421	19 Sep 1818	William James	Chelmsford	Mr Banister
422	18 Mar 1819	William James	Chelmsford	James Allen
423	18 Mar 1819	William James	Chelmsford	Mr Banister
424	31 Mar 1819	Benjamin Hewitt	Whitton [Suffolk]	Overseer
425	11 Aug 1819	William James	Chelmsford	Mr Banister
426	23 Sep 1819	Benjamin Hewitt	Whitton, Suffolk	Overseer
427	[6 Oct 1819]	T[homas] Mills	[*no place*]	Mr Robinson
428	12 Apr [1820]	Benjamin Hewitt	Whitton [Suffolk]	Overseer
429	23 June 1820	William Harvey	Gosport Barracks [Hampshire]	Revd William Marsh
430	29 June 1820	William James	Chelmsford	Mr Swinborne
431	6 July 1820	William Harvey	Gosport Barracks [Hampshire]	Revd William Marsh
432	10 Sep 1820	William James	Chelmsford	Mr Swinborne
433	19 Oct 1820	Thomas Mills	Wethersfield [Essex]	Mr Swinborne
434	30 Dec 1820	William James	Chelmsford	Mr Swinborne
435	11 Jan 1821	William James	Chelmsford	Mr Swinborne
436	25 Feb 1821	J[ames] Tracey	Chelmsford	[*no addressee*]
437	29 Mar 1821	William James	Chelmsford	Mr Swinborne
438	5 Apr 1821	William James	Chelmsford	Mr Swinborne
439	31 May 1821	William James	Chelmsford	James Allen

No.	Date	Sender	Place of sender	Addressee

St Peter, Colchester (contd.)

No.	Date	Sender	Place of sender	Addressee
440	19 June 1821	George Rowe	[Great] Coggeshall [Essex]	Overseer
441	31 July 1821	James Howell	Ely	[no addressee]
442	6 Aug 1821	George Rowe	[no place]	[no addressee]
443	30 Aug 1821	William James	Chelmsford	[Josias] Bryant
444	5 Sep 1821	William James	Chelmsford	[Josias] Bryant
445	25 Sep 1821	William James	Chelmsford	James Allen
446	13 Oct 1821	James Howell	Ely	Overseers and churchwardens
447	18 Oct 1821	William James	Chelmsford	[Josias] Bryant
448	1 Jan 1822	William James	Chelmsford	[Josias] Bryant
449	13 Mar 1822	George Rowe	[no place]	Overseer
450	27 Mar 1822	William James	Chelmsford	Josias Bryant
451	20 May 1822	William James	Chelmsford	John Cooper
452	25 May 1822	William James	Chelmsford	John Cooper
453	28 May 1822	William James	Chelmsford	James Allen
454	29 July 1822	William James	Chelmsford	[James] Allen
455	July 1822	James Howell	Ely	Overseers and churchwardens
456	5 Aug 1822	James Howell	Ely	Overseers and churchwardens
457	30 Sep 1822	William James	Chelmsford	John Cooper
458	[13 Dec 1822]	Mary Martin	Ipswich	[no addressee]
459	10 Jan 1823	George Rowe	Bocking [Essex]	Overseer
460	20 Jan 1823	Benjamin Hewitt	Whitton, Suffolk	Overseer
461	25 Feb 1823	William James	Chelmsford	James Allen
462	26 Feb 1823	William James	Chelmsford	[James] Allen
463	21 Mar 1823	George Rowe	Bocking [Essex]	Overseer
464	25 Mar 1823	William James	Chelmsford	Mr Hayward
465	5 May 1823	Joseph Thorough-good	London	Robert Alden
466	6 June [1823]	Benjamin Hewitt	Whitton, Suffolk	Overseer
467	17 June 1823	Benjamin Hewitt	Whitton, Suffolk	Overseers
468	25 June 1823	William James	Chelmsford	[no addressee]
469	30 June [1823]	Benjamin Hewitt	Whitton, Suffolk	[no addressee]
470	16 July 1823	George Craddock	Westminster, London	Robert Alden
471	4 Aug 1823	James Howell	Ely	Overseers and churchwardens
472	28 Sep 1823	William James	Chelmsford	[James] Allen
473	8 Nov 1823	George Rowe	[Great] Coggeshall [Essex]	[no addressee]
474	16 Nov [1823]	George Rowe	[Great] Coggeshall [Essex]	Overseer
475	14 Dec 1823	William James	Chelmsford	Robert Alden, overseer
476	19 Jan 1824	George Craddock	Westminster [London]	Robert Alden
477	24 Jan 1824	William James	Chelmsford	Robert Alden, overseer
478	7 Feb 1824	William James	Chelmsford	[James] Allen

No.	Date	Sender	Place of sender	Addressee
St Peter, Colchester (contd.)				
479	1 Mar 1824	William James	Chelmsford	Robert Alden, overseer
480	23 Mar 1824	Benjamin Hewitt	Whitton, Suffolk	Overseer
481	30 Mar 1824	William James	Chelmsford	Robert Alden, overseer
482	16 Apr 1824	James Howell	Ely	Parish officers
483	19 Apr 1824	Joseph Thorough-good	Bermondsey, London	[Robert] Alden
484	Apr 1824	William James	Chelmsford	Robert Alden, overseer
485	11 May 1824	Richard Player	Chatham, Kent	Overseers
486	25 June 1824	William James	Chelmsford	Robert Alden
487	24 July 1824	James Howell	Ely	Overseers
488	27 Sep 1824	William James	Chelmsford	Robert Alden, overseer
489	6 Oct 1824	George Craddock	Westminster, London	Robert Alden
490	6 Dec 1824	Mr Player	Rochester [Kent]	Mr Halkin
491	28 Dec 1824	William James	Chelmsford	Robert Alden
492	5 Jan 1825	George Rowe	[Great] Coggeshall [Essex]	Overseer
493	21 Jan 1825	Mary Martin	Ipswich	[no addressee]
494	23 Feb 1825	George Craddock	Westminster, London	Robert Alden
495	13 May 1825	Benjamin Hewitt	Whitton, Suffolk	Overseer
496	22 June 1825	William James	Chelmsford	Robert Alden
497	13 July 1825	George Craddock	Westminster, London	Robert Alden
498	22 July 1825	James Tracey	Bishop's Stortford, Herts.	Robert Alden
499	1 Aug 1825	George Craddock	Westminster, London	Robert Alden
500	[17 Aug 1825]	George Craddock	Westminster [London]	Robert Alden
501	[5 Sep 1825]	George Craddock	Westminster [London]	Robert Alden
502	26 Sep 1825	William James	Chelmsford	Robert Alden
503	[5 Oct 1825]	George Craddock	Westminster [London]	Robert Alden
504	[22 Oct 1825]	George Craddock	Westminster [London]	Robert Alden
505	2 Nov 1825	William James	Chelmsford	Robert Alden
506	7 Nov 1825	Benjamin Brooker	Ipswich	Robert Alden, overseer
507	13 Nov 1825	Robert Gosling	Portsmouth	Robert Alden, overseer
508	29 Nov 1825	George Craddock	Westminster, London	Robert Alden
509	30 Nov 1825	William James	Chelmsford	Robert Alden, overseer
510	[before 2 Dec 1825]	[Benjamin Brooker]	[Ipswich]	[no addressee]
511	16 Dec 1825	William James	Chelmsford	Robert Alden
512	20 Dec 1825	George Craddock	Westminster, London	Robert Alden
513	11 Jan 1826	George Craddock	Westminster, London	Robert Alden
514	31 Jan 1826	George Craddock	Westminster, London	Robert Alden
515	16 Feb 1826	William Wilsher	Norwich	Minister
516	21 Feb 1826	George Craddock	Westminster, London	Robert Alden

No. Date	Sender	Place of sender	Addressee

St Peter, Colchester (contd.)

No. Date	Sender	Place of sender	Addressee
517 12 Mar 1826	William Wilsher	Norwich	[no addressee]
518 13 Mar 1826	George Rowe	[Great] Coggeshall [Essex]	[no addressee]
519 14 Mar 1826	William James	Chelmsford	Robert Alden
520 17 Apr 1826	Ann Craddock	Westminster, London	Robert Alden
521 [Apr 1826]	Benjamin Brooker	[Ipswich]	[Robert] Alden Overseer
522 19 July 1826	George Craddock	Westminster, London	Robert Alden
523 21 Aug 1826	George Craddock	Westminster, London	Robert Alden
524 30 Aug 1826	George Craddock	Westminster, London	Robert Alden
525 24 Sep 1826	George Rowe	[no place]	Robert Alden
526 3 Oct 1826	George Craddock	Westminster, London	Robert Alden
527 13 Nov 1826	William James	Chelmsford	Robert Alden
528 12 Dec 1826	George Craddock	[Westminster] London	Robert Alden
529 12 Dec 1826	William James	Chelmsford	Robert Alden
530 20 Dec 1826	George Craddock	[Westminster] London	Robert Alden
531 8 Jan 1827	Benjamin Hewitt	Whitton, Suffolk	[no addressee]
532 7 Feb 1827	George Craddock	[Westminster] London	Robert Alden
533 16 Feb [1827]	Benjamin Hewitt	Whitton, Suffolk	[no addressee]
534 17 Mar 1827	William James	Chelmsford	James Allen
535 20 Mar 1827	William James	Chelmsford	Robert Alden
536 28 Mar [1827]	George Rowe	[Great] Coggeshall [Essex]	[no addressee]
537 [24 Apr 1827]	Ann Craddock	Westminster [London]	Robert Alden
538 20 June 1827	William James	Chelmsford	Robert Alden
539 [4 Sep 1827]	Mary Death	Hacheston, Suffolk	Robert Alden, overseer
540 7 Sep 1827	William James	Chelmsford	Robert Alden
541 13 Sep 1827	William James	Chelmsford	Robert Alden
542 3 Nov 1827	George Craddock	Bishop's Waltham, Hampshire	Robert Alden
543 8 Nov 1827	William James	Chelmsford	Robert Alden
544 11 Dec 1827	Benjamin Hewitt	Whitton, Suffolk	[no addressee]
545 18 Feb 1828	Benjamin Hewitt	Whitton, Suffolk	Overseer
546 19 Feb 1828	Elizabeth Norman	St George in the East, London	Robert Alden, overseer
547 14 Mar 1828	Elizabeth Norman	[St George in the East] London	Robert Alden, overseer
548 23 Apr 1828	Elizabeth Norman	[St George in the East] London	Robert Alden, overseer
549 18 Sep 1828	George Rowe	Braintree	[no addressee]
550 28 Sep 1828	William James	Chelmsford	Robert Alden
551 8 Oct 1828	George Rowe	Braintree	[no addressee]
552 18 Dec 1828	Elizabeth Brigg	Brightlingsea [Essex]	Robert Alden, overseer
553 20 Jan 1829	James and Margaret Howell	Ely	Overseers and churchwardens
554 [Jan 1829]	Benjamin Hewitt	Whitton, Suffolk	[no addressee]
555 9 Feb 1829	George Craddock	Westminster, London	Robert Alden

No.	Date	Sender	Place of sender	Addressee
	Date	*Sender*	*Place of sender*	*Addressee*

St Peter, Colchester (contd.)

No.	Date	Sender	Place of sender	Addressee
556	17 Feb 1829	George Craddock	Westminster, London	Robert Alden
557	7 Mar 1829	George Rowe	Braintree	Robert Alden
558	11 May 1829	George Rowe	Braintree	Robert Alden
559	Feb 1832	Edward Mills	Brisley, Norfolk	[*no addressee*]
560	16 Apr 1832	Margaret Howell	Ely	Overseer
561	18 Sep 1832	William Wilsher	Norwich	Overseer
562	23 Sep 1832	Edward Mills	Brisley, Norfolk	Robert Alden
563	3 Oct 1832	Margaret Howell	Ely	Overseers and churchwardens
564	8 Nov 1832	William Wilsher	Norwich	Overseers
565	16 Jan 1833	James Howell	Ely	Overseers
566	29 Jan 1833	William Watson	[St Marylebone] London	Robert Alden, overseer
567	9 May 1833	Edward Mills	Brisley, Norfolk	Overseer
568	14 Oct 1833	James Howell	Ely	Overseers
569	28 Oct 1833	Edward Mills	Brisley [Norfolk]	Overseers
570	[1 Jan 1834]	William Wilsher	Norwich	Overseers
571	[2 Jan 1834]	Benjamin Hewitt	Whitton, Suffolk	Overseer
572	6 Jan 1834	Benjamin Hewitt	Whitton [Suffolk]	Overseer
573	20 Jan 1834	Ellen Broker	Leicester	Robert Alden
574	30 Jan 1834	James Howell	Ely	Robert Alden, overseer
575	13 Feb [1834]	Benjamin Hewitt	Whitton [Suffolk]	Overseer
576	20 Feb 1834	William Green	Ipswich	Robert Alden, overseer
577	23 Apr 1834	James Ludbrook	[*no place*]	Overseer
578	1 May [1834]	James Howell	Ely	Robert Alden
579	12 July 1834	James Ludbrook	[*no place*]	Overseers
580	22 Dec 1834	William Wilsher	Norwich	Overseers
581	2 Jan 1835	William Wilsher	Norwich	Overseer
582	19 Jan 1835	Benjamin [Hewitt]	Whitton [Suffolk]	Overseer
583	2 Mar [1835]	George Baynall	Romford [Essex]	Robert Alden
584	1 Apr 1835	James and M[argaret] Howell	Ely	Overseers
585	3 Apr 1835	George Rowe	Bocking [Essex]	[Robert] Alden
586	12 Sep	Mary Braig	Brightlingsea [Essex]	Overseer

Great Dunmow

No.	Date	Sender	Place of sender	Addressee
587	13 Oct 1818	Hannah Hoy	[Deptford, Surrey]	Mr Fuller Esq.
588	31 Dec 1818	Isaac Milbourn	Great Wakering [Essex]	Overseer

Little Dunmow

No.	Date	Sender	Place of sender	Addressee
589	10 Nov [1817]	Jemima Wetherly	Whitstable [Kent]	John Allen
590	[*no date*]	*Anonymous*	[*no place*]	[*no addressee*]

Halstead

No.	Date	Sender	Place of sender	Addressee
591	2 Aug 1835	E. Harland	Ipswich	[*no addressee*]
592	26 Aug 1835	William Gale	[*no place*]	Overseers and churchwardens

No.	Date	Sender	Place of sender	Addressee

Havering-atte-Bower

593	[16 Apr 1795]	Ann Garner	[Attleborough, Norfolk]	Mr Cook
594	18 Oct 1803	R[achel] Robson	[Gateshead, Durham]	Mr Waltom
595	3 Feb 1804	R[achel] Robson	[Durham]	Mr Waltom

Kirby-le-Soken

596	14 Nov 1818	John Snell	Bristol	Sarah Mayhew
597	6 July 1827	Mary Snell	[Great] Yarmouth [Norfolk]	[no addressee]
598	10 July 1827	Jane Pooley	Needham Market, Suffolk	[William] Daniels
599	30 July 1828	Mary Hill	[Great] Yarmouth [Norfolk]	Thomas Stone
600	26 May 1829	Mary Hill	[Great] Yarmouth [Norfolk]	Thomas Stone Esq.
601	22 Feb 1832	Mary Harris	Boyle [Roscommon, Ireland]	Willliam Daniels, overseer
602	18 May 1832	Mary Harris	Boyle [Roscommon, Ireland]	William Daniels, overseer
603	12 July 1832	James Davey	Colchester	[Robert] Mumford, overseer
604	14 Sep 1832	Mary Harris	Strokestow [Roscommon, Ireland]	William Daniels
605	12 Dec 1832	Mary Harris	Clonmel [Tipperary, Ireland]	Willliam Daniels
606	19 Feb 1833	Elizabeth Davey	Colchester	[no addressee]
607	3 June 1833	Mary Hill	[Great Yarmouth, Norfolk]	[no addressee]
608	20 June 1833	Mary Harris	Fermoy [Cork, Ireland]	William Daniels
609	18 Sep 1833	Mary Harris	Devonport [Devon]	William Daniels, overseer
610	5 Feb 1834	Mary Hill	Great Yarmouth [Norfolk]	Robert Mumford, overseer
611	3 Mar 1834	Mary Hill	[Great] Yarmouth [Norfolk]	Robert Mumford, overseer
612	10 June 1834	James Davey	Colchester	[no addressee]
613	23 June 1834	James Davey	Colchester	Willliam Daniels
614	23 Nov 1835	J[ames] Davey	Colchester	Mr Robert

Lexden

615	27 Feb 1834	Richard Kimberley	Torpoint, Cornwall	Overseers

St Mary, Maldon

616	22 Aug 1811	Jonathan Sewell	Portsmouth	Mr Francis, overseer
617	9 Dec 1811	Jonathan Sewell	Hilsea [Hampshire]	Mr Francis
618	16 Nov 1812	Jonathan Sewell	Portchester [Hampshire]	Mr Francis, overseer
619	2 July 1813	Ann Doubty	Wivenhoe [Essex]	Mr Baker
620	20 Aug 1813	Jonathan Sewell	Portchester [Hampshire]	Mr Francis, overseer

No.	Date	Sender	Place of sender	Addressee
Mayland				
621	29 Mar 1822	Isaiah Duce	St Bartholomew's Hospital [City of London]	William Duce
Mundon				
622	1 Mar 1816	James Taitt	Chelsea, London	John Bourne
623	9 Apr 1820	Ann Burder	[St Andrew Holborn, London]	John Bourne
624	3 Feb 1821	Ann Burder	[St Andrew Holborn, London]	[John] Bourne
625	1 Feb 1823	John Thurtell	Romford, Essex	Overseer
626	13 May 1831	John Thurtell	Romford [Essex]	Overseer
627	12 Aug 1831	John Thurtell	Romford, Essex	Richard Solly
628	2 Dec 1831	John Thurtell	Romford, Essex	[Richard] Solly
629	28 Oct 1832	Mary Keeling	Maldon [Essex]	[John] Sewell
630	8 Nov 1832	J[ohn] Thurtell	Romford [Essex]	Overseers
631	[21 Dec 1832]	Ann Burder	[St Andrew Holborn, London]	Churchwardens and overseers
632	25 Sep 1833	Ann Burder	[St Andrew Holborn, London]	Overseer
633	22 Oct 1833	John Thurtell	Romford, Essex	Overseer
634	22 Dec [1833]	John Thurtell	Romford, Essex	Overseer
635	12 Feb 1834	John Thurtell	Romford [Essex]	Overseer
636	[*no date*]	Mrs Brown	[*no place*]	John Sewell
637	11 Jan	A[nn] Burder	[St Andrew Holborn] London	Mr Bowen
638	21 Apr	A[nn] Burder	[St Andrew Holborn] London	[John] Bourne
Navestock				
639	8 Sep 1829	Ann Pepper	Rochford [Essex]	Overseers
White Notley				
640	6 May 1831	Mrs Wilkinson	Rickmansworth, Herts.	[*no addressee*]
641	18 May 1831	Mrs Wilkinson	Rickmansworth [Herts.]	[*no addressee*]
Peldon				
642	[*no date*]	James Wells	Stratford, Essex	Mr Artkey
Purleigh				
643	1 Feb 1822	William Thurtell	South Benfleet, Essex	Mr Sanders, churchwarden
644	3 Jan 1825	William Thurtell	South Benfleet [Essex]	Overseer
Rainham				
645	[2] Mar 1748	Mary Pavett	Rainham	Henry Pavett, Stratford
646	[19 Mar 1801]	Amy Hill	Deptford, Surrey	Mr Saunders
647	23 June 1804	[Mrs] Wall	[*no place*]	Mr Surig, churchwarden

No. Date	Sender	Place of sender	Addressee
Rainham (contd.)			
648 21 June 1805	Hannah Wall	Mile End [Colchester]	Mr Masters
649 [12 Dec 1805]	Amy Hill	[Deptford, Surrey]	Charles Leeds
650 27 Jan [1806]	Thomas Briggs	London Hospital [Whitechapel] London	Mr Hayser
651 24 Mar 1806	Thomas Briggs	London Hospital [Whitechapel, London]	Mr Hayser
652 [27 Mar 1815]	Amy Hill	[no place]	Mr Heathroat
653 [no date]	Ann Gossling	[no place]	Mr Lee
Rayleigh			
654 1 Oct 1809	Thomas Sagger	Springfield [Essex]	Mr Spinks
655 2 Nov 1809	Ann Prigg	Southminster [Essex]	Overseer
656 26 Feb 1825	Ann Benson	Rochford [Essex]	[no addressee]
657 10 Mar 1826	Richard Porter	Ashby-de-la-Zouch [Leics.]	Overseer
658 24 Mar 1826	Richard Porter	Ashby-de-la-Zouch [Leics.]	Joseph Markwell, vestry clerk
659 14 Aug 1826	Thomas Brown	Romford [Essex]	Churchwardens and overseers
660 18 Sep 1826	Richard Porter	Ashby-de-la-Zouch [Leics.]	Overseer
661 28 Jan 1828	Lucy Shuttleworth	Nottingham	Overseer
662 25 Mar 1828	Mrs E. Reilley	Westminster, London	Churchwardens and overseers
663 25 June 1831	Elizabeth Goodman	[Shoreditch, London]	Mr Clayton Esq.
664 3 Sep 1831	Elizabeth Goodman	[Shoreditch, London]	Joseph Markwell
665 26 Jan 1832	Elizabeth Goodman	[Shoreditch, London]	Joseph Markwell
666 26 Dec 1832	Elizabeth Goodman	[London]	Joseph Markwell, overseer
667 26 Mar 1833	E. Smith	Finsbury [Shoreditch] London	Mrs Menesfield
668 1 Oct [1833]	Elizabeth Goodman	[Mile End Old Town, London]	Joseph Markwell, overseer
669 23 Dec 1833	Elizabeth Goodman	[Mile End Old Town, London]	Joseph Markwell, overseer
670 19 May 1834	Elizabeth Goodman	[Mile End Old Town, London]	Joseph Markwell, overseer
671 28 Aug 1834	Elizabeth Goodman	[Mile End Old Town, London]	Joseph Markwell, overseer
672 13 Dec 1834	Mrs Smith	Chatham [Kent] overseer	Joseph Markwell,
673 18 Dec [1834]	Elizabeth Goodman	[Mile End Old Town, London]	Joseph Markwell
674 23 Dec 1834	Elizabeth Goodman	[Mile End Old Town, London]	Joseph Markwell, overseer
675 2 Mar 1835	Maria Hurrell	[no place]	[no addressee]
Rochford			
676 11 Feb 1803	Dinah Martin	Hayes [Mdx.]	Thomas White

No.	Date	Sender	Place of sender	Addressee
Rochford (contd.)				
677	1 May 1803	Joseph Skewer	Great Wakering [Essex]	[*no addressee*]
678	6 Nov 1803	Joseph Skewer	Great Wakering [Essex]	Overseer
679	12 Aug 1804	John Maseon	Crays Hill [Essex]	[*no addressee*]
680	8 Nov 1804	Mr W. Gepp	London	Revd [Joseph] Wise
681	13 Dec 1804	S. Gepp	Heathrow, Mdx.	John Bright
682	2 Nov 1806	Ann Rayner	Little Wakering [Essex]	Churchwardens and overseers
683	11 May 1807	Mary Craske	Thurston [Suffolk]	Revd [Joseph] Wise
684	27 May [1807]	S. Beckwith	[Clerkenwell] London	J. Round, overseer
685	26 Feb 1809	Mary Craske	Rushbrooke [Suffolk]	Joseph Wise
686	18 Apr 1809	Lucy Humphreys	Shipley [Sussex]	Overseers
687	24 Aug 1809	Dinah Martin	[Hayes, Mdx.]	Overseer
688	30 Sep 1809	Thomas Sadler	Great Wakering [Essex]	J[ohn] Bright
689	17 Nov 1809	Mary Brooks	Danbury [Essex]	Overseer
690	[*before* 4 Mar 1810]	Mary Brooks	Danbury [Essex]	Overseer
691	1 July 1810	Dinah Martin	Hayes, Mdx.	Overseer
692	8 July [1810]	Sarah Ateradge	Canewdon [Essex]	[John] Bright
693	25 Aug 1811	Robert Hoy	Sheereness, Kent	[John] Bright
694	8 Sep 1823	Daniel and Mary Gray	[Clerkenwell] London	Isaac Harvey, overseer
695	[12 Nov 1829]	Elizabeth Ann Manning	Islington [London]	Overseer
696	4 Jan 1830	Elizabeth Ann Manning	Islington [London]	Mr Camport
697	13 Jan 1830	John Sams	Chelmsford	[Isaac] Harvey, overseer
698	25 Feb 1830	Elizabeth Ann Manning	Islington [London]	Overseer
699	[*no date*]	Ann Benson	[*no place*]	[*no addressee*]
700	12 Nov	J. Borcham	[*no place*]	[*no addressee*]
701	30 Apr	John and Elizabeth Maseon	Crays Hill, Essex	[*no addressee*]
702	[*no date*]	S. Stearns	[*no place*]	[*no addressee*]
Stanford Rivers				
703	12 Jan 1824	Jane Hogg	Ingatestone [Essex]	Mr Andrews
Stanstead Mountfitchet				
704	19 Sep [1813]	Elizabeth Shepphard	[Leyton, Essex]	[*no addressee*]
Theydon Garnon				
705	13 Jan 1731	Mary Howe	[Theydon Garnon]	Mr Ranking
706	1 Sep 1736	Mary Marshall	[*no place*]	Churchwardens and overseers
707	5 Nov 1736	Sarah Stone	London	[*no addressee*]
708	12 July 1759	Widow Camp	Widford [Essex]	Mr Humerson

No. Date	Sender	Place of sender	Addressee
Theydon Garnon (contd.)			
709 1 Apr [1802]	Ann Wood	Bethnal Green, London	Mr Peggrim, church warden
710 [1808]	Elizabeth Mines	[Bermondsey] London	William Archer
711 18 Oct 1819	Hannah Collesson	Rye [Sussex]	Overseers
Theydon Mount			
712 30 Dec 1769	Elizabeth Brown	St Bartholomew's Hospital [City of London]	Churchwarden
713 21 Mar 1831	Harriet Baker	Plaistow [Essex]	Overseers
714 20 Apr [1831]	Thomas Kellnby	Springfield Goal, Chelmsford	Overseer
West Thurrock			
715 [1770]	George Oliver	[no place]	Mr Long, overseer
716 10 Feb [1809]	Eliza Farrant	Bromley, Mdx.	Overseer
Tolleshunt D'Arcy			
717 27 Apr 1801	Edward Abbott	London [Hospitalc Whitechapel, London	[no addressee]
Upminster			
718 11 Apr [1802]	Ann Sinclair	Northfleet, Kent	[Thomas] Talbot
719 5 Sep 1802	Ann Sinclair	Northfleet [Kent]	[Thomas] Talbot
720 25 Sep 1802	Ann Sinclair	Gravesend [Kent]	[Thomas] Talbot
721 29 Dec 1802	John Hicks	Cheshunt [Herts.]	[Thomas] Talbot
722 28 Apr 1803	Richard King	Gravesend [Kent]	[Thomas] Talbot
723 14 Aug 1803	Richard King	Gravesend [Kent]	[Thomas] Talbot
724 9 Oct 1803	Richard King	[Gravesend, Kent]	[Thomas] Talbot
725 13 Nov 1803	Richard King	Gravesend [Kent]	[Thomas] Talbot
726 2 Mar 1804	John Hicks	Cheshunt [Herts.]	[Thomas] Talbot
727 18 Mar 1804	Richard King	Gravesend [Kent]	[Thomas] Talbot
728 20 Mar 1804	John Hicks	Cheshunt [Herts.]	[no addressee]
729 22 Apr 1804	Richard King	Gravesend [Kent]	[Thomas] Talbot
730 1 July 1804	Richard King	Gravesend [Kent]	[Thomas] Talbot
731 29 Aug 1804	John Hicks	Cheshunt [Herts.]	[Thomas] Talbot
732 16 Dec 1804	Richard King	Gravesend [Kent]	[Thomas] Talbot
733 2 Jan 1805	John Hicks	Cheshunt [Herts.]	[Thomas] Talbot
734 9 Apr 1805	Richard King	Gravesend [Kent]	[Thomas] Talbot
735 10 June 1805	Joseph Rogers	London	[Thomas] Talbot
736 14 Oct 1805	Richard King	Gravesend [Kent]	[Thomas] Talbot
737 19 Nov 1805	Ann King	Gravesend [Kent]	[Thomas] Talbot
738 29 Nov 1805	Ann King	Gravesend [Kent]	[Thomas] Talbot
739 9 Feb 1806	Richard King	Gravesend [Kent]	[Thomas] Talbot
740 4 July 1806	John Hicks	Cheshunt [Herts.]	[Thomas] Talbot
741 2 Mar 1807	Mary-Ann Smith	[St Giles without Cripplegate, City of] London	Mr Banks
742 5 Mar 1813	Francis Freeman	Middlesex Hospital [St Marylebone] London	[no addressee]
743 5 Jan 1814	Mary[-Ann] Smith	Clerkenwell [London]	Overseer

No.	Date	Sender	Place of sender	Addressee
Upminster (contd.)				
744	10 Feb 1814	Mary[-Ann] Smith	[Clerkenwell, London]	Mr Banks
745	13 Mar 1819	J. B. Crowest	[Upminster]	Overseer
746	19 Aug 1834	Thomas and Mary Lutterell	Burnham Westgate [Norfolk]	Overseers
Little Waltham				
747	9 Oct 1768	Ann Clark	[Bermondsey, London]	Revd Dr Chambers
Wanstead				
748	1766	Timothy Woodward	[no place]	Mr Drake
South Weald				
749	28 May 1818	Rebecca Robinson	Woolwich, Kent	Mr Pollis
750	17 Oct 1818	Mrs Robinson	[no place]	[no addressee]
751	[4 Jan 1819]	Mary Lee	Dunton [Essex]	Overseer
752	4 May 1825	James Randall	St Thomas's Hospital [St Thomas, London]	Overseer
Woodford				
753	14 Nov 1836	William Rolf	Sudbury [Suffolk]	Mr Darwood
754	1 Dec 1836	William Boreham	Kilby [Leics.]	Mr Darwood
Wormingford				
755	30 Apr 1824	Ellen Humm	Isle of Wight	Thomas Hallum
756	10 May 1824	Ellen Humm	Isle of Wight	Mr Stannard
757	12 June 1825	Thomas Rush	[Bocking, Essex]	Overseers
758	18 July 1830	Thomas Rush	[Braintree]	Mr Hicks

INTRODUCTION

Chapter 1
Pauper letters as a historical source

The English poor law of the eighteenth and early nineteenth centuries was probably the most comprehensive system of public poor relief before the coming of the modern welfare state. Its remarkably wide coverage is mirrored in the extraordinary extent and variety of records which have emerged from its administration. They include letters to the overseers of the poor that came from the poor themselves. Some 750 of these pauper letters, all those presently known to survive in the county of Essex, are documented in this volume. Their importance to the social historian can hardly be overrated. They are of paramount interest to anyone concerned with the history of the English poor law, the history of the labouring classes, and the history of literacy. Each of these points deserves a brief exposition in its own right.

Pauper letters reveal the attitudes of the poor to the poor law: for example, what they made of the 'right to relief' and the duty of the overseers; or how they tried to use certain legal provisions in their own interest. Pauper letters are therefore essential for the proper understanding of the Old Poor Law in actual operation. We have always had the record of that system 'from above', as it is abundantly preserved in tens of thousands of overseers accounts and vestry minutes, in the standard documents relating to settlement and removal, bastardy and vagrancy, in legal handbooks and guides for magistrates and parish officers, and in numerous statutes, pamphlets and the economic and social literature of the day. Pauper letters, by contrast, represent the record of the poor law 'from below'.[1]

---

[1] Milestones of the older literature still worth consulting, though heavily biased towards records 'from above', include E. M. Leonard *The early history of English poor relief* (Cambridge, 1900; repr. London, 1965); D. Marshall *The English poor in the eighteenth century: a study in social and administrative history* (London, 1926; repr. 1963); S. and B. Webb *English poor law history, I: the old poor law* (London, 1927; repr. 1963). Outstanding older case studies drawing on local archives are A. W. Ashby, 'One hundred years of poor law administration in a Warwickshire village', in *Oxford Studies in Social and Legal History* ed. P. Vinogradoff (vol. 3 [no. 6]; Oxford, 1912) pp. 1-188; F. G. Emmison, 'Relief of the poor at Eaton Socon', *Publications of the Bedfordshire Historical*

Apart from their specific relevance to the student of poverty and welfare provision, pauper letters are also of interest to anyone more generally concerned with the social and economic history of England during the era of the industrial revolution in that they provide a first-hand record of the living conditions and experiences of ordinary people. This is because in the late eighteenth and early nineteenth centuries the boundaries between the 'labourer' and the 'pauper', between 'poverty' and 'indigence' were fluid. There is a neat linguistic expression of this in the contemporary notion of the 'labouring poor', which Eden, in a classic definition, described as 'those whose daily labour is necessary for their daily support' and 'whose daily subsistence absolutely depends on the daily unremitting exertion of manual labour'.[2] Thus, what ordinary people felt they had to say about their work or the lack of it; about the loss of a child or spouse; or about getting old - all this is revealed in letters from the poor, put down in their own writing, often under conditions of extreme necessity, privation and despair.

As an early record of the practices of writing among ordinary people, pauper letters deserve a special place in the history of literacy. For the period in question, they represent the lowest level of recorded written communication, which is to be understood in a double sense. First, of course, in terms of social class, since the people who wrote these letters belonged to the lowest strata of society. Second, however, pauper letters represent the lowest level of literacy or, more precisely, of the competence of making yourself understood by putting pen to paper. Their his-

---

Record Society 15 (1933) pp. 1-98; E. M. Hampson *The treatment of poverty in Cambridgeshire* (Cambridge, 1934). More recent case studies include M. Neumann, 'Speenhamland in Berkshire', in *Comparative developments in social welfare* ed. E.W. Martin (London, 1972) pp. 85-127; A. Digby *Pauper palaces* (London, 1978); K. Wrightson and D. Levine *Poverty and piety in an English village: Terling 1525-1700* (New York, 1979; 2nd edn Oxford, 1995); M. Neumann *The Speenhamland county: poverty and the poor laws in Berkshire 1782-1834* (New York, 1982); T. Wales, 'Poverty, poor relief and the life-cycle: some evidence from seventeenth-century Norfolk', in *Land, kinship and life-cycle* ed. R. M. Smith (Cambridge, 1984) pp. 351-404; T. Sokoll *Household and family among the poor: the case of two Essex communities in the late eighteenth and early nineteenth centuries* (Bochum, 1993).

[2] F. M. Eden *The state of the poor* (3 vols, London, 1797) i, p. 4. See R. W. Malcolmson *Life and labour in England 1700-1780* (London, 1981) ch. 1; P. Mathias, 'Adam's burden: historical diagnoses of poverty', in his *The transformation of England: essays in the economic and social history of England in the eighteenth century* (London, 1979) pp. 131-47. For the social discovery of the 'labouring poor' from a European perspective, see the brilliant discussion in V. Hunecke, 'Überlegungen zur Geschichte der Armut im vorindustriellen Europa', *Geschichte und Gesellschaft* 9 (1983) pp. 493-94 and 509-12.

toric 'place' is striking in this respect. They survive from a society which was sufficiently literate for the technology of writing to have diffused to an extent where it had become readily available even at the very bottom of society. This is not to say that everyone was actually able to write. On the contrary, it was still a society where most of the labouring people were not literate. But there were enough literate people around to ensure that anyone who wanted a piece of writing to be set out in his or her name did not have to approach a learned person (or a professional scribe), but could easily draw on someone within the labouring community itself. At the same time, the fact that society was not yet fully literate enabled labouring people to make a fairly open use of the technology of writing. As there was still no compulsory elementary schooling, illiterate or semi-literate people were not yet discriminated against, or not at least to the extent which was to be found later under conditions of universal literacy.[3] This means that they could claim to make themselves understood in writing even when they possessed or made use of only rather limited powers of alphabetic articulation. For once, therefore, the labouring poor were in a position where they could justifiably write just as they spoke.

The fact that pauper letters record the words of the poor in their own writing has important methodological implications. Given that historical reconstruction, at least of those societies whose members are now all dead, primarily rests on written evidence, the people of the past can only be counted as historical subjects in the strict sense when they have left their own written testimony behind. But this does not normally apply to ordinary people before the transition to universal literacy from the middle of the nineteenth century. Accordingly, whenever historians have previously referred to the 'language' of the lower classes in former times, they have mainly used the term in a metaphorical sense. Thus, in studies of social protest, riots and popular disturbances have been described as forms of collective articulation, the social grammar of which the historian has to decipher. Hence the emphatic sense in which social protest has been understood as the 'language' of the otherwise silent and inarticulate.[4] Other

---

[3] For a brilliant discussion of the cultural context in which English society passed from partial to universal literacy, with due emphasis on the heavy impositions on the labouring classes involved in this process, see D. Vincent *Literacy and popular culture: England 1750-1914* (Cambridge, 1989).

[4] Classic contributions include E. J. Hobsbawm, 'The machine breakers' (1952), in his *Labouring men: studies in the history of labour* (London, 1964) pp. 5-22; G. Rudé *The crowd in history: a study of popular disturbances in France and England 1730-1848*

scholars have gone a step further, in drawing on sources which do in fact take us as far as to the spoken word of ordinary people. Classic accounts of that type include those featuring the people of early fourteenth-century Montaillou or the late sixteenth-century Friulian miller Menocchio, though in both these cases the oral testimonies were actually recorded in Latin and not in the vernacular.[5] More recently, there has been a growing number of studies, using court records of the sixteenth to the nineteenth centuries, in which the oral testimonies of ordinary people do seem to have been recorded word for word and in their vernacular speech. The most notable contributions refer to France and Germany.[6] Comparable studies for England are rare, since English court records do not normally provide longer verbatim recordings of the statements made by defendants or witnesses. Exceptions are to be found among ecclesiastical court records (but not beyond the seventeenth century) and among criminal court records in depositions and special kinds of trial reports like the Old Bailey sessions papers.[7] But whatever the quality of court records with respect to the spoken word of the poor, in all these cases the written record as such remains - literally - second-hand.[8]

(New York, 1964); R. H. Tilly, 'Popular disorders in 19th century Germany', *Journal of Social History* 4 (1970) pp. 1-40; E. P. Thompson, 'The moral economy of the English crowd in the eighteenth century', *Past and Present* 50 (1971) pp. 76-136; E. J. Hobsbawm and G. Rudé *Captain Swing* (Harmondsworth, 1973).

[5] E. Le Roy Ladurie *Montaillou: the promised land of error* (London, 1978); C. Ginzburg *The cheese and the worms: the cosmos of a sixteenth-century miller* (London, 1980).

[6] R. Cobb *The police and the people* (Oxford, 1970); R. Cobb *A sense of place* (London, 1975); A. Farge *Fragile lives: violence, power and solidarity in eighteenth-century Paris* (Cambridge, Mass., 1993); L. Roper *The holy household: women and morals in reformation Augsburg* (London, 1989); U. Rublack *The crimes of women in early modern Germany* (Oxford, 1999); D. W. Sabean *Power in the blood: popular culture and village discourse in early modern Germany* (Cambridge, 1984); D. W. Sabean *Property, production, and family in Neckarhausen, 1700-1870* (Cambridge, 1990); R. Schulte *The village in court: arson, infanticide and pouching in the court records of upper Bavaria 1848-1910* (Cambridge, 1994). Petitions for pardoning may also be mentioned in this context. Here again, the modern classic relates to France: N. Z. Davis *Fiction in the archives: pardon tales and their tellers in sixteenth-century France* (Stanford, 1987).

[7] For studies exploring that kind of material with a view to the words of ordinary people, see, for example, M. Ingram *Church courts, sex and marriage in England, 1570-1640* (Cambridge, 1987); L. Gowing *Domestic dangers: women, words and sex in early modern London* (Oxford, 1996).

[8] For the general question as to what extent the statements of ordinary people were recorded word by word in early modern records, see also P. Burke, 'Introduction', in *The social history of language* ed. P. Burke and R. Porter (Cambridge, 1987) p. 10.

In pauper letters, however, the utterances of ordinary people have also gone through their own hands, as it were, and these were often poor hands indeed. Numerous examples in this volume may be said to represent oral pieces of writing, produced by people who were quite obviously acting along the boundaries between the spoken and the written word. These pauper letters read - and look - like first attempts at alphabetic articulation. The writing is tentative, hesitant, evasive; or, on the other extreme, coarse, rough, rude, clumsily offensive. In this last case, they show a certain resemblance to that other early source of genuine lower-class literacy which is documented on a massive scale - the threatening letters. But the threatening letter was always anonymous, whereas the pauper letter was always written in the pauper's name. And their social contexts are different. The threatening letter, as E. P. Thompson has shown, is to be understood as the literary offshoot of social protest and collective action during food riots and early industrial disputes.[9] The pauper letter always derives from the specific circumstances of an individual case.

Despite their obvious importance, then, not just for the social history of poverty and the poor law, but also for that of the labouring classes in general, pauper letters have received very little attention in previous research. This is all the more surprising since this type of record has been known (or should have been known) to students of English social history for a long time. As early as 1934, Ethel Hampson, in her pathbreaking case study of the old poor law in Cambridgeshire, quoted from pauper letters, though only in one or two places; and in 1946 William Tate, in his *Parish Chest*, that classic guide to the study of English parish records, printed three excellent pieces in full, at the end of the chapter dealing with the records of poor law administration, under the title 'records left by the poor themselves'.[10] But apart from these notable exceptions and the odd article buried in a local historical journal,[11] and despite the fact that other sources coming from the labouring people themselves, like working-class autobiographies or threatening letters, have been given the appropriate

[9] E. P. Thompson, 'The crime of anonymity', in *Albion's fatal tree: crime and society in eighteenth-century England* ed. D. Hay et al. (Harmondsworth, 1977) pp. 255-344.

[10] Hampson *Treatment of poverty in Cambridgeshire* pp. 141, 143, 146-7, 150; W. E. Tate *The parish chest: a study of the records of parochial administration in England* (3rd edn, Cambridge, 1969; repr. London, 1983) pp. 237-41.

[11] For an example from Essex, presenting but a few examples from an antiquarian interest rather than with historical understanding, see A. P. Hutchings, 'The relief of the poor in Chelmsford 1821-1829: case histories and paupers' correspondence', *Essex Review* 65 (1956) pp. 42-56.

authoritative treatment for some time now,[12] work on pauper letters is still in its infancy. The scene may be said to have been set by Keith Snell with his *Annals of the Labouring Poor*, even though he did not himself draw on pauper letters (though he used letters from rural emigrants to North America), since it is only through his imaginative use of settlement examinations that we have become fully aware of the rich archive of personal testimonies which survive from the Old Poor Law.[13] Research on pauper letters as such, the most compelling type of record within that collective archive of the English poor, has since taken its first proper steps. James Taylor and Pam Sharpe have used pauper letters for individual case histories, the former with a strong narrative impetus, the latter from a more thematic perspective, while the present writer has attempted to follow a more analytical approach.[14]

The present volume is a fruit of this new interest in the historical study of pauper letters, and it is the first edition ever in which a large number of them have been assembled. Doing editorial justice to this unique source requires the most scrupulous and detailed discussion of the full range of problems encountered in the historical documentation of these documents. For this reason, the remaining parts of this introduction seek to provide a systematic platform of source criticism, not least in the hope of laying the ground for future research in the field. However, for the most part it

---

[12] For threatening letters, see Thompson, 'Crime of Anonymity'; for working class autobiographies, J. Burnett *Useful toil: autobiographies of working people from the 1820s to the 1920s* (Harmondsworth, 1977); J. Burnett *Destiny obscure: autobiographies of childhood, education and family from the 1820s to the 1920s* (Harmondsworth, 1982); D. Vincent *Bread, knowledge and freedom: a study of nineteenth-century working class autobiography* (London, 1981). An Essex example is to be found in the memoirs (written in 1871) of John Castle, silk weaver in Coggeshall and Colchester, in *Essex people 1750-1900: from their diaries, memoirs and letters* ed. A. F. J. Brown (ERO Publications, 59; Chelmsford, 1972) pp. 116-32.

[13] K. D. M. Snell *Annals of the labouring poor: social change and agrarian England, 1660-1900* (Cambridge, 1985).

[14] J. S. Taylor *Poverty, migration, and settlement in the industrial revolution: sojourners' narratives* (Palo Alto, Cal., 1989); J. S. Taylor, 'Voices in the crowd: the Kirkby Lonsdale township letters, 1809-36', in *Chronicling poverty: the voices and strategies of the English poor, 1640-1840* ed. T. Hitchcock, P. King and P. Sharpe (London, 1997) pp. 109-26; P. Sharpe, '"The bowels of compation": a labouring family and the law c. 1790-1834', *ibid.* pp. 87-108; T. Sokoll, 'Old age in poverty. The record of Essex pauper letters, 1780-1834', *ibid.* pp. 127-54; T. Sokoll, 'Selbstverständliche Armut. Armenbriefe in England, 1750-1834', in *Ego-Dokumente. Annäherungen an den Menschen in der Geschichte* ed. W. Schulze (Berlin, 1996) pp. 227-71. The Kirkby Lonsdale township letters have also been used by L. H. Lees *The solidarities of strangers: the English poor laws and the people 1700-1948* (Cambridge, 1998) pp. 166-76.

refrains from the substantive exploration of the material.[15] Thus, after a consideration of the institutional context (chapter 2), there is a quantitative assessment of the structure of the sample (chapter 3). This is followed by a qualitative investigation (chapter 4), which forms the basis for an outline of the editorial policy (chapter 5).

---

[15] The substantive interpretation of the entire body of Essex Pauper Letters will be found in a study in preparation by the present writer, under the title *Voices of the labouring poor*. For the time being, see T. Sokoll, 'Negotiating a living: Essex Pauper Letters from London, 1800-1834', in *Household strategies for survival: fission, faction and cooperation* ed. J. Schlumbohm and L. Fontaine (International Review of Social History, Supplement 8; Cambridge, 2000); 'T. Sokoll, 'Voices of the poor: pauper letters and poor law provision in Essex, 1780-1834', in *Poverty and relief in England from the sixteenth to the twentieth century* ed. A. Digby, J. Innes and R. M. Smith (Cambridge, forthcoming).

Chapter 2
Institutional context:
the practice of non-resident relief

Under the Old Poor Law, that is up to 1834, all parishes in England (or townships in the northern counties) were statutorily required to relieve their poor. By European standards, before the coming of the modern welfare state in the later nineteenth century, this was a remarkable achievement. As a system of public welfare provision, the English poor law was distinctive, first, in its comprehensiveness and uniformity.[1] Second, in its comparative generosity. In 1802-3, for example, total poor relief expenditure in England and Wales amounted to £4.1 million (1.9 per cent of the national income), with just over 1 million people or 11.4 per cent of the population relieved. This was equivalent to £3.92 per recipient (or £0.45 per head of the population), a figure whose weight is readily appreciated from the estimated national income per head of £23 for the same time.[2] The massive overall scale of income transfer of which the system was capable must not, however, make us overlook the small compass of its actual operation. For the third distinctive feature of the English poor law was its parochial foundation both in administrative and, most particularly, in financial terms. Practically, it was a 'welfare state in miniature' (Blaug), consisting of more than 15,000 parochial units, three quarters of which had a population of less than 800 people.[3]

To the beneficiaries of the system this meant that a person seeking assistance did not have to apply to a remote bureaucratic authority but

---

[1] P. M. Solar, 'Poor relief and English economic development before the industrial revolution', *Economic History Review* 48 (1995) pp. 1-22.

[2] PP 1803-4 XIII *Abstract of answers and returns relative to the expense and maintenance of the poor* p. 715; P. Slack *The English poor law, 1531-1782* (Cambridge, 1995) p. 22; W. A. Cole, 'Factors in demand 1700-80', in *The Economic history of Britain since 1700* ed. R. Floud and D. McCloskey (2 vols., Cambridge, 1981) i, p. 64; P. H. Lindert, 'Unequal living standards', in *The Economic history of Britain since 1700* ed. R. Floud and D. McCloskey (2nd edn, 3 vols; Cambridge, 1994), i, pp. 382-3.

[3] M. Blaug, 'The poor law report reexamined', *Journal of Economic History* 23 (1963) pp. 229-45.

could approach the overseers of the poor of his or her parish. In terms of space, this would normally not extend beyond two or three miles, which means that the overseers were in most cases within half a day's journey at most. Moreover, these parish officers were typically elected from among the leading farmers or shopkeepers within the local community, that is from groups within the 'middling sort' of society at large, and they were often personally known to the applicants. With the increasing appointment during the 1820s of salaried assistant overseers, who would stay in office for years, their personal familiarity to the poor must if anything have become even more pronounced.[4] Why, then, should that system have generated pauper letters?

In answering that question it is important, first of all, to point out that it is indeed not at all to be expected that people in need - sometimes people who were hardly literate - should have taken the trouble to write to their overseers, but that they would normally simply have called on them. In fact, it is absolutely clear (and also mentioned in many of the letters themselves) that most people who applied for relief approached the overseer, the churchwarden or the vestry meeting in person. An application in writing might be made by someone who lived outside the parish in which they were settled, while people residing 'at home' did not normally have any reason to write to their overseer and indeed hardly ever did so. This also explains the way in which pauper letters have come down to us: as part of the overseers' correspondence of the parish to which they were sent - and apart from a few exceptions, pauper letters were always sent from elsewhere.

That people should have left 'their' parish and gone somewhere else, whether in search of work or for their marriage or for whatever other reason, is hardly surprising. Early modern England was a highly mobile society, even if migration was typically over relatively short distances and longer-distance mobility seems to have declined during the second half of the seventeenth and the first half of the eighteenth centuries.[5] While the

---

[4] For a nuanced picture of the persistent importance of the parochial foundation of the Old Poor Law in the final fifty years of its existence, see D. Eastwood *Governing rural England: tradition and transformation in local government 1780-1840* (Oxford, 1994) pp. 99-165.

[5] *Migration and society in early modern England* ed P. Clark and D. Souden (London, 1987); A. S. Kussmaul, 'The ambiguous mobility of farm servants', *Economic History Review* 34 (1981) pp. 222-75. For internal migration in the first half of the nineteenth century, see A. Redford *Labour migration in England, 1800-1850* (London, 1926; 2nd edition, Manchester, 1964); E. H. Hunt *British labour history 1815-1914* (London, 1981)

traditional view that mobility was greatly obstructed, if not prevented, by
the settlement and vagrancy laws has proved untenable in the light of
modern research, it is nevertheless clear that the settlement laws in particular influenced migratory behaviour, by providing an institutional framework for inter-parochial movement within which people might choose
between various options. [6]

By the end of the seventeenth century, there were five major routes for
labouring people to move from their parish to another (specified) place
under the law of settlement. First, they could travel with a settlement
certificate, in which the overseers of their parish acknowledged them as
being legally settled in that parish and promised to 'receive back' those
people in case they applied for relief in the parish of destination. Second,
they could go to another parish to work there as a servant for one year.
Third, younger people could serve an apprenticeship in another parish,
which usually lasted seven years. The first option meant that they retained
their original settlement but could only be removed from the parish of
destination when they applied for relief (in legal terms: when they
'became chargeable'), while under the second and third options they
'earned' a new settlement in the chosen parish, with responsibility for
their relief shifting to that parish. A new settlement could also be obtained,
fourth, by renting property above the yearly value of £10 in another parish; and, fifth, by paying local rates in another parish.[7]

It is obvious that the extent to which people might take advantage of
these possibilities was not so much a matter of their own free choice as of
the co-operation of parish officers and other interested parties. For example, a settlement certificate had to be obtained from the overseers of one's
parish. However, these officials could not provide the certificate themselves but had to arrange for it to be issued by two magistrates. For hiring
and service or an apprenticeship in another parish, one had to find a master

pp. 144-57; C. Pooley and J. Turnbull, 'Migration and mobility in Britain from the
eighteenth to the twentieth centuries', *Local Population Studies* 57 (1996) pp. 50-71.
[6] The best account of complicated provisions and the practical effects of the settlement
laws is J. S. Taylor, 'The impact of pauper settlement 1691-1834', *Past and Present* 73
(1976) pp. 42-74; and Slack *English poor law* 27-31, for the pre-1795 situation. See also
W. E. Tate *The parish chest: a study of the records of parochial administration in England*
(3rd edn, Cambridge, 1969; repr. London, 1983) pp. 198-205, 221-6 (and plates XI-XV,
after pp. 206, 222), with useful extracts from (and facsimiles of) settlement certificates,
settlement examinations, removal orders and (pauper) apprenticeship indentures.
[7] There was the further possibility for gaining a new settlement by serving a parish office
in another parish. But this was normally of little importance for the people we are concerned with here.

in that place. Even if the overseers of one's own community were prepared to help with this or indeed arranged for children to be put out to masters in other parishes in order to 'export' potential future claimants, the overseers of those parishes might in turn try to obstruct such arrangements to prevent strangers from gaining a new settlement there.

For anyone not willing to use these institutional channels of migration, there was of course the further option simply to move about without them. But this was risky in itself, especially before 1795 when people leaving their parish without a settlement certificate ran the danger of being sent back home immediately, since up to that year parish officers could remove any newcomer who was 'likely to become chargeable' (technically speaking, by obtaining a removal order for that person, after his or her examination as to the place of settlement, from the nearest magistrate). That threat of removal on mere suspicion was no longer given after 1795, when the privilege of the 'certificate traveller' of being 'removable only if chargeable' was extended to all migrants. In effect, settlement certificates became superfluous. Nevertheless, once people did become chargeable to a parish in which they were not settled they were still supposed to be sent 'home' and to be relieved there.

The fact that parish officers enjoyed wide-ranging discretionary powers in the administration of the settlement laws has led to a reconsideration of the practical impact of pauper settlement in recent research. Some scholars have stressed the selective use of the law by parish officers and suggested that it served as an effective instrument for the regulation and 'monitoring' of people's migration. Others have been less prepared to accept this view and cast doubt on the notion of a close 'surveillance' of the movements of the labouring poor by local vestries. The issue is still under debate, and this is not the place to carry it any further.[8] But most

---

[8] N. Landau, 'The laws of settlement and surveillance of immigration in eighteenth-century Kent', *Continuity and Change* 3 (1988) pp. 391-420; N. Landau, 'The regulation of immigration, economic structures and definitions of the poor in eighteenth-century England', *Historical Journal* 33 (1990) pp. 541-72; K. D. M. Snell, 'Pauper settlement and the right to poor relief in England and Wales', *Continuity and Change* 6 (1991) pp. 375-415; N. Landau, 'The eighteenth-century context of the laws of settlement', *Continuity and Change* 6 (1991) pp. 417-39; K. D. M. Snell, 'Settlement, poor law and the rural historian: new approaches and opportunities', *Rural History* 3 (1992) pp. 145-72; R. Wells, 'Migration, the law, and parochial policy in eighteenth and early nineteenth-century southern England', *Southern History* 15 (1993) pp. 86-139; B. K. Song, 'Agarian policies on pauper settlement and migration, Oxfordshire 1750-1834', *Continuity and Change* 13 (1998) pp. 363-89; B. K. Song, 'Landed interest, local government, and the labour market in England, 1750-1850', *Economic History Review* 51 (1998) pp. 465-88.

would probably agree that it was one of the chief effects of the settlement laws 'to deter the migrant poor from claiming relief - for fear that they might then be moved out'.[9]

However, this deterrent effect was not necessarily all that powerful, given that there was still an alternative to the removal of the claiming migrant, which was in fact of immense practical importance. Out-parish relief could be paid to those resident elsewhere. This meant that people who resided in another parish than that of their settlement were *not* removed but supported at that place, on the basis of informal arrangements between the two parishes concerned. There were two forms. Either the overseers of the 'host' parish advanced the necessary payments, possibly at their discretion, and had them reimbursed by the 'home' parish; or the home parish made the payments itself, whether directly to the recipient or through the hands of others.

In order to appreciate the function of non-resident relief, it is important to understand that parishes which agreed on such arrangements effectively circumvented the legal provisions under the settlement laws. These in principle did not contemplate the relief of a pauper *in* a parish other than that of his or her settlement, even if in practice exceptions were possible, for example under a suspended removal order.

Why parishes should have chosen an alternative route is perhaps best explained by considering their various options as a kind of game, assuming that the major target for both parochial parties was to minimize costs. Let us further assume that on the whole the host parish provided better employment opportunities than the home parish; that the pauper, being the third party, had changed places precisely for that reason; and that his aim was to stay in his host parish, even if he was currently suffering from lack of work, illness or for whatever other reason he had applied for relief.

Under these conditions, both parishes might share the pauper's interest in not being removed and thus be willing to let him stay where he was. The host parish would thereby save the removal expenses, which could easily amount to £8 or more, while the home parish might find it easier to pay him non-resident relief than to have him back, given that his support 'at home' might well have been more expensive.[10] Against this, each party

---

[9] Slack *English poor law* p. 30.
[10] For the cost of removal, not including the considerable fees charged for the settlement examination and the removal order, see K. D. M. Snell *Annals of the labouring poor: social change and agrarian England, 1660-1900* (Cambridge, 1985) p. 18, n. 5. It should be noted, however, that this estimate can only be regarded as an average figure since the actual costs would vary according to the distance between the removing and the receiving

would of course also have to beware of risks and possible countermoves from the other side. For example, if the host parish advanced relief to the pauper, the home parish might take a long time or altogether fail to reimburse it. Conversely, in relying on the assessment by the host parish of the pauper's needs, the overseers of the home parish might find the relief bill unusually high and wonder what part of it had not been paid out to the pauper himself but rather pocketed by the overseers of the host parish.

It is as yet impossible to determine to what extent parishes preferred non-resident relief to removal, since the entire issue remains one of the most serious lacunae in current research on the English poor law. Nevertheless, for our purposes there are two observations which are worth making here. First, the Essex Pauper Letters collected in this volume have nearly all emerged from cases where non-resident relief was involved. Second, the letters themselves, and even more so the correspondence between the overseers and vestry clerks of the parishes concerned with these cases, provide ample evidence of the possible advantages of the practice of non-resident relief. More specifically, the material allows remarkable insights into the motivations and interests of the various parties using the system, and especially into the negotiating power of the poor themselves. In the light of this material the entire issue of the social control of the movements of the labouring poor by means of the settlement laws will have to be reconsidered.

It will be understood that this is not the place for the latter point to be developed any further. It is appropriate, however, to round off the discussion of non-resident relief by briefly summarizing our present knowledge about that practice.

Research in this field has mainly been concerned with the northern counties. There it was found that labourers from rural areas who had moved to the industrial districts were not removed when hit by unemployment during periods of trade depression but received support from their home parishes, since the latter preferred such limited relief payments to the constant burden which returning out-migrants would have imposed.[11] It is highly

---

parishes. At any rate, from 1795 on, all removal expenses were to be met by the removing parish. The fact that they had previously fallen on the parish of settlement need not concern us here, since virtually all Essex Pauper Letters date from after 1795.

[11] M. E. Rose, 'The administration of the poor paw in the West Riding of Yorkshire (1820-1855)' (Univ. of Oxford D. Phil. thesis, 1965) pp. 278-82; J. S. Taylor, 'A different kind of Speenhamland: nonresident relief in the industrial revolution', *Journal of British Studies* 30 (1991) pp. 183-208. There is also a brief discussion in G. R. Boyer, *An economic history of the English poor law, 1750-1850* (Cambridge, 1990) pp. 257-9.

significant in this context that the practice of non-resident relief, despite the fierce disapproval of the Poor Law Commission, was continued under the New Poor Law, most particularly in the northern industrial counties. Thus, in 1839-46 some 20 per cent of those relieved in the West Riding of Yorkshire were non-resident paupers, and in 1855, relief to irremovable paupers made up 37 per cent of total relief expenditure in Lancashire and 33 per cent in the West Riding (after 1846, non-settled paupers could not be removed after five years residence in their host parish).[12]

For the rural areas of the south, however, not only is the extent of non-resident relief unknown, but the whole issue is still largely unexplored. This is perhaps not all that surprising given that the context is more complicated, with the comparative advantages of the parishes concerned being much more difficult to determine.[13] Even so, some evidence, if only for individual years, may be gathered from parochial pauper lists which include non-resident paupers, mainly people receiving regular relief. Fortunately, among the lists surviving for Essex, there are some from parishes with major collections of pauper letters, namely Braintree and Chelmsford (Table 2.1). These admittedly limited figures suggest an order of magnitude of between a fifth and a quarter for the proportion of non-resident paupers among the outdoor poor, which is not unlike the proportions quoted for the northern counties.

It remains to be seen whether these findings will stand in the light of future research. They would seem to provide sufficient evidence to suggest that non-resident relief was by no means an unusual practice, but rather a fairly widespread form of parochial poor law policy. The most important point for our purposes is that it is to this institution of non-resident relief that we owe such pauper letters as we have. Without these inter-parochial arrangements *below* the level of the costly procedures stipulated in the settlement laws, we would have no access whatever to the words of the labouring poor.

---

[12] M. E. Rose, 'Settlement, removal and the new poor law', in *The new poor law in the nineteenth century* ed. D. Fraser (London, 1976) pp. 35-6; D. Ashforth, 'The urban poor law', *ibid.* pp. 144-6; D. Ashforth, 'Settlement and removal in urban areas: Bradford, 1834-71', in *The poor and the city: the English poor law in its urban context, 1834-1914* ed. M. E. Rose (New York, 1985) pp. 58-91.
[13] The best discussion is that in Wells, 'Migration, the law, and parochial policy'.

Table 2.1. Non-resident relief in selected Essex parishes, 1820-32

Parish	Year	Size of sample (cases)	Proportion of paupers residing elsewhere (%)
Braintree	1821	189	22
Chelmsford	1819-20	269	19
	1822-3	267	23
	1826-7	273	17
	1828-9	289	26
Wakes Colne	1821	107	26
Great Dunmow	1832	159	17
Thaxted	1821	165	21
Waltham Holy	1822	116	19
Wanstead	1820	73	21

Note The sample sizes refer to the number of entries on each list, not to the number of people. While the lists do include information on people's spouses and children (the printed ones even in special columns), that information was found to be provided so inconsistently that any attempt at converting the recorded cases into real people would have been subject to large margins of error. For this reason, a simple count of cases was preferred.

Sources ERO D/DO 08, Braintree, 'Poor Book', 1821; D/P 94/18/53, Chelmsford, list of out-door poor, 1819-20 (draft MS); D/P 94/18/55, Chelmsford, list of out-door poor, 1822-3 (printed); D/P 264/18/31, Chelmsford; list of out-door poor, 1826-7 (printed; copy in Braintree overseers' papers); D/P 36/28/3, Chelmsford, list of out-door poor, 1828-9 (printed; copy in Great Coggeshall parish records); D/P 88/18/5, Wakes Colne, pauper list, 1821; D/P 11/18/9, Great Dunmow, pauper list, 1832; D/P 16/12/20, Thaxted, pauper ledger, 1821; D/P 75/18/22, Waltham Holy Cross, pauper list, 1822; D/P 292/8/16, Wanstead, select vestry minutes, April 1820.

Chapter 3
The sample of Essex Pauper Letters
1731-1837

The sample of Essex Pauper Letters which form the body of the present volume does not exist as a physical archive of its own. Rather, it is an artificial collection, drawing on the records of the overseers of the poor of all Essex parishes held today at the Essex Record Office (henceforth ERO) in Chelmsford and at the ERO branches at Colchester and Southend.[1] Other parish records have also been consulted, and material from those other records has been incorporated in the apparatus of the edition. Thus, what now constitutes the final corpus of Essex Pauper Letters and the apparatus is the result of a complex process of assembling and collating thousands of records of various provenances. In order to appreciate the notion of pauper letters as a distinct historical source, it is necessary to place them within the wider field of parish records and then to see where precisely they have survived.

For the years up to 1834, the parish records surviving from the administration of the poor law usually comprise overseers' accounts, rate books and settlement papers (including bastardy and parish apprenticeship papers) of the overseers of the poor, along with vestry minutes when they contain resolutions on poor law matters, orders of poor relief and the like. In addition to these standard records, the keeping of which was statutorily embedded within the control of the justices of the peace, parish records may also contain miscellaneous overseers' records of various types, such as copies of the parochial returns for the first four national censuses (1801-1831), the more detailed of which have featured prominently in modern research into household structure. Another, less well-known type of record is overseers' correspondence, which normally consists of bundles of the letters received by the overseers of the respective parish.[2]

---

[1] Technically speaking, the collection draws on all parish records which are listed in the mammoth Catalogue of Essex Parish Records at the Essex Record Office in Chelmsford.
[2] The classic general survey of the records of parochial poor law administration is W. E. Tate *The parish chest: a study of the records of parochial administration in England* (3rd

Records of overseers' correspondence survive for 55 of the 415 parishes belonging to the historic county of Essex. Taken together, they form a body of evidence comprising some 5,000 pieces, which consists mainly of letters received by the overseers of these parishes from their colleagues (or other parish officers) in other places. For 40 parishes, these records include letters from the poor themselves, which add up to 758 letters dating from 1731 to 1837. That sample of 758 letters, however, is distributed extremely unevenly both between places and over time. It is the purpose of this chapter to describe the structure of the sample in some detail.

Chronological distribution

Beginning with the distribution of the sample over time, the most striking feature is the massive concentration of the material in the 1820s and early 1830s (Figure 3.1). No more than 13 letters (less than 2 per cent) date from before 1800, and only for individual years which are so erratically scattered over time that these pieces must be regarded as isolated cases. From 1801, pauper letters survive from each year, but until the end of the Napoleonic wars there are still rather few. The bulk of the sample falls in the years from 1817 to 1835 (more than 10 letters in each year), which add up to 632 letters (or 83 per cent), with peaks in 1818-19, 1823-9 and 1831-4 (years with more than 20 letters).

It might be tempting to read this chronological pattern as an indication of growing distress, or at least of publicly acknowledged poverty, during the final years of the Old Poor Law. For example, the up-surge in the number of pauper letters after 1817 coincides with the post-war depression. In

edn, Cambridge, 1969; repr. London, 1983) pp. 162-75 (vestry records) and 188-241 (overseers' records). See also W. B. Stephens *Sources for English local history* (Cambridge, 1981) pp. 77-80, 99-113. For Essex in particular, see E. J. Erith, 'Introduction' to *Catalogue of Essex parish records 1240-1894* ed. F. G. Emmison (ERO Publications, 7; 2nd edn, Chelmsford 1966) pp. 13-16 (vestry records) and 20-32 (overseers' records). Strikingly enough, Erith's excellent survey of Essex parish records does not mention any records of overseers' correspondence, let alone pauper letters. Copies of early census returns found among Essex overseers' records include those for Horndon on the Hill 1811 and Braintree 1821 which were used as early as 1969 in Lalsett's first general investigation into mean household size in England: P. Laslett, 'Size and structure of the household in England over three centuries', *Population Studies* 23 (1969) pp. 199-223, revised and extended as P. Laslett, 'Mean household size in England since the sixteenth century', in *Household and family in past time* ed. P. Laslett and R. Wall (Cambridge, 1972) pp. 125-58.

Essex, as in other southern agricultural counties, poor relief expenditure remained at a high level throughout the 1820s and early 1830s. But an explanation along these lines is hardly convincing. For if we were to assume that the volume of paupers' correspondence increased during times of high prices, food shortages and particular economic hardship, we should expect the highest numbers of letters to be in the years 1795-6, 1800-2, and 1811-13, whereas in fact only very few letters survive for these years.[3] It might be argued, of course, that growing distress did not immediately translate into an increase in pauper letters, but only with a certain time lag and after the recurrent experience of crisis years. But the problem is that the original volume of pauper correspondence is not known. All that we have are the numbers of pauper letters *surviving* in our 40 sample parishes.

Figure 3.1. Essex Pauper Letters 1731-1837: number of letters per year

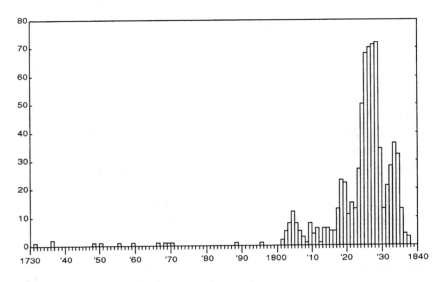

Source Appendix, List A.3.

[3] D. A. Baugh, 'The cost of poor relief in south-east England, 1790-1834', *Economic History Review* 28 (1975) pp. 54-7; T. Sokoll *Household and family among the poor: the case of two Essex communities in the late eighteenth and early nineteenth centuries* (Bochum, 1993) pp. 130-41, 149-53, 213-28; D. Eastwood *Governing rural England: tradition and transformation in local government 1780-1840* (Oxford, 1994) pp. 134-41.

Within that sample, however, the distribution of pauper letters over time is not even across the 40 sample parishes (Table 3.1). The earlier pieces mainly relate to those places for whom only a few pauper letters have survived, which is particularly true of the pre-1800 letters (except for the 1755 letter to St Botolph, Colchester). The middle-sized collections of Rochford and Upminster are also heavily skewed towards the years before 1815. By contrast, in Braintree, Chelmsford and the two Colchester parishes of St Botolph and St Peter, which are the parishes with the largest numbers of pauper letters, the material is most heavily concentrated in the 1820s and 1830s. However, even in the latter cases record survival is by no means even over time. In the two Colchester parishes, there are conspicuous gaps in what might originally have been continuous series. In Chelmsford, the largest of all parochial samples, we find 1 letter in 1820, 3 letters scattered across the first half of 1823, and then, beginning in November 1823, an extremely dense sequence of letters which covers virtually every month but suddenly breaks off after June 1829.[4]

The explanation of this erratic pattern of record survival is scarcely straightforward. That there were good reasons for the overseers to keep the letters they received from paupers residing elsewhere, at least in those cases where such people were supported, should be clear from our discussion in the foregoing chapter. But there is no reason why records, however well they were kept originally, should be expected to have survived to the present day. On the contrary, as every student of English parish records knows only too well, there are lots of documents which are incomplete or defective, while lots of others have been destroyed or otherwise lost. This is particularly true of such types of record as settlement certificates, removal orders, settlement examinations or indeed letters received by the overseers, whether from paupers or other people, all of which seem to have been kept in files of loose papers of various physical types (on pins, in bundles, boxes etc.), whereas overseers' accounts and poor rate assessments or vestry minutes were normally entered in proper books. Files of loose papers were sometimes bound up into books, and occasionally the overseers made lists or registers of the papers of a particular type. Thus, for some Essex parishes we possess lists of the settlement or apprenticeship papers which they received or issued over a

---

[4] For details, see the List of Essex Pauper Letters at the beginning of this volume.

Table 3.1. Essex Pauper Letters, 1731-1837: distribution by parish of receipt and dates

Parish of receipt	Total number of letters	Chronological spread of letters		Number of undated letters
		1731-99[a]	1800-1837	
Aveley	9	-	1825, 1831-3	1
Great Bardfield	3	-	1835-6	1
Braintree	68	-	1823, 1828-35	2
Steeple Bumpstead	13	-	1816-17, 1825/37	-
Great Burstead	4	-	1833-4	2
Canewdon	1	-	1825	-
Chelmsford	180	-	1820, 1823-9	-
Great Chishall	1	1788	-	-
Great Coggeshall	1	1750	-	-
Colchester, St Botolph	116	1755	1813-21, 1826-30, 1833-6	2
Colchester, St James	15	-	1810-11, 1813-14, 1817, 1833	2
Colchester, St Peter	175	-	1817-29, 1832-4	1
Great Dunmow	2	-	1818	-
Little Dunmow	2	-	1817	1
Halstead	2	-	1835	-
Havering-atte-Bower	3	1795	1803-4	-
Kirby-le-Soken	19	-	1818, 1827-9, 1832-5	-
Lexden	1	-	1834	-
Maldon, St Mary	5	-	1811-13	-
Mayland	1	-	1822	-
Mundon	17	-	1816, 1820-1, 1823, 1831-4	3
Navestock	1	-	1829	-
White Notley	2	-	1831	1
Peldon	1	-	-	-
Purleigh	2	-	1822, 1825	1
Rainham	9	1748	1801, 1804-6, 1815	-
Rayleigh	22	-	1809, 1825-6, 1828, 1831-5	4
Rochford	27	-	1803-4, 1806-7, 1809-11, 1823, 1830	-
Stanford Rivers	1	-	1824	-
Stansted Mountfitchet	1	-	1813	-
Theydon Garnon	7	1731, 1736, 1759	1802, 1808, 1819	-
Theydon Mount	3	1769	1831	-
West Thurrock	2	1770	1809	-
Tolleshunt D'Arcy	1	-	1801	-
Upminster	29	-	1802-7, 1813-14, 1819, 1834	-
Little Waltham	1	1768	-	-
Wanstead	1	1766	-	-
South Weald	4	-	1818-19, 1825	-
Woodford	2	-	1836	-
Wormingford	4	-	1824-5, 1830	-
TOTAL (no. of letters)	758	13	724	21

[a] Within this column, there is one letter for each given year, except 1736 for which two letters survive.

particular period.[5] But not a single case has been found in which a file of overseers' correspondence was bound up; neither does any register of such correspondence or letter-book survive. All that survive are a few references to individual pauper letters in parish records, as in those cases where the payment of the postage of a received letter has been recorded in the overseers' account books (**281, 299, 753**); or where a letter is explicitly mentioned in the vestry minutes (**314, 316, 320, 332, 337, 351, 623**). One pauper letter has come down to us only in the form of a copy made by the overseer (**656**), and another which does survive in the original was also copied into the vestry book in full (**80**).

The parish records do not, however, give any clue as to why pauper letters should have survived in large numbers in one case but not in another. For example, in none of the vestry minutes consulted is there any record of resolutions or agreements relating to the question of how the files of overseers' correspondence, let alone the pauper letters within them, should be handled. In other words, it would seem that pauper letters have survived as erratically as other types of parish records. As to their chronological spread, the fact that the vast majority of them survive only from the 1820s and early 1830s may be explained by the growing professionalization of poor law administration. Following the 1819 Vestry Act (59 Geo. III, c. 22) which, interestingly enough, also ordered the proper keeping of parish records, parishes increasingly came to establish select vestries and to appoint salaried assistant overseers and vestry clerks.[6] Thus, it is probably no accident that some of the largest samples of pauper letters come from parishes which made great efforts to improve administrative efficiency. For example, the select vestries of Braintree and St Peter, Colchester, were extremely active and conscientious in the business of poor relief, as is neatly witnessed in the painstaking detail with which the decisions on many individual applications have been recorded in their books. These include several cases of paupers living elsewhere, some of whom had

---

[5] Registers of settlement certificates include those for All Saints, Colchester, 1723-1800 (ERO, D/P 200/13/1A-B) and Harwich, 1693-1801 (ERO, D/P 170/13/1). Apprenticeship registers include those for Holy Trinity, Colchester, 1723-1800 (ERO, D/P 322/14) and Manningtree, 1800-35. There is a settlement examinations book for St Runwald, Colchester, 1818-32, which is a calendar of the examinations taken in that parish in those years (ERO, D/P 77/13/4), and a settlement and apprenticeship register for Wivenhoe, 1689-1819 (ERO, D/P 277/13).

[6] Eastwood *Governing rural England* pp. 34-42, 175-8.

actually sent a pauper letter.[7] It is also striking that the parishes with large samples of pauper letters seem to have had particularly diligent and long-serving parish officers. Among these, the most notable ones are Robert Alden, overseer of St Peter in Colchester, who is in evidence as an addressee of pauper letters from May 1823 to April 1835; James Read, vestry clerk in Chelmsford, in evidence from June 1824 to May 1829; and William Chisolm, overseer in St Botolph, Colchester, in evidence from August 1826 to August 1828. But again, this point must not be taken too far, as even in these cases record survival may be uneven. For example, the conspicuous gap from June 1829 to January 1832 in the pauper letter sample for St Peter in Colchester falls right in the middle of Robert Alden's long term of office.[8]

The fact that pauper letters run out after 1834, is of course due to the end of the Old Poor Law with the Poor Law Amendment Act of 1834. The 20 pieces surviving from the years 1835 to 1837 (less than 3 per cent of the sample) are odd survivals of the old system. This is not to say that there were no pauper letters under the New Poor Law. On the contrary, such letters do exist, apparently in considerable numbers, among the papers of the poor law unions and the correspondence of assistant poor law commissioners and inspectors, the administrative bodies established in 1834. But they have not been considered here, for the simple reason that the present volume is restricted to pauper letters under the Old Poor Law. The equivalent records under the New Poor Law deserve research - and editorial effort - in their own right.[9]

[7] In the present edition, such traces of pauper letter writers in other parish records, most notably in overseers' accounts and vestry minutes, have all been documented in the historical-critical apparatus underneath the respective letter. See chapters 4 and 5 below. For the poor law policy of the select vestry in Braintree, see Sokoll *Household and family among the poor* pp. 230-5.

[8] The number and chronology of pauper letters addressed to these or other people are readily visible from the List of Essex Pauper Letters at the beginning of this volume.

[9] The material is to be found within the files of the Department of Health at the Public Record Office (PRO, M.H. 12 and 32). See Stephens *Sources for English local history* pp. 107-111, for a brief summary of poor law records after 1834. For an illuminating case study, with a full transcript of four letters from the PRO files, see G. C. Smith, "'The poor in blindness": letters from Mildenhall, Wiltshire, 1835-6', in *Chronicling poverty: the voices and strategies of the English poor, 1640-1840* ed. T. Hitchcock, P. King and P. Sharpe (London, 1997) pp. 211-38.

Geographical distribution (i): places of receipt (and archival survival)

The distribution of the sample of Essex Pauper Letters is not only extremely uneven over time, but also between places (Table 3.1). There are 12 parishes for whom only one letter survives, 13 parishes with 2-4 letters, and another 4 parishes with 5-9 letters, which together hold no more than 77 letters (10 per cent), while the remaining 11 parishes with 10 or more letters share between them 681 letters (90 per cent of the sample). It is noticeable that the latter, henceforth referred to as the Master Sample of Essex Pauper Letters, relate almost exclusively to larger places. Colchester, featuring with three of its most populous parishes (St Botolph, St James and St Peter), was the most important (and oldest) Essex town, Chelmsford the administrative centre of the county. Braintree was an old market town and, like Colchester, a former centre of the woollen cloth industry. Rayleigh and Rochford, both on the old road from London to the latter, were also old market towns, if of lesser importance. Upminster was a growing residential parish about 15 miles from London; and Steeple Bumpstead a large village on the road from Saffron Walden to Sudbury in the neighbouring county of Suffolk. Only Kirby-le-Soken and Mundon were remote villages, both on the coast (Map 3.1).

On the face of it, it seems plausible that the sample of Essex Pauper Letters should be heavily skewed towards larger places. Other things being equal, one would expect a populous town to carry a larger number of paupers than a small village, which would entail a larger body of overseers' correspondence, and therefore a larger number of pauper letters. However, given that nearly all pauper letters came from people who lived in another place than the one they wrote to, the association would appear to be less straightforward. In fact, on the assumption that their senders were primarily people who had chosen to move elsewhere in search of better employment opportunities (and to stay there after having become chargeable), we might as well expect the opposite pattern of pauper letters typically being sent *from* larger towns into small remote villages.[10]

---

[10] There is one letter in the sample which was not received in the parish in which it has survived (Great Coggeshall), but was sent from there *to* the parish of St John the Baptist in Hereford (**280**). For the sake of simplicity, it is not distinguished from the remainder of the sample in the ensuing discussion even though, strictly speaking, it ought to be excluded when referring to the places of receipt or the places of sender within the sample.

Map 3.1. Essex Pauper Letters, 1731-1837: places of receipt

Source Table 3.1.

Therefore, in trying to assess the possible causes of the geographical distribution of the sample, three factors need to be considered. First, to what extent had the senders of pauper letters been 'pulled' to the places in which they resided? Second, were the conditions in the parishes in which they were settled really so bad that they had been 'pushed' out? The conditions 'at home', however, would not only involve economic factors like high rents or unemployment but also the extent of welfare provision within the community. For example, people might have been more inclined to move elsewhere when they knew that their home parish was prepared to give relief to non-resident paupers (or at least was not opposed to it in principle). Third, therefore, we also want to know what the poor law administration in the home parishes was like.

However, before we go into the details, it should be stressed that the consideration of these points must not be taken too far. Apart from the fact that we simply lack the data for any of the three factors to be assessed conclusively, it would be dangerous to expect that the evidence of labour migration and poor law policy could ever be sufficient to explain the distribution of pauper letters across our sample. This is because the sample of those non-resident paupers whose letters happen to have survived can in no way be regarded as representing a cross-section of all Essex paupers who had moved elsewhere.[11] This is not to deny that there are numerous examples, especially in the letters from London, which clearly reveal migratory motivations which may readily be accounted for in terms of either 'pull' or 'push' effects; while others, no less clearly, show the influence of the poor law, for example in that the overseers were trying to 'export' paupers to more affluent places in the hope thereby to reduce their relief expenditure. Against these, however, stand lots of other examples where the circumstances of the case remain completely unclear so that they cannot be subsumed under any category other than mere contingency. Therefore, if the ensuing discussion involves a certain amount of speculation about some of the factors which might conceivably have influenced the geographical distribution of the sample of Essex Pauper Letters, it must always be borne in mind that it is basically meant to serve as a simple statistical description of that sample and not as an explanatory account of migration patterns.

Let us return, then, to the 40 parishes for which pauper letters have survived, and to the question of their economic condition and poor law regime. As already said, a conclusive answer is impossible, since there is only very little and imperfect statistical evidence - unemployment figures, for example, are not available at all. Nevertheless, some crude demographic and poor-law measures may be obtained from the census data for 1801 (and 1831) in conjunction with the *Abstract of the Returns relative to the Expense and Maintenance of the Poor* for 1802. The data of the latter source, though its reliability has often been questioned, provides the most comprehensive set of official poor law statistics before 1834, which are of particular interest for our purposes in that they distinguish not only between 'indoor' and 'outdoor' paupers (and the corresponding heads of expenditure), but also between 'permanent' paupers, 'occasional' paupers,

---

[11] The same is true of settlement certificates and removal orders which survive in far higher numbers than pauper letters. All attempts at using such records for the analysis of migration are severely restricted by the completely erratic patterns of record survival. The records may survive by thousands. But as long as we do not know the original number of documents (in statistical terms: the record population 'at risk'), which unfortunately is the rule, there is no way of telling how much is much.

and 'persons relieved, not being parishioners'.[12] The proportion of indoor paupers (and, by implication, of indoor relief) may be regarded as an indication of social control in the administration of the poor law, in that a high proportion would suggest a stronger tendency towards the application of the 'workhouse test' in the parish concerned, while high proportions of 'occasional' and 'non-parish' paupers would point to a more lenient approach. Similarly, it would be reasonable to expect that a parish strictly opposed to hosting out-parish paupers was likely, in order to set examples, to spend large amounts on removals or on law suits regarding the relief of paupers whose settlement was disputed between the parishes concerned, which would involve a high proportion of legal expenses in total poor law expenditure. Needless to say, these are extremely crude measures the interpretation of which must not be carried too far. There is also the problem that is not clear to what extent the returned figures of occasional and non-parish paupers are subject to faults resulting from double-counting. On the other hand, there does not to be any reason to believe that they are systematically distorted. The ratio between permanent and occasional paupers, for example, has been shown to be consistent on a county basis, which suggests that the figures are more reliable than previously thought.[13]

It is convenient to begin with the average figures for the entire sample compared to those for Essex and England (bottom panel of Table 3.2). Like other predominantly agricultural counties, Essex had a comparatively high proportion of paupers. Roughly speaking, one in six of her population was on relief in 1802, as compared to one in eight in England at large.[14] With an overall mean in *per capita* poor law expenditure of £0.81 and an average poor rate of 6s (30p) in the pound, Essex lay 62 and 40 per cent above the national average. However, expenditure per pauper (£4.84) was only 16 per cent higher, and with respect to the proportions of indoor

---

[12] PP 1803-4 XIII *Abstract of answers and returns relative to the expense and maintenance of the poor*. The problems of this source, which was first dismissed as unreliable by S. and B. Webb *English poor law history, II: the last hundred years* (London, 1929; repr. 1963) statistical appendix, have probably been exaggerated in previous research. It is striking that a proper numerical assessment of the data is still lacking.

[13] K. Williams *From pauperism to poverty* (London, 1981) pp. 37-42 and 147-55.

[14] The figure for Essex was just above the average for the agricultural counties. There were six counties in which the proportion of paupers in the population exceeded that for Essex (by order of magnitude: Sussex, Wiltshire, Berkshire, Oxfordshire, Buckinghamshire and Suffolk). See Williams *Pauperism to poverty* pp. 149-50, Table 4.2. The slight discrepancies of Williams's figures from those given in our Table 3.2 are due to the fact that his category of poor law expenditure excludes all administrative and other expenses which were not strictly applied to relief purposes.

Table 3.2. Essex sample parishes: measures of population and poor law administration, 1802-3

	Population in 1801	Population increase by 1831	Indoor paupers as proportion of all paupers %	Indoor relief as proportion of poor law expenditure %	Non-parish paupers as proportion of all paupers %	Legal expenses as proportion of poor law expenditure %	Proportion of paupers in the population %	Poor law expenditure per pauper £	Poor law expenditure per head of population £	Poor rate s/£
		(1801 = 100)								
Master sample										
Braintree	2821	121	12	27	17	5	26	3.06	0.78	14.8
Steeple Bumpstead	787	137	-	-	1	2	18	6.19	1.09	8.5
Chelmsford	3755	145	13	65	46	2	29	1.97	0.57	9.5
Colchester, St Botolph	1709	150	3	18	8	4	15	2.42	0.37	7.0
Colchester, St James	1058	136	10	18	8	0	13	4.71	0.59	11.5
Colchester, St Peter	1358	135	8	32	7	4	17	4.82	0.84	20.0
Kirby-le-Soken	664	146	9	12	4	3	12	7.47	0.88	6.3
Mundon	283	96	-	-	10	-	14	7.72	1.06	4.6
Rayleigh	879	152	4	28	29	9	19	4.64	0.90	8.2
Rochford	1228	124	27	10	14	2	9	10.02	0.90	7.3
Upminster	765	135	15	56	4	2	26	4.17	1.08	4.5
Comparative figures **Means**										
Essex sample (40 parishes)	1050	136	8.5	25.4	19.6	4.2	15.0	5.01	0.75	6.8
Essex	545	139	6.6	22.3	15.0	3.8	16.8	4.84	0.81	6.0
England	578	157	7.0	24.5	16.1	4.4	12.0	4.15	0.50	4.3

Source PP 1803-4, XIII, *Abstract of the returns relative to the expense and maintenance of the poor*; PP 1802, VII, *Census 1801*.

Note The numbers of paupers on which the figures are based include indoor paupers, outdoor paupers, paupers relieved occasionally, and 'persons relieved not being parishioners'. While the inclusion of the latter group is important with respect to the poor law policy of the individual parishes, it would lead to distortions on the overall sample and county levels, and certainly to double-counting on the national level. For this reason, non-parish paupers have been excluded in the comparative figures in the bottom panel for the proportion of paupers in the population and poor law expenditure per pauper.

(6.6 per cent) and non-parish paupers (16.1 per cent) and the respective heads of expenditure (22.3 and 3.8 per cent) the differences between the county and national averages were only marginal.

The overall means for the 40 sample parishes with pauper letters are in turn not very different from those for the whole of Essex, though they are all (except poor law expenditure per head) somewhat higher. Only in population size do the sample parishes tend to be atypically high, being nearly twice as populous as the average Essex (and English) parish. This, however, is hardly surprising, given the heavy weight within the sample of Braintree, Chelmsford and the three Colchester parishes. The higher sample values for the poor rate and for the proportion of non-parish paupers might suggest that the sample parishes were perhaps more 'open' towards arrangements of out-parish relief, but the proportion of paupers in the population is lower than the county average.

Turning to the figures for the 11 individual parishes of the Master Sample (top panel of Table 3.2), there is, of course, bound to arise more variation than on the aggregate levels of county and national averages. This is especially true of the measures derived from the returns for the numbers of paupers in the various categories, which, as already said, must be treated with caution. For example, it is highly questionable that almost half of all paupers relieved in Chelmsford should have been people who were settled elsewhere. Similarly, it seems difficult to believe that indoor relief in Chelmsford amounted to 65 per cent of all poor law expenditure, when only 13 per cent of the paupers were indoor paupers, even if we allow for the fact that indoor relief was notoriously more expensive than out-relief (roughly speaking, £12 per pauper as compared to £3).[15] The same discrepancy is in evidence for Rayleigh and Upminster, while Rochford poses the opposite puzzle, with a large proportion of indoor paupers and a small value of indoor relief.

The financial data are probably far more reliable than the numbers of paupers in the various categories, not least because at the time they were much easier to determine than numbers of people. In fact, both expenses and poor rates must, in most cases, have been readily available in the accounts and rate books of the overseers which were settled and audited at half-yearly intervals. For this reason, the most robust measures supplied in Table 3.2 (apart from the population data in the first two columns)

---

[15] J. R. Poynter *Society and pauperism: English ideas on poor relief, 1795-1834* (London, 1969) p. 189.

are probably those for poor law expenditure per head and for the poor rate (in the last two columns). Interestingly enough, it is precisely here that we encounter the most striking findings.

Most of the parishes within the Master Sample suffered from very high poor rates. Only in Mundon, which was exceptional also in that its population declined, if only slightly, between 1801 and 1831, and Upminster, did the poor rate fall below the county average, while it was just above average in Kirby-le-Soken. All other places had poor rates well above the Essex average of 6s (30p) in the pound, most notably the three big towns of Braintree, Chelmsford and Colchester (except the parish of St Botolph, which is somewhat surprising), with values between 11.5s (57.5p) and 20s (£1). This is all the more remarkable since these three towns had comparatively modest *per capita* poor law expenditure. The low expenditure for the three Colchester parishes may perhaps be explained by the fact that the proportion of paupers in the population was relatively modest, whereas Braintree and Chelmsford had very high proportions of paupers (with an exceptionally high proportion of non-parish paupers in the latter case). At any rate, it is the combination of low to average poor law expenditure with very high poor rates, whatever the relative size of the group of paupers, which is of particular interest, since this suggests that the financial burden of relief was shouldered by a comparatively small section of the community.[16]

It might be argued, therefore, that the substantial householders who made the major financial contribution towards the parochial welfare fund, and who were often the dominant members of the vestry, had good reason to 'push' their paupers to more prosperous places. It would nevertheless be rash to conclude that this was the reason why the Master Sample parishes received so many pauper letters. While a certain proportion of their paupers resided elsewhere, a certain proportion of their own resident population were in turn paupers from other places, a number of whom even sent letters to their home parishes.

[16] See the discussion in Sokoll *Household and family among the poor* pp. 224-5, where it is shown, on the basis of an examination of poor rate assessments in conjunction with census data, that in Braintree in 1816, only about 5 per cent of all householders shared between them some 75 per cent of the poor rate. Unfortunately, apart from a similar discussion for the agricultural village of Ardleigh in 1796 (*ibid.*, pp. 124-30), no further analyses of that kind have as yet been undertaken.

Geographical distribution (ii): places of sender

In order to carry this point further, we may now turn from the places in which the letters have survived to those from which they were originally sent. In so doing we will also widen our perspective, since most letters came from outside Essex, some from as far away as Gibraltar. But we begin with locations within Essex, since they provide a convenient connection with our discussion in the previous section.

Within the sample of Essex Pauper Letters, 231 letters (30 per cent) came from 44 places within Essex (Map 3.2). The distribution of letters across those places is rather uneven, with 177 letters (77 per cent) coming from only 8 places (the ones from which 5 or more letters were sent).

Map 3.2. Essex Pauper Letters, 1731-1837: places of sender within Essex

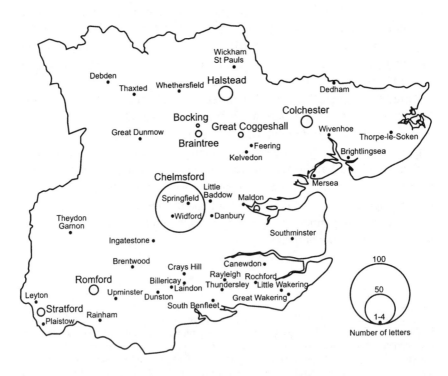

Source Appendix, List A.1.

They include Bocking, an industrial village adjoining (and, in social and economic terms, effectively belonging to) Braintree, and Coggeshall and Halstead, two old market towns, which had all been important woollen cloth producers in the seventeenth and eighteenth centuries; Romford, a market town close to London; and Stratford which was gradually being absorbed into the London area. While those five places did not receive pauper letters themselves, the remaining three did. These were Braintree, Chelmsford and Colchester, which in fact belong to the Master Sample of the recipients.

In all, just over half of the 231 pauper letters from Essex (117 letters) came from places belonging to the Master Sample, 80 per cent of which (92 letters) were sent in turn to places within the Master Sample. Chelmsford, for example, was not only the largest recipient of pauper letters, but also the place within Essex from which the majority of them were sent (83 letters). Thus, there was a fair amount of circulation of letters within the Master Sample, which means that at least within Essex the notion of pauper letters having been sent from poorer to more prosperous places does not make much sense. However, the exchange of letters between places was actually more limited than must appear from these overall figures. On closer inspection, it turns out that the movement of letters between individual places was rather uneven, while the amount of exchange looks somewhat different when allowance is made for the numbers of senders. Thus, there were 23 letters from Chelmsford to St Botolph in Colchester, but only 4 in the opposite direction; but the former came from only three people (John Hall sent 15 letters, his daughter Sarah Hall 7, and Thomas Strutt 1 letter) and the latter from two (Lucy Nevill and Harriet Twin, with 2 letters each). There were 54 letters from Chelmsford to St Peter in Colchester, but again from only two people (William James with 53 letters and James Tracey), and none at all in the opposite direction.[17]

Turning to the regional distribution of all places of sender, it is prudent to make the same distinction between a simple count of letters by place of sender and an alternative count which allows for the number of senders in each place, county or larger region. This is because the distribution of letters between senders was extremely uneven (Table 3.3). Nearly two thirds of all senders provide just one letter, but this total is less than a quarter of all letters, whereas the small group of senders with 7 letters or more (9 per cent of all senders) produced nearly half of all letters (47 per

---

[17] For details, see List A. 1 in the Appendix.

cent). Moreover, it is important to note that a sender is not necessarily one person.[18] There are several couples with letters under alternating names, like Davey and Susannah Rising in Halstead who sent 10 letters to Chelmsford from February 1824 to January 1827, of which 1 was written in his name (**108**), 2 in hers (**131, 185**), and the remaining 7 in the names of both, where his name was given first in 3 (**112, 129, 208**) and hers in 4 cases (**142, 153, 169, 202**). Regardless of who signed as responsible for any particular letter, it is their common case which is stated throughout all letters. For this reason, married couples have been counted as *one* sender. So have couples where the husband died and the widow, even though she wrote on her own behalf, effectively took up the case from her husband (as with James and Mary Smith, writing from London to Braintree in 1828-9: **28, 34**). For similar reasons, two pairs of siblings have also been counted as one sender each (Samuel and James Moore: **324, 329, 331, 336, 337**; Phillis Webb: **21, 22, 31**, and her brother William Webb: **33**). In all, a quarter of all letters came from couples and pairs of siblings.

Naturally, married couples consist of men and women. When the remaining individual senders are distinguished by gender, it appears that the shares of male and female senders are almost equal (Table 3.4). This may seem surprising, given that literacy rates were considerably lower for females before the mid-nineteenth century.[19] But pauper letters were not necessarily written by the senders themselves. The problem of the social practice of literacy which is involved here will be discussed in the following chapter. In present context, it is sufficient to say that the fact that about as many pauper letters came from women as from men suggests that women who could not write do not appear to have had particular problems in finding people to write a letter for them.

Returning to the geographical distribution of letters and their senders, it is noticeable that, for all necessary specifications, the emerging picture is nevertheless remarkably clear-cut (Table 3.5, Map 3.3). Multiple letter writers were particularly common in London, as can be seen from its significantly lower proportion of senders than of letters. The southern, midland and northern counties tended to host senders with rather fewer letters, which explains why their proportions of letters were lower than

---

[18] For the following examples, see also List A. 2 in the Appendix.
[19] R. S. Schofield, 'Dimensions of illiteracy, 1750-1850', *Explorations in Economic History* 10 (1972-3) p. 445. For the converse pattern after 1860, when women were ahead of men in most of the southern counties, see D. Vincent *Literacy and popular culture: England 1750-1914* (Cambridge, 1989) pp. 24-5.

Table 3.3 Essex Pauper Letters, 1731-1837: number of letters by type of sender

Number of letters	Type of sender				Letters from		
	Individual	Married couple	Both types		Individuals	Married couples	Both types
Detailed breakdown							
1	162	4	166		162	4	166
2	38	5	144		76	10	86
3	11	2	13		33	6	39
4	10	4[a]	14		40	16	56
5	2	2[b]	4		10	10	20
6	6	-	6		36	-	36
7	5	1	6		35	7	42
8	2	-	2		16	-	16
9	1	-	1		9	-	9
10	1	4	5		10	40	50
11	1	-	1		11	-	11
13	-	1	1		-	13	13
15	2	-	2		30	-	30
17	1	1	2		17	17	34
18	2	-	2		36	-	36
27	-	1	1		-	27	27
34	-	1	1		-	34	34
53	1	-	1		53	-	53
Summary				%			%
1	162	4	166	61.3	162	4	166	21.9
2-3	49	7	56	20.7	109	16	125	16.5
4-6	18	6	24	8.9	86	26	112	14.8
7-9	8	1	9	3.3	60	7	67	8.8
10+	8	8	16	5.9	157	131	288	38.0
TOTAL	245	26	271	100.1	574	184	758	100.0
%	90.4	9.6	100.0	-	75.7	24.3	100.0	-

[a] Including one brother and sister (William and Phillis Webb); Ann Bacon and Sarah Davis are counted within this group under their first marriages as Ann Lester and Sarah Withnall.
[b] Including two brothers (Samuel and James Moore).

Source Appendix, List A.2.

Table 3.4. Essex Pauper Letters, 1731-1837: gender of senders

	Letters from London		Letters from elsewhere		All letters	
	Number of senders	%	Number of senders	%	Number of senders	%
Male	30	38.0	89	46.4	119	43.9
Female	33	41.8	81	42.2	114	42.1
Couple/siblings	12[a]	15.2	14[b]	7.3	26	9.6
Unknown	4	5.1	8	4.2	12	4.4
TOTAL	79	100.1	192	100.1	271	100.0

[a] Includes one pair of two brothers.
[b] Includes one pair of brother and sister.

Source Appendix, List A.2.

Note Following the breakdown of senders in Table 3.3, joint letters from married couples and pairs of sibli
are counted in a separate category.

those of senders. This apart, however, there were only minor discrepancies so that the overall distribution is more or less the same on both counts. The overwhelming majority of the Essex Pauper Letters (91 per cent, with 85 per cent of all senders) came from Essex, London, the other home counties and East Anglia.

The comparatively large number of letters from Suffolk would seem to reflect the close links of Essex with her neighbouring county within the woollen textile industry of East Anglia in the seventeenth and eighteenth centuries. The same may hold, though to a lesser extent, for Norfolk, where the common industrial background is actually in evidence in the references to weaving in letters from Norwich (**66, 515**).[20]

Kent features mainly in respect of places along her border with Essex or on her northern coast. Most places of sender in the southern counties are also on or pretty close to the coast. Several of their senders were soldiers or mariners or the wives of such people, which is also true of the letters which were sent from Ireland (**601, 602, 605, 606, 608**, all from Mary Harris) and from Gibraltar (**95**), the furthest away of all places of sender.

As to the midland and the northern counties, it is noticeable that, although there are a few letters from Nottingham, Sheffield, Leeds and Gateshead (the southern outpost of Newcastle), the biggest industrial centres like Birmingham, Manchester and Liverpool have none at all. This, however, is hardly surprising, given the patterns of internal migration in England in the first half of the nineteenth century. People from the southern agricultural counties did not migrate to the industrial regions of the north to any large extent. Those few who did move there may well have prospered well enough not to be forced to apply to their home parishes for relief. Otherwise, for people who wanted to leave Essex, by far the most obvious destination was London.[21]

[20] See G. Unwin, 'The history of the cloth industry in Suffolk', in *Studies in economic history: the collected papers of George Unwin* ed. R. H. Tawney (London, 1926) pp. 262-301; P. Mantoux *The industrial revolution in the eighteenth century* (London, 1928; repr. 1964) pp. 50-4; D. C. Coleman, 'An innovation and its diffusion: the "new draperies"', *Economic History Review*, 2nd ser. 22 (1969) pp. 417-29; D. C. Coleman, 'Growth and decay during the industrial revolution: the case of East Anglia', *Scandinavian Economic History Review* 10 (1962) pp. 115-27; M. J. Daunton *Progress and poverty: an economic and social history of Britain 1700-1850* (Oxford, 1995) pp. 151-3.
[21] A. Redford *Labour migration in England, 1800-1850* (London, 1926; repr. Manchester, 1964); S. Pollard, 'Labour in Great Britain', in *The Cambridge economic history of Europe*, vol. 7: *The industrial economies: capital, labour, and enterprise* ed. P. Mathias and M. M. Postan (Cambridge, 1978) pp. 105-12; P. L. Garside, 'London and the home counties', in

Map 3.3. Essex Pauper Letters, 1731-1837: places of sender

Source Appendix, List A.1.

Table 3.5. Essex Pauper Letters, 1731-1837: regional distribution of places of sender

	Number of places	Number of senders[a]	%	Number of letters	%
Essex	44	87	30.7	231	30.5
London	1	79	27.9	270	35.6
Home countries (less London and Essex)					
Hertfordshire	4	6		17	
Middlesex	5	5		8	
Surrey	3	5		6	
Kent	9	15		42	
Subtotal	21	31	11.0	73	9.6
East Anglia					
Cambridgeshire	3	5		23	
Suffolk	13	25		64	
Norfolk	6	13		29	
Subtotal	22	43	15.2	116	15.3
South					
Sussex	3	3		3	
Hampshire	6	5		10	
Gloucestershire	1	1		1	
Devon	1	2		2	
Cornwall	1	1		1	
Subtotal	12	12	4.2	17	2.2
Midlands and North					
Leicestershire	3	3		5	
Nottinghamshire	1	1		1	
Yorkshire	3	3		4	
Durham	3	3		3	
Subtotal	10	10	3.5	13	1.7
Overseas					
Ireland	4	1		5	
Gibraltar	1	1		1	
Subtotal	5	2	0.7	6	0.8
Unkown	-	19 (25)[b]	6.7 (8.8)	32	4.2
TOTAL	115	283	99.9	758	99.9

[a] Including double counts of senders writing from places in different counties.
[b] Six senders with unknown place for whom other letters with known place have survived.

Source Appendix, List A.1.

London was indeed the most important of all places of sender, contributing more than a third of the sample. As already said, it hosted a large proportion of people who sent numerous letters, including George and Ann Craddock and David and Sarah Rivenall, the most prolific of all letter-sending married couples (with respectively 27 and 34 letters).[22] It is also interesting that the percentage of letters from women was a little higher in London than in the remainder of the sample (Table 3.4).

London was of course conspicuous by its sheer size, not just in terms of its estimated population of nearly 1.4 million in 1820, but also in terms of space, with an abundance of parishes even when those within the City are not counted individually, so that it is in a way misleading to treat it as a single place of sender. Chelsea and Kensington were entirely different from Bethnal Green or Spitalfields. In order to relate the letters to the social topography of the metropolis, particular care has therefore been taken to identify the location of senders in London (Tables 3.6 and 3.7).[23]

The fact that some people sent more letters than others again leads to discrepancies in the regional spread between senders and letters which are, of course, particularly noticeable when comparing individual parishes (Table 3.6). For example, there are 20 letters each from the parishes of Christchurch, St George and St Thomas in Southwark on the one hand, and from Shoreditch and Bethnal Green in the East End on the other, but they came from 4 people in the former case, as compared to 12 people in the latter. Another complication arises from the fact that some letters were sent by people in institutions. The letter from the parish of St Thomas, for example, came from James Randall who was in St Thomas's Hospital at the time (**752**). His normal address is not known, since no other letter from him has survived, so that we cannot even be certain that he lived in London. The same is true of six other senders in London hospitals (**126, 621, 650-1, 712, 717, 742**). For others, however, we do know the normal residences. For example, David Rivenall sent one letter from

---

The Cambridge social history of Britain, vol. 1: *Regions and communities* ed. F. M. L. Thompson (Cambridge, 1990) pp. 489-507. Migration patterns with respect to London did not much change in the later nineteenth century. See D. Baines, 'Population, migration and regional development' in *The Economic history of Britain since 1700* ed. R. Floud and D. McCloskey (2nd edn, 3 vols; Cambridge, 1994) ii, pp. 51-5.

[22] See List A. 2 in the Appendix.

[23] Nearly all London addresses could be traced by means of *The A to Z of Regency London* introd. P. Laxton (London Topographical Society, 131; 1985), based on Richard Horwood's 32-sheet map of London (1799, revised by William Faden, 3rd edn, 1813) and *The London Encyclopaedia* ed. B. Weinreb and C. Hibbert (revised edn; London, 1993).

Table 3.6. Essex Pauper Letters, 1731-1837: letters from London, detailed breakdown

		Number of senders	Number of letters	%
West				
Chelsea		1	1	
Kensington		1	1	
St Anne Soho		2	8	
St George Hanover Square		1	1	
St Giles-in-the-Fields		1	1	
St Martin-in-the-Fields		1	5	
Westminster		4	31	
	Subtotal	11	48	17.8 [18.6]
North				
Islington		1	3	
St Marylebone		6 [5]	10 [7]	
St Pancras		2	8	
	Subtotal	9 [8]	21 [18]	7.8 [7.0]
Central				
City		8 [6]	10 [8]	
Clerkenwell		5 [4]	9 [8]	
St Andrew Holborn		2	7	
St Luke Old Street		1	4	
	Subtotal	16 [13]	30 [27]	11.1 [10.5]
East				
Bethnal Green		6	10	
Mile End		3	8	
St George in the East		4	37	
Shoreditch		6	10	
Spitalfields		1	1	
Stepney		1	2	
Whitechapel		8 [4]	13 [8]	
	Subtotal	29 (27) [25 (24)]	81 [76]	30.0 [29.5]
South				
Bermondsey		6	12	
Christchurch		1	16	
Lambeth		4	7	
Newington		3	5	
St George		2	3	
St Saviour		2	2	
St Thomas		1 [0]	1 [0]	
	Subtotal	18 (16) [17 (15)]	46 [45]	17.0 [17.4]
Address not specifiable		17	44	16.3 [17.1]
TOTAL		100 [91]	270 [258]	100.0 [100.1]

Source Appendix, List A.1.

Note Figures in square brackets exclude letters sent from people in institutions (hospital, prison). Figures in round brackets correct double counts of people who sent letters from various parishes. That correction, however, was only made for each part of London, which means that people writing from various parts of London still count for each part.

the house of correction in Clerkenwell (**116**) and another one from the London Hospital in Whitechapel (**251**), whereas all the other 32 letters from him and/or his wife came from the parish of St George in the East. William Holden, on the other hand, sent one letter each from the Middlesex Hospital and the Western Hospital (**243, 263**), both in St Marylebone, but his normal address whence his previous two other letters were sent was in the same parish (**228, 230**). In order to control the distortions arising from such cases, Tables 3.6 and 3.7 have also been supplied with alternative figures excluding the letters sent from paupers in institutions.

A further problem is that in one out of six letters the sender's address is just given as 'London', without further specification, though most of these are from people for whom there are other letters with a specified address. On the assumption that their letters lacking a specified address of sender were sent from within the same part of town as the others, most can be classified accordingly, while 7 letters remain where the sender's residence cannot even be guessed in that way since the 6 people concerned have not left other letters behind (right-hand part of Table 3.7).[24]

Despite all necessary qualifications, then, the emerging picture is relatively clear. Not surprisingly, the East End was the most prominent area from which pauper letters to Essex parishes emerged, followed by the south, whereas central, north and west London were of less importance (though there was an exceptionally high number of letters per sender in the west).

To conclude our long discussion in this chapter, the major features of the sample of Essex Pauper Letters 1731-1837 may be summarized as follows. First, the majority of the letters survive from the final years of the Old Poor Law or, more precisely, from 1820 to 1834. Second, they were sent from more than a hundred places, most of which were situated in the

---

[24] The grouping of parishes follows that suggested for 1861 by G. Stedman Jones *Outcast London: a study in the relationship between classes in Victorian society* (Oxford, 1971) pp. 352-3, a study which is indispensable for the social topography of Victorian London. For earlier times, see O. H. K. Spate, 'The growth of London, 1600-1800', in *An historical geography of England before 1800: fourteen studies* ed H. C. Darby (Cambridge, 1936) pp. 529-48; E. J. Hobsbawm, 'The nineteenth-century London labour market', in *London: aspects of change* ed. R. Glass (London, 1964) pp. 3-28; G. Rudé *Hanoverian London 1714-1808* (History of London, 1; London, 1971) chs. 1, 5 and 7; F. Sheppard *London 1808-1870: the infernal wen* (History of London, 2; London, 1971) chs. 1 and 3; Garside, 'London and the home counties', pp. 480-4; H. Clout, 'London in transition', in *London: problems of change* ed H. Clout and P. Wood (London, 1986) pp. 23-32, and the classic account by M. D. George *London life in the eighteenth century* (London, 1925; repr. Harmondsworth, 1976).

Table 3.7 Essex Pauper Letters, 1731-1837: letters from London, with alternative grouping of letters lacking specified address of sender to presumed address of sender

Part of London	Actual distribution of letters				Distribution of letters with those lacking specified address of sender assigned to presumed address of sender			
	Number of senders	%	Number of letters	%	Number of senders	%	Number of letters	%
West	11	11.5 [12.4]	48	17.8 [18.6]	11	12.9 [14.1]	48	17.8 [18.6]
North	9 [8]	9.4 [9.0]	21 [18]	7.8 [7.0]	9	10.6 [11.5]	28 [25]	10.4 [9.7]
Central	16 [13]	16.7 [14.6]	30 [27]	11.1 [10.5]	16 [13]	18.8 [16.7]	31 [28]	11.5 [10.9]
East	27 [25]	28.1 [28.1]	81 [76]	30.0 [29.5]	27 [24]	31.8 [30.8]	108 [103]	40.0 [39.9]
South	16 [15]	16.7 [16.7]	46 [45]	17.0 [17.4]	16 [15]	18.8 [19.2]	48 [47]	17.8 [18.2]
Address not specified	17	17.7 [19.1]	44	16.3 [17.1]	6	7.1 [7.7]	7	2.6 [2.7]
TOTAL	96 [89]	100.1 [99.9]	270 [258]	100.0 [100.1]	85 [78]	100.0 [100.0]	270 [258]	100.1 [100.0]

Source Appendix, List A.1.

Note Figures in square brackets exclude letters sent from people in institutions (hospital, prison).
For the alternative grouping of letters lacking a specified address of sender those letters were assumed to have been sent from the same part of town in those cases where that sender's letters with specified address are all from the same part of London. Where a sender sent letters from various parts of the town, his or her letters without specified address are assumed to have been sent from that part from which most of his or her other letters were sent.

home counties and East Anglia. No less than 35 per cent of the letters came from paupers in London, mainly from those residing in parishes in the East End. This geographical distribution largely corresponds to the migration patterns to be expected for people from Essex at that time. Third, over 80 per cent of the senders of paupers letters sent up to 3 letters, but those with 4 or more letters sent nearly 75 per cent of them. Fourth, the share of men and women among letter writers was almost equal. Among senders in London, most were women. Fifth, the pauper letters were received by the overseers of 40 Essex parishes. But more than 70 per cent of them went to the three major towns within the county: to Braintree and Chelmsford, and to the parishes of St Botolph, St James and St Peter in Colchester.

These last-named parishes were extraordinarily painstaking in their poor-law administration, which also seems to provide part of the explanation of the peculiar shape of the sample of Essex Pauper Letters itself. Naturally, whatever pauper letters may originally have been sent to Essex parishes, we can only talk about those which are today to be found in the surviving files of overseers' correspondence. It may well be, therefore, that our sample contains so many pauper letters for Braintree, Chelmsford, and the three Colchester parishes not only because these were the Essex parishes which in fact received most pauper letters at the time, but also because the pauper letters sent to these parishes were better preserved than those sent elsewhere.

Chapter 4
Source criticism

For a critical assessment of the specific properties of pauper letters as a historical source, it is essential that the reader, before delving into their substance, should have a clear idea of their physical and formal features. For this reason, this chapter begins by examining in detail 14 individual pieces which are also presented as facsimiles (Plates I-XX). According to the order in which they have been placed, the discussion will proceed from simpler and more familiar to more complex cases, which does not, however, imply any typological intention. Rather, as a first step in the source criticism of pauper letters, it is basically a descriptive exercise, though it is also meant to serve as an illustrative platform for the second step, the systematic assessment of the physical, graphic, scriptual and literary properties of the entire sample of Essex Pauper Letters. The third step in source criticism aims at what might be called the personal 'heart' of the matter: this is the question of who wrote the pauper letters. The fourth step concerns the issues of factual 'truth' and credibility.

Exposition: examination of individual pieces (plates I-XX)

In appreciating the individual examples, it has to be borne in mind that there is no such thing as 'the' typical pauper letter but rather a number of different types. It is in this sense that some of the chosen pieces represent typical examples (examples of particular types), while others are decidedly untypical and exceptional. Between them, however, they may be said to convey an idea of the wider range of the material within the sample.

Plate I. It is convenient to begin with a pauper letter which displays the basic elements and layout of a modern standard letter as we know it today and as we ourselves would write it. In the chosen example, a letter from Arthur Tabrum (**179**), these elements are: (a) the place of sender (here without full address) and the date in the top right-hand corner of the page; (b) the salutation of the recipient ('Hon^d Sir'), placed against the left-hand margin; (c) the body of the letter, with the first line indented; and (d) the closing of the letter, comprising the valedictions ('I remain Your Humble S[ervan]t') and the sender's name, which are given in separate lines under the main body of the text, in the bottom right-hand corner of the page. The handwriting is also familiar to the modern eye: it is a neat round hand, the common ordinary script in England since the eighteenth century.

The only fundamental difference from the standard type of letter we know today concerns the distinction between 'inside' and 'outside'. Before the general use of envelopes which only emerged after the introduction of the penny post in 1840, the letter or, more precisely, the sheet of paper on which it was written was folded (several times, if necessary) in such a way that the text was inside and the recipient's address outside on the front, while the entire piece was sealed on the back (the aerogramme is the modern equivalent). In the present case, the postal address of the recipient appears on the page facing the letter as such. Both pages are written on the same side of the sheet while the back is left blank. The postmark is clearly visible above the recipient's address. Below the latter, reversed and written against the edge where the sheet was folded in the middle, there is a note from the receiving parish officer, giving the sender's name and the date of receipt. The wax mark just above that note and the missing bit in the middle of the top edge of the sheet indicate where the letter had been sealed.

Plate II. Some pauper letters fall below the familiar modern standard in that certain features are not properly displayed or lacking altogether. In the letter from Mary Mitchel (**300**), the opening salutation ('Sir') is incorporated in the body of the text. It is also obvious that the writer was less experienced than the one in the previous example (plate I). The handwriting is poor. Although the individual letters are clearly discernible, the letterforms are somewhat clumsy, and there is some irregularity in size and shading. It is also striking that 'B' and 'L' are used as capitals within words. Some of the letters are formed so idiosyncratically that they look like others (for example, 'u' is drawn like 'w'). The spelling is slightly phonetic. Nevertheless, there is a clear if simple graphical organization of the letter in that the opening and the closing are placed in centred lines and thus distinguished from the main body of the text.

The three other pieces, however, might be said to fall short of the normal type of letter, not least because they are so small. They are written on tiny slips of paper and indeed form the smallest pieces in the entire sample of Essex Pauper Letters. The second one from the top does give the date and the sender's place and name, but not the address of the recipient (**629**). The bottom one bears the sender's name, but neither place nor date (**410**). The one at the top lacks all these elements and is simply a very brief text with a mark at the end, possibly from the anonymous sender (**590**).

Plates III-VII. While some pauper letters fall below the basic standard, others bear witness to high epistolary expertise. These include the two chosen letters from William James in Chelmsford, the most prolific of all Essex pauper letter writers, from whom no less than 53 letters have survived, covering the period from July 1818 to September 1828. The first example, written in 1821, shows the neat copperplate handwriting and elegant layout (including paragraphs with indentation of the first line) which are characteristic of nearly all his letters (plates III-IV: **445**). It is only in his final two letters, the latter of which is given as the second example (plates V-VII: **550**), that the handwriting is somewhat larger and broader, with some irregularity in the shading, due to his 'Eye sight so much impar'd', as he puts it himself. Both letters are also interesting in that in addition to the full postal address of the sender, given at the end after his signature, alternative channels of delivery are named.

Plate VIII. The next two pieces also come from one and the same hand. Unlike the two letters from William James, however, they lack all characteristic elements of a normal letter and give no more than the body of the text. The very simple letterforms, the poor line direction, the heavy phonetic spelling, and the crude corrections in the longer piece suggest that for this person writing was hard work. Interestingly enough, in the longer letter the writer does show some graphical sense in that he made line breaks which may have been meant to indicate paragraphs (**510**). Both pieces can roughly be dated from notes which the receiving overseers made on them in order to document the amounts of money sent to the sender. In the first case (**377**), this appears below the letter, in the second (**510**), on the back of the piece (not shown) which is otherwise blank. In that second case, the note includes the sender's name. It is Benjamin Brooker, whose handwriting is so characteristic that the first letter could be identified, even though it gives no name of sender and has survived in a completely separate archive. This is because Brooker sent the first letter to the parish of St Botolph in Colchester, but the second to St Peter in the same town. He is the only pauper in the entire sample known to have written to and to have received assistance from two different parishes, though the nature of that twofold claim remains obscure. Sarah Finch also wrote to two parishes, from St George in London to St James, Colchester, in 1814 (**402-3**), and from Chatham in Kent to St Botolph, Colchester, in 1836 (**394**). But in her case it is not clear whether she was actually supported from both places.[1]

Plates IX-XII. As some of the previous examples have already shown, pauper letters often contain not just the original letter itself, but also additional textual matter from later (or earlier) hands. On the letter from George Smee (**14**), comprising four pages on one sheet, no less than five different hands are in evidence. Taken together, these have turned it from a simple letter into a rather complex file documenting the entire process of application for relief and the response from the overseers of both the host and the home parish. Six steps of that process can be distinguished.

(1) The pauper letter as such is from George Smee (plate IX). Its layout is neat, and the handwriting suggests an experienced writer, who uses a slightly older form of round hand as may be seen especially from the lower case 'e' characteristic of the secretary hand.

(2) Next, there is a brief note from an unknown hand, placed opposite the closing of the original letter and saying that 'The above was sent by Post & recommend'd by Mr J[oh]n Webb'.

(3) At the bottom of the page and running on to the middle of the second page (plate X), we find a note from John Webb, overseer of the parish in Norwich where George Smee resided, dated 9 May 1826 and supporting the latter's request. That note ends with a postscript ('Pray give an answer to the above').

(4) Below the postscript, another unknown hand has put down, in pencil, the amount of '1/6' (1s 6d = 7.5p).

(5) The third page (plate XI) bears a copy of the answer from Jeremiah Wing, overseer of the parish of Braintree where George Smee was settled, dated 15 May 1826.

(6) The fourth page (plate XII) gives the recipient's name and address, though with a wrong first name ('Joseph' mistaken for 'Jeremiah'). This last page was also written by John Webb. The postal address formed the outside front once the letter was sealed. The edges where the piece was folded are clearly visible. So are the point where it was sealed (above the recipient's name, on what had become the top of the front outside) and the postmark (on the left-hand side of the front outside).

---

[1] If she did receive relief from both parishes, she might, of course, have gained a new settlement in the parish of St Botolph by 1836, given the long period of time which had elapsed since her two letters of 1814 to the parish of St James.

The presumed sequence of action in which this letter turned into a file may be described as follows. The letter from George Smee was written first. Next, John Webb wrote his note to give his official support, folded and sealed the letter, wrote the recipient's address on the outside and sent it off to Braintree. At Braintree, it was then (we may assume) opened by Jeremiah Wing, who laid it before the select vestry to decide on how to proceed with George Smee's case. Finally, he wrote an answer to Norwich, presumably to John Webb, and made a copy of his answer on the blank page of the inside (the third page in our above count).

It is not clear who supplied the short note directly underneath the letter from George Smee (step 2 above). The handwriting might be that of Jeremiah Wing. In that case the note would probably have been intended as a briefing for the select vestry, which would mean that it was put down before he wrote his answer to Norwich. There is no clue as to by whom and precisely when the entry in pencil underneath the postscript to the recommendation from John Webb ('1/6') was made, except that it must have been made after John Webb had written his note. Given that the amount of 1s 6d (7.5p) corresponds to the increase of the allowance of 2s 6d (12.5p) to 4s (20p) as agreed by the select vestry, it would seem reasonable to infer that the entry was made in connection with the proceedings in Braintree.

Plates XIII-XIV. The next example also shows several hands, but decidedly *not* that of the sender herself. It is one of the very few cases where a pauper letter takes the 'official' character of a formal petition (**133**). It was obviously written by a professional scribe, as is witnessed by the rather pompous wording, the elaborate layout and the model copperplate handwriting. The petition as such appears on the third page, or the right-hand side of the inside (plate XIV). It is preceded by a formal certification on the first page (plate XIII), which is undersigned by fourteen local residents, with the signatures running on to the second page (plate XIV). The fourth page (plate XIII), which forms the back outside of the entire piece, bears a brief postscript in the same hand as the petition. Given that it was quite clearly neither written nor composed by Ann Marsh, whose case is reported in the third person, this petition is an exceptional case within the sample. It is nevertheless counted as a pauper letter because it was signed in her name, though again certainly not from her own hand.

Plates XV-XVI. This is one of the few cases where a letter sent out *to* a pauper has survived because the answering pauper letter was written on the same piece of paper which was then sent back to the parish from which it had come **(156)**. Thus, as in the case of George Smee (plates IX-XII: **14**), the pauper letter as such forms part of a larger file in which the hands of several parties are in evidence. On 13 May 1825, James Read, vestry clerk of Chelmsford, wrote to Mrs Halls at Mr Alexander's (her son-in-law's) in St Nicholas, Ipswich, requesting her to send 'a Certificate, signed by the Minister and Churchwardens that you are living', to state her age and to acknowledge the receipt of her allowance up to 26 March 1825 (plate XV). Apparently, this letter was given to the parish officers of St Nicholas, Ipswich, who turned it over and gave the requested testimony on the right-hand side of the blank back of the sheet. Next, the answer from Susan[nah] Halls was put down underneath on the same page and signed in her name. Finally, the full letter was addressed to James Read in Chelmsford on the remaining blank left-hand page (of the original back) facing the answers. It was folded, sealed and sent back to Chelmsford (plate XVI), where it has survived within the huge file of overseers' correspondence. As we know from other evidence in that file, it was not written by Susannah Halls herself, but by her daughter (or her son-in-law).[2]

Plates XVII-XVIII. While all previous examples are letters addressed to the parish officers of the place where the sender was settled, this one is a private letter, from John Barnes to his mother (**17**). He was a servant in Billericay and apparently supported by the parish of Braintree. Presumably his mother showed the letter to the acting overseer (this was Joseph Garrett, as we know from external evidence), who then kept it as proof of what he allowed Barnes, making a brief note to that effect at the bottom of the second page ('Granted 2ˢ for a New Shirt & 5ˢ to Buy Brushes etc. J. G.'). This explains why it has survived within the correspondence of Braintree's overseers even though it was not originally sent to them. The blotchy appearance of the letters would suggest that Barnes had as yet little technical experience in putting pen to paper, but the vivid description of his situation shows that he certainly knew how to write. Intimate accounts of personal circumstances, however, are also given in many pauper letters addressed to the overseers, though his evocation of the 'beatiful Leg of mutton roasted' he had 'dined of' is unique. As a private letter it is particularly interesting in that it does not show any specific features in

---

[2] For an account of her case, see T. Sokoll, 'Old age in poverty: the record of Essex pauper letters, 1780-1834', in *Chronicling poverty: the voices and strategies of the English poor, 1640-1840* ed. T. Hitchcock, P. King and P. Sharpe (London, 1997) pp. 127, 130-3.

layout, wording or style which are altogether lacking from ordinary pauper letters. This letter may thus be regarded as providing independent evidence of the rather familiar tone in which many paupers addressed their parish officers.

Plates XIX-XX. The final piece is one of the earliest pauper letters surviving in Essex (**281**). Apart from the fact that the handwriting, as one would expect, represents a slightly earlier type of the round hand, it shows no substantial differences from the previous examples, which suggests that the basic features of the pauper letter, as indeed the 'familiar letter' in general, were well established by the early eighteenth century and did not change during the whole period covered in this volume.

Systematic assessment

Having gone through a small selection of individual pauper letters in detail, we may now turn to a more systematic assessment of the physical, graphic, scriptual and literary properties of that type of record, drawing on the entire sample of Essex Pauper Letters. It goes without saying that in doing so it is impossible to do full justice to the immense variety and sheer richness of the material. Nevertheless, by means of more extended references it will be easier to appreciate the wide range of expressions and experiences encountered in this unique corpus of evidence and at the same time to obtain some idea as to which kinds of letter fall within the band of common epistolary practices and which are the exceptions falling outside that band.

Physical properties. Writing requires particular materials and techniques. In the present case, the people who wrote pauper letters used a metal pen, black ink and white paper. Ink and pen were also used for most of the notes which the receiving overseers or other users put on the letters, though some of these notes were made in pencil (e.g. **14** [plate XIV], **68, 335, 623**). A pencil was also used by three letter writers for drawing ruled lines (Marian Nevill: **392**; Edward Mills: **559, 567**, Elizabeth Manning: **695, 696**), but this was exceptional. All other pauper letters are written on plain white paper. This was not necessarily blank on both sides. Three people, including Susannah Halls, as we have seen, used the back of letters they had themselves received from the overseers of their home parishes (**156** [plates XV-XVI], **289, 379**). Another letter was written on the blank back of a printed form (of a medical certificate from White House in Bethnal Green: **349**). Most people used writing paper of good quality and of a standard size for letters, which means that they wrote on a square sheet of a size between what is today known as A4 and A3, folded in the middle to make four pages of which the inside ones carry the text of the letter, while the outside bears the address of the recipient. Exceptions to this conventional practice are rare. Occasionally, as in the larger letter from Benjamin Brooker (plate VIII: **510**), the whole inside was used upright as a single page; some pieces, three of which we have also encountered (plate II: **410**, **590**, **629**), were not letters in the strict sense, being mere slips of paper, with the back left blank, which suggests that they were not sent by post but handed over in person.[3] While pauper letters were sometimes of a smaller than standard size, there were no oversized ones.

Due to the fact that pauper letters were normally written on high quality paper, most of them survive in good condition. Quite a number of letters, though, have small holes or tears from the pins on to which they were fastened, as clearly visible in the middle of the pages of the letters from George Smee (plates IX-XII: **14**) and from John Barnes to his mother (plates XVII-XVIII: **17**). There are very few pieces where the text suffers from heavier physical destruction through worn-out edges or torn-off parts of the page, or because the paper is so heavily water-damaged that the ink has become virtually illegible (**19, 28, 32, 75, 401, 402, 595**). One letter from Susannah Halls literally fell to pieces under the hands of the present writer (**109**). There were also some papers within the files of overseers' correspondence which were so defective that they had to be left out altogether.

Layout. The physical shape of a letter also bears on its graphic organization. For example, because of the common practice of folding the original sheet of paper in the middle to form four pages, the text as such normally begins on the second page, or even, especially when the text is short, only on the third page, with the second page left blank. The most important influence on the layout, however, is the literary conventions concerning the standard elements of the letter and their positioning in relation to the

---

[3] Most letters were sent by post. For the postal services in late eighteenth and early nineteenth century England, see H. Robinson *The British post office: a history* (Princeton, N. J., 1948) chs 15-21; D. Vincent *Literacy and popular culture: England 1750-1914* (Cambridge, 1989) pp. 32-49.

main body of the text. This is not to say that these formal epistolary conventions leave no room for individual graphic expression, but they do set
certain rules. For example, the place of sender may be given at the bottom
rather than at the head of the letter (e.g. **11, 16**), but it is normally still set
off from the text. Likewise, the closing of the letter (valedictions and name
of sender) may be placed towards the left-hand edge (e.g. **20, 68, 234**),
in the middle (plate II: **300**), towards the right-hand edge (the most common position), or in a step-wise fashion across the page (e.g. **103, 145,
408, 555**), as long as it is separated from the body of the text.

Writing. The graphic expression in which the text is laid out on the page
is closely related to the performance of the individual hand in guiding the
pen to form letters into words and arrange them in lines. The handwriting
of most pauper letters is close to modern standards, with the script being
more or less the same as that used today. This is the round hand, that
mixture of the secretary hand and the italic (or roman) hand which had
become the standard form of handwriting in England by the late seventeenth century.[4] Only occasionally do older letterforms occur, mainly of
course in the earlier pieces (plates XIX-XX: **281**), but also in some of the
later ones (plate IX: **14**). A perfect round or copperplate hand as given in
contemporary copy-books is only found in the very few cases where a
professional scribe was obviously at work (plates XIII-XIV: **133**). All
other writers use the round hand in their own, highly individual form. The
writing may be poor (as that of Benjamin Brooker: plate VIII: **377, 510**)
or show certain idiosyncrasies (as in Mary Mitchel's use of capital 'B'
and 'L' within words: plate II: **300**). Nevertheless, the letter writers usually have an individual handwriting (just as people have today), most of
them writing in a fairly fluent hand, with an angle to the right and in more
or less straight lines, despite the fact that blank paper was used. An unusual
arrangement of lines occurs only once (**2**); in another case, the final part
of the text was written crosswise over the foregoing text, with the lines
going upright (**673**). In cases of people whose letters span a longer period

---

[4] See S. Morison, 'The development of hand-writing', in A. Heal *The English writing masters and their copy-books, 1570-1800: a biographical dictionary and a bibliography* (Cambridge, 1931; repr. Hildesheim, 1962) pp. xxxiii-xl; S. Morison, 'Calligraphy', in *Encyclopaedia Britannica* (14th edn; London, 1929) iv, pp. 614-18; L. C. Hector *The handwriting of English documents* (London, 1958) pp. 60-61; A. Gaur, *A history of writing* (British Library; London, 1984) pp. 158-60; H. E. P. Grieve *Examples of English hand-writing 1150-1750* (ERO Publications, 21; Chelmsford, 1954). See also H. C. Schulz, 'The teaching of handwriting in Tudor and Stuart times', *Huntingdon Library Quarterly* (1943) pp. 414-17.

of time, changes in handwriting are sometimes visible, as in the case of William James (plates III-IV: **445** as compared to plates V-VII: **550**). In the similar case of George Tye, this made possible the dating of a letter lacking the year (**384**).

Having dealt with the general physical and visual appearance of the pauper letter, we now turn to its individual formal elements, which are not only of interest with respect to the overall layout (as we have seen), but also show variations in their own right.

Place of sender. In most pauper letters, the sender's address is given as the place of his or her (private) residence. It is hardly surprising that most people writing from a village or small town give no more than the place name, whereas those writing from larger places tend to include house number and street and/or the name of the parish or part of town in which they reside, especially in the case of London. The place of sender, however, does not necessarily refer to a private address. There are also some institutional addresses, that is, people writing from hospitals (again, mainly in London) and prisons, and soldiers or their wives writing from barracks and ships of the royal navy. People also name inns or shops as places where letters can be sent 'to be left' for them (like William James: plate VII: **550**). This is especially true of coaching inns, and again of those in London in particular, like the Spread Eagle in Gracechurch Street (**110**) or the Cape of Good Hope in Lime Street (**285**), both near Leadenhall Market. Some people give both kinds of address (once again, William James: plate VII: **550**) or use addresses of various kinds on different occasions, like David and Sarah Rivenall, of whose letters 12 name their private address, 19 the King's Head, while one (from David Rivenall alone) refers to the Clerkenwell house of correction (**116**) and another to the London Hospital (**251**).

Individual mobility is also witnessed in pauper letters in that people moved about and addressed their home parish from various places, like William Holden who, in 1823, sent 2 letters from Hampstead (**101, 103**) and then, in 1827, another 2 from St Marylebone in London (**228, 230**); or Jonathan Sewell, who wrote from Portsmouth (**616**), Hilsea (**617, 618**) and Portchester (**620**). People also moved houses within London, like Arthur Tabrum, whose first letter, of June 1824, came from the parish of St Saviour (**120**), but the next one, in May 1825, from the parish of Christchurch (**157**). People did not only go from one place to another. 'Circular' mobility is also in evidence, as in the case of George Rowe, who moved about between Braintree, Bocking and Coggeshall, sending letters from each place, including one from Coggeshall in which he names Bocking as his place of residence and then gives two postal addresses, one with a collar maker in Coggeshall and the other one with the overseer of Bocking (**442**).

There are also letters, however, where the sender does not state the (precise) place. In most of these cases it has nevertheless been possible to identify it, either from the postmark or other evidence on the piece itself (such as notes from other people, as in the case of the letter from Susannah Halls from St Nicholas in Ipswich of 15 May 1825: plate XV: **156**), or to infer it from other letters from the same person or from other evidence. In all, there are only 19 letters (2.5 per cent of the sample) for which the place of sender has not been traced.

Date. There is less variation with the date. The general rule is that people either provide the full date, which is what most people do (though the normal order of day/month/year is sometimes altered); or, they do not date their letter at all. Incomplete dates are exceptional. As with places, however, most of the missing or deficient dates have turned out to be identifiable or inferable from other evidence, which again may either be found on the letter itself (postmark, note from another hand) or be given elsewhere (related correspondence). For one letter, as already mentioned, the missing year can be inferred from the particular stroke of the handwriting as compared to other letters from the same person (**384**), and for three others, from the place of the letter within the presumed chronological order of the original file of overseers' correspondence (**39, 74, 428**). Datings from postmarks or notes of receipt are, of course, only approximate, in that they provide the date after which the letter cannot have been written. The same is true of letters like that from Susannah Halls acknowledging the receipt of her last allowance on 5 February 1824, which means that it cannot have been written earlier (**111**). Editorial dating has been possible in 138 cases, while 21 undated letters remain (2.8 per cent of the sample).

Salutation. By the eighteenth century, an English letter did not require any particular formal address to the recipient, even if he or she was a local official, unless a member of the nobility, gentry or higher clergy was involved. However, the parish officers to whom pauper letters were normally addressed were not usually from these social groups. In most cases, therefore, the recipient was either addressed by name or, more often, with 'Sir' or 'Gentleman' (or 'Gentlemen'), or a slightly extended form of endearment ('Honoured Sir', 'Kind Sir', 'Dear Sir'[rare]). Occasionally, a more formal address was used, such as 'To the gentlemen of the parrish board' (**7**), 'To the Gentlemen of the poor' (**111**), or 'To the Parochial Authorities' (**406**). A more familiar form (other than in private letters) was only used once, when Elizabeth Lane addressed William Chisolm, the overseer of St Botolph in Colchester, as her 'gentlemen friend' (**355**). Again, only one writer, a certain Mrs Robinson, was so kind as to address both 'Gentlemen & Ladies' (**750**). There are also letters with no salutation at all, but these are exceptional and come from very few people. Some of these we have already encountered: Benjamin Brooker (plate VIII: **510**), Susannah Halls (**134**) and David Rivenall (**196**). The others are Sarah Manning and her husband (**195, 213, 226, 240, 255, 259, 268**), Mary Hill (**607**), Joseph Skewer (**677, 678**), John Hicks (**726, 728**) and Timothy Woodward (**748**).

Valedictions. As with salutations, most letter writers end with a conventional valediction ('Your humble/obedient servant'). But there are some interesting variations, in that qualifications or specifications are introduced, as in 'your unworthy but Humble servant' (**30**), 'your poor and needy servant' (**108**), 'Your unfortunate Humble Servt' (**385**), 'your most distress hum^l Servt' (**402**), 'your unfortunate And afflicted Most Humble And Obedient Servant' (**508**) or 'your trobbsom [*read*: troublesome] servent' (**753**). Another, perhaps more self-confident option is to replace 'servant' by 'petitioner' or 'parishioner'. John Hall, for example, signs nearly all his letters with 'your humble petitioner', and Susannah Halls signs as 'your poor humble parishner' (**123**). There is also 'your humble petiteoner William Marsh pauper on the parish of Brai[n]tree' (**68**); or, with a striking (deliberate?) slip of the pen, Ann Doubty, 'your poor afflicted Perrishner in Distress' (**619**). And there is James Davey who neither uses a closing phrase nor signs with his name, but ends his letter with the simple request 'Genteel men i BaG that You will think of me on saturday next' (**603**).

Name of sender. Being a piece of writing by means of which someone makes a personal claim on his or her parish, it is in the nature of the pauper letter that it should be signed in that person's name. This is indeed true of virtually all Essex Pauper Letters. In most cases, the name of sender is given at the end of the letter, following the valedictions, in the form of an individual signature in the same hand as the letter itself. Occasionally, the signature is found above the text or in the margin (**677, 678, 697**). In one case, it is in another, poorer hand than the text itself (**152**), while three letters are authenticated by the sender's mark, with the proper name written underneath (**224, 498, 607**). Whenever there is a named authentication, however, from whatever hand, it is always given as a clearly legible name, which corresponds to contemporary convention. The modern practice of signing with a personal, highly individualized cipher, which may well be completely illegible, dates only from the twentieth century.

There are very few exceptions to the general rule that the pauper letter bears the name of the sender. In his letter of December 1825 to the parish of St Peter in Colchester, Benjamin Brooker did not give his name, but apparently he assumed that his addressee, the overseer Robert Alden ('holden' in Brooker's characteristic phonetic spelling), knew from whom it came (plate VIII: **510**), either from the person who delivered it (there is no address of the recipient on the outside) or from the details of Brooker's case as spelt out therein (four weeks previously Brooker had already sent Alden a letter which did bear his name, though it was written in another hand [**506**]). Whatever may have been the case, Brooker's next letter to Alden (April 1826), from the same hand as the anonymous one, is duly signed with his full name at the bottom (**521**). When he wrote to the Colchester parish of St Botolph in July 1828, however, he again did not sign the piece. However, his surname is given in the reference to the allowance due to Mrs Brooker's boy ('mises Brooker Boyes muney', plate VIII: **377**).

Apart from letters giving no name of sender at all, there are others where the name is mistaken or, though originally given, is now missing. Thus, Benjamin Hewitt from Whitton in Suffolk mistakenly signed as 'Benjamin Whitton' (**582**), while in two letters from William King, the bottom of the sheet which must have borne his name is heavily damaged (**32**) or completely torn-off (**75**). In these cases, however, the two senders can be identified from their handwriting which was the same as that of all their other letters, so that the (correct) names of sender have been supplied in the heading of these letters.

There are only two letters in the entire sample which remain altogether anonymous, because the missing name could not be established from other evidence. Interestingly enough, each of them is also exceptional in another respect, because the name is not absolutely essential. One belongs to those small slips of paper which were not sent by post but presumably handed over personally (plate II: **590**). The other one is a private letter, which a young woman who had lost her husband wrote to her mother (**323**).

Composition and style. The epistolary components discussed so far not only concern the form of the letter, but are also closely related to its

substantive organization. As a standard set of formal elements they constitute an external framework, as it were, within which the substantive
elements are placed in an order in their own right. Again, as with the
arrangement of the formal components, that internal structure is not absolutely fixed, but it does follow certain conventions. To be more specific,
pauper letters, in their basic composition, rhetoric and gesture, may be
said to be bounded by two contemporary types of epistolary expression:
the 'familiar' letter on one hand, and the formal petition on the other.
Surprisingly enough, most pauper letters seem to show a closer resemblance to the familiar letter and *not* – as one would expect - to the petition.

Before examining the differences between these two types, however, it
is worth remembering that both are rooted in the same medieval model of
the letter (adapted from the Classical rhetoric scheme of the division of
speech), according to which the writer begins by greeting the recipient
(*salutatio*) and appealing to his or her goodwill (*captatio benevolentiae*);
then turns to an account of the particular case (*narratio*), which forms
the basis for a specific request (*petitio*); and closes by bidding the recipient farewell (*conclusio*). This is not of course to imply that the writers of
pauper letters would have remembered their Classics when they put pen
to paper. Neither is this to deny that, beginning with Renaissance writers
such as Erasmus, the ancient model had been subject to modifications, so
that those printed guides and text books of letter-writing which had emerged
in the sixteenth century, and which later became available in cheap popular editions, were actually a complex blend of various literary traditions.
Nevertheless, as any eighteenth-century exemplar of the *English letter-
writer* shows, the classical composition of the letter essentially remained
intact, providing the basic model. In following contemporary epistolary
convention, people reproduced that model even if the ordinary letter writer
would not normally have been aware of it. At any rate, the extent to which
many pauper letters retain the traditional rhetorical sequence is very striking.[5]

[5] See W. G. Müller, 'Brief', in *Historisches Wörterbuch der Rhetorik* ed. G. Ueding
(Tübingen, 1994- [not completed]) ii, cols. 60-76; R. G. M. Nikisch, 'Briefsteller', *ibid.*,
cols. 76-86; R. G. M. Nikisch *Brief* (Sammlung Metzler, 260; Stuttgart, 1991); G. Constable
Letters and letter collections (Typologie des Sources du Moyen Âge Occidental, 17;
Turnhaut, 1976) pp. 11-41; J. Robertson *The art of letter writing: an essay on the hand-
books published in England during the sixteenth and seventeenth centuries* (London, 1943);
K. B. Hornbeak, 'The complete letter-writer in English 1568-1800', *Smith College Studies
in Modern Languages* 15: 3-4 (1934) pp. i-xii and 1-150; K. B. Hornbeak, 'Richardson's
"Familiar Letters" and the domestic conduct books', *Smith College Studies in Modern*

Typically enough, the contemporary guides to the art of letter-writing relate almost exclusively to private or business correspondence and thus mainly provide examples of the 'plain style' that had become the literary standard of English letter-writing by the eighteenth century, characterized by clarity, brevity and an immediately appealing conversational tone. Some of the later guides contain supplementary material such as model petitions, which are predominantly petitions to the king and to members of the various ranks of the nobility and the higher clergy (hence the peculiar obsession with the correct forms of address). But some also provide model petitions to lower authorities, including those of the parish. Thus, in the 'Universal Petitioner', the final part of George Brown's *English letter-writer*, the following example of a petition 'From a poor Widow, soliciting for a Pension from the Parish' is to be found.[6]

To the Minister, Church-Wardens and Overseers of the Parish of

The humble Petition of A. B. *Widow.*
   Sheweth,
THAT your petitioner's husband was an honest industrious man, and lived many years in credit in the parish, where he served every office, and paid scot and lot; but dying in distressed circumstances, owing to his business having fallen off some years ago, she is left utterly destitute. In this unhappy situation she has presumed to address herself to you; and as she has a little work to do, whether the allowance of two shillings *per* week would not be better than going into the workhouse. Your petitioner humbly hopes that her case will be taken into consideration,
   And she, as in duty bound, shall ever pray. A. B.
Recommended by

Languages 19:2 (1938) pp. 1-29. For the eighteenth-century literary ideal of letter-writing, see J. Butt *The mid-eighteenth century* ed. G. Carnall (The Oxford History of English Literature, 7; Oxford, 1979) pp. 323-45; H. Anderson and I. Ehrenpreis, 'The familiar letter in the eighteenth century: some generalizations', in *The familiar letter in the eighteenth century* ed. H. Anderson, P. D. Daghlian and I. Ehrenpreis (Lawrence, Kansas, and London, 1966) pp. 269-82 and 297.
[6] G. Brown *The English letter-writer; or, the whole art of general correspondence* (6th edn; London, 1800) pp. 218-19. An earlier example is C. Johnson *The complete art of writing letters* (London, 1779). Model letters were also provided in more general guides like W. Mather *The young man's companion* (13th edn; London, 1727), which gives 'Letters upon several Occasions' (pp. 84-106), preceded by instructions on how to write (with specimen alphabets), and on how to make a pen, black ink etc. (pp. 73-83).

It is most obvious that the petition from Ann Marsh (plates XIII-XIV: **133**) was written along the lines of a model petition of this kind. But then it is all the more striking that there are hardly any other pieces among the Essex Pauper Letters which may be said to come anywhere near that type (**175, 246, 406, 408, 657, 743, 747**). This not only applies to the composition and literary quality of the letters in general but also to their individual elements. For example, as a closing of the letter, the prototypical petitionary phrase that the writer 'in duty bound shall ever pray' occurs only twelve times within the entire sample (**338, 404, 420, 439, 486, 673, 676, 696, 707, 715, 747, 755**).

While the petition as a literary genre does not normally bear on the form of the pauper letter, it may still be said to lie at the very heart of its substance, given that the major intention of the pauper letter is of course a particular request. Hence the frequent use in pauper letters of rhetorical devices, particularly in the opening gambits, which are replete with rather conventional apologetic phrases. Among the pauper letters chosen for the facsimiles on plates I-XX, for example, we find the following openings: 'it was far distant from my wish or thought to Trouble you [...] but Necessity impel me to ask you'(plate IX: **14**); 'I am sorry to trouble you so soon but being ill and not able to work...' (plate I: **179**); 'I trust you will Excuse me writeing to you' (plate III: **445**). Likewise, the request for help, which is often made after the account of the particular personal circumstances of the applicant, is typically tied up with deferential phrases: 'therefore Gent^n [I] hope you will have the goodness to take it into your most serious Consideration' (plate IX: **14**).

Deferential rhetoric, however, is by no means the only form of expression. On the contrary, many letter writers show a pretty self-confident attitude and address the overseers with surprising bluntness. Again, to quote only from the few examples which have been reproduced on the plates: 'I now make bold to write being your your poor yet humble Petitioner' (plate XIX: **281**); 'ihave taken the LeBety of riten to you' (plate II: **300**); 'ihave sent to you mister holden that i have no wark to doe and you must send me sum muney' (plate VIII: **510**).

In sum, then, it cannot be emphasized too strongly that in stylistic terms and from their overall scriptual habitus, most pauper letters do *not* normally follow the contemporary model of the formal petition, whatever conventional rhetorical phraseology may occur at certain 'strategic' places in the narrative. Rather, they are distinguished by a surprisingly informal, almost 'personal' tone. Moreover, as the examples in facsimile clearly show, pauper letters are characterized not only by their personal tone. They also 'speak' through their non-standardized, highly individual physical appearance, such as a particular stroke of the pen, and to the extent that this peculiar physical touch reflects a particular bodily expression, it seems appropriate to speak of the 'gesture' or indeed of the 'habitus' inscribed in these documents.[7] This is in sharp contrast to the experience of the labouring classes in other countries. For example, in nineteenth-century Prussia, the strict formal requirements of petitions were obeyed to an extent which suggests that not even minor local authorities would ever have accepted, let alone considered, informal pauper letters of the English type.[8] Unfortunately, comparative research into the social history of petitioning is lacking, so that it is impossible to continue along this line. The same is true of the history of letter writing in England, which has so far been concerned with epistolary notables like Lady Mary Wortley Montagu or Horace Walpole, but has not looked into the wider social use of that medium.[9]

In order to explain the extraordinarily personal use of the letter by the English poor, it would be well to remember that, whatever people may have made of letter-writers and other guide books, [10] the letter was simply a ubiquitous feature of eighteenth and nineteenth-century culture. Typically

---

[7] The term 'habitus' is here used following the suggestions by P. Bourdieu, in his *Outline of a theory of practice* (Cambridge, 1977) and *The logic of practice* (Cambridge, 1990).

[8] See J. Karweick, '"Tiefgebeugt von Nahrungssorgen und Gram". Schreiben an Behörden', in S. Grosse *et al. 'Denn das Schreiben gehört nicht zu meiner täglichen Beschäftigung'. Der Alltag Kleiner Leute in Bittschriften, Briefen und Berichten aus dem 19. Jahrhundert. Ein Lesebuch* (Bonn, 1989) pp. 17-87 and 188-89. The example of the applications for poor relief made in 1804-5 to the magistrate of the town of Essen (with a population of less than 4,000 at that time) is particularly instructive (*ibid*. pp. 32-40). See also O. Ulbricht, 'Supplicationen als Ego-Dokumente. Bittschriften von Leibeigenen aus der ersten Hälfte des 17. Jahrhunderts' and C. Ulbrich, 'Zeuginnen und Bittstellerinnen. Überlegungen zur Bedeutung von Ego-Dokumenten für die Erforschung weiblicher Selbstwahrnehmung in der ländlichen Gesellschaft des 18. Jahrhunderts', both in *Ego-Dokumente. Annäherungen an den Menschen in der Geschichte* ed. W. Schulze (Berlin, 1996) pp. 149-74 and 207-26.

[9] See, for example, the contributions in *Familiar letter in the eighteenth century* ed. Anderson, Daghlian and Ehrenpreis. For a perceptive assessment of the culture of correspondence among the middle classes of nineteenth-century Germany, see R. Baasner, 'Briefkultur im 19. Jahrhundert. Kommunikation, Konvention, Postpraxis', in *Briefkultur im 19. Jahrhundert* ed. R. Baasner (Tübingen, 1999) pp. 1-36. Work of this kind seems to be lacking for England.

[10] J. Fergus, 'Provincial servants' reading in the late eighteenth century', in *The practice and representation of reading in England* ed. J. Raven, H. Small and N. Tadmor (Cambridge, 1996) pp. 215-16, 218-20, deals with purchases of letter-writers by provincial servants.

enough, the very first modern English novel, Richardson's *Pamela*, was an epistolary novel, and it is a neat coincidence that it was written in that form because the author was bored at the prospect of composing yet another letter-writer he had been commissioned to produce.[11] People would also encounter letters in the political literature of the day, as in Arthur Young's *Farmer's letters*, or Burke's *Letter to the sheriffs of Bristol*; in periodicals and magazines, where the individual contributions were often in the form of letters, from the *Tatler* and the *Spectator* to the *Annals of agriculture*; and in newspapers, where the reports from other countries also came, typically enough, from 'correspondents'. Thus, by the end of the eighteenth century at the latest, even ordinary people must have been accustomed to the letter as a virtually universal type of literary expression, with a clear and unpretentious personal diction and thus capable of serving all sorts of private as well as public purposes.

Writing as social practice

Given that within the entire sample of Essex Pauper Letters the hands of professional scribes are in evidence in no more than a few exceptional cases and that in most letters, people appear to speak quite openly in their own words and with a highly personal tone, it is tempting to conclude that most paupers must also have written their letters themselves. In practice, however, the question of writing is more complicated. It raises a number of problems, which relate to the following three key factors: the act of writing, the person of the sender and his or her characterization as a pauper. It is convenient to discuss these points in reverse order.

First, then, who counts as a 'pauper'? In addressing this question, it has to be remembered that pauper letters, strictly speaking, do not exist as independent records, since they survive only as part of a larger corpus of evidence: namely, within the overseers' correspondence of the parish to which they were sent.[12] As a general rule, the only pieces of writing which

[11] Butt *Mid-eighteenth century* pp. 387-9. Richardson did publish his model collection of *Familiar letters* in 1741 (*Pamela* was published in 1740). See Hornbeak, 'Complete letter-writer', pp. 100-16.

[12] There are some private letters in our sample, such as that from John Barnes to his mother (plates XVII-XVIII: **17**), which had not originally been sent to the overseers. But their recipients had later given these letters to the overseers, some of them quite obviously at the sender's request. In all, there are 20 such private letters in the sample.

have been selected from those parochial files of overseers' correspondence and included in the sample of Essex Pauper Letters are those where
the text itself leaves little doubt - or where there is independent evidence
to prove - that the sender was actually in need or in receipt of poor relief.
There are a few cases, however, where this may be questionable. Samuel
and James Moore in St Martin-in-the-Fields in London received assistance from the parish of St Botolph in Colchester for boarding their
deceased brother's children, but do not seem to have themselves suffered
from want (**324, 329, 331, 336, 337**). Thomas Strutt, who wrote from
the debtors' prison in Chelmsford, was not given relief in the strict sense
but granted a loan of £10 to get back into business (**350**). Lucy Humpreys's
attempt at raising £20 to bail her husband out of an army contract (**686**)
and the claims made by Edward Mills (**559, 562, 567, 569**) and C.B.
Crowest (**745**) are also somewhat dubious. These letters might therefore
be said to fall outside the band of 'true' pauper letters. They have
nevertheless been included in the sample, because their senders were
either definitely assisted by the overseers or because, as extreme cases,
they may serve to illustrate the boundary between pauper letters and the
many other letters which people sent to the overseers for other reasons.

Second, the *sender* of a pauper letter, as the person in whose name it is
written and who authorized it, is not necessarily the same as the *author*,
the one who is actually speaking. In the letter from James Smith in Woolwich
of 8 February 1832, for example, the entire narrative is that of his wife,
with first-person references to her pregnancy ('until I am confined') or to
'My husband', but he is the one who signs at the bottom (**3**). Similarly, the
letter from Mary Ann Page from St Giles-in-the-Fields in London begins
by speaking in the person of her aunt Ann Trudgett, but then the narrative
subject changes precisely at the point where the text turns to the niece
(**85**). Reading the letter, one is tempted to imagine the situation in which it
was written, with Mary Ann Page at first drawing up what Ann Trudgett
told (or even dictated to?) her (or what she invoked her aunt to be saying
where in fact she was writing it all by herself?), and then explicitly continuing
in her own words.

Third, neither the sender nor the author has to be identical with the
writer as the person who physically put pen to paper. In our discussion of
the facsimile pauper letters, we have already encountered pieces which
are definitely not from the hands of their senders. The petition from Ann
Marsh (plates XIII-XIV: **133**) was evidently written by a professional
(though unknown) scribe; and the letter from Susannah Halls (plates XV-

XVI: **156**), which like all her other letters (in the same hand), was written by her daughter, Susan Alexander (or whoever wrote the letter in that name, announcing the death of her mother [**174**]). Judged by the extraordinarily neat handwriting and layout, the letters from Lucy Baley, Mary Keeling (plate II: **410**, **629**) and George Smee (plate IX: **14**) are also likely to have been written by other people, at any rate by fairly experienced writers. By contrast, the rather clumsy handwriting and heavy phonetic spelling of the letters from Mary Mitchel (plate II: **300**), Benjamin Brooker (plate VIII: **377**, **510**) and John Barnes (plates XVII-XVIII: **17**) would suggest that they were written by these people themselves. In the last of these cases, the record of the particular circumstances in which the piece was written, with the characteristic interruption at the end ('I cannot stay to write no more for I am called away to Dinner) [*continued later on*] I Dine^d of a beatiful Leg of Mutton ...') would lend further support to that conjecture.

Turning from these particular examples to the entire body of Essex Pauper Letters, the problem is that there is, on the whole, very little evidence which enables the actual writer of a pauper letter to be identified with confidence. Naturally, the text in itself is no help in this respect, since people do not normally say anything about the writing of their letters, except in the case of Jane Hills, who closes one of her letters with the telling confession: 'I can neither Read nor write and ham Abbot [am about] to Trouble Some body every Time to write' (**125**). The same confession was made, though not in words, by those people who (as already mentioned) did not sign but marked their letters (**224**, **498**, **607**) or supplied a signature which is from a poorer hand than the letter as such (**152**).

Thus, it is normally only the handwriting itself which may serve as evidence of actual writership, but this evidence is extremely rare. Positive proof of a letter having been written by a pauper himself is only provided once, for an undated letter from Robert Sewell, whose signature (in the same hand as his letter) appears in the select vestry book of Braintree, under an agreement by which he was appointed as a scribe (**80**). Otherwise, the strongest evidence of writership is in the negative, in cases where a pauper had his or her letter(s) written by someone else whose handwriting is found in clear independent evidence. For example, six letters from David and Sarah Rivenall, all in the same hand, were in fact written by their neighbour, Michael Howe, as may be seen from another letter in the same hand, which he wrote in his own name to support their case (**218**, **221**, **231**, **232** [with Howe's own letter quoted in the apparatus], **239**,

244). Other examples include letters which people arranged to be written for them by a close relative (**68**) or an acquaintance (**66**); by their master (**56**) or surgeon (**380**); by the vicar or minister (**657, 658, 717**) or by the overseer of the parish in which they resided (**81**, probably also **689, 691**).

To the extent that paupers may also have written letters for other paupers, the evidence of identical hands is, of course, of little use, since there is no way of telling to whom a particular hand belongs. For example, the 15 letters from John Hall in Chelmsford are all in the same hand as the first 4 letters of his daughter Sarah Hall. But whether she wrote them (that he wrote them is less likely) or whether a third party was involved, is not known. Indeed, her other 3 letters are in another hand.[13] The same is true of married couples who sent several letters in the same hand, where it is impossible to say whether it is the hand of the husband or that of the wife, as in the case of Thomas and Ann Cooper (with 10 letters); or of couples with all their letters in two hands, like Davey and Susannah Rising (also 10 letters); or, indeed, of couples with letters in numerous hands. Even when there appears to be some regular pattern in the distribution of hands, as in the case of the Mannings (again, 10 letters), whose first letter is from hand A, the following ones from hand B and the last one from hand C, we cannot identify these hands. David and Sarah Rivenall hold the record in commanding the hands of other people - their 34 letters come from 16 different hands. The opposite extreme is that where one and the same hand is in evidence in letters from several people, even from various places. Thus, Ann Sinclair, Richard King, Ann King and John Hicks sent between them 13 letters from Cheshunt, Gravesend and Northfleet to Upminster, between September 1802 and February 1806, all from the same hand (**719, 720, 722, 723, 724, 725, 730, 732, 733, 737, 738, 739**). But the same people (except Ann King) also sent further letters written from other hands.

For most Essex Pauper Letters, then, the actual writer is not known and will never be known. In many cases, however, it can nevertheless be presumed that people either wrote their letters themselves or had them written by someone who was close to them. This is particularly true of those paupers with numerous letters, all in the same hand but sent from various places and/or over a long period of time, where the use of others as scribes would require them to have had access to the same person on all their journeys or over all those years. Two such paupers we have

---

[13] For the individual letters in this and the following cases, see List A. 2 in the Appendix.

already encountered in the facsimiles: Arthur Tabrum (plate I: **179**) and William James (plates III-IV and V-VII: **445, 550**), the former sending 17 letters in all, covering the period from June 1824 to May 1829, the latter (as already mentioned) with 53 letters, ranging from July 1818 to September 1828. Other such senders include George Rowe, with 11 letters from Bocking, Braintree and Coggeshall between November 1817 and April 1835; Benjamin Hewitt, with 17 letters from Whitton, Suffolk, between March 1819 and October 1834; William King, with 15 letters from Bethnal Green, between November 1818 and October 1834; and Samuel White, with 11 letters from Halstead, between June 1824 and May 1829.[14]

It is obvious, then, that even in such cases the evidence of identical handwriting does not actually prove that these people wrote their letters themselves. But it would be wrong to overstress self-writership. For the real question is not so much whether people put pen to paper themselves but rather to what kinds of writers they would have turned for help or, more specifically, to what extent they would have had to look for help beyond the range of their kin, friends, neighbours and other people within the local community. In this respect, it is most striking that professional writers, as we have seen, were apparently only very rarely resorted to, and this not only affects the physical record of the writing, but also the language of the letters, their wording and their style. For example, there is not much difference in the wording and style of the 34 letters from David and Sarah Rivenall, despite the fact that 16 people wrote them. Judged by the literary record of the Essex Pauper Letters, it would seem that writing such missives did not involve a great deal of crossing of socio-cultural boundaries. It was for the most part performed within the social and cultural milieu of the labouring poor themselves.

It is worth pursuing this point a little further, since the implications for the social history of written expression are profound. In a programmatic essay on the social history of language, Peter Burke has declared that 'one of the most immediate tasks for social historians of language is to work out who, in a given place at a given time, used the medium of writing to communicate with whom about what.'[15] This implies a simple notion of written communication involving no more than two participants, the sender who produces a piece of writing which is issued to the recipient who then reads it. Judged from the evidence of Essex Pauper Letters, however, this

---

[14] Again, see List A. 2 in the Appendix for details.
[15] P. Burke, 'Introduction', in *The social history of language* ed. P. Burke and R. Porter (Cambridge, 1987) p. 10.

model is too simple, since communication as displayed in these records was by no means restricted to the sender and the recipient, but also involved other people at either end, thus extending both to the production and the reception of the letter as complex social practices. In other words, the fact that someone used the medium of writing does not necessarily mean that he or she used their own hand. It can also mean - and has indeed meant over long periods of history for which we possess written evidence - that, on whatever grounds and for whatever purposes, the hands of others were at their disposal. The power of writing was not confined to those who were themselves able to write. It also applies to any one who *had* a piece written in a given place at a given time. The same of course applies to reading.[16]

It is in this sense that the *scriptual power* of the labouring poor of late eighteenth and early nineteenth-century England, as witnessed in pauper letters, but also in similar pieces of writing such as threatening letters, resolutions and proclamations, needs to be seen as a complex cultural practice; or rather, as a spectrum of practices which can only be appreciated within the social context in which the documents were produced. Thus, a certain proportion of our Essex Pauper Letters may be assumed to have actually been written by the applicants themselves. That the poor should have been capable of writing may seem surprising. But in fact it is not, given that among labourers about a third of all adult males were literate in England by the end of the eighteenth century, a fairly high proportion by international standards.[17] However, even in the case of letters written

---

[16] For a perceptive general survey of problems confronted in the historical analysis of the dialectics of orality and literacy, see W. J. Ong *Orality and literacy: the technologizing of the word* (London, 1982). The best discussion for England at the time we are concerned with here is Vincent *Literacy and popular culture*. Comparative material is provided in L. Kuchenbuch, T. Sokoll *et al. Einführungskurs Alteuropäische Schriftlichkeit* (FernUniversität Hagen, 1988); R. Chartier, 'The practical impact of writing', in *The history of private life* ed. P. Ariès and G. Duby, vol. 3: *Renaissance to enlightenment* ed. R. Chartier (London, 1989) pp. 111-59 and 615-17 (the title is misleading, as Chartier is almost exclusively concerned with reading); R. Chartier, 'Leisure and sociability: reading aloud in early modern Europe', in *Urban life in the renaissance* ed. S. Zimmermann and R. Weismann (London and Toronto, 1989) pp. 103-20.

[17] R. S. Schofield, 'Dimensions of illiteracy, 1750-1850', *Explorations in Economic History* 10 (1972-3) p. 450. In counties like Essex, Suffolk and Norfolk, the level of literacy was of course lower. For eighteenth-century Essex, see P. King, 'Crime, law and society in Essex, 1740-1820' (Univ. of Cambridge Ph. D. thesis, 1984) p. 198, providing literacy rates of 13 per cent for labourers and 24 per cent for servants, based on a sample of Quarter Sessions depositions (N=367). For the nineteenth century, see W. B. Stephens *Education, literacy and society, 1830-1870: the geography of diversity in provincial England*

by their senders it does not necessarily follow that the people concerned composed them all by themselves. Many paupers must have had someone else to assist them in the writing. In some cases they must even have written no more than what their relative, friend or neighbour dictated to them. Conversely, for those pauper letters which were written by other people, it is equally important to envisage a broad spectrum of possibilities, with some paupers dictating their letters, while others had them written without much say in their composition and still others where the sender dispatched them without ever knowing what had been set down in his or her name.

Credibility

Whatever may have been the case in any particular instance, for the wider social historical interpretation of Essex Pauper Letters the question is therefore not so much who actually wrote these pieces as whether the poor would, on the whole, have agreed with the views expressed in these letters. This, however, seems very likely indeed. There is no indication that those paupers who sent letters were in any way peculiar. The conditions they describe correspond to the familiar 'face' of poverty at that time as known from other sources. There are the typical causes of poverty: unemployment, insufficient wages, debts, accidents, illness, infirmity, old age, death within the family. There are the common concomitants of destitution: want of food and clothing, ill health, bad housing. There is the economy of makeshifts in the daily struggle for survival: doing casual work of all sorts, peddling and tinkering, pooling incomes from all members of the family, drawing on additional resources from neighbours and kin. There are the familiar episodes of trouble with other people, such as the distress of household goods by the landlord for the arrears in rent. There is the shame of not being able to go out of doors since the coat is with the pawnbroker. There is the despair in the face of a dying child whose funeral cannot be paid.[18]

(Manchester, 1987) pp. 79-81; Vincent *Literacy and popular culture* pp. 22-6. For the European comparison, see C. M. Cipolla *Literacy and development in the west* (Harmondsworth, 1969) ch. 3 and statistical appendix; H. J. Graff *The legacies of literacy: continuities and contradictions in western culture and society* (Bloomington and Indianapolis, 1987) ch. 6.

[18] Some of these issues are dealt with in T. Sokoll, 'Negotiating a living: Essex Pauper Letters from London, 1800-1834', in *Household strategies for survival: fission, faction*

Naturally, the personal accounts given in pauper letters are highly subjective. Moreover, they are often tied up with strategic considerations. After all, these letters were written because their senders were seeking assistance from the overseers of their home parish. Therefore, in *what* people chose to say (and what not to say), they must to a certain extent have been guided by what they thought the overseers would want to hear. The same is true with respect to the question as to *how* their case might best be put. Hence the wide range of 'speech' forms encountered in pauper letters. Some letter writers use apologetic phraseology and deferential rhetoric, others prefer simple statements in plain prose. Some utter a desperate cry, while others engage in self-conscious protest. It is tempting, of course, to imagine that certain forms were more successful in obtaining relief than others. But that expectation is misleading for two reasons. First, it is typical for many letter writers not to opt for one particular form of writing but rather to combine defensive with offensive gestures. Second, even if those pieces which are clearly either defensive or offensive are compared with respect to the response they received from the overseers, there appears to be no clear-cut association. The modest request may be rejected, just as the most imposing demand can be granted. In fact, most letters seem to have met with success. It is conceivable, of course, that a higher proportion of successful rather than unsuccessful letters has survived, since successful letters were more likely to be kept by the overseers as evidence of why payments had been made.

Given the strategic interests inscribed in pauper letters, the question remains at to what extent they may be regarded as 'true' representations of their senders' circumstances. There can be no conclusive answer to this question, since it is impossible to check the individual accounts against external evidence for every single letter. But such independent evidence as we have suggests that on the whole pauper letters are indeed fairly credible. It will be sufficient here to refer once again to one of our facsimile examples discussed earlier on: the letter from George Smee of 9 May 1826 from Norwich to Braintree (plates IX-XII: **14**). He wrote to his parish 'to ask you for a Little more assistance as Can get no Employ Either for myself or family'. The statement was confirmed by the over-

and cooperation ed. J. Schlumbohm and L. Fontaine (International Review of Social History, Supplement 8; Cambridge, 2000); 'T. Sokoll, 'Voices of the poor: pauper letters and poor law provision in Essex, 1780-1834', in *Poverty and relief in England from the sixteenth to the twentieth century* ed. A. Digby, J. Innes and R. M. Smith (Cambridge, forthcoming).

seer of Norwich. For the overseers and the select vestry of Braintree, this was sufficient to increase his allowance until he found work again. They knew his case well, not only through the correspondence with their colleagues in Norwich, but also from their own experience. About a year before, Jeremiah Wing, overseer of Braintree, had himself been to Norwich and inspected all Braintree paupers residing there.[19]

That a pauper should have been visited by a representative of his home parish was perhaps somewhat exceptional. Parishes did not often take the trouble to organize such journeys, though occasionally they did, as the journeys from Braintree to Leeds (**58**) and from Chelmsford to London (**104, 106, 110, 118, 162**) show. But correspondence concerning non-resident paupers was normal. This correspondence was not only between the overseers of the parishes concerned. Letters on behalf of paupers were also sent by other people, such as relatives, neighbours and acquaintances. Another source of information for the overseers were those people whom they had authorized to pay out the allowances to paupers residing elsewhere. These could be coachmen or other people who regularly travelled between the parishes concerned, or residents of the host parish, such as local post officials.[20] Thus, the non-resident poor were subject to close scrutiny and control both within their host parish and from their home parish, which also helps to explain the high credibility of pauper letters. Most people who sent these letters were simply not in a position from which they might easily give false evidence.

In one respect, however, the views and attitudes expressed in pauper letters may have differed from those held by the labouring poor at large. This is the strategic position in which the pauper letter writers found themselves. They felt or knew that their removal to the home parish was unlikely, because it would cause more trouble for their home parish (and for their host parish as well) than the administration of non-resident relief. The disadvantage to the home parish of their 'coming home' was indeed the key strategic argument in their negotiations with the overseers. It was brought forward in various forms. People threatened to 'throw' themselves 'on the parish' or to send their family 'home'. Others stressed the better employment opportunities in the host parish, especially in cases where

[19] In the edition below, all that external evidence is reported in the apparatus underneath the text of this letter.

[20] For example, numerous letters sent to Chelmsford refer to Mr French, a coachman who delivered the allowances to several Chelmsford paupers in London. For details, see the name index at the end of this volume.

their present lack of work, due to illness or 'trade being dull' could be said to be only temporary. Some warned the overseers of the hassle and the expenses of the removal procedure itself. Elderly people expressed the wish to spend the remainder of their days in their familiar surroundings.[21]

Whatever arguments were put forward in the individual case, it is obvious that our pauper letter writers knew that the home parish basically shared their own interest in *not* being removed. In some cases, it might even be said that this peculiar convergence of interests led to a balance of forces between the overseers on the one hand and the pauper on the other. Whether or not one wants to go as far as this, the conclusion seems plausible that under the Old Poor Law, despite the discretionary powers of the overseers, the poor themselves had considerable room for strategic manoeuvring. The poor law was not only a measure of social control. It also provided an institutional platform on which people could effectively express their needs, pursue their interests and establish their claims. It is in this sense, then, that pauper letters may be regarded as a collective archive in which the experiences and attitudes of the labouring poor of late eighteenth and early nineteenth century England have been inscribed.

---

[21] People's threats to 'come home' feature in so many letters that it would be pointless to list detailed references here. They are provided in the subject index.

Chapter 5
Textual criticism and editorial documentation

Source criticism is not an end in itself. Its major practical purpose is to provide a firm basis for the editorial processing of the material and the documentation of the material within its historical context. As the discussion in the previous chapter should have made clear, pauper letters are rather complicated pieces of evidence. The text may be defective, the date, the place and even the name of sender may be missing, but at the same time the text may be surrounded by other written matter from various parties. As far as the pauper letters themselves are concerned, the editorial procedure therefore involved (a) the constitution of the *text* as opposed to (b) the documentation of the *circumtext,* that is the textual evidence (including postmarks) which falls outside the text as such, even though it is also found on the same pieces of writing.

These pieces of writing, however, are themselves surrounded by other ones, since pauper letters do not survive as sources on their own, but only as part of (and physically within) the overseers' correspondence of the parish to which they were sent (or otherwise incorporated). A good deal of that correspondence is in turn concerned with the same paupers, especially the letters from the overseers of the parishes in which they resided. For the standard editorial task of closing gaps in the primary evidence itself (such as identifying a missing date or place of sender), that correspondence was, of course, also used. The same is true of other parish records which were consulted, most notably overseers' accounts, pauper lists, settlement papers and vestry minutes. Thus, with respect to the evidence beyond the pauper letters themselves, the editorial work also involved a good deal of documentation under what has been termed (c) *related correspondence* and (d) *further evidence.*

In effect, then, the editorial process has led to a four-fold hierarchy in the documentation of the material. What that means in practical terms is spelt out in detail in a section of its own after the present introduction.[1]

---

[1] Editorial guide, pp. 79-87.

The logic of the editorial documentation, however, requires further explication. It rests on two simple decisions. First, the distinction between text and circumtext, which relates only to the pauper letters as such, but separates the words 'inside' the letter as authorized by the sender from whatever falls 'outside' that text; and second, the distinction between the edited text on the one hand, and the editorial and historical information provided in the heading and the apparatus on the other, which is based on both pauper letters and other material and concerns both textual criticism and historical documentation. The distinction between text and circumtext, which has been introduced by the present writer, should be seen as a modification of the standard rules of textual criticism and editorial documentation of modern texts and historical documents as adopted by the Centre for Scholarly Editions of the Modern Language Association and further developed by Fredson Bowers and G. Thomas Tanselle.[2]

Editorial documentation of the text

Text. The handwriting as such cannot of course be reproduced in print (nor, for that matter, can the physical features of the documents). The actual writing in terms of spelling and punctuation, however, has been retained in the present edition, including all idiosyncrasies of lettering, slips of the pen and phonetic spellings. Thus, with respect to the text of each letter the edition provides a strictly diplomatic transcription, without any correction or standardization, reproducing the original as it stands, except

---

[2] 'The Centre for Scholarly Editions: an introductory statement', *Proceedings of the Modern Language Association* 92 (1977) pp. 583-97; F. Bowers, 'Transcription of manuscripts: the record of variants', *Studies in Bibliography* 29 (1976) pp. 212-64; G. T. Tanselle, 'The editing of historical documents', *Studies in Bibliography* 31 (1978) pp. 212-64 (repr. in G. T. Tanselle *Selected studies in bibliography* [Charlottesville, Va., 1979] pp. 451-506). With respect to the logistics of the editorial process, the work of Bowers and Tanselle has been the single most important guide for the present writer. In more general terms, however, other influences have been no less significant. This is particularly true of the contrasting perspectives provided by scholars concerned with the critical documentation of medieval records and modern literary works, of whom but a few will be named here: M. T. Clanchy *From memory to written record: England 1066-1307* (2nd edn; London, 1993); L. Kuchenbuch, 'Ordnungsverhalten im grundherrlichen Schriftgut vom 9. zum 12. Jahrhundert', in *Dialektik und Rhetorik im früheren und hohen Mittelalter* ed. J. Fried (Schriften des Historischen Kollegs, Kolloquien 27; Munich, 1996) pp. 175-268; H. Zeller, 'Struktur und Genese in der Editorik. Zur germanistischen und anglistischen Editionsforschung', *Zeitschrift für Literaturwissenschaft und Linguistik* 19/20 (1975) pp. 105-26;

that underlined words are not printed as underlined but in italics (e.g. '*the Bearer*' in the letter from Mary Keeling [plate II: **629**]); and deletions or other textual alterations made in the process of writing are not reproduced within the text, but reported in the critical apparatus. The layout of each letter has also been retained, except that line breaks (and thus the division of words at the end of lines) and page breaks have been ignored. Otherwise, however, the printed text has been designed in such a way as to resemble as closely as possible the layout of the original, especially with respect to the placing of the formal epistolary components such as place of sender, date, and so on. Thus, where the place of sender is put in the middle of the first line in the original document, it also appears there in the printed text. It goes without saying that the aim of retaining the original layout has been subject to certain practical limitations and that the result is often only approximate.

Textual alterations. The documentation of the various kinds of textual alterations is best explained by means of the facsimiles. Thus, on the first page of the letter from John Barnes to his mother (plate XVII: **17**), at about the lower third on the right-hand side, there are two clearly visible *deletions*: 'and give ~~give~~ great Satisfaction' and 'for a ~~bottle~~ pot of black/ling/'. The first example shows the most common correction, the deletion of a word (here: by wiping it out) which was inadvertently written twice. The second example involves a substantive change, if only of minor importance, and in addition shows the most common form of breaking the regular linear flow of writing, the interlinear *insertion*. In this particular case, it was made at the very end of the line where the writer had run out of space. In fact, the word 'black/ling/' has been squeezed against the edge of the page in such a way that the final part is not clearly written out in individual letters so that its reading as 'ling' is an editorial suggestion, which is why it is placed in italicized square brackets in the printed text.[3]

H. Zeller, 'A new approach to the critical constitution of literary texts', *Studies in Bibliography* 28 (1975) pp. 231-64; J. Thorpe *Principles of textual criticism* (San Marino, Cal., 1972). The case for utmost historical scrutiny in all matters relating to the practices of (hand)writing may also be supported from the perspective of comparative linguistics. See F. Coulmas *The writing systems of the world* (Oxford, 1989).

[3] It may seem pedantic to distinguish two kinds of square brackets. With respect to the logic of editorial documentation, however, there is a major difference. Square brackets conventionally indicate that anything printed between them is not found within the original text (like a missing letter or word inserted by the editor). In the present case, however, the item in question is actually given in the original text. But it is not clearly legible as such so it is documented as an editorial reading, and this is indicated by italicized square brackets.

While an insertion like that, at the end of the line, might be said to interrupt no more than the physical course of writing, there is also the interlinear insertion which indicates an interruption of the mental process of writing in that the original text is being complemented by additional material which was inserted at a later point in time, if only a split second. An example of this is found on the second page of John Barnes's letter (plate XVIII: **17**): he first wrote 'and tell them that I will send them some money I cannot stay to write no more' (lines 6-7) and then added, after 'money', inserted between the lines, 'as soon as I can'. In this case, the insertion is simply made without indication, though it is absolutely clear from the text where it belongs. Normally, however, the precise place of where the additional text is to be inserted is indicated by means of a caret (or a stroke or cross), as with the 'and we Live' before 'very sparingly indeed' in the middle of the first page of the letter from William James of 25 September 1821 (plate III: **445**). In addition to deletion and insertion, which are often combined with one another, there is a third kind of textual alteration: correction through *overwriting*. This normally involves only one or two individual letters, often rendering the overwritten ones illegible, as in 'wark' in the middle of the third line in the longer letter from Benjamin Brooker (plate VIII: **510**). In most cases, overwriting is used to correct a mere slip of the pen, like 'b' written over the second 'p' in 'incapaple' (**662**). But it can also change the meaning. For example, when 'if you would send me one pound' is corrected to 'if you Could send me one pound' (**625**), or 'pay my Rent' into 'pay my Lodgens', with 'Lod' overwriting 'Rent' (**88**).

In the transcription of the pauper letters for the present edition, all textual alterations have been recorded. The form of documentation, however, depends on what the writer intended as the final text. Thus, a deletion is not reproduced within the edited text of the letter, but recorded in the critical apparatus, whereas an insertion is incorporated in the text and reported in the apparatus.

Most textual alterations do not matter much in substantive terms. Some, however, do make a difference. For example, towards the end of the letter from John Hall of 11 January 1827, it was first put down 'Sir I hope you will send', but then 'send' was ruled out and replaced by 'Take my Case into Concideration' (**341**). Amy Hill would not have applied for relief, 'Was it not for my Husband lying so heavy on my hands', but apparently she felt that this expression might in itself have been too heavy, for she altered the final words into 'lying so Ill' (**649**). In the letter from Elizabeth Baker, a woman whose husband had infected her with venereal disease and then run away, the original text says 'my desire is Gentlemen that you will make him allow me 4 or 5^s per week which is in his power to allow if he please to'. Here the final three words were deleted and 'you please to force him' was written above (**380**).

Historical documentation beyond the text

The problems discussed so far relate only to the text of the pauper letters as such. When their circumtext and other records are also taken into account, a number of further editorial problems are encountered. In considering these, we now leave the narrow field of textual criticism and turn to the wider one of historical documentation. This field is mainly covered in the other parts of the apparatus, but also extends to the headings of the pauper letters, the listings of all letters in the appendix (which were derived from the headings) and the indexes of names and places.

Inconsistent spelling of names. Personal names are sometimes given in various spellings, both by the senders themselves and between the senders and other people such as the acting overseers of the host or home parish. For example, one woman writing from Lambeth to Chelmsford signed her four letters as 'Munro' (**102**), 'Murrow' (**106**), 'Munrow' (**107**) and 'Monrow'(**117**). Similarly, there is a letter from Edward Horel from Leeds to Braintree (**58**), but in the select vestry minutes of Braintree he appears as Edward Orwell several times. In such cases, the following policy has been adopted for the editorial documentation. Within the text of the letters, each spelling is given precisely as it stands. In the headings, however, inconsistent spellings have been silently 'corrected' in order to avoid unnecessary confusion, taking the most frequent form to represent the standard against which other forms count as variant spellings. Thus, as the adopted standard spelling 'Orwell' appears in the latter example (even though the pauper himself did not use that form), and 'Munrow' in the former, since that is the most often used form in the related correspondence from the parish officers of Lambeth (though 'Munro' is also used in the notes made on her letters by the overseers of Chelmsford). Likewise, mistaken or incomplete names are retained as such within the text, but appear in the standardized form in the heading.

Where the name of the recipient is given on the outside (which is by no means always the case), it also appears in the heading, but since the outside of the letter is not regarded as part of the text (and thus not bound by the strict rules of diplomatic transcription), the name and/or title of the recipient are always given in their corrected or a standardized spelling. This does not, however, mean that they always appear in the same form, because with respect to the recipient the heading is meant to provide only the information found on the outside of the letter, except that missing first names have been added (in square brackets) where known from other evidence, again in order to avoid unnecessary confusion. Thus, Robert Alden, the overseer of St Peter in Colchester, does not appear in the heading of Benjamin Brooker's letter of December 1825 (plate VIII: **510**), because the outside of the letter does not bear a name, even though Alden must have been the recipient and is actually addressed as such at the beginning of the letter itself. In contrast, Alden's name does feature in the heading of Brooker's next letter, of April 1824 (**521**), as [Robert] Alden, overseer of St Peter, Colchester, since this corresponds to the information on the outside ('for mister holdon / oversear piters / piresh Colchester').

It goes without saying that names of senders have only been standardized on the basis of clear evidence. For example, Mrs Wall and Hannah Wall, who both wrote to Rainham in 1804 and 1805 (**647, 648**), may well have been the same person. The two letters are different in handwriting, wording and style, though this alone does not imply that they came from different people, since there are numerous paupers with letters from various hands. But there is no further evidence which would allow the question of the possible identity of the two Mrs Walls to be answered conclusively, so they have been counted as two people. The same applies to names of recipients, as with the two letters from Edward Roads in Sheffield to Steeple Bumpstead, one addressed to Mr Beans (**91**), the other one to Mr Baines (**92**), which may well be two spellings of the same name. But since no further trace of either name has been found in the parish records of Steeple Bumpstead, they have been taken as they stand, thus representing two people.

Occasionally, the outside of the letter bears not only the name (and office), but also the occupation of the recipient, as in 'Mr Boulton overseer Cimmist & Drugest' (**45**). According to the adopted principles of editorial standardization, such additional information is not represented in the heading of the letter, but may be reported in the apparatus at the discretion of the editor. The same applies to recipients like 'the Commetee of overseers Sitting at the workhouse' (**59**) or 'the Govner of the Grate poor house or The Present over Sear' (**123**), where the precise wording may be given in the apparatus, while the heading provides a standardized form ('overseer/s').

Place names. Within the text, place names are also given as they stand. In the headings, however, they appear in their modern spelling, regardless of any historic variants. For smaller places whose location may not be familiar to the general reader, the county has been added in the heading (in square brackets) when it is missing in the text. For letters from London, the parish or part of town is supplied. With London, there is of course the problem of where to draw the line demarcating it from the surrounding counties, the more so as the record of the letters themselves is not consistent in this respect. The same place may be given as belonging to London in one case but to Middlesex in another, and there are also double classifications like 'Christchurch Surrey London' (**212**). In the headings, however, such references have again been made consistent, with Christchurch, for example, always given as belonging to London, whatever the individual letter says.

EDITORIAL GUIDE

Editorial principles and transcription conventions

While the logic of the editorial process has been explained and justified in chapter 5 of the introduction, this section is intended to present its results in the form of a practical guide to the edition. It begins with an outline of the general principles which have guided the constitution of the text (nos. 1-4), followed by a descriptive account of the editorial documentation in the headings and the apparatus (nos. 5-6). Thereafter, the transcription conventions, the recording of textual alterations, idiosyncratic spellings and abbreviations are spelt out and exemplified.

Editorial principles

1. *Pauper hand = text*. Everything written or assumed to have been written by a pauper and/or said in his or her name, even when the actual writer is known to have been someone else, constitutes the TEXT of the pauper letter. The text is given as it stands, with all original spelling and punctuation or lack of punctuation retained. Within the TEXT, there is no editorial correction or standardization. Abbreviations are not extended.

2. *Other hand(s) = circumtext*. All other written matter found within or on the outside of a pauper letter but originating or assumed to originate from (an)other hand(s) is *not* part of the text but of the CIRCUMTEXT and is reported in the APPARATUS where this is regarded as appropriate.

3. *Clear text*. The TEXT is given as *clear text* and printed in normal type. It includes suggested or conjectured readings by the editor of illegible or destroyed parts which are meant to restore the original text. These editorial suggestions and conjectures are also printed in normal type, but placed within brackets. Brief editorial descriptions of longer missing, illegible or destroyed parts of the text may also be reported within the TEXT. They are also placed within brackets, but printed in *italics*. (See Transcription conventions.)

4. *Textual alterations*. The principle of clear text also means that the
TEXT records only the *final* text. Earlier stages of the text superseded by
alterations to the text made by the writer are not given within the TEXT
itself, but recorded in the APPARATUS.

5. *Heading*. The TEXT of each letter is preceded by a heading which is
printed in bold type. This is a standardized editorial text which is intended
to present the personal, locational and temporal features normally associated with a letter: the name and place of the sender; the name and/or
parish office and place of the recipient; and the date.

As far as possible, these pieces of information have been taken from the
letter itself. Any piece of information not derived from the letter is placed
in square brackets. Typically, all information regarding the sender and the
date are derived from the TEXT, whereas all information regarding the
recipient has been taken exclusively from the address on the outside of
the letter. This means that where the outside is blank or missing, no recipient is given, even if addressed in the letter itself or otherwise known. It
also means that the same recipient may not be documented consistently.
For example, his parish office might be given in one case but not in another.
However, the spelling of names and places has been standardized. For
smaller places, the location of which may not be familiar to the non-specialist reader, the county has been added. For letters from London, the
parish or common local name, such as Kentish Town, has been added
where it is given in the letter or could be identified from the sender's
address or from other evidence.

6. *Organization and scope of the apparatus*. The APPARATUS appears
after the TEXT of the letter. It is printed in smaller type and broken down
into various categories according to the kind of documentation involved.
The categories are organized consecutively, with their points of reference
spanning from the scriptual features of the letter itself to other letters and
external evidence of other kinds. Naturally, the full range of documentation covered by these categories applies to the textual corpus on the whole,
whereas for any individual letter the categories are only used where
appropriate.

TEXTUAL ALTERATIONS. This records *all* alterations which the writer made
to earlier versions of the text in order to attain the final text (corrections,
deletions, insertions).

SPELLING. For slips of the pen, such as 'sing' for 'sign', or spellings which
are so idiosyncratic that the reader may find it difficult to understand the

intended meaning, such as 'witsends' for 'wits' ends', a corrected reading is suggested.

ABBREVIATIONS. Unusual or idiosyncratic abbreviations which may be difficult for the reader to decode are extended. Common abbreviations, such as 'serv^t' for 'servant', are not spelt out individually but given in the brief List of common abbreviations below.

WRITING. This reports special features of the handwriting which cannot be reproduced in the printed TEXT, such as an unusual organization of the lines, or information on the hand of the writer, especially where he or she is known to have been a person other than the sender in whose name the letter is written.

DESTRUCTION OF TEXT. Where larger parts of the text have been physically destroyed, such as parts of the page having been torn off or eaten up by mice, silverfish or others, this is briefly mentioned.

NAME OF SENDER. Where a pauper's name occurs in different spellings, the spelling given in the editorial heading of the letter may differ from that found in the text. In such cases the editor's choice of the standard spelling as given in the heading is explained.

DATE. This explains the editorial dating of the letter where the text itself does not give a date or give a date which is inconsistent with other evidence. Where the letter has been dated from its postmark, this is not necessarily to be taken literally: strictly speaking, it means that the letter cannot have been written later than on the given date. In practical terms, most letters dated in this way should thus be assumed to have been written a day or two before the date reported.

PLACE. This refers to cases where the place of sender is not given in the letter but has been inferred from external evidence, or where a place name below the parish level is involved.

TEXT. This provides information on people or circumstances mentioned in the letter which is essential to its understanding. It should be stressed that entries under this heading have only been made where such information has been readily available from the records systematically consulted (other pauper letters and the records described under RELATED CORRESPONDENCE and FURTHER EVIDENCE). No attempt at ample (let alone exhaustive) coverage has been made.

CIRCUMTEXT. This records or refers to written matter which is found on the same letter but is not regarded as part of the TEXT, such as a note of receipt from a later hand. Such written matter 'outside' the text but in the same document is only reported when it provides additional information to the text which may be of interest to the specific case, whereas mere standard additions, such as endorsements by the receiving overseer which only repeat information already given in the text, such as the sender's name or the date of the letter, are *not* included. It should be noted that the CIRCUMTEXT can also include matter written in the same hand as the TEXT (pauper hand), such as an idiosyncratic form or spelling of the address on the outside.

RELATED CORRRESPONDENCE provides links to letters from other people, that is letters from relatives, acquaintances etc. of the sender on his or her behalf, or letters between the overseers of the parishes concerned. All these are normally found within the same parochial file of overseers' correspondence from which the pauper letters have been selected.

FURTHER EVIDENCE reports traces of the sender or of other relevant people in other parish records, notably overseers' accounts, vestry minutes and pauper lists of the place in which the sender had his or her settlement. Again, it should be stressed that such records, while searched and checked systematically, have not been exploited exhaustively.

Transcription conventions

[ ] Insertions of editorial text are placed within square brackets.

[ ] Suggested readings of ambiguous, indecipherable or illegible parts of the text are placed within *italicized* square brackets.

< > Conjectured readings of physically destroyed and irrecoverable parts of the text are placed within pointed brackets.

Anything placed within brackets and given in normal type is meant to restore the original text. Brackets of the appropriate type are also used for brief editorial descriptions of longer illegible, missing or destroyed parts of the text. Such descriptions are given in *italics*. Where no suggested or conjectured reading is provided, the approximate length in letters of the illegible or destroyed parts of the text is indicated by hyphens (one hyphen per presumed letter) within brackets of the appropriate type. Round brackets are always part of the text itself and never used as a transcriptive device.

Examples

[continued on outside]
send my allo*[wance]*
I am in g<re>at distress
I thought you had told Mr *[- - - - - -]* that my
brot<he>r had <- - - - -> for he is <*bottom line torn off*>
[5 March 1824]

Recording of textual alterations, idiosyncratic spellings and abbreviations

Textual alterations

All textual alterations made in the course of writing by the writer of the letter are recorded at the beginning of the critical apparatus below the letter, following the principles of textual criticism suggested by Bowers, Tanselle and others. After a line reference and a lemma followed by one square bracket, the alterations are briefly described. In these descriptions, all parts of the text or former text are printed in normal type and placed within inverted commas, whereas all descriptive matter is printed in italics.

Examples

2: means] *interl with caret.*
3: before] *after del* 'begore'.
4: overseer] 'r' *over* 's'

Abbreviations

interl	interlined
del	deleted
over	overwritten

Unless otherwise stated, 'interlined' or 'deleted' refer to that point of the text which is indicated.

Idiosyncratic spellings

Spellings which may be difficult for the reader to decode are recorded in a way similar to that of textual alterations. As a general rule, the reader may find that *reading aloud* is the best and most simple means to facilitate understanding.

Examples

2: sing] *read* 'sign'.
3: charricktor] *read* 'character'.

Abbreviations

Within the text, abbreviations are not extended, but given as they stand. Superscript letters are retained and printed in smaller type, while the full stop, dash or whatever other sign conventionally used in handwriting in connection with such superscription has been omitted. In cases where the non-specialist reader may be assumed to be unable to extend an abbreviation, the extension is given in the apparatus.

Examples

4: Affte] Affectionate.
5: M^r B] Mr Benson.

List of common abbreviations

acc^t	account
gen^n	Gentleman/gentlemen
hum^l	humble
ob^t, obed^t	obedient
ser^t, serv^t, ser^{vt}	servant
y^e	the
y^t	that

ESSEX PAUPER LETTERS
1731-1837

Aveley pauper letters

1   From Sarah Taylor in Deptford [Surrey] to [J. W.] Clover in Aveley, 31 May 1825

Deptford May 31ˢᵗ 1825

Mʳ Clover /

I Received your Letter wherein you said the Gentlemen would consider my case and would let me know but another month has elapsed and I have not heard any further from you I therefore have again taken the ₅ liberty of troubling you humbly hopeing the Gentleman will not forget to consider my case which I stated to you in my last Letter humbly intreating they will send me some releife or let me know what they would have me to do trusting in their goodness I remain with respect

their Obedient humble servant   10

Sarah Taylor

Wʀɪᴛɪɴɢ This letter was written by Sarah Taylor's presumed landlord, Mr Norris.

Rᴇʟᴀᴛᴇᴅ ᴄᴏʀʀᴇsᴘᴏɴᴅᴇɴᴄᴇ In a letter of 2 May 1825, J. W. Clover, vestry clerk of Aveley, had told Sarah Taylor 'that there is no Vestry to be held this *Week* but [...] that your case shall be taken into consideration as soon as there is one'. That letter was returned by post, with a statement (from the same hand as Sarah Taylor's letter) from Mr Norris, apparently Sarah Taylor's landlord, of 8 July 1825, saying that he had advanced £2 to her 'for rent due to me'.

2   From James Smith in Woolwich, Kent, to the overseer of Aveley, 5 September [1831]

September 5

Sir

I have taken the Liberty of Righting to you to inform you that my Wifes Freinds has got me A good Situation in Canterbury as Horse keeper providing I can get to go I have had only one weeks work since I was in esex ₅ it is here as it is every where they wont employ any one but there one I am very sorry to trouble the Gentlemen but I hope they will take it in to consideration and Send me A trifle to help to take my family down as I cant do here and I cant go whith out Some asistants for I have been obliged to make away with many of my things to help to keep my Children I ₁₀ would not trouble you if it was not force <i>f I cant get to go I shall be

obliged to bring My family home this quarter for I cant do any Longer it is
A thing I dont Like to trouble the parish that I am obliged at present I am
sure there is not many would gone through asmuch as I have done to keep
15 from A parish but if the Gentlemen will help me down I am in hopes that
wont be any more trouble to them for years if I do go I must be in Canterbury A Satuday the 10 of September for the other man Leaves on Friday
Night and I Should Like to embrace the opertunity for I may not have A
nother Chance again and My Friends as taken A deal of trouble in getting
20 the Place for me I hope the Sir you will do what you can for me for it takes
A deal to Suport 5 Children I can Say for this 16 weeks I have I have no
more to say not had 3 weeks work and there is no places here

direct for Jame Smith
Mr Evans Buildings Red
25   Lion Street Woolwich
Kent

TEXTUAL ALTERATIONS 11: go] *interl.* 14: to] *after del* 'as'.
  WRITING The confusion at the end of the letter (ll. 21-2) is due to the fact that the writer
placed the text in two blocks without leaving proper space between them, misleading the
reader into the wrong word order. The intended word order is: 'it takes A deal to Suport
5 Children I have no more to say I can Say for this 16 weeks I have not had 3 weeks work
and there is no places here'.
  DATE Year from postmark.

3   From James Smith in Woolwich [Kent] to Mr Sewell in Aveley, 8 February 1832

Febuary 8 1832

Sir I have rote these few Lines to You to infrom you of our distress in our
family My Husband as been Sick a long wile and not able to work for his
family and wee are very bad of I expect to be confined before long and I
5 am quit unprepared for it for I have not things nesary for my use for I
have not been able to Get them I have put it very week thinking that My
Husband would be able to Get work that I might <be> able to Get A few
things for my use wee have been obliged to make away with every article
that would fetch A Shilling for to Get Bread for the Children for wee
10 have been very bad of this winter I Should have come over and Stated the
Case to the Gentlemen but I have not Got Shoes that will bring me so far
and My Husband is not able to Come wee have had A deal of Sickness
this winter wee have done as long as wee posible can without troubling

the Parish wee have A large family to keep wee have had deal of Sick- ness lately and I have one that very ill cant run alone wee have 5 Children 15 and buried 3 in woolwich without any ones help wee have no one to Give us a penny and I hope that the Almighty will Soften the Gentlemens hearts towards us that they will Send us A trifle as soon as they Can for wee are greatly in need of it at present for to Get common nesarys for our use that I Cant do without wee have Children that has not A bit of shoes to there 20 feet at all wee would not trouble You if wee was not forced to do it I hope the Gentlemen will Send us A trifle as it is not often that wee do trouble them I would not know only for the Sutation that I am in and not things for my use but if the Gentlemen will not Send us any thing I must come home and remain there untill I am confined My Husband would have 25 come with his family before but wee are so much in dept that wee cant Get away from this I hope Gentlemen that you will send u<s> A little to help us through our trouble and to Get us A few things that cant be with- out and I hope you will send as soon as p<ossible> please God wee will not trouble again f<or> one wile for the summer is coming a<nd> I shall 30 be able to work often that Get over my trouble I am not afraid of work to help keep my family

Your Humble	direct for James Smith
Servant	Mr Evans Buildings Red
James Smith	Lion Street Woolwich	35

TEXTUAL ALTERATIONS 17: will] *interl*. 18: will] *inserted in left-hand margin*. 20: wee] *after del illeg*. 24: Gentlemen] *interl below after del* 'Gent^m' *at end of line*. 25: confined] *after del illeg*. 27: hope] *interl*. 27: send] *interl*. 28: and] *after del illeg*. 28: cant] *interl*. 29: will] *interl*.

WRITING It should be noted that this letter, while signed in the name of James Smith, is written in the person of his wife. Whether this means that she put pen to paper we do not know. At any rate, the letter is from the same hand as all (other) letters from James Smith (**2, 4, 5, 8**).

4   From James Smith in Woolwich, Kent, to the overseers of Aveley, 6 September 1832

September 6 1832

Gentlemen
I must be so troublesome to the Parish for A little asistance for I have been Laid up this 5 weeks very bad and I have one boy that is very ill at Present and My Wife is in a poor state of health and as been since She 5

was confined I have 6 Children and not one of them able to Earn A Penny
and that makes it very hard for us My Wife earns A little at her needle
when she is able it is very little that I Can earn for I am not fit for hard
work know I have had so much Sickness and if I trouble this Parish they
10 will Send My Family home because there is so much Sickness in Woolwich
know I am very bad of for I have been obliged to make away twith all I
have to Support My Family I will take it as A great favour if the Gentlemen will asist me a little for I Cant do any longer without some little to
help me and if the Gentlemen will not do any thing for me I must trouble
15 this Parish and Come home I dont whant to be so troublesome but I have
done as long as I Can do if I Come home I Cant do Feild work and there
is no thing els to do and here I am so much known that I Can Sometimes
Get A Job in the Stables when I am able to do it I Cant well Leave woolwich
for I am so much in Dept I hope the Gentlemen will do A Little for me as
20 soon as they Can for I am in great distress the Children are very bad of for
Clothing and Shoes and that is very bad to go without Shoes I hope You
will Rite by return of Post
                    so no more Your Humble
                    Servant James Smith
25   direct for James Smith
                    Mr Evans Buildings
                    Red Lion Street
                    Woolwich Kent

TEXTUAL ALTERATIONS 8: fit] 'i' *over illeg.* 12: Support] 'up' *over illeg.* 14: trouble] 'ro'
over illeg. 15: whant] 'n' *over* 't'. 17: no] *after del illeg.* 19: Dept] *after del* 'Dbebt'.

**5   From James Smith in Woolwich [Kent] to the overseers of
        Aveley, [25 September 1832]**

Sir I am very sorry that the Gentlemen would not Send me A trifle to asist
me and my Family as I am in great need of it for I have 6 months rent to
make up by the 29 ofand thats is on Satuday nex at 2 Shillings per week and
if I Cant pay it I Shall Lose what few things I have and what little <---> I
5 have got and then I am sure I Can<t> Get any more I am sorry to trouble
you but I Cant do without I do make all the Shift I can before I do trouble
you I wish I Could do without it I Should be very Glad but my Fanily is so

Large and So much Sickness that I Cant Avoid it but I hope that the Gentlemen will do A little for me and I wont trouble them all the winter no more

so no more 10
Your humble
servant
James
Smith

direct for   15
James Smith
Red Lion Street
Mr Evans
        Buildings
        Woolwich

TEXTUAL ALTERATIONS 2: in] *interl.* 5: more] 'o' *over illeg.* 8: and] *after del* 'tha'.
DATE Date of postmark.

6   **From Mary Wood in Mile End New Town, London, to Mr
       Sewell in Aveley, 13 December 1832**

1832
December 13

London
    Sir I am Sorry to have to Trable You Whith this date But I Do not
Know what to Do With the Gall As Her is So Bad of for Cloths Sir I Did   5
Come to Romforde on Wednesday Last and I Could not See you Sir I
Saw Mr Chamblin at Romforde and Him Saide that Whould Name it to
you Sir I Should Be much ablidg To you if Whould Send me A Trifle Of
Monny I Should Be much Ablidge to you for So Doing and if not Send
mee an answer Sir and I must Came Down Sum how But I hope Sir You 10
Will consider About it and Send Mee A Little Monny

I am your hum^l Servant
Mary Wood

Sir Derect to me
at No 5 King Street   15
Mile End New Town
        London

FURTHER EVIDENCE Mary Woods in Whitechapel had received 1s 6d per week for her illegitimate girl from March 1825 to March 1831 (ERO, D/P 157/12/10-11, Aveley overseers' accounts).

7   From Elizabeth Sheepard in Lambeth [London], to Mr Sewell in Aveley, 18 February 1833

Surry Feby 18th 1833

To the gentlemen of the parrish board of Aveley, in the County of Esex
Gentlemen

I am Sorry to inform you that I am at this time in grate distress Owing
5 to a bad State of health for above 4 months and my daughter is Still worse
being aflicted with fitts worse than Ever which is a grate trial to me and
my Boy is waigting his turn for the admision to the School so that it has
Caused me to part with Every thing that I could make a Shilling of to
keepe Us rather then become trublesom to my parish and Gentlemen I
10 have Not given you any trouble for above thirteen months therfore gentlemen I hope you will take my pityful Case into your kind Consideration and
Releive my distress

Gentlemen

I Remain your most

15   humble & Obed^t Servt

Elizth Sheepard

N 7 Winmill Row

Eaton St Newcut

Lambeth

20   Surry

TEXTUAL ALTERATIONS 2: board] *inserted in left-hand margin.* 4: that] 'a' *over illeg.* 5: for]
'f' *over illeg.* 6: than] 'a' *over illeg.* 6: Ever] 'E' *over illeg.* 6: trial] 'a' *over* 'l'. 7: the] 't'
over illeg. 7: School] 'h' *over* 'o'; *second* 'o' *over* 'l'. 9: and] 'nd' *interl.*

8   From James Smith in Woolwich [Kent] to Mr Sewell in Aveley, 21 March 1833

March 21 1833

Gentlemen

I am sorry to be So troublesome but I Cannot avoid it for I have been
Laid up with the rumatick Gout and not been able to do any thing for this
5 3 months My Pention is not much to keep 6 Children and our two Selves
I have been obliged to draw my money weekeley to keep us and that is
very little I am not able to work in the winter but in the summer I Can do
without troubleing the Parish I do as long as I Can before I do I pay 2

shillings Per week for one Room and that I have to Pay A quarters rent on
the 29 of this Month and I have not Got it to Pay if the Gentlemen will 10
will be so kind as to Send me A trifle to help me to Pay it or els I shall
have what few things taken away from us and then I am sure I Can never
Get any more and then I must come home but dont whant to Come for I
know the Workhouse will be my Portion for I am not able to work in the
feilds and in the summer I Got about for one and the Others as I am so 15
much known I hop Sir You will asist me this time as I will Give you my
word that I wount trouble you any more untill next Chrismas as the Summer is coming I Can do but in the winter I Cannot with my family for I
have not one to bring in any thing My Wife is Laid up with bad eys and
often is and can Get no care for them I should not trouble if I Could do 20
with I have been obliged to Make away with Last thing that will fetch A
Shilling for Bread for the Children if the Gentlemen will not be leive me
I Can show the doublicates My Wif would Come and state the Case to
you but her eys is bad and we have not Got the money to Come with I
hope You will do what you Can for me and if the Gentlemen will not asist 25
me in Paying of My Rent I hope you will Let me know and I must Sell
what few things I have to Pay the <rent> and Come home at You must
Consider that my Pention is not much to keep 3 of us and when I am Laid
up I whant Noureshment but I Cant have it I hope you will let me know as
soon as you can for the time is Short James Smith 30
Mr Evans Build^ng
Red Lion Street
Woolwich
I Received the last and much Obliged to You for Your kindness

TEXTUAL ALTERATIONS 6: draw] 'd' *over illeg*. 6: us] *after del* 'w'. 7: winter] 'n' *over* 't'.
13: dont] 'd' *after del illeg*. 14: know] *after del illeg*. 15: Others] 'O' *over illeg*. 18:
winter] 'n' *over del* 't'. 19: bring] *after del* 'thing'. 27: You] 'Y' *over illeg*. 29:
Noureshment] *after del illeg*. 29: let] *after del illeg*.

9   From E. Feild

Mr Joyner
    Sir
    I have sent to you as I am not able to Come myself to bag agreat favour
of you that is to now what the Gentlemen have agread to pay of my rent
and Likewise to now of you if I Sell part of my Goods and pay the 5

rammaner and pay for the futur Every week if you will grant me the favor
of having my house as usal as I have bing at the Expence of having an
oven bilt and making the place Comfortable pray Sir if posable dont Distress me of my house and home but pray send me word wether I must
10 leave it or not at mickelmas or seal or before pray Sir Grant me the favor
of stoping as usual I am your Hamble Servant
E Feild

TEXTUAL ALTERATIONS 4: the] *inserted in left-hand margin.* 8: Comfortable] 'table' *interl at end of line.*

FURTHER EVIDENCE Mrs Feild was granted 5s (per week) in December 1824, and 6s in March 1825 (ERO, D/P 157/8/3, Aveley vestry minutes, entries of 9 December 1824 and 25 March 1825).

Great Bardfield pauper letters

**10   From John Smith in Sutton, Surrey, to Samuel Dodd, over-
seer of Great Bardfield, 26 January 1835**

Sutton. Surrey. Jany 26th 1835.

Sir/

I am under the painful necessity of soliciting a little pecuniary assitance
in consequence of a long and dangerous illness - my Wife, with five children
&myself being all attacked with a violent fever, by which I was rendered   5
incapable of following my employment for 13 Weeks - during that period I
have not received any money from my employer (Mr Wm Amos) and
have been under the necessity of paying a nurse to attend my family for
eight weeks at 3^s/6^d pr Week - I am happy to state we are all getting better
but are still so weak as not to be able to keep about all day - I feel greatly   10
obliged for the assistance afforded me by the Parish &beg to state that
the supply has been stopped this fortnight. We are now greatly in want of
food, firing, &clothing & I therefore earnestly entreat &humbly trust you
will relieve our present necessity's, &you will confer a lasting obligation
on   15

Sir/

Your most distress'd Servt

John Smith

WRITING Professional hand.

CIRCUMTEXT Statement from William Amos on back of page: 'Gent^n this Letter is a True
Statement of Poor Smith Distress and any further Assistance that you Can Afford him
will be a Great Charity'.

RELATED CORRESPONDENCE In a letter of 13 March 1835, to the vestry clerk of Great
Bardfield, the overseer of Sutton (name illegible) said about John Smith and his family: 'I
am truly sorry the bill seems so large but i can assure you the family was in that state to
require so much nursing *[etc.]* that it could not be avoided'.

**11   From John Dennison in Debden [Essex] to the overseers of
Great Bardfield, 3 May 1836**

To the Overseers of Great Bardfield

Gentlemen

I am not possessed of any real or personal Property I live with my Son
who maintains me I made whatlittle property I had overtohim in a legal

5 manner before the present poor Law act came into operation consequently
there is nolaw which will compel me to maintain my Grandchildren

I am Gent[n]

Your obed[t] Serv[t]

John Dennison

10 Debden

3rd May 1836

TEXTUAL ALTERATIONS 4: i had] *interl with caret.*
WRITING Extremely neat hand.

12   From Jacob Brown in Laindon[-cum-Basildon, Essex] to Mr Smith in Great Bardfield

jintill min

iright to you but do not wish to fend you but to inform you that the
parish of landon that you gintill min of Bardfield brought me home too
and received me by the bond that m[r] waledy made with you thay

5 <r>eceived me and have releved me for thease twelve years and know
are agoon to bring me and my wife and seven children home to bardfield
but the gintil man is dead that i lived with and likewise the witness is
dead and and the parish of landon is a goon to make the san fo ny master
pay the hundred pounds for that is the bond and thay will bring me home

10 to Bardfield

i have Been before m[r] Bull squ[r] sunday last and examined and i always
will stand by it that i belong to the parish of landon and nother and i
should be glad of your advise how i an to pursead and like wise answer by
the return fo the post

15 Jacob Brown i maried the daughtor of nrs ann barker in great Bardfield

TEXTUAL ALTERATIONS 4: with you] *interl.* 9: pounds] 'ds' *interl at end of line.* 11: and examined] *interl.*

PLACE 'Landon' as given in the text is misspelt for Laindon, which was part of the parish of Laindon-cum-Basildon. The postmark is from Billericay, about 4 miles north of Laindon.

Braintree pauper letters

13 From Ann Hitchcock in Feering [Essex] to the churchwardens and overseers of Braintree, 22 December 1823

Feering December 22 1823

Gentelmen) I Ann Hatchcock)

Take the liberty of writeing to you To know wich way you intend to do,
for My creators have been to me for money and I tell them all that they
Must take my goodes For I have no money, for I cannot pay no Rent but 5
Gentlemen if I am to Come Home you must let me know for I may as
Well come as stop hear to be starved for my Boys cannot get no work so
how am I to do But if I come home you will have to buy me Goodes for if
I have to come home my Creators Will tak my goodes and chatels for
money due To them but Gentelmen if I remain here They will not desturbe 10
me, but I have, been A widow for 11 years I had a good Bed to Lay on I
shall take it very hard to have it Taken from me Gentelmen if I stop were
I am you must send me some shifen For I am great destress at this time
my Boys Haven no work is a great hurt to me I hope Gentelmen you will
Let me know What is to B done as soon as possebel 15

Gentelmen   I remain

your

most Ob^{nt} Hum

Ann Hatchcock   Ser^{vt}

TEXTUAL ALTERATIONS 5: no money] 'no' *followed by del* 'n' ('non'). 12: very] *after del*
'ye'. 14: my] *interl with caret.*

NAME OF SENDER 'Hatchcock' as given in the letter is regarded as a variant spelling.

FURTHER EVIDENCE In the overseers' accounts of Braintree, references to Widow Hitchcock
at Feering are to be found from the second quarter of 1827. At that time, she received a
weekly allowance of 5s which was paid to her son Richard Hitchcock and was apparently
meant to cover both of them. From the fourth quarter of 1829, the allowance was split into
one of 2s 6d for herself and of 2s for her son. The amount for the last quarter of 1829 was
handed out to her daughter, Elizabeth Hitchcock, who certified the receipt with her mark
in the overseers' account book. Within the same source, there are also some earlier references to Widow Hitchcock (alias Hitchercock) at Inworth from the second quarter of
1824, according to which she received a weekly allowance of 7s 6d until the first quarter
of 1825. From the places at which they were recorded within the quarterly accounts of
relief payments and the close proximity of the parishes involved - Inworth is less than two
miles from Feering - it would seem likely that the two widows Hitchcock were one and
the same person (ERO, D/P 264/12/31, Braintree overseers' accounts).

14* **From George Smee in Norwich to [Jeremiah] Wing in Braintree, 9 May 1826**

Norwich 9th May 1826

Gentⁿ

it was far distant from my wish or thought to Trouble you for an addition on the Allowance of what you are so good as to relieve me with but
5 Necessity impel me to ask you for a Little more assistance as Can get no Employ Either for myself or Family therefore Gentⁿ hope you will have the goodness to take it into your most serious Consideration for my Condition is truly Deplorable hope you will grant me Something Farther in Order to Alleviate the Distress my Family Labour under

10

am Gentⁿ

your Ob[/d]t

& Mst Hble Servt

G: Smee

TEXTUAL ALTERATIONS 11: Ob[/d]t] 'd' *over illeg.*

CIRCUMTEXT Note from other hand below text, facing valedictions: 'The above was sent by Post & recommend d by Mʳ Jnº Webb' (hand A). Statement from John Webb, overseer in Norwich, 9 May 1826, at bottom of page and on back: 'Mʳ Webb knows the writer of the above as an honest industrious Creature + really stands in need of some additional assistance from your Parish if that assistance is not afforded himself Wife + two Children woud indeed must return home to Braintree'(hand B). Underneath, note in pencil: '1[s]/ 6[d]' (hand C).

Copy of answer from Jeremiah Wing, overseer of Braintree, 15 May 1826, on next page: 'Sir The Gentlemen of the Select Vestry wish me to infome you that they will allow you to pay to George Smee 4/ per week from this day till himself and family gets Employment & when that is, will thank you to reduce it to the former Allowance of 2/6 will oblidge the Gentlemen of the Select Vestry of Braintree'(hand D).

Address on outside from hand of John Webb (hand B), 'Joseph' mistaken for Jeremiah.

FURTHER EVIDENCE A full copy of this letter, retaining the original spelling, and a copy of the answer from Jeremiah Wing are to be found in the vestry minutes of Braintree (ERO, D/P 264/8/10, Braintree select vestry, book of memoranda, 1817-36, entries of 9 and 15 May 1826).

In June 1825, Wing had visited the Braintree paupers living in Norwich. In his 'Statement of the poor at Norwich', where each family is given with the names (except for wives), ages and earnings of the individual members, George Smee (aged 53), his wife (49) and their children Eliza (14), James (9), and George (6) were reported as earning 11s 3d (George 7s, Eliza 2s 9d and James 1s 6d). 'The man', it was said, was 'very weakly & not [on] average the above earnings in winter time' (ERO, D/P 264/8/10, Braintree select vestry, book of memoranda, 1817-36, entry of 16 August 1827). George Smee had received a weekly allowance of 5s until Lady Day 1825. We do not know when it was reduced to the amount of 2s 6d referred to in the answer from Wing of 15 May 1826, since there are no detailed overseers' accounts for the time from Lady Day 1825 to Lady Day 1827. From the second quarter of 1827, George Smee received a weekly allowance of 4s (ERO, D/P

264/12/31, Braintree overseers' accounts). See also FURTHER EVIDENCE to his letter of 26 Februray 1828 (**19**).

15   From Thomas Elsegood in Norwich to the overseer of Braintree, 22 May 1826

Norwich 22nd May 1826

Gentlemen

I Am Sorrow to think that I am Oblidged to trouble you for a Greater Relief of Solomon Spooner for the distressendness of the times cause me so to do and also the loss of my Wife by Death make it still worse for I am   5
oblidged to get a Woman to do for him has he is so infirmed with age that he his not capable of doing any thing for himself for his age is 78 and Gentlemen your kindness at present for the Relief of him is 2ˢ/6ᵈ pʳ week but I hope you will be pleased to take it into your most Serious Consideration through the hardness of times and his infirmed Age that you will   10
be pleased to Allow him as far as You Possibly can he have had a very Servere illness and I have done for him all that laid in my power and also this Doctor I have paid but for the want of Employment for myself I cannot Assist him So well as I could wish therefore I ma<y> trust to Your goodness in doing the best y<ou> can you will be pleased to direct for   15
Thomas Elsegood to be left at the Sign of the Ship Sᵗ Micheal at Thorne Lane Norwich, Gentlemen

I Remain Your very Obedient
& Very humble Servent

Thomas Elsegood   20

CIRCUMTEXT Note from other hand below text: 'Answer to this Paid 9ᵈ' (hand A).
Note from other hand at bottom of first page: '3/0 wk from May 29' (hand B).
    Note of answer of 29 May 1826, from Jeremiah Wing, overseer of Braintree to Thomas Elsegood, on back of first page: 'Allowance to Solomon Spooner^{Senr} be increased from two Shillings to 3 Shillings per Wk from the 29 Day of May 1826'(hand C).
    FURTHER EVIDENCE In June 1825, Wing had visited the Braintree paupers living in Norwich. In his 'Statement of the poor at Norwich', where each family is given with the names (except for wives), ages and earnings of the individual members, Solomon Spooner (aged 78) was reported to live with his son-in-law (Thomas Elsegood?) and his daughter, being 'quite unable to do any thing'. Two years later, after another journey to Norwich, Wing reported that Solomon Spooner (80) lived on his own, 'Mostly confin'd to his Bed', and received a weekly allowance of 3s (ERO, D/P 264/8/10, Braintree select vestry, book of memoranda, 1817-36, entries of 23 June 1825 and 16 August 1827). As a matter of fact, Solomon Spooner seems to have received that allowance of 3s as early as 1824 and through to 1829 (D/P 264/12/31, Braintree overseers' accounts).

16   From Thomas Cleare in Braintree, 29 January 1827

Gentl^n

   I hope you will take it into Consideration to allow me something of the
back pay for the support of Greys family for I am unable to pay my rent &
my Land lord is going to Distress me he will wait no Longer & the whole
5 Family you must take for I have brought myself to poverty & sold my
Linnen off my back for their Support & now take it hard to be turned into
the Street & Loose my work for My Loom will be taken & my Master
will Give me no more & it is not my wish to bring any Expenc upon you
if I can avoid it for I have done to the utmost of my power & I trust Gent^n
10 that you cannot say but what I have behaved as a man hope you will
consider it & Let me know to day & you will Greatly Oblige your Obedient & Humble Servt

Thos Cleare

Braintree
15 29 Jany 1827

TEXTUAL ALTERATIONS 5: you] *interl with cross.* 5: have] *interl with cross.*

17*   From John Barnes in Billericay [Essex] to Mrs Digby in Brain-
   tree, 24 July 1827

   Briliricay July 24 1827
Dear mother this comes with my Love to you hopen to find you and my
Brothers and sisters all well as it leaves me at present thank God for it I
got here on sunday Evening about 9 o clock as wet as I could be but I
5 dried myself as much as I could but I Did not get quite Dry nor are my
trowses Dry now my master inquired wether I could Drive post and I said
no and then he said that I must go back again for I was of no use and he
wondered how Mrs Goodman came to bring me but she said that I should
Do in time so I went to work and give great Satisfaction Dear mother I
10 had to give 4 shilling for a set of brushes and 6^d for a pot of black/ling/
and 6 for a lock and key to lock them up again the Maids for here is 5
Maids house Maid cook waiter chamber maid and kitchen Maid so that I
could not buy a shirt and I Doubt I shall not get no great Deal of money
this week for the races are 3 Days but we had 3 travlers stopt here last
15 night and I got 9^d then Dear mother I wish you could send me my shirt on

friday for theres is a coach goes from our house to chelmsford than Give
my love to M^rs ward and m^rs Wright and tell them that I will send them
some money as soon as I can I cannot stay to write no more for I am
called away to Dinner) I Dine^d of a beatiful Leg of Mutton roasted and
some turnips &c &c   20

           So no more
           at present
           from your
           Loven Son
           John Barnes   25

TEXTUAL ALTERATIONS 9: great] *after del* 'give'. 10: pot] *after del* 'bottle'. 10: black[ling]]
interl at end of line. 15: night] *after del illeg*. 15: 9] *after del* '9'. 16: our] *after del* 'h'. 16:
chelmsford] 'ford' *interl at end of line*. 18: as soon as I can] *interl*.
   CIRCUMTEXT Note at bottom: 'Granted 2^s for a News Shirt & 5 to buy Brushes &c. J.G.'
This was from Joseph Garrett, overseer of Braintree, which also explains how this private
letter came into the hands of the overseers. John Barnes's mother must have given it to
them, requesting assistance towards his expenses for clothes and other necessaries.

18   **From Samuel Spooner in Norwich to [Jeremiah] Wing, over-
       seer of Braintree, 16 January 1828**

                        Norwich 16th Jany 1828

Sir
   On account of the scarcity to work I am obliged to apply to the parish to
which I belong and to state that I have had but very little to do for this
three Months, and also that I am now out of employ, and that the Chil-   5
dren can earn nothing and that we are in extreme distress; I have therefore to Solicit your kindness in recommending me to the Committee for
an increase to my Present allowance, and as I have Six Children entirely
to support I have to request that you will be also pleased to state to the
Committee that it will be impossible for me at present to support myself 10
and family without an addition of three shillings ^per Week to my present
allowance which if not granted I shall be obliged to return immediately to
to the Parish with my family, I shall be obliged by your having the goodness to acquaint Mr Webb as soon as possible with the result of my application   15
           I am
                  Sir
                Your most respectfull

and very obedient

20   humble servant

Sam¹ Spooner

Circumtext Address on outside 'Mʳ Whyn | Clock and Watchmaker | Overseer'.

Note from Jeremiah Wing, overseer of Braintree, on next page: 'The pay of Sam¹ Spooner Junʳ to be 6/ per week to commence from Satterday Next the 26 Inst[ant] - Mʳ Webb wrote to that effect'.

Related correspondence and further evidence In a letter from the overseers of Braintree to John Webb, overseer of Norwich, 12 February 1827, which was apparently delivered by Spooner, Webb was requested to pay Spooner 3s from 17 February 1827 on.

In August 1827, Wing had visited the Braintree paupers living in Norwich. In his notes on 'The State of the poor at Norwich' of 16 August 1827, where each family is given with the names (except for wives), ages and earnings of the individual members, Samuel Spooner (aged 50) appears with his children Mary (16), Solomon (14), Samuel (10), Ann (7), Sarah (5) and Hannah (3). 'His Famely earns nothing Call his Eranings 10ˢ-0ᵈ a week on Average.' He was said to receive a pension of 5s 3d and a weekly allowance 3s from the parish, which made a sum total of 18s 3d for the weekly family income (ERO, D/P 264/8/10, Braintree select vestry, book of memoranda, 1817-36). The allowance of 3s must later have been increased (though the overseers accounts give no clue), since in April 1828 Robert Medcalf, vestry clerk of Braintree, wrote to Norwich that the weekly allowance for Samuel Spooner was to be reduced to 4s 6d.

19   From George Smee in Norwich, 26 February 1828

Nor<wich> 26 Febʸ 1828

Honour'd Gentⁿ

In Consequence of my wife Labouring under a very Sore and grevious ku[-------------] afflion and have the three or four months Last past which have rendered her incapable of attending to the Family therefore Gentⁿ
5 hope you will have the goodness to spent me a Farther Supply for me and my Family than what is already allowed as my wife is not Likely to do any Better at present She having a <->estick fever accompanied with a very bad Cough which <h>ave brought her Exceeding Low hope Gentⁿ you will have Compassion on her and grant me my Request that She may
10 be able to get Something in Order to alleviate her present direfull Condition as it is not in my power out of the <Sc>anty pittance that I Can Earn to Render her any Relief in this her truly Deplorable State

am Gentⁿ

Your Obet

15   and mt Hble Servt

Geo Smee

CIRCUMTEXT Note from John Webb, overseer of Norwich, 26 February 1828, on back: 'Allow me to add that I believe Geo Smee an honest industrious man [*illeg*] by Afflictions of various kinds & *fully* deserving an addition to the allowance he now takes of me from your parish'.

DESTRUCTION OF TEXT The top of the page is heavily damaged, the left hand corner at the bottom is torn off.

FURTHER EVIDENCE and RELATED CORRESPONDENCE In August 1827, Jeremiah Wing, overseer of Braintree, had visited the Braintree paupers living in Norwich. In his notes on 'The State of the poor at Norwich' of 16 August 1827, where each family is given with the names (except for wives), ages and earnings of the individual members, George Smee (aged 56), his wife (52) and their children Eliza (17), James (12), and George (8) were reported as earning 14s 4d (George 8s, Eliza 4s and James 2s 6d) and receiving an allowance of 4s per week. In a letter of 23 August 1827 to the overseers of Norwich, Wing informed them that the select vestry of Braintree had decided 'that the pay to George Smee of 3/ per Wk is to [be] discontin[ue]d from last Satterday the 18 Inst'. By the second quarter of 1829, his weekly allowance had again been increased to 5s. In that quarter, he died, after which the same allowance was given to his wife and her two children, together with an extraordinary payment of £1, presumably for his burial. In the last quarter of 1829 the allowance to his widow was increased to 6s (ERO, D/P 264/12/31, Braintree overseers' accounts; D/P 264/18/34, list of the out-door poor of Braintree, 1829-1830).

20   From John Gibson in Little Baddow [Essex] to the overseer of Braintree, 18 June 1828

June 18 1828 from Little Baddow Jentelmen All i hope you Will not Be Angry of Me By Senden you these few Lines for i Bag the faver of you All that is i hope you Will Be So kind Jentelmen as to Grant Me a Pare of Shooes for three of My Children for three of them are Al<l> But Bare foot and M^r holmes hase hav Made Me Some and i do Not Know how to   5
Pay for them i hope Jentelmen you Will Not disepoint Me for i have Not Been Troubeelsom to you Jentelmen for this 3 yearrs Eany Thing for i have thought Jentelmen Many times that i Should Come home I hope Jentelmen you Will Be So kind as to Give M^r holems the order When he Brings you this Note i hope Jentelmen you Will Not desepoint Me being   10
as i have Not had Nothing from you for this 3 years for i Shoul have Com over and ask you the faver Jentelmen But M^r holemes Tould Me that he Would Give you the Note and i hope Jentelmen it Will Be 3 years More Be fore i Shall ask you for Eany thing More i Will Not in Less i am forst
i am your humble Servant   15

    John Gibson forom Littel
    Baddow

TEXTUAL ALTERATIONS 7: Troubeelsom] 'eslom' *interl with caret at end of line*. 12: Jentelmen] 'n' *over* 'l'.

CIRCUMTEXT Address on the outside (same hand as text): 'for the over Seer Brantr<e>e By Mr holeems feavor [*read:* favour]'. There is no postmark, so the letter may be assumed to have been delivered by Mr Holmes.

21   From Phillis Webb in Ipswich to James Joscelyne in Braintree, 14 July 1828

Ipswich July 14th 1828

Honoured Sir,

I write these few lines to inform you that I cannot keep my Brother with two Shillings a week I have also a Shilling to pay for lodgings therefore I
5 cannot keep him with 2 Shillings a week he has not got any Shoes to his feet nor any thing to wear and the People where I Lodge will not alow him to lode with me you did only send me only 8 Shilling for 5 Weeks and I cant afford to keep him out of that as I have to work for my living and work is very scarce I hav not heard of a place yet what will be the
10 most you can give if he gets a place please to send me word

I remain

Your Humble Servant

Phillis Webb

Direct for William Hitchccok

TEXTUAL ALTERATIONS 7: only] *above del* 'not'.

CIRCUMTEXT Address on outside: 'James Josling'.

RELATED CORRESPONDENCE and FURTHER EVIDENCE James Joscelyne, overseer of Braintree, had written to Phillis Webb on 1 July 1828 that she was to be given 8s for boarding her brother William Webb. On 21 July 1828, apparently answering her above letter, he wrote to her that she was granted an allowance of 3s per week as long as her brother stayed with her. The idea was that she should find a place for him, and she was told to write back in a month's time. On 18 August 1828 Joscelyne wrote to her again, confirming that the allowance for her brother was to be continued. 'They [the select vestry of Braintree] hope you will do all that you can to get him a place, You must write again in a month time and let us know whether you have got a place for him or not.' Apparently, she did not succeed in finding a place for him, for two years later it was recorded that William Webb 'lodges in Workhouse' and that he had received casual relief of £1 1s 6d in 1829-30 (ERO, D/P 264/18/34, list of the out-door poor of Braintree, 1829-30).

22   From Phillis Webb in Ipswich to James Joscelyne in Braintree, 13 September 1828

Ipswich Septem[r] 13 1828

Sir I am Sorry To write this but I am Forst Sir I have done my best Endeavor
to gett my Brother a plase but Trade is so Dull that I am sorry to \<say\>
that I cannot gett him one I \<---------\> I Could So Sir I have wrote to you
according to your wishes -   5
          Please to Dirct

                                                  For Phillis Webb
                                                            in Tanners Lane
                                                            Near Madam
                                                            Swales   10
                                                            Ipswich
                                                            Suffolk

TEXTUAL ALTERATIONS 2: Forst] 'st' *interl at end of line.* 3: Brother] 'r' *over* 'o'.

23   From Samuel Spooner in Norwich to [Jeremiah] Wing in Braintree, 20 September 1828

Norwich 20th Sep[t] 1828

Sir

  I most respectfully take the liberty to acquaint you that I have now very
little to do and that from the frequent attack of Rheumatism it is but little
that I am able to do, and also that such of my Children as could contribute   5
any thing towards a maintenance by working in the fields and gardens are
now also out of employ, I have therefore to solicit you to have the goodness to make my case known as early as possible to the Gentlemen of the
parish in order that an increase to my present allowance may be made,
which will much oblige.   10
                    Sir
                          Your most respectful
                            and very Obedient
                                  humble Servant
                                  Sam[l] Spooner   15

CIRCUMTEXT Address on outside: 'M[r] Whyn'

**24   From Samuel Spooner [in Norwich] to the overseer of Brain-
tree, October [1828]**

Oct^r *[- -]*

Gentlmen

In reference to my letter to Mr Wynn dated 20th ulto Soliciting that
gentleman to be pleased to lay my present distressed case before you in
5 order that you wold take the same in to your faverble considiation and
allow me an encrease to my present allowance from the parish and as the
result of my application has only obtained me sixpence per week to my
former allowance (vez. three Shillings) and also as my prevent debility
presents me from supporting a family of six children on that allowence I
10 have caused them to be forwarded to the parish they belong -

I further take the liberty to state for your information that if you will be
plesed to grant me the allowence I have hitherto received vez. six shillings per week for the winter half year and three shillings per week for the
summer half that I will endeavour to provide for them as long as I am
15 able and further that it will be imposseble for me to take Less to find them
Sufficent Bread -

with due respect
I remain
Gentlemen
20   your very
abident
humble
Servant
Sam Spooner

25   to the overseers
of the parish of
Braintree
Essex

DATE Year inferred from reference to Samuel Spooner's previous letter (**23**).
   PLACE Inferred from previous letter (**23**) and further evidence.
   FURTHER EVIDENCE Samuel Spooner in Norwich had received a weekly allowance of 3s
from Lady Day until Michaelmas 1827, and later, from Lady Day 1829 on, he received
6s. Unfortunately, due to the lack of records between those dates it is impossible to say
what he received at the time of the above letter. The same is true of the previous and
following letters from him (**23** and **25**). At any rate, his weekly allowance of 6s is in
evidence until Michaelmas 1830 (ERO, D/P 264/12/31, Braintree overseers' accounts; D/
P 264/18/34, list of out-door poor of Braintree, 1829-30).

25 From Samuel Spooner to the overseers of Braintree, 17 November 1828

17th Novr 1828

Gentlemen

I take the liberty to inform you that since I caused the part of my family to be forwarded to the parish of Braintree that I have been in the Country in order to obtain work to support the remaining part of the family and as 5 I have not been able to succeed I am obliged to return to Norwich again when I am promissed work to the am^t of five shillings per week during the winter that if you will comply with the request contained in my letter forwarded to you by my daughter Viz to allow me Six Shillings p^r week for the winter and three Shillings for the Summer I will endeavour to do 10 the best in my power to provide for them, I therefore take the liberty to request that you will be pleased to have the goodness to answer my letter and also that you will have the goodness to direct it to Mr Webb who will acquaint me of your decision, otherwise I shall be obliged to return to Braintree myself with the remaining part of my children 15

I remain
Gentlemen
Your Most respectfull
and very obedient
humble Servant 20
Samuel Spooner

TEXTUAL ALTERATIONS 8: the request] 'the' *above del* 'my'.

26 From William King in Bethnal Green, London, to [Robert] Medcalf in Braintree, 20 November 1828

London No^r 20th 1828

Mr Metcalf

I Beg the favour of you to Give this Letter to the Commity Next Monday if you will Be So Kind, the Gentlemen I Humbly Hope Will Condesend to aford Me Soum Relief as I am in Very Low Circumstances, and have 5 Refrained to trabble them till this time, Notwithstandg our Great Straits and Wants Before, I Now feel Myself Very Unfit to Coum Down as I am So Subyect to an asthma and other Complaints in My Boddy. When I was

Last theare I though I Should Never Get to London and in the Night I
10 thought I Must Destrub Mr Coots House But I yust Bore Up Under My
Gret affliction of Mind Partly owing to My Being obliged to trabble My
Parrish. the Little I had was Usefull to Me, I Greatly fear twill Be My
Sore trial Be on Soume Greater Dependence to My Parrish But I Hope
Not My work Such I Do is Now Very Slack, and We have Made the Most
15 trying Shifts till Now Let the Gentlemen Consider how Little I have
trabbled them and I Trust they will Behave with a feeling Spirit towards
it tis My hope Not to Send again till I am More than forced to do it. We
Keep our trabble from the World all we Can, But But have Been obliged
to Part with our Poor Cloase Such as they are to Get a Meal with Even
20 My Wifes Ring is Nearly the Last, My Girl is in Place we have only to
Mend her Cloathes I hope Shee will Be No Expense to My Parrish - My
wife is Very ill I Yust Now Brought Medecine from Shordith for her
from the Doctors, if the Gentlemen would But aford Me a Little Money
about two Pounds I Might Be able to do all the winter. I Long for the time
25 to take a House and Pay So Much for it for a Twlve Month as May Make
Me a Parrisoner in London, Pray Gentlemen Consider Me and if you Let
Me Know whom I Shall apply for what is Sent By a few Lines - or it May
Be Sent to My House I Shall Be Most thankfull, and I Shall Ever feel
oblidged to Such as are My friends in the time of Want
30   I am Gentlemen your Most Humble
          Servant Wm King
               Please to direct
                    To Wm King
               Shoe Maker N°22 King Street
35   Turk St^r Bethnal Green

TEXTUAL ALTERATIONS 6: Notwithstandg] 'g' *interl below at end of line.*
CIRCUMTEXT Note from other hand below text, 24 November 1828: 'Sent one Pound to
the Above'.

**27   From James Tidman in Farningham, Kent, to the church-
          wardens and overseers of Braintree, 27 November 1828**

                                        Farningham Novr 27th 1828
To the Churchwardens &c of the Parish if Braintree
     Gentlemen
          I have addressed these few lines to you to inform you that 3 weeks ago
5 there came two of your parishioners to my house a young woman named

Mary Spooner and a boy about 4 years old named Henry Spooner they
are the children of Sam¹ Spooner a Shoemaker whose wife was niece to
my wife they came to <m>e quite destitute and I have kept them ever
since we have now got a service for the Girl but she is d<e>stitute of
clothing and I am unable to get her any I have therefore made this appli- 10
cation to you to desire you to send her something to get her some cloathes
and then she may go to service and with respect /to the/ <boy I> cannot
keep him for nothing <I am hardly> able to maintain my own fa<mily
as> the case stands I have no objection to keep him if you will allow me
three Shillings a week with him so that I may receive the same quarterly 15
- if you will please to answer this as soon as possible I will thank you or
otherwise I shall deliver them both to Farningham Parish and let them
bring them home with an order - I hope you will send immediately and
enclose a Post office bill for the money you send and then I can receive it
at Dartford - Direct to James Tidman, Shoemake<r>, Farningham, near 20
Dartford Kent. Your speedy attention to this will much oblige

Gentlemen

Your Humble Servt

James Tidman

NB They came to me on wednesday <Nov>^r /1/2 - last   25

TEXTUAL ALTERATIONS 5: parishioners] 'io' *over illeg.*
    DESTRUCTION OF TEXT Right-hand edge in the middle and left-hand bottom corner of
page damaged. Therefore, the conjectured readings (except those of individual letters) are
no more than guesswork.

28   From James Smith in [St Pancras] London, to the overseer of Braintree, 30 November [1828]

James Smith   November 30 <---->
    Gentelmen Having stated <in> My last letter the distres in Which i was
in i need not mentin Any further about it since then i hav been obliged to
seek releef from the parish i now am in af Which i hav had releef and
unless i recive sum releef from you i shall hav to be past home by this   5
parish But gentelmen if you would extend your benovlance tewords me
your humbel Petitenar it will greatley relieve me for though my beeing i
have not been Abel to pay any rent and i expect to loose my things which
i hav about me <--------------> removng me from whare <---------------->
g/e/t work when i am abel to <-------> Gentelmen i anly ask releef th/a/t 10

i may be able to satesfy the demands of my landlord and asist me for a
week ar til im able to work wich i am in hops i shall be in in a few week
i remain your humbel petitner James smith taylor son of joseph smith if
you should forget me you will find my name by refaring to the books
15 about eleven yearback

5 Chapel Yard Camden
Town

TEXTUAL ALTERATIONS 5: sum] 'u' *over* 'a'. 12: hops i] 'i' *interl*.
  DESTRUCTION OF TEXT Right-hand top corner of page damaged.
  DATE Year from postmark.
  CIRCUMTEXT Note from J. Blackstone, surgeon, on back: 'I hereby certfy that James
Smith is confined with a disease of the Liver which is likely to continue some weeks
(before he is better) and I believe he is in want'. Underneath: signature of William Alston,
overseer of St Pancras.

29   From Hannah Porter in Chelmsford to Eliza Green in Stebbing, 2 December 1828

Decem^r 2^d 1828

Dear Sister
    I wish you to come over to Chelmsford Immediately for I have heard of
a place which I think will suite and if that does not there is a young woman
5 here will get you another so I wish you to come directly and what you
want done your Sister will do for you. be sure and come on Thursday at
the furtherst Wednesday if you can.

So no more from your
Loving Sister

10

Hannah Porter
New Street
Chelmsford

PLACE Stebbing is about 7 miles to the east of Braintree.
  RELATED CORRESPONDENCE Anonymous undated letter to Robert Medcalf, overseer of
Braintree: 'Sir Eliza Green has Sent to inform you that She has got a place of service if the
Gentlemen will be So kind as to Send her something to Support her there and to Clear of
her Lodgings where She now is which She must do before She can take her things away
She is disitute of any help of her own'.

30   From Maria Cousins [in Braintree] to the overseers of Braintree, 16 December 1828

16 Decem^r 1828
Gentlemen
   I beg as a great favour That you will allow My Mother to receive for
Mee the Money you allow Mee towards the support of my Child Samuel
as i Shall Safely and regularly receive it of her   5
from your unworthy
but Humble Servent
Maria Cousins

FURTHER EVIDENCE Samuel Cousins was an illegitimate child. Payments for him of 2s 6d
per week are recorded from Michaelmas 1829 until Lady Day 1830 (ERO, D/P 264/12/
31, Braintree overseers' accounts). As that source does not give a place for his residence,
it may be assumed that he and his mother lived in Braintree.

**31   From Phillis Webb in Ipswich to Mr Rebel in Braintree, 18
December 1828**

Ipswich Decb^r the 18 1828
Sir I sent to you last Week to you and I thought you whould have sent to
me before now for my brother have benn very Ill in dead and it do not
know how to do for him so if you do not send to me he must Call on the
Parish and that they must bring him hoom for he is all most Nacked and   5
i can not Cloth him nor find him things to Whare and I can not keep him
for they Will not trust me no longer so pray send me the monney for 8
Weeks you allways send me it by or in 6 Weeks i Want the monney to
Pay away so pray send to me as soon as you can so no moor from your
Humbell sarvent Phillis   10
Weebb

<direc>t to me
<Phillis> Weebb
Tanners lane
Ipswich Suffolk   15

32　From [William King] in [Bethnal Green] London to [Robert] Medcalf in Braintree, 30 April 1829

London Ap 30th 1829

Kind Sir

I Humbly Beg you to Show this Line or two to the Gentlemen, By which they will find that I am in Great Nead of Soum Little assitance
5　from them, <--> when I Last wrote I Was in Very Trying Circumstances Nor am I Now Less Neadfull, But I thought it Not alltogeather Neadfull to Enter into a Detail of My Wants for in truth I Was allmost ashamed to Lower the feelings of the Kind <Gentle>men with So Sorry <------------->
<notw>ithstanding I am Per/--/<--------------> in our Dwelling /--/<-----
10　---->ght By Reson o<f> our <--> of a Clear Dispasstition yet our Household is But Very Mean, My Wife is But a Poor afflicted woman and My Self am at times Very Bad in My Breath and other Complaits the Gentleman who Deliver out the Tickets for Bread to the Destressed have Given Us three or four Lovis this W<i>nter though we Do Not Blong to Bethnal
15　Green when you Sirs Sent Us the Last Pound it was Remarkd how Kind you where by a Gentleman who was in My house when I Resivd it and <-
---> the Most of it I w<a>s <--------------->/-------/ider the most tr<------
-->/lost/ My Chilldren in a <--------> would Not trabble My Parr/ish/ <-
---------->ough I was gre<a>tly Blamed <-------------> My Sean of
20　wreachedness apeared in the News and in a Small track Likewise wich I Now Can Produce if Neads be, and am Happy to Say My Carricktor will Bear Looking into Under thease Circumstances. I Humbly Beg the Gentlemen to Remember there old Townsman and Consider My days May be few I Shall No More want the things of Time and Sence, I Know the God
25　Bless you Sir, is Very Cheap for in Most of the Low and Depraved Sort of Men <-----> it I Beleave the Prayers <----->/Curses/ of Gods People in his <----------> Establish his *truth* <-----------> Gentleman /I oftener think I/ <---------->/lys/ and I Love you all /--/<--------->and beg Pard<on> if I have offended /--/<--->
30　<*most of bottom line destroyed*> H<umble> Servt W<illiam King>

Textual alterations 3: Beg] *inserted.*

Spelling 19: Sean] *read* 'scene'. 21: Carricktor] *read* 'character'.

Destruction of text The text comprises three pages, each of which is heavily stained and damaged in the bottom third on both sides.

Writing Although the sender is not given, the style, phraseology and spelling, the context, and above all the handwriting identify him as William King.

CIRCUMTEXT Note on outside from same hand, across left-hand margin: 'I Humbly thank Mʳ Hayward for his Kindness'. Mr Hayward (alias Haywood) was a coachman who delivered the allowances to several Braintree paupers residing in London. The meeting place was a public house, the Three Nuns in Aldgate High Street (see letters from Maria Godfry, **65**, **73**).

PLACE Inferred from text (ll. 12-15).

33   From William Webb in Ipswich to Mrs Fish in Braintree, 7 July 1829

Ipswich ᵗʰᵉ7 july 1829

Mrs Fish

have the goodness to oblige me & send my jacket & trowes to the Angel
Inn witham by the Maite to be Left for Mr Turner Driver of Burys Waggon
& I Shall be much oblige to you for I am Liveing with my sister Phillis now   5
the Kellsey Peop[le] are now expecting me home as halfe my time is out
so you must do as you Please aboaut sending me home as there is only
halfe the Money paid so be so good as to write to my Sister to let knowe
what you intend to do directly if you please direct Phillis Webb Tanners
Lanners Lane Ipswich Suffolk   10

So I remain your
Humble servant
William Webb

TEXTUAL ALTERATIONS 3: goodness] *interl.* 6: Peop[le]] *interl after* 'Kellsey' *followed by del* 'Peplel'. 9: Phillis] *after del* 'Tanner'.

CIRCUMTEXT Address on outside: 'Braintree poor house'. The addressee was probably the wife of John Fish, the poorhouse master.

34   From Mary Smith in [St Pancras] London to the overseer of Braintree, 25 July 1829

Camden Town July 25ᵗʰ 1829

Gentlemen

My present distress has urged me once more to write to you, for 5 month
past my Children have been afflicted with the small pox and a bad fewer.
and have lately lost one which Mʳ Meccup the overseer when in town   5
pro[m]ised I should <ha>ve one pound given me towards the expenses
of the funeral which he has never sent - and I really cannot do without it.

the undertaker will take the remainder of his bill as I can pay it under such circumstances, I beg you will send it to me, when you send my weekly
10   allowance (Friday next)

Gentlemen Mr Leach of the post Office Camden Town has kindly offered to receive my money, if you will make your payments to him, instead of where you do now, and it will save me a deal of trouble and I should esteem it as a great favour you will make my payments so as I can receive
15   them weekly instead of once a fortnight and of my last money I had to pay 16^s rent besides my Bakers bill. my distressed situation I hope you will take into consideration, and send me the £1 which Mr Meccup kindly said I should have and please to write to Mr Leac/h --------/ to pay me on or before Friday so that I may receive my next payment of him. will greatly
20   oblige your

M<os>t obedient & humble
servant Mary Smith
widow of Ja^s Smith

WRITING Professional hand.

CIRCUMTEXT Note from other hand at bottom of page refering to payment £2 2s for burial expenses (hand A, though possibly same hand as text). Underneath, note in pencil from other hand: 'was allowed Augt 15th 1829 J Wing J Garrett R Springett'(hand B). Note on back, from same hand as text: 'This is to certify that during the last Five Month Mary Smiths [fam]ily have been afflicted by illness during which I have attended them for Mr Blackst[one]', countersigned 'Geo. Brodle' (hand C).

FURTHER EVIDENCE On the list of the out-door poor of Braintree, 1829-30 (ERO D/P 264/18/24), Widow Smith, Camden Town, with 5 children, is said to have received a weekly allowance of 10s, or a total of £26 10s during that year. In the overseers' accounts (ERO, D/P 264/12/31) that allowance is also in evidence from Lady Day 1829 until Michaelmas 1830, though that source records her with 6 children. On 6 May 1833 the overseer of Braintree sent a letter to Mr Leech, Camden Town, requesting the allowance for Mrs Smith be reduced from 6s to 4s (copy of letter in ERO, D/P 264/8/10, Braintree select vestry, book of memoranda, 1817-36).

35   From William King in London to [Robert] Medcalf in Braintree, 5 August 1829

London august
5 1829

Kind Sir

I Humbly Beg the favour of you to Lay thease Lines Before the Gentle-
5   men on Monday Next they will thearby Perhaps take into Consideration

My Neady Situation if I Where Not in the Greatest Nead of a Little *assistance* I Should Not have trubbled them, But of Late we have Been Grately Put to it to obtain a Liveing, and in order to Obtain a Meal at times we have Been obligded to Make off with that which we had obtained to Wear by Going *without a Meal* the Last Donation wich the Kind Gentle- 10 men Sent Us was Reseved with Unexpresserble Gladness, I Nor My wife Cannot Be thankfull too Much for the Goodness of My Overseers, But if they would Be So Kind as to Do Me the favour of alowing Us a Little Stoteadly it would Greatly Elivate that Gloom wich So often Bows Down the Spirits of Sach a Poor Man as *My Self* it would Pain the Gentlemen to 15 Lern the wreached Shifts that I am Obligded at times to Make and I have had My Girl at Home Many Weeks But is Now, Last Nigh Gon I hope to a Place again - I will Only Beg once More that I May Wait on Mʳ Hayword on the forepart of Next Week and again find that Benevolent Suply wich they will No Doubt feel Disposed to afford, 20

the Gentlemen My Be Shure tis Not willingly that I trubble them
I Am theare Most
Humble Serᵗ Wᵐ King

CIRCUMTEXT Note from same hand on outside below address: 'By the favour of Mʳ Hayward'. This, together with the fact that there is no postmark, means that the letter was handed over to Hayward, the coachman travelling between Braintree and London, who delivered it to the overseer of Braintree.

Note from other hand at bottom of last page: '10/ Allow'ce Augᵗ 15 1829 J. Wing J.Garret & R. Springett'.

36 From Elizabeth Watty in Chester-le-Street [Durham] to the overseers of Braintree, 11 February 1830

ChestleStreet Febʸ 11ᵗʰ 1830

Gentlemen

I am under the Nessity of wrighting to you to let you know that I am no more able to pay my Rent out of my Weekly Allowance 3 Shillings per week, for I am in a very poor state of health I am not able to earn myself 5 1 Shilling on account of an affliction in my hands, I hope you will excuse me for wrighting to you but I am realey in great want at this time and my Rent will be Due before this reach you and it is 2 £per year and I am indetted half a year at present I hop you will answer my letter by Return of Post or as soon as possible 10

I remain your Humble Ser^t
Eliz. Watty Widow

Please to Direct
for Elizabeth Watty
15 South Side of the Burns
ChesterleStreet

RELATED CORRESPONDENCE On 8 May 1831 Charles Scott, overseer of Chester-le-Street,
wrote to Mr Shaw, overseer of Braintree, presenting an account of payments advanced to
Widow Watty, with the request of remittance. Similar letters date from 20 February and
30 October1832.
   Two years later, the overseer of Braintree received a letter from William Smith, London, St Giles: 'Having rec^d a letter from my poor sister Watty of Chester le Street County
of Durham Deploring the unfortunate situation she is placed In through the alteration of
the Poor laws act so that she is left quite destitute I have taken this liberty of adressing you
Dear Sir on her behalf I am a Journeyman tailor Married and a fammily I feel for her
wants and wish to relieve them as much as lays in my power To do so I will remit to her
Parish Quarterly a Shilling per week which tho little is as much as I can Possibly spare
from my Earnings in the in the hope that the Gentlemen of your Honourable Board will
reconsider her unhappy Fate and restore her to a part of her former Stipend is the prayer
of you humble Servt and Petitioner &c'(letter of 2 December 1834).
   FURTHER EVIDENCE From Lady Day 1824 until Michaelmas 1830, Elizabeth Watty (alias
Watley/Wattley) received a weekly allowance of 3s (ERO, D/P 264/12/31, Braintree overseers' accounts; likewise ERO, D/P 264/18/34, list of the out-door poor of Braintree,
1829-30: total of £7 19s). Back in 1825, her case had briefly been dealt with at a meeting
of the select vestry (ERO, D/P 264/8/10, Braintree select vestry, book of memoranda,
1817-36, entry of 13 June 1825).

**37   From William King in London to [Robert] Medcalf in Braintree,
       25 February 1830**

London feb^y
25 1830

Kind Sir
   Perhaps you will have the Goodness to Lay thease few Lines Before
5 the Gentlmen of the Commita on Monday Next. I am waiting Under the
Greatest Distress and anxierty for Soume Relief. Dureing the winter Both
My Wife and Self have Suffered Undeerble Trubble and Want and
Great affliction Every Little Kind of Charity has Escaped Us and we have
Not had Even one Loaf - Every Little Debt is Now Looked Up for and I
10 am ashamed to Pass the doors Where I owe the Money. My Girl is Kept
By My Brother at Camden Town as She is out of Place and he Gives her
a Home for a wile. I Cannot Give her a Dinner work is Greately over with

Me Nor is theare Enny to Be Got But what Little I have is Mostly My friendship wich hangs on a Very Brittle thread. My Head is - I fear - too Unable to alow My Coming Down Unless to abide theare for Good. I 15 Humbly Hope thease things will have a Place in the feelings of My Benevolent Townsmen that they will Come to a Conclution to Do a Little More Perminent for Me as I have Bourn the Heat of the Day of forty years Trubble and Painfull Distress. Without Being Chargerble to My Parrish wich Must have Cost Meny Pounds had I aplied as I was often 20 told to do. But I wait for ward Under hope. Now age and in firmity have over taken Me I Can only Seek a Lasting help from you My Worthy friends and Gentlem<en> Pray Sirs Let Mr Haywood Bring Us Soumething that will inable Me to Go on and to feel the Good of for My Comfort. I Most Candidly ashure the Gentlemen I will Make the Most of it and Keep 25 from Trubbleing them as Long as I Can. But if we are Oblidge to Come down things Might Be otherwise - I am told By two or three friends they would Sign the Names if I took this to them. But I trust theare is No Nead of it too true and Painfull for Me -

Under all Circumstances I 30
am Gentlemen your Most
Humble and Obed^t
Servant Wm King

We Live about one Mile and Half from the 3 Nunns. Meny Ca/rd/ and furney to See if Eny thing Comes in Hunger and Nakedness 35

CIRCUMTEXT Note on outside from same hand, facing address: 'By the favour of Mr Hayward' (see **35**).
    FURTHER EVIDENCE On the list of the out-door poor of Braintree, 1829-30, William King, London, is recorded to have received a casual allowance of £2 (ERO, D/P 264/18/34).

38   From William King in London to the overseer of Braintree, 12 March 1830

London March 12 1830

Honer^d Sir

I am oblidge to Beg Your attention to My Distress wich is Very Great Perhaps the Gentlemen had Not Oppertunity Last Meeting to Consult My Case or they would have S<en>t to My assistance. tis My Misfortun<e> 5 thurs to Be So Pressing But I Cannot Do without Soume Help. Every

thing of My Wearing apparell and Even My wifes Ring is Put of to Procure food and I am Not able & I fear to Get Down by My Self. I have
Very Hevey inward Complaints and My Shoes are Nearly of My feet. I
10 have Mended them till they are Got No foundation to work Upon - I Get
a Little work ore we Should Starve But I Know Not How Long that will
Last Yet as the Summer is Comeing I feel of Hope that if I was Set a
Little for ward I Might Mend ore Make a few Slop womans Shoes and So
hold out the Season. But Not as things are My Nakedness and Hunger
15 will Not Permit. Nature failt. Haveing Shure Stated the Simple truth to
My Kind Townsmen and Gentlemen I Must Leave My Case in thear Consideration. I trust they will Never forget Poor King Next Monday

I Remain Sir

your Most Hum^b Ser^t

20   Wm King

My wife is Now Going to Get M^r H to Bring this and we have had No
Dinner Nor hardly Ever Know where the Next Meal will Come from -
Pray Gentlemen Do Not forget Me I will Make the Most of your Kind-
ness -

TEXTUAL ALTERATIONS 8: Down] *interl below at end of line.*
    ABBREVIATIONS 21: Mr H] Hayward alias Haywood.

39   From Adam Turthing in Chelmondiston, Suffolk, 4 June [1830]

Chelmonsdiston 4 June

Sir

I Beg to inform you that it is my wish to Marry Mary Sperman widow
belonging to your Parish if you will promise me by letter that you will
5 send me the mony that you usly give to a person that take a woman of
your parish upon my sending to you our Marriage lines - The woman is in
the family way and we are twice published - I belong to Chelmonsdisten in
the Hundred of Samford

I intend to keep her Child with me please to ans^r this imidately

10   your Obedient

Servant A Tur

My Address is Adam

Turthing Chelmonsdiston

Suffolk

TEXTUAL ALTERATIONS 3: you will] *after del* 'you will'.
DATE Year inferred from the place of the letter within the broad chronological order of the archive.

40   From Stephen Linzell [in Cheshunt, Hertfordshire] to the overseers of Braintree [27 September 1830]

To

The Gentlemen Overseers of the parish of Braintree I hope you will Allow me Something A week to maintain my family with During the time I am unable to work I have 5 children to Support & Only Did 2 days work last week if you do not allow me Somethings to Keep them I must   5
go to the parish were I am Yours &c

Stephen Linzell

TEXTUAL ALTERATIONS 3: me] 'e' *over* 'y'
CIRCUMTEXT Note from Thomas Sanders jun., surgeon in Cheshunt, 27 September 1830 at top of page: 'This is to certify that Stephen Linzell is under my care, very Ill and requires relief'(hand A), countersigned 'Weston'(hand B).
Note on back, reversed, from William Coote, vestry clerk of Braintree: 'to authorize Overseers to allow 5/ or 7/- p^r Wk', with note of answer, 11 October 1830.
FURTHER EVIDENCE At the select vestry meeting of 6 June 1830, it had been reported that Stephen Linzell 'has been reliev'd this day on the promise that he will go to London & try get a place. And will certainly not return for 6 months to come'(ERO, D/P 264/8/10, Braintree select vestry, book of memoranda, 1817-36).

41   From Sarah Smee in Colchester to the overseers of Braintree, 12 November 1830

Colchester Nov^m the 12 1830
To the Gentlemen of the Parish of Brantree Essex I Bag leave to trasspass a Few minuts On your time well knowing that you are always Ready to attend to the complaint of the Poor, and -
Gentlemen, the complaint that I Have To Lay before you is the keeping   5
of the Poor Chield that belongs to my Husband Tis Not mine, Gentlemen.
I have Keept the Poor little boy, tell I cannot Keep Hime No longer without Releafe From the Parish the chield is almost Blind and I am sure that
I cannot tell the Expence I have been out for doctering for the Chields Eyes, But I cannot Do it any longer <an>d Gentlemen, It is of No ususe to   10
ask <th>e chield Farther for any Releave for hime Because the lasst time

He was In Colchester to take his Pension He Spent Every Shilling and Never left Mee Nor the Chield a Single Penney So I Most Humbley Bag that you will look To the case, and takett In to your Consideration And
15 By So Doing You will For Ever Oblidge Your Humble Servant Sarah Smee
Gentlemen Pleces to Derect for Sarah Smee

Angle Lane Colchester

TEXTUAL ALTERATIONS 7: Releafe] *after del* 'leave'. 9: any longer] *interl below, with caret, at end of line.*
CIRCUMTEXT Note from other hand on back: 'this is to say from Mr Smee that I have Made the Best of the 5 Shilings that I Recevd of Mr John Garard one Pair of Shoes 3^{s}3^d one Pair of Soed 1^{s}0^d One Pair of Sockx 0^{s}6^d one threepence to keep him since the time'.
FURTHER EVIDENCE Joseph Smee (presumed husband of Sarah Smee) had appeared before the select vestry of Braintree on 13 December 1829 and promised that he had given his wife £1 15s since July (ERO, D/P 264/8/10, Braintree select vestry, book of memoranda, 1817-36).

42   From William King in London to the overseer of Braintree, 9 April 1831

London Ap^l 9 1831

Kind Sir

I Am Oblidge^d again to Beg of your Kindness to Ward Me, I Humbly thank the Gentlemen with your Self for the Last 10 Shillings, it was But
5 Very Little But we have Suffered Much Since that time Rather than Be trubblesom to you, I am Perswaded if you Sir and the Gentlemen Knew alltogeather My Situation they would Not So Delay in Affording Me Soum thing Moor than what they have Done, we Strive to the Utmost to Get a Liveing tis But a Sorry one after all I hope to Get through this Summe<r>
10 and Must Leave the Painfull Prospect of another winter to its Nearer approach Upon Us This amanst Meny others has Been a Most trying one to Me. Now we are Very Bare in Regaurd of Cloaths, they are Not in our Keeping what few we have. and they where Given to Us. we owe 12.6 for Rent and Unless I Pay I Cannot Live Much Longer where I am. I Sorry to
15 Say I owe Meny Shilling wich I fear will Never Be Paid By Us Pray Sir have the Goodness to Do the Best for Me you Can and Not oblidge Us to Trubble Mr Haywood So Menny Times as our feelings Under Such Distressing Circumstances Cannot be hid from your feelings. I Must Now

Humbly hope an Benevolent Result of My Best friends, (and Gentlemen
to whome I Ever feel the Greatest Regaurd and thankfullness   20
                    I Remain your
                         Most Hm
                                        Ser^t Wm King

TEXTUAL ALTERATIONS 20: thankfullness] 'ness' *inerl below at end of line.*
CIRCUMTEXT Note from other hand at bottom of page: 'To be sent 1 £'

43   From Joseph Brand in Brentwood [Essex], 15 April 1831

                                   Brantwood 15 Aprill 1831
Kinde Gentlemen I have written to you to say that my wife is Still confined
to her bed and that i am obliged to keep a woman in the house Stil there
fore i have written to you by the order of Mr Wright and other gentlemen
unles a weekly alowance is Setled upon us as Long as she is ill you must   5
expect to see us come home as the Malting is over and the wages are but
ten Shillings per week and I have changed the Doctor and he is in hopes
She will get the better of it but he Says that it will be a Long time first you
must think gentleman this afliction is beene very Great therefor you must
Render me Some asistance and Likewise send an answr of what mean to   10
do as have work a plenty if any more is ReQuird imply to M^r wright or M^r
Richardson Surgeon of Brentwood
                    your Obedient Severant
                    Joseph Brand

TEXTUAL ALTERATIONS 5: as Long as she is ill] *interl.* 5: you] *over illeg.*
RELATED CORRESPONDENCE Joseph Brand had received an allowance, though it is unclear
from what date, from the overseers of Brentwood, which they reduced from their debit to
the overseers of Braintree for the second half of 1830 (letter from overseer of Brentwood,
31 December 1830). A week after the above letter the overseers of Braintree were
informed that Brand's wife was still ill (letter from overseer of Brentwood, 23 April 1831).

44   From Stephen Linzell in Cheshunt [Hertfordshire] to the over-
        seer of Braintree [18 April 1831]

Gentlemen
    I hope you will Concider my Situration and please to Allow me as much
per week as you think proper to enable me to Support my Family which is

5 Children now and my wife expecting every day to be Confined again my
5 Club when I have paid the Expences is not more than 7 Shillings per week
which is impossable to support 7 people I not wish to be forced home to
my parish as I Can jest get A living when I am well and never trouble you for
any thing but at this time my Case is distressing my Accident happened
when I was fetching my master Horses up out of the field I was on one and
10 the other turned and Kicked me my Leg is Shiverd in A shocking manner
Your H.S.

Ste^p Linzell

Cheshunt

TEXTUAL ALTERATIONS 5: per week] *interl below at end of line.* 6: wish] 'is' *over* 'h[i]c'. 6: be]
over illeg. 9: when] 'w' *over illeg.* 9: master] *interl after* 'my'. 10: Kicked] 'K' *over
illeg.*

CIRCUMTEXT Note from Thomas Sanders jun., surgeon in Cheshunt, 18 April 1831, at top
of page: 'This is to certify that Stephen Linzell is under my care with a compound
fractured Leg'.

**45   From George Whitaker in Cambridge to [William] Boulton,
overseer of Braintree, 3 June 1831**

Cambridge June 3 1831

Gent/

I have got a place in Cambridge but my Earnings are but Small at preasent
if you Would be so kind as to render me Sum assistance to get my familey
5 Down to Cambridge and to pay my rent that is now Due at Standon so as
I Can get away from thaire I hope never to be aney moore truble to you
Wich if my rent is paide now at Standon I Shall belong to that parrish and
all my familey together as my Landladey has raised my rent to 10 pounds
p^r yeare so that I must belong to that parish I Can accept the notice for the
10 10 pounds p^r yeare or I Can Stand at 8 guineas p^r yeare and belong to
Braintree parrish Wich you please but I Should think you Would rather
get rid of me alltogether and most to your advantage When I Was at
Braintree Last Shoved mr Nottage my notice for to pay 10 pounds pr
yeare and he Saide that I Could Except it or not I Could Do as I pleased
15 about it and mr Nottage Saide that he thought that you Would Do Sumthing
for me to get me of of your parrish Gent I hope you Will Excuse me in
Writing to you as I Cannot get Enough for me and my familey to Live upon

much moore to get them Down to Cambridge and being apart it makes So
much Diffrence I am oblidged to go to Standon Every Satterday to take
them What Little I get I have Been at Cambridge amonth and I am in 20
hopes that I Shall do verry Well When the gentlemen Cum back to the
Colleges again Wich Will not be untill octber next Wich is along Wile to
weight gent I hope you Will you Will take it into Consideration and assist
me this once So as I Shall not be aney moore truble to you if I Can pay the
rent at Standon I must pay the Six months rent as I have not given notice 25
to Leave gent I leave it intirley to your kindness to assist me hoping you
Will as You have others I hope and trust you Will me this time pray help
me this once as you Cannot Do a greater Charritey at the preasent time as
I Dont Wish to Leave the town of Cambridge if I Dont have Sum assistance I Shall be oblidged to Leave Direct for me as under George Whitaker 30
at mr Grouts Garlick faire Lane Cambridge if <you> Send to me pray pay
the postage as I Cannot get moore then 10ˢ or 12ˢ pr weake

TEXTUAL ALTERATIONS 22: untill] *after del* 'not'. 31: Grouts] 'G' *over illeg.*
   CIRCUMTEXT Address on outside: 'Mʳ Boulton overseer Cimmist & Drugest'.
   RELATED CORRESPONDENCE From a letter of 13 April 1831, from the overseer of Standon,
requesting relief for George Whitaker and his family, it appears that Whitaker's family
lived at Standon, Hertfordshire.

46   From James Gray in [Shoreditch] London to [William] Boulton
in Braintree, 11 June 1831

Gentlemen
   In consequence of your not compling with my request of so moderate a
sum which I solicited, it has been the means of loosing my passage, and
passage money - Through the Kindness of the Secretary and Captain of
the Owners, I shall in about three or four weeks be at sea, but fear in the 5
mean time that my wife may tumble to pieces, and being drained, as you
Gentlemen must Naturally expect, must be under the painful necessity of
sending her home, unless Gentlemen, you are so good as to bear out such
expences My expences are indeed great, as you will know - I have not
any thing here to do, that can possibly earn me a shilling, and unless you 10
are good enough to assist us with two pounds by Mʳ Haywood the Coachman. I will attend at the Three Nuns, at Aldersgate to answer any questions you Gentlemen may think proper, on Tuesday next

If Gentlemen, I cannot have my request granted by Tuesday, We shall
15 be compelled to have a pass to our Parish. I trust you will not think my
request very great, as it is the last on this Earth, we shall ever *have* or
make. May Almighty God, protect you Gentlemen, and prosper my dear
beloved Parish, ever fervently and devoutly prays

                                        Gentlemen
20   Your most Obidient
                                        Humble Servant
                                        James Gray

June 11th 1831
4 Pimlico Walk Hoxton London
25 to Mr Bolton &c &c Braintree

TEXTUAL ALTERATIONS 7: Naturally] 'Na' *over illeg.* 13: on Tuesday next] *added in right-hand margin.*
    WRITING If the letter of 2 July 1831 from James Gray to his wife (**48**) was written by Gray himself, then this one was not, as the hands are different.
    RELATED CORRESPONDENCE In his letter of 18 June 1832 to the overseers of Braintree, James Waddell, who offered an emigration scheme to North America in collaboration with Messrs Carter and Bonus of Leadenhall Street in London, requested £7 for the passage of Edward Grey, on board of the ship 'Ocean', to North America. His brother William Grey was reported to be with him on the same boat.

47   From William Goodwin [in Norwich] to [Samuel] Shave in Braintree, 1 July 1831

                                                    July 1 = 1831
Sir
    I am sorry that I am under the painful necessity of writing to you in
consequence of my health being so very bad I have been ill for a year and
5   a half and have depend troubling you but my Wife being unwell I am at
length compeld to trouble you I earnesly hope you will take my case into
consideration and assist <me> as early as possible as it is a very pressing
one) I am Sir your Humble servant William Goodwin Lower Heigham
Norwich Norfolk) Son of Thomas and Elizabeth Goodwin
10   Sir I sent my affidavit by Mr Webb

CIRCUMTEXT Notice from John Webb, overseer in Norwich, to Samuel Shave, overseer of Braintree, dated 2 July 1831, on back: 'I know the writer of the annexed & from the total incapacity of himself & his wife from Sickness they are unable to do any work I recommend their case to your consideration I hope you will order me to allow them 3 or 4

Shillings a week for the present as soon as they are able to do any Work the allowance shall cease'. Address on outside from John Webb's hand.

48 From James Gray in [Shoreditch] London to Phoebe Gray in Braintree, 2 July 1831

Hoxton 2nd July 1831

My Deare Wife

I arrived in safety yesterday about twelve oClock and this day I have been to Chelsea and have seen the Pay Master who behaved very kindly to me and enquired very kindly after you and our dear boy; I find that 5 there is a Ship which will sail about the 20th of this Month and I have spoken with the Captn and aggreed with him for our passage and board as well as bedding for £18..5/- of which I have recovered back from Mr Richardson £8..17..6 and I hope to get the remainder which is stop't for our provissions on board the Mint, when we arrived out at Quebeck as the 10 Pay Master has promised to give me a Note to th<e> Captain requesting him to do so on my arrival <when> there. Dear Wife I have spoken to the P<ay Master> respecting some more money and he desi<red me> to write to the Secretary and he has no <-----------> that he will grant it me; I shall do this on next Monday as it is too late this day; I find that this business 15 will take me a longer time than I expected therefore I shall not be able to come down before the end of the next week at soonest. If you should want any Money before I come down you must apply to the Parish and if they insist upon it I must repay them when I get my Money which I cannot do untill all my business is gone thro' in a regular way, and if they 20 dispute my word tell them that they can write up to the Pay Master at Chelsea who will give them every satisfactory information respecting my busines; Dear Wife I beg you will not make yourself in the least uneasy as you may depend upon <my> doing every thing in my power to get my <-----> settled as soon as it possibly *lies in my* <power> 25

Dear Father & Mother and Sister Ann <----> to you that if any thing should happen to my Wife during my absence that you will do all that you promised me and that you will do your best endeavours to make both her and my dear Boy quite comfortable and I shall be happy to repay you for all your trouble when I come down. Your Sister Rebecca begs you 30 will give her kind love to William and tell him that she is very sorry to think that he did not get things settled before her Brother came away but

she hopes that he will get every thing done before he comes down again
which will <be> some time n<e>xt week so th<a>t he may come up with
35 them as she th*/------/*<----->g till she sees him. Mr Andrews desires <---
> respects to Ann and hopes she will keep her <spi>*/r/*its up, and says if
he were at Braintree he would take good care that she should take some
Gin down

I am my dear Wife
40   Yr Affte Husband
James Gray

Mr Coote/
    Sir I hope you will accom<any> my Wife as you promised me during
<the time of my> absense and I will repay you as soon <as possible>
45   I am Sir Yr Mo^t Hb <Servant>
James Gr<ay>
[*At top of outside, reversed*] the reason that I have engaged with aonther
Ship is that Mr Richardson is not a going to send any more Ships this
Season the Name of the Ship we are going in is the James & Henry
50 Cumming.

TEXTUAL ALTERATIONS 24: in] 'i' *over* 'o'. 28: you will do] *interl with caret*. 37: would]
above del illeg.
ABBREVIATIONS 40: Affte] Affectionate.

49   From Joseph Brand in Brentwood [Essex] to Mrs Boullin in Braintree, 18 July 1831

18 July   Brentwood 1831
    Kinde Gentlemen I <wr>ite to you to informe you that my wife is a litle
beter but i my Self am verry ill not abele to worke there fore i thought it
proper to Let you know it for wee cannot do without assistance i am Sorry
5 Gentlemen that I am Obligde to trouble you but afliction is that witch none
of us can out stand but I trust you will send us Something as soone as you
can for if I have not support it is impossible for me to Go to worke

I Remain
Youre Humble Sarvant
10   Joseph Brand

TEXTUAL ALTERATIONS 6: will] *interl after* 'trust'

RELATED CORRESPONDENCE Half a year after this letter Joseph Brand was reported to have had an accident and to be in need of an extra allowance (letter from Thomas Wright in Brentwood, to the overseers of Braintree, 7 December 1831, with note of answer from Braintree that 6s were allowed).

50 From S[tephen] Linzell [in Cheshunt, Hertfordshire] to William Coote, overseer of Braintree, 24 November 1831

Nov 24.1831

Sir

I am sorry to be any trouble to my parish I thank them for the relief they Orderd me in my illness and I now beg the favour of them if Chose to pay my Club which I Cannot out of my wags which is 12 Shilling per week 5 and I have 5 Children and Another near at hand to maintain I never wish to be troublesome to my parish but I am greatly behind now for my Club and I have nothing to pay it with if the Gentlemen do not think proper to pay It I must be Excluded please to give the Answer to my Mother

Your H S S Linzell 10

TEXTUAL ALTERATIONS 4: beg] *over illeg.*

CIRCUMTEXT Note on pencil on back '1/7 p^r Month club Meeting next Monday at the Horse & Groom'. Underneath, note from William Coote, overseer of Braintree, 29 November 1830 'One Month Club Money Paid 1/9'.

RELATED CORRESPONDENCE In his letter of 22 November 1831 to William Boulton, overseer of Braintree, Robert Crawler, vestry clerk of Cheshunt, had complained that despite various reminders there was still an outstanding bill of £9 10s for relief given to Stephen Linzell, 'which to say the least of it, is not the way that one Parish should act towards another and particularly so, when at your request the Officers here took upon themselves the relieving of your parishioners that you might not be put to the expence of a removal by Order of Magistrates'.

It is unclear whether Stephen Linzell's mother, mentioned at the end of the above letter, was the wife or widow of Joseph Linzell to whom earlier letters (6 and 11 January 1830) from the parish officers of Cheshunt relate.

51 From William King in London, 16 December 1831

London De^r 16 1831

Kind Sir

I Humbly thank you and the Gentlemen of the Commitie for the Last 20 Shillings wich I Receved of Mr Haywood I Could have wish it had Been More, as My Neady Circumstan Could only feel a Temporary Relief. But 5

I Must again Express My thanks for the Same. I am But Very ill and My
wife the Same we Live in a Poor Cold Mean Place I hope Soon to Get out
wheare I May Get a Little More Jobing on My own acount. But I owe
Menny a Shilling Round the Places and our few Cloaths a Mostly all out
10 or My wife Might apear More tidey. I Lost My Best Coat a week or two
a Go wich was in for 1^S..6^d and Unless we Can Get a Littl Money we
Must Suffer More Loss and other Painfull feelings. Let Me Beg of you
Sir to Be a Kind to My feelings as you and My well Disposed Gentlemen
where Last time. Perhaps you will Be Better, tis Chrismas. I hope to have
15 a Merry heart of thankfullness. to you Sirs, and to him on whome all our
hopes Should Hang for Chrismas in Substance.

Yours Most Respectfully
Wm King

TEXTUAL ALTERATIONS 6: Express] 'ess' *interl below at end of line.*
CIRCUMTEXT Note from other hand across left-hand margin: 'Directed to Send £1.0.0'.

**52   From James Smee [in Norwich] to Mr Browne in Braintree
[22 May 1832]**

To the Overseers of bralt/r/y
    Sirs having received a severe kick from a horse at my employ and being
unable to work for this fortnight past i am forced to call for assistance or
i must be past home and that directly. James Smee.

CIRCUMTEXT Address on outside from hand of John Webb, overseer in Norwich.
    Statement by John Webb, dated 22 May 1832, below text: 'This Case of Jam^s Smee
deserves your immediate Attention I have seen the Surgeon who has been obliged to
attend him he fully confirms the above statement I hope you will allow him 3/ a Week for
a few weeks [until] the moment heis able heis willing to return to his work where he has
been earning 5/ a week & I will undertake to see that you shall not allow him anything
longer than dire necessity requires'.

53   From William King in London to the overseer of Braintree, 18 July 1832

London
July 18 1832

Kind Sir

I feel Greatly oblidged to you and the Gentlemen of the Vestry for the Last 20 Shillings which they Sent Me by Mr Hayward. My wants Comple   5 Me to Beg of you Sir to Speak on My Be half, as tis By Your United Goodness and other Little Helps of Providence wich Carry Me through Notwithstanding the Meney Doubts and fears wich I am the Subyect of, the winter wich is Past has Been a Most Suffering one to Us. By Reason if a Cold and Shattered Covering But we have Remooved to a Better   10 Dwelling though Under Much *Imbarisments* Sirs tis with the Greatest Humility and Respect that I thurs Apeel to you But tis to My own Beloved Birth Place on wich I think with P/ecular/ Delight Under a Mind Sometimes Bent down with Sadness and Distress. My Towns Gentlemen though I have Not the Pleasure of Knowing them I have the Happyness of 15 a heartfelt Respect to all and Every one of them.

{ I Must Beg theare forgiveness for all th/eay/ See a Mis in I am theare Unworthy But Very Humbl
    Ser^t Wm King

CIRCUMTEXT Note from other hand: 'Boy for Mr Lacey to assist the Bricklayer's'.

54   From William King in London to the overseer of Braintree, 18 October 1832

London   Octobr 18 1832
    Sir

I Humbly thank you and the other Gentlemen, for the Last 20 Shillings which was Sent by Mr Hayward, But Must assure you our Sufferings Where Very Great on account of haveing So Menny times to Go to the   5 Coach, if Sir you Realy Knew our wants and feeling you and Most of the other Gentlemen would Be anxious to assist Us, I Must Beg you Sir as a friend to aquaint the Gentleme who Compose the Vestry of My Present Neady Circumstances as I find it hard to Get along from one Day to another. and Was it Not for the assistance of My Parrish I Must Sink, But   10

we have a few old Cloaths Given to Us Now and then, and I am Sorry to
Say they are Mostly out at this time. My old Great Coat wich hides the
Rufull tokens of want and Poverty - will take 2/6 to Redeem, our Blanket
and Meny other things are away By Reason of want, I have the Happy

15 ness to Say that Every act of Thurs. Putting them away will Bear Reflection - No Drunkness, No Disorderly Life. Let Me Beg of My worthy
overseers Not to forget Us Next week as My wife has faithfully Prommised
to Pay Several Little Detps. I am your Very

Hum^l Ser^t Wm King

20 I am glad My old Townfolks had a fine fair I Should have liked Been
ab<l>e to Coum down and Seen it with My Wife and Girle I Still feel as
it whre the Pecular Secrets of the old fair, when Mrs Redhead Lived at the
Green Man and old Mrs Bush at the Books head - you Perhaps will Smile
Sirs, But I am Perswaded will Not be ofended. May the old Town florish

25 and the People Be among Theese who are Called the Exerlent of the Earth.

Even So -

TEXTUAL ALTERATIONS 15-16: Reflection] 'tion' *interl at end of line.* 21: feel] *after del
illeg.*

CIRCUMTEXT Address of sender (same hand as letter) on outside: 'Nova scotia gardens No
2'. Note from other hand '1 pound'.

55   From Maria Godfry in [St Pancras] London to the overseers in Braintree, [23] October 1832

London Octr 24th 1832

Sir,

Having lost the best part of Three Days at the Pancrass workhouse about
the Child John Stibbings money I was told I could not receive it thare and

5 as I am a lone woman and having a family of my own you will oblige me
much if you will send me an order to receive it at Barkleys Bank once a
month - be goodenough to send me an answer as soon as possible

with due respect

I remain &^{c}

10   Maria Godfrey

N° 41 Litle Albeny St North

DATE Postmark: 23 October 1832.

56   From Abraham Stuck in Upminster [Essex] to the churchwardens and overseers of Braintree, 2 November 1832

Upminster 2nd Novr 1832

Gentlemen,

I am sorry to be under the necessity of troubling you again, but I can get no sort of employment, and am destitute of ncessaries. - During the Haytime and Harvest I have been employed by Mr Lee, a Gentleman in 5 this parish, who has no more for me to do now. I have walked all round this part and cannot get a Job. The fact is, there are so many poor who belong to the parishes, that those who do not can get no work; There is an opening here now, which if I had a trifle to begin with, I think I could maintain myself and family, at least thro' the winter, and then I hope I 10 should not have to trouble you again, It is by buying and selling small wares such as Skins &c Oysters Henings &c as it is a considerable neighbourhood; If I can get nothing, I must with my wife and children come home. Gentlemen I wait your answer, and am

Your obedient, humble servant, 15
Abraham Stuck

CIRCUMTEXT This letter was written by Stuck's master. Below, there is a note from the same hand: 'Abraham Stuck has worked for me as stated, and has conducted himself properly, but I have no farther employ for him at present. Jos^h Lee'.

57   From John Spearman in [Whitechapel] London to Mr Taylor in Braintree, 25 November 1832

London November 25 1832

Gentelmen

I Send you this letter to inform you that our weekly money has been Stoped and as I have not yet got imployment I make this application for the Continuance of that Small weekly alowance to enable me to Surport 5 my family for A Short time longer hopeing that era long I Shall be able to find employment and maintain my family with out being A burden to Others which gives me Great pain to be Compeled to do at this time Gentlemen trusting to your kindness I hope you will be so good as to Sent up to the parish Officers To Continuer the alowance for A little longer 10

I am Gentlemen
Your very humble Serveant
John Spearman

PLACE Inferred from postmark: King Street, Tower Hill.

**58   From Edward Orwell in Leeds to James Joscelyn in Braintree,
        [3 December] 1832**

1832 Wheat Sheet No 23 york Road Leeds

Genttlemen it is with the greatest sorrow that I write to you, to inform
you that I have been now for a Long time out of imploy, and have not
been able to support my Familey, and also my children have had No work
5 for more than ten weeks, for that all Kinds of work has been very dead
every since the Chorlera commenced in Leeds, and we have had a great
deal of Sickness in our Familey, I myself have been for the last month so
Ill and still am very Ill, that if I had work to go to I am not able to work,
Genttlemen, the money that you gave me when I was over I have paid
10 where I owed it, and I am now six months bad in my Rent and my Family
is very poorly off for clothing and we have no means to get any, Genttlemen
I have not appled to any wheare for relief, but according to your derections
I thought it most proper to state to you our rent want and I hope you will
send Me somthing to Releive me at this time,
15   your humble needful
                    Edward Horel

TEXTUAL ALTERATIONS 3: you] *interl with caret.* 8: had work] 'k' *over illeg.* 10: bad] *after
del* 'in'.
CIRCUMTEXT Address on outside: 'John Joshlen'.
NAME OF SENDER 'Horel' as given in the letter is regarded as a variant spelling.
DATE Date of postmark.
FURTHER EVIDENCE In October 1831, on his journey to inquire into the condition of the
Braintree paupers living in Yorkshire, Joseph Garrett, overseer of Braintree, had also
been to Leeds where he called on Edward Orwell (aged 51), his wife (31) and their children Joseph (13), Edward (11), Charlotte (9), Jane (7), James (5), Richard (2) and William
(7 months). Garrett had reported to the vestry that Orwell had been a soldier for 22 years,
for which he received a pension of 1d per day, had then been a watchman for four years at
between 13s and 15s weekly and was now 'jobbing'. The vestry had agreed to send £2 to
Raymond Brown, overseer in Leeds, to pay Orwell a weekly allowance of 5s. In March
1833, Edward Orwell came down to Braintree and 'applied in person [...] at the Vestry for
some further assistance stating that at present he could get but little work to do, but hop'd
soon to be in full employ - the Vestry granted him £5.. with the understanding that he
would not apply again unless he should be in very great distress' (ERO, D/P 264/8/10,
Braintree select vestry, book of memoranda, 1817-36, entries of 15 October 1831 and 19
March 1833).

**59   From John Spearman in [Whitechapel] London to the over-
seers of Braintree, 8 December 1832**

London December 8 1832

Gentlemen

I am Compeled to trouble you with this Letter to inform you that I have
not had any Comunication from you Since I Sent the Letter to Mr Taylor
and that I have not had any releif this fortnight in Consequence Gentle-   5
men I and my family are in Compleate poverty and cannot live without
assistance for A time and I hope A Short time but till I can get employment I must throw myself upon the parish as the only means of preventing Apsolute Starvation and I hope you will Order my Small alownance
to be payed again as I cannot do with out it if you Do not Send up orders   10
to that effect I must apply to the Lord Mayor to get my family passed
Down and put them all in the house as I Cannot Support them without
work and as I told you before as Soon as I Get work I will not trouble you
one Day longer Gentlemen I Shall await your will till thursday next which
is the day on which we have been paid at whitechaple and if payment is   15
not Ordered to be renewed you will be Burdened with my family on
Saterday next

I am Gentlemen

your very humble

Servant   20

John Spearman

TEXTUAL ALTERATIONS 4: any] *interl with caret.* 7: Short] 't' *interl at end of line.* 14: await]
after del illeg.

CIRCUMTEXT Address on outside: 'to the Commetee of overseers Sitting at the workhouse'.

RELATED CORRESPONDENCE On 15 December 1832, John Smith, vestry clerk of St Mary
Whitechapel, wrote to Mr Ware, overseer of Braintree, requesting £1 6s for payments
made to John Spearman (nine weeks at 4s from 4 October to 29 November 1832) to be
remitted.

**60   From John Spearman in [Whitechapel] London to the over-
seer of Braintree, 5 April 1833**

London April 5 1833

Gentlemen

I am Sorry to trouble with this Letter but as you have not Sent me any
answer to my Last Letter which I Sent you A fortnight ago I am Compeled

5 to Send you this to Assertain if it is your intention to Do any thing for me
I do not wish to be burdensome to the parish but the pressure of the time
are so bad that I Cannot get Employment and am Oblidge to Appeal to
the parish very much - against my will Gentlemen I hope you will take
my Case into your Consideration and give me Some tempory releif as I
10 have not have A Stroke of work these 8 week Gentlemen if you Do not
Send me Some releif by Thursday next I Shall Consider your Silance to
be a refusal to releive me and must Come with my family into the house
                    I am Gentlemen
                         your very humble
15   and Obedent Servant
                                John Spearman

No 19 Swallows Gardens
Chamber Street Goodman
feilds London

CIRCUMTEXT Address on outside: 'For the Committee of Overseers Sitting at the Workhouse'.
    FURTHER EVIDENCE On 22 April 1833, the select vestry of Braintree agreed to allow John
Spearman 4s per week for two months. The money for one month was to be advanced
straight away, 'the remainder to be paid thro' Mr S. Heyward's hands', and J.W. Goodale,
the overseer, ordered to send Spearman a letter to that effect (ERO, D/P 264/8/10, Braintree
select vestry, book of memoranda, 1817-36).

**61   From John Spearman in [Whitechapel] London to the over-
         seer of Braintree, 8 May 1833**

                                        London May 8 1833
Gentlemen
    it is with regret that I have to trouble you with this Letter but as I have
no prospect of any work yet I am Oblidge to do it Gentlemen if you
5 would let me have about 3 pounds at once I think I Could manage to get
in Something where by I might get Surport for my family without
troubleing you any more by going to the Markets and buying things and
then Selling again as I know three or four Do so in my trade since it as
been so bad for I am sick of walking about Doing nothing Gentlemen if
10 you Should be inclined to let me have it Depend I Shall make the Best use
of it in my power

I am Gentlemen with
Submission your very
humble Sarvant
John Spearman   15

N0 19 Swallows Gardens
Chambers St Goodmans fields
London
to Save you the postage Gentlemen with your permission I will wait upon
Mr Hayward for your answer on We<dnesday> Next   20

CIRCUMTEXT Note from other hand at bottom of letter: 'Administration & Operation of the Poor Laws - Published by authority. 4/-'.

**62   From William King in [Bethnal Green] London to the over-
       seer in Braintree, 11 May 1833**

London May 11 1833

Kind sir

I Must Beg of you to Speak on My Behalf to the Gentlemen of the Vestry Next Monday, as we are in the Greatest Want of Soume assistance I and My wife and Daughter had Been Very ill with the affliction wich 5 has Carryed of So Meny of our fellow Creatures of Late and I Can do But Little work and My Calling is one of the worst to afford us Eny Supply what to do I Know Not for we have Not one farthing to go on with it would Be Very Painful to you to witness our Distress I Know you and the other Gentelmen would Be Not Slow to afford Me Soum Relief I do 10 Keep from Sending till the Last Moment and of times wish I was at Braintree that I Might fare a Little Better I owe Menny Shillings to My Nabours and Do Humbly wait your Sending Us the Useal Sum at furtherst this week after Next the 21ˢᵗ insᵗ Pray Sir and Gentlemen do Not Disopoint Me as tis Both Dangerous and Painfull to Go So often to the Coach office 15 Beleave Me your Tryd and Humble Serᵗ Willᵐ King -
[*Note on outside across margin, folded in:*] We have had the Parrish doc-
tor Mʳ Luff of Bethnal Green he is a Very Skilfull Man and has don My wife Much Good

TEXTUAL ALTERATIONS 15: Dangerous] 'ous' *interl at end of line.*
    CIRCUMTEXT Note from same hand on outside below address: 'By the favour of Mʳ Hayward'.
    PLACE Parish inferred from text (l. 18).

63   From John Smoothy in Whethersfield [Essex], 19 May 1833

May 19th 1833

Sir^s, I have taken Leaf to right to you to inform you that my son Tho^{ms} Smoothy have had a vary havy trial his wife have been Confind nerly five weeks and she had a vary bad brast and is fost to keep a woman in the
5 house all the time for she cannot sit up but avary littel at a time and she cannot maintain the cous so he stand need of sum help from the Preish so he hope that you will spiek for him at the commetty if you plese
    your humble sarvent
    John Smoothy
10   Weathersfield

TEXTUAL ALTERATIONS 6: Preish] *after del* 'Presh'.

**64   From John Spearman [in London] to [John] Goodale, over-
seer of Braintree, 8 June 1833**

June 8 1833

Sir

I trouble you with this letter to Acknowledge the receipt of your Note and the tow pounds from Mr Hayward and I regret I was not at home
5 when you Called had I been at home I would have taken you to my Marsters Who would have Confirmed my - Statement respecting the want of Employ ment the reason my wife did not - know of me have the money was this I had Borrowed from time to time of A freind to the amount of 18 Shillings this I had to pay 9 Shillings I had to pay the Baker from where I have had
10 My Bread till lately this Made 27 Shillings out of the tow pounds leveing me 14 Shillings out of which I have laid out about 5 Shillings Dureing this last fortnight for food for my wife and Children the other nine Shillings I have Still Got and the Day you Called I - Bought Some things for the first time and whent all the way to Arcot Races A Distance of thirty miles to
15 Sell them from which place I arrived last Night just Sixpence out of pocket by the journey had I told my wife that I had the Money it would have Been Gone at once for me owe so much Rent and She is so anxious to Get it payed that it would have Gone at Once for that Purpose I Shall econmise with wath I have left with all my power

I am   20
Sir your very
humble
Servant
John Spearman

TEXTUAL ALTERATIONS 6: Confirmed] 'C' *over illeg.* 9: where] 'ere' *over* 'om'. 20: I am] *followed by del* 'Gen'.
 SPELLING 14: Arcot] *apparently misspelt for* 'Ascot'.
 CIRCUMTEXT Note on outside from same hand: 'per Mr Heyward'.

65   From Maria Godfry [in St Pancras, London] to Robert Joscelyne in Braintree [18 June 1833]

Sir

I hope you wont fail in sending Stebbings childs money as I have had a havy hand with the poor child for this two months he had this enfluency first and then he had an Absess formed in the throat the doctors gave him over I could not go out to one days work if you could let me have it on   5
saturday instead of tuesday you would greately oblige me as I am in the greatest distress at this time I have a family of my own and a widow for this eleven years If you will give it to haywood I will be at the 3 Nuns on Saturday its a long way from my place near 4 Miles

your hble Ser[t] 10
Maria Godfry

41 Little Ablany St
North

SPELLING 8: haywood] *variant spelling of* 'Hayward'.
 Mr Hayward, a coachman, delivered the allowance to several Braintree paupers residing in London. The meeting place was the 'Three Nuns' in Aldgate High Street, a busy coaching inn.
 DATE Date of postmark.

66   From Susan Spooner in Norwich to [John] Goodale in Braintree, 21 June 1833

Norwich June 21, 1833

Gentleman I take the liberty of writing to you has Mʳ Wells informs us that we are not to be allowed any longer I hope Gentleman that you will Consider when I state the situation that Elizabeth Spooner his in she has been
5 bedred for this Last 9 months with a bad Nepser Sore on her back with 5 Holes Continnual Discharghing with make her not able to move therefore she must be allowed -

Susan Spooner I hope Gentleman you will allow me as usal for I have no way of getting of a living for I ham so very lame for I cannot wok if
10 not I must Come home then my sister must have some body to do for her therefore it will be more expence to you she cannot be alone nor cannot be moved I have expected her death for several weeks

TEXTUAL ALTERATIONS 5: Last] *over* 'one'. 6: not able to] 'to' *interl.* 8: for] *over illeg.* 9: ham] *interl after* 'I'.

SPELLING 9: wok] *intended lexeme unclear; both* 'walk' *and* 'work' *possible.*

WRITING This letter was written by William Muskett of Norwich.

CIRCUMTEXT Address on outside from hand of John Webb, overseer in Norwich.

RELATED CORRESPONDENCE About four years ago, Robert Medcalf, overseer of Braintree, had received a letter from Norwich on behalf of Susan(nah) Spooner (and from the same hand as her above letter): 'Gentleman I William Muskett take the liberty of writen to you for Susanar Spooner single woman aged 48 weaver She has not had any work for the last 3 months beg to be releived for she is in great distress and cannot get through any longer for she is not able to do any other employment on the account of being lame if not allowed something she must come home' (letter of 20 February 1829). This was followed by a statement from John Webb (from his hand), addressed to Robert Medcalf, in answer to a letter from him received the day before, concerning Samuel Spooner and his child. It went on: 'Susannah Spooner has applied to me to represent her Case to your Parish which I believe to be truly distressing from a variety of untoward circumstances. I hope you will allow her something & if she coud get work [s]he woud not apply for Relief at all she is lame in her Knee & in other respects stands in need of your Assistance'. As in the case of the letter from Susan Spooner herself, the address on the outside of this one is from the hand of John Webb.

FURTHER EVIDENCE. Susan Spooner had received a regular weekly allowance of 2s since Michaelmas 1829 (possibly even before that date: there are no surviving records from Michaelmas 1827 until Lady Day 1829), and her sister the same amount since Christmas 1830 (ERO, D/P 264/12/31-32, Braintree overseers accounts). The money was sent to the overseers of Norwich by bank order and then handed out to them. In a report of a visit to the Braintree paupers at Norwich by a representative of the select vestry of Braintree who inquired into their condition and checked on whether their allowances were still appropriate, it was said about Susan and Elizabeth Spooner that one of them had a lame knee and that 'both weave Silk but can get very little to do - a complaint general throughout the trade' (ERO, D/P 264/8/10, Braintree select vestry, book of memoranda, 1817-36, entry of 22 July 1831). See also Sokoll, 'Old age in poverty', pp. 140-2, 153.

67   From William King [in London] to the overseer of Braintree, 17 July 1833

July 17 1833

Sir

    I Must Beg the favour of you to Make My Request Known to the Gentle-
men of the Vestry on Monday Next, I Return Both you and them My
Sincear thanks for the Last 20 Shillings, at this time I am Still in Very   5
Great wants and have Been Soum how Kept Up Under the Greatest trubbles
as My work Being So Bad and I So Unable to do what Might do to Make
Us a Little Better off. My wife is the Subyect of Much illness Moreso
then My Self though I am at times allmost turnd over in My Mind how to
Get a Liveing the Little Help from you Sirs I feel Very thankfull for, as it   10
for the time Pays Part of My Little Detps wich I am oblidged to Contract
as to My few old Cloaths I Seldom Can Redeem and thearby I Slip out on
the Lords day in the Most Private way I Can, and feel thease things and
the want of a dinner when I Return Very hard, I have Now Look over My
tickets and my Poor wifes Ring went Last for Support. as to drink I Never   15
Sit down in a Publick house Exsept Called Upon So to do By a friend
once Perhaps in a Twelve month. Let Me Humbly Beg the Gentlemen to
Send it By Mr Hayward at once at the opointed time as tis So hard and
Unpleasent to him and all Partys to Go So far. I Make Not Doubt But the
Gentlemen will Grant Me thus favour Not Being willing to ad Repeatd   20
Disopointment to one who is all most drivn to dispair. that the Kind officers
May do this I Purpus to attend M^r H^d on Tuesday week the 30th in^t. as My
Sincear and Best Respects Extend to My worthy overseers they will Not
disdain Me,

                                     theare Most   25
                                     Humble and
                                     obedient Servant
                                     Wm King

ABBREVIATIONS 22: H^d] Hayward.

    CIRCUMTEXT Note from same hand on outside below address: 'By the favour of M^r
Hayward'. Note from other hand on outside, reversed, recording relief payments sent by
John Goodale, overseer of Braintree, on 20 May 1833: £1 to William King, £1 16s to
[John] Spearman, and £1 19s to Widow Cole.

    PLACE Inferred from paratext and William King's other letters.

68   From William Marsh in Devonport [Devon] to the overseer of Braintree, 22 September 1833

Devonport Septr 22nd 1833

Sir

　youl have the goodness to state to the gentlemen of the Commity in concequence of the order my agent recieved from them to cut my weekly
5　pay one - Shilling per week wherein I rather Expected they would have augmentid one shilling haveing ane more added to my family and all liveing on me - the two Eldest that might be getting samething to help me are always sick and have been along time under the doctors hands which is very Expensive - therefore gentlemen If you do not think proper to
10　plase me on the former allowance at best, I shall be under the nesesity of coming home, it was very hard living on the former pay with 7 childeren now I have 8 and not one of them getting one penny, therefore gentlemen If you cannot grante me my former allowance - youl have the goodness to let me know by what conveance we can best come by, - and youl very
15　much oblidge your

　　　humble petiteoner William Marsh
　　　pauper on the parish of Braitree

TEXTUAL ALTERATIONS 16: petiteoner] 'o' *interl after* 'te'.
　WRITING This letter was written by William Webb, the father-in-law of William Marsh.
　CIRCUMTEXT Note in pencil from other hand at bottom of page: 'Continue the same'.
　RELATED CORRESPONDENCE In a long series of 18 letters running from March 1828 to November 1834, William Webb addressed the overseers of Braintree (whom he always knew by name) on behalf of William Marsh (letters of 11 March 1828, 24 Dec 1830; 3 April, 21 June and 11 July 1831; 23 June, 6 July, 26 Sep, 14 Oct, 27 Oct, 4 Nov and 20 Dec 1832; 5 Jan, 20 Jan and 7 April 1833; 17 March and 16 Dec 1834). Some letters requested relief in more general terms, others were specific to the point of eccentricity, like those of 3 April and 21 June 1831 in which Webb first announced that Marsh's boat needed repairing and then asked for the sum of £1 he had advanced for that purpose to be remitted. While it is not clear whether that request was met, repeated complaints about delayed bank transfers suggest that by December 1830 Webb received regular payments into his bank account on behalf of Marsh.
　William Webb also seems to have received letters from the overseers of Braintree (copy of a letter to him with £1 enclosed for William Marsh, 4 April 1828). Nevertheless, for some years they seem to have been at a loss as to his position, wondering whether he was an overseer or not. Answering a letter from Braintree of 18 April (not found), Richard Ellis, assistant overseer at Devonport, wrote to John Goodale, overseer at Braintree, 'that we have not or ever had any Overseer called Webb, neither have we ever paid any person by the name of Marsh, on your account, or have we any demand upon you for any Paupers. I remember a long time since receiving a similar letter from you but not knowing any of the parties or hearing again from you no notice was taken of it. - Should there be any thing unproper in the application to you, I will assist you to trace it out, if you wish it'

(letter of 28 May 1833). A week later, after another letter from Goodale (not found), Ellis reported: 'I called on Webb - and found that he is the Father to Marsh's Wife - I have also visited the Family and find all right, they state they have received the 18/. & 16/. from Webb, and I really think they are much in want of the relief You give them - they have Eight Children'. He also gave the children's names and ages: Sarah Ann (aged 18, 'very sickly'), Amelia (14), Mary Ann (12), Elizabeth (10), William (8), James (5), Robert (2 1/ 2) and Susan (2 months) (letter of 6 June 1833).

FURTHER EVIDENCE Whatever individual payments are mentioned in that correspondence, from the overseers' accounts of Braintree, it appears that William Marsh received a weekly allowance of 4s from the second quarter of 1827 until the second quarter of 1829 and then of 6s from the fourth quarter of 1829 until the third quarter of 1830 (ERO, D/P 264/12/31, Braintree overseers' accounts). Unfortunately, there are no detailed overseers' accounts after the third quarter of 1829 so it is impossible to tell what precisely he received at the time when the above letter was written or thereafter (for the same reason we do not know what he received during the third quarter of 1829).

69   From Maria Godfry in [St Pancras] London to [John] Goodale, overseer of Braintree [23 September 1833]

Sir

I hope you wont fail in Sending Stebbings childs money by Mr Haywood as I shall be obliged to go down for it this time myself as my children is Ill I must loose half a day work to go down for it it is a long way from my place be so kind as not to led me have my Journey for nothing on Thurs-   5
day

your hble Servt
Marie Godfry
41 Little Abony
Street North 10
Regents Park

DATE Date of postmark.

70   From Maria Godfry in [St Pancras] London to [John] Goodale, overseer of Braintree, 25 September 1833

London   September 25th *1833*

Sir I hope you will Excuse the liberty I now take in sending for the Money for the child as thinking that quarter day was on thursday I promised my landlord his money & as I now owe him two quarters Rent he has just now put an Execution in & will not be prevaild on to wait any longer   5

& unless I can pay him on Friday I shall be turned into the street with My
Children Destitude of every thing if you will have the kindness to forword me the money By that time I shall ever feel Grateful & thankful to
you for the same Sir I am sorry I have not the money to pay the Postage of
10 the letter but will thank you to stop it out of the money - your very
Hum^{ble} Ser^t
Maria Godfry

Little Aboney street north
41 Regents Park

TEXTUAL ALTERATIONS 1: *1833] interl below at end of line.* 2: now] 'ow' *over illeg.* 9: the
money] *after del* 'that'.

71   From John Spearman in London to the overseers of Braintree, 8 February 1834

London Feby 8 1834
Gentlemen
   I am obliged to Trouble once more for Some releif for my family but I
am in hopes this will be the Last time for Some time to Come and I
5 Should be very Glad if was the last for Ever I am expecting Some work
about a week or A fortnight time but the most of my tools are in pledge
and I hope you will be so kind as to let me have A trifle as Soon as
possible to redeem them and keep my family with for A little longer and
believe me Gentleman as Soon as I get my work me nor my family Shall
10 not be A Trouble to the parish of Braintree any longer I must Conclude
Gentlemen by thanking you for the past relief I have had at your hands
and by emploreing you to Send me as Soon as you Can the Present request
I am Gentlemen with
all respect your very
15   humble Servant
John Spearman

PS I will call upon
Mr Hayward in the
Middle of the week
20
TEXTUAL ALTERATIONS 8: little] *interl with caret.*

72 From William King in London to the overseer in Braintree, 4 March 1834

London March 4 1834

Honoured Sir

I Humbly Beg the favour of you to aquaint the Gentlemen of the Vestry that I am in Very Distress^d Circumstances. I Most Heartly thank you all Sirs for the Last 20 Shillings But am Sorry I had to Be So Very 5 Trabblesome to M^r H^d By haveing to Go So Meny times to white chapple, Did you Know Sir what Either I or My wife Suffer By it you would No doubt Pervent it. Pray Gentlemen Do Let Me Receive it at once as the Little Detps wich we are Obligded to Contract Depend Much Upon it, as allso My Name and word, I Now Get in years and feel the Nead of what 10 I Cannot obtain, Both Past and Present Afflictions Lay hold on Me and My wife She Poor woman is a Good wife and when She Can Get a Shilling By Eny Imploy wich She Can do it Comes Very Sweet, But that is Not often, Such as Respect her Give her an old Garment Now and then as to Me Likewise, and tis one Comfort to Us that we are thought worthy for 15 our Wishing at Least to do that wich will Bear Refliction. I am Glad My wife is Better in helth than She was I wish it May Last, But I am So Much Subyect to asthma and Rehmatism that I Get But Little Sleep. But I forbear Speaking More But will trust to the Benevolent feelings of the Gentlemen - if Mr Hayward Brings this for Me I will Not apply to him for what the 20 Parrish Send Me till the week after Next as I would Not Give Eny ofence, Nor Suffer the Painfull feelings wich Lay hold on Us when our Jurneys Prove fruitless. Nor Would Eny of the Gentlemen with Me So Much Sinking of Spirits theare Spirits I Boldly hope are of Noble^r Birth.

I Conclude Gentlemen 25

By asking your forgiveness

for Every thing Amis in My

Poor Supplycations to you

and I Remain your

Very Humble 30

Servant Wm King

I think it Best Not to Seal the Letter as I Saw in a Printed Paper a Great deal of what would Result from the Law in Such a Case

TEXTUAL ALTERATIONS 7: Know] *interl.* 32: in] *interl.*
  ABBREVIATIONS 6: H^d] Hayward.

CIRCUMTEXT Note from same hand on outside below address: 'By the favour of Mr Hayward'.

73   From M[aria] Godfry in [St Pancras] London to the overseers in Braintree [21 April 1834]

Sir

I should esteem it A perticular favour if you will let me have little stebbings Money on monday instead of tuesday my children is Ill I shall have an Opportunity of going myself on monday as I have no washing to
5 go out to but shall have the 2 next days it is a long way to go from my plase so I will be down at the 3 Nunns white chappel so If you will be so greatful as to send it down Mr Haywood stage coachman he will be happy to bring it to me

your Hble
10   Servt
M Godfry

31. little Abbony
street north

DATE Date of postmark.

74   From William King in London to the overseer of Braintree, 31 July [1834]

London July 31^t

Kind Sir

I am Sorry to Be oblidged to Send By Post to you But it is through the Great Want of Soum Reliaf, it was My hope that Mr Hayward Might have
5 Brought the L for Us By wich I Could have Paid Soum Little Detps wich I have Contracted on the Ground of My Little Allowance, Perticklar My Landlord who is But Poor as he Says - to Morrow is the Day I Beg^d for You Sir I Beg will feel for Me for My Circumstances are to Us Most Distressing. My Little work will Not Carry Me through. I Get in years
10 and feel the failings of Nature to Be Very alarming Not only in Boddy But in Mind allso Long Years of Trubble have Bowed Me down as it wheare But Sir you will I trust Use your Good word on My Behalf to the

Kind Gentlemen of the Select Vestry I will attend M^r H on Saturday Next
though it apears Not Very agreeble to him to Be So Repeatedly applyed to
But alas My feelings are far More *Deposed*, I Return Very Disconsolate   15
Pray for give Me Sir and Not Disopoint your Humble Ser^t

Willm King

I will Not Put this in the Post till I See wither Mr Hayword has it for Me.

TEXTUAL ALTERATIONS 11: Me] *interl.* 15: are] *inserted.*
    ABBREVIATIONS 13: H] Hayward.
    DATE Year inferred from the place of the letter within the broad chronological order of
the archive.
    CIRCUMTEXT Endorsement: 'had £1.0.0 from Mr Goodale 20th May last'.

75   From [William King] in London, September 1834

London Sep^r
1834

Honnoured Sir

   I am again oblidged to Beg your Kind assistance as My wants are Most
Pressing. I thank you and the Gentlemen of the Vestry for the Last 20   5
Shillings. I Beg the one Kindness to Me as the Prince is So Near and My
Neady Circumstances oblidge Me to Call forth your Benevolent feelings.
I have thursfor Been Supported in the Way through Meny Trubbles Known
only to Myself - Perhaps Sir I May have to Coum Home and tis a Pleaseing
Reflection Mixed with Humble thankfullness that I have Ever Such an   10
Asylum My old Birth Place till then Sirs I Must Beg and Rely on your
United feelings of Kindness and Help. No Doubt Sir you will acquiesce
in My Doing the Best I Can to Pick Up a Bit of Bread as Long as I Can.
But I am Not able to Do as formerly - I feel Great weakness and Sinking
Such as I am Perswaded all People feel who are told 60 years - My Poor   15
wife Suffers Much But She Soume times Gets a Litte by her Relations we
Do the Best we

TEXTUAL ALTERATIONS 7: Call] *inserted in left-hand margin.* 10: thankfullness] *interl below at
end of line.*
    DESTRUCTION OF TEXT Bottom of page torn off.
    WRITING Same hand as all other letters from William King.

76   From William King in London to the overseers of Braintree, 2 October 1834

London
Octo^r 2 1834

Honourd Sir

as Mr Hayward is Not yet Brought My allowenc I am Greatly Put to the
5 Most Painfull feelings. Perhaps Sir you will Use your Best Endevour to Send
it this week, as My Promis is Much Depended on as I have Depended on
the Little Sum wich the Kind Gentlemen whar Pleased I /Se/ttle -

as to the New Laws I am informed have No Efect on My Poor Donation at Present. Let Me Thearfore Humbly Beg of you Sir and the Gentle-
10 men who Compose the Vestry to Deal Kindly with Me, and to Consider
My Low Estate My Meney fould Sufferings and Perhaps as Men of Benevolence and Charity they will Notwit<hhold> that Small triffle wich in
Pa<rt> will Raise the Spirits wich Deeply Opressd, I Rely on the Kindness of you Sirs, and Still hope to hold out My epointd Days wich are Now
15 on the decline Tis October with Me {

you will Pardon what May Be found Amis in your Most Humble Servant Willm King

Permit Me to wait on Mr H on Saturday or Tuesday at furtherst

TEXTUAL ALTERATIONS 13: will] *inserted in left-hand margin.*
ABBREVIATIONS 18: H] Hayward.
CIRCUMTEXT Note from same hand on outside below address: 'By the favour of M^r
Hayward'.

77   From Henry Spearman in [St Botolph without Bishopsgate in the City of] London to the overseers of Braintree [1834]

Gentleman

I hope you will excuse the Liberty i have taking in addressing these few
lines to you to inform you David Spearman has not at Present been Fortunate
Enough to procure a Situation wich he appears very anxious to obtain and
5 there is no doupt Gentleman that he will obtain a Situation particular as M^r
Jackson has been so kind as to give him a Character. Gentleman as a
brother i have assisted him for Nearly - 6 Weeks since he left Braintree
and Gentleman i have a Wife and 3 Children to Support and i am sure you
are aware that it must be by making sacrifice that i am enabled to support

him as i have greatly Distressed myself to assist his brother John from 10
time to time Gentleman if you would be so kind as to render him some little
assistance it would be very thankfully received as it Really is Gentleman
out of my power to support him in toto as he is Obliged to go Out to Lodge
and it is as bad as two Rents to me in fact it is such Gentleman you can if
you Please refer to Mr Jackson as he has been twice called upon for 15
Davids Character but is knowledge as a footman is not sufficent and he is
now trying For a Grooms Place

I Remain Gentleman

Your Obedient

Servant   20

Henry Spearman

^{No} 53 Skinner Street
Bishopgate Without
London

DATE Year from postmark.
    CIRCUMTEXT Address on outside: 'To the Committe of Gentleman Sitting at the Work-house'.

78   From John Cardinal in [Great] Dunmow [Essex], 29 June 1835

Dear Sir   Dunmow June 29 1835
    I hope that you will excuse My takeing the liberty of writeing to you As
i cannot get information who the Gentleman is that is overseer at this
time And as you are the only Gentleman that I know of to write to as a
friend of mine I thank you sir if you would be so kind As to send this to 5
the overseer i send this requesting the gentleman to send the quarters
Allowance as now is the time that i have To pay my rent please to send it
on Monday next by the errant Cart man Direct it to be left for john Cardinal Att Mr Suckling Dunmow My wife is some what better but not able to
do any thing as yett   10
    I am sir your humble supplicent
    John Cardinal

CIRCUMTEXT Note from other hand below text: 'to be sent by Hodges last Monday £1.6s-d is quarterly paid in quarterly pay Book'.
    RELATED CORRESPONDENCE About a year before, James Suckling, overseer in Great Dunmow, had written to Joseph Garrett, overseer of Braintree: 'Dia Sir I am persuaded you will excuse my troubleing you with a case of extreme distress which you would oblige me + the

Pauper John Cardinal by laying before your Parish he has been Ill with a Billious Fever nine Days Confined to his Bed in a very redused state the docter has orderd him into a Seperate Room + there Poverty is such that thay have not a Change of Sheets +c without Borrowing + it is not to be wonderd at Considering his Wife has been Confined to he Bed princepaly for the last 7 years + the pay being reduced to 3/ per Week has very much Insured them + haveing a Daughter to maintain who is Obliged to be at home to take care of her Mother the Boy who was earning 3/ per Week only is now laid aside Ill the Man to his Credit has paid his Rent up to Lady Day indeed he allways left it in my hand Weekly for his Landlord as early assistance would be thankfully recd as I can vouch for it that they have not a penny to help themselves but what is lent them and also for the last Week' (letter of 10 April 1834).

In two further letters from Great Dunmow (undated) the overseers of Braintree were informed that John Cardinal's wife and son were ill and that on one occasion they had been given 5s in addition to the 10s they had received according to the order from Braintree.

FURTHER EVIDENCE John Cardinal is recorded to have received a regular weekly allowance of 2s from 1824 and of 4s from Lady Day 1829 at the latest (D/P 264/12/31, Braintree overseers' accounts). He was also recorded on the list of the out-door poor of Braintree, 1829-30 (D/P 264/18/34).

79   From Thomas Cleare [in Braintree]

Gent^n

I hope you will take it into Consideration & find employment for the Boy Grey for it is not in my power to maintain him for the small trifle he have brought me in Lately about 1^{s}6^d p^r week & my Wife is unable to go
5 about after work for him for it is not in my power to keep on my credit at the high [price of] bread & rent Mr Cousin [----------] hand says he believe the boy would do better now if he had Constant work it is not my wish to give you any trouble if i can help it but it has been very hard upon me, hope you will take it into consideration for the Long Cold winter will
10 without an alteration oblige me to quit the Field I rem^n
Gent^n you obedient and
humble Servt
                    Thos Cleare
The boy his barefooted if he can get work & find him Shoes it is not in
15 my Power for I Cannot get any for myself

TEXTUAL ALTERATIONS 3: him] *interl with caret.* 9: consideration] 'on' *interl at end of line.*
PLACE Inferred from sender's letter of 29 January 1827 (**16**).

80   From Robert Sewell [in Braintree]

Gentlemen

I hope you will excuse my writing as I this morning had the misfortune
to hurt my knee insomuch that I can not come if it was for a Guinea the
reason of my application is as my wife was confined on Saturday morning last and I am unable to support the cause as my small income does not   5
exceed five shillings per week, therefore Gentlemen I beg some assistance until she may be able to get about again - I would not have troubled
you but I am compelled by necessity

I am Gentlemen

your humble   10

Servant

Robert Sewell

P.S. What you Gentlemen please to let me have give to the Workhouse
Master if you please and he will send it to me

FURTHER EVIDENCE Robert Sewell, who lived in Braintree, received a weekly allowance of
2s 6d from mid-1824 until the third quarter of 1830 (ERO, D/P 264/12/31, Braintree
overseers' accounts). Since there are no detailed overseers' accounts beyond that period
of time, we do not know what he received before or afterwards. In 1829, he lived at Pump
Yard in Braintree (ERO, D/P 264/18/34, Printed list of Braintree out-door poor, 1829-
1830). In 1833, the select vestry appointed him as a scribe, ordering that he 'shall do all
the writing the Parish shall require of him for 4^s p^r Sewell to find Pens - Ink & Paper'. His
signature in the vestry minute book is in the same hand as the above letter (ERO, D/P 264/
8/10, Braintree select vestry, book of memoranda, 1817-36, entry of 22 July 1833).

Steeple Bumpstead pauper letters

81 From Joseph Wright in Braintree to Mr Jackson in Steeple Bumpstead, 6 December 1816

Braintree 6th dec[r] 1816

Gentlemen

Not recieve[g] no answer from the letter I sent some time ago, I am oblid[gd]
to trouble you again hoping you will have the goodness to remitt half
5 years rent due to the Rev[d] B. Scale otherwise our goods will be tak[n] for
payment of the same, I hope I shall not trouble you again as my Husband
is got employment at present the *sum is two pounds*

Your hb[l] Serv[t]

Joseph Wright

10 NB-

I gain a Settlement
by living with the
Rev[d] Stewart two years

please to direct for M[r] Johnson
15 Overseer Braintree & I shall have
it safe -

WRITING This letter was written by William Johnson, overseer of Braintree.

RELATED CORRESPONDENCE On 6 November 1816, William Johnson, overseer of Braintree, had written to the overseers of Steeple Bumpstead that Joseph Wright 'has been out of employ some time, and his wife newly put a Bed by which means he stands indebted for half Years Rent to the Rev[d] B Scale; which is two Pounds begs your assistance for the same otherwise he must sell his goods and come home'. On 25 February 1817 Johnson wrote that Wright 'has got employment but is in a very poor State of health, and not able sometimes to hold at his work'. Both letters are from the same hand as that from Joseph Wright.

82 From Thomas Turner in Newmarket [Suffolk] to Mr Jackson in Steeple Bumpstead, 11 January 1817

Sir/

It is now a fortnight since I apply[d] to M[r] Stevens & rec[d] no Answer - I
once more write to beg of you to send me word directly wether you mean
to do any thing for me or not - I have a child under the doctors hands & no

one can be more distress^d if therefore I do not hear from you directly - I 5
shall apply to this Parish to Pass us home at once for I can no longer live
such a wretched life -

Y^r hum^ble Ser^vt

Thos Turner

Newmarket   10
Jan^ry 11th 1817

RELATED CORRESPONDENCE There is some later correspondence between Messrs Norton &
Co. in Newmarket and the overseers of Steeple Bumpstead about outstanding bills for the
medical treatment of Mr (Thomas?) Turner and wife (letter from Norton to Edward Fitch,
7 April 1825; letter from John French in Steeple Bumpstead to Norton 8 June 1825,
saying that the bills will not be paid as nothing was ever promised; letter from Norton to
overseers, 27 August 1825).

83   From William Trudget in Ingatestone [Essex], 24 February 1817

24 Feby 1817

Gentlemen

I take the Liberty of wrigthing to you conserning my Son Edward that
hath been bad with abad leg & hath not been able to Do any work for 6
months his leg is healded & he is able to walk about, but not able to do 5
any hard work. Mr Butler says that he never will be able to do any more
hardwork with his lege Mr Butler order me not to put him to hand work or
if he Got with he though it would be as bad or worst then it wase before.
Mr Butler says that you had better put him apprentice, as he never will be
able to Get his Living at Day labour - Mr Nunn a shoemaker hath Room 10
for apprentice in this Town, & will Take him if you Gentlemen will be so
Kind as to advance a bout 12^£ 0^s 0^d for I am not able to do any thing for
him my self for one of my Daughters that hath fits had a fall about 3 week
sence & hath not been able to Get out of bed sence if he is Bound to an
apprentice it will settle him so that he will be no more Expence to Your 15
parish - I shall be much ablige to you to Send me an answer in a few Day
as Mr Nunns sath if he Dont have my son he shall take nother

from Your Humble Servt &c &c

Wm Trudget Ingate<stone>

TEXTUAL ALTERATIONS 4: any] *interl with caret*. 8: if he] *interl with caret*. 8: be] *interl with
caret*. 8: worst] *after del illeg*. 9: says] *after del illeg*. 19: Trudget] 'd' *over* 'g'.

RELATED CORRESPONDENCE On 11 April 1816, Charles Elvin in Ingatestone had written to the overseers of Steeple Bumpstead, requesting an increase in the allowance of William Trudget. On 22 November 1816, he had written again, presenting an account for William Trudget's child, and asked to remit the payments for Trudget's family (84 weeks at 1s for 27 March 1815 to 18 November 1816). He had said that 'the Family is very much destrest and beg you to allow them sumthing'; that the son (aged 18) had a swollen heel which prevented him from work; and that the girl for whom 1s had been allowed 'has Fits so frequently that the Mother cannot go out to earn a Shilling'.

84   From G. Allam in London to Mr Jackson in Steeple Bumpstead, 28 July 1817

London July 28 1817

Sir I have taken oppurnity of writing these few lines to you to let you know that I am very bad off at present I should wish to know of you which is the best way to do wether to come down to Bumpstead or to stop up in Lon-
5 don and be starved for I am almost at this time for I have no were to go to at Nights to sleep and no work of a day time for I have been for 3 days without food I have not had aplace since I have been up this time and but very little work to do and if the parish will send me a trifle up I shall be very much oblidge to them if you send to me

10   G Allam

at Mr Shallness No^r 11
Zoar Street Gravel Lane
Borough

TEXTUAL ALTERATIONS 5: almost] *after del* 'a'.

85   From Mary Ann Page [in St Giles-in-the-Fields, London] to John French, vestry clerk of Steeple Bumpstead, [27 September 1825]

Sir

I Humbley Beg pardon for taking this Liberty of writing to you and the gentelmen To Inform you and that the gentelmen of Saint Gileses parich allways Paid me 3^s 6^d pur week sins th time that you gentlmen Sent M^r
5 Erl th order to pay me and If you gentlmen plese to Send a order to Mr Erl to Pay me as Before I will try And do with it as Before and If not I The gentelmen of Saint giles parish must Carrey me home to you Emelditley

for I Canot live hear and Starve as I am a Poor Ofliced woman and Cannot work for my Living and likewise that my Nece has to dress and un dress me and has had for years gentelmen Mary ann page I am Ann 10 Trudgett Nese I have don for my Poor ofliced old ant for years with Your assistance I have Borded lodg wash and Every othe thing that Laid in my Pour for 6^d per day and I will leve it to you gentelmen whether that has Been Cefesent for me I went to Mr Erl for the money that was due to me for the keep of my Aant which th gentelmen Honrehell Paid me and I was 15 informed that you doe Not know my aunt ann Trudgett the wife of Edwerd trugett witch you dad doun with you 3 quarters of a year when you gave hur th order for 3^s 6^d for wich I Canot tell how yoa gentelmen Canot know hur unless Mr Erl made a misstaike in Speling th Name th gentelmen had my aunt in th house 10 dayes for to Cum home or a order to pay as 20 usell Plese to send Mr Erl order to pay as usel or else She must Bee Cared home dierectley

TEXTUAL ALTERATIONS 7: must] 't' *interl at end of line.*
DATE Date of note of receipt.
PLACE Inferred from text.

86   From Hannah Mansfield in Wickham [St Pauls, Essex], 5 January 1827

Mr Hills
   Sir/
   I am sorry to come to trouble you but my Poor Mother has been very bad for 3 months and not been able to do any thing for herself and has bein some weeks confined to her bed she has the ague very Bad I hope 5 you will send her something more than her allowance or she will be obliged to be brought home as I cannot keep her with that I should have come to you before but myself and husband are both ill and have the ague that we could not Either of us come I hope you will please to send her a pice of Cloth to make her a shift 10
                          from your Hannah Mansfield
                          Daugh^t of Wi^d Dodd
1827
Jany 5 W Wickham

TEXTUAL ALTERATIONS 5: weeks] *over illeg.*

87   From Ann Trudgett [in St Marylebone, London] to Mr Howes in Steeple Bumpstead, 23 October 1831

october 23 1831

Gentelmen

Ann Trudgett the Wife off Edward Trudgett Now a widdow I went to
Mr Deeds For my money as he was so kind to pay me and to my surprise
5 Mr Deeds told me the gentlmen ware not satsfide that he had Paid me I do
a sure you gentelmen that I ded Receive off Mr Deeds 3^s pur week sense
Last Ester up to the 8 off october gentelmen iff you do not a low M^r deeds
to Pay me as usell i must through my self on the Parish and Bee Brough
home as i am a Poor oflicted woman not able to work for my Living i am
10 Sixty 1 years old and iff it was not for my Nece i Could not do at all and
she is hevely oprest hur self with a large familey off 7 Children

Ann Trudgett

London

I hope gentelmen you will Consider
15 my Cace and plese to Send Mr Deeds your
order to pay me

WRITING Same hand as letter from Mary Ann Page of 27 September 1825 (**85**).
  PLACE Inferred from related correspondence.
  RELATED CORRESPONDENCE and FURTHER EVIDENCE On 16 November 1831, Mr Hoskins,
magistrate at the Police Office of St Marylebone, wrote to Mr Holmes in Steeple Bumpstead
that Anne Trudgett had complained that her money (which was brought by Mr Deed) had
been withheld. 'She is much distressed, & I beg you will be So good & remit the arrears
immediately & *answer this letter by the post*'. It looks as though the overseers of Steeple
Bumpstead were trying to ignore her case, or determined to make her come home if she
needed assistance, for in a further letter from St Marylebone Police Office they were told
that Ann Tredget (alias Trudgett) was too old to be removed and that her allowance ought
to be continued (ERO, D/P 21/16/4, Steeple Bumpstead overseers' settlement correspondence, letter of 12 December 1831).

88   From Joseph Derham in Brighton to Mr Fitch in Steeple Bumpstead, 19 March 1833

Mr Fitch

Sur ihoumbell Beg your parden in teaken the Liberty of Writen to you
sur Bout iam sory to in form you that My Wife is dangrest ill and With
the small pox and 2 of My Cheldren and ihave Not earened Bout 10
5 shilengs sins isen you sur and iam fraid that ishall have My things sold to

pay My Lodgens and they thriten mee and iam all Most starved and Clearly
in the greates of Destrest and if the over sears and you Could send Mee
pound or the seam as you gave Mee When iWas thear ishould Return you
thousen thanks and if icould Roub Long 2 Months Mor fishen is Comon
inn and Markerell seasen and ihave got to pay the Docter 12 shelings and 10
god Noes how or Whean and if you Canot send Me the trifwell Wee Most
Com home to the paresh M^rs stevens Canot Dou Mee eany goud in My
Destrest Ceast her have sist Mee sins isen you sur and ihope you Will
send eit oupt By the Havrell Coch inn small parsell By Mondy Next and
there the Brighton Cochman Will Call for eit at Mrs Nelsons Bouell in 15
Aldgeat street and pray sur Bee our frind ons More and ihope that Wee
May Not Com to troubell the paresh No Mor and eit tis hard for Mee and
pray sur send Word Where or Now and then ishall Now What to Dou as
the Cochman Will Call on porpos and eit tould Com seaft to Wee By him
and if you send By the the Havrell Coch 20

     Derect eit for Joseph Derham
     to Bee
     left at Mrs Nelsons
     Bouell inn aldgeat street
     till Call for 25
      Leat serveant to M^r stevens
     Esq. god Bles you all
         Joseph Derham

Brihton
March 19 30
1833

TEXTUAL ALTERATIONS 6: Lodgens] 'Lod' *over* 'Rent'. 25: till Call for] *interl below at end of line.*

89 From Thomas Albion in Cambridge to the overseers of Steeple Bumpstead, 9 November 1833

         Cambridge Nov 9th 1833
To the Overseers of Steple Bumstead. In the County of Essex
 Gentlemen I am sorry to say that the Unfortunate situation Which I
have been placed In since the Loss of my Wife, being left with Four
Small Children and no person to take care of them, but by Hiring a Woman, 5

and having to Maintain her has hadded much to my present difficulties,
When I was last at Steple Bumstead on the 5th day of November 1832. I
had hopes and Flatter'd Myself that with your Allowance of Three Shillings and Sixpence a Week I should be Enabled to Support My Family,
10 but to My Grief and Misfortune after Twelve Months Trial, I am worse
off than Ever for I am in debt and my best part of Clothes are in pawn. My
Money which I earn is not sufficient to Maintain My Self and One Child,
without paying rent -

    Now Gentlemen, not being able to support them with your Allowance
15 nor Even with double the sum It is My Intention that the three youngest
of My Children shall come home to the parish, I have found by some
means by Gods help and pawning always a Belly full of Victuals, but for
Clothes I am not able to due it, as for to get Credit that is Impossible, as
Every Tradseman that knows my Circumstance knows well. It would be
20 Never be in My power to pay them, I will keep and Clothe the Eldest
Girl, I should hope and Expect you will send me a Letter by the Carrier as
next Saturday, for me to send the three youngest Home by Him If not I
shall be forced to Earn what little works I have, and Bring my Self a
Burthen on the Parish with all the Children. If you agree to this, probable
25 something may happen which I hope it will, then I shall be enabled to
send a Trifle to help my Dear Motherless babes I shall expect an Answer
by the Carrier as Next Saturday directed to me at the Black Lion Silver
Street Cambridge

I am Gentlemen with Humble Submission
30   Your Obedient Servant to
Command Thomas Albion

RELATED CORRESPONDENCE Over the previous year, the Revd Faulkner of St Sepulchre,
Cambridge, had sent several letters to the overseers of Steeple Bumpstead on behalf of
Thomas Albion. On 8 February 1832 he made his first request for an allowance for Albion,
whose settlement in Steeple Bumpstead he said he had gained in 1822, when he had
worked as a groom for E.A. Stevens Esq., Bower Hall, an etstate in that parish. Albion
had four children and 'his distress arisis from the long continued Sickness of his Wife
who is rendered totally helpless'. He was in work at 12s per week, and 'the woman who
was the Widow of a Soldier killed in Waterloo has £10 p^r annum - but yet nowithstanding
all this there is very great distress in the family solaly through the heavy Sickness of the
poor Woman'. On 21 February 1832, Faulkner wrote to Thomas Goldstone, the vestry
clerk, repeating his request to support Albion, and then again on 17 May 1832 to the same
effect, saying 'his Wife remains in the same afflicted state as before' and 'he is again in
much distress & want'. On 14 August 1832, Faulkner informed Goldstone that Albion's
wife had died on the 24 June and that by now he earned only 10s per week, 'his children
[the eldest of whom was only 8 years old] requiring the constant attention of a female
while he is at work'.

90   From Mary Pannel in Hertford to Charles Pannel in Steeple Bumpstead, 22 December 1835

Hertford Dec 22 1835

Dear Brother

I hope these few Lines will find you on good Health buy my present afflicted Circumstance press me to write to ask th favor of you if you can do any thing for me with th Gaurdiens of th Parish as they have taken of   5
all my pey and I am now left intirely Distitute of any means of support for myself and the two poor helpless Children in additions to to me now Ill in Bed and another that hes had no employ for nearly six Months and as I find it Impossible to exist in the <su>ffering state I shall take it as a great kindness if you would be so good as to see them and to know what they   10
would wish me to do, if they would allow me but a small sum I would indeavour to do with it and if not myself and the two Children must come home to the parish which I shall be very sorry to do and then I dont know how I can possibly get there but necessity and distress has now compeled me to take some step as I have made different applications by Letter and   15
it has had no Effect I thought they mig<ht> attend to it by your mentioning it to them and shall be glad of an answer as soon as you can conviniently send one - my son Thomas and wife are in a middling state of Health but th two Children are very much afflicted so that they cannot give me any assistance I conclude with my kind Love to you and yours and am your   20
poor afflicted sister

Mary Pannell

NB I still live in st Andrews Parish Hertford

RELATED CORRESPONDENCE Three years before, an unsuccessful attempt had been made at removing Mary Pannel. In a letter of 19 April 1832, Mr Swaddle and Mr Hills in St Andrew's, Hertford, had informed the overseers of Steeple Bumpstead that the parish had obtained an order for the removal of Widow Mary Pannel and her three children to Steeple Bumpstead, which had been suspended 'in consequence of the Illness of the Woman [...], but as soon as she is able to travel we will send her to you'. On 10 May 1832 Mr Munday, vestry clerk of St Andrew's, Hertford, sent a copy of Mary Pannel's settlement examination (4 April 1832 marked, not signed) to Thomas Goldstone, vestry clerk of Steeple Bumpstead, according to which Mary Pannel was the widow of Joshuah Pannel whom she had married about 24 years ago and who had belonged to Steeple Bumpstead by birth, and of whom she had three children: Sarah (15), William (8) and Elizabeth (4).

At about the same time, Bernard Gilpin, rector of St Andrew's, Hertford, had approached the overseers of Steeple Bumpstead, requesting the repayment of the allowance his parish had granted to Mary Pannel and her children, and suggesting to them a reconsideration of the question of her removal. 'It strikes me, that considering the illness of the

the daughter [spine injury], and that the mother here by takeing in lodgers & other means is able to do a little for herself, more perhaps than in a place in w^h she was not known - it would not be worth while nor indeed expedient to insist on her removal. She is a very quiet, steady, respectable person, & fully deserving the support which her destitute case seems to require. Should your Parish, taking these things into consideration, agree to award her a fixed allowance, & to empower our overseers to pay the same weekly, I think it would be very well' (letter of 3 May 1832). The answer is not recorded, but a month later he wrote again, to W. Goldstone, vestry clerk of Steeple Bumpstead, giving a detailed account of the expenses for Mary Pannel: the overseers of his parish had allowed her 7s for eight weeks, and then given 5s for four weeks as ordered by Steeple Bumpstead, which, together with 3s 4d for the postage of the letters sent so far, came to the total amount £3 9s 4d. He said that apart from the children living with her she also had three sons who were 'able to earn their own bread, tho' not (in the case of 2 of them) without some further charge to their mother'. Her daughter Sarah was suffering from a 'severe injury in the back, & is likely to be very tedious, if indeed she ever recover. The mother's time is much taken up by attendance on her. On the whole therefore 7^s/ appeared to our overseers not more than a fair allowance and I would earnestly request that while her daughter continues so ill as she is at present, that allowance might be granted. If however her present allowance of 5^s/ be abridged, of course she must be passed home, & her daughter too when she is able. They wish me to say, that certainly they cannot object to this, if it be the plan you wish them to adopt, but it will be attended with serious inconvenience, as they will have to give up many advantages (especially for the 3 sons) w^h here, from their connexions &c they are able to obtain - and also, it is to be feared that on the most moderate computation, the expense to you of maintaining them at home, w^d considerably exceed 5^s/ or indeed 7^s/ weekly'. Again, we do not know the answer from Steeple Bumpstead, but there is a further letter from Gilpin and John Davies, surgeon in Hertford, of 12 July 1832, with a request to increase the allowance for Mrs Pannel and a medical certificate for her daughter.

Whatever the overseers of Steeple Bumpstead decided, Mary Pannel obviously stayed in Hertford. More than two years later (and about a year before her above letter to her brother), William Taylor, assistant overseer of St Andrew's, Hertford, wrote to the overseers of Steeple Bumpstead, answering their request to report what she did for her living: 'I dont belive she dows any thing besides plating some weeks she his some & others she his none [...] she is rather a weekly woman that I dont belife she is able to go about Washing' (letter of 29 December 1834).

After Mary Pannel's letter to her brother, the overseers of Steeple Bumpstead were approached, on her behalf, from St Andrew's, Hertford, on two further occasions. On 18 February 1836, Thomas Nunn asked them to allow her 3s per week (with note of answer: allow 2s till Lady Day). And on 7 September 1836, Thomas Booth requested the remittance of her allowance during the last six months. 'For the future,' he added, 'please forward the money to me once a quarter by Mr Sharp of Cambridge who comes to Hertford once a fortnight.'

91   From Edward Roads in Sheffield to Mr Beans in Steeple Bumpstead, 1 January [1837]

Janury 1 1834

Sir

  i take the liberty of writing to you to let you now that i have got no work to nor as had any since Mr Baker call upon me we are straving if you would be so good as to lend me atwo pound i should be very much obliged 5
to you i will be sure to return it again in the summer for i have got the proimese of a summer work for myself my wife and children we have had a great deal of illness and i have got a large doctors bill to pay wish i must pay and i expect to have my thing taken from me every day for rent i have wrote to my daughter but she cannot releif me for she have been 10
very ill if you do not releif me i shall be oblig to come home next week i should be much obliged to you send me word what i am to do so no more from your humble servant Edward roads longford yard little Sheffe
  Sheffeild yorkshire

TEXTUAL ALTERATIONS 12: much] 'm' *over illeg.* 12: you] *interl.* 13: servant] 't' *interl at end of line.*
DATE Correct year from postmark.

92   From Edward Roads [in Sheffield] to Mr Baines in Steeple Bumpstead, 12 January 1837

Jan 12 1837

Dear sir

  i return you many thanks for your kindness and ham happy to say that i received the money safe we should have had to come this next week if i had not have has it did i ham glad to say that i have got a fortnight work 5
at oult park my wife as been very bad but thank god she is geting better Mrs Goerge Shocks will employ me this next summer so as soon as i Get into good work i will be sure to send the money back the weather is so very bad if i could Get the work to do i could not do i have to walk 6 mile morning and night to my work i must conclude with my thanks to you all 10
gettenlmen an i remain yor humble and obliged
  Servant Edward Roads

TEXTUAL ALTERATIONS 3: i] *after del illeg.* 3: happy] 'h' *over* 'p'. 5: glad] 'g' *over* 'h'.
PLACE Inferred from Edward Roads's previous letter (**91**) (both from same hand).

93   Thomas Albion in Cambridge to Mr Brooks, 26 March 1837

Mark 26 Cambridge 1837

Mr Robenson pay ofeser haverell I have to in form you I hav Bean very
an Well for the Last 5 Weeks Im veary sory that it due Not Lay in my to
due for my familay More then I have dun I hope it will be In a Short time
5 be in my pour to have my dauhgter harrat to Cambridge about May I hop
thay are all Well I Will never tirn my Back an my Childran I Will due all
I Can forw them

     So no mor from me
     Thomas Albon Cambridge

TEXTUAL ALTERATIONS 4: be] *inserted in left-hand margin before* 'In'.

Great Burstead pauper letters

94 From James Willson in Springfield Gaol [Chelmsford] to Sarah Willson in Billericay, 31 October 1833

Springfield Gaol October th31 1833

Dear wife I write these few lines to you to let you know that I shall not be out of prison til this day fortnight and I am very glad to hear that you and the children are all well and I have to let you know that I am t<o> put in my own bail to keep the peace for six months <from> the expiration of my months imprisonment you may tell the overseers of the parish that the clerk fees will be 8 or 9 shillings for putting my own bail in and you can tell them if I have not the money they will keep me for six months and you can come here if you like the day as I come out so no more at preasen<t>

from your loving husband James Willson

CIRCUMTEXT Note from other hand below: 'allowed Nov 4 1833 Daniel Richardson'. Address on outside (same hand as letter): 'To be left at Mrs Cricks at the poorhouse Billericay for Sarah Willson'.
PLACE Billericay was a chapel within the parish of Great Burstead.

95 From George and Mary Pateman in Gibraltar, 7 June 1834

Gibraltar

June 7th 1834

Dear Mother Brothers and Sisters

I embrace the earliest Opportunity of writing to let you know of the Safe arrival of my Wife and Children here after A Passage of Sixteen Days. We are all well with the Exption of my eldest Son who is badly in his bowels

I went to the Colonel with her and Shewed the Caracter She received from the Overseers and told him that she was Sent out by the Parish he said that there was the Complement of werran came out With the Regiment But the first Vacancy that there Was she should have the Indulgence the same as Another woman. the Colonel Said that they Should not have sent her out so Soon and he wanted me to send her home Again Giving her A free Passage home But I thought that She had been a great deal of trouble

15 to the Parish already. A woman undergoes so much trouble and
inconvienence on board a Ship be so good as tell the Gentlemen that I
have to Pay for lodgeings in this town at the rate of 10 shillings a month
which I cannot afford without that the Gentlmen Send me Some releif for
A short time if that they do not send Assistance to me a little I shall be
20 Obliged to send her home again to the Parish which I Do not wish to do if
I can without I am forced so to do I can Manage every thing else but the
lodgeings that runs so very high I can Get A Free Passage Home at any
time in Vessels leaving this Port if they Please to send me a small trifle by
the Next Packet I shall be much Obliged to them the Regiment is Greatly
25 in debt first coming out on a Foreign Station and they Pay is so Very small.
if they will Obliged me thus far I trust that it will be the last time that I shall
trouble them if that they do not grant me this favour I shall be Obliged to
Send he home by the next Transport as it is Impossible I can Pay the rent
I am Very Sorry to trouble as they have been to a great Deal with my
30 family but this is a case of Necessity which cannot be avoided
      Dear Mother Give my best respects to my Brothers and Sisters and to
all Inquireing friends
            So no more at Present forom your Affectionate
            Son & Daughter
35   and Children
                  George Pateman
                  Mary Pateman
Dear Mother be sure to show this to the Gentleman
      Dear Mother the Fruit and wine is Very cheap But were confined to
40 Barracks all Day till near Sunset in Summer the Garrison is Strongly
Fortified all round there is Gallery Bored in the rock were the cannon is
mounted and some Very Pretty large Caves on Saint Michael and another
Saint Georges there is Jews turks Moors Greeks and Soldiers and Sailors
of all Natons the Natives are very fond of Oil and Ga<rli>c and fish the
45 wemen Dress Very handsome <-------------> Great pr<i>de in their hair
they are mostly <----------->s Portuguese &c
      Fowls are Very cheap a<------->s fish which is here in Abundance we
shall soon have the grapes in there very cheap and so are figs Oranges
Peaches Apricots Water and Mash Melons Pomegranites there is Pota-
50 toes they sell at about six shillings to eight shillings a hundred Weight
                  Please to write by return
                        of Post

TEXTUAL ALTERATIONS 11: first] *interl*. 19: send Assistance to] 'send' *and* 'to' *interl*. 30: Necessity] 'ce' *interl below*.

DESTRUCTION OF TEXT There is a big hole in the middle of the last page of the text. This is also why the address on the outside is missing.

FURTHER EVIDENCE The vestry of Great Burstead decided that George Pateman should 'Not [be] relieved, on account of his having earned 8ˢ/ pʳ week'. But his mother, Widow Pateman was on regular relief (ERO, D/P 139/8/8, Great Burstead vestry minutes).

96   From William Catt

Honourᵈ Geenteelmen

I am verry Sorry that I have to trouble you for assistance But I Cannot Do without any Longer for I am Not abel to Do any thing at Present and I have No money Nor any thing to take to my 4 Children are all verry Bad with the Small Pox and I Cannot Get any thing for them without your   5 assistance So geenteelmen I hope you will Send me Sum money for my Support for I have Spent all my money that I had and have Not 1 penny to help myself So I must Lay at your mercy to Give me what you Please But I Do Ashure you that I Stand in Need of Relief And hoope that you Relieve me for I have Not Done any work for one month   10
                    Wᵐ Catt

TEXTUAL ALTERATIONS 9: Ashure] *after del illeg*.

97   From William Pryor in Spitalfields [London]

N° 2 farthing Hill
Spittlefield

Hᵒⁿʳᵈ

Gentlemen

of the Committe -   5

your Humble Servant William Pryor beggs pardon for the Liberty that he is now about to take my Wife is now Confined and very much in want would be much Obliged to your kindness for A few Shillings Extra to help me over the next week

                    I Remain Honᵈ   10
                    Sⁱʳ your Humble
                    Ser<vant> William Pryor

Textual alterations 1: Hill] *interl at end of line*.

Circumtext Note in pencil from other hand interlined after 'William Pryor': '5^{S}0^D Granted'.

Further evidence In 1823 and early 1824 Widow Pryor at 8 Bath Street, Tabernacle Square, received regular relief of between 2s 6d and 3s per week, until her death on 10 February 1824 (ERO, D/P 139/8/8, Great Burstead vestry minutes).

Canewdon pauper letter

**98   From Sarah Albon in Horringer, Suffolk, to Mr Lodwick Esq.
[21 September 1825]**

Horringer

Sir

Sarah Arbon will thank you to send James Arbons Money as the time is
expired and I should be Glad of it Sir if you Could send as quick as
possible   5

Sarah Aarbon
Horringer Near
bury St Edmunds
Suffolk

to be left   10
at Mr Armstrongs
Grocer Abeyate Sret
Bury

CIRCUMTEXT Note from other hand on back: 'This is to certify that James Alborn is now
living, and at present residing in the Parish of Horringer' (hand A). Signed by W.C.
Cherry, curate of Horringer (hand B) and Thomas Gardiner, churchwarden (hand C), 21
September 1825. Note from further hand (D) below: '£1:6:0'.

DATE Inferred from circumtext.

NAME OF SENDER 'Arbon' and 'Aarbon' as given in the letter are regarded as variant
spellings of 'Albon'.

FURTHER EVIDENCE In 1821 and 1822, Sarah Albon had received an allowance of 1s for her
illegitimate boy (ERO, D/P 219/12/45, Canewdon overseers' accounts).

Chelmsford pauper letters

99 From William Ardley in Kelvedon [Essex] to the overseer of Chelmsford, 15 October [1820]

S^{ir}

I am Sorry I am Under the Obligation of troubling you for some Relief, but my poor Children are in a Naked Situation and me and one of my Children have the Ague every third day and have had for this five Weeks
5 which have brought me verry weak and Low so as I can Scarcely do my Work S^{ir} I hope you will ask the Gentleman to be so kind as to send me a trifle by the Retu<rn> of post for if the Gentleman do not Consider me a trifle I cannot think what I am to do -

S^{ir} I Remain Your Humble Ser^t
10   Wm Ardley Horsekeeper
Octr 15th Angle Inn Kelvedon
Essex

TEXTUAL ALTERATIONS 2: Obligation] *first 'i' interl with caret.*
DATE Year from note of receipt on outside.
FURTHER EVIDENCE Since Christmas 1819, William Ardley, who was then reported as aged 41 and having three children, had received payments of £7 (ERO, D/P 94/18/53, List of the out-door poor belonging to Chelmsford, for the year from Christmas 1819).

100 From William Ardley in Romford [Essex] to the overseer of Chelmsford, 17 January [1823]

Sir

Mr Dillemore the Overseer at Romford Wrote to you for some Relief for me and he have not Receiv^d no Answer; for my Wife and Child have been bad with the Bad Fever for some Weeks and I stand in great need of
5 some Relief from you, Mr Carruthers the Doctor which attends my Family gave me a Note and I gave it to Mr Dillomore and he knows my Family want some Assistance more than I Can do for them I hope S^{ir} you will send me a trifle of Money, if you please you can send it to the Overseer at Romford for I have been Obige to have a Woman to do for my Family and
10 I cannot pay my way without your Assistance when I left Kelvedon I was out of place a fortnight before I got a place at Romford which makes me

in poor Circumsteance so I hope you will Consider me and send me some Relief -

S^{ir} I Remain Your humble Servant

Wm Ardley Horsekeeper 15

Romford Jany 17th}

TEXTUAL ALTERATIONS 3: have] *after del* 'have'. 10: pay] 'p' *over* 't' *and del* 'get'. 14: Servant] *interl at end of line.* 16: Romford] *above del* 'Romford'.

CIRCUMTEXT Filing note on outside: 'Mr Delamere respecting Wm Ardley a pauper at Romford'.

DATE Year from filing note on outside.

RELATED CORRESPONDENCE and FURTHER EVIDENCE In two letters of 2 and 21 August 1824, Mrs Palmer in Romford suggested taking Mary Ardley (variant spelling: Ardleigh) into her service if the overseers of Chelmsford provided for her clothes, to which they agreed. On 8 August 1824, they allowed £1 'to Mary Ardley on going to Service' (ERO, D/P 94/12/17, Chelmsford overseers' accounts, pauper ledger). On 10 December 1825, Mr Thompson in Romford wrote to them that he had taken her sister Sarah into his service and requested clothes for her 'in the same way', pointing out that Mary Ardley 'has now procured a Settlement by her Service in her own right'. The overseers of Chelmsford answered on 30 December 1825 and sent him a £1 note.

101   From William Holden in Hampstead to John Stokes in Chelmsford, 29 July 1823

Hampstead July 29th 1823 -

Sir

Mr Stokes I hope you will parden the liberties I ha<ve> Taking in Directing these few lines to you hoping att the Same time you will Oblige Me with answer -   5

Sir I have to inform you i have Rote four letters To Chelmsford 3 to Mr Wiffen and one to Mr Goimer Requesting answer My request Not Being Complyd With in their Not answering any One wich has Put Me att a loss how to act Not knowing wi<ch> Way to Make the Money up I have put it off from time to time in expecting of answer in some One way or another 10 I Sir have taking the liberty off directing to you earnestly Beggen you will Condesend to Releve My troubled Mind in letting Me know in Some one way or another In So doing you will Ever Oblige your Obedent Humble servan<t>

William Holden 15

Flask walk Hampstead

Middlesex

to M^r Ab. John Stokes
Chelmsford
20 Essex

TEXTUAL ALTERATIONS 12: My] *after del* 'y'. 16: Hampstead] 'ad' *interl at end of line*.
CIRCUMTEXT Filing note on outside: 'a Pauper to borrow Money on his Pension'.
FURTHER EVIDENCE William Holden, a shoemaker with two children, had received a
weekly allowance of 4s from the parish of Chelmsford from Midsummer 1821 (ERO, D/
P 94/12/36, Chelmsford overseers' accounts). In addition, he had received occasional
cash payments to the amount of £2 5s 6d in 1823 (D/P 94/12/17, Chelmsford overseers'
accounts, pauper ledger). He also received a pension from the Office of Ordnance, on
which the overseers of Chelmsford tried to establish a claim (see **103**).

**102   From Mary Munrow in Lambeth [London] to Joseph Wiffen,
overseer of Chelmsford, 9 November 1823**

Lambeth Novr 9 1823

Sir

I hope you will excuse the liberty I take adressing these few lines to you
but having made frequent application to Lambeth Parish concerning my
5 unfortunate Daughter mary teece who I am sorry to say is wholy incapable of getting her living owing to the dreadful malady she had and praying
you would allow her some trifle or I must be obliged to send her to the
Parish being unable to support her myself

Sir Please to answer by return of Post and you will much oblige your
10   Humble Servant
                                                Mary Munro
                                    N° 2 Glasshouse Court
                                        Glasshouse Street
                                                Vauxhall

TEXTUAL ALTERATIONS 5: unfortunate] 'nate' *interl at end of line*.
CIRCUMTEXT Filing note on outside: 'Mary Munro respecting Mary Teece a Letter from
the Parish Officers of Lambeth was answered some Time back requesting them to use
their own Discretion respecting Mary Teece.' Mary Munrow's daughter, Mary Teece,
was mentally ill. She had been removed to Chelmsford in September 1822 but apparently
gone back to Lambeth later on. See letters from Mary Munrow of 29 January and 4 June
1824 (**107** and **117**).

103   From William Holden in Hampstead to Mr Goymer, overseer in Chelmsford, 15 November 1823

Hampstead 15th 1823 -

Sir

Mr Goymer in answer to a letter Received from Chelmsford Dated the 12 Instant Respection the Money that Remains Undrawnd I have to asure You Nothing Would Give Me More Plesure then to Draw the Money and   5 Remit it down to Chelmsford with Adishanal alowance every quarter Where I in Prossion of My instructions Wich is att this time in the Hands of Mr Archer and it is Curtain I Can Not draw the Money with out it If the Genteelmen thinks proper for Me to draw the Money they will Surify to same By emeditly Admiting By return of post My Instrictions with a let- 10 ter to produce Att the Bord

I am sir your Obedent

Humble Servt

Wm Holden

Flask Walk   15

Hampstead

Middlesex

To Mr Goimer

Oversear of the

poor Chelmsford   20

Essex

SPELLING 7: Prossion] *read* 'Possession'.

CIRCUMTEXT On outside, note of answer, sent 28 November 1823, requesting William Holden to send the 'necessary Affidavids'.

RELATED CORRESPONDENCE Apart from his weekly allowance of 4s from Chelmsford, William Holden also received a pension of 3s 6d per week from the Office of Ordnance, which the overseers of Chelmsford managed to claim. Following a magistrate's order they had obtained, the pension was paid to them for the period from 1 January to 30 June 1824 (letter from the Office of Ordnance to the overseers of Chelmsford, 3 May 1824).

104   From David Rivenall in St George in the East, London, to Joseph Wiffen, overseer of Chelmsford, 5 December 1823

23 London Terrace London Decr 5th 1823
St Georges East Commercial Road

S^r

I am under the necessity of again adressing You - having no answer
5 from the letter I addressed to you on the 21st of Last month, nor will M^rs
Nelson give me any Acc^d why the mony is Stop^d - it will be 3 weeks next
monday Since I Rec^d any from Mrs Nelson which has thrown me into the
greatest Distress possible & If Releif is not afforded me immediately I
must apply to the parish I now Exist in for means to keep me & my
10 numerous almost destitute family from Starving & the officers will soon
discover which way I Am to be Releived. Mrs Nelson will not assign any
reason for witholding the mony, I hope you will afford me Redress
Speedley or we Shall be Starved alive, Your most H^ble & ob^t Servt

David Rivenall

TEXTUAL ALTERATIONS 7: from] 'f' *over illeg.* 8: not] *interl with stroke.* 8: immediately]
'diately' *interl at end of line.* 9: to] *interl with stroke.* 12: reason] *interl with caret.*

FURTHER EVIDENCE Early in December 1823, John Sheppee, on behalf of the select vestry of Chelmsford, had visited several Chelmsford paupers residing in London. According to his report of 13 December 1823, David Rivenall (aged 42) had a wife and seven
children (four boys aged 12, 11, 2 and 5 months, the eldest of whom was 'in the Charity
School', and three girls aged 8, 7, and 5). Rivenall had 'had his Goods distrained upon for
3 Weeks Rent at 3^s 3^d p^r Week in consequence of not receiving his allowance as he
formerly did; - the expences incurred were 10 Shillings; - I gave him £1, and told him all
the allowances were stopt for the present, and that he must not expect so much as 5^s/ per
Week for the future; - The Family look in a very deplorable state; - it appears the Children
are shut up in the house all day, as the Wife keeps a Stall and the Husband acts as a Porter
in the day time and carries Oysters about in the Evening; - They appear to me to be both
fond of Dram drinking' (ERO, D/P 94/18/42, Report of John Sheppee on his journey to
London, 13 December 1823). Rivenall had received a weekly allowance of 6s in 1819/20,
which had been reduced to 4s in 1822/23 (D/P 94/18/53, List of the out-door poor belonging to Chelmsford, for the year from Christmas 1819; D/P 94/18/55, List of the out-door
poor belonging to Chelmsford, for the year from Lady Day 1822). After Sheppee's report,
Rivenall's allowance was reduced to 2s 6d, and this was paid until Michaelmas 1825 (D/
P 94/12/36, Chelmsford overseers' accounts).

105 From William Day in Thorpe[-le-Soken, Essex] to James Read in Chelmsford, 7 December 1823

Thorpe Dec[r] 7 1823

Sir I write this as an answer to your request I have 9 shillings per week when I work the week my eldest girl aged 17 do for me and my family the next Boy aged 15 has 6[d] per Day when he work but has not alw<a>ys Employment one Boy aged 13 has been out three weeks for his Board I   5
have to find him all his Cloathes the two youngest the one aged 9 the other 5 years

I am yours
W[m] Day

CIRCUMTEXT Note of answer of 9 January 1824 to the overseer of Thorpe-le-Soken at bottom of page, ordering the weekly allowance to be reduced from 4s to 2s 6d.

RELATED CORRESPONDENCE and FURTHER EVIDENCE William Day, a labourer with five children, had received a weekly allowance of 5s since Christmas 1819 (ERO, D/P 94/18/53, List of the out-door poor belonging to Chelmsford, for the year from Christmas 1819; D/P 94/18/55, List of the out-door poor belonging to Chelmsford, for the year from Lady Day 1822). On 15 October 1824, Mr Bentfield in Thorpe-le-Soken wrote to the overseer of Chelmsford on behalf of Day, saying that the latter had found a place for his son, John Day, with Nathaniel Saunders, a fisherman at Harwich, and that he 'wants your assistance in binding the boy'. He mentioned the sum of £6 for 'fitting out an Apprentice with Clothers', which Chelmsford seems to have met (note of answer to a further letter from Mr Bentfield to James Read, 24 December 1824).

106 From Mary Munrow [in Lambeth, London] to Joseph Wiffen in Chelmsford, 18 December 1823

December 18th 1823

Gentleman I am Sorry to Be So Troublesome But as I have not heard any further from you I thought Proper to write to inform you that My Daughter is in a very Bad way and it is imposible for me to Support her without Some alowance from the Parish as I have Distressd my Self to the utmost   5
for her I wish to know if I am to Bring her Down against the Commite Day But if I Could Be alowed any thing in reason I Should wish to See to her myself as She Requires Particular atention and She is Likewise in want of Clouths of ever Discription

your humble Ser[nt]   10
Mary Murrow

TEXTUAL ALTERATIONS 3: thought] 'ht' *interl at end of line.*
CIRCUMTEXT Filing note on outside: 'Mary Munrow respecting Mary Teece'; underneath, note of answer, 24 December 1823: allowance 2s weekly.
PLACE Inferred from further evidence.
FURTHER EVIDENCE Early in December 1823, John Sheppee had visited several Chelmsford paupers residing in London on behalf of the select vestry. He had also called on Mary Teece (alias Teace, aged 17) and reported that 'her mother Mary Munrow no 4 Glasshouse Court Lambeth, near the Workhouse, intends applying to the parish of Lambeth, if immediate assistance is not given; - she wants something settled upon her Weekly; - she thought 2^s/ or 2^s/6^d per Week; - I told her not to expect so much as that; but if the Overseers were disposed to allow any money Weekly, a Letter would be written to her after Monday next; - I consider her to be an object of Charity, but I think less than than 2^s/ pr week would prevent her from coming home'. As it appears from a marginal note against the report, the vestry decided to allow 2s (ERO, D/P 94/18/42, Report of Sheppee on his journey to London, 13 December 1823).

107 From [Mary] Munrow [in Lambeth, London], 29 January [1824]

January 29 [1824]

Sir

I took the Opportunity of writing to you About my Daughter for to Acquaint you that She is verry Bad again and that I have made Applica-
5 tion <to t>he Gentlemen of the Parish and they <tell> me that they Exspected you every day for they Said they Could dwo nothing till you came to London She has been verry Bad for this Month Past and that She his a great Exspence and that my husband & me Cant get no Rest Night nor day And I Should wish to know what his to be done and If you will be
10 so good has to Send me word by the Return of Post So no more at Present from me
Please to direct for me at N° 4
Glashouse Court Vauxhall London

Mrs Munrow

TEXTUAL ALTERATIONS 4: is] *interl with carret.* 10: has to] *interl.*
CIRCUMTEXT Filing note on outside: 'Mrs Munro respecting her Daughter Mary Teece'.
DATE Year from circumtext.
RELATED CORRESPONDENCE Two weeks before, the overseers of Chelmsford had been informed by the parish of Lambeth that Mary Teece was in 'that state that her Friends cannot keep her longer' and that she had to be sent home. In his answer, the vestry clerk of Chelmsford requested that additional relief be advanced to Mary Teece 'till a Parish officer calls, which will be during the week' (letter of 12 January 1824 with note of answer). Apparently she was not removed, for on 29 January 1824, Lambeth reported that she was 'in a very alarming state and represented as dangerous to those about her'.

108 From Davey Rising in Halstead [Essex] to the governor of the poorhouse of Chelmsford, 1 February 1824

Halstead Febuary the 1 1824

Honoread Gentellmen I am sory I have To wright to you the Second time and Sory I am to inform you my husband is no Buter And is not Likely to Be no Butter At present I wish he was I am Sory to Aquaint you Gentellmen I had no moneay sataday Night and if my marster had not Sent me A   5 Trifull my Wife no my Children would not Ahad Abit of witells to Eat and I have not But my hand up to my mouth this Four days And I do not know when when I shall we have nothing to take to not untill you Gentellmen please to Send which I hope will Be By the Return of post I Sent to you Last Tusday And Sory I am to think I Recievead neither Let-   10 ter nor moneay theirfore pray do Answer my neady Request

    your poor And neady Servant

    Daveay Rising

WRITING The letter was apparently written by Davey Rising's wife Susannah. It is in the same hand as all other letters from Davey and/or Susannah Rising (except **185**).

CIRCUMTEXT Note from overseer of Chelmsford: £2 allowed, to be advanced by Mr Wyatt, overseer at Halstead, at his discretion; pair of blankets to be sent. Note of answer to Mr Wyatt to the same effect, 2 February 1824.

FURTHER EVIDENCE Davey Rising was a tanner and had six children. He had received a weekly allowance of 5s in 1819/20 and of 3s 6d from Lady Day 1822, which was paid until May 1825 (ERO, D/P 94/18/53, List of the out-door poor belonging to Chelmsford, for the year from Christmas 1819; D/P 94/18/55, List of the out-door poor belonging to Chelmsford, for the year from Lady Day 1822).

109 From [Susannah] Halls in Ipswich to the overseer of Chelms- ford, 1 February 1824

1824 Ipswich febry 1st from widow Hall

    Sir I shall toke it as a grate favour if you <will send my> pay as i have not Recd any <since> the 16 of october 1823 to the 7 of this month will be 16 <w>eeks widow Hall will be oblight to you to send it as soon as possible for she is wanting of it from yours &c widow   5

               Halls

plese Direct for widow Halls at

Ja^s alexanders friers Road

<S>t N<icho>las Ipswich

  Su[ff]   10

TEXTUAL ALTERATIONS 5: wanting] 'i' over 'g'.
WRITING This and all other letters from Susan(nah) Halls are from the same hand as that from her daughter Susan Alexander of 16 November 1825 (**174**).
CIRCUMTEXT Note from other hand at bottom: 'Wᵈ Halls must write herself or send a Certificate that she is living'.
Address: 'the present over Sea or the Govner of the poor hous' in writer's hand.
RELATED CORRESPONDENCE On 5 December 1823, Mr Grimsey, overseer of St Nicholas, Ipswich, had written to the overseers of Chelmsford and confirmed that Susannah Halls 'lives opposite to me and I am almost daily in the habit of seeing the old Lady'.
FURTHER EVIDENCE Susannah Halls lived in Ipswich, possibly with her son-in-law's family. She had received a weekly allowance of 2s 6d since Lady Day 1822. That allowance was continued until her death in November 1825 (see **174**). It was paid, by bank order, to her son-in-law James Alexander, normally at quarterly intervals in advance. Occasionally, the payments were delayed, as in the present case. For further details, see Sokoll, 'Old age in poverty', pp. 127, 130-3.

110   From Samuel Hearsum in St Marylebone [London], to Mr Goymer in Chelmsford, 5 February 1824

Mʳ Goymer

According to promise I Expected a line from you before now to lit me Know Wether the Gentⁿ of the Committee pease to allow me a small Trifle weekly, I think it very hard as I have payᵈ so much into the poors
5 fund to be Forsed in to the Workhouse for the Triflon sum of 1ˢ:6ᵈ per week, which I will Endevour to make shift with, Gentalmen If not I hope you will be so good as to let me know wether you would pay Mʳ French to bring me Down or to Appley to Marylebone Parish to Pass me home which will be very Expenceiv as I Am not Able to Walk I Almost killed
10 my self when I Came Down last, and I never should have reached home If I had not meet with a Good Friend I send by Coach to save Expencess which I hope I shall have an Amswer by retrun of Coach and a few Shillings as I Am in great Distress

                please to Direct for me to be left
15   at the Sprid Egell Grate Church Sᵗ
            Coach Office your Most Humble
        Obed/i/ent Servᵗ Samˡ Hearsum
Febʸ 5ᵗʰ 1824
26 Sattford Sᵗ
20 S marylebone

TEXTUAL ALTERATIONS 3: Gentⁿ] *after del* 'C'. 3: allow] *over illeg.* 11: with] *interl.*
SPELLING 3: pease] *obviously a slip of the pen; read* 'please'.

CIRCUMTEXT Note of answer on outside, 17 February, 'acquainting him that the Parish would not consent to any Allowance'.

FURTHER EVIDENCE Early in December 1823, John Sheppee had visited several Chelmsford paupers residing in London on behalf of the select vestry. He had also called on Samuel Hearsum (then aged 71) on whom he gave the following report: 'he has been in the habit of selling Tea by Commission about London, two days in the Week which brought him in about 4^s/ pr week - but he is about £11 in debt with his late master. - is now selling for another Person. - he earns upon an average about 6^s/ per week; his rent is 2^s/6^d per Week. - the money he receives of this Parish is not for his present support, but he pays it to his former master in part for the Debt he contracted while in his Service. - I told him that as I did not consider that the Parish of Chelmsford were bound to pay his debts, no further allowance would be given him. - his answer was "Then I must come down." - from appearances I think 1^s/ pr week would prevent him from coming home'. As it appears from a marginal note against the report, the vestry decided to discontinue his allowance (ERO, D/P 94/18/42, Report of John Sheppee on his journey to London, 13 December 1823).

111   From Susannah Halls in Ipswich to Mr Goymer, overseer of Chelmsford [*after* 5 February 1824]

To the Gentelmen of the poor Chelmsford

I Susanah Halls receved my Last alowence very Safe and do return you all Gentelmen my Sincer thanks to all For your kindness to me a poor helpless Feabel Creature I Can but Just Creep About I been very bad indeed I receved my Last alowence 5th Feby 1824 and am much oblidght   5
to you all Gentelmen I remaine your poor parishner Susanah Halls
plese Sir to Direct For me at James
alexanders Friers road St Nicholas
Ipswich Suffolk

CIRCUMTEXT Address: 'to Mr Goymer present over sear'.
DATE Inferred from the date referred to in the text.

112   From Davey and Susannah Rising in Halstead [Essex] to the overseer of Chelmsford, 15 February 1824

Halstead Febuary the 15 1824

Honoread Gentellmen I once more threw Necesity am Forsead so to Do I am Sory to inform you we have Nothing to take Two And pray take our destressead Case into Considerrashion And Earnestly think what me And my husband And Family Can do had not Mr Wyatt Lent me 2 Shiling we   5

Could not have Broak our Fast But we Cannot Exspect to think our marster
Can or will Lend us money And my husband Not Able to Do no work nor
I do not know when he will and if you most wordy Gentellmen Do not
think proper to Answer our needy Request we must Be Brought home For

10 wheare no money Can Be Earnt no Living Cannot Be had therefore pray
Answer our needy Request And Answer our needy Request with Speed
And you will Ablidge your most obedant Servants Davey And Susanaha
Rising
pray think and Answer our Needy

15   Request

TEXTUAL ALTERATIONS 6 not] *interl.*

RELATED CORRESPONDENCE On 27 February 1824, John Cardinall, overseer of Halstead,
wrote to James Read, vestry clerk of Chelmsford, that Mr Wyatt had advanced £2 to
Davey Rising, in addition to the weekly allowance of 3s 6d, 'since his affliction Continued'.
On 23 March 1824 he reported that David Rising was better: 'he thought himself Strong
Enough to work and did so all yesterday; am sorry to say he is much worse to day and is
obliged to apply to the Docter again he is an object of Pity and is in much need of your
Further support'. Cardinal told Read that Wyatt had increased the weekly allowance for
Davey Rising to 8s, and in a further letter of 14 April 1824 he said that Rising was still
'Quite Incapable to attend to Business'.

113   From Mary Hearsom in [St George] London to [Thomas] Archer in Chelmsford, 10 March 1824

N° 4 Minon Place King S^t
Boro' road Southward
10th March 1824

Sir

5   I beg to take the liberty of writing to you to request that you will be so
kind as to speak to the gentlemen of the Committee and inform them that
I cannot yet get my money and really do not know what to do and therefore to beg of them to send me some as I am much in arrear of rent and
other things which would require about five pounds which if I dont have

10 in a few days I must be remove to Chelmsford as I shall not be permitted
to stay here any longer

And you and they will confer
a great obligation
On Sir your most Humble Servt

15   Mary Hearsom

Mr Archer

CIRCUMTEXT Address in the same hand as letter: 'Mr Archer Attorney at law'.
Note of answer on outside, 16 (March 1824) 'saying that her application will be considered at Easter'.

114 From John Argent in Bethnal Green, London, to the overseer of Chelmsford [28 April 1824]

Gentlemen

I write to Inform you My Wife Eliza Argent received from Mr J. Read your Vestry Clerk the last Quarters Allowance which we thank you for on Account of her Daughter Mary Barker and hope you will have the goodness to Continue it a few Quarters Longer as she Stands more in need of it   5
now more than Ever being near Six years old and I am not able to Do what I would for her, being in ill health so must beg of you to Continue it a while longer or I must take her to the Poor house of Bethnal Green Parish as Soon as I find it discontinued that they Support her or Pass her home

   Gentlemen I am your very Obedient Servant   10

           John Argent

N° 5 Half Nichols Street
    Bethnal Green

TEXTUAL ALTERATIONS 7: for] *interl with caret*.
CIRCUMTEXT Note in pencil from other hand at top of page: '1^s/6^d a week'(hand A). Note across left-hand margin: 'Information to be sent that no further relief is to be given'(hand B). Note of answer on outside 'that the Vestry could not comply with the Request'.
DATE Date of note of answer.
FURTHER EVIDENCE Elizabeth Barker had had an illegitimate child before she was married to John Argent (ERO, D/P 94/18/36, Chelmsford overseers' accounts, including lists of illegitimate children).

115 From David Rivenall in [St George in the East] London to the overseer of Chelmsford, 4 May 1824

           London May 4th 1824

Sir

I am under the Necesity of writing to You again As not having an Answer from the last I sent You respecting the interment of my Child Which is out of my power to do I hope You will Answer this by return of post   5
And send mee some money that I may bee able to get it put in the ground

or Otherways I must apply to the Parish Where I am for relief I expect to
loose two more every hour I am

Sir Your most Ab^{dt} hbl St

10 Davy Rivenell

Please to direct to mee
Kings head Comersiael Road

116   From David Rivenall in the [Clerkenwell] House of Correction, London, to the overseer of Chelmsford, 29 May 1824

London
May 29th 1824

Sir

   It is with much regret that I have to inform you that I am now in the
5 House of Correction for the County of Middlesex, for a Debt of Two
Pounds which I contracted in the Year 1822 during that hard Winter, and
from having so large a family, have not had the possible means to pay the
same. I am truly sensible of the great obligation which I am under and
shall ever feel most grateful for the same, and if Sir, you will under my
10 distressed situation, be pleased in some measure to alleviate the demand
against me, be assured that the gratitude of myself my Wife and family
will never cease but with our lives. With all Deference, & respect

I am Sir Your most Ob^t Servant
David Rivinall

117   From M[ary] Munrow in Lambeth [London] to the overseer of Chelmsford, 4 June 1824

Lambeth June 4 1824

Sir I have taken the Liberty of Writing afew Lines to you to inform you
that I Dont think my Daughter Will ever be any better While she is at
hogsdon I think if she was put to the New Bedlem that she would be much
5 better Dun by - I Go evry Week Where I am able - to see her and I still
find her Geting much Worse - if she was at the New Bedlem there would
be much better Means used to her then there is Whare she is Now - therefor
I hope you will have No objections to remove her as soon as possible -
because I Dont think that she is by any Means Dun by as she oaght to be

- I have been there to See if thay will take her in aGain and thay veary 10
aGreeable to take her aGain if you will have the Goodness to w[rite] me
afew Lines as I Dont wish to Give you any troble in Moving her I have
Got the paper to sine ready and I have been so ill Concerning her Myself
I Dont think that she will ever be any better Whare she is and I Consider
it my Duty to Do the Best I Can by her I am With all Due respect M. 15
Monrow

pleas to Derict N° 4 Glasshouse
Cort Near voxhall

TEXTUAL ALTERATIONS 8: her] *interl above* 'remove'. 13: to sine] *interl above* 'ready'. 13: and] *after del* 'sind'.

CIRCUMTEXT Note of answer, 8 June 1824, 'acquainting her that her Request could not be complied with'.

RELATED CORRESPONDENCE Mary Teece had been admitted to Hoxton House, a private lunatic asylum in Shoreditch, on 8 February 1824, at a rate of 9s per week to the account of the overseers of Chelmsford (letter of same date from Hoxton House).

FURTHER EVIDENCE Mary Teece received a regular allowance of 9s per week until 1827 (D/P 94/12/36 Chelmsford overseers' weekly accounts).

118   From Isaac Harridge in [Newington] London to the overseer of Chelmsford, 10 June 1824

Honoured Sir

London June 10th 1824
This is to Inform you I have sent Two letters before - wich I am suprised
I have not Receved anney Ansur This is to Inform you I cannot stop Anney
longer without you send the Monney - as I am tormented by the Peple that 5
I ow it two - pray Sir be So kind as to send as soon as Possable - as I am In
great Destress For want of at - or I must Come Down - pray Sir Cosider
wat trouble And Expence it will be for me to Come It is Seven Deus last
Saturday the 5 June Wich I hope you will not fale Sending it by Mr French
as I am In great wants of it - 10

In so Doing you
Much Oblige me
Isaac Harridge

Isaac Harridge
No 2 Littel Trafalger Place 15
Lacks Fields Near the Kent Rode

CIRCUMTEXT Note from other hand at bottom: order of payment of £1 4s for eight weeks up to 12 June [1824].

FURTHER EVIDENCE From Lady Day 1822, Isaac Harridge had received a weekly allowance of 6s, which had been reduced to 4s early in 1823 (ERO, D/P 94/18/55, List of the out-door poor belonging to Chelmsford, for the year from Lady Day 1822). In December 1823, John Sheppee, on his journey to the Chelmsford paupers residing in London on behalf of the select vestry, had also called on Harridge (then aged 60) and his wife (70), and given the following report: 'Mr Harridge receives 6d per week for circulating Notices of immediate Cure of a disagreeable Disorder, and of Quack Medicines; - his Wife is a Char Woman and gets upon an Average about 2s/ per Week; - he pays 3s/ per Week for Lodging; - he has his health quite well, but his Wife is frequently troubled with the Rheumatism; - No Person has ever visited him from Chelmsford since he has been at Trafalgar Place, which is above two years; - From appearances 4s/ per week is too much to allow them'(D/P 94/18/42, Report of John Sheppee on his journey to London). The allowance was indeed reduced to 3s as from January 1824 and continued until December 1826 (D/P 94/12/36, Chelmsford overseers' accounts).

119   From S[arah] Manning in Stratford [Essex] to [James] Read, overseer of Chelmsford, 11 June [1824]

Sir

    According to your request i have sent the names of the Children and their fathers the Boys father is name feccit and the Girls Thornshill i have three shillings per Week With the Girl and one and sixpence With the
5 Boy i have sent the last note i receive Of Mrs Goymer Have the kindness to answer this and send by M^r french On monday By so Doing You Will much Oblige

        S Manning

Stratford June 11th

TEXTUAL ALTERATIONS 6: french] 'h' *interl at end of line*. 7: much] *interl at end of line*.

CIRCUMTEXT Note from other hand at bottom of page, detailing outstanding allowance: 24 weeks due on 19 June 1824 at 4s 6d per week, totalling of £6 10s 6d. Note from other hand on outside: 'for the Allowance due to the Children of Sarah Facey a Boy & Girl 4s/ 6 weekly [...] Send it by French'.

DATE Year from circumtext.

FURTHER EVIDENCE The two illegitimate children of Sarah Manning (née Facey) were Henry Facey (born 25 December 1813) and Louisa Facey (born 5 May 1815). Their fathers were Capt. Fawcett and Lt.-Col. Thornhill (ERO, D/P 94/18/36, Chelmsford overseers' accounts, including lists of illegitimate children).

120 From Arthur Tabrum in [St Saviour] London to the overseer of Chelmsford, 11 June 1824

Hon^d Sir

I wrote to you on the 3rd of May Concerning the Money that is due to Me for Arthur and have receivd no answer I have been several times to the Coach which is very inconvenient, as I have to be so far away from home to my Work at Times that my Employers take Notice of my losing 5 Time What I wrote concerning of Arthur in my last Letter to you I think is no more than right as the Boy is in want both of Shoes and Cloathes too which I am not able to get for him, as I can not keep my Wife and myself and Child desent, I bought him a suit of Clothes and Shoes too about eight months ago, which very near took all my Weeks wages, and you know 10 that there is the expence of wear & tare besides, as you know what Children are I say now as I said before that the Committee must do something more for me or else they must keep him as I know it takes almost as much to keep him as it does me, as he is getting on for 6 years old now. I do not want to impose upon them, only to have what is wright and necessary 15 they cant deny what I ask and I think I have been as Little trouble to them as a many, but I suppose they think they have got rid of me and so they will do as they like, but I hope they will not be against what I have wrote for, as it is his mother wish for me to write as I have done it is now 18 weeks 20

> I remain
> Your humble Servt
> Arthur Tabrum

We Live at N° 20
Zoar Street G^t Guildford St 25
Southwark London at Mr Herwoods Slater
I should be much obliged to you if you would write to me to Let me know when I may expect it, as I am at no certanty of being at home

TEXTUAL ALTERATIONS 18: against] 's' *interl with caret.* 26: at] *interl with caret.*

CIRCUMTEXT Note from other hand at bottom: '19 Weeks due 19th June at 1^s/6 [totalling] £1.8.6'. Note on outside: 'to Ann Tabrum's Child'.

FURTHER EVIDENCE Payments of the weekly allowance of 1s 6d for Ann Tabrum's child are in evidence until Lady Day 1829 (ERO, D/P 94/12/36, Chelmsford overseers' accounts). His name was Arthur Good (see later letters from Arthur Tabrum, esp. **171** and **189**), and he had been born as an illegitimate son of Ann Good before her marriage to Arthur Tabrum (D/P 94/18/36, Chelmsford overseers' accounts, including lists of illegitimate children).

121   From R[ody] Jolliff in Hertford, 12 June 1824

Hertford

12 June 1824

Sir

    I received your and I am very sorrey the Gentlemen will not add to my
5 Allowance - but will be much Oblige To You to Send me what I have got
comeing To me on Friday by Mr Chymist as he Keep the Markett Every
week - and mr Wiffen or to Send If by him

                      I am Y^r Humble Ser

                        R Jolleff

CIRCUMTEXT £1 6s ordered 21 June 1824 (being 26 weeks at 1s), 'to 12 June on which Day the Allowance was discontinued'.

FURTHER EVIDENCE Rody (alias Rhoda) Jolliff had received a weekly allowance of 1s since Michaelmas 1821. If payments were stopped with effect from 12 June 1824 as suggested in the circumtext, this must have been a temporary measure. Despite interruptions, the allowance was never discontinued altogether. With the constant amount of 1s per week, it is in evidence until Rody Jolliff's death on 3 August 1827 (ERO, D/P 94/12/36, Chelmsford overseers' accounts).

122   From Lucy Nevill in [St Botolph] Colchester, 16 June [1824]

S^r

    you wish to know wether my Child was living. it is alive and well. it
was born upon the 12th Janury 1821. but if you wish to see the Child. and
you will have the goodness to pay my Carriage .. I will come over with it.
5 if not any Gentleman come up from Chelmsford may see it by calling at
my House in Black Boy Lane No 22 shall be oblige to you to send the
money back by the Carrier

        your Humble S^t

        Lucy Nevell

10 Colchest^r June 16

CIRCUMTEXT Note of receipt of 13s for Lucy Nevill's child, signed Edward Moore, on outside.

DATE Year from note of receipt on outside.

FURTHER EVIDENCE Lucy Nevill (alias Nevile) had an illegitimate son (born 12 January 1821) for whom she received a regular allowance of 2s 6d per week until January 1828. The parish was reimbursed by his father, Abraham Jacobs (ERO, D/P 94/18/36, Chelmsford overseers' accounts, including lists of illegitimate children; likewise D/P 94/18/53, List of the out-door poor belonging to Chelmsford, for the year from Christmas 1819; D/

P 94/18/55, List of the out-door poor belonging to Chelmsford, for the year from Lady Day 1822).

123 From Susannah Halls in Ipswich to the overseer of Chelmsford, 21 June 1824

To the Genteelmen of the poor Chelmsford

Honnerd Genteelmen

I Susannah Halls am very Sorrey to Troubel you with this as I Sent before And once troubeled the Church warden to Write to you to Say I am Still Living But have had no answer to either I was Afraid thay miscaried 5 Genteelmen you Can not Think how bad I have wanted my Weekley alowence I have bean very bad in Deed not abel to keep up and am So now Genteelmen had I got my alowen now Hear I Can Truley say not one Farhing is mine I have Got in Det think Gentelmen on my Age is very Grate I think I am 88 years old I think I Shall not Trouble you much 10 longer I am so very feable but Gods will be done I Must wate my apointed time let It be Long or Sort

Genteelmen I receved my Last alowence very Saft up to Febuary 5th 1824 and I do retrun you all my Sincer Thanks for all your kindness to me apoor helpless Creature I hope Genteelmen you will be So kind as to 15 write as Soon as posebl you Can you now not how Much I wante it Tho its not in my power to reward you Genteelmen I Sincerley beg of God to retrune it to you Ten fould I remaine your poor humble parishner Susannah Halls

please Genteelmen to Direct for me 20
at James alexanders Friers road
St Nichoals Ipswich Suffolk
June 21st 1824

TEXTUAL ALTERATIONS 7: not] *after del* 'a'. 10: you] *interl.* 12: time] *after del illeg.* 14: I] *after del illeg.*

CIRCUMTEXT Address on outside, from same hand as letter: 'To the Govner of the Grate poor house or The Present over Sear'. Note on outside from other hand: '£2.7.6 sent by Mr Andrews' on 22 June 1824.

124   From Jane Hills [in St John, Westminster, London] to the overseers of Chelmsford [29 June 1824]

Sir/

be pleased to Send the Mony up by the Chelmsford Coach and I will
Meat it in Gracechurch Streete on Monday next

your humble

Servant

Jane Hills

5

DATE Date of postmark.
RELATED CORRESPONDENCE In a letter of 23 April 1824 to the overseer of Chelmsford,
James Davies, parish officer of St John, Westminster, had reported that Jane Hills (aged
73) was 'in very great distress and in a declining state of health she have for many Years
received a Quarterly payment from the Overseers of your parish by the Coachman who
brings it to Gracechurch Street'. He went on that she would have to be passed home if
there were to be no reply to her request: 'this is the 5th application made this quarter'.
   FURTHER EVIDENCE Jane Hills lived with her daughter (aged 36) and had received a
weekly allowance of 2s from Lady Day 1822. It was continued until Lady Day 1827
(ERO, D/P 94/18/55, List of the out-door poor belonging to Chelmsford, for the year
from Lady Day 1822; D/P 264/18/31, List of the out-door poor belonging to Chelmsford,
for the year from Lady Day 1826 [kept among Braintree overseers' papers]).

125   From Jane Hills [in London] to the overseer of Chelmsford [7 July 1824]

Sir/

be so good as to send the Money up by the coach & I will meet it at
Gracechurch St on Friday next will you have the goodness to send it as I
can neither Read nor write and ham Abbot to Trouble some body every
5 Time to write

Your Humble

Servant

Jane Hills

TEXTUAL ALTERATIONS 3: St] *interl at end of line.*
DATE Date of postmark.

126 From Hannah Death in London Hospital [Whitechapel, London] to Dr Prichard in Chelmsford [8 July 1824]

Sir

I your Afflicted hand maid do humbly beg your assistance in sending me a little money to help to bury him as it is not in my power to do it myself, Sir I hope you will have Compassion and lay it before the Gentlemen he is dead and must be buried therefore I hope you will take it into 5 Consideration and pity your

Humble Ser^{vt} Han^h Death

Please to direct for Han^h Death
Talbots Ward London Hospital

CIRCUMTEXT Enclosed statement from London Hospital of 8 July 1824 that Thomas Death had died in the evening of the previous day. Note of answer, 9 July 1824, on outside, 'inclosing a Pound Note'.

FURTHER EVIDENCE In 1819 Thomas Death had received relief payments of £3 18s 6d (ERO, D/P 94/18/53, List of the out-door poor belonging to Chelmsford, for the year from Christmas 1819). His widow with two children received an allowance of 4s per week from Lady Day 1826 to Lady Day 1828 (D/P 264/18/31, List of the out-door poor belonging to Chelmsford, for the year from Lady Day 1826 [kept among Braintree overseers' papers]; D/P 36/28/3, List of the out-door poor belonging to Chelmsford, for the year from Lady Day 1828 [kept among Great Coggeshall overseers' papers]).

127 From Rachel Brown in [Clerkenwell] London to [Thomas] Archer in Chelmsford, 26 July 1824

Charter House London july 26 1824

Mr Archer

Sir I beg pardon for thus troubleing you but Being informed you are in office in the parrish I write to beg the favour of you and the Rest of the Gentelmen to faver me with A few Shillings to buy me A p^r of Shoes And 5 Some linnen as i am much is wants and my Fathers income is not Suffitiant To provide me with foode and Cloathing as he wants many nesserrys the House does not Alow and i am obliged to pay the Nurse Nevertheless for my being here As he is quite helpless and not fit to be left If my Request Can be Granted A Line Dirrected to A^{bm} Brown Charter House I will 10 meet Mr French any day you Think proper to name I Remain Your Humble Servent Rachel Brown

TEXTUAL ALTERATIONS 3: beg] *interl.* 7: nesserrys] *second* 's' *over* 'c'.

FURTHER EVIDENCE Rachel Brown had received occasional cash payments of 10s on 24 May and 21 July 1823. Possibly as a consequence of this letter, she received another 10s on 3 August 1824 (ERO, D/P 94/12/17, Chelmsford overseers' accounts, pauper ledger).

128   From Ann Marsh in London to Robert Marsh, 26 July 1824

1824   London July the 26
Dear Brother & Sister
   I hope this will find you all well we are but verry poorly here I Received
Your Letter and was Glad to here You were then well Thos Marsh is
5 Married and is no assistance watever to Me I hope You will Go to the
Committe and You will Show them the oth<er> Side I Can asure You if
Somthing is not d<one> I must Come to the parish I hope You will rite an
answer as Soon as You Can
   Ras[on] Desire thir Love To You and my Duty to My Mother and Love
10 to all
                           from Y^r
                                 Ann Marsh
[*Next page*]
To the Oversears of Chelmsford
15   Gentelmen Since the time that I was down at Chelmsford I have tried all
in my power to Maintain my family wich is Six fatheless Children the
Littel work I have is not Suffient to find them in Bread I have been Obliged
to part with the Chief of my things for our Support Gentelmen I hope You
will take this into Your Serious Consideratton and allow Somthing as in
20 Your wisdom may think proper Towards the maintainance of so Large a
family if Somthing is not Done I must with my family apply to to be Sent
home to My parish
                  Gentlemen I Remⁿ Your &. Ann Marsh
                  London July 26 1824

TEXTUAL ALTERATIONS 5: no] *interl with stroke*. 8: You] 'u' *altered from* 'y'. 15: I have] *after del* 'all in my'. 20: so] *interl*. 21: to be Sent] *after del illeg.*
   CIRCUMTEXT Note in pencil from other hand at bottom of second page: 'Not attended to'.
   FURTHER EVIDENCE In May 1824 Ann Marsh had received 10s. In October 1824, she received another 10s (ERO, D/P 94/12/17, Chelmsford overseers' accounts, pauper ledger).

129   From Davey and Susannah Rising in Halstead [Essexc to Mr Gimore, overseer of Chelmsford, 1 August 1824

Halstead Agust the 1 1824

Honoread Gentellmen I hope you will Take my Destressead Case into
Considerashion And Be So kind And So Good As to Send me Some Cloth
For my husband And myself And my Children Are Allmost without And
none we Can Get For we have Nothing to Do to Earn Alittle moneay to   5
By Any with For Braiding is of no use For it Fetches Nothing when it tis
Done worth Speaking on And if you most wordy Gentellmen do not please
to Send me Some Cloth we shall Be Spoilt For we hant Got none nor non
we Can Get Theirfore I hope you will Consiader our Great Destress And
want And need And pray not For Get us For our Destress is Great And our   10
Dear Gentellmen Can if thear please help us And hoping theea will I wish
to Remain your obeedant Servants
Davey And Susanah Rising
pray do not Forget to Send as Soon As you Can
Halstead Essex   15

TEXTUAL ALTERATIONS 3: Considerahion] 'shion' *interl at end of line*.
    RELATED CORRESPONDENCE On 21 June 1824, John Cardinall, overseer of Halstead, had
written to James Read, vestry clerk of Chelmsford, and given a detailed account of various payments advanced by Mr Wyatt to Davey Rising and family, totalling £12 18s (15
weeks at 8s; 19 weeks at 3s 6d; chemist's bill [enclosed] of £1 16s 6d).

130   From David Rivenall in St George in the East, London, to [John] Shepee in Chelmsford, 2 August 1824

August 2nd 1824

Mr Shippy

Sir

In Consequence of one of my young Ones now laying dead I am under
the necessity of Soliciting you for a trifle to inable me to Bury it, as it is   5
not in my power without your kind assistance having 5 Children now left
and one still remains very Ill. And neither able to Earn one Shilling towards their Support. If I am not assisted I must be under the necessity of
applying to St Georges East for the means for to Bury it by Complying
will Confer a Lasting Obligation on   10

Yours Respectfully
David Rivenall

N° 23 London terrace
Saint Georges East

CIRCUMTEXT Note from other hand on outside: 'I will Attend Marrch to Night Because I have not a Coffin to put the Child In'. Note of receipt of £1 for David Rivenall, 3 August 1824.

131   From Susannah Rising in Halstead [Essex] to the governor of the poorhouse in Chelmsford, 27 September 1824

Halstead September The 27 1824
Honoread Gentellmen I once more make Free to wright to you And I hope you will Answer my needy Request For I am in Great Destress And Trouble and none of us hant Got no Lenen I Sent A letter to you Some
5 weeks A Go And Sory I am that I have to Inform you that I Recievead No Cloth nor no letter But prey do Dear Gentellmen take my destressead Case into Considerrashion And Answer my Needy Request as Soon as you Can And if you did Believe my Destressead Case you Certainly would have pity and Compashion on us And Answer our needy Request Susanah
10 Rising pray Gentellmen Consider us And wright as Soon as you Can

CIRCUMTEXT Note from other hand at bottom: '£1.0.0 sent by Post Oct 1st 1824'. Note on outside: 'Send them Informed & Say they will be called on'.

132   From Phebea Joice in Ingatestone [Essex] to James Read in Chelmsford [11 October 1824]

Spread Eagle Ingatestone
    Sir/
    I am Sorry to Trouble You With Letter But I am Inform.d By a friend That Mrs Taylor that Has My Child That she Intends to Trouble Me at My
5 Place But if You Can Possable Prevent her Comeing You Will Greatley Oblige Your humble Servant as I am Comfortly Situ/v/ated and My Intention is to Do all in My Power to for My Child While I am in the Situvation as I now am I Do not Whant the Parish to find him any Cloaths I will furnish him With What he Wants and as I Understant she is a Woman
10 of Drunking Habits and always having the Child With her in her Ramble.s I Wish to se the Child Well Done By and I Wish to Do all in My Power for the Woman if she Would But Conduct herself toward him and Not Pawn

his Cloths the Parish as so Bountyfully Giving him as I Understand that is
the Case I hope Sir You Will linder all these Evils You Will try and furnish the Boy With a Light Place to go With Errands and Make himself 15
Usefull and I will Buy him What Cloaths I Possable Can as he may stand
in nead of I Cannot Possable Come Personly Myself as My Mistress has
Not at home But as soon as I Possable Can I will Come at settle all Things
With you and By so Doing You Will Grately Oblige

    Your humble Servant 20

    Phebea Joice

TEXTUAL ALTERATIONS 8: Whant] 'n' *over* 't'. 10: Drunking] *after del* 'be [?] of'. 14: Evils]
after del illeg.

CIRCUMTEXT Note at bottom of page that the boy (aged 10) is boarded with William
Taylor at Willingdale. Note of answer on outside, 14 October 1824, saying that 'her Child
is Well taken Care of by Mrs Taylor'.

DATE Date of note of receipt on outside.

FURTHER EVIDENCE Phebea Joice had an illegitimate son (born 1814) for whom she received a weekly allowance of 1s 6d until April 1828 (ERO, D/P 94/18/53, List of the out-
door poor belonging to Chelmsford, for the year from Christmas 1819; D/P 94/18/55, List
of the out-door poor belonging to Chelmsford, for the year from Lady Day 1822; D/P
264/18/31, List of the out-door poor belonging to Chelmsford, for the year from Lady
Day 1826 [kept among Braintree overseers' papers]; D/P 36/28/3, List of the out-door
poor belonging to Chelmsford, for the year from Lady Day 1828 [kept among Great
Coggeshall overseers' papers]; D/P 94/12/36, Chelmsford overseers' accounts). Occasionally, she had received additional payments for his shirts, stockings and shoes (£1 15s
in 1823, £1 7s in 1824). In January 1826, she received £1 3d (D/P 94/12/17, Chelmsford
overseers' accounts, pauper ledger).

133* From Ann Marsh in [Shoreditch] London, [11 October 1824]

To the Churchwardens & Committee of the Parish of Chelmsford

    This Humble Petition of Mrs Ann Marsh of Sugarloaf Court Long Alley
Moorfield Sheweth

    That your poor Petitioner is a Parishioner of Chelmsf^d and is left a Widow
with 7 Children 6 of whom are dependent on the poor pittance; which the 5
kindness of a few neighbours supply her with; by sending her a few
Cloathes to Mangle for them which at present is so trifling that they are
now literally half starving; and in winter time she knows from past experience her supply will be near wholly cut of, as her few employers do not
Mangle in the Winter season as in Summer So that she has now a long 10
dreary Winter to look forward to with numerous infants whom she fears
will be crying to her for Bread; which it will not be in her power to provide.

She therefore is impelld humbly to beg your pity & humanity to assist her
utmost endeavour; this Winter, to provide for her numerous infant charge,
15 (without which) She never can keep them from Starving,) 4 of them being
under 9 years of age which She hopes will claim your kindest Sympathy,
which She will ever acknowledge with grateful thanks to her kind
benefactors

Your very Humble Supplcant
Ann Marsh

TEXTUAL ALTERATIONS 1: Chelmsford] 'rd' *interl at end of line.*
WRITING Professional hand and layout.
CIRCUMTEXT The entire piece consists of four pages, with the letter itself on the third
page. The first page bears the following statement (from the same hand as the letter): 'The
truth of the Statement in this petition is assertain'd and verified by the Undermention[d]
respectable inhabitants of the Parish of S[t] Leon[d] Shoreditch where your poor Petitioner
resides who beg leave to recommend her distressing Case to your kind Consideration'.
This is followed by fourteen signatures, covering the lower half of the first page and the
top of the second page. The signatories include Joseph Price, churchwarden of St Leonard,
Shoreditch, and the first signature, by Charles Loosely, suggests that he was the writer of
the letter. The fourth page bears the following statement (again from the same hand as the
letter): 'The person who presents this petition will undertake to forward to your poor
Petitioner whatever your kindness may assist her with weekly'. There is no address, only
a note of receipt from another hand.
DATE Date of note of receipt on back outside.
FURTHER EVIDENCE Apparently as a consequence of this letter, Ann Marsh received a
weekly allowance of 5s from 21 November 1824 until Midsummer 1825, and of 4s from
then until Midsummer 1830 (ERO, D/P 94/12/36, Chelmsford overseers' accounts; likewise D/P 264/18/55, List of the out-door poor belonging to Chelmsford, for the year from
Lady Day 1826 [kept among Braintree overseers' papers]; D/P 36/28/3, List of the out-
door poor belonging to Chelmsford, for the year from Lady Day 1828 [kept among Great
Coggeshall overseers' papers]).

134   From [Susannah] Halls in Ipswich to the overseer of Chelms-
ford [4 November 1824]

I
widow Hall have not Receved any pay since June the 25 she will be
oblight to send Directly

5   at Ja[s] alexanders
friers Road Nicholas
Ipswich

TEXTUAL ALTERATIONS 1: I] *followed by del* 'wid'.
CIRCUMTEXT The text of the letter covers the bottom third of the page. It is preceded by
the following statement from another hand: 'This note is sent to certify that Susan Halls

Widow is now living in our Parish and incapable of maintaining herself', signed by Lawrence Patrick, presumed overseer of St Nicholas, Ipswich, and dated 4 November 1824.
    DATE Date of circumtext.

**135   From Susannah Halls in Ipswich to Mr Andrews, overseer of
        Chelmsford [November 1824]**

                                          To the Genteel men of the Poor
Chelmsford
    I Susanah Halls
    Do Genteel men return my Sincer Thanks for all your kind ness to me
apoor helpless Creature I receved my last allowence very Safe you wear   5
So kind as to Send by Mr Prentis he Told me if I Got the over Sear to write
a Few Lines That wold be Quite Sefishent I Did So Genteel men I am very
Sorrey to trouble you with this I receved my Last June 25th Genteel men
its not in my power to Do eany work now I am Grown So Inable
    I remaine your poor humble parishner S Halls plese Sir to Direct   10
for me at James alexander Friers road
                                          St Nicklars parish Ipswich
                                                            Suffolk

TEXTUAL ALTERATIONS 6: So] *interl.* 9: eany] 'e' *over* 'C'.
    DATE Date from filing note on outside.

**136   From Sarah Baynes in Thaxted [Essex] to Mr Marrion, church-
        warden of Chelmsford, 18 December 1824**

                                          Thaxted Decr 18 1824
Gentlemen/
    I beg leave to informe you I have receiv.d a very extraordinary Bill
from Mr Brooks Apotecary [&c] of this Town, for Medicines and Attendance upon my Daughter, longin^g from April 27 : 1824 to Augst 19 1824 of   5
4$^£$ 12^S 4^D the Items which compose this Bill are, as Irregular as the amount,
and supposing you have already been Charged by Mr Brooks, I think it
unjust any demand should be made upon me; perticularly as I am unable
to Discharge it, having an allowance of only 2^s p^r Week from this Parish,
and am entirely oblig^d to be in attendance upon my daughter I shall feel   10
extremely oblig^d by an answer P^r return of Post, informing me what had

better be done in this matter, for should Mr Brooks Streniously insist upon
this new Charge, I hope and trust You Gentlemen will either look into the
Justness of his demand, or discharge the same, I must still continue to
15 think the Bill extraordinary as I am inform.d he has already been paid by
you, a Bill of 8 or 12 £s which I consider much longer then could have
been expected;

       I am with Due Submission
       Gentlemen, Yr most Hum Ser^vt
20   Sarah Baynes

TEXTUAL ALTERATIONS 11: oblig^d] *interl with caret.* 11: had] *after del* 'I'.
RELATED CORRESPONDENCE On 7 December 1823 John Fry, vestry clerk of Thaxted, had
written to James Read, vestry clerk of Chelmsford, on behalf of Sarah Baynes's daughter
Mary Baynes, saying that 'the state of Health of the poor young Woman is very debilitated & declining'. James Read answered, requesting 'a Certificate from a Medical Man
what her Complaint is' (note from his hand on Fry's letter), and received a letter from Mr
Brooke, surgeon in Thaxted, saying that Mary Baynes was 'suffering from deseased lungs'
(27 December 1823).
    FURTHER EVIDENCE Mary Baynes had received a weekly allowance of 3s since Lady Day
1822. It was continued, though possibly with interruptions, until 1829 (ERO, D/P 94/18/
55, List of the out-door poor belonging to Chelmsford, for the year from Lady Day 1822;
D/P 264/18/55, List of the out-door poor belonging to Chelmsford, for the year from Lady
Day 1826 [kept among Braintree overseers' papers]; D/P 36/28/3, List of the out-door
poor belonging to Chelmsford, for the year from Lady Day 1828 [kept among Great
Coggeshall overseers' papers]).

137   From Thomas Smith Carritt in [Newington] London to the over-seer of Chelmsford, 21 December 1824

                         December 21 1824
To the acting Overseer of Chelmsford
  Sir
    It is with seveere regret that I must now address you on a subject - the
5 most galling and distressing to my feelings I allude to immediate pecunary
assistance - on Saturday last M^rs C was put to bed of a fine Girl and is not
doing so well as at former periods - I have been out of employ for about a
month and no prospect at present to meet with any thing likely to assist us
- we have pledged what furniture we can possibly spare - and likewise a
10 great part of M^rs C's and my own wearing appearel - all our Silver Spoons
and my Watch - we are now quite aground - the entire of the money being
gone - besides a few shillings in Debt since saturday we have now Six
Children to provide for and nothing coming in - I think I need not say

more to convince you we have not applyd before it was absolutely
neccessary - indeed it must have come to this before now - had not a few 15
Friends through the hand of M[r] T. Durrant made us a very acceptable
present your speedy reply to my address as at foot will greatly oblidge

Your mo[t] ob[t] hble Ser[t]

Tho[s] Smith Carritt

T.S. Carritt   20
10 Wellington St
Newingtoncauseway
Southwark
London
P.S. The petition to the Freemason girl school lays there - for ballotting 25
for I am told she is not likely to get in for another 6 or 12 months - I wish
it may, be soon

**138   From Thomas Cooper in Woolwich, Kent, to the overseer of
         Chelmsford, 10 January 1825**

Jan[y] 10 1825

Gentelmen/
   I am sorry that I am under the Necesssity of Stateing to you that I am
know Confined to my Bed with an Inflamation on my Chest and under the
Doc[rs] Hands I have been very ill this Month and was foth to truble you but   5
know am Obligateed as I am in no Club to render aney support for my
family I have 4 Children and I have Stopt thinking I should get better till
I have Pledged all our things that is worth any thing of wereing Apparel
therefore I hope Gentlemen you will take this into Consideration to send
me a Present Relief or else I shall be Oblidge'd to Apply to the Overseers 10
of Woolwich Parish and as soon as I get better be passed home which may
be Avoiead as I hope to get better for I have work to do as soon as I am
Able to do it and Possable I my shortly return to it again but some relief I
must have for we have spent the Last farthing Please to send an Answer as
soon as Possable.   15

from Your Humble Ser[t]

Thomas Cooper

Collar Maker

Please to direct to Thomas Cooper
Collar Maker   20

at Mr Lunns House Near the fortune of War
New Road Woolwich Kent

TEXTUAL ALTERATIONS 8: Pleged] *after del* 'not'. 20: Maker] *followed by del illeg.*
    WRITING This letter is from the same hand as those from Ann Cooper.
    CIRCUMTEXT Note from other hand on outside: 'Answ^d requesting Mr Stone to give him
£1.0.0'.
    FURTHER EVIDENCE Thomas Cooper was the husband of Ann Cooper. From January to
March 1825, they received cash payments, mostly £1 at a time, to the total amount of £5
10s (ERO, D/P 94/12/17, Chelmsford overseers' accounts, pauper ledger).

139   From David Rivenall in St George in the East, London, to Mr Shepping in Chelmsford, 12 January 1825

London January 12th 1825

Sir
    I am very sorry to have to write to you concerning what I have to say, as
my Wife has been very ill for some Time and has been obliged to have a
5 Doctor and two of the Children are very ill at present and Mrs Nelson has
Stopped The Money in consequence of not hearing from you and I expect
to loose any few things every Day if I do not recieve some help

Yours &c
David Rivenall

10 Direct for me at No 23
London Terrace
St Georges East

140   From Lucy Nevill [in St Botolph, Colchester], 15 January 1825

Jany 15 1825

S^ir
    this is to certify that my Son Abraham is alive and well and is as four
Years Old the 17th of last Jany I would have come over with him but being
5 in service I can not leave my place hope therefore you will send the money
by the Carrier and you will oblege your Humble Ser^t
sign^d
    Lucy Nevill

CIRCUMTEXT Brief note from Mr Jennings, overseer of St Botolph, Colchester, at bottom of page, confirming statement in the letter; note to the same effect by Mr Hoblyn, minister of St Botolph, Colchester, enclosed.

RELATED CORRESPONDENCE Three years later, Messrs Church & Sons of St Botolph, Colchester, wrote to James Read, vestry clerk of Chelmsford, on behalf of their parish, referring to a letter of 4 January 1828 from Chelmsford to Lucy Nevill in which she had been informed that Mr Jacobs, the father of her illegitimate son, was no longer willing to pay for his maintainance: 'Mr Jacobs is laboring under a very erroneous impression if he imagines he is not bound to maintain the Child beyond 7 yrs old - he is by Law liable to maintain it till it can get its own living, and therefore he must be called upon to do so - The Mother is living in service and cannot contribute any part of her small earnings towards its suppport and the Child is now living with its Grandmother, who is extremely poor, and almost under the necessity of applying for relief for herself - & therefore totally unable to provide for the Child - Unless therefore the Parish Officers of Chelmsford continue to send the weekly allowance as heretofore she will be obliged to apply to the parish Officers of the parish she is residing in to relieve the Child, who will do so, and it will be removed to Chelmsford as the place of its legal Settlement We trust the parish Officers of Chelmsford will not render this course necessary, but will punctually transmit the accustomed allowance -'(letter of 3 February 1828).

141   From Ann Cooper in Woolwich [Kent] to the overseer of Chelmsford, 22 January 1825

Gentelmen/

I am sorry that I am under the Necessity of trubleing you the Second time for Relief My Husband still Continues very ill Confined to his room not Able to go about Gen^m I Return you many thanks for the Pound I Rec^d of Mr Stone the Post Master I have made it go as far as I Could which is   5 know Expended I am very sorry we are so truble^m but it would not have been if my Husband had not been ill but we must have some relief and we thought it most Prudent to send Again to you which I hope that you will Answer as soon as Possable the doctor will give Mr Stone every Satisfaction in regard to My Husbands Illness that we are not Imposing upon the   10 Parish

   Gentelmen I Remain Your
    Humble Servant Ann Cooper

Woolwich
Jan 22^d 1825   15

TEXTUAL ALTERATIONS 9-10: Satisfaction] 'c' *over* 't'.

142　From Susannah and Davey Rising in Halstead [Essex] to the governor of the poorhouse in Chelmsford, 27 January 1825

Halstead January 27 1825

　　Honeread Gentellmen I once more make Fre<e> to wright to you hoping
you will Excuse my Freedom A<n>d parding the liberty I take in So do<in>g
As Necessity Forsess me So to do And the Furder Contents of my wrighting
5　is to Inform <you> that my Husband Is Weary Bad And Cannot help himself No more then A young Child And Cannot go Across the house if he
Could gain <A th>ousand pound Neither Can he Go to bead nor Get up
without A man to help him to Bead And From Bread I Cannot shift no for
Now my husband is laid Aside All is Laid Aside with me therefore I must
10　Surmit <your> Ge<nteel>m<en> mercy For if you Gentellmen do not please
to help us we must Give up housekeeping For out of nothing thear Ca<n>
<------> Done Consider our Destress and Send us Speedy help if you pleas
　　　　Your humbells Servants Susannah
　　　　And Davey Rising

143　From Thomas and Ann Cooper in Woolwich [Kent] to the overseer of Chelmsford, 28 January [1825]

　　　　　　　　　　　　　　　　　　Woolwich Jany 28/ <-->

Gentelmen/

　　I was under the Necessity of riteing to you last Monday Requesting
some relief as My Husband Conti<nues> very ill and unable to work but
5　<I> have recieved no answer I am very sorry to say that we must have
some relief from woolwich Parish if you do not take it into Consideration
and send us some and we shall be oblidged to Come Home as may be
prevented as my Husband as got Constant work to go to when He gets
better Gentelmen My Husband as been ill this 6 Weeks and we Had done
10　without trubleing you till the Last till we Could not do without as I said
before we have 4 Children
　　　　from your Humble Servants
　　　　Thomas & Ann Coop<e>r

TEXTUAL ALTERATIONS 3: riteing] *after del* 'of'. 9: My] *over del* 'you'.
　　CIRCUMTEXT Note from other hand at bottom: 'Allow^d 20/. to have Medical Certificate'.
Note of answer on outside, 31 January 1825: 'written to Mr Stone of Woolwich request-
ing him to give Cooper another Pound'.
　　DATE Year from note of answer on outside.

144   From Sarah Baynes in Thaxted [Essex] to Mr Marrion, church-warden in Chelmsford, 2 February 1825

Thaxted Feb 2 1825

Gentlemen/

I beg leave to trouble you with these few lines in consequence of my being refused the weekly allowance of my poor Daughter; by Mr Bond of this place on my applying for it on Saturday last I thought it my duty to   5 inform you of it; as the distressed state of ill Health she still continues in; makes it impossible for her to do without support and the situation I am in; it is impossibel for me to do it without the assistance of you Gentlemen; as I am ignorant of the cause of its being refused I hope and trust you Gentlemen will condescend to look into the matter so that my poor Child 10 does not suffer for the want of necessaries. I am Gen^t with due submission; your Most Hum^{le} Ser^{vt}

Sarah Baynes

TEXTUAL ALTERATIONS 11: not] *interl with caret.*

CIRCUMTEXT Sarah Baynes's daughter referred to at the beginning was Mary Baynes (filing note on outside).

RELATED CORRESPONDENCE On 4 February 1825 James Read, vestry clerk in Chelmsford, wrote to Sarah Baynes in Thaxted that he had been informed 'that you are Come into property, consequently you have no Claim on the Parish for your Daughter's Maintenance'. That letter was returned with a covering letter from John Fry, vestry clerk of Thaxted (dated 3 March 1825 and also signed by the churchwarden and the overseer) which pointed out that 'the Widow Baynes *is by no means in circumstances adequate to the Maintenance of her helpless and afflicted Daughter* - It is true that the poor Woman has recently come into possession of some property but *that is* at present *insufficient for her own support* and she is now actually receiving weekly allowance from the Overseer of this Parish'. This caused Chelmsford to give in, for on 14 March 1825 the chairman of the select vestry made a note on the returned letter: 'allow^{ce} continued for the moment'. As it turned out, it was probably not only for the moment. Sarah Baynes seems to have received further support for her daughter. On 12 April 1826, Mr Braind and R. Fitch, churchwarden and overseer in Thaxted, wrote to the overseer of Chelmsford that Mary Baynes 'continues in a very debilitated & declining state of Health' and that she was 'an object requiring and deserving your bounty'. A further letter to the same effect was sent from Thaxted to James Read on 16 April 1828.

FURTHER EVIDENCE Mary Baynes had received a weekly allowance of 3s from Lady Day 1822 to Lady Day 1823. Unfortunately, we do not know to what extent she was supported in 1824 and 1825. But from Lady Day 1826, the weekly allowance of 3s is again in evidence, and this until Lady Day 1829 (ERO, D/P 94/18/55, List of the out-door poor belonging to Chelmsford, for the year from Lady Day 1822; D/P 264/18/55, List of the out-door poor belonging to Chelmsford, for the year from Lady Day 1826 [kept among Braintree overseers' papers]; D/P 36/28/3, List of the out-door poor belonging to Chelmsford, for the year from Lady Day 1828 [kept among Great Coggeshall overseers' papers]).

145   From Ann Cooper in Woolwich [Kent] to [James] Read, over-seer of Chelmsford, 11 February 1825

Woolwich feb^r 11 1825

Gentelmen/

    I am very sorry that I am under the Necessity of trubleing you again for Relief as my Husband Continues very ill Confined to his room Therefore
5 I hope you will have the goodness to send me furthur Assistance as we cannot do without as the Pound we last recieved is know Expended as we have no other means of Subsistance

from your

Humble Servant

10   Ann Cooper

CIRCUMTEXT Statement from W. Harris, surgeon, at bottom, confirming that Thomas Cooper was still 'Under Medical Treatment and incapable of Work' (12 February 1825).

146   From David Rivenall in St George in the East, London, to the overseer of Chelmsford, 22 February 1825

London Feby 22nd 1825

Sir,

    I am extremely sorry that it is my case to ask your Assistance, but necessity makes me require your kind assistance my Wife has been now
5 under the Doctors hands for this last 3 Week with an inflamatione, and expects every day to lie in therefore if you do not assist me, I must through nessessaty apply to the Parish I now reside in, I should not have troubled you but every thing is so bad and in fact my Poor Boys have not sufficiant to cover them and it lays out of my power to cover Them

10   Yours &c

David Rivenall

Direct for me at Mr Gardners Kings
Head Comercial Road St Georges East
London

CIRCUMTEXT Note from Thomas Archer, chairman of the select vestry of Chelmsford, at bottom: 'Send a pound'.

**147 From Ann Cooper in Woolwich [Kent] to [James] Read, over-
seer of Chelmsford, 25 February 1825**

Feby 25 1825

Gentelmen/

Iam Extreemly sorry that I am under the Necessity of your further
Assistance as My Husband still Continues very ill unable to do the Smallest
thing towards the Support of our Family as the Pound you was so kind as 5
to send us the Last fortnight is now Expended as Provition is very dear in
this Place as my Husband wants a deal of Nurrishment to gain his strenght
again Please to send me an answer as soon as Possable for I am know in a
great straight

from your Humb Servt 10

Ann Cooper

TEXTUAL ALTERATIONS 8: as Possable] 'as' *interl.*
CIRCUMTEXT Statement from W. Harris, surgeon, at bottom, confirming that Thomas
Cooper was still weak, though recovering, and that 'by a nourishing diet, he has Every
Prospect gaining strength'.
Notes from Thomas Archer, chairman, and James Read, vestry clerk, at bottom and on
back, ordering Mr Stone to allow 10s.

**148 From A[nn] Cooper in Woolwich [Kent] to the overseer of
Chelmsford, 3 March 1825**

Woolwich March 3^d 1825

Gentelmen/

I am sorry that I am Oblidged to truble you with another letter as I sent
one on friday last requesting your Assistance Acquanting you that my
Husband was something better but have received no Answer with A 5
Citificate from the Doctor of the Royal Arsneal which he is know under
he as been Confined at home for nine weeks to Morrow and we must have
relief from either you or woolwich which of the tow you think proper if
we have not an Answer by the return of Post as we Pledged every thing
that we had before we truble you thinking he would get better in a week or 10
tow we are know in the greatst of Distress not a farthing in the world

from your

Humble Servant A. Cooper

TEXTUAL ALTERATIONS 8: relief] 'l' *over* 'f'.

149 From A[nn] Cooper [in Woolwich, Kent] to the overseer of Chelmsford, [12 March 1825]

Gentlemen/

I am sorry that I am under the Necesity of trubleing you with this Letter
to Inform you that my Husband is much wors than he was and not likely
to be able to work for some time he is not able to sit up a whole day so
5 therefore Gentelmen I must beg of you to send us some relief I return you
maney thanks for the 10 shillings I receivd last week but I hope that you
will take it into Consideration and send us more for that is not suffition
for our family as we have 4 Children or Please to send word what we are
to do for we are in very gerat distress which you are welcome to Inquire
10 into if you think proper to Appoint aney person to come to see
from your
Humble servant A Cooper
Please to turn over for the doctors Certificate

DATE Date of postmark.
CIRCUMTEXT Certificate by Mr Harris, surgeon in Woolwich, on next page. Note of
order of £1 on back.

150 From A[nn] Cooper in Woolwich [Kent], [27 March 1825]

Woolwich March
Gentelmen/

I am very sorry that I am again Oblidged to truble you with another
Letter as my Husband still Continues very ill unable to do aney thing for
5 the maintainence of our family I was in hopes that I should not have had
to have trubled you again Gentelmen I return you thanks for what you
was so kind as to send me last I am sorry that we want your further relief
at this time I hope that you will Consider our Case and send us relief as we
have no other subsistance

10
from your Humbl
Servn A. Cooper

CIRCUMTEXT Statement from surgeon at Royal Arsenal at bottom, dated 27 March [1825],
saying that Thomas Cooper was still unwell and unable to work.
DATE Postmark: 27 March 1825.

**151   From Rachel Brown in [Clerkenwell] London to [Thomas]
Archer in Chelmsford, 18 April 1825**

London April 18th 1825

Mr Archer

Sir I am Sorry to be so Troublesome To you but not knowing who to
Apply to So well as yourself I again take the liberty of beging The favour
of the Gentelmen to Send a few Shillings as i am in wants Of Nessorys   5
wich i Cannot Get As my Father is now very infurm and Cannot now Eat
what is provided by The House wich is A Great disadvantage To us If this
Request Can be Granted A Line to A Brown Charterhouse I will meet Mr
French

I Remain your Humble Servent 10

Rachel Brown

TEXTUAL ALTERATIONS 3: Sir] *after del illeg.* 7: what] 't' *over illeg.*

**152   From Mary Hearsom in London to Thomas Archer, Esq. in
Chelmsford, 18 April 1825**

No 11 Agnes PLace
Waterloo Road

Sir/

I have taken Liberty of Writing to you Sir to beg your Interference with
the Overseers of your Parish to Render me the assitance of Two Pounds to   5
Enable me to get my Money Out of Chancery Court Rec^d a letter Since I
saw you Sir and it will and it will Require the Sum above named to make
the necessary application to get what is now due to me Your Kind Interference in this matter will most particularly oblige Your in the greatest
Destress   10

Mary Hearsom

April 18/1825
I would thank you for an answer Sir as Soon as Convenient

WRITING The signature is from a hand which is different from and less educated than that
of the letter.

**153   From Susannah and Davey Rising [in Halstead, Essex] to the
overseer of Chelmsford, 24 April 1825**

Apriel the 24 1825

  Honoread Gentellmen I Hope you will Excuse my Freedom And parding
the Liberty I Take in wrighting to you As Necesity Forsess me So to Do I
Furder Sory to Aquaint you That my Son Thomas is weary Bad with The
5 hucking Coff And Quite uncapabell of Doing Any work And I am in
Aweary poor State of helth myself And uncapabell of doing For myself or
Family I theirfore Hope you will Answer my needy Request as Soon As
Conveanant I Sent to you A fortnett Ago And Sory I am that I Recievead
Neigher Letter nor Nothing to help me in my destress And Trouble which
10 is Great And Forses me To Crave your help and Assistance which I hope
you will willingly do And By So Doing you will Greatly Ablidge your
most obeadant Servants Susanah And Davey Rising pray do not Forget
me this time But Answer my Needy Request

CIRCUMTEXT Note from other hand below: 'to come home if they want more Relief'.
PLACE Inferred from other letters from Susannah and/or Davey Rising.

**154   From Thomas Smith Carritt in [Newington] London to the over-
seer of Chelmsford, 7 May 1825**

To the acting Overseer of Chelmsford
  Sir/
  By laying this before the select Vestry on monday next you will much
oblidge
5   Your mo obt Ser^t
                                                     Tho S. Carritt
To the Chairman and the Gentlemen of the Select Vestry
  Sirs/
  It is with great grief and sincere regret - that I am again oblidged to
10 apply to you for pecuniary aid - in consequence of my being so much out
of employ since I was last at Chelmsford - we are again quite aground - in
some instances I have had only 2 or 3 days in a week - and sometimes not
as many - our privations have been very great - such as my going from 8
O'Clock in the morning until 9 O'Clock in the evening with only a Crust
15 of Bread - and having but a small portion of Bread at home for the Children and their Mother - for Months past my earnings have not been sufficent

to find us in victuals of the coarsest fare - independent of Clothing Coals
Rent &c &c - I am very desireous of hiting upon some plane to need as
Little assistance as possible - but am quite at a loss to know how to act for
the best - *could you advise*?   20

I hope to hear from you in a post or two

Interem

I am Gentlemen

Your most obt & hble Ser^t

Thos Smith Carritt   25

10 Wellington St
Newington causeway
May 7th 1825

<small>TEXTUAL ALTERATIONS 17: victuals] 'vi' *over illeg.*
   WRITING 20: could you advise] *twice underlined.*
   CIRCUMTEXT Note of answer, 19 May 1825, on outside, 'inclosing a Pound Note'.
   FURTHER EVIDENCE The payment mentioned in the circumtext was recorded in the over-
seers' accounts on 21 May 1825. Thomas Carritt had received £5 on 14 March 1825
(ERO, D/P 94/12/17, Chelmsford overseers' accounts, pauper ledger).</small>

155   From Daniel Rust to Charles Rust in Chelmsford, 8 May [1825]

May 8th
   Dear Wife I rite to you hopeing this Will find you and the famely all Well as
it Leaves me at Present I should wish you to show this to the Gentlemen at the
Committy Gentlemen I adress this to you Being a Por Man with a familey
you Gentlemen well Now that MySelf Wife and 5 Children Could not Exist   5
on 11 shillings Pr Weak and you Gentleman Promised Me fair to My face at
the committiy Before I life the Poor house that If I strove to the Best of My
Industry My famely should not Want you Promised that what Ever My wagers
was defichant you would make it up to 15 shillings p^r Weak which I stated to
you Every statement of my later Imployment Was But a 11 shillings p^r Weak   10
which I told you Gentlemen that I ad starved Enaf all Redey you Gentlemen
must no that I to Make shift have goon to Work the hole day With 1 Peneworth
of Bread Rather then take it from the Children when 5 have Been Redy to
drop Gentlemen I Rite this to Inform you of My Princeples of a man I am very
sorry thay you Gentlemen of th committy should Cause a man like me from   15
my famely which I love my children a dear as you do But for a man to be
lockd & Bard from his Wife does a way with all word of god for dam^d is he
that Parteth Man & Wife for nothing will Bring on disstruction sooner

Gentlemen I hope you will not think that I have forgot my famely no I am In
20 Imploy at 1.0.0 pʳ Weak But I wand Shirts and Shoes and when I am suppliey
with them I will allow 8 shillings pʳ Weak during the time she is there til she
has got over her laying In which you no it is of no use for me to have her with
me in a strange Place with out anything to do with

I dont Mean to Give you any more troble than I am forst to do I am Willing
25 to send you 8 shillings pʳ weak I have 26 to Pay for lodgings I waist nothing
But what is fair My Meaning is not to incroch on the Parrish no more than I
can help

as soon as My Wife is over her troble I will take them from you and I Will
Pay you 8 shillings pʳ Weake tel that time and by that time I may be able to get
30 a Place for her and the family

> so No More From
> Mʳ Daniel Rust

TEXTUAL ALTERATIONS 8: Industry] 'u' *over* 'y'. 19: In] *interl at end of line*.
DATE Year from filing note on outside.
FURTHER EVIDENCE Daniel Rust (aged 55) had received occasional payments to the amount
of £8 2s 10d in 1824, and received payments to the amount of £13 19s in 1825 (ERO, D/
P 94/18/55, List of the out-door poor belonging to Chelmsford, for the year from Lady
Day 1822; D/P 94/12/17, Chelmsford overseers' accounts, pauper ledger).

156* From Susan[nah] Halls in Ipswich to James Read, overseer of Chelmsford [15 May 1825]

Honnard Genteelman

I Susan Halls do sincely return you all Genteelmen My Thanks for all
your kindness to me I receved my Last alowence very Safe up to 26ᵗʰ
March 1825
5 Genteelmen
My age is Either 88 or 89 I Cannot Say Whitch I remaine your poor
Humbel parishner Susan Halls

TEXTUAL ALTERATIONS 3: very] *after del illeg*. 3: up] *after del illeg*. 6: or] *after del* '8'. 6: I
remaine] 'I' *after del* 'I'.
CIRCUMTEXT The letter is preceded by the following statement, dated 15 May 1825 and
signed by M.G. Edgar, minister of St Nicholas, Ipswich: 'I hereby certify that Susan Halls
is living'. Underneath, there are two further signatures from Thomas Bradlaugh, churchwarden, and Edward Chapman, overseer. Edgar's certificate and the three signatures take
up the top third of the page. Neither of the three hands is identical with that of the letter.
The entire piece is written on the back of a letter from James Read, vestry clerk of
Chelmsford, of 13 May 1825, to Susan Halls at Mr [James] Alexander, her son-in-law, in

St Nicholas, Ipswich, requesting her to send 'a Certificate, signed by the Minister and Churchwardens that you are living', to state her age and to acknowledge the receipt of her allowance up to 26 March 1825.

157   From Arthur Tabrum in [Christchurch] London to James Read, vestry clerk of Chelmsford, 17 May 1825

London May 17th 1825

Sir

I do not understand your meaning by sending that answer back, if you or any of the Parish thought that the Boy was not alive why not have come yourself or some one that knew the Boy and satisfied yourselves about   5 that, I think that you cannot understand common writing yourself to say that I have sent for 11 Weeks when there is only 6 Due which I wrote as Plain as I Possibly could do you say there is only 5 But I will Prove there is six on the 26th of Febuary I receivd 18^s Shillings Due on that Day and from that Day to the 14 of May is 11 Weeks and I have receivd 5 Weeks   10 Money 7^s6^d out of that and if you are not satisfied you may find me at ^{No}39 St John Street Holland St Blackfriars Road Near the Bridge the same Directions as you have had a time or two before and so that is no excuse, if I had not been out of Work I would not have troubled myself about it, as the Parish is very greatly oppressd by allowing a Poor Man 1^s6^d per Week   15 to Maintain a Boy 6 years and a half old, I suppose they would sooner give their friend in the House 4^s6^d and would not think so much about that as they do to allow me 1^s6^d but perhaps they may have three at that Price to Pay for it I do not get on as I certainly shall send them down as to getting the Certificate signd by the Minister was a very ignorant expres-   20 sion for to make, for a Strange Woman to take a Child before a Person they never knew or saw to say that was her Child People in London know better than to do such things or at Least the Ministers do I have had a Deal of trouble as I am a Stranger if you will send on to Morrow by Mr French my Wife and the Boy shall both be there although he has not a bit of Shoe   25 to his feet

Your humble St

Arthur Tabrum

I have been ever since Last Saturday a getting a Certificate Next Saturday will be 7 Weeks The Beadle of the Parish got the certificate for me or I   30 could not have got it myself

TEXTUAL ALTERATIONS 1: 17th] '17' *interl below del* 'th'. 5: knew] *over del illeg.* 10: the 14 of May] *interl above del* 'this'. 10: and] *after del* 'D'. 18: to] *interl with caret.* 24: to Morrow] *interl above del* 'Monday'. 24: by Mr French] *interl.* 26: his feet] *after del* 'Wear'. 30: the] 'th' *over* 'a'.

158   From Susan Bright in Mildenhall [Suffolk] to James Read, vestry clerk of Chelmsford, 19 May 1825

Mildenhall May 19th 1825

Mr Reade

According to your Request I Have sint you my age is 42 Yeares Robt Bright 16 Years James Bright 15 Years Susin Bright 13 Years Sarah Bright
5 10 Years Mary Bright 7 Years Neither of the Girls do not Earn a haf penny but are at the *[------------]* School Ja^s Bright has 2 shilling & sixpence per Wheek when in Imployment a he do not belong to this parrish some Time has work and some Time none -

Mr Gill stop^{d £}1^s15 out of My pay for Rates 1 shilling per wheeke for 35
10 whekes

Gentlemen I hope you will A low me widows pay if you doe nott I shall be a bliged to Come home

Susan Bright

TEXTUAL ALTERATIONS 6: but are at the *[------------]* School] '*[------------]* School' *interl in two lines with caret.*

CIRCUMTEXT Between the text ad the signature of Susan Bright there are two signatures from other hands: 'H.G. Phillips Vicar' and 'James Read Churchwarden'. It is not altogether clear whether the signature of Susan Bright is in the same hand as the letter.

RELATED CORRESPONDENCE Answering a letter from Chelmsford, Mr Gill, overseer of Mildenhall, had written to James Read, vestry clerk of Chelmsford, on 13 February 1823. He had called at Widow Bright's house and given the following report on her condition. She had four children: James (12), Susan (9), Sarah (7), and Mary (4), of whom only the boy was occasionally employed, but not more than three days per week at 3d, whereas 'the other children had no employm^t & the widow but seldom - as our parish is very populous & we can not find employment for our own poor'. Her rent, he went on, was £4 14s per year, and she had to pay poor rates of 6s 6d per quarter. 'I believe the Widow is anxious to continue here because she has a very aged mother - and a Brother or two residing here who occasionally assist her / they are journeyman tradesman excepting one who is a master but he has a very large family - her children are sent to School by Lady Bunbury'.

FURTHER EVIDENCE During the year up to Lady Day 1823, Susan Bright had received a weekly allowance of 9s (ERO D/P 94/18/55, List of out-door poor belonging to Chelmsford, for the year from Lady Day 1822). We do not know to what extent she had been supported during the following year or so, but from June 1824 to Midsummer 1825 she received 6s per week (ERO D/P 94/12/36, Chelmsford overseers' accounts).

159 From Daniel Rust to Sarah Rust in Chelmsford, 25 May [1825]

May 25

Dear wife i Received your Letter and in arncer to it i have sent to Let you
Know whot i intend to do you must Content your selfe ware you are till
arfter your Lying in and then by that time i shall be able to get a few
things to gether to Put in to a Room for you to Come to you Can not think 5
of Coming hare till you are able to take a Journey Mr Reed Rought a
Letter wich i Received saying that i was to send 8 shillings p^r week for
your beign in the house but that i Cannot do if i do i shall not be able to get
a few things to put in to a Room for you to Come two and if i do N Not do
that you Cannot Come Hare till I Can do it you Know that you have Not 10
Got but a verry few things to bring with you You Know the situation i was
in when i Left you i have been forst to buy a Pare of New shoose and a
Cupel of shirts & stokings for you Knew i had None now i shall Save all
i Can to by a few things to Put in to a Room one bed i must by and beding
wich by the time you will be able to Come i Shall Get them this is a verry 15
good Place for wourk thay Pay well for it woman are Paid better hare then
men are at Chelmsford if you was hare and well you might yarn 9 or 10
shillings p^r week the Pore men tell me that this is a verry good Parrish and
that thay Pay thare Pore men with famelys 3 shillings p^r day and if i should
be so Luckey i will trie and settle my selfe thare 20

Pray make your self as Happy as you Can so I Conclude your Ever
Efectunate Husband

Danl Rust

TEXTUAL ALTERATIONS 5: to] 't' *over* 'S'. 5: not] *interl at end of line*. 9: Not] *after del illeg.*
20: so] *after del* 'and if i should be'.
DATE Year from filing note on outside.
FURTHER EVIDENCE Daniel Rust received an allowance of 7s per week from May 1826,
and of 5s from May 1827 (ERO, D/P 94/12/36, Chelmsford overseers' accounts).

**160 From Sarah Manning in Stratford [Essex] to James Read, ves-
try clerk of Chelmsford, 26 May 1825**

Sir

In Anwsering your letter that I Receved yesterday you wished me to send
you word the Names of my two Children that I Receved the Money for the
Oldest Henry and the youngest Luezer Facy and the Age of one is Eleven
and the Girl is Nine years Old the Father of Henry his Name is Henry Fosset 5

and the Father of Luezar was William Thornhill and you wished me to send
you word - how the Children were Employed and there Earnings as to that
Sir I Can assure you that they have Never Earned one Shilling since I had
them for they Both go to School at the Pressent and have took the two
10 Children with me for the Churchwarden &c to see them from

your humble Servant
Sarah Manning
Stratford Essex
May 26 1825

TEXTUAL ALTERATIONS 5: Name is] *interl.* 8: one] 'o' *over illeg.*

CIRCUMTEXT Note from vicar and churchwarden of West Ham, that Henry Facey and
Louisa Facey are Sarah Manning's children, on next page, dated 28 May 1825.

RELATED CORRESPONDENCE Sarah Manning (née Facey) had two illegitimate children for
whom she received regular payments from the overseers of Chelmsford. The latter in turn
received payments towards the maintenance of the girl from her father as late as 1828
(letter of 1 September 1828).

The evidence provides no clue as to when she left Chelmsford (and got married). For
about a year after the above letter, the overseers of Chelmsford thought she had gone to
Stratford-upon-Avon. On 13 May 1825 they sent a letter to her at that place, which got
into the hands of the overseers there who answered that they knew nobody by the name of
Mrs Manning (letter from James Payton, assistant overseer in Stratford-upon-Avon, to
James Read, 20 May 1825).

161   From S[usan] Bright in Mildenhall [Suffolk] to J[ames] Read in Chelmsford, 29 May [1825]

Mildenhall May 29th

Sir I Rec[d] your Letter wich I was much surpris[d] What I said A Bout the
Rates I Declare it to Be the truth and I have Six Shillings Now to pay this
week or I shall Be Dristresd for it & Gentelmen A Bout my family I have
5 But One that have Any Inployment and he Is at work at the Lime Keln for
2[s]6[d] p[r] week when In work And the three girls do Not Bring me In Any
thing And as for my Self I have No Employment But to do for my family
the Room that I Require for my family is 2 Shilling p[r] week to Be Paid
Out of Allowance
10   And Gentlemen James Bright Belong To Chelmsford As the three Girls
A Bove mentiond this I Hope Gentlemen you will think A Sufiant
Answer to your Letter

I Remain

Your &

S Bright 15

TEXTUAL ALTERATIONS 4: Gentelmen] 'n' *over* 't'.

DATE Year from filing note on outside.

RELATED CORRESPONDENCE Apparently the overseers of Chelmsford had told Susan Bright that they were not (or no longer?) prepared to pay for her poor rates due at Mildenhall and threatened to discontinue her allowance altogether. On 15 June 1825 Thomas Adams, overseer of Mildenhall, wrote to James Read, the vestry clerk of Chelmsford: 'I understand from her that you have been acquainted with the earnings of herself and family: her allowance of 6ˢ per week (granted by your parish) has been regularly paid - but I find from a letter she brought me this morning that you will not continue it after Midsummer. I think it will be impossible for her to remain here if you do not continue her allowance & pay her Poor Rates. [...] I made enquiries respecting her character, circumstances, &c and find that she is deserving your notice'.

FURTHER EVIDENCE Susan Bright received an allowance of 6s per week until November 1825, when it was reduced to 3s (ERO, D/P 94/12/36, Chelmsford overseers' accounts). It was further reduced to 2s as from Lady Day 1828, by which time she had only two (coresident) children (D/P 264/18/55, List of the out-door poor belonging to Chelmsford, for the year from Lady Day 1826 [kept among Braintree overseers' papers]; D/P 36/28/3, List of the out-door poor belonging to Chelmsford, for the year from Lady Day 1828 [kept among Great Coggeshall overseers' papers]).

162   From Ann Herbert in [Bermondsey] London, 1 June 1825

June 1ᵗʰ 1825

Sur

I recived your letter and I am still Living and I am now entered in my 6.3 year I git my Livelehood by plain Knedle work and on a Fair Calculation I Can say truly it will not a mount to more than 3 Shillings pʳ Week -   5
as my Helth is in a very precerous State - and I am very unwell at the present But having my Daughter with me tho she has very Bad state of Helth that renders her - Incapable of servitude to Gether by industry and What you are Kindly allowing wee G[ett] Due - this is a Just and true Statement - you may Depend on - I am Sur - With great respect   10

yours ann Hurbert

TEXTUAL ALTERATIONS 1: 1825] '5' *after del illeg.*

CIRCUMTEXT Confirmation from overseers of Bermondsey workhouse on next page.

FURTHER EVIDENCE From Christmas 1819 to Lady Day 1823, Ann Herbert had received a weekly allowance of 2s 6s per week (ERO, D/P 94/18/53, List of the out-door poor belonging to Chelmsford, for the year from Christmas 1819; D/P 94/18/55, List of the out-door poor belonging to Chelmsford, for the year from Lady Day 1822). Early in

December 1823, by which time her allowance had been reduced to 2s, John Sheppee had visited her, on his journey to several Chelmsford paupers in London in behalf of the select vestry. She lived with her daughter (aged 31), and Sheppee reported that she 'considers that if herself and daughter get 6 Shillings in One Week, it is a good Weeks work, but they generally get about 4ˢ/, as her daughter has a very bad state of health; - their employment is Needle Work; - they bear a very good Character and have been in the present Lodging 15 years, - they pay 2/6 pʳ Week for One Room, - From Appearance I think they are deserving of some allowance, as one or the other is constantly unwell'(ERO, D/P 94/18/ 42, Report of John Sheppee on his journey to London, 13 December 1823). Following that report, the allowance of 2s had been continued, but from 1 July 1825 it was reduced to 1s, which Ann Herbert received until 1829 (D/P 264/18/55, List of the out-door poor belonging to Chelmsford, for the year from Lady Day 1826 [kept among Braintree over-seers' papers]; D/P 36/28/3, List of the out-door poor belonging to Chelmsford, for the year from Lady Day 1828 [kept among Great Coggeshall overseers' papers]; D/P 94/12/ 36, Chelmsford overseers' accounts).

163   From Thomas and Ann Cooper in Woolwich [Kent] to the over-seer of Chelmsford, 20 June 1825

Woolwich June 20ᵗʰ 1825

Gentlemen/

I am sorry that I am under the Necessity of writing to Inform you that my Husband is very ill and is discharge on account of his illness from the
5 Kingsworks as the Doctor is pronounced him unable to do his work and in a decline and we must come home for we have nothing here to subsist upon Gentelmen I have taken the Lberty of riteing this Letter to ask you wether we are to Apply to woolwich Parish to be past home or wether you think Proper to send us up something to bring us down as my Husband is
10 able to Come at this time but Possable in a little time may not we thought it the Properest way to let you know of it as we do not want to run the Parish to greater expences than needs must pleast to send us answer as soon as Possable as we are in great distress and adrove it of till the Last we have 4 Children
15   from your Humbl Serᵗ
                                                    Thomas & Ann Cooper

Please to direct to Thoˢ Cooper Collarmaker
Near the fortune of near new road Woolwich

TEXTUAL ALTERATIONS 9: something] *after del illeg.* 13: till] *after del illeg.*
WRITING Same hand as letters from Ann Cooper.

**164   From Samuel White in Halstead [Essex] to Mr Joselyne in
        Chelmsford, 20 June 1825**

Halsted June 20 1825

Sir/

Haveing (with many privations) made shift so long time without Parish
relief I am unable to do it any longer as I have six Children two of them in
arms, my wife in Confinement and a Nurse in the house, besides - which   5
I have had three Children bad with the Measles and the youngest but one
is left in such a weak state as to be not likely to walk alone this six Months
if ever, I have been obliged to Employ a Docter for them and my Wife,
the expence of which is more than - two Pounds of which I have nothing
to Pay - I have had - one Death and two Births in the house since I had any   10
assistance - and flour and other nessecerais <----------> dearer - I therefore hope the Gentlemen will *[t]ea[k]* <m>y Case under there serious
Consideration and grant me some Present relief and a trifle Per week while
my Children Continue so small.

I have taken the Liberty of writing to you Sir as not knowing any other   15
Gentleman of the select Vestry and to spare the exspence and loss of time
in Coming to Chelmsford = hope you will be so kind as to do what you
Can for me in so Doing you will Confer a real favour upon Sir your obedient

Humble Servant   20
Sam¹ White

my own wages 15/= Per week
Eldest son — 1/= Do
no other able to earn any thing

TEXTUAL ALTERATIONS 8: have] *interl with caret.*
   CIRCUMTEXT Note of answer, 8 July 1825, on outside, 'including a Pound Note'.
   FURTHER EVIDENCE During the year up to Lady Day 1823, Samuel White had received
occasional relief payments to the total of £4 5s (ERO, D/P 94/18/55, List of the out-door
poor belonging to Chelmsford, for the year from Lady Day 1822).

**165   From Jane Hills [in London] to the overseers of Chelmsford
        [27 June 1825]**

Sir/

Please to send Mʳˢ Hills Money up by Mʳ French on Monday next and I
will Meet it Thire witch is Due on the 24ᵗʰ of this Month the Last Money

there was 2ˢ Shorts I am Sca*[rce]* able to walk up & Down Stairs you add
5 need put More or then Take it off

I am your Humble Sᵗ
Jane Hills

DATE Date from filing note on outside.
PLACE Inferred from text and Jane Hills's other letters.

166   From Ann Cooper in Woolwich [Kent] to the overseer of Chelmsford, 1 July 1825

Woolwich July 1ˢᵗ 1825

Gentelmen/
    I am sorry that I am under the Necesity of trubleing you with this Letter
to Inform you that My Husband is in Guys Hospital we thought it the
5 most prudent way that He might get restre'd to his Health to support his
family he went in Last Wednesday he was Oblidge to be Carreid in the
Coach he is so bad. Gentelmen I hope that you will Consider my Case and
have the goodness to send me A support dureing the time my Husband is
bad for my family as I am in very great distreess he as not hearnt a penny
10 this 3 weeks I hope that you will not Compel me to Come home and my
family till I see wether he gets better for I am Oblidge to keep him in
Cleane Linnen and I have no one to do it for him I have 4 Children one 11
years old one 6 years one 3 years one 10 months If you will have the
goodness to Consider my Case I Can take it of this Parish if not I must
15 Apply to the Overseers of this Parish as I have no means of subsistance
and they will Immediately take me and my Children home and my Husband will be Oblidge to Leave the Hospital as he will have no one to find
him in Cleane Linnen

from your Humble Servant
20   Ann Cooper
Please to direct Ann Cooper
Near the Fortune of War *Woolwich*

TEXTUAL ALTERATIONS 5: way] *interl with caret.*
    CIRCUMTEXT Note from other hand in left-hand bottom corner of page, facing valedictions: 'We the undermentioned Parishioners of Sᵗ Marys Parish Woolwich in Kent Certify the above Statement to be true'. Signed Andrew Duncan, Phillip Pank ('victular'), Thomas Mills (baker).

RELATED CORRESPONDENCE On 9 July 1825 the vestry clerk of Woolwich wrote to the overseer of Chelmsford that Ann Cooper was the wife of Thomas Cooper who was ill and currently a patient in Guy's Hospital. They lived at New Road and had four children aged 11, 6, and 3 years, and 10 months. Her examination showed they had been removed from St Mary Cray (near Orpington, south east London) to Chelmsford about three years before and stayed in Chelmsford poorhouse for a year before they had come to Woolwich. He suggested 'that this Parish will give them such relief as may be required on receiving your order - but should you decline such arrangement they will be forthwith removed'.

FURTHER EVIDENCE Three months later, Thomas Cooper was dead. On 13 Octber 1825, the overseer of Chelmsford remitted the overseer of Woolwich £16 7s 6d for the funeral expences. Ann Cooper was left a widow with four children and received a weekly allowance of 8s from 20 October 1825 till May 1828. By 1826, she had moved to Chelmsford, where she lived in Duke Street. Her allowance was reduced to 7s in May 1829 (with three children at home), to 6s in May 1830, and to 5s 6d in September 1830 (ERO, D/P 94/12/17, Chelmsford overseers' accounts, pauper ledger; D/P 94/12/36, Chelmsford overseers' accounts; D/P 94/18/55, List of the out-door poor belonging to Chelmsford, for the year from Lady Day 1822; D/P 264/18/55, List of the out-door poor belonging to Chelmsford, for the year from Lady Day 1826 [kept among Braintree overseers' papers]).

167   From Jane Hills [in St Sepulchre, City of London, 14 July 1825]

Sir

will you have the goodness to send Mr Hills money up by m^r French on monday next in Gracehurst Street and her Daughter will meet it Thire as She is not able to go her Self Sir if you will have the goodness to Allow her a triffle more, as She is not able to do any thing   5

I ham your Humble Servant

Jane Hills

CIRCUMTEXT The letter begins on the second page. The first page bears a certificate, dated 14 July 1825 and signed by William Edwards and John Hill, churchwardens, and W[illiam] Rippon and Charles Walsturn, overseers of St Sepulchre, City of London, 'that Mrs Hill is living at N° 25 White Horse Alley in this parish'. Note from Charles Count, chairman of the select vestry of Chelmsford, dated 28 July 1825, below text: 'Pay the Allowance as before'.

RELATED CORRESPONDENCE On 1 July 1825, James Davis, parish officer of Westminster, had written to James Read, vestry clerk of Chelmsford, that Jane Hills was helpless and lived with her son's widow who had a large family (with note of answer from Chelmsford: 'To be visited by one of the Parish Officers').

168   From Jane Hills [in London] to the overseers of Chelmsford, 1 October 1825

Sir

if you Please to send Mrs Hills Money up by Mr French Coachmen on monday Next in Gracechurch St and I will meet it Thire witch was Due on
5 the 29th of Septr Last
            I ham your Humble S^t
                    Jane Hills
Saterday Octr 1st 1825

TEXTUAL ALTERATIONS 3: St] *interl at end of line.*
    CIRCUMTEXT Note from other hand at bottom: '10 Weeks will be due on the 8th October'.
    PLACE Inferred from text and other letters from Jane Hills.

169   From Susan[nah] and Davey Rising in Halstead [Essex] to the overseer of Chelmsford, 4 October 1825

                                    Halstead october the 4 1825
Honoread Gentellmen I have to Inform you I am in Great Destress Concearning my Rent I have A Great Sum of moneay to Raise For to pay my Rent which I am Not Able to to Raise I theirfore Hope you wordy
5 Gentellmen will Be kind And so Good As to Send me Alittle money to help me to pay my Rent or Eals them will Take my ould Lumber pray wright to me as Soon as you Can your humble Servents Sasan And Davay Rising

TEXTUAL ALTERATIONS 6 Eals] 'l' *over* 't'.
    FURTHER EVIDENCE Davey Rising's weekly allowance of 3s 6d had been discontinued at the end of May 1825 (ERO, D/P 94/12/36, Chelmsford overseers' accounts).

170   From Jane Hills [in London] to the overseers of Chelmsford, 5 October 1825

Sir

will you have the goodness to send Mrs Hills^s Money up by Mr French on Saturday Next in Gracechurch Street and I will meet it Thire witch was Due on the 29th of Last Month as she is quite destitue of money as She as
5 nothing but what she is Oblight to Borrow

I ham your Humble St
Jane Hills
Wensday October 5th 1825

TEXTUAL ALTERATIONS 6: St] *interl at end of line.*
PLACE Inferred from text and other letters from Jane Hills.

**171   Arthur Tabrum in [Christchurch] London to James Read, over-
seer of Chelmsford, 16 October 1825**

London Oct 16th 1825

Sir

I take this opportunity of Writing to you concerning Arthur Goods
Money, as you wrote saying that you was not to Pay any more to me or
any of My Family, because that I spoke the Sentiments of my mind a little   5
Harsh, which I have acknowledged to Mr Baker twice but never receivd
no answer I have therefore wrote to you, as the Poor Fellow is almost
Naked, and whilst I Keep him I shall expect to be Paid for it, and If I do
not receive any remuneration, I shall take him before the Lord Mayor,
and see what is to be done, and whilst you make me keep him you are   10
imposing upon a Man that is hardly able to support his own, it was the
agreement of the Parish to allow the 1^s6^d if I took him therefore I have a
right to it, untill such time they take the Boy away, I have no Business to
send him away, without one of the Guardians of the Parish he belongs to
comes & receives him from me, And I shall expect the Money for him as   15
Long as I have and if the Parish Does not Pay me I shall put it into Court,
as I have had advice about it, I submitted myself to Mr Baker & acknowledged what I said in the Letter to you, but I do not see that I was in fault
because I did not speak without a very great reason, when I am keeping
all the expense i can of the Parish and working hard for a Living, not to be   20
assited in a small trifle more to maintain that I have no business to Do
myself, I shall not trouble myself no more, but I shall apply elsewhere as
there is redress for me as well as other People

Your Humble St
Arthur Tabrum   25

TEXTUAL ALTERATIONS 15: &] *inserted in left-hand margin.* 23: there] *first* 'e' *interl with caret.*

172 From Susannah Halls in Ipswich to the overseer of Chelmsford
[*before* 8 November 1825]

To the Genteelmen of the poor Chelmsford
   Honeard Genteelmen
   I Susana Halls
   Do return my Sincear Thanks to you all Genteelmen For all your kind-
5 ness to me apoor feable Creature Genteelmen I am Quite Confind to my
   bed I receved My Last allowance very Safe up to 23ᵈ July 1825 Genteelmen
   I am in Grate want
   I remaine your Humbel parishner
   Susana Halls
10 Please Genteelmen Direct for me at James
   alexander Friers road St Nicholas
   Ipswich Suffolk

TEXTUAL ALTERATIONS 1: Chelmsford] 'd' *interl at end of line*. 6: up] *after del illeg*. 11: St] *after del* 'S'.
DATE Inferred from circumtext.
CIRCUMTEXT Note from other hand at bottom of page: 'Cheque on Crukitt' 8 November 1825.

173 From Arthur Tabrum in [Christchurch] London to James Read,
vestry clerk in Chelmsford, 13 November 1825

London Novʳ 13ᵗʰ 1825
Honᵈ Sir
   I receivd your Letter Yesterday and we are much obligd to the Gentle-
   men for their Goodness, and if you will be so good as to send by Mʳ
5 French on Wednesday Morning Either My Wife or Myself will be there
   to receive it, as it is very acceptable to us as every thing is very Dear in
   London and it is as much as we can Do to Live,
                                             I remain Your Humble
                                                         Servant
10   Arthur Tabrum
   Nº 39 John Sᵗ
   Holland Sᵗ
   Blackfriar Rᵈ
         London

TEXTUAL ALTERATIONS 9: Servant] 'e' *over* 't'.
CIRCUMTEXT Note from other hand at bottom: 'Sent £1.19.0 by Mr French Novr 16, 1825'.

174 From S[usan] Alexander in Ipswich to James Read in Chelmsford, [15 November 1825]

Honnerd Genteelmen
This is to inform you that Susan Halls died this Moring I wold be So
much abldight to you if you Will be So kind as to Send what the parish
alowes For bering She is had avery heavey afflicton We wear obldight to
have Two to do for her Her paines was So grate one Could not do for her   5
alone that maid it So very heavey for me and bissnes so very Dull or I
wold not asked you but you may depend that is the Truth Genteelmen I
return my Sincer Thanks to you all for all your kindness to My poor old
Mother I remaine your Humbel S alexander
pleas Sir Direct for J. alexander   10
Friers road Ipswich Suffolk

TEXTUAL ALTERATIONS 3: what] *interl.*
WRITING This letter is from the same hand as all letters sent in the name of Susannah
Halls. Her daughter Susan was married to James Alexander in Ipswich, St Nicholas.
DATE Given on outside, below address, in same hand as letter.
FURTHER EVIDENCE This letter was received in Chelmsford two days later: the payment
of the postage of 7d is recorded in the minute book of the select vestry. James Alexander
was allowed £1 towards the burial expenses for Susannah Halls, which was sent on 18
November 1825 (ERO, D/P 94/8/6, Chelmsford select vestry minutes; D/P 94/12/17,
Chelmsford overseers' accounts, pauper ledger).

175 From David and Sarah Rivenall in [St George in the East] London to the overseer of Chelmsford, 15 November 1825

London Novr 15th 1825
To the Gentleman *Churchwardness* and *Overseers* of *Chelmsford* in the
County of Essex The Humble *Petition* of *David* & Sarah *Rivenall* Showeth,
that your Pettioners Are in very grate distress, the heavy family thay *Have*
to Provide for, and their rent, to Pay, has bean The *means* of *Throwing*   5
them into grate *Distress* from ther falling off in the little Way of *Buisness*,
thay not being Able, to raise A Stock, of goods, for Sale, that would be the
means of doing. Better for them Selvs, Humbly *Beg* that you *Gentleman*
will Consider their *Case* They are very thankful for what thay do and

10 Have received from *you*, and *Hopes* that you You will remit them Something, In *addition*, they Beg to Inform you, thay have An Oppertunity, Of
Appentising David the Eldest Son to a very Respectable *Man* in the City,
but they have to give And undertaking for bearing a *Part* of the *Expences*
that would would have bean done this day But they have not the money to
15 do it *with* therefore it is Put of till this day *Week* When we hope you will be
Kinde Enough to have Taking our Case into *Consideration* and Something
done, we are in Arrears of *Rent* to the Amount of 15ˢ Shllᵍ, and are threatned
with Being *Siezed uppon* from the Aforesaid Want of Assistance But Should
you Gentleman remit us Something, we will not Press uppon you in So
20 Short a time again, as I have got my health In a grate measour restored, So
as not to be under the Care of the Sergeons of the Hospital, but Still remain
very Week, for Want of *Nourishments* your Kindness Gentleman we Shall
be Ever Bound to Pray for your goodness and

                                        Subscribe our Selves your
25   Obedint and Humble Servents
                                        David & Sarah Rivenall

Witness James Riddel
[*Continued on next page, written crosswise*]
Address to D Rivenall
30 at the Kings Head
         Commercial
              Road

TEXTUAL ALTERATIONS 12: the eldest son] *interl with stroke above del* 'has they have'. 17:
Amount] *after del* 'Amount'.
   WRITING 18: Siezed uppon] *twice underlined.*
   FURTHER EVIDENCE Possibly as a consequence of this letter, David Rivenall's allowance
of 2s 6d, which he had received since December 1823, was increased to 4s with effect
from 5 November 1825. This was paid until Michaelmas 1826 (ERO, D/P 94/12/36,
Chelmsford overseers' accounts).

**176   From Rachel Brown in [Clerkenwell] London to [James] Read,
         overseer of Chelmsford, 27 December 1825**

                                            London Decʳ 27 1825
Mʳ Reed
    Sir I hope you will pardon the liberty i Take in writiing to you but as i am
in wants Of Som Cloathing as my Fathers income Is not Enugh to Supply
5 us Both with Nessarys as he is very infurm and want Great Suport I therefore Beg the favour of you to Solisset the Gentelmen for me If they would

have the Goodness to send ne 1$^£$0^{S}0^D i Should be very thankfull as i want A gown and other nessurys wich i know not how to do without If this favour Can be Granted A line Directed to A^{bn} Brown Charterhouse or my Brother will Meet Mr French when you think proper to name From your humble   10
    Servent Rachel Brown

TEXTUAL ALTERATIONS 5: want] *over del* 'a'. 6: Solisset] *after del* 'S'. 9: Brother] *over del illeg.*
    CIRCUMTEXT Note of answer in top left-hand corner of page, 30 December 1825, 'and a Pound given to Mr French for her'.
    FURTHER EVIDENCE In the following year, Rachel Brown received another pound (ERO, D/P 264/18/55, List of the out-door poor belonging to Chelmsford, for the year from Lady Day 1826 [kept among Braintree overseers' papers]).

177   From Jane Hills in Westminster, London, to the overseer of Chelmsford, 29 December 1825

Sir/
    if you Please to send Mrs Hills Money up by Mr French the coachmen in Gracechurch St on Monday next and I will Meet it there as you Particularly wish to no more Mrs Hills is removed So it is to William Huntley N° 27 Market St Horseferry Road westminster   5
        I am your Humble S^t
            Jane Hills
Thursday Decr 29th 1825

TEXTUAL ALTERATIONS 6: S^t] *interl at end.*
    CIRCUMTEXT Note from other hand at bottom: '£1.4.0 Sent by Mr French on Monday Jany 2nd 1825 [mistaken for 1826]'.

178   From Rody Jolliff in Hertford to James Read in Chelmsford, [2] January 1826

Hertford Jan^y *[2^d]* 1826
Sir
    I should be much oblige to you if you will let Mrs Cobbin draw my Money what I have comeing to me as it will be a great Kidness as soon as the Gentlemen think proper to Grant it   5
            So I remain
            Yours &
            Rody Joliff

TEXTUAL ALTERATIONS 3: draw] 'n' *del from* 'drawn'.

RELATED CORRESPONDENCE Half a year before, the Revd Thomas Lloyd of Hertford had inquired why the weekly allowance of 1s for Widow Jolliff had been discontinued (letter of 23 May 1825 to the Revd W. Warden in Chelmsford).

179*   From Arthur Tabrum in [Christchurch] London to James Read, vestry clerk in Chelmsford, 5 January 1826

London Jany 5th 1826

Hon^d Sir

I am sorry to trouble you so soon but being ill and not able to work myself & Family are badly off, and should esteem it a great favor if you
5 would send the trifle that is due for my Wifes Child, by Mr French on Saturday Morning, as we have not wherewith to help ourselves, and my wife shall be there to receive it, as I am not able to go out of Doors myself, I believe you will find from the 12th of November I receivd the last Payment to the 7th of January 1826 is 8 Weeks Due I should not have Troubled you so soon, but under a case of real Necessity, as I am scarcely able to write this to you for it

I remain Your Humble St
Arthur Tabrum

180   From Samuel White in Halstead [Essex] to James Read, overseer of Chelmsford, 26 January 1826

Halsted Jan 26 1826

Sir/

as I am now able to write myself I thought I would not impose on the kindness of Mr Bass by troubling him to write to you again
5   I am so far recovered as to hope to be able to begin to work again next week though from weakness fallen into my legs I am unable to stand long at a time - I would not have applyed for releif again at Present if I had not received from my Doctor a bill for Familly illness amounting to £1..4..0 and which I have no means of Discharging as since my illness I have
10 spent a few shillings laid up towards it - and as the Fiorm of Gibson & son is about to be Dissolved it is requested that the Bill be Paid soon - if the Gentlemen will be so kind as to send me one Pound more I assure them that I will not trouble them again unless some serious affliction should again happen

I am Sir your most obedient 15
Humble Servant
Saml White

TEXTUAL ALTERATIONS 10: Spent] 'Sp' *over del illeg.* 10: Fiorm] 'Fio' *over del illeg.* 13: serious] *after del* 'heavy'.

CIRCUMTEXT Note from James Bass below: 'I know the above to be true case having seen the Bill'(hand A). Note of relief order from other hand at bottom: 'allowed one Pound'(hand B).

RELATED CORRESPONDENCE On 23 December 1825, James Bass in Halstead had written to James Read, vestry clerk of Chelmsford, that Samuel White was ill with severe fever ('it is feared it may prove typhus'), and that his wife and six children needed relief (with note of answer from Chelmsford, 30 December 1825, including £1). On 8 January 1826, he had written again, acknowledged the receipt of £1 and reported that Samuel White was recovering but still in distress (with note of answer from Chelmsford [no date]: 'To send another Pound').

FURTHER EVIDENCE During the year from Lady Day 1826, Samuel White received further cash payments to the total amount of £6 16s (ERO, D/P 264/18/55, List of the out-door poor belonging to Chelmsford, for the year from Lady Day 1826 [kept among Braintree overseers' papers]).

181   From David and Sarah Rivenall in [St George in the East] London to [Thomas] Mr Archer, churchwarden of Chelmsford, 30 January 1826

London 30th Jany 1826

Gentlemen

To the *Church Wardens* and *Oversears of Chelmsford* in the County of *Essex* your *Petetioner* David & Sarah *Rivenall* Rivenall Beg to Inform you that, I Call^d at Mrs Nelsons; In White Chapple, for your Weekly 5 Assistance that Is allowed me, and my Family, was yesterday Stopd By Mrs Nelson Saying Shee Should not Pay me any more money, the little i Was to receive was all I had to go to Market With It Being Saturday it has Now Gentleman Thrown us into the Greatest distress and From the Frost being So Sharp their was no Work to be got, therefore you Gentlemen 10 will have the goodness to Indeavour to render me And my Family that Assistance you have Bean doing for us, and Likewise wee have to thank you for your kindness Towards my Son *david Rivenall* that was to have bean Apprenticed to Mr Simpson of the 3 Tons in Billingsgate he having declined Taken him for Mr Simpson Says *now* 7 *years* is a long time to 15 Serve in that Line of *Buiseness*, I have the Whole of the 7 Children at home and Gentlemen you will be Kinde Enough to let me Know where I

am to Call for the money As Mrs Nellson Says She will not Pay any more
and Allow us to Subscribe our

20   Selves David and Sarah Rivenall
                              of No1 Bath Place Comm^l Road
Letter to Be Addressd to me and left At Mr Gardners Kinghead
Comm^l Road

TEXTUAL ALTERATIONS 4: Essex] *after del illeg.* 4: Rivenall] *interl at end of line, above foregoing 'Rivenall'.* 15: him] *after del* 'as and'. 21: No1] *interl with caret.*
    CIRCUMTEXT Note from other hand at bottom of page: sent £1 by post, 10 February 1826, 'to pay up to 4th March'.

182   From Samuel White in Halstead [Essex] to James Read, overseer of Chelmsford, 25 February 1826

                                  Halstead Feb 25 = 1826
Sir
    I wrote a few weeks since to you to inform you that I had a Docters bill
of one Pound four Shillings which I had no means of Discharging and
5 requesting the Parish to Discharge it - for me I have now to inform you
that I have been obliged to begin another account as my eldest son is very
bad and I have been obliged to Call in Medical assistance in addition to
that exspence I am loseing the trifel that he earns and must therefore earnestly request that some assistance be given me to Defray the last years
10 bill - I hope the gentlemen will Consider what it is to be Deprived of a
Parish Docter as I am and with such an Afflicted Familly as mine - I have
only had in five years with the loss of my wife & 2 Children and my own
illness - seven Pounds while if I am rightly informed there is a Familly in
this Place that is receving more than Double that sum from your Parish
15 every year although there youngest Child is working in a tan yard at
Chelmsford and I myself saw in your Printed list of out Door Poor for
1821 the following item „David Risen resident at Halsted 5^s/0^d per week,
Casual Allowance £3..18..0 altogether more than £16 in the year
    I have no wish to be burdensome to the Parish and therefore will never
20 trouble them but when absolute nescessity Compels me therefore hope I
shall soon be enabled by you to Discharge my Bill - and I am Sir with -
thankful acknowlegements for what I have already received your Humble
Servant
                                    Saml White

TEXTUAL ALTERATIONS 10: I] *after del illeg.* 14: receving] 'vi' *over illeg.* 20: nescessity] *corrected from* 'nescicessity'.

CIRCUMTEXT Note from other hand below: 'Answ^d 26th Feb^y'.

TEXT David Risen (alias Davey Rising) referred to at the end of the first paragraph did live in Halstead and was also relieved by Chelmsford. The reference to the list of the out-door poor of Chelmsford for 1821 could not be substantiated since no copy of that list has been found, but David Rising does appear in the printed list for the following year 1822 (ERO, D/P 94/18/55, List of the out-door poor belonging to Chelmsford, for the year from Lady Day 1822) as well as in that for 1819 which has only survived in manuscript form (D/P 94/18/53, List of the out-door poor belonging to Chelmsford, for the year from Christmas 1819). There are numerous letters from Davey Rising and his wife Susannah themselves.

183   From David and Sarah Rivenall in [St George in the East] London to James Read, vestry clerk in Chelmsford, 27 February 1826

London 27th Feb^y *1826*

To the Churchwardens and Oversears of Chelmsford in the County of Essex

Gentleman I have Acknowled the receipt of your remittance of the 10th Instant for Wich we are very much obliged to you for the Same having   5
Come at an Acceptable Time for My *Rent* Gentleman you would be Kinde Enough to Make my Payments At *Charles Savill Cheesmonger &^{c} Commercial Road*, or if you fell disposed to Sent me up a Pound at a Time as you Remitted the larst that will be the Same And do me more good, your dates of times of receipt from Mrs Nellson Exactly Corresponds With my   10
receipts Your Obedient Servants

David and Sarah Revenall

To be left at Mr Gardners
King head Comm^l Road

184   From Samuel White in Halstead [Essex] to James Read, vestry clerk of Chelmsford, 27 February 1826

Halsted Feb 27 = 1826

Sir,

I this Morning received your Letter stateing you had sent me a Pound Note on the 10th of this Month but which I had not received I immeadatly made applycation at the Post Office and found they had got one Directed   5

James White Halsted (which you will find on the other side) and they Did
not know such a Person but they never enquired of me nor my Familly
supposeing you Sir would like to have it acknowleged I have written by
return of Post Beging Parden for the trouble I have given you

10   I remain Sir with grateful
                              acknowlegements your Humb¹ Servant
                                                   Sam¹ White

CIRCUMTEXT This letter is written on the back of a letter, dated 10 February 1826, which
James Read, vestry clerk of Chelmsford, had sent to Samuel White: 'Sir I am instructed to
send you another Pound Note which is inclosed and to acquaint you the Parish will not
listen to any other Application for Money'. The original letter was folded inside out, and
the new address was written on that page of the former inside which had been left blank.

**185   From Susannah Rising in Halstead [Essex] to James Read, ves-
         try clerk in Chelmsford, 1 March 1826**

                                            Halstead 1 March 1826
Gentlemen
    I am extremely sorry to inform you that I very ill and am afraid I shall
loose the Use of one side and my daughter is also is very ill and is incapable
5 of doing any Work, I would not have troubled you If I could have any
ways have avoided it if you would be pleased to Send me Somthing I
should be much oblig'd to you

                                                  I am Gentlemen
                                    Your dutiful & Obᵈᵗ Servant
10   Susannah Raison

TEXTUAL ALTERATIONS 5: Work] *over* 'thing'.
    WRITING This is the only letter from Davey and/or Susannah Rising which is not in the
same hand as all others. Note also the clear differences in style, wording, and spelling.
    RELATED CORRESPONDENCE On 17 January 1826, John Cardinal in Halstead had written to
James Read, vestry clerk of Chelmsford, that David Rizon (alias Rising) was in great
distress, and had asked him 'if you can assist them with a little to Purchase Firing and a
few other things to warm and Protect them from the severity of the wether' (with note of
answer from Chelmsford, 28 January 1826, requesting Mr Wyatt to advance David Rising 10s). On 3 May 1826, Cardinal told Read that, according to a report from Wyatt,
Susannah Rising was suffering from ague (with note of relief ordered from Chelmsford:
10s through Wyatt). On 26 July 1826, Cardinal wrote again, saying she was still ill and
needed further relief.

186 From David Rivenall in [St George in the East] London to the overseer of Chelmsford, 13 March 1826

London Mar 13th 1826

Sir

I am under the Necessity of informing You that I And 7 Children Are at this time in the greatest distress And I have nothing to go to market with to Obtain Any relief for us there is three weeks money due on Saturday 5 next And I hope You will bee so kind As to Advance mee a fortnite forward so that I may bee able to go to market to do my best for us if you dont think good to Comply with this whe Certainly must all Come to You Imeadietelly When You Answer this please to direct to Mr Gardner Kings Head Comersieal Road London 10

I Am Sir Your Most
Ob^{dt} Hble St
Davy Revenel

TEXTUAL ALTERATIONS 7: go] 'g' *over* 'd'. 9: Kings] *after del* 'Queens'.

187 From Jane Hills in Westminster, London, to the overseer of Chelmsford, 28 March 1826

March 28 1826

Sir

Will you have the Goodness to send Mrs Hills Money up by Mr French the Coachman to Gracehurst street on Thursday next And i will meet it There 5

I am your humble
Servant
Jane Hills

Irizine at William Hentley N° 27
Market Street Westminster 10
Horsefrey Road

SPELLING 9: Irizine] *read* 'I reside'.

188   From Sarah and David Rivenall in [St George in the East] London to James Read, vestry clerk of Chelmsford, 28 March 1826

London 28th March 1826

Sir

having not received the remittance Of the monthley allowance that was promised, But they do not Like to advance Before hand, in the Immediate
5 time we Are Still Kept in Arrears, for Rent, As Well, as not having money to go to Market in the morning, and that hinders Us from Getting a *Shilling* or *Two* that may be made if i had money to go to market with, By yo remitting up 2 £ on this remmittance to Mr Charles Savill N° 4 Cheesmonger Comm^l R^d he will take Care to pay the money regular
10   We Subscribe Ourselves

your Obed Parrishoners

Sarah & David Rivenall

TEXTUAL ALTERATIONS 8: M^r] *inserted in left-hand margin.*
PLACE Inferred from previous and following letters from the Rivenalls (**186, 190**).

189   From Arthur Tabrum in [Christchurch] London to J[ames] Read, assistant overseer of Chelmsford, 29 March 1826

London March 29th 1826

Hond Sir

I should be much obligd to you if you would send the Quarters Money Due for Arthur Good My Wifes child from the 7th of January to the 1 of
5 April, which I believe is Correct as I am very much in Distress at this Present time, If you would be so good as to send it by Mr French and my Wife if she is able will be there to receive it if not if Mr French will be so Good as to Leave it at the Bar of the Tap I will come up on Saturday Night as I have no other time that I can come
10   for through Sickniss and My Wifes troubles I am hardly able to keep open Doors If you will be so good as to send on Saturday I shall take it a very great Favour

to Your Humble S^t

Arthur Tabrum

TEXTUAL ALTERATIONS 5: Distress] *first* 's' *inserted.* 8: come] 'me' *over illeg.*

190   From David and Sarah Rivenall in [St George in the East] London to [James] Read in Chelmsford, 26 April 1826

London 26th Ap^l *1826*

Gentlemen of Oversears and and Churchwardens of Chelmsford in the County of Ex I Beg to Inform you that I have at this Present Time One *Child one,*} of the *Twins* Now Lying *dead* and Expects that therre will be Two more *dead* by the Time the Poste Comes Off To you If you Gentle- 5
man Will have the Kindness to remit a Little Extra Assistance at this present Time you will be the means of Paying for the Funeral In Part as I have bean at a grate Expence According to my means they have the Measles; a Deseas Quite Previlent in London And We Subscribe Our Selves

David and Sarah Revinell   10
turn over [*continued on next page*]
Letters Adressd to DR
At Mr Gardners Kings Head
Comml Road

WRITING 4: dead] *underl twice.* 5: dead] *underl twice.*
CIRCUMTEXT Note from other hand at bottom: 'to have 1£'.

191   From David and Sarah Rivenall in [St George in the East] London to the churchwardens or vestry clerk of Chelmsford, 10 May 1826

London 10th May 1826

To the Churwardens Overseers and &^c of Chelmsford in the County of Essex

Gentlemen pardon the Liberty we take in Writing to you so Often but Necessity obliges Us to do So from the grate distress we are in having 5
Buried the Child that we Inform'd you was *dead,* and Since that on Tuesday, Another died and we are in HOur'ly Expecting the death of Another Child which will Make 3 *dead* then We are unable to pay the Expences of the funeral unless you will Gentleman Remit us the Means of getting them laid In the ground and for which we Shall be Ever bound to thank 10
you for the Kindness

Your Obedient Servents
David and Sarah Revinall

Batty Gardens
15 Bath St Commercial R^d

TEXTUAL ALTERATIONS 7: HOur'ly] 'H' *interl before* 'Ourly'. 10: for which] *interl with cross*.
WRITING 6: dead] *underl twice*.
CIRCUMTEXT Note from other hand across left-hand margin: 'Answ^d 12th May acquainting him I sent a Pound Note on the 5th directed for him at Mr Gardiners Kings Head Commercial Road'.

192   From David Rivenall [in St George in the East, London] to the overseer of Chelmsford [May 1826]

Sir
   I have remitted the Amount of the two Childrens death for your inspection And Am sorry to pres upon Your kind favours for A further remittance of payments for the Same As it is Not in my power to do I have to inform
5 You I Recive My Weekly money from A Gentelman whom You may pay it Quarterly to by
   Directing to the Kings Head
Commercial Road as formal letters
   Pleast to Comply with this Request And I hope I shall not be under the
10 necessity of troubling You for a Length of time

I am Dear Sir
Yours Gratefully And Most
Respectfully Sir
Davy Revenell

TEXTUAL ALTERATIONS 2: Childrens death] *interl with caret*.
CIRCUMTEXT The text is preceded by a detailed bill (from another hand) for the funeral of Alfred and Edward Rivenall which takes up the top two-thirds of the page. The items include the two coffins, pillows and bed, hood and scarf, and the total amount comes to £2 9s. Between the bill and the text of the letter there is a note from Thomas Marshall, chairman of the select vestry of Chelmsford: 'Allowed £1.0.0' (and a note of answer on the outside to the same effect dated May 1826).

193 From Samuel White in Halstead [Essex] to James Read in Chelmsford, 16 June 1826

Halsted June 16 = 1826

Sir/

I have thought it right to inform you that my Poor boy who has been ill so long Departed this Life last Saturday - and as the select Vestry have been allowing me 7^s/= a week from the 10 of April last I return them my 5
- sincere thanks for there kindness and hope they will Continue it a few weeks longer to help me out with the Funeral exspences - which I suppose are about 30^s/= - my wife has not recovered her late atack she has not the full use of her left arm and her mental faculties are in a very weak state so that although her health is something better she is unable to do for her 10 Familly I am obliged to have a woman about two Days in a week I hope the Gentlemen when they take of the 7^s/= a week will be so kind as to allow me something till my wife is able to manage her own Concerns though I am almost afraid that will never be -

I requested Mr Wyatt to write but he had not opportunity said I had 15 better Do it myself

I am Sir your Humble Servant
Saml White

TEXTUAL ALTERATIONS 12: will] *interl with caret.*

CIRCUMTEXT Note from other hand at bottom: 'See Minute Book April 6. 1826 7^s/ allowed weekly'. Note from other hand on next page: 'To be discontinued'.

FURTHER EVIDENCE Whatever the acting overseer decided at the time, Samuel White received assistence to the total amount of £6 16s during the year from Lady Day 1826 (ERO, D/P 264/18/55, List of the out-door poor belonging to Chelmsford, for the year from Lady Day 1826 [kept among Braintree overseers' papers]).

194 From David Rivenall in [St George in the East] London to the overseer of Chelmsford, 18 July 1826

Sir

I am sorry to bee under the necesity of Once moor troubeling you with A letter respecting the remitance of my money which you neglect to make there is £3.0.0 due From 7th April to 15 July And as I am in the greatest distress for the want of money I hope you will not fail to Imeadietly remit 5 it by directing to Mr Gardners Kingshead Comersieal road I expect to have an execution upon mee everry day for rent, I am Sir

Your Most Ob^t hble S^t
David Revenell

10 London July
18th 1826

WRITING 4: 3.0.0] *underl twice.*

195   From Sarah Manning in Stratford [Essex] to James Read, vestry clerk of Chelmsford, 26 July 1826

July 26 1826
Mrs Manning would be much Oblige to Mr Read if he would send her the
Money for her Children as she wants it as there is six Months due the 7th
of August as it will be thankfully Recevd

5   Sarah Manning
                      Startford Essex

TEXTUAL ALTERATIONS 3: as there is] *after del* 'to'.
CIRCUMTEXT Note of order of relief at bottom: 26 August 1826 'Sent £6.15.0. by M^r
French'.

196   From David Rivenall in [St George in the East] London to the overseer of Chelmsford, 29 July 1826

London July 29th 1826
I feel geatelly Suprisd At You Not Answering Any of My letters As You
Must Now I Am in great wants of My Money I Can only inform You in
Ca<se> You pay no regard to this I must Imeadietelly Apply to the parish
5 I Am in Without further delay

I am Yours &c
Davy Revinell

PLACE Inferred from previous and following letters from David Rivenall (194, 201).
RELATED CORRESPONDENCE On 26 July 1826, Charles Savill in London had written to
James Read, vestry clerk of Chelmsford, requesting him to remit the money paid to David
Rivenall (£ 2 4s for the allowance of 4s per week from 7 April 1826 to 16 June 1826),
while at the same time he left no doubt about his opinion of him: 'I think it a great Shame
that you Should allow Such People money. For they Both are tipsey From Monday morning to Saturday night.'

**197   From Samuel White in Halstead [Essex] to James Read, over-
        seer of Chelmsford, 3 August 1826**

Halsted August 3ʳᵈ 1826

Sir

I neither expected nor desired to have seven shillings a week Continued
long after it Pleased God to take away my Poor boy, but I did hope it
would have been kept on a few weeks longer to have enabled me to Pay   5
the Docter and the Funeral expences which I am utterly unable to Do
without your assistance as my wife still Continues unable to Do for her
Family and in such a state of stupidety and forgetfulness as makes it almost unfit for her to be left alone, it was but last Monday her Cloathes
Caught Fire and were burnt very much but through Mercy it was Put out   10
before it Burnt her body -

I Paid the Doctor one Pound, and about 12 shillings towards the Funeral
exspences while I was receiving the allowance but on that been with-
drawn I was obliged to stop, I exspect I owe the Doctor one pound ten and
for my Poor sons Coffen 20 shillings - I must intreat the Gentlemen to   15
enable me to Discharge this Debt as they know it is no Common Affliction that I have been exercised with as four of us were ill at one time

leaveing this to the serious Consideration of the select Vestry I remain
Sir with grateful acknowledgements for Past favours your Humble Servant
Samˡ White 20

Tᴇxᴛᴜᴀʟ ᴀʟᴛᴇʀᴀᴛɪᴏɴꜱ 9: left] *after del* 'a'. 9: last] *after del* 'the'.
    Cɪʀᴄᴜᴍᴛᴇxᴛ Order of relief from other hand at bottom: 'Ansᵈ requesting Mʳ Wyatt to let
him have a Pound'.

**198   From Rody Jolliff in Hertford to James Read in Chelmsford,
        15 August 1826**

Hertford Augᵗ 15. 1826

Sir

I should take it as great favor if you will pay to Mʳˢ Cobbin what money
i have got comeing to me the first oppertunity and the Gentlemen please
to Grant it Sir I should be Sincerley oblige to you if you will leave the   5
money with Mʳˢ Cobbin and she will send it to me so I remain

Your humble
Servant
Rody Jolliff

199   From Eliza Jackson in [Kensington] London to the overseer of Chelmsford, 27 August 1826

agust the 27 1826
Gentlemen I ham sorry to be under the necitey of trubling you I threw
myself on Chelera porreg in my illness was in the house 5 weeks as soon
as i was able to be removed they Discharged from that parrich and gave
5 me to understand that I Cam Claim no other parrish bt Chelmsford i ham
still not able to gett my breead nor am i likley to Do Itt i have left the
house a fortnight without a shiling to soport myself with should be verey
much oblidge to you to send me trifel to soport me a few weeks untill i
ham able to Do somthing to geet be a bitt of bread if not i must be pass^d
10 home as i have no nececras of soport whatever

gentlmen yours
most obedent
Eliza Jackson
once Eliza Willson
15 Mrs Jackson
N^r 8 prospect Row
Old Brompton
near Knigtsbridge
London

TEXTUAL ALTERATIONS 5: bt] *inserted.*
  CIRCUMTEXT Note from Henry Chinnock, surgeon at Brompton Square, enclosed, saying that (Eliza) Jackson had suffered from a 'very severe attack of Typhus Fever, and Cholera Morbus' and been attended for six weeks.

200   From Arthur Tabrum in Christchurch, London, to James Read, vestry clerk in Chelmsford, 3 September 1826

London Septr 3rd 1826

Hon^d Sir

I have taken this Opportunity of writing to you for the Allowance due for Arthur Good, I receivd the Last Payment 27th of May, which now makes 14 Weeks Due to me, I should be much obligd to you if you would   5
send it by Mr French by Wednesday, as I exspect to be going out of town again, as I am most always out at Work and very Little opportunity to see to anything for myself If you will be so kind as to send it by there you will much oblige your Humble
    Servt Arthur Tabrum   10
at Mr Freemans
N° 2 Mitre Place
Broadwall Christ Church
Surry

TEXTUAL ALTERATIONS 4: I] *after del* 'my'. 6: exspect] 's' *interl with caret*. 10: Servt] 'e' *over* 't'.
    CIRCUMTEXT Note at bottom: 16 September 1826 given to Mr French £1 2s 9d for 15 weeks due 9 September 1826 for Anna Tabrum's child.

201   From David Rivenall [in St George in the East, London] to the overseer of Chelmsford, 27 September 1826

Gent^n

I hope you'll pardon the liberty I take in troubling you, but being greatly distressed it as induced me to trouble you having a Child now laying in a dying state and I myself for this last Six Weeks through a severe attack of Illness not being able to do any work. I most humbly hope that you will   5
remit me the allowance which is due from the 17 of June last for my Children having all Five of them at Home. and it is quite out of my power to get them any Situation or employment on account that they have not any Wearing apparel of any discription whatever that they can appear in. on Account of my Illness and every thing being so very dull and provision   10
so very dear, I also beg leave to say that I am very much in Arrears for my Rent, and my Landlord has inform^d me that unless I do immediately pay up my Rent he will instantly distrain upon me for the same. and if you dont please to have the goodness to grant my request by remitting the

15 mony which is due for my Children, I myself Wife and Family must declare upon the parish which we now reside in for we are actually in want
of necessaries. Waiting your answer per return

I am

Gent^n

20   Your mo ob^t Servt

David Rivenall

King Head
Commercial Road
Septr 27th 1826

CIRCUMTEXT Followed by statement (in different hand) from neighbour (name illegible) to 'testify as to the truth of his Distress and Poverty'. Note on outside: 'not to be answered'.

202   From Susannah and Davey Rising in Halstead [Essex] to the governor of the poor house in Chelmsford, 4 October 1826

Halstead october the 4 1826
Honoread Gentellmen I hope you will Excuse my Freedom And parding
my Liberty I Take in wrighting to you As want and Necesity Forsess me
So to Do I am Sorry to inform you I have been weary Bad For this 4
5 munths And not Able to Do Any Thing For myself Nor My Family nother
I hope Gentellmen you will take my Destressed Case into Considerashion
And Send me Some moneay For I am in Great Destress And Trouble if
you will Please to Send me Alitill moneay I will Try Ashift Alitill Longer
And if you do not I must Come home I hope you will Answer my Needy
10 Request By Return of post And By so doing you will Blidg your humble
Servants
Susanaha And Davey Rising Halstead

CIRCUMTEXT Note on outside: 'not to be answered'.

203   From David Rivenall [in St George in the East, London] to the overseer of Chelmsford [12 October 1826]

Gen^n

    It is with sincere regret that I am under the most distressing necessity of
writing you, I took the liberty a short time ago of addressing you in hopes
that you would have taken my destress condition at that period into your

kind consideration, but since then, I beg to inform that by your not complian   5
with my request in forwarding the amount of which I most sincerly hope
was due to me for my Children my Landlord did distrain upon me for my
Rent which I inform'd you in my former letter of and I am with my family
turnd out of Doors and if it had not been for a friend who was so kind and
benevolent knowing my distress'd case took compassion on me & my   10
family I must have been past d immediately to the parish of Chelmsford
were you perfectly will know I belong to, but it does not lay in his power
to let me reside with him any longer than Monday next, also my Wife is
not allowd, to set in the Street to earn anything towards supporting our
most destress ed state, I also beg to inform you that my Child is still under   15
the Doctors hands and it is out of my power to get her nourishment to
enable her to get about or out of her deplorable place which She is obliged
to lay upon through my not been able to earn anything, I hope and trust
that your goodness of Hearts will take my case into consideration and by
return if possible remit what in your opinion you may in your wisdom for   20
a distressd family think fit & proper and by so doing you will relieve in
his sad deplorable condition
    Your most ob^t & very hble Servt
    David Rivenall
Mr Gardner   25
Kings Head
Commercial Road
St Georges East

TEXTUAL ALTERATIONS 5: consideration] 'a' *interl.* 12: it] *after del* 'he'. 16: out] *after del*
'qu'.
 CIRCUMTEXT Note of answer on outside, 20 October 1826, 'acquainting him that no
more would be allowed'.
 DATE Date of postmark.
 FURTHER EVIDENCE David Rivenall's allowance of 4s per week, which he had received
since November 1825, had been discontinued from Michaelmas 1826.

**204 From Arthur Tabrum in [Christchurch] London to James Read,
  vestry clerk of Chelmsford, 11 December 1826**

         London Decr 11th 1826
Sir
 I should be much obligd to you if you would send the Money Due for
Athur Good, you will find 14 Weeks due on the 16 as I was Paid up to the

5 9th of September last time, if you can send it by Mr French on Wednesday
Week the 20th I should be very much obligd to you

Your Humble St
Arthur Tabrum

CIRCUMTEXT Note at bottom from other hand, saying that Mr French was paid £1 1s on 17
December 1826.
PLACE Inferred from previous and following letterss from Arthur Tabrum (**200**, **212**).

**205   From David Rivenall in St George in the East, London, to the
overseer of Chelmsford, [15 December 1826]**

Gentⁿ/

I am sorry to be under the most distressing circumstance of informing
you that unless you do grant me relief that I must under the most poginant
Grief send my Dear Wife and family down to the Poor House at Chelms-
5 ford as they are totally distitude of being able to earn anything on Account of wanting Shoes Stokings &^c and unless you will take my most
distressing case into your kind consideration by remitting A Trifle as to
procure them things necessary to go after employment to earn towards
their support they will be on the parish as I is my wish to go to Sea for I
10 cannot bear to see my Children Want as well as my Dear partner

Waiting your reply

I am
Gentⁿ
Your ob^t Servt
15   David Rivenall

Kings Head
Commercial Road
St Georges ye East
London

TEXTUAL ALTERATIONS 8: them] *after del* 'ht'. 10: my] 'm' *over* 'f'.
DATE Date of postmark.
CIRCUMTEXT Note in pencil on outside, listing ages of members of the family: David
Rivenall (44), Sarah (42), David (15), William (14), Mary (10), Sarah (9), James (7).

206   From Rachel Brown in [Clerkenwell] London to James Read in Chelmsford, 15 January 1827

Charterhouse London January 15 1827

Mr Reede

Sir

I hope you will Excuse the liberty I take in writing to you but I do not know who To apply to. I Should be greatly obliged to you If in your 5
power to beg the gentelmen to Send me 1$^£$ if it is not out of Reason As i am much in wants of Shoes and Linnen and other nessarry

I hope they will not think me Troublesome as Cannot them and would Not Send if i Could help it If my request can be granted i will meet Mr French as before if you Will be so Good to give me a line Directed to the 10
Charterhouse

From your humble Servent

Rachel Brown

please to give my respects to Mr Ramball and Family

TEXTUAL ALTERATIONS 7: nessarry] 'rry' *over illeg.* 9: help] *over illeg.*
    CIRCUMTEXT Note at bottom, from other hand: 'to have a Pound'.

207   From Samuel White in Halstead [Essex] to James Read in Chelmsford, 22 January 1827

Halsted Jan 22 = 1827

Sir/

I am sorry to be again under the Nescesity of applying for assistance as my wife is now Confined in Child bed and as I have had so much afflic- tion in my house I have been unable to Provide any thing towards such an 5
exspenceeve time I have in the Past year Paid my Docter 2£ 4 shillings besides the Funeral exspences of my Poor boy more than 30 shillings I have now a Docters Bill of one Pound six for the Past year unpaid in addition to the Present Lying in which is one Pound one more add to which I have now 6 Children and a woman in the House and am obliged 10
to keep two Fires in this inclement season of the year -

my wife has not recovered of her Late attack her Left hand is but little use to her as she is unable to hold any thing fast and if it was not for my Daughter about 12 years of age I must absolutely keep a woman Con- stantly in the house to Do for my Family - I have not rec^d anything since 15

august Last when I immeadiatly took it to the Carpenters to Discharge the Bill for my Poor boys Coffin - I would not have applyed now if there had not been absolute nescessity for so Doing - I hope the gentlemen will send me a Pound towards my Docters Bill and some thing at least to Pay the
20 Nurse as I am not like Poor men in this Parish who have Docter and Nurse Paid by the Parish

I am sir your most obed^t
Humble Servant
S White

CIRCUMTEXT Note from other hand at bottom: 'to have one Pound 5ˢ/'.

208   From Davey and Susan[nah] Rising in Halstead [Essex] to the governor of the poorhouse in Chelmsford, 24 January 1827

Halstead Essex January the 24 1827
    Honoread Gentellmen I hope you will Excuse my Freedom And parding the Liberty I Take in wrighting to you As Necesity Forses me So the Reason is my husband has But weary Litill work to do And he has but
5 weary money For what he does do For his job of work he does he knows But Little About tis Allmost As bad As no work Atorl And we Cannot Shift without Lowance No Longer we would willingly try Afew weeks if you would Asist us And Send us Alitill money to help us Afew weeks untill we Can See our master Does his work Come in Again And if his
10 work Comes in Again in Afew And you Are please to Send us Alitill money to Asist us Alittil For Afew weeks I hope we Make Shift without Troubling you Gentellmen Any Furder After After my husband has Gat his order marster and his order work Again I must Leave All to him That Can do more And Buter For us then we Can Ask or thank or Are wordy to
15 Recieve Davey And Susan Rising pray Send or Come as you Can For our Destress and Trouble is Great

WRITING 5: weary money] *read* 'very [little] money'. *The foregoing* 'weary Litill' *is written in the previous line, right above* 'weary', *so the writer might have confounded the two lines at this point.*
    CIRCUMTEXT Note of answer to Mr Bryant in Halstead, 26 June 1827, requesting him to give Davey Rising £1.
    FURTHER EVIDENCE Davey Rising received occasional relief payments to the amount of £2 5s in the year from Lady Day 1826 (ERO, D/P 264/18/55, List of the out-door poor belonging to Chelmsford, for the year from Lady Day 1826 [kept among Braintree overseers' papers]).

209   From David Rivenall [in St George in the East, London] to the overseer of Chelmsford, 25 January [1827]

Jany 25

Sir

I hope you will excuse the liberty I take in adressing myself to you,
but the pressint time being so severe is the cause of my thus troubling
you I am, so curcumstanced as it respects my rent, that I shall lose my   5
goods next monday without your usseal goodness would extend so far, as
to render me a little assistance I should not trouble you were we not in the
great distress and for which act of Kindness we will ever pray
Your Ob^t St David Rivenall
Please to direct   10
to Mr Gardiners
Kings Head
Commercial Road

DATE Year from postmark.   15

210   From R[ody] Jolliff in Hertford to James Read in Chelmsford, 2 February 1827

Hertford Feby 2 1827

Sir

I should be Glad if you would be so obligeing as to send me what money
I have got comeing to me Sir I am sorry to say I have got a very bad breast
it has been coming nearly this three years and I am Nothing else to expect   5
but what it is a cancer and I am not been able to do any thing for a month
and I hope the Gentlemen will consider my affliction and send me a little
money on account as it will be a great Kindness to me please to send it as
you did before and I return you many thanks for your Kindness I remain
            Your humble Servant   10
            R Jolliff

TEXTUAL ALTERATIONS 5: else] *inserted in left-hand margin.*
RELATED CORRESPONDENCE and FURTHER EVIDENCE Rody Jolliff had received a weekly
allowance since Michaelmas 1821. The money was always sent to her niece Mrs Randel
at Hertford. Half a year after the above letter, the Revd Thomas Lloyd wrote to the overseers of Chelmsford that Rody Jolliff had died on 3 August 1827, and asked them to settle
the outstanding payments which had been advanced by her niece Mrs Randal 'who is

most justly Entitled to it for her unceasing attentions to her Aunt & who has been put to Expence in various ways in keeping her'. He also requested a contribution towards the funeral costs (letter of 12 August 1827, with note of payment at bottom: £2 sent 29 August 1827, for 24 weeks at 1s plus 6s).

211 From Mercy Poole in [St George, Hanover Square] London to [James] Read, overseer of Chelmsford, 12 February 1827

London Fabrury 12th 1827

Sir/

 your humble servent Mercy Poole Bags the faver of you to send her the Child Money up to her Every 12 week witch thar is 2 week Due lerst
5 saturday and Mercy Poole is on asike Bad and the Child is with her and she hopes you well send the Money or let her no wher I Can receve it at aney other Parish in London if you Pleas you can send it up by Mr Mourrell the Chelmsford Choch men and I hope you well not think it tow much trubel to let her no how she is to receve it as I am aservent in London and
10 ean not afored to Com Down

 Pleas to Dract for Mercy Poole ar Mr Sewell 39 south molton street oxford street Londen

 MP Bags for aletter Before long as she is very Ill and is afrad she well Be forst to Give up her Plase/   I Remane your hombel
15   servent Mercy Poole

TEXTUAL ALTERATIONS 4: Money] *interl below at end of line.* 4: Due] *after del illeg.* 7: Mourrell] *interl at end of line.* 8: the] *after del* 'Me'. 11: 39] *inserted in left-hand margin.* 11: molton] 'l' *over* 'u', 'n' *over illeg.*

FURTHER EVIDENCE Mercy Poole received a weekly allowance of 2s 6d for her illegitimate child (born about 1820) until Lady Day 1827 (ERO, D/P 94/18/55, List of the outdoor poor belonging to Chelmsford, for the year from Lady Day 1822; D/P 264/18/55, List of the out-door poor belonging to Chelmsford, for the year from Lady Day 1826 [kept among Braintree overseers' papers]).

212 From Arthur Tabrum in Christchurch, London, to J[ames] Read, vestry clerk of Chelmsford, 18 February 1827

London Feby 18th 1827

Hond Sir

 I should be much obligd to you if you would remit the Money Due for Arthur Good, we was Paid up to the 14th of Decr which on Next Saturday

will be 10 Weeks due, if you would be so kind as to send it by Mr French 5
My Wife will be at the office on Saturday Morning, I should not have
troubled you quite so soon, but this hard Weather every thing is so dear,
that we have a hard matter to struggle on

I remain
Your Humble Servt 10
Arthur Tabrum

No 2 Mitre Place
Broadwall
Christchuch
Surry London 15

TEXTUAL ALTERATIONS 6: at the] 'at t' *over* 'there'.

213 From Sarah Manning in Stratford [Essex] to James Read in Chelmsford, 19 February 1827

Startford Feb 19 1827
Mrs Manning would be much Oblige to Mr Red to send her the Children
Money as there is six Months due to day and she would be glad to have it
as soon as possible as she is been very Ill this ten weeks and is wants of
her Money 5

Sara Manning

CIRCUMTEXT Calculation from other hand at bottom, resulting in £6 17s 11d.

214 From Isaac Harridge in Newington, London, to Mr Swardley, overseer of Chelmsford, 19 March 1827

Honoured Gentlnen

London March 19th 1827
This is to Inform you I am In A Badd Situation at Present As I have Had
Scarsley anney Anney anney thing thing to Doe since, I left Chelmsford I
hope Mr Maridge and Rest <o>f the Gentlmen will Consider me Mee an 5
Object of Charity wich I hope you Gentlmen will Concider I will bee as
favourlbe as Possible I can But Please to Rember I had Six Shillings p^r
Weeke for a Long wile After I Came Out of the white House Wich I

should wish to bee as Reseble With youth you as I Can but I You Gentlmen
10 will Consder me As a Man that Doe not wish to Impose apon your Parrish
so I hope You will Consider me worthey of your Considration to alow me
my Salery As I had wich is three Shillings Per Weeke or if you Gentlmen
will Advance Few Pounds I will no More trouble to You my Wife is
Seventy there Years of Age wich You Cannot Expect but wee must be
15 Troublson to the Parrish

I Remain Youre
Isaac Harridge

Please to Direct to me at
No. 4 Colitch Place Cross Street
20 Newington Surrey London

TEXTUAL ALTERATIONS 12: if] *after del illeg.*

215 From Jane Hills in London to the overseer of Chelmsford, 28 March 1827

London March 28 1827

Sir

Please to send Mrs Hills^s money up by Mr Frenchs Coach on Saterday
wich was Due on the 25 of this month and I will be Thire to meet it
5

I Ham your
Humble Servant
Jane Hills

CIRCUMTEXT Note from other hand at bottom: £1 6s sent by Mr French, 7 April 1827.

216 From Arthur Tabrum in Christchurch, London, to James Read, assistant overseer in Chelmsford, 18 April 1827

London April 18th 1827

Hond Sir

I should be much Obligd to you for to send the Little Money that is due
for Arthur Good, if you would be so good as to send by Mr French on

Next Tuesday my wife will be there to meet the Coach I was paid up to 5
the 17th of Feby from that to the 21st of April will be 9 Weeks due,

I have been going to write to the Gentleman of the Committee several
times, to ask them to assist me to get me on to another Parish as it is not
my wish if ever any thing happened to me ever to have to trouble them, if
I had had Household Furniture of my own I would have belongd to 10
another Parish a Long while ago, if the Gentlemen think Proper to do any
thing for me, I shall go about it directly, as things are so very precarious in
London at this time, that very like in the course of another Year or two, I
may be obligated to do that I never wish to do no more, and as my Bread
lays in London I never wish to Leave it again, or become troublesome to 15
Chelmsford Parish no more if you think Propper to shew what I have
wrote or think it any use I should be much obligd to you if you would do
it

Your Humble St
A Tabrum   20

Mrs Freeman
At N° 2 Mitre Place
Broad Wall
Christ Church Surry
London   25

TEXTUAL ALTERATIONS 7: to write] *interl with caret.* 8: assist] *final 's' over 't'.* 13: time]
after del 'th'.

**217   From Mercy Poole [in London] to [James] Read, overseer of
        Chelmsford, 30 April 1827**

Aprel 30th 1827

Sir/

your humble servent Mercy Poole hops you well Be so kind as to seend
her the Childs Money up By Mr Murrel the Chelmsford Chochmen as I
am in great want of it and if you well Be so kind as to seend it up to Satday 5
next that well Be one Pown and if you well give the Money to Mr Murrel
I well Corl at his house for it and he well Bring it up quit saft

Pray sir seend it up to night if you Can for My Child is very ill with the
smorl Pox and I have not aney Money to go on with I am your humble

Servent Mercy Poole 10

TEXTUAL ALTERATIONS 8: night] 'ht' *over del* 't'. 8: you] *from* 'your' (*del* 'r'). 10: Servent] 'r' *over illeg.*

PLACE Inferred from previous and following letters from Mercy Pool (**211, 220**).

218 From David Rivenall [in St George in the East, London] to the overseer of Chelmsford, [15 May 1827]

Friday morning

Sir In Concerquence of your Not answering my last letter though the Great-est of trouble Was the Cause of my Sendin to trouble the Genteelmin I have Got the Broker in my Place and Wont leave till I Can Give him
5 Sattisfaction Wich his Not in my Power to Give I have Not the means to doe it and unless I have assistence I must apply to Saint Goergius parish and my family must Come Home to Chelmnsford the Broker Was Sent Thursday about 4o/ Clock the Expences allreadey his Run to Rather above the Pound this have Caused the Greatest disstruction in my Family let me
10 Bage of the Genteelmin to answer this and Releave me of this trouble as I am Not able to Git throu With out their assistence and hope the Genteelmin Will take it into Conciдеration and Send as Soon as Possable to Prevent the Expencis Runing Farther I have Not had any thing to Goe to markit With if I had Been able to lay in astock of things I then might have done
15 Better the trifill the Genteelmin Give me I had to Pay away and if the Genteelmin Will

Send to me I Shall be thank full as Soon as Possable as it his acase of disstress

david Rivernill Nº 3 Grove Place
20 Grove Street Commercial Road

TEXTUAL ALTERATIONS 2: letter] *interl.* 6: assistence] 'nce' *altered from* 'd'. 6: parish] 'ar' *over illeg.*

WRITING This letter was written by Michael Howe, a neighbour of David Rivenall (see **232**).

DATE Date of postmark.

219   From Isaac Betts in Mitcham, Surrey, to the overseer of Chelmsford, 17 May 1827

Mitcham 17^{May} 1827

Gentlemen

having for some time past suffered severely by Ill health the Consequence of old Age I am reduced to the Necessity of applying to you for
some pecuniary Assistance rather than come down I would - Gladly put   5
up with almost any thing I therefore hope you will not delay sending me
an answer Imeadeately as I must Otherwise Come home -

I am Gentlemen Your Ob^t

H^{bl} Servt

Isaac Betts   10

please to address -
Carpenter &c near the Swan Mitcham Surry
NB. it may be Nessary to state my age is between 77 & 78 - }

220   From Mercy Poole in London to [James] Read, overseer of Chelmsford, 18 May 1827

London May 18th 1827

Sir/

your humbel servent Mercy Poole wishes to inform you that she most
seend her Poor Child down under your Cair as I am very ill and have been
out of Place for this 4 Months and I have nothing to support us with therfore   5
if you well take Carge of her as her Pashes is in Chelmsford you well
Receve her to day By Mr Morrels Choch as I most go in the hospitle on
Mounday therfore she well have ahome but I hope you well find ahome
for her

your hunble servent 10

Mercy Poole

TEXTUAL ALTERATIONS 3: servent] 'n' *over* 't'. 3: most] 't' *interl.* 8: therfore] 'e' *interl.* 8:
she] *after del illeg.* 8: you] *inserted in left-hand margin, before del* 'she'.

221   From David Rivenall [in St George in the East, London] to the overseer of Chelmsford [18 May 1827]

to the overseers

Sir I am Not able to doe any thing for the Suport of my Family at Present and Should be thank full to have atrifil to helpe me in my Present disstress Sir the Stuff you told me of have Been a deal of Good to my foot and
5 Should be thankful to be able to doe for my family if the Genteelman Would be So Good as to Releave me With the Small Sum of one Pound I Would Not trouble them any more if I am Spard if this Should Not meet the Genteelmins approbation to let me know and I must Come home With my family as I have Not a Shoe to my foot and Was oblidged to Pay 6
10 Shillings to my landlord for Rent out of the triffil the Genteelmin Was So kind as to Give me or I must have lost all my things I Still owe him 10 Shillings Wich I must Pay him I hope the Genteelmin Will attend to me as if Would Not have Sent if I Could have done With out it

and by So doing you Will
15   oblid your Humble Servint
david Rivarnell
N° 3 Grove Place
Grove Street
Commercial Road

TEXTUAL ALTERATIONS 4: Sir] *interl*. 19: Road] *interl below at end of line*.
WRITING This letter was written by Michael Howe, a neighbour of David Rivenall (see **232**).
DATE Date of filing note on outside.

222   From Robert Griffith in Dedham [Essex] to the overseer of Chelmsford, 25 May 1827

To the Overseers & Gentlemen of the Parish of Chelmsford

Gentlemen/ I am again compelled to ask your Assistance in my Rent as I have at this time a Distress in my house for the Sum of 6£7s10d & my Goods will be sold on monday next if not paid & any portion that you
5 may think proper to send me will be thankfully received & feel myself very much obliged to you for the 1£ I received through the hands of Mr Chalk to Mr Swinborne I hope Gentlemen you will take my Case into your serious Consideration as you must think it has been a very hard one with me to have so much Affliction in my house with Wife & 4 Children

ever since a fortnight before Christmas only myself & 1 Child have 10
escaped & likewise expect my Wife to be confined next month I intended
to have come myself but a Gentleman came & took me to a house to paper
for him throughout & a Prospect of Work for some time which I hope will
enable me from troubling you more when my rent is once clear which is is
very much against my Wish troubling you & I hope Gentlemen you will 15
be so good as to let me have what you may think proper before Saturday
Afternoon 4 OClock on Sunday's Post as I shall have to go to Ipswich if
I can settle it which I pray you will assist in &

I remain Gentleman,
Your very humble Edward Moore   20
Robt Griffith

Dedham Friday 25th May
1827
P.S. My Brother will give you my Direction if by Coach

TEXTUAL ALTERATIONS 14: troubling] *interl with caret*. 15: against] *after del* 'much'.
  CIRCUMTEXT Note from other hand at bottom: 'To have a pound'.
  RELATED CORRESPONDENCE On 6 January 1827, George Witheat in Dedham had written
to Mr Baker, churchwarden of Chelmsford, on behalf of Robert Griffith 'who has requested
me to write, His living very near me enables me to speak with confidence of His Character
and earnest endeavours to maintain His family He works hard and is himself but a weakley
man added to which His Eldest daughter has been exceedingly ill this has thrown Him
back [...] He is deservedly respected here and with some assisstance will I think do'.
  FURTHER EVIDENCE Robert Griffith had received occasional relief payments to the amount
of £1 in the year ending on Lady Day 1827.

223 From Arthur Tabrum in Christchurch, London, to James Read, assistant overseer of Chelmsford, 26 May 1827

London May 26th 1827

Hond Sir
  I should be much oblidg to you if you would be so kind as to send the
allowance Due from the 14 of April to the 26th May for Arthur Good I am
sorry to trouble you soon but I have been ill a Long time and very little
help at this time, you sent no answer concerning what I wrote to you 5
about in my Last, if the Gentlemen would do any thing I mean to act
honourable in what I there said, If you will be so good as to send it next
Saturday by Mr French I should be much obligd to you

10   Your Humble St
                                                    A Tabrum

   at Mr Freemans
   No 2 Mitre Place
   Broad Wall
15 Christ Church Surry

<small>TEXTUAL ALTERATIONS 8: good] 'g' *over* 'd'.</small>

224   From Isaac Wright in St Alfege, [City of] London, to the over-
        seer of Chelmsford, 31 July 1827

                                                    Philip Lane
                                                    London Wall
                                          London July 31th 1827

   To the acting overseer of Chalmsford Paresh
5 Sir/
   Having been very bad for 6 Months Last & tossed three fingers of my
   right hand, and reduced to very low circumstances or I should not have
   troubled you - had I not been forced too it through real necessety I hope you
   will therefore lay my case before the committee - and that they will render
10 me as much assistance as possable - I was at Chelmsford on saturday the 28
   Ins^t & saw Mr Perry & Mr Cheff who informed me that my case must be
   layed befor the committee but I had not the means of remaining there until
   they meet - I hope therefore the Gentlemen of the Parish will spare me the
   expense of again returning to chelmsford. the two Gentlemen alluded too
15 will be able to inform you that I cannot do anything in my trade, I am Sir
                          your very humble & obd Servant
                                  Isaac Wright X

   address N° 9
   Philip Lane
20 London Wall   N.B. Parish of
   London   St. Alphage

<small>TEXTUAL ALTERATIONS 1: Lane] *after del* 'Wall'. 11: informed] *after del* 'will', *which had*
been interl with caret. 11: me that my] 'me' *above del* 'you' *and* 'my' *above del* 'your'.
   WRITING From other hand. The 'X' after the signature is apparently Isaac Wright's
mark.
   CIRCUMTEXT Countersigned at bottom from other hand: 'John Harley Overseer of Saint
Alphage London Wall'. Note of answer on outside, 11 August 1827, 'saying that he must
be examined to his settlement'.</small>

RELATED CORRESPONDENCE In January 1827, Isaac Wright had injured his hand through 'a cut into a joint with a Piece of Copper' and since been treated by Mr Kingdon, surgeon (certificate of 27 July 1827).

225 From David Rivenall in Cold Bath Field Prison [Clerkenwell] London, to the overseer of Chelmsford, 24 August [18]27

London August 24th 27

Gentlemin

It is with the most profound Sentiments of respect and gratitude that I take the liberty of adressing you Humbly Imploring your Charitable aid for myself and helpless distressed family at this unfortunate *period* when 5 I am deprived of my liberty or the mains of doing any thing for them - I have been labouring under the greatest distress for some time past being quite out of Employm^t, but did not wish if possible to trouble my Parish as I was in hopes that when the oyster season would commece that I should be able to get round and provide for my poor family by selling of oysters 10 in which I have been always Tolerably Lucky but Just as the season began I was taken and put in prison for a the small sum of twelve shillings and Six pence which I had no mains on earth of paying so that I now remain in Confindment and Know not what will will become of my poor wife and Childrens I have also the unhappiness to State that I have been very lead 15 in my health for a long time and are severely troubled with fits I have had several since I came to this Prison and in the Prison chapple on sunday I had a severe one and was obliged to be taken out in the middle of the service by two men Believe me *Gentlemen* that it is very painfull to me to be under the necesaty of troubling you but the want of my health being 20 deprived of my liberty and the extreme destress of my family is such that I most humbly beg of you to do something for me at this unhappy time and I shall ever feel a Just sense of gratitude for your goodness I remain Gentⁿ your ever obliged and obd^t Humble Ser^t

David Rivenell 25

Debtors yard Colebath Fields London
Please Direct to Mr Gardners
King^s Head

Comercial Road
St *Georges East* 30

For D *P[ur]mell*

TEXTUAL ALTERATIONS 14: poor] 'r' *over del illeg.*

226   From Sarah Manning in Stratford [Essex] to James Read, 28 August 1827

Stratford Essex Aug 28 1827

Mrs Manning would be Much Oblige to Mr Read to send her the Childrens Money has she has not Recvd any Since the 17 of February last and would Be glad if Mr Read would send it By Mr French on Satturday or as Soon
5   as Possible as she <is> Really in wants of the Money By so doing she will feel Greatly Oblige

Sarah Manning
Stratford

Mrs Manning will Meet the Coach on Satturday Morning Next

CIRCUMTEXT Note in pencil from other hand (possibly that of James Read, vestry clerk of Chelmsford) to complete the postscriptum (written on same line): '- Turnpike Row near the Yorkeshire Grey -'. Further note across left-hand margin: '30 weeks 17 Feby to 15 Sep^t 1827 @ 4/6 = £6.15.0'.

227   From P[hilip] Noon in Colchester to the overseers of Chelmsford, 24 September 1827

Colchester sep^t th24 1827

Sir

I take the liberty to write to you on a Curcumstance I am under the nessessity of asking your assistance that is my son Philip Noon is now in
5   Clarkenwell Prison for Entering the East India Company service and not attending there to this occurrane took place 2 years ago and was an intire secret to me till Last tuesday when an information was Leyid against him by A Man who formerly live in Chlemsford a shoemaker by the Name of Boyles who Work for Mr Wiffin therefor I hope you and the Gentleman
10   of the parish will take it into your most searious Consideration and Render me sum assistance in Gitting him of as his family is in London with out my Maintanace and his wife in a state of pregnancy I have being to London once on the /Bestins/ I went to the India House and I was there inform I Could not have his Liberty for No less then 20$^£$ ponds I will do all that in
15   my power with your assistan but I am not able to git all therefore I must Call on you in a day or two

y Humble servnt
P Noon

TEXTUAL ALTERATIONS 4: nessessity] 'ty' *interl at end of line*. 9: Work] *after del illeg*. 15: all] *after del* ' the what'.

FURTHER EVIDENCE In 1819, Philip Noon, shoemaker at Colchester, had received occasional relief to the amount of £1 (ERO, D/P 94/18/53, List of the out-door poor belonging to Chelmsford, for the year from Christmas 1819).

228 From William Holden in St Marylebone, London, to James Read in Chelmsford, 1 October 1827

London October 1st 1827

Genteelmen

I wish to state in a few Lines to you Of my sitiration wich i am sorry to say Is rather Deploreable My few things wich I Could Call Mine are now impounded to My Landlord Who is waiting the result of an Answer wether 5
this quarters pention is to Be Drawn By Me if not I wish to have your Opinion in which Way to act as i shall Have no resedence their is no altermative But I must except of Colage or Be past Home to My parish I have a letter for the Horspital But quite Deficent of every necery of Life and nothing But what i stand in keeps me from going in I have strugled 10
through 15 months Illness through the asistance Of My frinds wich will not Be in town till After Christmas My disorder is gaining fast on me and in adition I have the Rumities in the Hip Joint wich renders Me unable to do anything

I remain Genteelmen with   15

Due respect your obedent

Humble servant

Willm Holden

Edwardst portman

Square   20

Marylebone London

PS Genteelmen I trust your goodness will allow Me to draw this quarter to appease My Landlord wich i have every reason to Believe Will Be the Last

TEXTUAL ALTERATIONS 22: Me] *after del* 'to'.

CIRCUMTEXT Note from other hand in left-hand margin: 'Nothing to be done for him'.

FURTHER EVIDENCE Whatever the acting overseer had in mind, William Holden continued to receive his weekly allowance of 5s, which he had received since Michaelmas 1826, until April 1830 (ERO, D/P 94/12/36, Chelmsford overseers' accounts).

229 From Arthur Tabrum in [Christchurch] London to James Read in Chelmsford, 4 October 1827

London Octr 4th 1827

Hon Sir

I should be much obligd to you if you would remit the trifle that is due
for Arthur Good, which will be 8 Weeks on Saturday the 6th as i was paid
5 to 11 August Last but I was paid only up to the 14th of April when I
receivd 12^s for 8 Weeks, and on the Second of June I receivd 10^s 6^d for 7
Weeks therefore if you will have the Goodness to look over your Books
you will find that there is a Weeks money back on Last Decr I receivd $^£$1-^{s}1
14 Weeke money up to the 16th Day of Decr Feby 17th 16-6 9 Weeke
10 April 14th 12-6 8 Weeke June 2nd 10-6 7 Weeke Augt 4th 11th there was 10
Weeke Due and I receivd 9 Weeke money 13^s 6^d

I remain your Humble
Servt Arthur Tabrum

My Wife will come on up to the Spread Eagle on Monday to meet Mr
15 French if you will be so good to send it

TEXTUAL ALTERATIONS 8-9: $^£$1-^{s}1] *interl above* '14'. 9: 16-6] *interl above* '9'. 10: 12-6]
interl above '8'. 10: 10-6] *interl above* '7'.
CIRCUMTEXT Note of answer from other hand at bottom: 26 February 15s sent by Mr
French 'for 10 Weeks to 24 Feby he says 13^s/6^d'.
PLACE Inferred from previous and following letters from Arthur Tabrum (**223**, **234**).

230 From William Holden in [St Marylebone] London to James Read in Chelmsford, 22 October 1827

London October 22^d 1827

Genteelmen

I hope you will excuse My Beggin an answer to My letter on the first of
Octr as i am excending ill and Unable to work That you Might not think it
5 an alusion In what i stated in My fore going letter I have Troubled My
Landlord to state That i am in arears with him

I remain your Obedent
Humble
Servant Wm Holden

CIRCUMTEXT Confirmation by landlord James Walker (hand A) underneath. At bottom,
note from other hand (B): 'Not to be noticed'.

PLACE Inferred from previous letter from William Holden (228).

231   From David Rivenall in [St George in the East] London, 25 October 1827

London october 25 1827

Genteelmin I am obliged through Real distress to apply for Releaf as you Will See I dont decerve you my fits have been Such as to dissable me from Workin to keep my Family the 10 shillings you Was So kind as to leave me I Put it to the Best use I Could you are Well aware how far Such 5 a Sum of money Will Goe I Was ordrd By this Parish to Send to you the Gentleelmin Was So kind as to Give me 2 Shillings I have 7 in family With my Wife Self and No house to Be in I am distresst Beyound and all I Ever met With and hope the Genteelmin Will take this in to Considera- tion and Releave me if Not I am Come to So much disstress I must Come 10 Home With my Family if I Was Settled and had my few things I Would try and do all I Could Not to trouble you as I am much better in Helth if I had applid to you for my Rent this might have Been Prevented But I Was in hops I Could have done With out troublin you an answer to this Will be thankfulley Recevd by David Rivernell   15

Direct to Mr Howe
4 Grove S^{tr}
Commercial Road

TEXTUAL ALTERATIONS 7: 7] over '8'.
    WRITING This letter was written by Michael Howe, who lived at the same address as David Rivenall (see RELATED CORRESPONDENCE to the following letter, 232).

232   From David Rivenall [in St George in the East, London] to the overseer of Chelmsford, 31 October [1827]

October 31

Genteelmin Not Recevin an answer to my letter I feel my Self Werry much disstresst and hope you Will doe Something for me to Restore my few things again Mr Pirkins Calld on me on Tuesday and Promised me if I Could Pay him a Pound in Part he Would take the Remaining Part at 5 Sixpence atime I have Not it in my Power to Pay him and hope you Will take it into Consideration and answer this and doe Something for my disstresst family his my Sincer and Earnist dissire

David Rivernell

4 Grove Street

TEXTUAL ALTERATIONS 6: atime] *after del* 'at'.
DATE Year from postmark.
RELATED CORRESPONDENCE On 5 November 1827, Michael Howe in London wrote to the overseers of Chelmsford (same hand as six letters from David and Sarah Rivenall from May 1827 until July 1828: **218, 221, 231, 232, 239** and **244**): 'Jenteelmin knowin david Rivernalls distress, I advanced him the money to Releave his things and Shall be Glad if you Would have the Goodness to Convay it to me by Mʳ Murrell that drive Mʳ Frenches Coach as I Shall Want it as Soon as Possable I did it as I Could Not Bare to See Such Real distress and hope you Wont fail to Send it by So doing you Will obleidge me'. On 23 October 1827, the goods of David Rivenall had been distrained by his landlord Mr Perkins to cover arrears in rent of £1 17s (inventory on printed form, kept among overseers' correspondence).

233   From Hugh Constable in Halstead [Essex] to James Read in Chelmsford, 23 November 1827

Halsted Novʳ 23ʳᵈ 1827

Sir

I hope you will not be offended at my troubling you concerning an affair that I wish very much to have settled I am under the nessesity of writing to you on Susan Risons account who I am sorry to Say is Likely to be confined in a Short time and I am very willing to Marry her but am quite unable to defray the expences of marrying or Getting a few Household Goods I am published to the young woman and have been some time and if the Gentlemen will advance a little money to finish furnishing a place it is my intention to marry if I possibly can raise Sufficient money I wish to have an answer before the young woman swears it as I do not wish to put you at any trouble and thought best to consult you about it as it will take the young woman quite off your hands an answer to this will much oblige your

Hugh Constable

Please to direct
For Hugh Constable
near the Bull
Halsted Essex

PS if the Gentlemen think proper they may send the money over by a 20
person who may see us married as any day will be convenient to me but it
must be shortly or the young woman will be obliged to come to Chelmsford

TEXTUAL ALTERATIONS 10: it] *after del* 'and'.
RELATED CORRESPONDENCE and FURTHER EVIDENCE Susan Rison alias Rising was the daughter
of Davey and Susannah Rising in Halstead. She had had an illegitimate son from William
Newton in Halstead. The child had been born on 20 February 1825 and died on 20 October 1826 (ERO, D/P 94/12/36, Chelmsford overseers' accounts). On the next day, James
Cardinal in Halstead had written to James Read, vestry clerk of Chelmsford, that Susan
Rising needed assistance for his funeral. Newton had been required to repay Chelmsford
the allowance they gave Susan Rising for her child. Apparently he had run into trouble
with the parish for not paying regularly, for on 29 March 1825 he had written to Chelmsford, requesting that his 'business' with Susan Rison be settled by the payment of £4 2s
without appearing before the Quarter Sessions.

234   From Arthur Tabrum in Christchurch, London, to James Read in Chelmsford, 28 November 1827

London Novr 28th 1827
Sir
I should be much obligd to you for the trifle that is due for Arthur Good
from the 6 Octr to next Saturday will be 8 Weeks, I have had a very Bad
accident by a fall and have been under the Docters hands ever since Last 5
Monday Fortnight, and not able to go to Work, and When I can do no
work there is no Money for me, If you would be so kind as to ask the
Committee for a five Shillings to help me at this time I should be very
thankful If any one doubts my words in respect to my Accident, or of my
wants, if they will apply to Dr Bridgman Stamford Street Blackfriars Road 10
he will fully satisfy there Enquiries or if you would be so kind as to advanc
me 2 or three Months of the Boys Money I should be very thankful, My
Wife will meet Mr French on next Monday if you will be so kind as to
send
    I remain your   15
    Humble St
    Arthur Tabrum
N° 2 Mitre Place
Broad Wall
Christ Church   20
Surry

CIRCUMTEXT Note from other hand at bottom of first page: '13ˢ/6ᵈ by Mʳ French on the 2ⁿᵈ
Decʳ to 8ᵗʰ Decʳ'.

**235   From Hugh Constable in Halstead [Essex] to the governor of
the poor house of Chelmsford, 2 December 1827**

Halstead Decr 2 1827

Sir

I take the liberty of writing to you *[concerning]* Susanah Rising as I
Received no answer to the one that I sent on the 26 but I hope that you
will answer this as soon as posible as the Overseer of this Parish say
5 unless we are married she will be forced to sware it on Friday next and so
I wish for an answer before then as I think it will save you the trouble of
coming after me that is if you will do as i stated in the letter that I have
allready sent you and I think that my Request is very Reasonable as for I
Shall take her wholely of of you hand and if you Dont think proper to
10 consent to it I Shall not trouble my self no Farther if you will be so good
as to answer this buy the 6 I shall be much oblight to you
        I Remⁿ your
        Humble Servant
        Hugh constable
15 Direct for Hugh constable Near the BUll Halstead

TEXTUAL ALTERATIONS 8: after me that is] 'that is' *interlined between* 'after' *and* 'me'. 9:
for] *unclear whether* 'for' *has been ruled out.*
    TEXT The letter of 26 (November 1827) referred to at the beginning has not been traced.
Presumably Hugh Constable confused it with that of 23 November 1827 (**233**).

**236   From Isaac Wright in [St Alfege, City of] London to the over-
seer of Chelmsford, 10 December 1827**

London, December 10 1827

Sir

In consequence of the money I was allowed being expended, I am under
the necessity of again applying to the Parish, I have done the best in my
5 power to live upon 5 shillings a week for myself and wife, with the trifle
that I earn at fitting Tea Kettle Handles, &c which amounts to 3 or 4
shillings weekly,

Your's &c
Isaac Wright

PLACE Parish inferred from letter from Isaac Wright of 31 July 1827 (**224**).
FURTHER EVIDENCE In the year from Lady Day 1828, Isaac Wright received occasional relief to the amount of £1 (ERO, D/P 36/28/3, List of the out-door poor belonging to Chelmsford, for the year from Lady Day 1828 [kept among Great Coggeshall overseers' papers]).

237　From Robert Tapple in Ipswich to the overseer of Chelmsford, [30 December 1827]

Ipswich

Gentlemen

I lay Under the Nescessity of writng to you Respecting My Mother In law which Is now Rezedeing with me and she have not aney work to do As such She Is in great Distress and we hope You Gentlemen be so good　5
as to allow her a Trifle to live on with her daughter In Ipswich and if not she will be obidged to fling herself on One of thase Parishes And be Past home And If you will allow the widow Susan Jefferson Something She now live In Mary Elms Parish Near the Black Hors - - -
Answear from these few Lines Is required As Soon as you Can　10
I Am your Robt Topple

TEXTUAL ALTERATIONS 3: writng] 't' *interl*. 6: daughter] 'ter' *interl at end of line*. 7: obidged] *final* 'd' *interl at end of line*.
CIRCUMTEXT Filing note on outside: 'Tapple'.
DATE Date of postmark.
RELATED CORRESPONDENCE On 12 March 1828, the overseer of St Nicholas, Ipswich, wrote to Chelmsford that Susan Jefferson (aged 65) was in need of relief.

238　From Arthur Tabrum in Christchurch, London, to James Read, assistant overseer of Chelmsford, 31 March 1828

London March 31 1828

Hond Sir

I should be much obligd to you if you would remit to me the trifle of Money that is due for Arthur Good I was paid up to the 16th of February and to next Saturday will be 7 Weeke due if you will be so kind as to send　5

it on Next Monday I should be much obligd to you and my Wife will be
there to meet Mr French

I remain Your
Humble St

10

Arthur Tabrum

N° 2 Mitre Place
Broad Wall
Christ Church
Surry

**239   From David Rivenall in [St George in the East] London to the
overseer of Chelmsford, 4 April 1828**

London April 4th 1828

Genteelmin once more I am under the Real Necessity of troubling you as
I am Severley afflicted With my fits I am Not able to Git my living by
Real Hard Worke I am Perswaded by Severil Genteelmin In the Commer-
5 cial Road to deal in fish as I am Compleat master of that Bussness and
they Will doe all in their Power to Encourage me as I have Been So many
years in the Road Mr Dinch have Promised No one Shall Have a Stall
against me my 2 Boys are at Place I have 3 to Keep and my Helth his
Werry Bad or I would Not trouble you I Wish you to understand I Cannot
10 Git into this Way unless the Genteelmin Will Send me Something to
Begin With I think I Shall doe Well in that line as So many Genteelmin
Wish me to try and Promis to Encourage me I hope this his the last favour
I Shall ask and Hope the Genteelmin Will Send me an answer as Something must be done I am Not able to doe for my Family Sittuated as I am
15 and Shall Relie on your favourable answer as I Should be thankfull to Git
into a Better Way of living at the Present I am in a Starvin State and my
Children are Naked in a manner of Speakin your answer Genteelmin Will
be thankfully Recevd by your Humble Servant David Rivernell

Grove Place Grove S^t

20

Commercial Road

TEXTUAL ALTERATIONS 1: 4] *over* '3'. 16: Starvin] 'r' *over illeg.*
    WRITING This letter was written by Michael Howe, a neighbour of David Rivenall (see
232).

**240   From Mr Manning in Stratford [Essex] to [James] Read, ves-
       try clerk of Chelmsford, [14 May 1828]**

Stratford Essex

Mrs Manning will feel greatly obligid to Mr Read laying this letter before
the Comitee of Chelmsford Parish when they Meet to let them Know that
since they have takeing the pay of that he has being in the Habit of Recveing
for the Support of his Wife Child a Boy he Wishes to let the Gentleman   5
Know that he Cannot afford to Keep him without Some allowanc as he has
got a young Family of his own to provide for that he would be Oblige to the
Gentleman if they would take it in Consideration and place him out so that
he may be Enabled to get his future living or Else he will be Oblige to send
him to them to take Care off has he has no Employment nor Cannot get any   10
for him to doo by so doing he would Be v[er]y thankfull

                                                          Maning Blacksmith
                                                                  Stratford
                                                                     Essex

                                                                              15
TEXTUAL ALTERATIONS 9: send] *interl.*
DATE Date of postmark.

**241   From Samuel White in Halstead [Essex] to James Read, vestry
       clerk in Chelmsford, 21 May 1828**

                            Halsted May 21 1828
Sir/
       Haveing been favoured with Pretty good health in my own Person and
Family I have not made any application to my Parish for about sixteen
Months and if Providence had Continued the Blessing I would still have   5
kept from so doing - but I am sorry to inform you that I am ill and unable
to work I have been Poorly for serveral weeks but Continued to work till
the Doctor informed me I should not get better till I left off - I am in a
Clubb and receive 10/6 per week but that is not near enough for the support of eight of us - especialy as I am recommended by the Docter to take   10
nourishing things which it will be the interest of the Parish to enable me to
get that I may be the sooner restored to health and strength any sum the
select vestry may be Pleased to allow me till that Period will be thankfully
received by Sir your

15   Humble Servant
                                                          Sam¹ White

Mr Wyatt will Pay me any sum you Please to order

TEXTUAL ALTERATIONS 4: application] *after del* 'any'. 6: ill and] *interl with caret*.
CIRCUMTEXT Note from Benjamin Gilson, surgeon, at bottom of page: 'The above representation of Sam¹ Whites case is correct'.

242   From Samuel White in Halstead [Essex] to James Read in Chelmsford, 30 May 1828

                                                          Halsted May 30 = 1828
Sir/

I have seen your Letter to Mr Wyatt this Day in which you are so good as to order me a sovereign for which I return my sincere thanks and
5 inform you that I am better and my work being easeer in summer than winter I began to Do a little yesterday and through your kindness hope to be able to Continue - my own age is 39 years my wife 35 my eldest Daughter Elizebeth 13 of a weakly Constitution and I fear Consumptive Thomas aged 8 Maria 6 Martha 4 Henry Kirk 3 and Hannah 1 Year and a Quarter
10 and not able to bear more on her feet than when first born my wife also about 6 Months towards another which with the effects of her Paralattic attack Prevents her been able to earn any thing
                                  I remain sir your obliged Humble Servant
                                                          Sam¹ White

TEXTUAL ALTERATIONS 5: easeer] *final* 'e' *over illeg*. 9: Henry] 'n' *over del illeg*. 9: Hannah] 'na' *over del* 'ah'.
FURTHER EVIDENCE In the year from Lady Day 1829, Samuel White received relief payments to the amount of £2 (ERO, D/P 36/28/3, List of the out-door poor belonging to Chelmsford, for the year from Lady Day 1828 [kept among Great Coggeshall overseers' papers]).

243   From William Holden in Middlesex Hospital [St Marylebone, London] to the overseer of Chelmsford, 2 June 1828

                                                          Middlesex Hospital
Sir

at the time Mʳ Reed called on me it was out of my power to go to the Office But I have Since then been Removed to this Hosp¹ & have Suffered

much from indisposition Since I have wrote to the Board concerning it 5
And they have forwarded me two Certificates by Coach Please let me
know if you have Received the money If not I have an Opportunity of
getting Any Certificates Signed by one of Mary-le-bone Magistrates Who
attend this Hosp¹ as Treasurer your Answer as soon as possible Will Much

Oblige Sir   10

your Most Obᵗ
Servant
William Holden

June 2nd 1828
Please pay the Postage when you write to me   15

WRITING Professional hand.

RELATED CORRESPONDENCE William Holden received a pension from the Office of Ordnance which was claimed by the overseers of Chelmsford towards the defrayment of their
relief expences. However, Holden was apparently not prepared to accept that. Writing on
his behalf, Messrs Greenwood & Castle in London addressed the overseers of Chelmsford concerning the pension for the last quarter of 1827 and the first quarter of 1828,
wondering 'if it will require the whole of the mans pension for the above periods to satisfy
your claim, as the Pensioner seems to be in a distressed state', and suggesting that 'some
arrangement consequently should be made if possible to give him a portion of the pension' (letter of 13 March 1828, with postscriptum: 'You will be so good as to return us the
mans letter'). Two months later, the Office of Ordnance answered a letter from the vestry
clerk of Chelmsford of 7 May 1828 in which he had stated that the parish was unable to
obtain William Holden's pension even though the payment had been directed 'in consequence of his having suffered his wife and children to become chargeable to the parish'.
It was said that according to 59 Geo III, c. 12 s. 31 'the man's affidavit and receipt is
required to be produced in proof of his being alive and entitled to the pension' and that for
the time being 'all the assistance the Board can legally afford the parish is to continue to
withhold the pension' (letter of 21 May 1828).

**244   From Sarah Rivenall in [St George in the East] London to the
overseer of Chelmsford, 3 July [1828]**

London July 3ᵗʰ

Genteelmin I am truly Sorrey to trouble you again But I have No means of
doing for my family any longer for my Husband have his fits So bad I
Cannot doe any thing With him and last Night he Was Quite delaries this
morning he his much Worse I have Got him into the london Hosppittle I 5
did for him as long as I Could But have No other means But applying to
you or this parrish as my Children are in a Starvin Condition and hope
you Will Send me Some Releaf as I dont think he Will Come out a live I

hope Genteelmin you Wont fail to help me as I have Stated my Real Case
10 to you and shall Expect your answer as Soon as Possable pray dont fail to
send to me as I Cannot Sup*/sist/* any longer With out your Help I doe
Earnestly Bage for my dear Childrens Sake you Will Send Soon as I am
disstresst to the uttermost

Sarah Rivenell
15 Grove Place Commercial
Road

TEXTUAL ALTERATIONS 5: london] *final* 'n' *interl at end of line.* 11: Sup*/sist/*] 'sist' *interl at end of line.*
CIRCUMTEXT Year from filing note on outside.
WRITING This letter was written by Michael Howe, a neighbour of David and Sarah Rivenall (see **232**).

245   From Arthur Tabrum in Christchurch, London, to James Read, assistant overseer of Chelmsford, 10 July 1828

London July 10th 1828
Sir
I should be much obligd to you for the trifle that is due for Arthur Good
from the 23rd of May to 12th of July just 7 Weeks if you will be so kind as
5 to send by M[r] French on Monday My Wife will be there to receive it

I remain Your
Humble St
Arthur Tabrum

N° 2 Mitre Place
10 Broad Wall
Christ Church
Surry

246   From Samuel Hearsum in St Marylebone, London, to the overseers and parish officers of Chelmsford, [11] July 1828

To the overseers and offises of the Parish of
Chelmsford
Sheweth that I Samuel Hearsum late of the Little farm of Moulsum Common rated Fifty Pounds a year have Lost in the year 1813 and Optained

my Livlyhood by Labour in the Regents Park untill afflicted with a fill of 5
apable etery the 12 of May 1820 and near 76 years of Age which renders
me incable of geting a Livelyhood, Should be very Thankfull for a small
Trifle of Money If it is only 2 Shillings per week, and am Gentlemen your
most Humble Obedeint Servant.

Sam¹ Hearsum 10

July 1828 26 Stattford Street
Lisson grove
St. Marylebone

CIRCUMTEXT At bottom four signatures (W. J. Hutchins, Charles Chambers, Lloyd, William
Holland), the first one being that of the curate of Christ Church, St Marylebone. Note of
answer, 25 July 1828, on outside, 'desiring him to send down his examination'.
DATE Day from filing note on outside.
FURTHER EVIDENCE Possibly as a consequence of this letter, Samuel Hearsum received a
weekly allowance of 2s from August 1828 to Midsummer 1830 (ERO, D/P 94/12/36,
Chelmsford overseers' accounts).

**247 From John Wybrow in Lambeth, London, to [James] Read in
Chelmsford, 18 August 1828**

Lambeth Augest 18 1828

Sir
I have Made free to Trouble you and the Rest of the Gentlemen With a
few Lines to Inform you that I am Not In Constent Employe and By that
Means I Cannot Come Down to Take My Wife Up to London at present 5
for I Do Not now from Wone Weak to a Nother But I Shall Be Oute of
Work and have to Come Down to Chelmsford My Self for Work Is Like
to Be very Scase Heare
Sir If any thing Is Required of Me By the Gentelmen Pleas to Be so
Kind anuf to Send Me a few Lines By the Poast 10
NB Pleas to Drect to My Son John Wybrow Chain Maker at Nᵒ 14
Lambeth Mark and he Will Lett Me Know
from Yours John Wybrow Cooper

TEXTUAL ALTERATIONS 6: a] *inserted in left-hand margin.* 6: of] *interl.* 9: so] *interl.* 11: NB]
inserted in left-hand margin.
SPELLING 12: Mark] *mistaken for* 'Walk'.
FURTHER EVIDENCE Some time after this letter, John Wybrow must indeed have come to
Chelmsford, for on the list of out-door poor for the year from Lady Day 1828 he is
recorded as living in Chelmsford workhouse and having received occasional relief payments to the amount of 17s (ERO, D/P 36/28/3, List of the out-door poor belonging to

Chelmsford, for the year from Lady Day 1828 [kept among Great Coggeshall overseers' papers]). In 1819, he had received occasional relief payments of 17s (D/P 94/18/53, List of the out-door poor belonging to Chelmsford, for the year from Christmas 1819).

248   From Isabella Weeden in [St George in the East] London to James Read in Chelmsford [3 September 1828]

N° 10 Forton St Commercial R^d

London

Mr Read

Sir.

5   I have wrote to inform you that my boy George his getting worse every day at this time my Life is not safe therefore shall expect he will be taken away Immediatly I am very unwell having kept my bed for five weeks & he being along with me makes it very unsafe your attention will oblidge

Your Obediant S^t

10   Issabella Weeden

DATE Date of filing note on outside.

249   From David Rivenall [in London Hospital, Whitechapel, London] to the overseer of Chelmsford, 12 September 1828

Sep^{tr} 12 1828

Gentlemen of the Parrish of Chelmsford David Rivenall Sends these few lines to inform you that he now here in the London Hospital Under the Cure of Dr Frampton on account of having my fits so bad ever Since the

5   Last Letter I sent to you I hope Gentlemen you will have the Kindness to Send me A trifle to Help to Surport my wif and three Children for they are in bad State for Clothing Gentlemen I Could get my two Girls Places if you would Send them a pair of Shoese a Peace

the Place of

10   Direction

At Mr Gardner Kings head

Commarcile Road

TEXTUAL ALTERATIONS 4: on account of having my fits so bad] *interl in two lines.* 11: head] *interl at end of line.*

250   From Thomas Smith Carritt [in London] to James Read in Chelmsford, 13 September 1828

L<ondo>n 13 September 1828

Mr Reed

Sir/

I have been unfortunate hitherto in not being enabled to get into employ - and my funds are quite expended - I have Frinds in 3 or 4 places who 5 promise to do something for me - & I do hope in afew days some one of them will be enabled to get me into some Kind of employment - I trust you will be Kind enough to assist me in the Money way - I will await the Arrival of Mr Frenchs Coach on monday morning - when you can either give the money to the Coach Man or make a parcel of it - I will write you 10 again in time for the Committe on thursday - could you see Mr Bacon - he had something in view for me

I am Sir Your m^t ob^t Ser^t

Tho Smith Carritt

251   From David Rivenall in London Hospital [Whitechapel, London] to the overseer of Chelmsford, 20 September [1828]

London Horspitel Se^p 20th
John^s Ward

Gentelmen

I ham Sorey that i ham Under the Nesetey Of trubling you for Sum Relefe and as i have Not Been abel to do aney work for this larst 3 mounths 5 and my famley Are Verey bad of for the want of a littel Assistenc to perches a fue things from Market From which thay would be abel to do for their Selves Thearefore Gentelmen i hope you will Take it into Considarration as Soon as porsibel or otherwaes My wife will be Obliged to aply to the Parish whare she Now lives, Sir i ham a del Better then i was 10 and i hope in a Short time i Shall Be Abel to Doe for them my Self as before

I Remain your Humbel Servent

David Rivenall

TEXTUAL ALTERATIONS 5: as] *interl with caret.*
DATE Year from date of circumtext.

CIRCUMTEXT Confirmation from apothecary at London Hospital on next page, saying that David Rivenall has been admitted as an in-patient, and that his case is 'strongly recommended' for 'an early consideration'.

252   From S[amuel] White in Halstead [Essex] to James Read, vestry clerk of Chelmsford, 3 October 1828

Halsted Octr 3 = 1828

Sir/

Haveing had within the last fortnight an addition to my family, together with the rapid advance of Flour I am again Compeled to make an applica-
5 tion for some releif we have now nine in the Family and a - nurse in the House - my eldest Daughter who is now fit for service is (much against her inclination) obliged to keep at home on account of my wives inability to Do for the Family as our Child more than a year & half old is still unable to stand alone - I hope the Gentlemen will Consider my Case and
10 send me something to Defray the exspence of Docter and Nurse, and if flour gets Dearer I shall be obliged to apply for some regular allowance as I am quite unable to feed and Clothe so many by my own earnings - I am sir your Humble Servt

S White

TEXTUAL ALTERATIONS 3: addition] *first* 'd' *interl with caret.* 5: for some] 'for so' *over del illeg.* 11: to] *inserted.* 12: I am quite] 'I' *over del* 'as'.

253   From Thomas Smith Carritt in Cambridge to James Read in Chelmsford, 14 October 1828

Cambridge 14th Octr 1828

Mr Reed Sir

By laying this before the Committe on Thursday you will much oblidge

Your mot obt Sert

5   Tho. S. Carritt

To the Chairman & the Members of the select Vestry

Gentlemen

Mr Reeds of the 19th Ultimum with 10/- I duly received and for which I return You my most sincere thanks - I should have been in Chelmsford as
10 therein express'd but got into employ - I left Chelmsford on September

5th from which time to the 26th I had not an oppertunity of earning a
shilling a period of three weeks

I then went to Gravesend, and should have wrote you from there on the
tuesday previous to the last Committe day but had not oppertunity - being
engaged in Stock taking from 6 OClock in the morning untill past twelve   15
at night - I left Gravesend on a Saturday afternoon for London and came
off to this place on sunday morning how long my continunance may be
here I cannot at present say - nor do I yet Know what my salary will be
wither 21/- 25/- or more per week that depending upon circumstances -
but soon as I can come to an Arrangement with Mr Tarrant I shall send   20
Mrs Carritt all I can possibly spare - and if I can get into permanent employ
I will if possible get off the parish books intirely - Mrs C. writes me her
allowance is *all* taken off - Gentlemen you cannot but come to the conclusion, if you seriously think - it is a great cruelty - she has not means
sufficent to get them bread - it is a heart rending sight to see her children   25
starving around her, in a Christian Country & in a Land of plenty -

I do hope and trust that you will enable her to buy Bread for her little
ones untill I shall have it in my power to send her assistance - surely
Benevolence, Charity, and all the better feelings of the Christian, have
not taken a retrograde motion in Chelmsford -   30

I am Gentlemen Your mo ob^t hble Servt

Thomas S. Carritt

**254   From Thomas Smith Carritt in Cambridge to James Read in
Chelmsford, 26 October 1828**

Cambridge 26th Octo^r 1828

Gentlemen

It gives me much pleasure and satisfaction in announcing to you - that as
long as I am in employ - we shall be ennabled to get off and Keep off the
Parish Funds - for past assistance (*which was not applied for unnicessarily*)   5
I have to beg the Committe to accept my most grateful and sincere thanks

I am

Gentlemen

Your most obt Ser^t

Tho. Smith Carritt   10

255   From Sarah Manning in Stratford [Essex] to [James] Read, vestry clerk of Chelmsford, 27 October 1828

October 27 1828

Mrs Manning has wrote to Mr Reed to have the Goodness when the Comittee Meets to let them Know that her husband is been bad for 10 Week and Not been able to doo any thing worth Speaking for a living and
5   that they Must doo something for her Boy as he has Not Got any thing to doo to earn any thing and she Cannot Support him and would be Oblige by the Gentleman allowing her something for his Maintenance by so doing she will Feel very thankfull

Sarah Manning
10
Stratford Essex

256   From Mary Mason in [Stepney] London to the overseer of Chelmsford, 21 November 1828

London November the 21 1828

Gentelmen with sorrow I lay my distreced Case before you and implore you to take it into your concideration and render us Asistance at this time as my Hursband W^m S Mason have been wary bad ever since Mitchalmas
5   have had the Typus fevor and it have left him in sutch A weak state that he cannot walk Alone and as his Afliction have been so long I have expanded all that I have therefore I must beg for Asistance from you as we have not gained aney settlement aney were since we left Chelmsford and my Hursband is so bad that he cannot be removed neither can I leave
10   him therfor Gentelmen I hope you will send us sum surpo/rt/ untill my Hursband is better which I fear will be A long time as we have nothing to subsist on but what few things we had if not I must apply to the Pirrish we live in but would not wish to do as we live in Lumehouse feilds East feild Streeat No 36 near Stepney Chirch and I am Gentelmin
15
your humble survant
Mary Mason

TEXTUAL ALTERATIONS 1: the] *above* '21'.

CIRCUMTEXT Confirmation by attending surgeon at bottom.

RELATED CORRESPONDENCE On 8 July 1824, Charles Carron, vestry clerk of Stepney, London, had written to the overseer of Chelmsford, saying that John Mason had become ill and inquiring whether the parish was prepared to reimburse any relief payments advanced to him. The note of answer from Chelmsford is apt: 'Pay the Pauper as if your own & let us know & send acc^t'.

257 From David Rivenall in St George in the East, London, to the overseer of Chelmsford, 22 November 1828

London 22^d Novr 1828

Gentlemen

I am sorry that my particular distress forces me to trouble you for relief as I am very ill and not able to do any work for this long time which has caused me to be in the greatest distress and misery having a wife and three 5
Children and nothing to support them with - - my wife has been the only means of Our support for this long time by keeping a little stall in the street of the Commercial Road selling fruit and other little things but is now prevented by the interference of the Police Officers who will not allow it so that I am now Quite destitute which the enclosed Order will 10
more particulary give proof to what I have stated, - I have two Little Girls One ten & the Other Eleven years of age which I could to service but am prevented for want of Clothing as they are nearly naked and to add to my distressing situation the broker has Come in to seize what little things I have got for arrears of Rent, but seeing my distress as given me another 15
week to try if I can get them some money as I am in arrear 12^s/- Gentlemen I hope you will take into your Kind Consideration and send me some relief and if it is not thought proper - to be soo good as to send me word how I shall do to remove my self and family to Come down into the Parish House, as some thing must be done immediately if God pleases to 20
restore my health, and I had the two little Girls off my hands I think that me & wife would be able to do for ourselves & the Child, provided we could Obtain some assistance for the present - and hope should not be troublesome any longer - Gentlemen I have delayed applying to you as long as I positively Could until hunger & extreme want has forced me for 25
which I am very sorry

I remain
Gentlemen
Your Very Obed^t Humble S^t
David Rivenall 30

NB please to write me answer directed to the Kings Head Commercial Road St Georges East London -

258   From William and Mary Mason in [Stepney] London to the overseer of Chelmsford, 30 November 1828

London November the 30 1828

Gentilmen I receivd your kind letter where in you was so good as to say you would send me A sovren by Mr French which I acknowledge the recept of the same but yet am sorry that I should have to trouble you but as
5 Mr Masons Afliction have been so wary great that I could not doe aney longer as I rote to Mr Poarter to remit me sum Money on my dividand but he would not or I should not have troubled you and it will be sum time before he can do aney work as yet but will doe with as little as possible from you and as you was please to menchen the doctors bill he had no
10 right to say aney thing of the kind as I have paid for near all the medicine as I had them and I hope I shall not have to trouble you A bove once more therfore Gentilmen I will trust our selfs on your goodniss and with our dutey to you for your kind attencion to our distress and conclud and we remain your humble servants
15 W^m S and Mary Mason

TEXTUAL ALTERATIONS 1: the] *above* '30'. 2: as] *after del* 'sta'. 8: as yet] *inserted in left-hand margin, after del illeg at end of previous line*. 8: doe] *interl*. 12: trust] *after del illeg*. PLACE Parish inferred from previous letter from Mary Mason (**256**).

259   From Sarah Manning in Stratford [Essex] to [James] Read, vestry clerk of Chelmsford, 4 December 1828

Stratford Dec 4th 1828

Mrs Manning would be glad if Mr Reed would send her the Childrens Money as she really wants it she also begs to Say that she and her Biggest Girl is very Ill with and Inflamation and Oblige both of them to Keep
5 there Bed and are under the Doctors hands and have been for this last Month and her husband being out of Employment and her Son have Nothing to doo to bring in any thing for a living therefore she Must have some Support for the Children therefore as a Mother she thinks it her Duty to let the Comittee Know how she and the Children are Suitated as they belong
10 to that Parish and they Must take Care of them for it is not in her Power by so doing she will be very thankfull   Sarah Manning

TEXTUAL ALTERATIONS 3: and] *after del* 'is'. 9: Comittee] *interl*.

**260   From Arthur Tabrum in Christchurch, London, to James Read,
overseer of Chelmsford, 23 December 1828**

London Decr 23rd 1828

Hon^d Sir

I should be much obligd to you if you would remit the Money that is
due for Arthur Good which will be 6 Weeks on Saturday Next, and should
be much obligd to you if you would speak when the Committee meets 5
again, about him as my Family is increasing I find it very hard to support
him, and unless they can afford me something to find him in Cloths so
that I may make him a little decent to get him into a Place off my Hands I
must and will send him down on the Parishs Hands, as I am not able to do
it myself, as he gets a great Boy now and if some means are not taken to 10
get him some where I am afraid worse will become of him, therefore his
Mother & myself are determined to send him if the Gentlemen of the
Parish do not think Proper to do something for him as it takes more to
keep him now than it does myself, and as for Clothes I can hardly find my
own I have done my Duty by him ever since he was born as you may say, 15
and I am sorry to say I cannot do it any Longer If you will be so good as
to speak or shew what I have wrote I should be much obligd to you, and if
nothing is done I shall get him Passd Home to his Parish If you will send
on Next Monday By Mr French and send me an answer as soon as you can

You will Much blige 20
Your Humble St
Arthur Tabrum

No 2 Mitre Place
Broad Wall
Christ Church Surry   25
London

**261   From Harriet Twin in Glemsford, Suffolk, to [James] Read,
overseer of Chelmsford, 31 December 1828**

Suffolk
Gelmsford Decr 31st 1828

Sir/

This is to inform you of the death of Mr Twin on the 22^d of Decr and the
Consequence of that death is that I am reduced to the very lowest, having 5

not sufficient to defray the funeral Exspence am obliged to part with some
of my Effects, and am now involved in debt for the carriage of the sams
from Chelmsford to this place, Doc^{tr} Mr Crumers bill is not paid and two
or three other persons are in exspectation of receiving remittances from
10 me which I am sorry to say is not in my power to send, you are aware of
my family 4 Children oldest 8 years next 4 and one not 2 years old the
baby is only 8 weeks old, you also know that we belong to Chelmsford,
and my insufficency of supporting these 4 Children and my self with out
assistance from the Parish if you do not send me some relief, shall apply
15 to this parish to be brought to Chelmsford for maintenance, having no
other source you may asurtain of Mr Crumer and Mr Barnes at Lion &
Lamb that we belong to Chelmsford and I am entirely destitude of money
to procure the necessaries of life Trusting you will make my Case known
to the Gentlemen and send me some relief immidiately as there is no relief
20 for me from the Board of Excise, as soon as death takes place all is ended,
and it is well known that My Husbands Sallary was dropt on the 3 of
September last and we living up to 22 of Decr as we could without any
thing earning in his protracted Illness increased as much that we were
quite reduced and Chelmsford such an enormous dear place we thought to
25 remove to this his native place, and if it had pleased God to have spared
him should have had a pension but he is taken away before that pension
was fixed, and I and family at the mercy of Chelmsford
                    Hoping you will receive this statement
                    as true I remain Yours Respectfully
30   H Twin
                            Glemsford
I hope You will answer this immediately

TEXTUAL ALTERATIONS 6: some] *after del illeg.* 8: Doc^{tr}] *interl.* 16-17: Lion & Lamb] *interl
below with bow.*

262   From David Rivenall in [St George in the East] London to the
    overseer of Chelmsford, 12 January 1829

                                        London 12th Jany 1829
Gentlemen
    I return you my most sincere thanks for your kind remittance of One
Pound which I rec^d By the Coachman Mr French which did give me and

family great relief it is now two months ago an I am sorry to inform you   5
that my little stock is again exhaust[ed] as our family has had nothing else
to support us on up to this time

Gentleman I have Obtained a place to stay and sell a few Articles [a]tt
the Corner of Union Street Commercial Road provided you would again
assist me to raise a little stock which you may depend upon me making 10
the best of it in my little way as to making it hold out as long as possible
I can I am obliged to remark to you since I last troubled you that I have
been Obliged to sell my bed from under me to Pay my rent Otherwise I
should have lost bed stead and all I am likewise almost naked without
scarce a shoe to my foot I am in the geatest distress that any poor man & 15
family can possibly be in and Gentleman as for the truth and Correctness
of my statement I refer you to my landlord Mr Perkins Little Turner Street
Commercial Road which I hope you will be so Kind as to ascertain in
Order that I may meet with more speedy relief from my present unhappy
and misserable state please to Consider my and send me an answer with 20
some Relief as speedy as possible in whatever shape you may think most
proper

> I am Gentleman your
> most Obd^t Humble Servt
> David Rivenall   25

Please to direct
to the Kings Head
Commercial Road

TEXTUAL ALTERATIONS 6: has] 'h' *over* 'ar'.
  SPELLING 8: [p]tt] *read* 'at' *or* 'past'.
  CIRCUMTEXT Note from other hand on outside: 'to have a Sovereign'.

263   From William Holden in Western Hospital [St Marylebone, London] to [James] Read, overseer in Chelmsford, [10 February 1829]

Western Hospital Nutford place
  Sir
Mr Read I Beg you would present these few lines to the parish athorites
that they would Be plesed or advised means for me to Come home to
Chelmsford - as it is not in my pour to defray the expences of My Jurney   5
as i am not able to walk one mile of the Way I Must Leve this place on

friday next the 13 instant and i am totley Unprowided with Lodgins and Must be under the necesity of proceiding Home emeditley as the Doctors Can do no more for Me

10   I remain sir your
    obedent Humble servant
    Wm Holden
    Western Hospital Bryentson sq^r

I Beg you woudl Not send a Unpaid letter as i am Not abell to pay for it

TEXTUAL ALTERATIONS 8: Doctors] *after del illeg.* 13: Bryentson] 'son' *interl at end of line.* DATE Date of postmark.

264   From Samuel White in Halstead [Essex], 19 February 1829

Halsted Feby 19 = 1829

Sir/

As I have somehow managed to get through the winter without assist-ance I should not now have Presumed to have ask'd for any were it not I

5 have an offer of a situation for my Eldest Daughter which Promises to be of service to her, if I can send her out a little respectable as it is to be introduced into a shop - which it is not in my Power to do without runing into Debt which I have no Desire to Do as I have already incurred as much or more than I shall be able to get through all summer - if the Gentlemen

10 will have the goodness to send me 20 or 30 shillings for this Purpose I shall esteem it a great favour as it will most likely be the last for the Girl as she is going to Messing in Essex and if she Continues there a year will no longer belong to you - I am sir your Humble Servant

                                       S White

15 PS I should have said I have still 2 Children unable to walk although the oldest is nearly 2 ½ years old and the Docter informs me the youngest never will walk as it has some Disease in the Back

TEXTUAL ALTERATIONS 3: somehow] 'how' *over del illeg.* 9: or] *after del* 'as'; 'o' *over del illeg.* 11: great] 'ea' *over* 'at'. 12: if] *interl with caret.* 16: me] *interl with caret.*

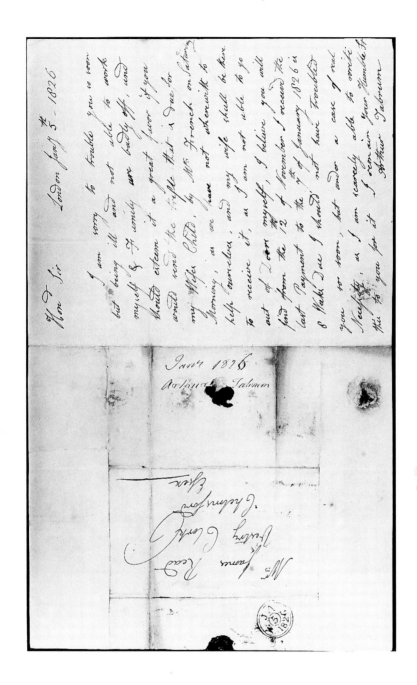

Plate I: Simple standard
ERO D/P 94/18/42 Pauper letter from Arthur Tabrum in [the parish of Christchurch in] London to James Read, vestry clerk of Chelmsford, 5 January 1826 (**179**)

Original size: 185 x 217 mm (each page 185 x 108.5 mm)

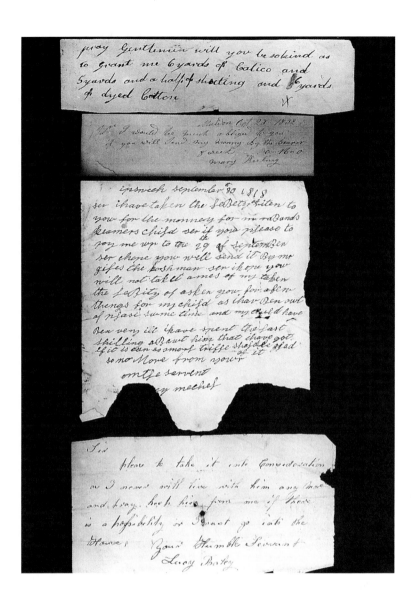

Plate II: Deficient pieces

ERO D/P 95/18/3 Anonymous pauper letter surviving from Little Dunmow (**590**); ERO D/P 238/18/1 Pauper letter from Mary Keeling in Maldon [Essex] to [John] Sewell [overseer] of Mundon (**629**); ERO D/P 203/18/1 Pauper letter from [Mary] Mitchel in Ipswich [to the parish of St Botolph, Colchester] 30 September 1818 (**300**); D/P 138/18/11 Pauper letter from Lucy Bayley [in the parish of St James in Colchester] (**410**)

Original sizes: 48 x 201 mm (**590**), 40 x 160 (**629**), 165 x 160 mm (**300**), 92 x 181 mm (**490**)

Chelmsford Sep.t 25 = 1821

Sir,

I trust you will Excuse me writing to you, but as you told
me, when I was last time with you, if any thing occured in which
I wanted Advice or Relief, to let you know, and not suffer myself to be
in distress, nor put myself to the trouble, or Expence, of coming to
Colchester, but to write to you, as that would do as well, and that you
would do, what was in your power for me, provided I did all I could on
my part, to procure a Livelyhood, indeed Sir, this I have done, but as I
stated to Mr Bryant, that work from time to time having been so
very slack, & Illness together, have put it out of my power, to go on
as I could wish, and work have continued in the same dead state, as
when I wrote last to Mr B— , I have Earned, but 15 Shillings,
since that time, five of which I Expended, for Materials, to do the
work with . and the most part of what Mr B— had the goodness,
to send me, I paid where I had been Credited, and what remained,
was Expended, for Immediate, necessaries of Life — it will be Vain to
repete over again what I wrote to Mr B— on our distressed case,
I would refer you, Sir, to those Letters, I can only say, things are with
us, as they then were, and we live very sparingly indeed, and I can now say, we have
not, so much, as one Shilling, to help ourselves with, nor a Job in view,
at present, (in this I am not worse off than my Neighbours,)

I must say, my Rent is behind, the Allowance made for my
Daughter, which I Applied to that purpose, I have now been under
the necessity of useing, for to provide the necessaries of Life, and
am now in Expectation every day, of the few things we have, to be
seised on, and taken from us, indeed Sir, we are truly Miserable

I do find that without some Assistance, tis Impossible for me, to
recover myself — to stand my ground, or support ourselves, had I Regular
Employ I could do it, but in this dead state of Employment, I find it
Impossible — what to do I know not, nor how to apply for relief,
your past friendship, and what you said to me, Induces me to ask
your Advice, what is best for me to do, I know not, to whom to Apply
but yourself and I hope to receive your Advice, I much wish, and
would do all in my power, to Avoid coming home to my Parish, as I
do think, I can do much better here, than to do that, but I cannot
Procure, common necessaries, without some further Aid, for which I

Plate III: Highest standard
ERO 178/18/23 Pauper letter from William James in Chelmsford
to Robert Alden [overseer of the parish of St Peter] in Colchester,
25 September 1821 (**445**)
Original size: 228 x 181 mm

make no pretence of Claim, but ask as a favor — I am thankfull
for the Allowance given us, it is a help, but not Competent, in our
present state of things — will you, Sir, be so kind, to do what
you can for us — to write to me, what step to take, what you would
have me do — If you wish me to Apply in any other way, or to
any other person, I will follow your Instruction — I hope Sir some-
-thing will be done for me, to stop the threatining proceedings
of my Landlady, to take away the Comfort, of our few goods from us
in which cage, I see no remedy, to keep us from utter ruin = I am Indebted
to her 4=10=0, up to Michaelmass; and more Expence, will follow
such a step, — I must Leave my case with you, trusting you will be my
friend, as you have ever been — I humbly ask pardon, for troubling
you, and as humbly Intreat your advise, and Answer =
    I have Intreeded with my Landlady, to give her an Answer, on
monday or tuesday next, you will do me a great favor, if you
will condesend, to write to me, by that time, then I can give her
an Answer, — Pray Sir Excuse me,

                My Wife and Daughters Duty to Mr & Mrs Allen, &c
                    I am Sir Your Obedt, Humble Servt
                            Wm James

            If by post
        Wm James — Bell-hanger
        Near the Windmill Inn
            Moulsham   Chelmsford   Essex
        _____
            If by Carrier — as Usual   —

Sir I would have pd the postage of this, but really, have not six pence to do it

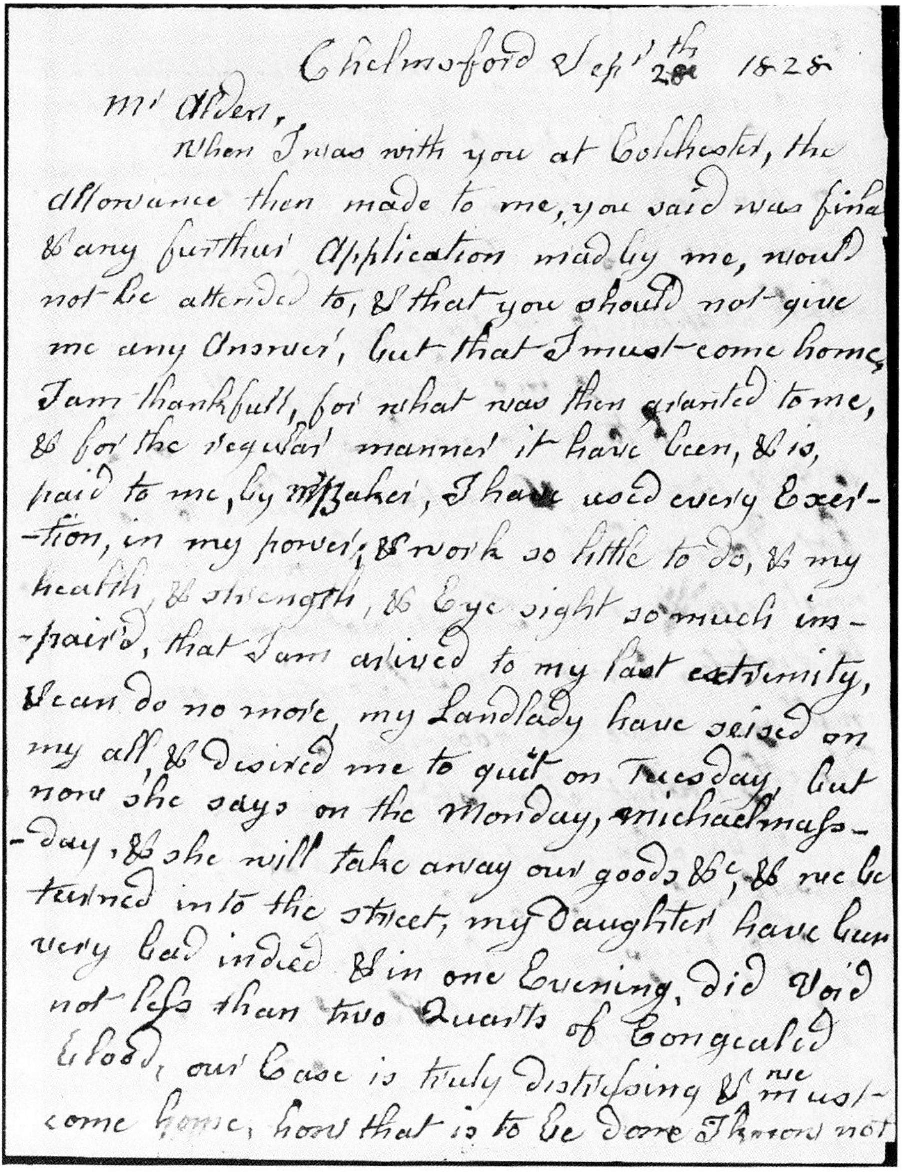

Chelmsford Sep'r 28th 1828

Mr Alden,

When I was with you at Colchester, the
allowance then made to me, you said was final
& any further Application mad by me, would
not be attended to, & that you should not give
me any Answer, but that I must come home,
I am thankfull, for what was then granted to me,
& for the regular manner it have been, & is,
paid to me, by Mr Baker, I have used every Exertion, in my power, & work so little to do, & my
health, & strength, & Eye sight so much im-
prair'd, that I am arrived to my last extremity,
& can do no more, my Landlady have seised on
my all, & desired me to quit on Tuesday, but
now she says on the Monday, michaelmassday, & she will take away our goods &c, & we be
turned into the street, my Daughter have been
very bad indeed & in one Evening, did Void
not less than two Quarts of Congealed
Blood, our Case is truly Distressing & me must
come home, how that is to be done I know not

Plate V: An older hand

ERO 178/18/23 Pauper letter from William James in Chelmsford
to Robert Alden [overseer of the parish of St Peter] in Colchester,
28 September 1828 (**550**)

Original size: 204 x 160 mm

I can truly say we have been living a half starving Life, & now have very little to subsist on, only the 4 Shillgs you allow us, for if I had a Job come in, I could not do it, & now, Sir, 'tis come, that, I must do something, shall I apply to the Parrish Chelmsford, for Relief & bring me home, or will you send me Relief to gett our'selves home, or send to Mr Baker, & impower him to do it for you, which I believe he would do, on your writeing to him, I wish not, nor do I presum to dictate, I cast myself entirely on you, will you have the goodnefs to write to me directly, what I must do, home I must come, but I have not the means of doing it in myself, I hope not to Offend, far be it from me, so to do, Necefity (real Necefity) Compel me to write, & with the deepest humility, & Thankful-nefs, I have done, I am your Obedt Humle Servt Wm James

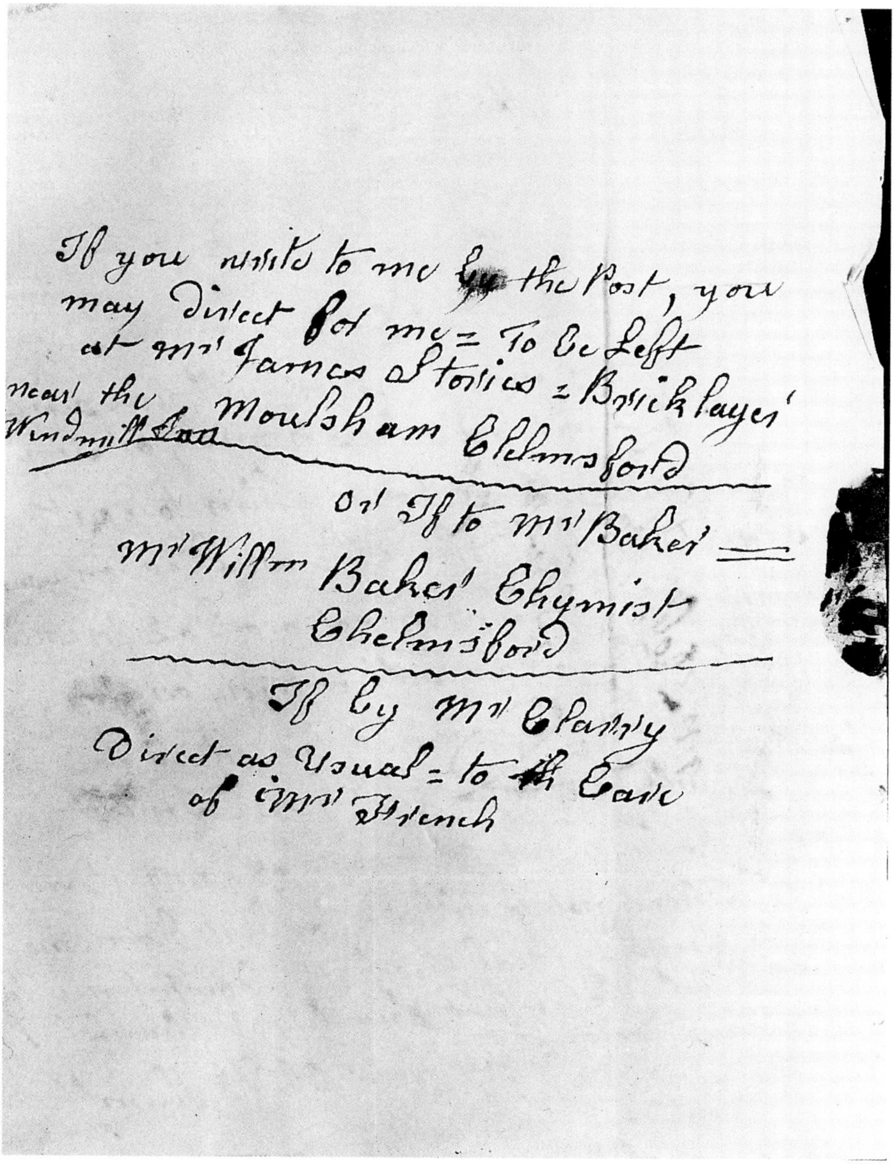

If you write to me by the Post, you
may direct for me = To be Left
at Mr James Stories = Brick layer'
near the Moulsham Chelmsford
Windmill Lane

Or If to Mr Baker —
Mr Willm Baker' Chymist
Chelmsford

If by Mr Clarky
Direct as Usual = to the Care
of Mr French

Plate VII
550 contd.
Original size: 204 x 160 mm

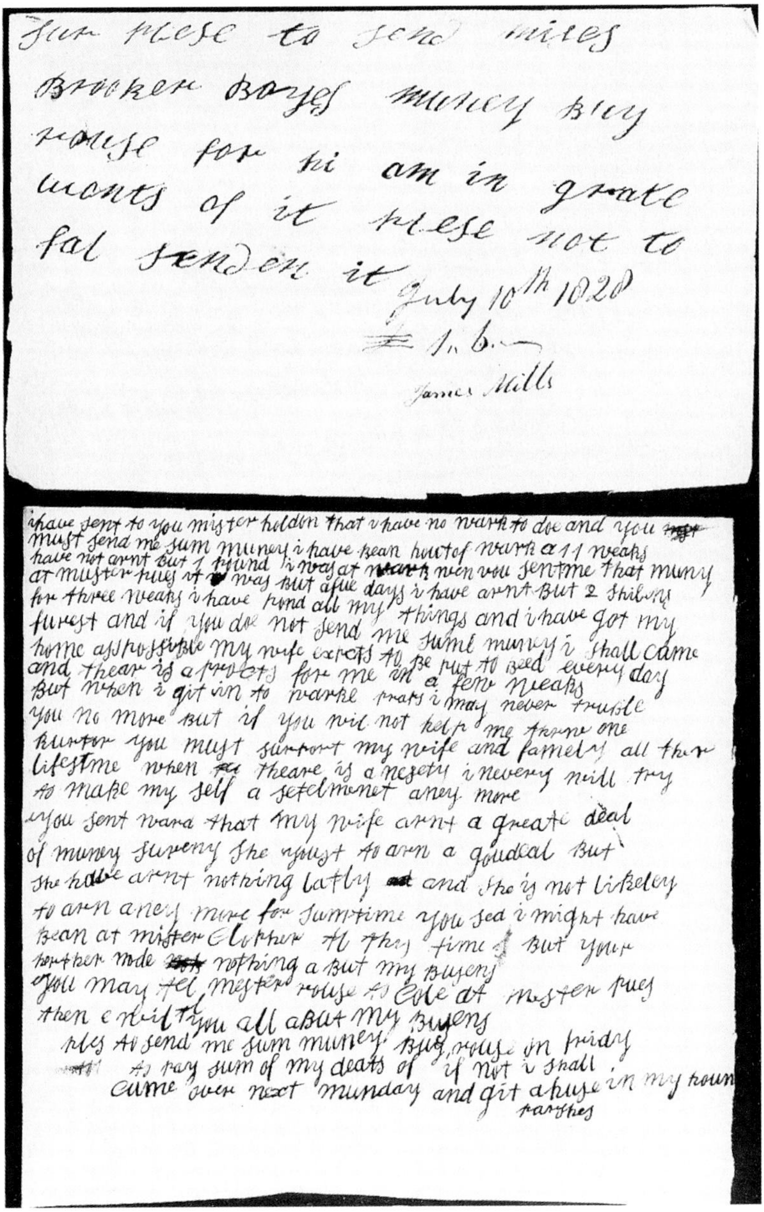

Sur plese to send miles
Brooker boyes muney by
rouse for hi am in grate
wonts of it plese not to
fal sendin it July 10th 1828
£ 1.. 6..
James Mills

i have sent to you mister holden that i have no wark to doe and you
must send me sum muney i have bean hout of wark a 11 weaks
have not arnt but 1 pund i was at
at muster pugs it was but a fue days i have arnt but 2 shilins
for three weaks i have pond all my things and i have got my
furest and if you doe not send me sume muney i shall came
home as possible my wife expects to be put to bed every day
and thear is a prospects for me in a few weaks
but when i git in to warke praps i may never truble
you no more but if you wil not help me throw one
winter you must support my wife and famely all thr
lifestme when theare is a nesety i neverey will try
to make my self a setelment aney more
you sent ward that my wife arnt a greate deal
of muney surenty she youst to arn a goudeal but
she haste arnt nothing latly and she is not likeley
to arn aney more for sumtime you sed i might have
bean at mister Clarker at thes time but your
brother made nothing a but my bisens
you may tel mester rouse to cole at mester pugs
then e will tel you all abut my bisens
ples to send me sum muney by rouse on friday
to pay sum of my deats if not i shall
came over next munday and git a huse in my oun parishes

Plate VIII: Oral writing

ERO D/P 203/18/1 Pauper letter from [Benjamin] Brooker [in Ipswich to the parish of St Botolph in Colchester, 10 July 1828] (**377**); ERO 178/18/23 [Pauper letter from Benjamin Brooker in Ipswich to Robert Alden, overseer of the parish of St Peter in Colchester, before 2 December 1825] (**510**)

Original sizes: 127 x 207 mm (**377**), 196 x 183 mm (**510**)

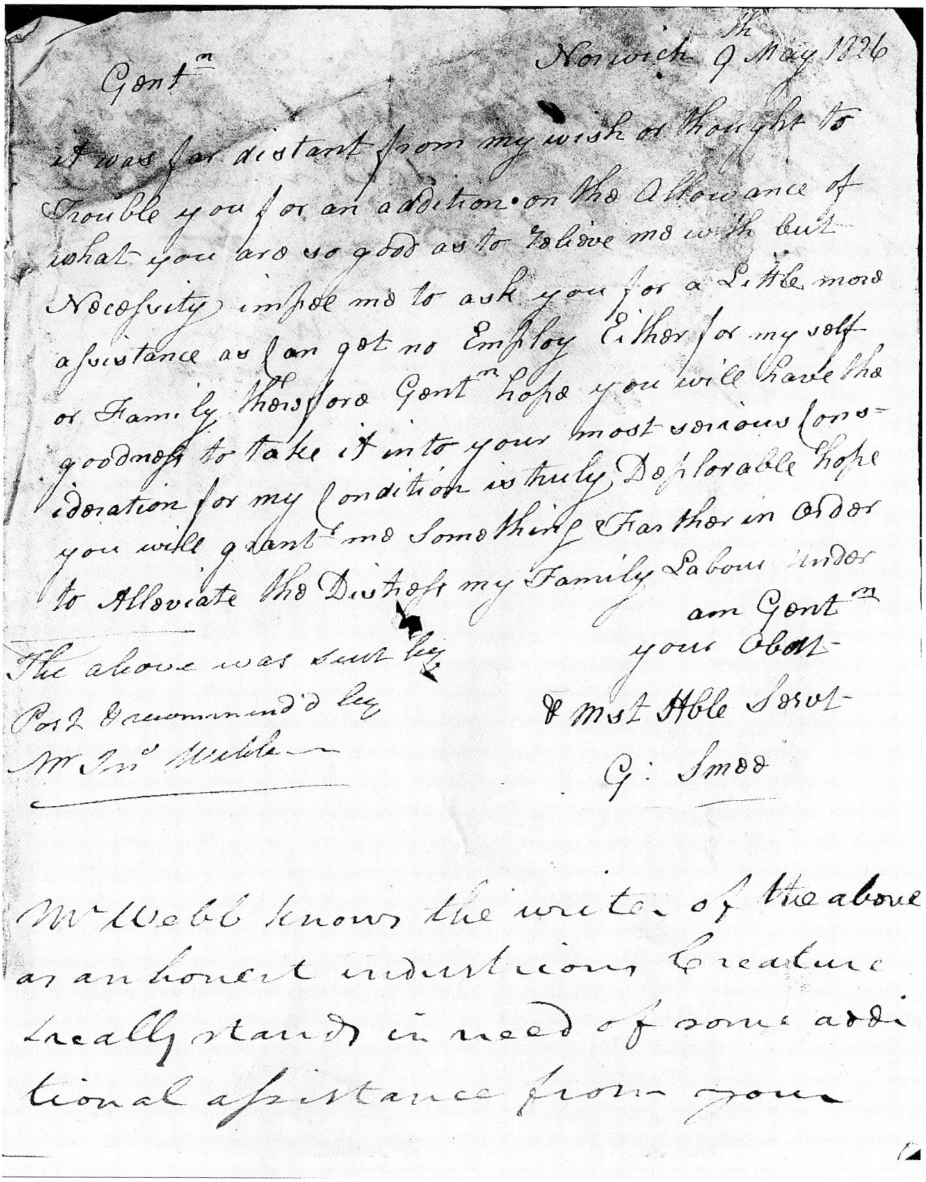

Gent[m]   Norwich 9 May 1826

it was far distant from my wish or thought to
Trouble you for an addition on the Allowance of
what you are so good as to relieve me with but
Necessity impel me to ask you for a Little more
assistance as I can get no Employ Either for my self
or Family therefore Gent[n] hope you will have the
goodness to take it into your most serious Consideration for my Condition is truly Deplorable hope
you will grant me Something Farther in Order
to Alleviate the Distress my Family Labour under
                                           am Gent[n]
The above was sent by   your Obdt-
Post & recommend'd by   & most Hble Servt-
Mr In[o] Webb   G: Smee

Mr Webb knows the writer of the above
as an honest industrious Creature
& really stands in need of some addi
tional assistance from you

Plate IX: Letter turned into file
ERO D/P 264/18/42 Pauper letter from George Smee in Norwich
to [Jeremiah] Wing [overseer of] Braintree, 9 May 1826 (**14**)
Original size: 223 x 182 mm

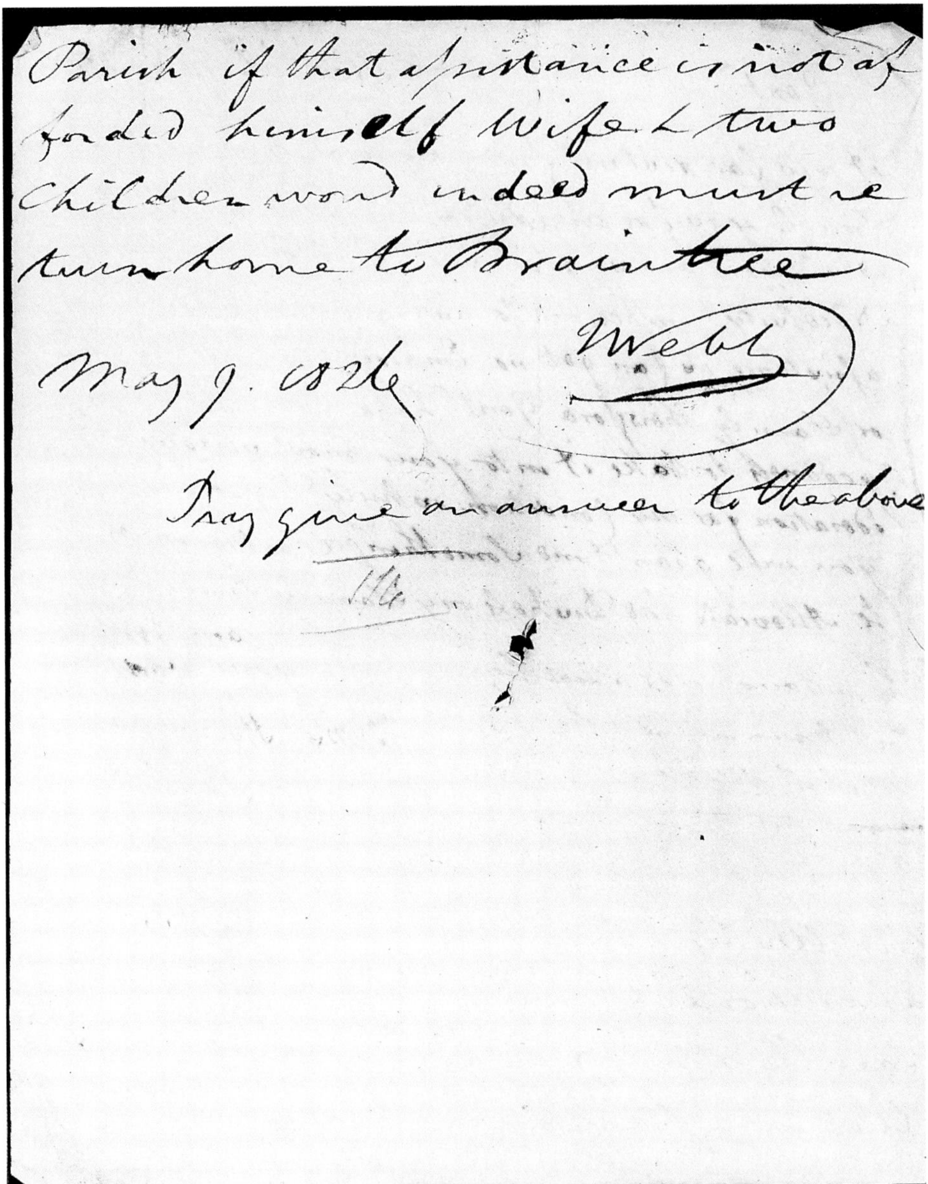

Parish if that assistance is not af
forded himself Wife & two
Children would indeed must re
turn home to Braintree

May 9. 1826   Webb

Pray give an answer to the above

Plate X
14 contd.
Original size: 223 x 182 mm

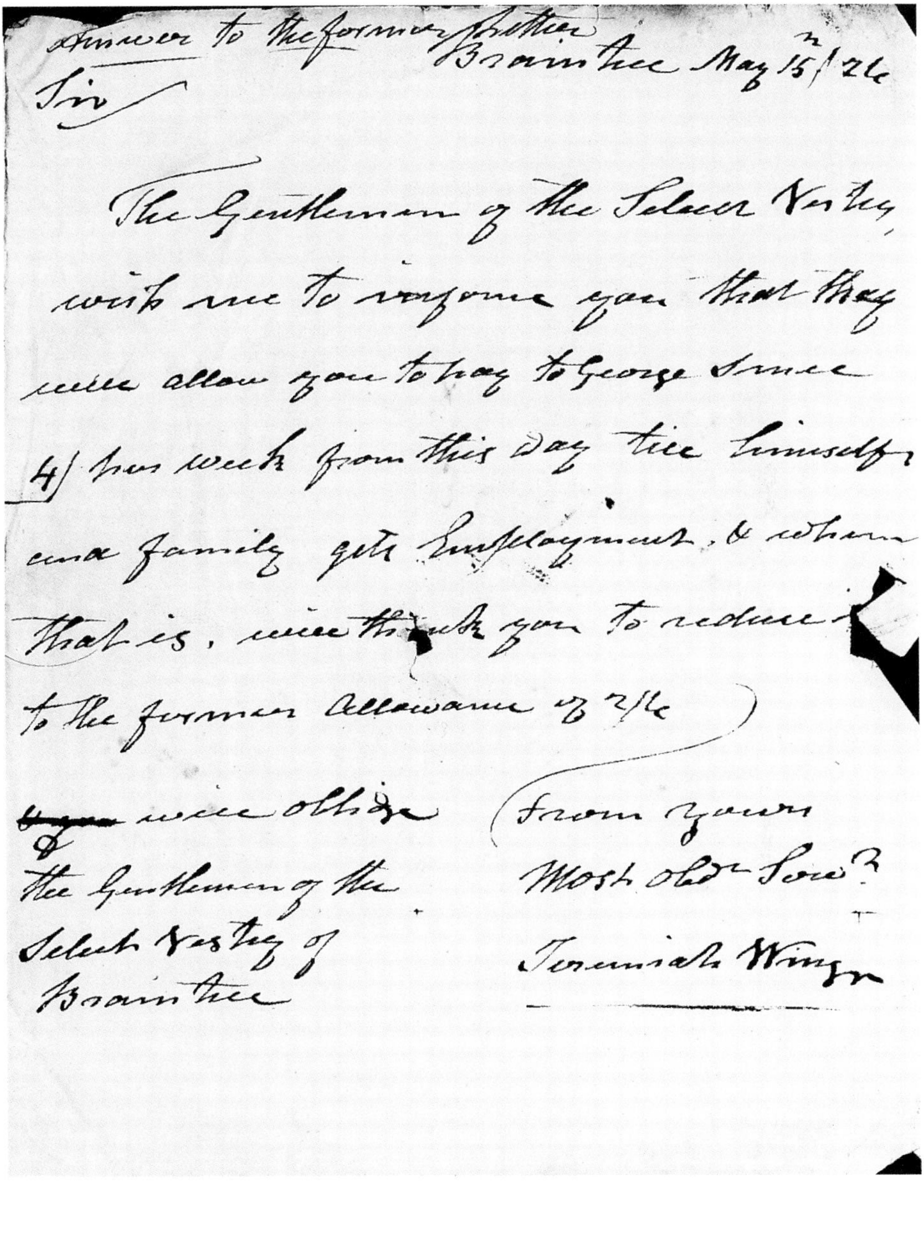

Answer to the former Brother

Braintree May 15/26

Sir

The Gentlemen of the Select Vestry, wish me to inform you that they will allow you to pay to George Smee 4/ per week from this day till himself, and family gets Imployment; & when that is, will think you to reduce it to the former allowance of 2/6

you will oblige
the Gentlemen of the
Select Vestry of
Braintree

from yours
Most obed Serv?
Jeremiah Winge

Plate XI
14 contd.
Original size: 223 x 182 mm

Plate XII
14 contd.
Original size: 223 x 182 mm

Plate XIII: Formal petition
ERO D/P 94/18/42 Pauper letter from Ann Marsh [in Shoreditch]
in London to the churchwardens [and overseers] of Chelmsford
[11 October 1824] (**133**)

Original size: 226 x 372 mm (each page 226 x 186 mm)

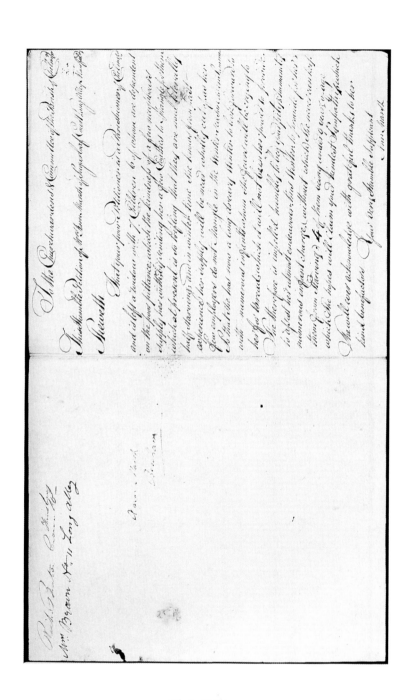

Plate XIV
133 contd.
Original size: 226 x 372 mm (each page 226 x 186 mm)

Plate XV: Return of post

ERO D/P 94/18/42 Pauper letter from Susan[nah] Halls in
Ipswich to James Read, overseer of Chelmsford [15 May 1825]
(**156**)

Original size: 226 x 372 mm (each page 226 x 186 mm)

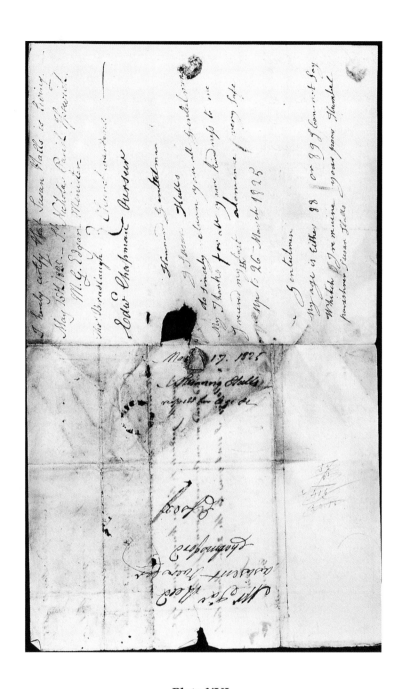

Plate XVI
156 contd.
Original size: 226 x 372 mm (each page 226 x 186 mm)

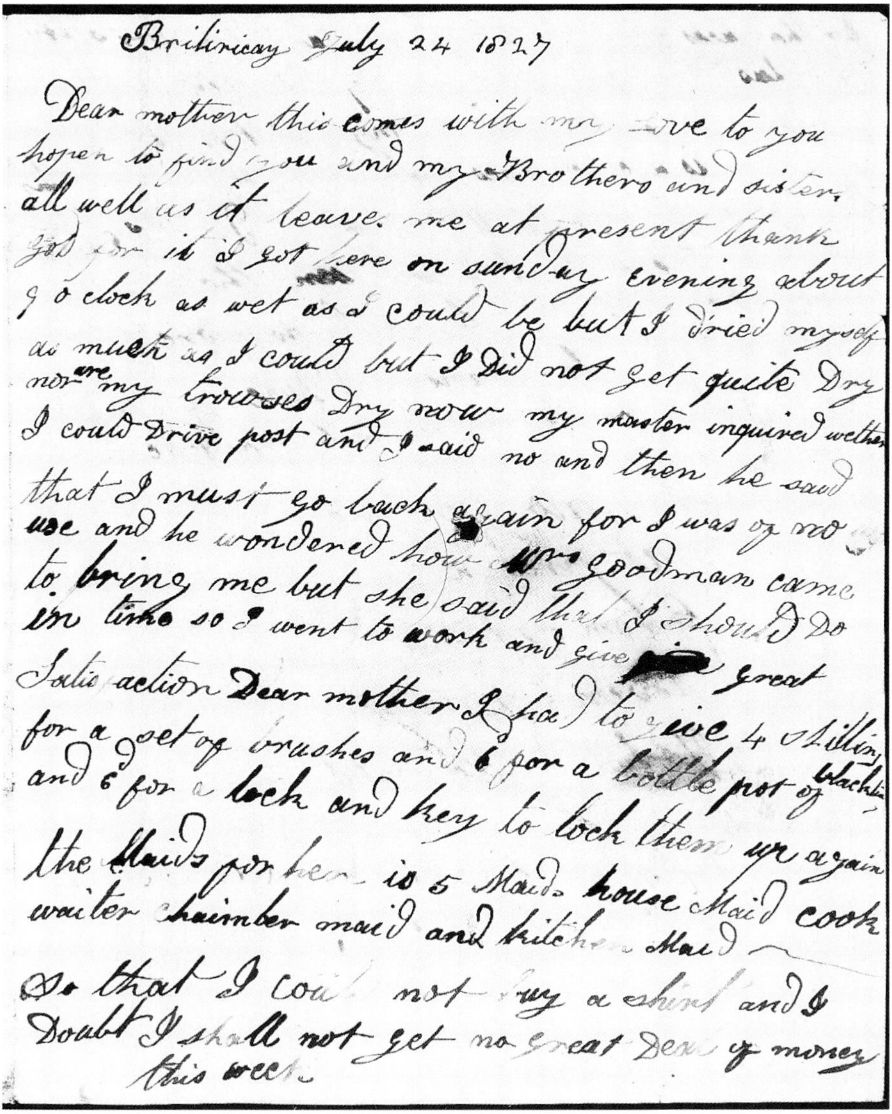

Brilricay July 24 1827

Dear mother this comes with my love to you
hopen to find you and my Brothers and sister
all well as it leaves me at present thank
God for it I got here on sunday evening about
9 o clock as wet as i could be but I dried myself
as much as I could but I did not get quite Dry
nor are my trowses Dry now my master inquired wether
I could Drive post and I said no and then he said
that I must go back again for I was of no
use and he wondered how Mrs goodman came
to bring me but she said that I should do
in time so I went to work and give great
Satisfaction Dear mother I had to give 4 shilling
for a set of brushes and 6 for a bottle pot of blacki
and 6 for a lock and key to lock them up again
the Maids for her is 5 Maids house maid cook
waiter chamber maid and kitchen Maid
So that I could not buy a shirt and I
Doubt I shall not get no great Deal of money
this week

Plate XVII: Private letter
ERO D/P 264/18/42 Pauper letter from John Barnes in Billericay
[Essex] to [his mother] Mrs Digby in Braintree, 24 July 1827 (**17**)
Original size: 224 x 187 mm

for the races are 3 Days but we had 3 travelers stopt
here last night and I go to them Dear mother
I wish you could send me my shirt on friday for
for ther is a coach goes from our house to chelms
then give my love to Mrs ward & Mrs Wright
and tell them that I will send them some
money I cannot stop to write no more for I
am called away to Dinner) I Dined of a beautiful
Leg of Mutton roasted and some turnips &c &c

So no more
at present
from your
loven Son
John Barnes

Granted 2s for a New Shirt
& 5s to buy Breeches, J— G—
&c

Plate XVIII
17 contd.
Original size: 224 x 187 mm

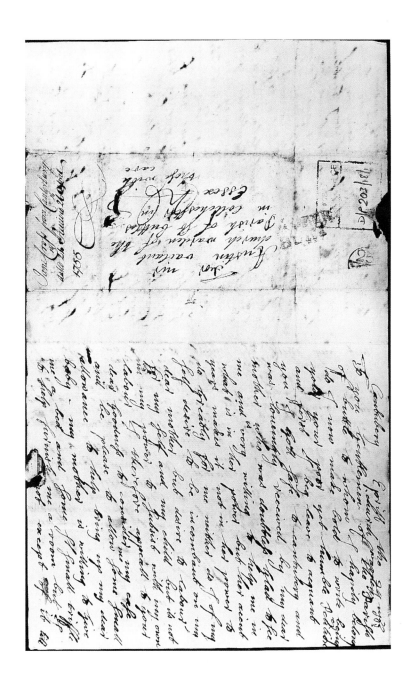

Plate XIX: An early piece
ERO D/P 203/18/1 Pauper letter from Jane Cross in Canterbury
to Austin Vailant, churchwarden of the parish of St Botolph in
Colchester, 24 April 1755 (**281**)
Original size: 190 x 304 mm (each page 190 x 152 mm)

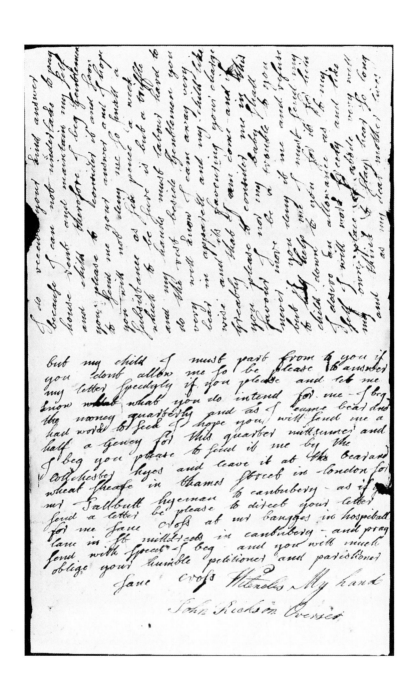

Because I can not undertake to pay house rent and maintain my self and child therefore I beg gentlemen you; please to consider it and I hope to send me your answer and I hope you will not stay me so long a week Subsistance as for presse a week which to be sure is but a triffle to the rest beside Gentlemen your very well drawn I am come and if that directly that I am come and if that you please to conduct me by that direckly I no; my trouble to you never more to be a trouble to you but if you help me I must send 1739 child down to you for to fetch him I adore for allowance as the self I will would speedy very well my own, place (if I stay I may so long) and thick as my dear mother

but my child I must part from to you if you dont allow me so to be please to answer my letter speedyly if you please and let me know what what you do intend for me — I beg the money quarberly and as I came beat and had work to feed I hope you will send me a half a Geney for this quarber midsumer and I beg you please to send it me by the Colchester hyes and leave it at the bearand wheat sheafe in thames streeb in London for mr Sallbutt hycrman to canbubery — as if I send a letter be please to direcb your letter for me Jane cross ab mr bangges in hospiball lane in St millstreeb in canbuberg — and pray send with speed I beg and you will much oblige your humble petitioner and parisshioner

Jane cross Witeness My hand

John Rickson Overseer

Plate XX
281 contd.
Original size: 190 x 304 mm (each page 190 x 152 mm)

**265   From Sarah Rivenall in St George in the East, London, to the
       overseer of Chelmsford, 25 February 1829**

London
25th February 1829

Gentlemen

I return you many thanks for the last remittance you were so kind as to
relieve our family with thro the hands of Mr French. and were in hopes it   5
would have been the last time we should have troubled you, But I am sorry
to inform you that my husband David Rivenall is again suffering under is
Old Complaint he has several severe fits of late which has left him in so low
and melancholy state that requires some one constantly to mind him which
prevents me entirely from endeavouring for support for my Children would   10
therefore be extremly Obliged if you would send him some relief weekly or
as you may judge proper. as it is impossible for us to survive any longer
without some relief which is required as speedy as possible Gentlemen if
any doubt ar/ises/ in your mind the truth of this statement can be Obtained
by Mr French on is next time that you may think proper to send - Gentlemen   15
belive me we are in the utmost distress - but are still in hopes thro Gods
goodnes will soon sooth our present misery

I remain
Gentlemen your Obedient
& very Humble Servant   20
Sarah Rivenall

Please to direct to the
Kings Head
Commercial Road
St Georges East   25
London

CIRCUMTEXT Countersigned from other hand below valedictions: 'Corn^s Bland Assistant
to Mr Dale Surgeon'.

**266   From Harriet Twin in [St Botolph] Colchester to [James] Read
       in Chelmsford, 29 March 1829**

Sir

You will please to present my thanks to the Vestry for the favour they
granted me in February last.

This will inform them that I and my family have left Glemsford, and are
5 now at Colchester, where I have hired a small house with an intention of
keeping a school having done so while Mr Twin lived there I thought my
former friends would assist me again, but you are aware, it will take some
time to establish myself in it, and as my children are so small and sickly
they want all my attention I therefor humbly hope you will consider my
10 case as being very *hard*, and allow me not less at present than *2^s pr week
each*. If I should suceed in my undertaking, I should be glad to be less
burdensome to the Parish, sorry indeed am I that Poverty obliges me to
trouble them now, having been obliged to sell even the Cloathes of my late
husband to defray the expence of moving here and the Rent of the house we
15 inhabited at Glemsford with other expences having left only a few things to
furnish a small house at 3^s and 6^d per week, trusting you will give me that
support you think needful to suppo<rt> the wants of 4 small children

I Remain Gentlemen
your humble Petitioner
20 Harriet Twin

Colchester, March 29 1829
St. Botolphs Stret
Near Mr Shepherds Brewery

CIRCUMTEXT Note from other hand at bottom: answered 3 April 1829 'including a Pound
Note'.

FURTHER EVIDENCE Possibly as a consequence of this letter (her previous one [261]
apparently having been ignored), and further to the pound note sent on 3 April, Harriet
Twin received a weekly allowance of 5s from 25 May 1829 until Michaelmas 1830 (ERO,
D/P 94/12/36, Chelmsford overseers' accounts).

267 From Jane Wall [in Mile End Old Town, London] to the overseers of Chelmsford, 29 March 1829

March 29, 1829.

Gentlemen,

I write to inform you, that I am the widow of the late Samuel Wall, who
belonged to your Parish, and who was formerly Tall Keeper at Chelms-
5 ford Market, and resided in Baddow lane and who died in the Poorhouse
a few years ago. I have for Several years been enabled to Support myself
as a nurse, but owing to my advanced age, being nearly Seventy years of
age, and in addition being very lame, I am unable to do anything towards

Procuring the means of Subsistance: under these Circumstances, I am
Compelled to Solicet assistance from the Parish; and hope I shall not be 10
deemed obtrusive in humbly requesting that I may recieve any Sum the
Parish officears may think Proper to allow, at my Present Place of abode,
as I am near my Children, though thay are not able to contribute to my
necessities, being in distressed Circumstances themselves. I beg to add,
that I have delayed making this application till the last extreme and that I 15
have no other resourse but becoming an inmate of your Poorhouse. I Con-
fidently Challenge the strictest envestigation into my case; and remain,
with Great respect, Gentlemen, your

very humble Servent,
Jane Wall. 20

At Mr Kills, Dogson,
Mile End, Corner
of John Street.

Please see other side.

CIRCUMTEXT Note from John Tunstall, No.1, Swan Place, Sidney Street, Mile End Turnpike (same hand as letter) on next page, countersigned by R. Hearson, overseer: 'I beg to
certify, that the foregoing case is correctly stated; the Applicant has nursed my Wife with
two children, during which times she conducted herself in a remarkable sober and steady
manner, and in every respect gave great satisfaction.'

**268   From Sarah Manning in Stratford, Essex, to [James] Read, ves-
        try clerk of Chelmsford, [13 April 1829]**

Stratford Essex
    Mrs Manning has sent these few Lines to Mr Read to say that she is very
Sorry to trouble him so but she would be much Oblige to him if he would
send her a Little Money to Buy her Son Some Cloathes and Shoes as he is
quite distress for he has no shoes hardly to his Feet and he is such a Great 5
Boy Now and has not got any Employment to earn any thing at that she is
Compell to send for Something and hop[e] you wont fail of Sending some
thing or else she shall be force to Come down to Chelmsford herself M^r
Manning would not have Sent but she is been Ill all the Winter and her
Husband has been troubled all the Winter with the Rheumatick Gout that 10
he has not been abl to doo any work and a family to Maintain besides that
all gether she is under the Necasty of Sending for Something

Sarah Manning

DATE Date of postmark.

269   From Elizabeth Philbrick in Wivenhoe [Essex] to the overseers of Chelmsford [14 April 1829]

To the Gentlemen Churchwardens and Overseers of the Parish of Chelmsford I Elizabeth Philbrick the Widow of Thomas Philbrick Hair Dresser
served his time to Mr Wiffen of Chelmsford I do hear Protest that I have
Lived 38 years in the Parish of Wivenhoe and brought up a Famaly and
5 paid Rates and Taxes till now I am 68 years old and am not able to do it no
Longer I am now Oblight to Call on the Parish I have bean a Widow 14
years next May I have a Daughter that will take me if you Gentlemen will
be so good as to allow me something a week and by so doing I shall
Esteem it a great favour I am your Humble Sarvent
10   Elizabeth Philbrick of Wivenhoe

TEXTUAL ALTERATIONS 2: Hair] 'ir' *over illeg.*
     DATE Date of circumtext.
     CIRCUMTEXT Letter from the overseers of Wivenhoe to the overseers of Chelmsford on
back of page, dated 14 April 1829, confirming that Elizabeth Philbrick is the widow of
Thomas Philbrick who gained his settlement at Chelmsford through service with Mr Wiffen
(hairdresser) some 10 years ago, and concluding that 'the Overseers [of Wivenhoe] will
be happy to spare Chelmsford any trouble; and trust that Chelmsford are disposed to do
the same by them'.

270   From Sarah Albra in [St Andrew Holborn] London to Mr Crimer in Chelmsford, 16 April 1829

London 16th April 1829
Sir
    I have taken the liberty of Addressing those few Lines to you hopeing
you will not feil it to much Truble to lay befour your honourabl Bord I
5 Sarah Albra Wife of James Albra of Chelmsford Bookbinder My husbarn
has bin ill 3 mounth not bin able to harn a fathen and I am Left destude
with 4 yong Children and back with my Rent and in the Great Drestress
my husbann is at Chelmsford With i<s> mother at the Royal Oke in the
Back Street Ware you Can Inquire And if you dute Wot I Say if you any
10 Gentleman in town to inquire I Live at N° 12 Dorrington Street Brooks
Market Holborn or at my Landlords Mr Holmes N° 10 in the Same Street

Which i how for Rent 1-10-0 which I hope Si^r you and the rest of the
Gentleman will do Same think for me or Else I Shall be Compell to Come
Down With my Children and throw myself and Children on the perish So
Si^r I Wait your answair   15

I am

You^r Humble Ser^t

Sarah Albra

I hope Mr Crimer you will Do Some think for me

TEXTUAL ALTERATIONS 7: yong] *interl.* 8: Chelmsford] 'm' *interl.* 10: inquirec *after del* 'if'.
14: With] *after del* 'W'.
  FURTHER EVIDENCE James Albra had received occasional poor relief payments to the
amounts of £1 9s in 1823 and of 19s 6d in 1824 (ERO, D/P 94/12/17, Chelmsford overseers' accounts, pauper ledger).

**271   From William and Sarah Duke in Kentish Town [St Pancras],
        London, to the overseers of Chelmsford, 20 April 1829**

To the Overseers of the Parish of Chelmsford Essex
  Gentlemen
  I am very Sorry that I am under the Nesessity to Inform you that I am
very Ill and Confind to my Bed for this week past and not able to help
myself to any thing my wife also has been very bad for a fortnight Past   5
and not able to do any thing for herself but through mercy is Slowly
Recovering, but not able at Present to do any work that by Both of us
being Ill together all means of Supporting ourselves or our three Children
is at Present Suspended
  We therefore your Humble Petitioners most Humbly Pray your assist-   10
ance by Some Speedy Relief for the Present and sincerely hope that a few
weeks will Enable us to Provid for ourselves and Family with the Weekly
allowance which we Recieve from you for Which we are very Thankful
and that you may not think this an Imposition on the Parist The Reverend
Minister of this Place and the Medical Gentleman who attends us both   15
have been Plased to Give their Signatures
  we therefore Gentlemen Humbly Beg your Speedy assistance whatever
it may be will be most Thankfully Recievd by Gentlemen your very Humble
and Thankful though afflicted Servants
Willm and Sarah Duke   20
N° 11 Mansfield Cresent

Kentish Town London
April 20th
1829

TEXTUAL ALTERATIONS 14: think] *interl.*
CIRCUMTEXT Two signatures below: Johnson Grant, minister of Kentish Town (hand A) and G.O. Heming, surgeon (hand B).
FURTHER EVIDENCE William Duke had received a weekly allowance of 4s 6d and occasional relief payments to the amount of £1 4s 6d during the year ending on Lady Day 1829 (ERO, D/P 36/28/3, List of the out-door poor belonging to Chelmsford, for the year from Lady Day 1828 [kept among Great Coggeshall overseers' papers]).

272   From Arthur Tabrum in [Christchurch] London to James Read, overseer of Chelmsford, 6 May 1829

London May 6th 1829

Sir

I should be much obligd to you if you would send the trifle of Money that is due for Arthur Good, and to allow me some relief as I have had a
5 verry bad misfortune as you will see by the Surgeons signature, and are very bad off there is six of us in Family, if you will be so kind as to send by Mr French on Monday My Wife will meet him

I remain Your Humble
A Tabrum

10 No 2 Mitre place
Broad Hall
in Lambeth Parish

TEXTUAL ALTERATIONS 12: in] *inserted in left-hand margin.*
CIRCUMTEXT The Text is followed by a certificate from Henry Appkins, surgeon, 54 Stanford Street, Blackfriars: 'This is to certify that Arthur Tabrum has had the misfortune to break the small bone of the Leg and is of course unable to provide for his family'.

273   From Harriet Twin in [St Botolph] Colchester to [James] Read, overseer of Chelmsford, 13 May 1829

Sir/

I should be thankful if you would inform me whether the General meeting has taken place, and also whether the gentlemen have considered my Case, and what the maintenance is to be as they must be aware that I

cannot go on with out their assistance in an uncertainty, any longer, hope   5
they will please to send to me, as soon as convenient.

   I Remain Sir
     Yours Respectfully
      Harriet Twin

Colchester Essex   10
May 13th 1829
St. Botolphs St
Near Mr Shepherds Brewery
PS I received with thanks the 1£ note on the 3^d of April

**274 From Thomas S[mith] Carritt in Cheapside [City of London]
to the overseer of Chelmsford, 18 May 1829**

          26 Friday Street - 18 May 1829
To the Acting Overseer of Chelmsford
 Sir/
Not having one day employ since 11st January last it is with extreme
regret that I am compell'd to apply for pecunary aid - I hope you can so   5
arrange that I may receive a weekly Stipend until I again git into employ
- when you shall immediately hear from me it will give me as much satisfaction to get off your funds, as it now grieves me to be compelled to
come on them I have put off waiting to the very last extremity and we are
now in very distressed circumstances and quite destute of money, *Food*,   10
or any thing to pledge to procure *food* - an early reply or at foot
    will much oblidge Gentlemen
      Your mo^t ob^t Servt
         Tho. S. Carritt
a lettert or parcel   15
will find me at
26 Friday Street Cheapside

FURTHER EVIDENCE Thomas Carritt had received occasional relief payments to the amount
of £14 5s during the year ending on Lady Day 1829. But he does not seem to have received relief after that date (ERO, D/P 36/28//3, List of the out-door poor belonging to
Chelmsford, for the year from Lady Day 1828 [kept among Great Coggeshall overseers'
papers]).

275 From David Rivenall in St George in the East, London, to [Joseph] Wiffen in Chelmsford, 19 May 1829

London May 19th 1829

Dear Sir

I am Sorry that necessity Compels Mae to make Nown My Unfortunate Settuation to You As I hope You will Make Nown to the Rest of the
5 Parishioners that my Wife is at this moment Confind of Two Boys on Saturday last And from such a Serious Oppression it is not in my power With every exertion to meet that support Wich nature requires With Out Your Concideration of Assistance I am Obligd to have A Nurse from St Georges in the Ast And Necessity Requires me to apply to them for Relief
10 I hope Sir You Will Not delay Making Your Consideration As Speedy As possible As My Wife is in a dangerous state And relief is momentary Required I am Dear Sir

Yous Most Respectfully

David Rivenall

15 Please Sir to not lose the site of this Application As Necessity Compells me to make Nown to you

[*Continued on next page, reversed*]

Please to Direct to David

Rivenall the King Head

20 Commercial Road S[t] Georges

for the East

TEXTUAL ALTERATIONS 1: May] *above del* 'March'.
CIRCUMTEXT Note of answer on outside, 20 May 1829, £1 enclosed.
FURTHER EVIDENCE David Rivenall had received occasional relief payments to the amount of £6 during the year ending on Lady Day 1829 (ERO, D/P 36/28/3, List of the out-door poor belonging to Chelmsford, for the year from Lady Day 1828 [kept among Great Coggeshall overseers' papers]).

276 From Sarah Manning [in Stratford, Essex] to [James] Read, vestry clerk of Chelmsford, 21 May [1829]

May 21 182<->

Gentlemen

I should be much oblidge[d] to you if you would send me my Money as soon as It is due I receive[d] my last money on the fifth of December my

half years pay will be due on the fifth on June Gentlemen I should take it 5
as a particluar favour if you could do something for my boy for as I have
had a very trial with him this winter for I Could got nothing for him to do
I remain your Obeint Servant

Sarah Manning

CIRCUMTEXT Filing note on outside: Sarah Facey.
DATE Year from filing note on outside.

277   From Sarah Rivenall [in St George in the East, London] to the overseers of Chelmsford [May 1829]

Gentlemen

It is with extreme reluctance that I again make bold to solicit your
assistance, in consequence of the continued Severe illness with which my
Husband has been afflicted for the last 3 months, & which has reduced us
to the lowest ebb of poverty   5

We shall be most grateful therefore if you will please to repeat that
charity which y^r Goodness was pleased to confer some time since as it
will not only assist us in our present dreadful emergency but thereby we
shall be enabled to give our 2 daughters that *covering* (being at present
almost without clothing) by which means they will be capable of obtaining 10
some Employment.

The Sale of Oysters being the only means from which can derive
anksistence & next Wednesday terminating the Season thereof We shall
be truly grateful to hear from you *pevious* to that time, for a little purchase
made on the above Day will produce a considerable advantage -   15

I am Gentl^m
Y^r most Ob^t & Grateful Servt
Sarah Rivenall

1 Grove place
Grove S^t 20
Commercial Road

TEXTUAL ALTERATIONS 9: to give] *interl with caret*. 13: thereof] *interl with caret at end of line*. 15: made] *interl with caret*.
DATE From filing note on outside.

278   Henrietta Carritt in Cheapside [City of London] to Mr Creamer, silversmith in Chelmsford, 10 June 1829

Mr Creamer/ will thank you to lay the following before the committe
Sirs/
Since my Husband wrote Mr Creamer the other day, I have seen a M^{rs}
Harris a Friend of ours, where our eldest Daughter is learning the Dress-
5   making &^{c}. M^{rs} H- says she will do all she can for her, she is receiving 2/
6 per week and has victuals, and as she improves she is to receive more
M^{rs} H- has not room for her to sleep.
should we be compell^d to enter the House - our Dear Girl will loose the
only oppertunity she may ever have - of bettering herself -
10   on my own account I have great dread as to going in the House, I well
strive all in my power to get Bread - at the wash tub or in any way that
may occure - I have got the promice of one Ladys washing - my aversion
is such, that if I must go to the House I must sink under the punishment I
could not survive it - nither could I die happy to have my Dear little Chil-
15   dren without protection, my Husband is also desirous of doing as he can
he is now trying to get a porter's place should he not get this one he is
after - Mr Tarrant says he will do all he can for him - should we come to
Chelmsford we shall also loose what little furniture we have altho worth
but little, yet we can make do for us - I have most earnstly to entreat that
20   you will not be so cruel and hard hearted as to compell us to our utter ruin
- but to allow us a little longer to struggle against the tide of adversity and
I trust we may be more successfull to sum up in a few words, my horror of
the House is as great as a man can have of Death and I am confident will
be the Death of me, and in a short time - I do hope the Revd Mr Mildmay
25   will be my Friend in the above

I am Sirs
your Obedient ser^{vt}
Henrietta Carritt

26 Friday St Cheapside
30   June 10th 1829
I write this in the absence of my Husband, who is in the City seeking for
employ

TEXTUAL ALTERATIONS 1: committe] *interl at the end of line.* 3: M^r] *over del* 'you'. 24: me]
over 'us'.

Great Chishall pauper letter

**279   From Thomas Bray in Edmonton [Middlesex] to the church-
wardens and overseers of Great Chishall, 12 March 1788**

To the Church Wardens & Overseers of the Poor of the Parish of Chisel
    Gentlemen
    I am Sorry I should have Occasion to trouble you but Necessity Obliges
me, having had the Misfortune of two fitts of illness as you may see by the
Apothecaries Bills, as well my Wife has been ill some time not able to do   5
anything which has greatly Distressd me, as I never have been any ways
troublesome to you for any Relief before, I hope you will be so kind to
take it into Consideration, as the Apothecary is so very Pressing upon me
for his Money, and it is not on my Power to pay him any without Selling
what few things I have which if I should be Oblig'd to do, I and my Wife   10
must be Oblig'd to Come to you for Relief, I hope you Gentlemen will be
so kind to Advance the Money for the Payment of these Bills, as my Long
illness greatly Distress'd us, for a support, or I should not have troubled
you, be so kind to Order the payment soon as I am greatly Distresst on
Acouunt of it, I am   15
              Gentlemen
                    Your Afflicted & Distress'd
                    Servt
                      Thomas Bray
Bury Street Edmonton   20
March 12 1788

TEXTUAL ALTERATIONS 21: March 12] over 'Feby 24th'.
  WRITING Professional hand.

Great Coggeshall pauper letter

280 From Thomas Morse in [Great] Coggeshall to the churchwardens and overseers of St John Baptist, Hereford, 12 March 1750

Coggeshall March ye 12 1750

<Gen>tleman

    This with my humble Service returning many thanks for all favours: to
Inform you that the Overseers &c of the Parish have been with me and
5 desired I would write to You forthwith relating to the Money which they
Disbusted to me and which I have Recev^d from their hands though since
the Receving of Your letter have been Obliged to Shift without - through
the Goodness of some Friends and of my Son who has been a Servant
here and is out of his time But the Gentlemen have given me Notice that
10 Unless their letters be answered to their Satisfaction within 14 days they
will get an Order & bring me home and as I am settled here & through the
Help of Some friends Capable of getting my Bread better than if I should
come home and as you must be Sinsable it will be a great Expence for two
People so far advanced in Years to Come so far I hope you will therefore
15 take it into Consideration and so Order the matter that wee may be Continued where we are which will Greatly Oblidge Gentleman

Your Obedient & humble Servant
Thomas Morse

PS. Gentlemen

20   I should be glad to Receive your answer please to Direct for mee the
Bull In Coggeshall Essex

TEXTUAL ALTERATIONS 10: their letters] 'ir' *over* 're'. 10: answered] 's' *over* 'd'. 12: Help]
over del illeg. 20: Receive] 'eceive' *over illeg.*

WRITING This letter was written by Edward Powell, overseer of Great Coggeshall. It is
a copy of a letter sent to Hereford.

RELATED CORRESPONDENCE About two weeks before, Edward Powell, overseer of Great
Coggeshall, had written to the churchwardens and overseers of St John Baptist, Hereford
(same hand as letter from Thomas Morse), stating that 'an Account was Sent to you in
September Last of the releif Rec^d by your Parishioner Thomas Moss residing here (by
Virtue of your Certificate) to the Sum of two Pounds thirteen shilling<s> and Eleven
Pence Particulars of which You then Recev^d and Some Letters Since are all unanswered;
Wee now Remind You that, You will be more just to Your Parrishioners, and Your own
Characters - by Your immediate Discharge of the Presant Bill, than incurring a further
charge which will be the Consequence of Your disregard hereof' (copy of letter of 23
February 1750). He gave a detailed account (Thomas Morse had been advanced a weekly

allowance of 1s 6d), but apparently the letter remained unanswered. Thus, on 11 March 1750, Edward Powell approached the parish officers of St John Baptist, Hereford, again: 'On the 23^d of the last Month by my letter You had an Account of the Releif of Your parishioner Thomas Morse to which You have gaven no Answer, Now I tell You if this [is] not answered in fourteen days Yer shall see Your Parishioner at Your Expence' (copy of letter). This time he received an answer. On 18 March 1750, Thomas Hodges wrote from St John Baptist, Hereford: 'By orders of our officers I am to acquaint you that they Re^d your letter of ye 11th instant to their great surprize, they having paid ye money to your order when they sent you word, tho they had no receipt for it till since they rec^d your last, so they hope ye money is now paid. they having a receipt from your carrier as we suppose <----> like wise they Rec^d a letter from Thos Morse dated ye 12th <----> he have rec^d no more from you since our letter. therfore I hope this will put a stop to any farther trouble'.

FURTHER EVIDENCE When Thomas Morse was examined on 7 May 1750 he said he was born in St John the Baptist, Hereford, and had served an apprenticeship there, as a cordwainer, for seven years.

St Botolph, Colchester, pauper letters

281* From Jane Cross in Canterbury to Austin Vailant, churchwarden of St Botolph, Colchester, 24 April 1755

Cantubery   Eprill the 27 1754

To you Gentlemen church wardens of the Parish of buttle to whom I
hapily belong do I now make bold to write being your your poor yet
humble Petitioner and first I beg leave to acquant you I Gott safe to
5 cantubery and was loveingly received by my dear mother who was doubt-
less Glad to see me and is very willing to help me in what is in her power
but her acent years makes it not in her power to do Greatly for me neither
do I of my self desire to be incombant on my dear mother but desire to
labour for my self and my child but its not in my power to subsist with
10 my own labour I therefore appeall to your dear Goodness to consider my
case and be please to allow me some small allowance to help bring up my
dear baby - my mother is willing to Give me a bed and some sl small
triffle to help furnish me a room but I <can> <n>ot except of it till I do
receive your kind answer because I can not undertake to pay house rent
15 and maintain my self and child therefore I beg Gentlemen you please to
consider it and soon to send me your answer and I hope you will not deny
me so small a subsistance as six pence a week which to be sure is but a
triffle and my hands must labour hard to do the rest beside Gentlemen
you very well know I cam away very bear in apparell and my child like
20 wise and its favouring your charge Greatly that I am come and if you
please to consider me in this favour I nor my baby shall never more be a
trouble to you but if you deny it me and refuse to help me I must send my
child down to you for its for him I desire an allowance as to my self I will
work freely and like my own place of abode very well and think to stay
25 hear so long as my dear mother lives but my child I must part from to you
if you dont allow me so be please to answer my letter speedyly if you
please and let me know what you do intend for me I beg the money quarterly and as I came bear and had work to seek I hope you will send me a
half a Geney for this quarter mittsumer and I beg you please to send it me
30 by the Collchester hyes and leave it at the bear and wheat Sheafe in thames
street in london for mr Tallbutt hyeman to cantubery - as if y<ou> send a
letter be please to direct your letter for me Jane cross at mr bangges in

hospitall lane in st milldreds in cantubery - and pray send with speed I beg
- and you will much oblige your humble petitioner and parishsoner
Jane cross   35

TEXTUAL ALTERATIONS 2: church wardens] *interl.* 4: Petitioner] 'er' *interl at end of line*. 6: is
very] *'is' interl.* 11: me] *interl.* 18: Gentlemen] 'G' *over* 'S'. 20: am] 'a' *over illeg*. 22: help]
after del 'helf'. 27: what] *after del* 'whtat'. 34: parishsoner] *second* 's' *interl.*
    CIRCUMTEXT Note from other hand below text: 'Witenells My hand John Rickson Overser'.
Note of receipt on outside: 26 April 1755.
    FURTHER EVIDENCE 'Postige for a Letter from Jane Cross from Canterbury' (ERO, D/P
203/12/4, St Botolph, Colchester, overseers' accounts, entry of 26 April 1755).

**282   From George Watson in Shoreditch, London, to Mr Bugg in St
Botolph, Colchester, 24 April 1813**

London April 24th 1813

To Mr Bugg/
and Gentlemen of the Parrish of St Botolph
After a Period of Near two Years with the Greatest Regret under Affliction
and the Greatest Distres I am Compelld to write to you Gentⁿ I have   5
Struggeld to the Present Moment to Support my family under such Difficulties that I Believe few familys in Town or Country have done Because
I would not Trouble you Gentⁿ But Now it is Come to the Worste Gentⁿ
the Troubles I have Encounterd this Last Winter to Give my Family (I may
say) half Support. I cannot Describe nor would I wish to Trouble you with   10
a Relation. I have Little Else but My Warehose Money to depend upon as
Sometimes I have a Little Work and sometimes none & my Warehous
Money will but Just Procure us Bread if we had a full supply I have often
Given my Landlord a few Shillings for Rent & have not had a Bitt of
Bread for my Chilldren or means to Gett it to keep him from Takeing my   15
few things (wich are not worth is Taken) and Turning us in the Street as I
owe him best Part of 2 Pounds. a Person I dealt with for Bread Last
Winter has Serv^d me with an Execution on my Goods when the [G]entⁿ &
his two Men Came into my Place and saw me Ill and my Chilldren almost
Naked Looking Round at they Things says he Those things are not worth   20
my Taking I must Gett and Execution and Take you and it appears To me
you will be as Comfortable in Jail as in your present Situation this Gentⁿ
was a few days agoe and I am very Ill at This Time the Whole of my
family have been very Ill we have scarce a Bitt of Bread and This day

25 Landlord has been abuseing me his Money he will have Sickness of Fam-
    ily is Nothing To him he will be Rob^d no Longer he says This Gentle^n is a
    True Case of my Present Destrest Situation I have no other Refuge than
    to Submitt my Case to your Human Considertation and I do most humbly
    Sollicitt you Gent^n in Behalf of my Poor family. Gent^n I do not know
30 before tomorrow night we may be Turnd Into the Stret or I Takin to Jail as
    I Lye Intirely to Their Mercy Gent^n I am with

                                          the Greatest Respect
                                          George Watson

    N° 8 Dukes Court Long alley
35 near Worship St Shoreditch

TEXTUAL ALTERATIONS 8: Worste] 't' *interl with caret.*

283   From John Hall [in Chelmsford] to the overseer of St Botolph, Colchester, [8 December] 1814

                        <--------------------> 1814
    <--------------------> me to Write to you for Relief <-------------------->
    you Since last Feb^y [&] March <--------------------> Time & I Owe A
    Debt Ever <------------------> Been in my Power to Pay it <--------------->
5   Benefited Much by the Piece for <----------> been As Deer as Ever taking
    Every thing <----->er I Expect to be Put in Count of Court for the money
    that I Owe Sir I have kept from Troubleing you As Long As i Could So I
    hope you Will Consider my Case & Send me Relief At this Time I have
    Something In View that I hope I Shall Not Be Any Trouble to Much
10 Longer Sir I Am your Humble Petitioner

                                          John Hall

DATE Day and month from note of receipt on outside.
    DESTRUCTION OF TEXT Top left-hand corner of page torn off.
    FURTHER EVIDENCE John Hall (born 1767) lived in Chelmsford where he had worked for
    Thomas Johns, fellmonger at Baddow Lane, since 1782. In 1788 he married Elizabeth
    Seabrock with whom he had nine children, three of whom have left letters of their own:
    Sarah (**291, 293-5, 313, 315, 321**), Thomas (**339, 340, 342, 344-7**), and Elizabeth, who
    wrote to John Hall himself (**390**). John Hall's letters were probably written by his daughter
    Sarah - they are all in the same hand as her letters surviving from 1817 (**291, 293-5**). For a
    detailed reconstruction of the case of the Hall family, see Sharpe, 'Bowels of compation'.

284 From Sarah Withnell in Bethnal Green, London, to [James] Cole in St Botolph, Colchester, 2 October [1815]

London octr 2
Mr Cole

Sir/

I will thank to present my Case to the gentlemen and my Settuvation at present is wery Tryan for the money I had at First when i had got her and buying but 2 or 3 things to put in to a Room My money was gon and having My 2 Children to Surport And work is sCarce here that i have been oblidge to get much In deat I owe £3 and I should be much oblidge to the gentlemen to advance with what I had When I Came make it up to three Quarters I shall no dout have a hard tryal to get throug the winter but I hope if I live till Next summer I shall get more knowing and get more bisness And then I hope I shall recover My self - I hope you will send to Me as soon as posible as I am Much destresd)for you may Rely on my word I will Not trouble you any more then I can posibel help) and I should be glad if Mr Cole or Mr Mason Would Call on me when they Come to London - but when you Send the money or a lether Where to draw it you will
pleas to derect
Mrs Sar^h Withnell
No 25 Hair St
Brick Lane Bethnellgreen
    your Humble Serven
    Sarah Withnell

TEXTUAL ALTERATIONS 6: things] *interl*. 9: gentlemen] *final* 'en' *interl below with bow at end of line*. 13: Rely] *after del illeg*. 14: you] *interl*.
DATE Year from postmark.

285 From John Seowen in [the City of] London to [William] Mason in St Botolph, Colchester, 18 October 1815

London Oct 18 1815

Gentlman

I am sorey to say what I ham Goin to you that I am very bad of my old Complaint of my feet and hands So that I Canot Work at hard work to Maintain my famley But wea Canot get no Relif heair because heaving

onley a room it Will Not Settle us heair they wold give us an order to Cum
home but wea do not wish that But sumthing Most Be dane for wea heave
been Living upon the Spoail for this five Weeaks and I am Sorey to Say it
that it Will soon all Be Mead away With But still we Could Live in London
10   with a little assistans so asto hire a house to owar Selves - But we Cano<t>
<he>av without five or Six Pound Expencise then that wold Settell us so
asto by and Sell as theair is a living to be got as I Canot Stand hard Work
and I ham very sorey for it But I Most heav relif heair or theair and if we
heav Not Relif we most be Broght home Witch I ham Sorey to Say But if
15   you Wold Be so Good as to furnish us With ten Pounds to Set us forid in
Sum little trade as I canot Work hard But we Canot think of taeing aney
house to Settle us Withoute Sum relif and we Canot teak a house Without
5£ or 6£ Pounds for fixters &c and if you think Proper to furnish us With
that Sum we Can teak a house Dyrectly and Be No More trouble to you
20   But I Shall s<-------->t to you Genteel Min all Witch way you think Best of
it But I am very sory it Should hapen So that wea Should Be Broft so Low
as to Want that assistans But I Canot help it and I turn you Maney thanks
for all Past feavours But I think I Can Live in London With alitle help But
I Canot Put My Sellf fored With Nothing to Be Givn With Gentlann I
25   Should be Abliged to you for answeair one Way or the other as Soon as
Convenand to Let me no What I ham to doa for I ham very unhapey about
my famley to now Wat is to Be Cum With them as the Winter is Cumin on
So What to doa I Canot tell But to Leav it to you to doa the Best you Can
for Me I ham Sorey to trouble you for it
30   from yours
                                                          John Seowen

Pleas to drect Mr Seowen to
Be Left at the Ceap of Good hope
tavern Lime St Liden hl Market London
35   [*Postscript written crosswise in the middle of the sheet between the two
inside pages:*] Mr Mason I hoap you Still keep the Books till you heairs
from Mea again

TEXTUAL ALTERATIONS 1: Oct] *interl.* 9: still] 't' *interl.* 14: Broght] 'g' *over del illeg.* 15: us]
after del 'you'. 20: all] *inserted between* 'Min' *and* 'Witch'. 22: assitans] *second* 's' *over
illeg.* 23: feavours] 's' *interl below at end of line.* 31: Seowen] *interl below del* 'John'.

286 From Sarah Withnell in Bethnal Green, London, to [James] Cole in St Botolph, Colchester, 11 December [1815]

London December 11

Sir)

This is the third Letter I have Sent To trouble you for my pay and as I have had no answer and am much distressd I am oblidged to send to you)for releafe I must have from some were) you told me when I left you 5 would Send Me a Quarters pay when the first monay Was out)and as I hoped you would have Been so considered of my sittuation) A Wider with 2 Children in a strang place)it was a great favour for any one to girve me Credate - but as I owe so much and the mony not coming As I promsed I am ashamed to ask any forther neither do the person like To 10 trust me as the money has not Come according to my promise I Should be very sorry indeed to give the gentelmen any troublle but as I am so much deruld I hope you will have The goodness to send the pay up To Ester and pray do send immediatly One of my Children has been ill for some time and help either I must have from you or the parish were I am which I 15 should be wery Sorry indeed to do

I am you Humble Servent
Sarah Withnell

pleas to Derect
No 25 Hair Street 20
Brick Lane Bethenell green
Sir) if you have any friend I Could take it of I Should be Thankful to have the expence of the post spear^d

TEXTUAL ALTERATIONS 6: monay] *above del illeg.* 7: you] *over del illeg.* 11: Should] *after del illeg.* 14: immediatly] 'iatly' *interl below with bow at end of line.* 15: I must have] *interl below.*

DATE Year from postmark.

287 From Sarah Withnell in [Bethnal Green] London to [William] Mason in St Botolph, Colchester, 19 December 1815

London De^r 19 1815

Sir/

I receved your letter and the pound Note for which I am oblidge to you Thow it Caused me much Sorrow of Hert to find I must carry my letter

5 And the pound Note to the person That has been so Kind as to give me
Credit more then £4.0.0 regely trusting Me allmost ever sence I have
been here or I must have been Scerved and my Children or I must have
been Brought home to the parish And i could only appeas the person By
telling them you could not do much Without Consulting the parish meet-
10 ing Thew I did hope Sir you would have done that bifore - for I would Not
have the person loose the money herdly for my life do pray Sir for god
Sake help me at this time or it will So destress Me I think it will break my
Heart - for if you do not See the Consevenc that must follow
Sir/
15   I So far as the Silk Weaven is So bad I can get but little Work at present
I)must give up My room and throw my Self upon the parrish to bring me
and the Children home which I should be greved to my hert to do for
various Reasons) for as the Silk Weaven is expected to go much better In
2 or 3 months I should not fear but I shall get more work but this step
20 would take it out of my power of geting bread for My self or helping my
Children Another Reason I should be truly Sorry to put the parrish to that
Expenc) for beleave me *Sir* I am of That Disposion I do not like to be
beholden to other men to Feed my Fatherless Children thow I am A Widow
I should feel A pleasure to work for my Children if I could get it to do
25 and if ever I can see that day I will not troube the Gentelmen for I have no
dout but They are much burdand - *Sir* if you Belief you paid me 3 weaks
after Whitsentide And if you will have the goodness To send me £4 0 0
more and the the one I have had will fill the pay up to easter as I ricken it
just £5 do pray *Sir* show my letter to the parrish meeting and I have no
30 dout But they will Consider my Situation and will send me the Pay) from
your Humble

Servent Sarah Withnell

TEXTUAL ALTERATIONS 3: Note] *interl below with bow at end of line.* 9: not] *interl.* 9:
Without] 'out' *interl.* 9: Consulting] 't' *interl.* 10: I would] 'I' *interl.* 11: money] *over
illeg.* 16: room] *interl.* 16: upon] *after del* 'on'. 16: the] *interl after del illeg.* 18: expected]
'p' *interl.* 20: self] *after del illeg.* 21: I] *after del illeg.* 22: me] *interl.* 23: Children] *interl.*
25: and] *after del illeg.* 26: dout] *after del illeg.* 26: burdand] *first* 'd' *over illeg.* 26:
Belief] *second* 'e' *interl.* 27: Whitsentide] 'sentide' *interl below with bow at end of line.*
28: just] *after del illeg.* 28: £5] *interl below at end of line.*
PLACE Parish inferred from previous letters from Sarah Withnell (**284, 286**).

288 From Samuel Balls in Hull to [James] Cole in St Botolph, Colchester, 14 January 1816

Hall Jany 14th 1816

Gentlemen

I have taken the Liberty of Informing you of my sircumstances at present my wife has been bad those four months I have labourd to supoart hir under a bad state of Ealth my self I Did not make my Case nown untill I had Pledged all our weairing Aparril and Even my wifes Ring being thus Destressed and No further Imploy to be had I have Aplied to the Parish of skullcoates for Reliefe my wifes Ilness is ocaisoned by our Jurney from Colchester she was braut to bed on the tenth of this month being 7 months gone with Child she is Attended By Dr Ayers of the Hull infermery at present I aplied on those Circumstances to the Parich of sculcoate as I reside here and I here Inform you what relief thay have

given us saturday 6th Rec^d 2^s:0^d
monday 8   Rec^d 3:0
wedensday 10   Rec^d 3:0
saturday 13   Rec^d 1:0

I have given you a true state of my afairs and if your Gudness would be so kind as to furnish us with £2:0:0 I think I Could Get on without further trubling you as I have promis of a Constant place of work

the parish of scullcoates thretens to pas us home Next week but my wife is not in a state to be removed at present

    Gentlemen I Remain your
    Humble servent sam^l Balls
    shoe maker Lees Row Milk street
        Hull

TEXTUAL ALTERATIONS 5: Did] 'i' *over illeg.* 13: 6] *over* '5'.

RELATED CORRESPONDENCE On 11 January 1816, Joseph Marsh, one of the Guardians of the Poor in Sculcoates (near Hull), wrote to the overseers of St Botolph, Colchester, that Samuel Balls, with wife and two children, had applied for relief, saying that his settlement was in St Botolph and 'that his family was relieved by you about 7 or 8 months ago'. Marsh went on: 'I visited his habitation this Day which is a very poor one indeed and therefore beg that you will have the goodness to consider his Case and order them some relief immedeately'.

289   From Mary Rabey in [St John, Westminster] London to [William] Mason in St Botolph, Colchester, 16 March 1816

London March 16th 1816

Mr Mason

You Desired me to Let you know the Names and ages of my Children James Six years Old the 25th of November Last and Jesse 4 Years the 24th
5 of December Last and not able Either of them of any Employment Whatever and i myself Get their Living and mine by going out to washing Sometimes 3 Days in a week and Sometimes 4 and out of that Pay Eighteen Pence a week for their being taken Care of You Likewise Say that as i am married I Cannot Belong to that Parish but my Husband is an Irish-
10 man by birth and therefore i Can claim no other Parish but that but i Do not ask you for any thing for myself So as you will assist me in keeping the Children When i married i did it in a view of bettering myself Likewise my Family but my Husband was Called away on Foreign Service where he has been 2 Years the 24th of Last November Where he is Like to
15 remain i hope you will Send as Soon as Soon as you receive this For i Cannot Do any Longer

Please to Direct as before to No 9 New
Rye Streat at Westm London

Your Humble Servant
20   Mary Rabey

CIRCUMTEXT Attested below text by signatures of Mathew Jenkinson and John Slater, churchwardens of St John, Westminster, and John Simpson, overseer.

Mary Rabey's letter is written on the second and third pages of a letter she had received from William Mason, overseer of St Botolph, Colchester, dated 9 March 1816, in which she was informed 'we should not releive you any longer unless you sent us your Adress and the Names and Age of your Children and their employment and how situated and such Letter to be Signed by the Curchwardens and Overseers of the Parish where you live Until that is done you will not here from us and as you are married you cannot belong to the Parish of St Botolph'. On the back of that page, there is a statement by Robert Moody, 19 March 1819: 'This is to Certify that Mary Raby is a Lodger of mine and her Husband as been on Forigen Service a Consirable Time and that She is a poor woman as Tow Children and works verry Hard For a Living!'

FURTHER EVIDENCE Six years later, Mary Rabey appeared before the select vestry of St Botolph, Colchester, and 'Brought her son James Barker (who is just come out of the Duke of Yorks School) from London in order to obtain some weekly allowance for him'. It was resolved to allow her 2s per week 'until a place be provided for him and that his mother be requested to provide a master for him as early as possible', the money to be paid through Mr Dodd's brother. She was also given 7s 'for her expenses to return to London with her son'(ERO, D/P 203/8/2, St Botolph, Colchester, select vestry minutes, entry of 11 May 1822).

290 From John Hall in Chelmsford to [William] Mason in St Botolph, Colchester, 6 May 1816

Chelmsford May the 6 1816

Sir

I Beg Leave Once More to Infirm you Concerning the Doctors Bill I Expect to be Trouble^d for it Every Day So I hope you Will take It Into Concideration & Settle it for me As I have had Nothing of you for 5 Almost three year & I hope I Shall have no Ocation to Trouble you Without Any thing happings to Me In Affliction Witch I hope Will Not by the Blessing of God you know Sir Every Poor has a Doctor Allowe^d them But I have not Trouble^d you for Any thing of the kind A Long time & I hope you Will do it for me this time or I dont know What I Shall do My Daughter is been 10 Verry Ill But thank God is A deal <b>etter & the Child Grows A Grate Boy She Did not know Where to Apply For her Money When Mr Miles Was gorne She Went 2 or 3 times Before She Could get Any Intiligence But She haves it Now & We turn you All the Gentlemen & Mr Danniels Many thanks for All your Kindness to her & She Acknowleges the Same 15 With gratitude

So I Remain Sir your Humble Petitioner John Hall

TEXTUAL ALTERATIONS 7: Witch] 'i' *over* 'h'. 13: Went] *interl with caret.*14: All] *after del* 'you'.

291 From Sarah Hall in Chelmsford, 4 March 1817

Chelmsford Ma*[rch]* 4 1817

Sir

I have Sent you A Letter in Return of yours & for What We know Or Can hear he is At his fathers At Latchendon I Sent Word so Before Sir I hope You Will Settel the Money So as it dont Put Me to Any Expence to 5 Get it for I Cant Afford it as I Want it for Support it Cost Me 2^S6^D When My Brother Came for it & 1^S for the Letter that you Sent there is 2^s0^d more due Last friday Besides the Pound Note you Sent Sir I hope you Will Settle it So As I Can have it Weekly for I Cant do Without it Sir I am Yr Sarah Hall 10

TEXTUAL ALTERATIONS 6: Want] *after del* 'Wat'.

RELATED CORRESPONDENCE On 29 February 1826, the overseer of St Botolph, Colchester, had written to Chelmsford, requesting them to advance 3s per week to Sarah Hall for her child.

FURTHER EVIDENCE Sarah Hall (born 1797) was the daughter of John Hall (see **283**). In January 1816 she had left service and given birth to an illegitimate son for whom she received a regular allowance of 3s per week. She and her son seem to have lived with her parents in Chelmsford. The boy's father referred to at the beginning (l. 4) was Charles Ellis, a carpenter at Latchingdon near Purleigh. For further details, see Sharpe, 'Bowels of compation', p. 92.

The four letters from Sarah Hall surviving from 1817 (the present one and **293**, **294**, **295**) are in the same hand which is the same, in turn, as that of the letters from her father, John Hall.

292   From John Hall in Chelmsford to [William] Mason in St Botolph, Colchester, 19 March 1817

Chelmsford March the 19 1817

Sir

I Am under the Obligation of Writing to you Concerning the Childs Money for I Stand in Grate need of it it is 8 Weeks Next friday he Was at
5 Fathers at Latchendon Some time ago & brought a Months Money And I thought he Woud do the Same again I Sent three Letters to him And Could get No Answer & I Should be glad if you Will take it to Hand to get the Money for us I Expect he is at his fathers Now At Latchindon Sir I Am your Humble Servent John Hall

TEXTUAL ALTERATIONS 8: Expect] *after del illeg.*
TEXT The child referred to was the illegitimate son of John Hall's daughter, Sarah Hall (see **291**).

293   From Sarah Hall in Chelmsford to the overseer of St Botolph, Colchester, 31 March 1817

Sir

My Present Necessity Obliges me to Send you Another Letter Concerning My Money for I Am in great Disttress For it My Parents Cannot Aford to Maintain me & the Child Without my Alowance for I Cant get
5 Anything To Do I Am in Vew of A Place in Chelmsford But I Cant go to it Without the money to get me A thing or tow to go in for i am in Wants Of things & I Shall Be Oblige to you to get the money for me or I Shall

Not know What Cource to take Sir I Shall be Oblige to you to Send me An
Answer by the Return of Post

Sarah Hall 10
<Che>lmsford March
the 31 1817

TEXTUAL ALTERATIONS 7: Oblige] 'i' *interl with caret.*

294   From Sarah Hall in Chelmsford to Mr Arthur, overseer of St
Botolph, Colchester, 24 April 1817

Sir

I have taken the liberty to write to you I hope you will excuse me But I
would wish to know What I am to do Concerning the allowance for My
Child I have not heard any thing of Elliss Nor yet had any money since
my brother Was at Colchester I should wish to know how I am to receive 5
my money and were I am to receive it for if I dont have it regular I cannot
support my Child therefore I must be oblidged to come home to my parrish
as I cannot stop here and parrish and it is out of my fathers power to
maintain me and my Child I hope Sir you will favour me with a few lines
to let me know what I am to do if I dont here from you I must Come 10
imeadately

your humble serv^t
Sarrah Hall

Chelmsford
April 24 1817   15

TEXTUAL ALTERATIONS 5: how] *interl.*

295   From Sarah Hall in Chelmsford to John Rudkin in St Botolph,
Colchester, 20 May 1817

Chelmsford May 20 1817

Sir

I hope you Will Excuse my Writing to you but Necessity Obliges me to it
for Times is So hard that I Cannot do Without Receiving the Childs Money
Weekly So I hope Sir you Will Take it into Consideration & Appoint Some 5

Person in Chelmsford to help me to it my Child grows a fine Boy he only Wants a Good father my Pay is a 11ˢ0ᵈ Next Friday & Sir I hope you Will Send me an Answer to this Letter & I Shall turn you Many thanks Sir I Am Yˢ

10   *Sarah Hall*

TEXTUAL ALTERATIONS 10: Sarah] 'r' *over illeg.*
CIRCUMTEXT Copy of answer from St Botolph, Colchester, at bottom of page: 'Mʳ Palmer a Person of the name of Sarah Hall who lives in Badder Lane at Chelmsford has to receive 3ˢ/- Weekly from our Parish & there will be due to her Eleven Shillᵍˢ next Friday which please to pay her & evry Friday after that 3/. pʳ Week till Midsumʳ Day & send us an accoᵗ we will receive the money here & place it to your accᵗᵗ.

296   From John Hall [in Chelmsford] to [John] Rudkin in St Botolph, Colchester, 5 June 1817

<Chelms>/[f]/<ord>June the 5 1817
Sir
   The Present Presure of the Times Obliges me to Send to you for Some Assistance for I Cannot Support my family Bread is So Verry Dear I
5 Cannot Get it & I am Callᵈ Upon for a debt Of £2-0-0 and if dont Pay it Directly my Creditor Says he Will Put it into the Lawers hands & have my things out of My House Sir I dont Trouble you Often So I hope you Will grant My Request & Send me A Some thing to Wards the debt or I Shall Not know what to do to have my fue things taking Away Will be a
10 Sad thing for me So I hope you Will Answer My Letter Without Troubling you Any further & Sir I hope I Shall Not be Oblige to Trouble Any More yet Awile
                              Sir I Am your
                              Humble Petitioner
15   *John Hall*
PS
   Sir I Beg Lieve to Inform you I have to Pay to the Rates and the Parrish Some Time Ago Settled them for Me But is Not for Some Time I Should Not Have Troubled you if Flour had Not got up So high for that is the
20 Debt I Owe

TEXTUAL ALTERATIONS 8: grant] 't' *interl at end of line.*

297   From John Hall in Chelmsford to John Rudkin in St Botolph, Colchester, 26 August 1818

Chelmsford August the 26 1818

Sir

I Beg Lieve to Inform you that I have been Verry Ill and Not Able to Work and I Stand in Need of your Assistance at this Time for I am Verry Back in my Payments I dont Often Trouble you So Sir I hope You Will   5 give my Present Distress a Thought Sir I Was Verry Bad Some time Back and I did Not Trouble you then for Any thing then but my Present Nessesity Obliges me to do it at this Time I Wish it doe Not So Sir I hope you Will Sind me a Something at this Time and I hope I Shall Not have Occation to Trouble You Any More So Sir I Am your Humble Petitioner   10

John Hall

298   From John Hall in Chelmsford, 9 September 1818

Chelmsford Sepr the 9 1818

Sir

I Beg Lieve to Trouble you With Another Letter and hope you Will Send Some Relief for I Stand in great Need of it for I have been Verry Ill of Late I have the Rates to Pay to and my Work is fell Verry Short All at   5 Once for I have Notthing to do this Week as yet And am Unable to Pay What I have Run back Without Some Assistance and if you Will be So good as to Send me Relief At this Time it Will be thankfully Reciev^d and By the help Of the Lord I Shant Trouble you Any More Sir I Do Remain Your Humble Petitioner John Hall   10

TEXTUAL ALTERATIONS 3: hope] *after del* 'h'.

299   From John Hall in Chelmsford, 24 September 1818

Chelmsford Septr the 24 1818

Sir

I According to your Request I have Sent you a Line to Let you Know I have Recieved your Letter & the Contentis & Am Humbly Thankfull for

5 the Same & by the Blessing of God I hope I Shall Have My health &
Shant Trouble you no more At Present
    Sir I Do Remain your Humble Servt John Hall

FURTHER EVIDENCE The postage for a 'Letter from John Hall of Chelmsford' was paid by the
overseers of St Botolph, Colchester, on 25 September 1828 (ERO, D/P 203/12/41, St
Botolph, Colchester, overseers' accounts).

300* From [Mary] Mitchel in Ipswich, 30 September 1818

                    ipswech septembr th30 1818
ser ihave taken the LeBety of riten to you for the monney for mr raBands
keamers chiLd ser if you pLease to pay me up to the 29th of septemBer
ser ihope you will send it By mr giLes the korshman ser ihope you will
5 not takit ames of my taken the LeBity of asken you for afew things for
my chiLd as ihav Ben out of pLase sume time and my child have Ben
very ill ihave spent the Last shilling aBaut him that ihave got if it is evn
as smorL trifLe shaLl be gLad of it
                    so no More from your
10   ombLe sarvent
                      <mar>ey mecheL

TEXTUAL ALTERATIONS 2: of] *interl.* 8: of it] *interl below.*

301   From James Haxell in Colchester to the overseer of St Botolph, Colchester, 10 December 1818

                                Colchester 10th Decr 1818
Gentlemen,
    Having this morning made application to Mr Rudkin for relief by one
of my Daughters, was desired to attend this meeting, but not being able
5 myself to attend, I have made bold to write these few lines, I have now
been confined nearly sixteen weeks, and it has cost me some weeks to the
amount of 2^s/6^d out of my income for herbs for fomenting &^{c} that the
Subsistance I have had cume to my share has been very trifling - If I
continue to live as I have for this last seven weeks the time will be long
10 before I shall ever be able to labour again for my family, I ought (as I am
I trust in a state of Convalescence) to allow my self half apint of Porter

every Day, as that would do my Deseasd Limb more good in one week, than all the Medical application I could apply in one Month, I trust the Gentlemen will consider my cirumstances and do the best they can for me, resting assured I will not trouble them any longer than I am able to 15 work, in case it cannot be granted I must on Saturday next, be removed to my Quarters and there remain untill I am able to work for my family (Mr Dodd stated the other Day that my Wife & Daughter worked at Needle work, but that is but very little as we are not able to purchase materials to work with,) but should the Gentelmen be so condecending as to do for me 20 what they may Judge requisite as far as is Portable it will be received with gratitude from their obedient Servant to Command

James Haxell

To the Gentelmen
of the Parish   25
of St *Botolph*
PS Should any enquiry be wanting respecting the Ages of my Children
there are 1 female -   17^{yrs}
- one D^o -   14
   one D^o -   4   30
   one D^o -   2
   one Male -   4

TEXTUAL ALTERATIONS 6: been] *inserted in left-hand margin.*

302   From John Hall in Chelmsford, 11 December 1818

Chelmsford Decr the 11 1818

Sir
My Present Occation Obliges me to Send you this Letter for I have No Work to do at this Time & I have Two Lads at home have Nothing To do and What to do We Cannot Tell So Sir I hope you Will take our Present 5 Distress into Consideration for We Cannot Get Bread Sir I Am A Certifi- cate Pirson to Chelmsford So I hope you Will Send a answer To my Petition or I Shall Be Oblige to go this Parrish for We are In Great Want Sir I am your Humble Petitioner John Hall

TEXTUAL ALTERATIONS 5-6: Certificate] 'c' *interl with caret.* 8: Great] 'r' *interl with caret.*

303   From John Hall in Chelmsford, 21 December 1818

Chelmsford Decr the 21 1818

Sir

Our Present Distress Obliges me to trouble you With Another Letter
for I did Not do but two Days Work the Week before Last & but three
5 Days Work Last Week & that Will not maintain my family & have to Pay
the Rates the Parrish Settled the Rates for me Some time back When
Times did not go With me as they do now for my Work is Verry Short
And I have to Maintain the Lad that Come down to you for Work and but
Verrry Little for the other to do & I Shall have but three days Work to Do
10 this Week So I hope Sir you Will take my Case into Consideration at This
Time for We must have Support from Some Quarter for We Are drove to
the Lowest Degree So Sir I Am your Humble Petitioner

John Hall

304   From Sarah Mitchel in Ipswich to [John] Rudkin in St Botolph, Colchester, 29 December 1818

Ipswich December 29th 1818

Sir/

I take the present opportunaty of writing beging the remitance of the
Money allowed for my Child by the bearer as I greatley want it being at
5 this time out of place - and unless you concider my situation and allow
me something from the parish I must put him into the House - for my
Wagers is bearly enough to find myself when in place -

yours &c

Sarah Mitchel

10 PS the amount of the Money Due to me is one pound 12^s6 -

TEXTUAL ALTERATIONS 6: him] *interl with caret.*

305   From Elizabeth Hines in [St Anne] Soho, London [1818]

Sir

i thake this opertunity of writing to you Concerneing my Money i hope
you will Send it as Usewell you wish me to Explain my meaneyng wich

you know my Meaing for the Quarter is out you Payd me up to 17th September i hope you will have the Goodness to Send it me as usell for i 5 Cannot do without when this Quarters is out Mr Bishop will pay it me if you have the Goodness to Lett him do i hope you will Send up next weake or up By the Post for it wold Be much Better of my Baker Expct his money i Cannot do without it

Elesbeth Hynes dirict 10
for Me at kinks Street
Shoo

TEXTUAL ALTERATIONS 6: is out] *inserted between* 'Quarters' *and* 'M^r'.
DATE Year from filing note on outside.
RELATED CORRESPONDENCE This and six other letters are assumed to have come from the same person, even though the scriptual record (various hands, variant spellings of sender's name) and provenance are not altogether conclusive. Five letters are from poorer hands: two definitely from the same hand (**353, 356**), two possibly from another (same) hand (the present one and **306**), one from yet another hand (**361**). The remaining two letters are from (different) professional hands (**312, 375**). Nevertheless, the poorer letters (without dates) agree with the properly documented ones in their references to Elizabeth Hines's daughter suffering from fits and to Mr Bishop, a presumed contact man in Soho. Elizabeth Hines wrote from London and Ipswich, though there is no clue why she wrote to both places at the same time (see **306**). It also remains unclear whether she moved from London to Ipswich or travelled between the two places. While only two of her letters come from Ipswich (**353, 356**), the only pieces of related correspondence refer to that place. These are a letter of October 1818, from Ipswich (no parish given) to Colchester, the precise direction of which is not clear, with reference to the advanced payment of '16 weeks pay' to Mrs Hines; and a letter from Ipswich, 27 March 1833, saying that Elizabeth Hines's daughter, Eliza, was married to James Mills of St Helen's, Ipswich (with copy of marriage certificate from curate of St Helen's).

306 From [Elizabeth] Hines in [St Anne, Soho] London to Mr Dodd in St Botolph, Colchester [1818]

Mr Dod

I have wrote to you and likewise to Ipswich and have had no answer from near a place I hope you will see about it as I am in great Distress and have no home to put my head in as the Family where I was at is come to town and I must get a lodging and if you would grant me a quarters money 5 I should be very glad and if not I must come down next Thursday as I must have some money I dont want to come but I must if you dont send me some money but if you would send me my pay I can do very well you must consider I have 2 Children to keep and they and myself are half

10 starved and if you would seend it up to the Ipswich arms in Coullum Street
is a parcell and Direct it to me at No 81 Deon Street Soho Square with out
Delay to Mr Dobyell Painter
     I remain Yours &c
     H Hines

TEXTUAL ALTERATIONS 11: Street] *after del illeg.*
WRITING Possibly same hand as that of previous letter, from Elizabeth Hines (**305**).
DATE Year from filing note on outside.

307 From Sarah Mitchel in Ipswich to [John] Rudkin in St Botolph, Colchester, 4 January 1819

Ipswich January 4th 1819

Sir/
    I received the parcel you sent by Mr Child the Coachman containing
1[£]7^s6^d but it was not the sum I Should have had by five Shillings, - the
5 former payment that I received from you was 1[£]5^s0^d from July 22nd up to
September 30th which was quite right and from the 30 of September to
the 30 of December must undoubtedly be 13 Weeks - for which time
1[£]12^s6^d must certainly be the sum. - I therefore hope you will send it - be
assured I cannot afford to Loose it - being out of place and have everry
10 necessary to find the Child from my wagers. -
               your Humble Servant
               Sarah Mitchel

TEXTUAL ALTERATIONS 9: have] *after del* 'and'.

308 From Sarah Davis in Whitechapel, London, to Mr Dodd in St Botolph, Colchester, 25 January 1819

London

Sir/
    As you was so good as to promise To Cloth my boy my Husband expects
to go in A few Day and Will be much oblidged to you To send as soon as
5 poseble I hope Sir you will not send me less Then £3.0.0 as you know he
is Allmost naked and must be Doubell Clothed -

your Humbl
Servent S^a Davis
Late Sarah Whitnell

Pleas to derect 10
No 161 Brick Lane
White Chappel

25 Jan 1819

TEXTUAL ALTERATIONS 6: naked] *after del* 'of'. 11: Lane] *interl with bow at end of line.*

309   From John Hall in Chelmsford, 5 February [1819]

Chelmsford Feb^{ry} the 5 1719

Sir

My Present Situation Calls for further Assistance for my Work is verry
Short I have been with my Master this 36 year and Never Expirence^d
Such a time before for I Cant Clear my way At no Rate for I Cant get 5
enougf for bread So I hope Sir you Will Consider our Cace and Send us
further Support Sir I am Sorry to Trouble you So Soon but Necessity
Obliges me as I have No Other friend but you to go to for Any thing I
have a Lad to maintain That works With me but He has nothing to do
Now and i have him to Maintain now so it goes verry hard with me Sir I 10
am your

Humble Petitioner John Hall

TEXTUAL ALTERATIONS 7: am] *after del illeg.*
DATE '1719' is obviously a slip of the pen.

310   From John Hall in Chelmsford, 11 February 1819

Chelmsford Feby the 11 1819

Sir

I hope you Will Excuse Me for Troubleing you with Another Letter But
I am Oblige to It for Necisity forces me to It for We are at A Verry Low
Ebb I Dont know where to get Another Weeks Bread Without Some 5
Assistance So I hope you Will Answer this Litter Or I Must Apply for
Relief At this Parrish & that I Shall Not Like to do But I Cant do without
I Wish I Could But As I Tould you in my Letter of my Work being so Short

that I Cannot do without Some Assistancce Witch I hope you Will Grant
10 At This Time or I Shall Not know What to do Sir I kindly Thank you for All
Past favours So i Remain Your Humble Petitioner
John Hall

TEXTUAL ALTERATIONS 11: Remain] 'in' *interl at end of line.*

311   From Sarah Mitchel in Ipswich to [John] Rudkin in St Botolph, Colchester, 30 March 1819

Ipswich March 30th 1819

Sir/
I take the present opportunity of beging the remitance of my Money -
as the time is Expired. necessity Oblige me to be exact to the time as the
5 person have calld on me for some Money that have the Child to Keep, but
could not let her have any till you send me some, - but I hope their will be
no mistake this time fom the 30th of December to the 30 of March is 13
Weeks - the sum due to me at three shillings p^r Week is 1[£]19^s0^d -
Sarah Mitchel

312   From Elizabeth Hines in [St Anne] Soho, London, to Mr Dodd in St Botolph, Colchester, 9 May 1819

Sunday May 9 - *1819*

Mr Dodd
I Shall take as a grate faviour if you would Send me a little Money if
you could Send me the quarters money it would be very Excepable and if
5 you cant please to Send me a pound I have been very bad and was not
able to pay the last quarter rent as I am a pound behind hand and they
begin to be very impatiose for it you told me if I wanted a favior to aploy
to you please to give it to Thos Bisshop and let it not be Book^d for it will
cost me 1^s4^d
10   I am your Humble
Servant Elizth Hines

I shall go to Bisshop on Satuardy morning
Elizth Hines
N7 King Street
15   Soho

TEXTUAL ALTERATIONS 5: cant] *interl.* 6: a] *interl.* 8: not] *interl with caret.*

313 From Sarah Hall in Chelmsford, 21 June [1819]

Chelmsford June 21

Sir

  i write this to inform you that my childs money is stopt i should be glad if you will send me word sir ware i ham to take it m^r hadmer says he will pay me if you please i should be glad sir if you will send a anwser to this   5 for i want the money Sir i ham sorry to trouble you

your humble

Servant

Sarah Hall

TEXTUAL ALTERATIONS 4: he] *after del illeg.* 5: i] *after del illeg.*
DATE Year from filing note on outside.

314 From S[arah] Mitchel in Ipswich, 29 June 1819

Ipswich June 29th 1819

Sir

  please to send my Money by the Barer Mr Childs which is due on the 30th ove June the sum is 1$^£$19^s Shillings the last I receivd was on the 30th ove April if you will you'l grately Obligh Yours Humbl   5

Sarvent S Mitchel

TEXTUAL ALTERATIONS 6: Sarvent] 'v' *interl.*
FURTHER EVIDENCE In April 1821, after having received several letters from Sarah Mitchel 'requesting a further Sum of 1/- per week in addition to 3/- she had been receiving for her Bastard child', the select vestry of St Botolph, Colchester, decided 'that it be not Granted'. A month later, she came in person and stated 'that Mr Osborne the Late Overseer had promised her an extra Shilling per Week'. Again, it was decided 'that *but 3/- per week* Could be allowed for the child as herefore', and she was given £3 18s up to 24 June 1821 (ERO, D/P 203/8/2, St Botolph, Colchester, select vestry minutes, entries of 16 April and 14 May 1821).

315   From Sarah Hall in Chelmsford, 2 July 1819

Sir/

In answer to your Rec^d this morning I have to inform you that it is not
my intention to part wit my child as Chas Ellis request - for as I have been
able to bear through With him in I should wish to have the care of him in
5 futir I have been to a Magistrate to day & he says that If the Pay for my
child is taken of he will have it put on again for he cannot demand him
from me - I hope that you will inform Charls Ellis of the same

I Remain

With due Respect

your Oblig^d St

Sarah Hall

10

Chelmsford

July 2^d 1819

316   From James Clark in [St George in the East] London to the overseers of St Botolph, Colchester, 9 July 1819

London 9th Juley 1819

Gent^lmen

I am Sorey to truble but my wife has Wrote two Letters and has had no
answer Concerning hir Weekley Pay from the Parish - Gent^lmen be
5 asshured if it was in my pour to Suport a Sickley Wife and 5 Smal Children i ould not truble you but not haveing any Settled Employ it is not in
my Pour to Suport them my Wife has lain in about two months and when
we had the last letter from you you mentoned that when you Com to
London you ould Gett Some person to Pay hir Weekly mony Regurlarly
10 and wee Depended on it Acrording to your word to assist in Paying the
Expence of hir Laying inn and we are now in grate truble I am only a
temprery man in the Inde Cmp^ys Employ and only Employd when the
Tee Flit is in and they have Comenced paying them of in the first of this
month 100 a week and we will be all off by the 24th of this month I begg
15 Gent^lmen you will have the goodness to answer this letter as ther is no
Remadey for me but to have my Wife and famley Reglurly passed hom
as I have taken advice on the Subject Gent^lmn I hope you will censider
this letter as I Do not wish to be more trublsum then I can help or to put
the prish to my Extre Expence

Gent^lmen your 20
ob^d Hub^l Servt
James Clark

N° 4 Bettey Streat Bettey Place
Comershell Road London

TEXTUAL ALTERATIONS 24: Comershell] *after del* 'NB'.
FURTHER EVIDENCE On 16 April 1821, having received a letter from James Clark's wife
Rachel 'Stating her Great Distress & prays for 6/- per week to be allow^d She having been
receiving 3/- per week', the select vestry of St Botolph, Colchester, decided 'that 3/- per
week be allow^d till further orders, & that some Person be requested to wait on the Parish
Officers in London & Beg them if the Husband James Clark be forced to pass them home
to Scotland' (ERO, D/P 203/8/2, St Botolph, Colchester, select vestry minutes). The letter from Rachel Clark of April 1821 has not survived. But there are letters from her from
London from 1826 (**327, 332, 333**), which suggests that the attempt of St Botolph's select
vestry at removing the family to Scotland failed.

**317   From William and Ann Lester in Sudbury [Suffolk], 30 August
1819**

Sudbury August 30th 1819
Gentlemen
I am now Compelld to address you with a Line Informing you I have
Been verry Lame with one Foot for a Nine or Ten Days and I am alltogether
Indifficent and my Dear Chilldren are all Poorly Particular my youngest   5
Child is verry Ill my Case is Deploreable and in a word Distressing I
must acknowledge your Favours have Been Great and Necessity Compell
Mee to Be Troublesome Gentlemen I have not Cloathing Enough to Cover
my Nakedness it is true the weather have Been warm and Cloathing have
not Been so Much wanted But the weather will Soon Be Colder and as   10
there is a Long winter fast approaching I Hope the Gentlemen will Render
Mee Some Extra assistance to get Some Cloathing for myself and Chilldren
for my Chilldren are allmost Naked and on the other Hand I am now
Indebted Half a years Rent this Mickalemas which will take Place on 29th
of September and as wee do not Belong to Sudbury wee are Put into the   15
Rates. and that will Be Three Shillings a Month Gentlemen I must once
more Peray you to Compassionate Our Present Distress
      and Remain your most Humble Petitioners &^c &^c Willm and Ann
Lester

TEXTUAL ALTERATIONS 15: do] *interl.*

FURTHER EVIDENCE Apparently in response to this letter, William Lester was allowed the sum of £1 (ERO, D/P 203/12/41, St Botolph, Colchester, overseers' accounts, 25 September 1819). A year-and-a-half later, he told the select vestry of St Botolph, Colchester, that his rent was due and it was ordered that £1 2s be paid through Mr Oliver in Sudbury (ERO, D/P 203/8/2, St Botolph, Colchester, select vestry minutes, entry of 9 April 1821).

318   From John Hall in Chelmsford, 6 September 1819

Chelmsford Sepr the 6 1819

Sir

   I Beg Lieve to Iform you that I Stand in further Assistance for I Am Lame in my Leg through A Strain & am unable To Work so Sir I hope
5 you Will Not think it Ill of my going to this Parrish for Relief for my Club Box is Shut Up & have No feind to go for any thing But you I have two Children that is Not able to do any thing So Sir I hope you Will Send An Order to the Oversears of Chelmsford for they dont Like to Any thing Without your Order So Sir I Am your Humble

10   Petitioner *John Hall*

RELATED CORRESPONDENCE Thomas King, surgeon in Chelmsford, had written to St Botolph, Colchester, on 4 May 1819 that John Hall and his wife had 'both been very ill of a Fever', and that, while John Hall had since 'got to work again', 'the Woman tho recovered from the fever is still in a very low and debilitated state of health & requires more nourishment than her husband can procure her'.

319   From John Hall in Chelmsford, 12 November 1819

Chelmsford Nov^{br} the 12 1819

Sir

   I Beg Lieve to Inform you that I have been Verry Ill And as my Club To Shut Up I have been Under the Painfull Necessity of Applying to this
5 Parrish for Some Little Relief As I have been So Ill that I Could not Follow my Work Sir the Overseer Told Me to Acquaint you of the Same As my Work has been So Short I Was Oblige to go to the Parrish Which Sir I hope you Will Not take it Amiss but thank God I Am better Which I hope by his Blessing I hope I Shall Remain So I Remain Your Humble

10 Ser^{vt} John Hall

320 From George Watson in [Shoreditch] London to Mr Osborn in St Botolph, Colchester, 21 February 1820

London Feb 21ˢᵗ 1820

Sir

I humbly beg leave to Submitt the few following Lines to your Consideration having no Intention Either to Dictate or offend you. I must beg leave to Inform you *Sir* I was Greatly Surpriz·d at my Daughters Comeing 5 home Six Weeks after her Lying In and that without any Prevous Notice I with a Wife on a Sick bed and 3 Chilldren about me and no Conveneince for her and her Child haveing only one room for us all and no bed to Lay her on if *Sir* I had Preveously Known of her Comeing I should have Prevented it if Possible at Least untill I was better Prepar·d to Receive her 10 she is my Daughter *Sir* and if it was In my Power I would assist her in her Unfortunate Situation but it is not I have brought one family up and have at this Time 3 Chilldren and a Poor Afflicted Wife Confin·d to her Room tho Illness by the 6 Months Together Labouring under a Severe Asthmatic Complaint it Surprizes me that a woman with an Infant Child only 15 6 Weeks old and that In the middle of Winter should take such a Journey it is a Providence she has not Suffer·d Siverely for it if *Sir* she has House room with me it is as much as I can do for her she and her Infant is Sleeping along with 2 of my Girls on a very small bed I may say all of them Crippled I would Get her a Lodgeing if I was able to pay for it but I 20 am not If Sir you will have the Goodness to assist me with the means I will Get an old flockbed and and old Blankett or 2 and make her up a bed but without you do *Sir* I cannot as she is with us we must do as well as we can it is a thing I little Expected In those Cases In London they Keep the Woman if the Child lives 9 Months in the Poorhouse At Present *Sir* I am 25 not Troublesome to you nor any body Else but with more Incumberance than I have it is the way to bring us all to Trouble for it is with the Greatest of Strugle I can Keep my head above water. My Daughter Informs me *Sir* you have Propos·d allowing her 4ˢ Per Week with Respect I beg leave to say that she and the Child Cannot Subsist on it. she has tried it since 30 she has been home it will Scarcely Procure her half support as she ought to have as a Woman Suckling a Child if *Sir* you will Please to allow her another Shilling she will be humbly thankfull In Respect of Recvᵍ the Allowance *Sir* I do not Mean to Dictate I only give it as my Oppionion I think the Best way and will be attended with the Least Ilconveinence will 35 be if it meets with your aprobation is to Inclose a Note in a Lettʳ the

greatest Ilconveinence will be in having 1ˢ4ᵈ to Pay for Postage as a Double Lettʳ if it is not your Pleasure to Pay *Sir* she must out of her money. I beg leave to say my Daughter has made the greatest of spare with what
40 you Gave her Paying her Carriage up and a little suport on the Road and since she has been home and a Trifle she Laid out for an old Cradle for her Child she has Chang·d her Last Shilling humbly begging Pardon if I have said any thing to Offend as it is not my Intention I humbly beg the favour *Sir* if you will have the Goodness to awnswer this as soon as you
45 Can Conveinently as I shall have her to support untill you do thanking you *Sir* for all favours I am with all due Respect
George Watson

Please to Direct G. Watson
Nᵒ 8 Dukes Court Long alley
50 near Primrose Street
London

TEXTUAL ALTERATIONS 19: Sleeping] *first* 'e' *over* 'l'.
FURTHER EVIDENCE George Watson's daughter, Hannah Watson, and her illegitimate child had further difficulties with their parish. On 16 April 1821, the select vestry dealt with a letter which had been written on her behalf, and with a man (no name given) who had come up from London 'in Order to Lay the Matter Before the Parish upon examination of which it proved to have been a piece of Gross Misconduct of Mʳ Osborn the Late Overseer in not paying the allowance to the Infant Son of [the] said Hannah Watson'. She was granted her outstanding allowance, and her unnamed friend from London was given 15s for his expenses. Osborn was later charged with fraudulent record-keeping during his term of office. On 17 December 1821, the select vestry attended to a letter from Hannah Watson (not found), according to which her allowance (3s 6d per week) was due up to Christmas, which suggests that she had not received it since Michaelmas. James Cole, the overseer, was ordered to settle it. On 22 January 1822, she applied for an increase in her weekly allowance of 1s, which was granted (ERO, D/P 203/8/2, St Botolph, Colchester, select vestry minutes).

321   From Sarah Hall in Chelmsford, 15 March 1820

chelmsford <---->
Sir
<I> am Sorry to trouble you but mʳ palmer will not pay me aney more money till he has further orders Sir if you will be so obligen as to return a
5 few Lines i Shall be very thankfull as i have to pay for my child and i do not know how to do it without money Sir i am Sorry i have to truble you

for if i could do without money i would but i cannot So if you will be So
kind Sir as to Send afew Lines by return of post I shall be very thankfull
your humble
Servent Sarah Hall 10

march 15 1820

TEXTUAL ALTERATIONS 5: Lines] *after del* 'L'. 6: Sir i am] *interl.* 6: you] 'u' *over* 'y'.7: i
cannot] 'i' *after del* 't'. 9: your] *after del* 'y'.

**322 From Mary Taylor in Hadleigh [Suffolk] to [James] Cole in
St Botolph, Colchester, 9 May [1821]**

Hadleigh May y 10
Mr Cole
Sir I really when I was at Colchester thought you weare my friend by
your behaver to me when theire but indeed Sir I find you are not - or you
would not distress a poor helpless widow with such a family as I have got 5
by keeping me out of the little pilliance that I have allowed me from the
parish I really am in such a distress^d situation that I know not how to
exsist as I am kept from the money which is my due as I have always such
a trouble to git what I have due to me you know Sir it is an exspence to
me as warren cant wait of me for nothing - you - told him you would 10
faithfully send me the money by Mr James on Monday but did not as he
would bring it me for nothing he said he went three Times on Tusday and
that they promised him the money should be sent to his quarters to bring
on Wednesday I went last night to him he said it was cruel usage to me -
you Sir when I was at Colchester promised me I should have the money 15
sent regular every fortnight now it will be three weeks to morrow - you
promised me Sir to send me a peice of cloth to make my Children some
shirts and a trifal to buy them some shoese as They have none to theire
feet but yet Sir you did not perform your promise I have now sixteen
shillings to pay for rent what am I to do - but I am determined to come 20
home into the House then instead of paying me eight shillings a week you
will have to pay four or five shillings a head or us - I have ask^d the advice
of my Superiors who have told me how I am to procede but perhaps in a
few days the Gentlemen will heare more about it - not from me but from
some other quarter who will compel them to do Justice to the father^less & 25

widow - I dont lay all the blame on you Sir as I think by what I saw of you
that you was inclined to do me justice I am Sir your distressed
Mary Taylor

as I am told by those that know better than myself that even if I had a
30 pound a week comeing in they could not compel me to support my children as after my poor Husband was dead the Family all belonged to you
- but I have been only too quiet for my own intress^d just such a case was
tried a few years back a Bury Assices and the parish lost the cause

TEXTUAL ALTERATIONS 12: for] *after del illeg.* 13: his] *over del illeg.* 29: even] 'n' *over* 'r'.
DATE Year from filing note on outside.
FURTHER EVIDENCE Mary Taylor had received weekly payments of 5s on average from
May until August 1817, and casual relief on numerous occasions thereafter. By April
1821, she was again receiving a weekly allowance of 4s, the payment of which, however,
seems to have been somewhat irregular. From 13 July 1821 until 24 June 1825 she
received regular relief of 8s per week which was later reduced to 6s (July 1825 till August
1826) and then again to 4s (August till December 1826) (ERO, D/P 203/12/41- 44, St
Botolph, Colchester, overseers' accounts).

323   From [a female Anonymous] in Woolwich, Kent, to James Upshire in St Botolph, Colchester, 29 March 1826

Woolwich March 29th 1826

Dear Mother this Comes with My love to you All hopen to find you all
weel as it Leaves me very porly at this time and i took it very uncind of
you that you did not answer the Letter i Sent to you afortnight ago but i
5 see now ihave Lost my husband ihave Lost all but Dear Mother when
isent to you idirect it for john to be Left at your house to Spear you paying
the post for now i Cannot git it frank now he is away Dear Mother iwill be
forst to Come to the parish for icanot do for Myself for iam expecting to
be Confined every day and iam not able to do for Myself and my Child
10 for it Cost Me all the Money ihad to come from irland to englan and iwill
not git any from my husband till next june so Dear Mother if you will try
if you can git any thing for me iwill be much oblidge to you you may tell
them that i go to this parish for sume help for i cannot Come to them till
igit better and then imust Come home for iwill not be able to do for my
15 Children ihope you will send to me as soon as you git this Letter for ihave
been very unhappy to think you did not Send to me before So ihave no
more at present but remain your Loving daughter
When you rite to me

Direct it to Richard
wolfinetine 7 Batt   20
Majour leavens Company
Barrccourt woolwich Kent

TEXTUAL ALTERATIONS 1: 1826] '6' *interl at end of line*. 8: Myself] *after del illeg*. 9: day] *after del illeg*. 13: cannot] *after del* 'g'. 14: and] *after del illeg*. 14: imust] 't' *interl at end of line*. 20: 7] *after del illeg*. 21: leavens] *after del* 't'. 21: Company] 'C' *over del illeg*.

324   From S[amuel] and J[ames] Moore in [St Martin-in-the-Fields] London, 7 June 1826

Sir/

I Recd your letter dated May 31st 1825 with an Order for the sum of £15.3.- being up to April 15th 1825 we have not Recd any money from you since the Above Date & should be much Obliged to you to you if you could make it convenent to settle up to April 15th 1826 being 52 Weeks at   5
7^s/6^d viz £19.10^s.-^{d} I Also have the pleasure to inform you that we do not expect any further Allowance for the two Girls but hope you will Allow as much as possible for the Boy Beeing Only eight years of Age A Remitance of the money soon as Possible will much Oblige your Ob^t Ser^{ts} 10

                                        S & J. Moore
London June 7th 26 1 West Street St Martins Lane

TEXTUAL ALTERATIONS 6: not] *interl at beginning of line*. 8: eight] 'e' *over* '8'.

CIRCUMTEXT Note from other hand at bottom of left-hand margin, written crosswise: £23 5s 0d up to Midsummer.

FURTHER EVIDENCE According to an agreement made with the select vestry of St Botolph, Colchester, on 11 May 1824, James Moore, carver and gilder in London, had taken care of the three children of his deceased brother James Moore, who had been a carpenter in Colchester, St Botolph. Moore had 'to cloath & provide them with every necessary & Maintenance', for which he received an allowance of 2s 6d per week for each of the children from the parish (ERO, D/P 203/8/2, St Botolph, Colchester, select vestry minutes).

325   From George Little in Rayleigh [Essex] to the gentlemen of the parish of St Botolph, Colchester, [26] July 1826

Rayleigh July 1826

from George Little

to the Genteelmen of the parish of Saint Botolophs Cholchester Essex
Genteelmen I hereby inform you I have lost my wife by deth she was
5 taken ill with A fever and in less than A fortenate died on friday June 30
1826 leaveing me with two small Children one about 2 years and half old
which has been very ill for som weeks and the other about half year old I
hope you will be kind enough to allow me some money to spport the
children and to pay medecial and funerel expencies which are more then
10 I can Pay

Textual alterations 9: medecial] 'c' *interl.*
Circumtext Note from Thomas Byass, surgeon, dated 26 July 1826, below text: 'I
hereby Certify the above is a True statement', with bill for £2 10s for medical attendance.
Related correspondence Some weeks later, the overseers of St Botolph, Colchester,
received a letter from Thomas Bishop, grocer in Rayleigh: 'I am agreable to pay Mr Little
the Bearer hereof whatever Collection you may think proper to allow him by a Line from
you Saying what Sum & when you wou^d like to have your Bill Sent'. He stated that Little
had two children, George (aged 3) and John (8 months) and that 'his wife is dead 3
months'(letter of 7 September 1826). Apparently, the parish agreed to that offer. There is
a series of nine letters from Bishop up until March 1835, which show that he advanced a
weekly allowance of 3s to Little and was repaid by the parish at quarterly intervals (letters
of 20 March, 20 April, 5 November and 17 December 1827, March 1828, 10 December
1832, 21 March and 26 September 1833, and 13 March 1835). Most of the letters simply
state the 'account' due to him, but some also give information on Little's situation. Thus,
on 17 December 1827 Bishop reported that Little earned not more than 7s per week, since
the farmers 'do not Consider him able to do a Day's work'.

326   From Sarah Challis in Chelmsford to [William] Chisolm, overseer of St Botolph, Colchester, 1 August 1826

Chelmsford Aug 1 1826

Honoured Sir

i hope you will excuese the Liberty i have taken in troubling of you but
i Should take you as a Great faveurd if you would be so kind as to Send
5 Me a trifull to put afue Clothes on my my Boy Back as he is allmost
naked i am Sorry to trouble you Sir but beleive me i had him to keep for
this 7 years and i find it very hard to find him food and Clothes and m^r
dewall promist me he would Send me a a pound if i Sent in a Short time

so i not wish to trouble the parsh with him but i Cannot take him home as
he is and if i do not have a Little assistence i Shall be oblidge to Send him 10
home again So i hope Sir you will Consider my Case and Send me a
trifull and i hope i Shall not be any more trouble to you for i do not wish
it but pray Sir Send it this time for i am in Great trouble and i am Just redy
to be Confined and i Cannot take him home till he has Something to ware
i remain your humble 15
Servant Sarah Challis

TEXTUAL ALTERATIONS 9: so] *interl.* 11: Consider] *after del illeg.* 13: Just] *interl.* 14: Con-
fined] *after del illeg.*

**327 From Rachel Clark in London to the overseers of St Botolph,
Colchester, 7 August 1826**

jentlmen i am sorray to be trabelsum But mr Cole informed mee last
Weeck When i went to him for my pay that it would be the last time he
could pay mee till you pay him for he have Not resived aney money from
you sense the 3rd of june i have all Ways resived my pay of him every
Week - kind jentlmen i have seeven Children all att home and my hus- 5
band have lately been out of work for 10 Weeks that i am in grate deet
with my Baker and the landlord for rent And my self so veary much
aflicted that i Cannot arn aney thing to suport my Children and my husband is onley a labring man he have no Constant work to do that i Cannot
do with out a sistance i have one that i Could geet out for an arand Boy if 10
i Could geet him sum Clothes But i Cannot geet them Clothes till i have
paid my reent i am a fraid they should take my few goods if i do not keep
paying my reent kind jentlmen i hope you will pay mr Cole and order him
to keep paying mee for if he do not i shall bee forsed to cum home in a
few days - for i do a shure you that i have a poore life with my husband 15
becaus i Cannot arn aney thing to help maintain our Children it is hard
work for my Weeack state of helth to do for seeven Children my self and
my husband for i have one at my brest 11 munthes old
i am your veary humbel searvent
Rachel Clark / London augst th7th 1826 20

TEXTUAL ALTERATIONS 2: When] *after del* 'whe'. 7: veary] 'r' *interl.* 9: to] *after del illeg.* 10:
sistance] *second* 's' *over illeg.* 13: kind] *after del* 'king'. 20: Rachel Clark] *below del* 'Rachel

Clark', *apparently in order to enlarge the Space between the two bottom lines.* 20: 1826] '6' over '8'.

CIRCUMTEXT Note from other hand on next page: 'Jm^s Cole who drive the Shannon Coach, always paid her four Shill^{gs} Pr Week she had her Money P^d every month C Heath.'

328   From George John Tye in [St Anne, Soho] London to the Revd Hoblen in St Botolph, Colchester, 19 August 1826

August 19th 1826 No 424 Oxford Road

To the Rev^d - Hoblen

Most Revd Sir - In humility and affliction I Beg your Remmembrance of George John Tye Som years a grocer In the Parish of Sn^t Botolph^s to
5 which I now belong - Haveing been Reduced by an unfortunate partenarship - with the unhappy young man Stephen Norman Deceas^d left Colchester have som years since lived in Flanders - 2 years last march past on my return to this Countrey was - again Reduc^d by an unfortunate Ship wreck on the Coast of Holland loosing Every thing I prossess^d -
10 Since which time I have had a little werk In the Kings works - which I left last Febuary as Master & Supercargo on Board a Sloop belongeing to London - for Cardiff in wales from whence I was to to proceed to Rouen in France - and from Thence on a Coasting Voyage Into the ports of that Countrey - on my arival at Cardiff I found a Change of Owners Owen to
15 Som unfortunate *failure* of my Employers Being Oblig^d to Resigne my Setuation - a few day^s after which I become Greatly afflicted with an Augue & Fever - my giting worse and haveing Nothing to Subsist on only from the Sale of my few Cloaths - I was Sent to Devonport by a vessle - ware laying Three weeks - not know to any Person - at most
20 times In a Delierious Fever - In A state of Starveation and Wrechedness I was Sent into the Exeter & Devon Hospital by the kind hand of Doct^r Collyns of Kenton of Devon - ware after being 9 weeks was Discharg^d the 4 - Ins^t - haveing nothing to Depend on by the way but the Small Allowance granted by the Midecant Society Arived in london on the 14th
25 In a most deplorable Condition - Oh Revd Sir the most wreched - Distitute of Every Common Neccessaire of Life - Since that time have been Supported - by Mr Jolly Baker formely a Resident of Sn^t Botolph^s He have been to me like the good Samaritan He have adminesterd to My Destress^d Setuation all the good in his power Had not I as a mercy of provedence
30 meet with this good man and his friendley wife - I Must of Dropt a wreched and forlorn vagabond in the Street and of been Brought Home to my

parrish - Revd Sir haveing before time Known the almighty god had Bless^d you with a Heart of Charity towards the Destress^d I Humbly beg you in Christs Name to Commiserate My Present Condition - praying you to represent - my Cace to the Churchwarden Overseer - praying your 35 Charityable Consideration of Sending me a triffle that I May Immedeatly git into Som little Imployment that I may Not be Sent whom as a Burdon upon the parrish trusting in god my health will be Soone Reinstated - Being Extreemly Sorry to Be Oblige through great Distress for this Intrusion - But with all Humility and prayer Humbly Submit Myself To your 40 goodness - kindness and Charity -

and and with gratitude and due respect

Most Revd Sir

Your Most obidient and Humble Servant

George John Tye   45

at Mr Jolly^s

424 - Oxford Street

London

TEXTUAL ALTERATIONS 7: march] *interl with caret*. 12: proceed] *first* 'e' *over* 'l'. 17: Nothing] 'No' *over illeg*. 42: and] *after del* 'although'. 42: with] *interl with caret*.

CIRCUMTEXT Note from T. Jolly below: 'this is to Certify that the a Bove Statement is Correct having Priviouely Recd a Let^r from an a tendent of the Hoshelell Before tyes orrivell NB and i witnesd his Destressed State on her arrivell from Holland as before Stated'.

329   From S[amuel] and J[ames] Moore in [St Martin-in-the-Fields] London to [William] Chisolm, overseer of St Botolph, Colchester, 24 August 1826

Sir/

On the 7th of last June we wrote to Mr Heath requesting the remitance of £19.10^s~^d Being 52 weeks at 7^s/6^d up to April 15th 1826 Also stating to him that we did not exspect any further Allowance for the two Girls but hope you will do the best you can for the Boy as he is Only 8 Years of 5 Age it Cost Us 5^s/6^d Per week for him including his Cloths if you will be Kind anough to send the Above sum by return of Post or an Order for the same at you Bankers you will much Oblidge - as there is a quarters money Due to Mrs Ward which we want to send to her

10   your early attention will much Oblidge
your Humble Servants

S & J. Moore

August 24th 1826

1 West Street St Marints Lane
15   London

330   From John Hall in Chelmsford, 3 September 1826

Chelmsford Sep^t 3 1826

Gentlemen

I Beg Lieve to Inform you that my Daughter is been to London & got A
Verry good Place but thro Bad Health Was Oblige to lieve it & Come
5 down in the Country Again for the Doctors in London Told her if She did
Not Lieve Town And Come in to her own Natural Are She Would go into
A decline She is been to Several Places in Chelmsford The People Would
have her but they All Told her She Was Not fit for Servise She Look^d So
ill I have Given Up house keeping & Sold all my things Except my bed
10 But if you Will Be so kind as to Send me A Something to buy her A Bed
I Will get A fue things & She Shall do for me or She Will have to Come
home to you & that be More Expence to you I I hope you Will Consider
it & Send me Word you Will Oblige your Humble
Petitioner John Hall

TEXTUAL ALTERATIONS 4: Was] 'W' *over illeg.* 9: keeping] 'ep *over* 'y'.
SPELLING 6: Are] *read* 'Air'.

**331   From S[amuel] and J[ames] Moore [in St-Martin-in-the-Fields,
London] to [William] Chisolm in St Botolph, Colchester, 4
September 1826**

Sir/

we sent a letter to Mr Heath on the 7th of Last June also a letter to you on
Augst 24th requesting a remitance of the money an anr^s will much Oblige
your Humble

5   Servants
S. & J. Moore
Sep 4th 1826

TEXTUAL ALTERATIONS 3: an] *over del illeg.* 7: 1826] '8' *over del illeg.*
CIRCUMTEXT Note from other hand below, stating senders' addresses (Samuel Moore, 5 Little Russell Street, Drury Lane; James Moore, 1 West Street, St Martin Street [St Martin-in-the-Fields, London]) and the names of the two girls and of their deceased brother who were living with them: Harriet (aged 16) and Mary Ann (14).

332   From Rachel Clark [in London] to the overseer of St Botolph, Colchester [5 September 1826]

honnd jentlmen i am truley Sorrey to trubel you a gain But mr Cole have not paid Me for last Weeck But told mee that you said i did not belong to you But i know I Belong to you for it is my maiden parish and my husband is a Scotchman he have no parish to take mee to And for the life i have with him i wish i was dead that the last time i Came home to the 5 parish i made a grate Vow in Deed i took a grate oath that if ever i had to Cum home a gain that my leegs should Brake under mee if ever i returned to him a gain i have a bad life with him with the money you alow me mutch moore with out it he says he will be damd if he work to maintain my damd Bodey with out i work for my self i can hardley do for my 10 Children i am so weeck jentlemen if you do not send me my money you may Expect to see mee down in a few days and if i am forced to Cum i will sooner lay in god save the king rather then cum Back to london a gain -

                                                            i am your humbel 15
                                                            Sarvent Rachel Clark

TEXTUAL ALTERATIONS 3: I] *over* 'i'. 6: oath] *after del* 'outh'. 16: Sarvent] 'a' *over* 'u'.
DATE Date of filing note on outside.
FURTHER EVIDENCE This 'impudent Letter from Rachel Clark threatening to return home to her maiden Settlem¹ in this parish unless an allowance was continued to her' was dealt with by the select vestry of St Botolph, Colchester, on 5 September 1826. It was resolved 'That suitable Enquiry be made for the husband So as to be able to apprehend him with his Wife & family to Scotland in the Event of her throwing herself & Children on this parish' (ERO, D/P 203/8/2, St Botolph, Colchester, select vestry minutes).

333   From Rachel Clark in London to the overseer of St Botolph, Colchester [5 September 1826]

honrd jentlemen i am soray to trubel you again so soon But to in form you that mr Cole told mee last Weack that he would not pay mee Another

farthing till you pay him he says you paid him for 8 Weacks and now he
have paid mee 4 weeks sense he says that he allways had money on
5 adwanse from mr heath and that he will not be paying money out of his
pocket to no one i went to him last night to hear if you had sent to him But
he said no so i am forsed to trubel you again for i Cannot do With out a
sistance -

i am your humbel searvent
10   Rachel Clark

TEXTUAL ALTERATIONS 2: Another] *after del* 'a'. 5: heath] *after del illeg.* 5: be] *after del*
'being'. 6: you] *after del* 'you'.
DATE Date of filing note on outside.

334   From George John Tye in [St Anne Soho, London] to William
Chisolm, overseer of St Botolph, Colchester, 7 September 1826

September 5th 1826
To Mr Willm Chisolm
Overseer of the parish of Snt Botolphs Colchester
Sir/ - I was favoured with your letter of the 30th of August - and am
5 Sorry To find the gentlemen of the Vestry haveing formd a Mistaken
Idea of my haveing gained a Settlement Elceware - I Certainly Hired a
Small House for the purpose of Buseness - as an Eating House - No 3
Queen Street Mint Square Borough - at the End of June 1818 - after my
Leaving Colchester - But in Three weeks finding it would not answer I
10 put it off to a papper lace Maker named Benjn Swindon - By Sinking the
money paid for fixtures &c - as by agreement with The person that took
the House - and to the Best of My Knowledge Did not Reside in prossession
of the House more then Six weeks at The utmost - I heve paid neither
Rent or Taxes nor Rates of Any kind whatsoever - all ware to be paid by
15 Benjn Swindon by the Consent of the Rent Collector - who Meet - Swindon at the house On the Accasion - In the august following I went over to
Bruges In Flander^s - and returnd to London in May 1819 - when the parish Of Sn^t Botolph ware kind Enough to give me there Certifigate - to
Endeavour to git a Setuation in the Customs - or to git placed on The
20 pension List of the Hon^{bl} Board of Ordnance - I Could not Succeed In
Either - I went out to Brussells in June the Same year - and was Employd
as a man Cook and Confectioner to verious English Famely^s passing and

repassing through that City - till my Return to This Countrey - and was
Cast away on the Coast of Holland - and Reduc^d to great Destress by
loosing all I prossess^d and was by the Favour of the British Consul of 25
Rottedan Sent whome a free passenger To London in April 1824 - Since
which time I have lived as a wanderer by my Industrey warever I Could
git Employ^d to the presant peirod - I Have not had a House nor hired a
House of aney Discription Since that in Queen Street Mint Square -
This Being a True Statement To which I will Make Oath -   30

George John Tye

September 7th 1826
To Mr Willm Chisolm
Sir/ on the recp^t of your letter I laid the above Statement before the
Magistrate at the Malboro Street Office - and He Derected Me to the 35
parish of Sn^t Georges - ware I was disired to attende a Select Vestry This
day - I have done So and am desired by the Clarke of the vestrey To
transmit to you the above Declaration for you to lay before your own
vestry or your own Magistrate - Saying If you Doubted my not Belonging
to Sn^t Botolphs - they Should on my next application take My Affidavit 40
and pass Me whome - under the presant Act and would of Done So this
Day had I been agreeable and would of ask^d relieff This under My presand
- needfull Curcumstances have placd me in great Emberisment as I am
anxious to git into Som Employment - Expecting my wife home from
Brussells ware She now remain in a veri Declining State of health - I 45
Could Certainly have My Eating and Drink at Mr Jolly^s for a fortnnight or
Three weeks free or till I Could git Som Situation But I Cannot pay my
Lodging I have apply^d to the National guardian Institution - No 46 Bed-
ford Row for Employment and as they are particular about my parish and
Settlement this curcumstance Is against me - I hope Sir and pray you will 50
be So good as to give me your reply by monday^s post if poseble - So that
if I Cannot be Relieved with a Triffle that I May be pass^d home - this I
beg to leave to the Comiseration of the gentlemen of the parish of Sn^t
Bottolphs

And am with Due Respect 55
Sir your Obedient Humble Servt
George John Tye
424 Oxford Street

TEXTUAL ALTERATIONS 14: to be] *interl with caret.* 18: Certifigate] *first* 'i' *over* 'y'. 28: not]
interl with caret. 35: He] 'H' *over illeg.*

CIRCUMTEXT Copy of answer from W[illiam] C[hisolm] of 8 September 1826 below text:
'Sir/ Your letter of the 5th ins^t has been received since which I have Consulted the Genlemen
of the Parish who disire me to inform you that your Statement has not removed the opin-
ion they had formed from information they possess and that they still believe your Settlement is in the Borough and that they therefore cannot relieve you as disired - Should you
think proper to make Oath to your Settlement for the purpose of being pass'd by Orders it
may be well for you to consider whither the Statement is quite corect before you make
Oath to it.'

335　From George John Tye in [St Anne, Soho] London to William Chisolm, overseer of St Botolph, Colchester, 11 September 1826

September 11th 1826

To Mr Willm Chisolm

　　Sir - I have been favour with your letter of the 8 Ins^t - Which I have
this day laid Before the parish Officers of Sn^t Georges - they remark that
5　your letters are *Couchd* in those tirmes that no magistrate will give me an
Affidavi^t with out passing me to my own parish which thay grant to be
Colchester and no other - and of Course the parish of Sn^t Geroges will
have no further Concerne with me As I Do Now and have Done Since I
have been in London Resided In the parish of Sn^t Ann^s Soho - for the
10　gentlemen of the parish To sit aside there Doubts In Respect to My Settlement - According to the *Information they prossess* - and to Save Expences
lett them wright To the Landlord a Mr Brownd West Square - and the
Rent Collector Mr Corsley Wine Street Near the Hero of Waterloo at the
foot of Waterloo Bridge - or to Mr Cannon House agent & Worker for the
15　partys - at the Lord Nelson Nelson Square great Surry Road - they will
find My Name Is Not So Much as on thire Books - as I had never a
Money transaction with them whatever - I wish to god I had or Could
Claim a parish in London - and be assured I Should never be troubleso<me>
to Colchester - as the Dye appear to be last I Shall be under the
20　Disagreeable Neccessity of Being pass^t whome the latter End of th<is>
week - and you are well aware of the Expences attending on the <------->
for Relieff &c and the Beadles Expences you will find will not be far
Short of £3 - a pound of this money would of make a man of me If you
Realy wish to See me in Sn^t Bottolphs workhouse - you must Be gretify^d
25　- What Ever Sorrow It must be to me - the parish may Probaly find me
Employment on a Situation - If So I shall be greatfully thankfull for Such
favour renderd me in a time of Age & neccessity - I Certainly am of an
Opinion you are a gentleman of to much *Candor* to withhold from me any

Information respecting my Settlement that you or the parish may have
recieved - as I *repeet* I am truly Sorry that I Belong to Colchester - Perhaps 30
you will be kind Enough to Informe me of Som Curcumstances I am not
aware off in that respect - But you may rest perfectly assured - of my
belonging to the parish of Sn^t Botolphs and no other - If you think propper
to give me a line previous to my Coming Down It will be greatfully received
By Yours veri Respectfully 35
& Humble Ser^t
George John Tye
424 Oxford Road
London

TEXTUAL ALTERATIONS 5: will] *inserted in left-hand margin.*
CIRCUMTEXT Note in pencil from other hand, written crosswise in lower half of left-hand
margin: 'March 16. 1818 10£'.

**336   From S[amuel] and J[ames] Moore in [St Martin-in-the-Fields]
London to [William] Chisolm in St Botolph, Colchester, 12
September 1826**

London Sep th12 1826
Sir/

We received a letter from you last Week Stating you did not think Yourself Justified in paying for the Support of me Late Brothers Children any
More than 2^s/6^d Pr Week in future or that We did not Aught to of Asked
the Parish for Any Money Until We had given an Account to the Parish 5
of the Produce of me Late Brothers Efects the Celect Vestry Was Informed at the time of his Death Me Brother was Insolvant before his
Death and Also What Use was Made of the Money his goods Was Valued at at the time the agreement toke place for the Parish to Alow With
the Children - the Whole of the Efects Was Valued by Mr Parker of Col- 10
chester at the Sum of 89 £ Sutch part of the Above Valued Effects as had
been had by Me Brother from different persons Upon credit Were
returned to them Again as far as possible Mr Hawkins Had What timber
& Deals there Was left and Verry Kindley gave Up the remaining part of
his Account Mr Tabor had Also Some of Utensals & Unmanufactor^d Stock 15
in trade & Money the Whole Amount of his Rent Workmans Wages Was
Paid also Physician Nurse Funeral Account & Expences Money Was

advanced to redeam Some goods then Pledged as Stated in the Above
Valuation and Small Accounts to Poor Persons Was also Paid -

20   What part of the goods We toke We Alowed the Same Price as they
have Valued at With the Endavour to make more of them & We did not
Make so Much of Some as they Ware Valued at therefore the Sum of
Money Expended Upon the Children & other Expences has been Considerably more than the Overplush of Money left of me Brothers Efects &

25   the Money had of the Parish - besides a Considerable Standing Debt own
to Both Up before me Brothers Death - & we Differ in opinion with the
Parish the Services of the two girls having been More Valuable than there
Board Lodgings & Cloaths if so Why did not the Parish Provide Places
for them

30   However We do not Wish the Parish to be Burthened With any More
expence than cannot be Avoided and now that Mrs Ingram there Grandmother has taken the two Girls the Boy is now the only one to Provide for
We have to State We find by letters received from Mr Heath the 6th &
31st of May 1825 an offer to Pay for one Quarter of a Year at the Usual

35   rate of 7^s/6^d Pr Week and 5^s/0^d Pr Week Up to Michelmas 1825 & So to
continue therefore the Sum at that rate from April 15th 1825 to april 15th
1826 the time Aplyed for Amounts to only £14.12.6 Instead of £19.10.0
Being for a Year - I hope this is Sufficiently explained both to you & the
Parish & that you Will Send Up a remitance as Soon as Possible having

40   money to Pay out of it for Board & he is Verry much in Want of Cloths -
Your earley Atention will Much oblige

I am Sir your Ob^t Ser^t

S. & J. Moore

TEXTUAL ALTERATIONS 9: Use] 's' *over illeg.* 36: 1825] '1' *over del illeg.*
CIRCUMTEXT Note from other hand below: 'See May 11th 1824'.
PLACE Parish inferred from senders' earlier letters (**324, 329, 331**).
RELATED CORRESPONDENCE In the letter referred to at the beginning, from the vestry clerk
of St Botolph, Colchester, Samuel and James Moore were informed that their letters had
been laid before the select vestry and the following position had been adopted: 'that the
Sum you demand will not be paid until the parish are satisfactorily apprized of what
became of the Valuable furniture & Effects left by your Brother - it being supposed that
great part thereof was removed by you and is still in your possesion and should of course
be appropriated to the support of the Children before the parish are called on to maintain
them - you have had the entire services of and which the parish consider to have been
valuable & quite equal to her maintainance & clothing and that you ought not for sometime past to have effects an allowance on her account. The Boy too appears to be placed
in a situation not very suitable to his condition & if the 2/6 a week is continued for him the
parish will on your making up the 4/6 as now paid for his support obtain some more

comfortable & proper place for him or at least will endeavour so to do & have no doubt of succeeding -' (copy of letter of 5 September 1826).

337 From S[amuel] and J[ames] Moore in [St Martin-in-the-Fields] London to [William] Chisolm in St Botolph, Colchester, 19 October 1826

London Oct 19 1826

Gentlemen)

I have been daily in Expectation for Above a Month time which time I wrote to you Before expecting hearing from you Concerning me Late Brothers Boy James Moore to know what terms the Parish have to offer for the Support of him in future if the Parish would wish Uss to do Any thing with them for his Support as Tiss Quite Impossible for Uss to Prov<ide> for him Ourselves I have Als<o asked> to have A remittance of t<---------------> Already due According to <-----------------> Offer by Letters on the 6th & 31st of May 1825 on offer to pay for one Quarter of a Year at the Usual rate of 7s/6d Pr Week & 5s/0d Pr Week to Michelmas & So to Continue Which Sum Amounts to for a Year from 15th April 1825 to 15th April 1826 to £14.12.6 - We are Much in Arears of Payments With the Woman he is with & I Understand the boy is Almost naked for the Want of Clothes An earley Complyance to this will Much oblige

Your Obt Servts
J & S. Moore

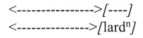

<----------------->[----]
<--------------->[lardn]

TEXTUAL ALTERATIONS 4: Late] 'l' over del illeg. 14: Understand] 'Un ' over illeg.

PLACE Parish inferred from senders' earlier letters (324, 329, 331).

RELATED CORRESPONDENCE Copy of letter from vestry clerk of St Botolph, Colchester, to Samuel and James Moore, 18 October 1826: 'I have laid your Letters before the Gentn of the Parish and also made the enquiry of Mr Parker to which you refared in your Letter but he cannot give any Account of the Furniture &c &c of the late Jas Moore he Says that he never took any Account of the Value of the Goods only of what he bought for himself. So the Parish is not Saitsfied with the Account which you have given. But in Order to Settle they have Ordered me to offer you £10 and out of that sum I am to Pay Mrs Ward what may be due for the Boy which you will please to State the Amount and the Balance what may then be left I will Pay to you or any one that you please to appoint The Parish will Allow 2/6 with the Boy and they hope that you will continue to Allow as you have done to his Support in order that he may not be put in the Workhouse'.

338   From Elizabeth Lane in St Luke Old Street, London, [12] December [1826]

London Dec 17th 18*[--]*

Gentle men i hum sorry to informe you i have been veury hill in the
horspital ever sence i was a tome and not ban able to earn one sixpence
never sence and i ham to be so troublesom to you and the Lameness of
5   my harm Gets wors so that i ham not able to do aney thing i must beg to
ask you the favour of Granting me a weekely a Lowance an i ham out of
the horspiteal and naked and must be past home plase to answer as soon
as Conveanent as i ham quite desstente of eveary means of support and
your piticoncer as in dutey Bound will ever pray

10   Elizabeth Lane

Dic^r to N° 3 James St
old st St Lucks London

TEXTUAL ALTERATIONS 7: and naked] *interl below*.
    DATE Day and year from postmark.
    FURTHER EVIDENCE On 11 February 1823, Elizabeth Lane had come from London before
the select vestry of St Botolph, Colchester. On the grounds that she 'has been absent from
Colchester 18 years', her settlement examination had been taken. She had been granted an
allowance of 1s per week, and the overseer to whom her case had been referred had given
her 16s 'to take her to London'. On 1 September 1826, that is three months before her
above letter, she had again come to Colchester and applied for relief, saying that she had
been 'obtaining her living by washing & which from an accident she is unable to follow'. It
was resolved 'that a Sum not exceeding thirty shillings be applied for the said Elizabeth
Lanes benefit & in payment of her conveyance back to London at the overseers discretion'
(ERO, D/P 203/8/2, St Botolph, Colchester, select vestry minutes).

339   From Thomas Hall in [Bermondsey] London to [William] Chisolm in St Botolph, Colchester, 20 December 1826

Dece^{r the} 20 1826

Sir I take the liberty of riten to you I hope you send me a trifel for I am in
grat Disstres for i have work to do but i am not able to do it for i have bean
very ill and my Wife is had a bad Brest and not able to do for her self and
5   famley and I am Sory to truble you for I am in Grate wants of sume
asistance and i hop the Gentlemen will send me something and if thae do
not I must go to Sant Gorges for my wife expcets to be Confind evry day
and i cant Get a nus or for les then 4 shilen a weak I should wish for one

of the Gentlmen to come and see me when thas come to London I live at
No 11 Weeb Stret Burmonsdey new Raad I am yur   10
    humbel Seravent Thos Hall

TEXTUAL ALTERATIONS 5: you] *inserted*. 7: expcets] 'c' *over del* 'et'. 9: when] *after del illeg.*
10: Weeb] *after del illeg.*
    CIRCUMTEXT Copy of answer from William Chisolm, overseer of St Botolph, Colchester,
of 22 December 1826, on back of page: 'T Hall/ I have Sent you a one Pound note which
will inable you to meet the extra expences of your wife's confinement I am Sure you
would be very uncomfortable was you to come home on account of your former conduct.
but I am satisfied you will not come home. If any of the Gentlemen should come to
London I will endavour to get them to Call'.
    FURTHER EVIDENCE Thomas Hall (born 17 October 1798) was a son of John Hall of
Chelmsford. In 1821 he had married Sarah Gowlett. In the summer of 1826, they had
entered the workhouse in St Botolph, Colchester, but Thomas Hall disappeared at har-
vest-time and was found working in Great Wakering. After being arrested in Colchester
gaol he managed to be released and went to Bermondsey, London, where he lived with
his family. For a detailed account of his case, see Sharpe, 'Bowels of Compation', pp. 97-
100.

**340   From Thomas Hall [in Bermondsey, London] to [William]
       Chisolm in St Botolph, Colchester, 4 January 1827**

                                     Janurey 4 1827
Sir i have taken the liberty to rite to you agane and I am in Grate trubel at
this time for my wife is confind and she is very ill for want of noureshment
if the Gentlemen will be so kind as to lend another pound to help me out
of my troubel and i will pay you agane i wold not have to trubelled you if   5
i had not have lost my time through Liven so bad in the Sumer now i have
got to work i feel it but i hope i shall troubel you no more and i should
wisch one of the Gentelmen to come and see me and that will satesfy the
Gentelmen that i am in want of sum relife i am your humbel servent Thos
Hall   10
    Sir i have received you Later and i return maney thanks for been so
kind to me for my wife wase Confind the same Day

TEXTUAL ALTERATIONS 5: to] 't' *over illeg.* 8: Gentelmen] *first* 'n' *over del illeg.*
    PLACE Inferred from previous and following letters from Thomas Hall (**339, 342**).
    CIRCUMTEXT Note from other hand below: 'not Granted by Select Vestry Jany 9th 1827'.

341 From John Hall in Chelmsford to [William] Chisolm in St Botolph, Colchester, 11 January 1827

Chelmsford Jany th 11 1827

Sir

I Beg Lieve to Inform you I Am in great Need of your Assitance At this Time for I have been Ill for Some time My Master Sent you A Letter of
5 the Same & thought you Would have Answer^d it for he know^d my Need And Sir I hope you have Not Shut up the Bowels of Compation Intierly Concerning me so I hope Sir you Will Send to me this Week or I Must Apply to Chelmsford for Relief I have a boy to Maintain and Cant do for myself So Sir I hope you Will take my Case into Concideration At this
10 Time or I must Apply to this Parrish for I Stand in Need of Immadiate Relief Sir I Remain your Humble Petitioner John Hall

TEXTUAL ALTERATIONS 9: take] *after del* 'Send'.
RELATED CORRESPONDENCE A week later, James Read, overseer of Chelmsford, wrote to St Botolph, Colchester, that John Hall 'has applied here for Relief and has received 5^s/ I therefore have to request that you will remit that Sum, & say what further Sum I Shall give him. - if I do not hear from you in a few Days [I] shall relieve him as we do our own Poor and send the Bill. - he has been relieved here several Times a few Years back' (letter of 17 July 1827). Colchester, however, ordered 'no relief to be allowed' (note of answer, 23 January 1827, at bottom).
FURTHER EVIDENCE This is the last letter from John Hall from Chelmsford. Some time thereafter he moved (or rather, was made to move) to St Botolph, Colchester. By 1829, he lived in St Botolph's workhouse where he received a letter from his daughter, Elizabeth Anderson (see **390**). For further details, see Sharpe, 'Bowels of Compations', pp. 95-6.

342 From Thomas Hall in Bermondsey, London, to [William] Chisolm in St Botolph, Colchester, 11 January 1827

Jenery th11 1827

Sir i have taken the liberty to wright to you and i hope the Gentlemen will send me a trifel for i am in Grate Destres for i have got a bad foot i run anail in it and i cannot do no Worke i an forste to go to the Guies Hospitle
5 as out pashent if thay do not imust go to sume other Parish for i must have relife frome sum ware for iham in grat Destres at this time pray Mr Chisolm to send me answer wether the Gentelmen will send me atrifel or not and my wife is very bad for want of nuresment and that is the truth

I ham your humbel Survent
10 Thos Hall No 11 Web Street New Roade Burmonsd*[sey]*

TEXTUAL ALTERATIONS 7: me answer] 'me' *inserted in left-hand margin.* 7: not] 't' *over illeg.* 8: my] *over illeg.* 9: Survent] 'n' *over illeg.* 10: No 11] *interl.* 10: New Roade] *interl below.* 10: Burmonsd/sey/] 'nsd' *interl with caret at end of line.*
CIRCUMTEXT Note from other hand on outside, 17 January 1827: 'Sent N° 74305 £1-Pound To Tho⁵ Hall 11 West Street Burmondsey New Road'.

343   From Edmund Cross in London to Edmund Cross in St Botolph, Colchester, 13 January 1827

London 13 Jany 1827

Couzin Edmund

I yesterday Receivd a letter from the Committy of St Lukes to inform Me that the Physician Went to the Hospital yesterday and Saw Miria and Declard her to Be No Better But that She Will Continue a lunitick and 5 that She Must Be taken out Next friday So that you or the Parrish officer Must Cume up to London on thursday Next and Bring A Strait Jackett to take her home With on the friday as She Cannot Be at My house one Night So I hope I shall Not Be disappointed In Seeing one of you as I Must Be there Next friday Morning at 11 o Clock there Will Be Some 10 Expencis to Pay But I Donot yet Know Wat

I Remain thine

Resp^ty Edmund Cross

TEXTUAL ALTERATIONS 4: Physician] 'y' *over* 's'; 'ci' *over illeg.*
CIRCUMTEXT Note from other hand at bottom of page: 'The Assistant Overseer is requested to Attend to the above application' followed by four signatures, presumably of members of the select vestry of St Botolph, Colchester.
RELATED CORRESPONDENCE Maria Cross was a patient in Holly House in Hoxton (undated bill for the care of three lunatics, including her). Six months after the above letter from Edmund Cross, Holly House informed the overseers of St Botolph, Colchester, that Maria Cross had 'Improved very much in her Health but her state of mind remains much the same' and that she was 'quite comfortable' (letters of 23 and 29 August 1827). On the former occasion, reference was also made to a letter from her father in which he had complained about her treatment.
FURTHER EVIDENCE When this case was discussed at the meeting of the select vestry of St Botolph, Colchester, of 23 January 1827, it was resolved that the overseer should obtain advice from the parish solicitor (ERO D/P 203/8/2, St Botolph, Colchester, select vestry minutes).

344   From Thomas Hall in [Bermondsey] London to [William] Chisolm in St Botolph, Colchester, 18 January 1827

Jenerry ^{the} 18 1827

Sir i hav taken the liberty of Writen to you agane to informe you that i am
out of worke i wors discharges last sadey night and if the Gentlman do
not alowe me a sumthing a weak til i can get on to worke agane we must
5 cune home agane that i do not wiche to do for i hope i Shall soon get into
worke agane send me answar as soon as you can if you Pleas

I remane your
Humbel Suvent
Thos Hall

TEXTUAL ALTERATIONS 2: taken] 'n' *over* 'r'. 4: til] *after del* 'i must'.
PLACE Parish inferred from previous and following letters from Thomas Hall (**342,
345**).

345   From Thomas Hall in Bermondsey, London, to [William] Chisolm in St Botolph, Colchester [25 January 1827]

Sir i have ret to you againe and i have beer to St Gorges Parish for relife
and thae say if thae relive me thae will bring us home if you do not send
me a trifel for i have no work to do i Expets a nother Place of worrk in
another fortnight i do not want to come home if i can helpe it but if you do
5 not send sumthing this week we must we are in great wants i hame your
humble Survent Thomas Hall
N 11 web Street burmonsdey New Roade

TEXTUAL ALTERATIONS 2: thae] 'a' *over del illeg.* 2: home] 'h' *over illeg.* 5: must] *after del*
'must'.5: i] *after del* 'Jan'.
DATE Date of postmark.

346   From T[homas] Hall in [Bermondsey] London to [William] Chisolm in St Botolph, Colchester, 28 January 1827

London Jany 28 - 1827

Sir

I recived your letter which intimates that you have sent me two pounds
I have recieved one pound on the 23rd December last and that is the Whole

I have received you state that you sent one pound on 17 January and I 5
have not informed you of it I have had the one pound but the last you sent
I have not recieved I hope to reciev it soon as I have no employ
    I Remain your humb¹ Ser^vt
    T Hall

TEXTUAL ALTERATIONS 5: one] *above del* 'two'. 7: have not] 'v' *over illeg.*
WRITING This is the only letter from Thomas Hall which is not from the same hand as his
other letters. Note also the different spelling, wording, and style.
CIRCUMTEXT Copy of answer from William Chisolm, overseer of St Botolph, Colchester,
29 January 1827, on back of page: 'Thoˢ Hall I am Suprised that you state in your Letter
of yesterday that you have not Received the Pound that I Sent on the 17ᵗʰ Inˢᵗ the N° of the
Note was 74305 Bank of England I hope you have made the necessary enquiry at the Post
Office and got it before this time'. Underneath, copy of letter from Chisolm to F. Freeling,
Esq.: 'Sir/ I Posted a Letter on 17ᵗʰ Instant with a one Pound note enclosed N° 74305 Bank
of England and I am enformed that it was not to come to hand on Satᵈ last it was Directed
as under - Thoˢ Hall 11 West Street Burmondsey new Road London'.

347 From Thomas Hall in Bermondsey, London, to [William] Chisolm, overseer of St Botolph, Colchester, [5] February 1827

Feb ᵗʰᵉ 8 1827
Sir I have taken the liberty of riten to you agane and i have found the one
pound that was lost i had it last tusday i was in deet for rent ten shilens and
i wors forst to pay it if i had not paid it we should all bean turned out of
dores and i hoed 6 shilens for Bread i paid it out of the pound and the 2 5
Leters cost me 2 shilens and 4 pence and i have no Worke to do pleas to
alow us sumthing a weeak til i get sum worke to do for i do not like to keep
riten so every weeake if the Gentelmen do not we must cume home agane
for we cannot live so no longer for the worke is bad in London for there is
nun to be got at present Sir i hope you will send as Soon as you can for i 10
have not a bit of Bread to give my Children and i do not know what do and
i Should not like to come home if i can helpe it for me and my Wife never
[break] our fast for too days i should like for sume of the Gentelman to
Cone tand my Destrs and thae will now that i am not Deciven of them
pleas sir <se>nd me word by the return of Poast what i shall do were i 15
shall Come home or not
    I reman your humbel
    Survent Thoˢ Hall
No 11 Webb St
Bermondsey New Roade 20

TEXTUAL ALTERATIONS 3: pound] *interl.* 4: had] *interl.* 11: what] 'h' *over illeg.* 14: now] 'w' *over del illeg.*
DATE Postmark: 5 February 1827.

348   From Elizabeth Lane in [St Luke Old Street] London to [William] Chisolm, overseer of St Botolph, Colchester, 7 February 1827

February 7th 1827

Sir as Necessity has Obliged me to apply through illness for some relief as having no Work iwas Obliged to part with my ᵐ[-] Clothes if the Gentlemen will allow me a trifle a Week ishall be very thankful for it if not ishall be
5 under the Necessity of being passed home Gentlemen idont wish to put you to that Expence Where ireside Iam in debt for Rent and can not stay any longer in it pray Gentlemen do not fail in Answering this letter as soon as possible

Your Obedient S[t]

10   Elizabeth Lane

No21[--] Featherstone Stt City Road London

SPELLING 3: ᵐ[-]] presumably intended as 'my', where the 'y' has not been completed and the letters have erroneously not been ruled out.

349   From Edmund Cross in London to [William] Chisolm in St Botolph, Colchester, 20 February [1827]

London Febu[y] 20

Respected Freind Chisem

    according to the Request of a letter I Recievd from the father of the Poore Girl that I took out of S[t] Lukes & Brought Down to Colchester A
5 few Weaks ago, I Went to the Comitty to See If Shee Could Be admitted a Gain as a Weakly Patient a Gain But Was informd She Could not as there Was Moore then five Hundred Now on the List and She had lost her turn By Not haveing her Name Put on the list that Day She Came out <---> <th>ey tould Me if it had it Most likely it W<ould> <be> 12 or 14
10 years Before it Would Come to her <--->t they advised Me to try Som Privett Madhous<e> they tould Me Bathlem Green Would Be as good a one as any So yesterday I Went to hear their turms Which Ware as under and they Gave Me this Sertifficate to Be feld up By the Doctor Church

Warden and overseers With their Signatuers then the Bill Would Be sent
harf yearly for to Be Paid then She Might Be admitted as Soone as you 15
Please the turms are these Nine Shillings Pr Weak, No Entrence Money
and if they found her With Cloths & Linen it Would Be four Pound P^r
year)) Sh<e Can b>e Visitted Every Day of the Weak Except Sa<turday
If you> Conclude to Send her I Would Come Down <-------------->er in
for 2 Pound & My Coach hire, I Co<----------------------> cts Yours & 20
C^t
Edmund Cross

<---------------->wn Court
<----------------->ore fealds Lon<don>

TEXTUAL ALTERATIONS 3: the] *after del illeg.* 5: If] *after del* 'I'. 7: Hundred] 'n' *interl with
caret*. 14: Warden] 'den' *interl at end of line*.

DATE Year inferred from previous letter from Edmund Cross (**343**) and related correspondence.

WRITING The letter is written on the blank inside of a printed form of a medical certificate from White House in Bethnal Green.

**350   From Thomas Strutt in Chelmsford Prison to Mr Harris Esq.
in St Botolph, Colchester, 20 February 1827**

Chelmsford

Dear Sir/

It Is With A Reluctance that That I Make free to Address You With this
letter But Necessitay Compells Me to Do that I Am almost Ashamed off
When I Compare the Present With the Past But a kind Providence has So 5
ordered It that We know not one Day What Another May Bring forth Sir
attempting to Solicit your Assistance I hope you Will Excuse Me And I
am Confindent In My Mind that you Will. I have No Doubt But you have
heard that I Am Now Confined In Prison for Debt and that I have got a
Very Large family And from Losses In Bussiness Expences of Family 10
And Dullness of Trade these Last three or four years Is the only Cause of
My Being there I Now Am about to take the Benefit of the Act That I
Might get home to My Family The Expenses of Doing it Are Very Heavy
But they Must Be Paid Before I Can get My Releasement And I Myself
Have No other Means of Doing it Without Calling on the assitance of the 15
gentleman of St Botolph^s To Subscribe their Mite to assist Me In My
Release and which if they Do I hope Will Ever Be on My Mind With

Feelings of gratitude Sir I have Made free to Write to you Because I know
you have great Interest Amongst the gentleman of the Parish The
20 Expenses of Filing My Schedule Will Be about 15£ But I Do Not know the
Exact Sum yet But Mr Wix of Chelmsford the Attorney for the Court Says
that It Will Be about that Sum your kind Assistance Would Be the Means
of My Liberty And without which I have No Means of getting the Money
whithout Selling what Little I have got allowed Me By the Act In Wearing
25 apparell And Furniture I have Sir but of the 15£ Rec^d 5£ from My Wife
Which Is all She will Ever Be to Let Me have Allow Me Dear Sir To
Inform you that Unless there Is Something of the Kind Done for Me So as
to Raise the Remainder 10£ I See Nothing Else But My Large Family
Must Directly Fall Upon the Parish and I Must Remain Where I Am Sir
30 your very Kind Consideration And Attention to this Letter Will Ever Be
Remembered Sir By your

obedient
Humble Servant
Thos Strutt

35 Chelmsford Prison
Common Debtors Side Feby 20th 1827

TEXTUAL ALTERATIONS 20: know] *over del illeg.* 29: Must] *after del* 'Be'. 29: Upon] 'U'
over illeg.

FURTHER EVIDENCE Thomas Strutt's case was dealt with by the select vestry of St Botolph,
Colchester, a week later. 'It appearing that he has a Wife & Eleven Children & his business standing still in his Absence', it was agreed that 'Ten Pounds the sum he requests be
advanced to him by way of Loan' (ERO, D/P 203/8/2, St Botolph, Colchester, select
vestry minutes, entry of 27 February 1827).

351 From [Mrs] D. Springet in [Romford, Essex] to [William] Chisolm in St Botolph, Colchester [March 1827]

Sir/

in great grief Iam taken this lisbyte to inform you that me and my five
Children are in inutterable distresst ihave no means Geting through my
distressedness but applying to you Ihope and trust you gentlemen will tak
5 up my Case; the famaly have had but one meal since yesterday, Ihave
been confined 5 weake and am now very ill it is truely hard to come into
Atown like this to be shut up to Starve, and no one to help. I beg of you
Gentlemen to render me some present help and then to Convay us to my
husband if you think it proper for him to stay

I Subcribe 10
myself your
Humbe Survent
D *Springett*

TEXTUAL ALTERATIONS 3: Geting] 'g' *interl at end of line*. 6: is] *after del illeg*. 9: if] *after del illeg*.
PLACE and DATE Inferred from further evidence.
FURTHER EVIDENCE This letter is presumed to be the same as that from Mrs Springet (alias Springett) 'requiring present relief & requesting to be removed to her husband at Romford' which was dealt with by the select vestry of St Botolph, Colchester, at the meeting of 27 March 1827. 'It appearing that her husband is in work & that she has already objected to be removed on account of illness', it was ordered that 'the Case be left to Mr Chisolm the assist^t Overseer'. About a month later her case was discussed again. Mrs Springet, whose husband was a journeyman miller at Romford, had become ill and gone into Colchester Hospital. Her five children were placed in the workhouse and it was resolved to write to her husband. In his answer (as summarized in the vestry minutes), Springet offered to take his children and his wife when they were better, provided the parish allowed him 3s per week and shoes for the children. The select vestry ordered the overseers to obtain shoes and send them to Romford. Springet was allowed 3s per week and 20s 'to purchase a Bed' (ERO, D/P 203/8/2, St Botolph, Colchester, select vestry minutes, entries of 20 April and 1 May 1827).

352 From George Watson [in London] to Mr Chisnall, overseer of St Botolph, Colchester [22 May 1827]

To the Gentlemen Overseers of the Poor of St Botolph. Colchester
Gent^n Mr John Goslin Informs me that at Lett^r I wrote to him begging the favour of him to Give it to Mr Chisnell has not been awnswerd I humbly take this Liberty in writing to you Gent^n In behalf of my daughter Hannah Watson and her Child. Gent^n it is now *[6]* Years Since my daughter Came 5 home to My Place Strongly Persuaded by Mr Osborn on Promise of Allowing her 4 Shillings Per Week and telling her Likewise she should have a few Shillings Now and then Independent of her Weekly Allowance to Gett a few things for herself and Child. how far Mr Osborns Word has been Kept I appeal to you Gent^n her Weekly allowance has been Reduc.d 10 from Time to time from 4 shilling^s to 2^s Per Week and as for a few Shillings Now and then she has Never had a Penny. she is Now and has been ever since she Left Colchester an Inmate with me and if it was not for me she & Child Must starve Gent^n I stated all things how I am situated in Life in that Lett^r I sent to Mr Goslins. M^r G Inform^d Me he had Given it to M^r 15 Chisnell and that it should be Laid before the Gent^n at a Vestry Meeting I

do now Gentⁿ Humbly ask the favour of you If you will in Goodness do
some Little for her and Child as they Are Nearly Naked Look at 2 Shillings Per Week it is not that I cand Receive a Months Money of 8 Shillings
20 without Paying 6^d wich makes it only 1^s.10 1/2 Week - it is not half Enough
to support the Child Gentⁿ I donot wish to send her and Child down to you
without first writeing to you and haveing y^r awnswer but if it is your Pleasure not to do a Little More for her they Must Come down I have not Got
it in My Power to help them Now as I have done Gent I did beg the favour
25 in the Lett^r I sent if you would Please to allow her 6^d a Week more and
send her a few shilling^s to Gett herself and Child a few Nessasaries
     Gentⁿ I shall not take y^r time up any Longer If it is y^r Pleasure to do a
little for her Mr Goslin will send it her Imeadeatly you Gives it him Gentⁿ
I shall Esteem it a Great favour if you will Let Mr Goslin Know y^r Pleas-
30 ure and he will send to Me. and than I shall Know what to do Gentⁿ I
Remain with all due Respect
                                   Y^r Obeid^t
                                        Geo. Watson

TEXTUAL ALTERATIONS 4: daughter] 'er' *interl at end of line.* 28: up] *interl.*
   DATE Date of postmark.

353   From E[lizabeth] Hines [in Ipswich] to the overseer of St Botolph, Colchester, [27 July 1827]

Sir I sent a note to you requesting a little money But you sent me an
answer Back that you was not to Pay till the quarter was out now I shael
thank you if you woud advance me up to Michelmas as I Can assure you
I an in the greattes Distress for the want of it as the my Daughter as had
5 another fit if you Do not send me an answer But I Shall Come on Monday
and show a Note from Me Doctor
I remain your Obliged E Hindes

TEXTUAL ALTERATIONS 4: my] 'm' *over* 'y'.
   DATE and PLACE From note of receipt on outside.

354   From Elizabeth Lane [in St Luke Old Street, London] to the overseer of St Botolph, Colchester, 20 August 1827

August 20th 1827

Gentlemen Iam sorry to trouble you but on account of illness Iam Obliged
to it as ihave been ill for some time through not being able to do any thing
ihave sent to you before iapply to St Lukes Middlesex where ireside
unless you do Something for me directly Ialso dread the Winter Comeing   5
as unless you do Something to assist me through it if not Ishall be obliged
to be to be sent home if you please to allow me something p^r Week
Iunderstand it may be done by the parish Ireside in idont wish to trouble
you longer than ican help pray send me an Answer as soon as possible
your Obedient St Elizabeth Lane   10
        21 Featherstone Stt City Road

TEXTUAL ALTERATIONS 6: it] *interl.*

355   From Elizabeth Lane in [St Luke Old Street] London to [William] Chisolm, overseer of St Botolph, Colchester, 23 August 1827

August 23rd 1827

Gentlemen friend Ireceived your letter at the present time ihave Nothing
to take to Nor any thing ican make Sixpence of only the kindness of my
landlady Assisting me my illness is an inward Complaint wich as afflicted me
5 months and of that nature that icant Explain to the Gentlemen and if they   5
please to send they will find what ihave Stated to be true and if the Gentlemen dont do something for me imust come home as my landlady cant let
me Stay any longer

Your Obedient St Elizabeth Lane
21 Featherstone St^t City Road London   10

TEXTUAL ALTERATIONS 6: if] *interl.*

356   From E[lizabeth] Hines in Ipswich to [William] Chisolm, overseer of St Botolph, Colchester, 27 September 1827

Ipswich Sep^t 27 1827

Sir I Should be verry much opliged to you if you would send me my Daughter money for it have Cost me so much for Doctor medicine that I Can scarcely make the money last But thank God She have not her fits so often and I
5 am still in hopes in time she will quite recover if You will send me the money by the Bearer I shall Feel verry thankful and I remain your humble serv

- *E. Hines*

TEXTUAL ALTERATIONS 1: 1827] *interl at end of line.*

357   From R. Springet in Romford [Essex] to [William] Chisolm in St Botolph, Colchester, 12 November 1827

Romford Novr 12 1827

Mr Chislom I Will be obliged to you if you Will Be So Kind as to Send me 3 Pounds to Pay the Rent as it Was Due Last Satuarday Which I had quite forgot till the Landlord Cold today I am Sorey to trubel you for So much
5 But I am under the Nessisity of telling you I Cant Doo Without it as My Wife have been So Expencive Since She have Been at Romford She Was ill a long time and after She Got well Shee had the misfortune to Let a Boiler which Contain 2 Pails of Boilen hot Water ove Boath Lags it Cost me 1..10..0 in a few Days and Now She is Confind With the 6 Child
10 Which make me in a Grate Deal of trubel Pray Doant fail in Sending me 3 Pounds as I Cant Do less on Saturday as I Promised to Pay on Sunday Pleas to Send it By the Wellington Coatch as it is quite Darke when Mr Cracknell Go By
Pleas to Dyrect it to the Last Mill Going out of Romford
15 I Remain yours Respectfuly
R Springet

TEXTUAL ALTERATIONS 5: you] *interl at end of line.* 9: With the 6 Child] *interl at end of line.* 11: 3] *after del illeg.* 11: as I Cant Do less] *interl at end of line.*
CIRCUMTEXT Note from other hand below: sent £3 per Wellington Coach, 17 November 1827.
FURTHER EVIDENCE R. Springet was the husband of D. Springet (see **351**).

358 From Ann Lester in Sudbury [Suffolk] to the overseer of St Botolph, Colchester, 13 November 1827

Sudbury Novr 13 1827

Gentlemen/

I am sorry to have exertion to write to you on this subject but my presant nessessities are so far beyond my means that I find it impossible to pro-vide for myself and family without some assistance from you beyond 5
what is already allow.d when you consider that my Family consists of six small children unable to provide for themselves and some of them afflicted with the hooping cough and verry unwell myself you must be aware of the Impossibility of my doing without your kind assistance in Cloathing more particularly we are verry much in wants a remittance 10
from you for that purpose will very much Oblidge

Your Humble Servant Ann Lester

TEXTUAL ALTERATIONS 4: means] *after del illeg.* 7: provide] *after del* 'for'.

CIRCUMTEXT Note from Oliver Byer at bottom of page: 'The Widow Lester has been very ill for a month past medical aid was necessay she is not able to pay for it the Children are much in want of Cloths' (hand A). Note from other hand on back of page: sent £1 by Mr Brag, carrier (hand B).

RELATED CORRESPONDENCE and FURTHER EVIDENCE According to an undated list which must have been made up by the overseer of one of the parishes concerned (that is, Sudbury or St Botolph, Colchester), William Lester and family had received medical relief (mainly 'powders' and 'mixture') to the total amount of £25 7s from November 1825 to April 1827 (kept among overseers' correspondence). William Lester himself must have died during that period, for on 11 July 1826 the select vestry of St Botolph, Colchester, had approved an application from Widow Lester 'for a small sum to enable her to purchase some linen & she has agreed to liquidate it by payment of 6^D p^r week' (ERO, D/P 203/8/ 2, St Botolph, Colchester, select vestry minutes).

359 From George Watson in London, 20 November 1827

Sir

I Recv^d y^r Friendly Lett^r by the Waggon with 1£. I humbly thank you for the 3 Weeks Money wich you have alow^d besides the the Months Money I can say *Sir* with truth it was due to My daughter you say Sir in ye Lett^r it would settle the 3 Weeks due and Get her bit of Linnen Sir With Respect 5
I beg Leave to say takeing the 3 Weeks Money 7.6. and the Months Money 10^s Wich was due there was but 2.6 Left *Sir* this is a small sum to gett a few Nessasarys such as a P^r of shoes for herself and child a bit of

Linnen and and a flanell Peticoat those are the things she wants. she
10 bought a P^r of shoes with the 2.6 and the other things she is at Presint
without. Sir with the Greatest Respect I beg Leave to say Next *Friday*
Novr 23rd the Months Money is due if *Sir* you could put a Little to it she
will be humbly thanfull to you and Get something for herself & Child as
they are both almost Naked and she Cannot Get it out of her Weekly
15 money as that will Scarcely Get them dry Bread. Sir bothe she and myself
Joins In Returning you and the Gentⁿ our humble and Gratefull thanks Sir
I shall Goe to the Waggon next Tuesday Nov 27.

G Watson

London
20   Nov 20 27

TEXTUAL ALTERATIONS 3: Months] 'th' *over illeg.*
    CIRCUMTEXT Note from other hand below: £1 sent, being five weeks' pay (up to 30
November 1827) 12s 6d plus extra allowance of 7s 6d, 29 November 1827.

360   From G[eorge] and Hannah Watson in London to William Chisolm in St Botolph, Colchester, 18 December 1827

London Decr 18th

To Mr Chisolam
Sir
    My Daughter & Myself Return Your our Gratefull thanks for 1 Pound
5 I Recv^d of Mr Russell Your Statement is *Sir* 5 Weeks Money due up to
Nov 30 - the other *Sir* she has Made the best use of *Sir* At this Time *Sir* I
humbly beg the favour if you will Please to Give Mr Russell 4 Weeks
Money wich will be due on Friday Decr 28

Humbly thanking you
& Gentⁿ for all favours
I am Sir with Respect
G & *Hanah Watson*

10

CIRCUMTEXT Note from other hand at botttom: 10s sent, for four weeks up to 28 December
1827.

361 From [Elizabeth] Hines in St Anne, Soho, London, to [William] Chisolm, overseer of St Botolph, Colchester, 1 January 1828

London Jany 1 1828

Sir

i hope you will Excuse the Freedom i have taken in Trubling you with these few Lines Respecting my Daughter Eliza Hinds who was Ill Ever since she Came to town hopes that you will take it into Consideration and 5
Asist me a Little and i shall be bound to pray for your Goodness and i hope that you will Remit me the Six Shillings that is Due to her in so Doing you will Greatly Befriend your Most Humble Servant <E> Hinds

No 6 King Stt

Sn^t Anns Soho 10

P.S. be so kind as to Send It by Greens Waggon

362 From Hannah Steward in Hadleigh, Suffolk, to Mr Orford in St Botolph, Colchester, 17 January [1828]

Jen 17

Dear frind this Come with my kind love to you and to inform you that my dear Child departed this life this morning about 5 oCloCk i humbly beg the favour as i have no other Earthly frind in this Case that you will dereCtly go to her overser and do all you posable Can for me as i know 5
not wat to do till i hare from you pray Send to me by return o<f> post wat thay will alow me to burey her from me Hanner Steward Hadglak Gorge Streat Suffolk

DATE Year from filing note on outside.

363 From Thomas Goody [in St Botolph, Colchester] to [William] Chisolm, overseer of St Botolph, Colchester [9 February 1828]

Si^r

it is painfull to my Feelings to State to you that my landlord Called upon me on Satarday last To inform me that Bisness being Settled Since The deceace of his Father The exSeceter^s Whould Call on me in 2 or 3 Weeks to receve The rent due from midsummer to Michaelmas and that he him- 5

self should Receive for the preasent quarter and After I told Him I was sorry to say I Was unprepard to meet Their demands I Therefore Beg of you Sir to State the Same to the gentelmen who in Consideration of my long affliction with my also Children Will I pray exstend their Compasion
10 and relive Me in my preasent destress

                                    Thomas goody

TEXTUAL ALTERATIONS 9: my also] *interl.* 9: exstend] 's' *interl.*
    DATE Date of note of receipt on back.
    PLACE Inferred from related correspondence and further evidence.
    RELATED CORRESPONDENCE Thomas Goody was admitted as an in-patient to the Essex and Colchester Hospital on 22 May 1828, on the recommendation of the overseers of St Botolph, Colchester, and discharged on 19 July (?) 1828 (letter from Essex and Colchester Hospital, date of second letter partly illegible).
    FURTHER EVIDENCE Thomas Goody received casual relief of 12s on 3 October 1828 (ERO, D/P 203/12/45, St Botolph, Colchester, overseers' accounts).

364   From George John Tye in Colchester to Mr Harris in St Botolph, Colchester, 11 February 1828

                           Colchester - Febuary 11th *1828*

To Mr Harris
  Sir/
  It is with a Trembling hand I beg to Intrude this Letter Being fearfull
5 you will think me Troublesom - and I acknowledg with all Humility I feel myselfe So after The great kindness and Bountyfull friendship Shown to me By the gentlemen of the Select Vestry of the parish of Sn^t Botolph at the time I was before them - I am Sorry to find Since by a more accurate Calculation on the means wareby To git a bit of Bread for the future - that
10 I had formd an Aronious Idea of my Situation to Obtain that much discred Object - Since that time I have made arangements on as Limited a Scale as poseble ware by to do my utermost Endeavours to git a Sustanance that I may not any more Be troublesom - which I humbly beg to Submit to thire Generious Consideration - I have made an arangement with M^r
15 Hagg - to carry out numbers of Such Books as I can git Sale for which will bring me in a triffle - Likewise - Could I but git a Retirn or Two of wrighting paper and a Couple of Hundred of Quills that I Could Cut into pens at My Leasure - with a few Sweets of my own makeing To make up a Load - and to take a regular Curent round Colchester - I feel great
20 Confidence I Could git a Livelyhood a pair of Scales - with Small weights

up to a pound I Cannot Do without - with a triffle of money in my pocket
to buy any thing that might benefit me by way of return - and not haveing
a friend in the world that I Can ask a Shilling off to help me - being thus
Ancumbranc[d] I humbly pray you to take my Cace into your generious
Consideration If you Can do a triffle more for me - It would Emancipate   25
me From real poverty - and give me a Chance to git my Bread Unshackled
- and that I may not be a Shackle hangen on as a Burden on *this* or any
other parish So Long as it Should please god I Can keep my health - that
when I know to what parish I may belong to be duly Sworn Before one or
more Magistrat[s] and receiving thire Certifycate I may pass through the   30
Country without any Cat Suit or Malestation of any person or persons
whatsoever - as I am privelidge[d] by Servitude by an Act of George 3rd
22nd June 1816 Chap[r] 67 - Humbley Submiting my Selfe to your goodness

      I am gentlemen with Due respect and gratitude   35
your Most Obedient Humble Serv[t] George John Tye

TEXTUAL ALTERATIONS 15: which] 'c' *over illeg.*
  FURTHER EVIDENCE At the meeting of the select vestry of St Botolph, Colchester, on 22
January 1828, it was decided to advance George John Tye £1 and 'that Enquiry be made
as to a Living in Southwark since he left Colchester' (ERO, D/P 203/8/3, St Botolph,
Colchester, select vestry minutes).

365 From R. Springet in Romford [Essex] to [William] Chisolm in St Botolph, Colchester, 18 February 1828

                           Romford Feby 18th 1828
M[r] Chislom
      Sir I am under the Nessesety of Trubling you for 2[£]10[s]0[d] to Pay my
Rent with as it was Due on the 10 of this Munth the Landlord has been
with me and said he shold Call for it on Wednesday it being Market Day   5
he Shold Waight till then Pray Doant Disopint me in Sending it by the
Same Convaince as before you will

                      Oblidge your omble
                      survent R Springet
I Recvd the Last Saft a few Days after   10

TEXTUAL ALTERATIONS 6: Shold] 'S' *over illeg.* 6: in] *interl.* 7: Convaince] 'i' *inserted.*

FURTHER EVIDENCE At the meeting of the select vestry of St Botolph, Colchester, of 19 February 1828, R. Springet was granted the sum of £2 10s 0d (ERO, D/P 203/8/3, St Botolph, Colchester, select vestry minutes).

366   From George John Tye to [William] Chisolm in St Botolph, Colchester, 18 February 1828

Febuary 18th 1828

To Mr Chisolm
- overseer of the parish Sn^t Botolph^s Colchester
Sir/

5   I am Sorry to find my Exertions as far as my power Can go toward^s giting a Livelyhood - will be of no avail - as my means I find are to Curcumscrib^d to bear me up against aproaching poverty - If the gentlemen that have already been So kind to me can render me a triffle more assistance I have Every reason to hope I Shall be able to Subsist without
10   any more trouble - If they would be kind Enough to advance me Sufficent to purchas a Ream & -/2 of paper - I would Do Every thing in my power to refund the Same at 9^d a a Shilling a week - as I Could git 5/ a week for takeing about numbers on this Sum I Could not Subsist haveing to take Long Journeys and as I find I might add to that Sum Consederable by a
15   Little paper & wareby I Should be able to get on - as I am now Confind to the townd - and So little to be pick^d up in So Confin^d Space that with 14^{/d/} for Rend and a few Coals Is as much as I Can get - and must in Conciquence quickly fall into Extreem want - I beg Sir you will be kind Enough To make this Statement to the gentlemen If they In thire goodness Can do
20   any thing more for me they will do me a Charity that will be greatfully remmembred
                I am Sir veri respectfully
                Your Obedient Humble Servt
                George John Tye
25 PS
        I would of call on you but have been veri Lame with a Swell^d food last week - that have hurt me veri much In not Being able to git out but Little

FURTHER EVIDENCE At the meeting of the select vestry of St Botolph, Colchester, of 19 February 1828, it was decided that casual relief be granted to George John Tye 'at the overseers discretion' (ERO, D/P 203/8/3, St Botolph, Colchester, select vestry minutes).

367 From George John Tye to William Chisolm in St Botolph, Colchester, 25 February 1828

To Mr Chisolm

  Dr Sir

I am certainly asham^d of the meny applications and trouble I am given you - But as I adress this *note* Exclusively To you - I hope you will pardon me for So doing - you ware kind Enough Last week to give me Eight- 5 een pence for which I beg my greatfull thanks although but a little was a great reliefe to me - I have known you for meny years - and I well know you are always ready to do good to those you think Deserve or need it - If you Could git those kind gentlemen of the parish to allow me Two Shillings and Sixpence a week for a few weeks I trust I Should be able to Do 10 for myself - I wish to God I Could now But it is So little that I Can pick up - as all sorts of Trade is So dead - it is not realy not Sufficient to keep life and Soul Together all last week I Did not git a bove Two Shillings - what can I do with that - after paying 1/2 for a room and a few Coals - god knows thare is Little left for Bread - I know Sir that thare is no gentlemen 15 In Colchester undersand the Expence of modern liven better then yourselfe Should I not belong to this parish - I hope you would git repaid from ware I Do belong - But in the mene time what Can I Do - I Cannot do for my Selfe I wish to god I Could - I git old and good for nothing and Cannot keep myselfe in any way to live - My Cloaths all Sold or nearly worn out 20 and In fast I am nearly a Compleet wreck - I humbly beg you to have Compassion on me and if you Can git me a triffle

            It will render me a Charity

               and will be greatfully

remmembd   25

         By Sir/

               Your Obedient Humble Ser^t

               George John Tye

PS/ I will take the Liberty to Call on you to morrow Evening - Febuary 25th 1828 -   30

T<small>EXTUAL ALTERATIONS</small> 6: although] 'l' *over illeg.* 12: realy not] 'not' *interl with caret.*

368   From George Watson in London, 10 March [1828]

London March th10

Sir

I Recv^d 10^s of Mr Russell wich was due on the 22 of Feb^{ry} Last I humbly beg the favour of you *Sir* if youl be so Kind as to Remitt me this
5 Months wich will be due Friday March 21 of this Month. and I Will attend for it Next Tuesday - 18 *Inst* -

Sir I beg Leave to say that the Revd Mr Smith of Pensance a very Popular Carecter in London Minister of the Marriners Church In Willclose square has Publish^d an Account of the Late Callamity of the Brunswick
10 Theatre with some very Good Observations on the Curcumstances attending the dreadfull Callamity: I have Instord the same If *Sir* the Reading of wich should afford you or any of your Freinds any Gratification I shall feel my self well Pleas.d I am Sir with

all due Respect Geo Watson

TEXTUAL ALTERATIONS 5: wich] *after del* 'due'.
DATE Year from filing note on outside.

369   From John Balls in Maldon [Essex] to Mr Bugg in St Botolph, Colchester, 25 March 1828

Maldon March 25th 1828

Sir

I am very Sorry that I am under the Nessesity of Troubling you. but our Trade is so bad that We have little or Nothing to Do Since I was at Col-
5 chester. and we realy are in Great Distress and Cannot Get Work enough for Nessasary Food and Oblidge to go without Bread or any thing frequently by the Day tolgeter, we would not have troubled You but Hunger is so very Sharp and we know not what Step to take we Humbley Pray that you and the Gentleman will have the Goodness to Grant us this Once
10 our Request to forward a Pound by the Burnham Van. I fear without Your favour we shall be Oblidge to Come to Colchester. I should have Come but am poorly and low and have heard that our Trade has been bad there. as well as it has in Maldon, I hope Sir You will send the above Mentiond or some Word what Step we may take, the Money I Recev^d of you befor

we pay^d it it where we owed mostly for Rent. but now have had so long 15
Vacation or we would not been no more troublesome

Your Obeident & Humble Servants
John M Balls

TEXTUAL ALTERATIONS 4: We] *after del illeg.* 6: for] *interl.* 7: tolgeter] 'g' *over* 'l', *second* 't' *over* 'r'. 9: and the] 'and' *interl.* 12: am] *interl.* 14: Step] 't' *over illeg.* 15: it where] *after del* 'where'. 15: mostly] 'l' *over* 'y'.

RELATED CORRESPONDENCE Some ten years before, the overseers of St Botolph, Colchester, had received three letters on behalf of John Balls at Maldon. On 13 August 1817, John Stow, overseer of St Mary, Maldon, had requested assistance for him for the burial of his deceased nine-year-old son. Two letters had come from G. Long in Maldon, the master of John Balls since 1806, reporting on his distressed situation and requesting assistance (8 May 1818; date of second letter destroyed).

370 From Ann Lester in Sudbury [Suffolk] to [William] Chisolm, overseer of St Botolph, Colchester, 1 April 1828

Sudbury April 1st 1828

Sir

I hope that you will Excuse my making so Bold as writing to you But I was along with Mr Syer this morning and Mr Syer told me that he had not Rec^d any Note from your hand according as you promised me last Thurs- 5
day when that I was along with you, You told me that you would Send me two Pounds last Saturday or otherwise write to Mr Syer so that I Could Receive the money of Mr Syer and If that you do not Send it so that I can Change my Situation Eight Shillings a week will not Keep mee and the Family for you must think that I Cannot do much myself 10

So I Remain yours &c
Ann Lester

TEXTUAL ALTERATIONS 11: &c] *interl below.*
WRITING This letter was written by Thomas Bacon.
CIRCUMTEXT Note from Thomas Bacon (same hand as letter) at bottom of page: 'Sir, If that you do not Send the two Pounds according to promise I will not have the Women let what will Happen'. Thomas Bacon was Ann Lester's future husband (see her next letter: **381**).

371   From John Balls in Maldon [Essex], 7 April 1828

Maldon April 7th 1828

Sir

I am Sorry to inform You that I am so very bad off that we are under the
Necessity of Troubling You at this present time. I forwarded a Note to M^r
5 Bugg Last weeke as you was not at home. I hope this will meet with You
and have the Goodness to Send us what I mentioned to You Gentleman
Last week. as I Declare to you I Did not Earn but 4^s7^d last week. a little
stir has been the forepart of this week. or I must have Come over. we are
in hopes that Trade will soon set in, and I certainly will Endeavour to
10 avoid of being so troublesome. but we now Stand in the Greatest Need &
we hope and pray Sir that you will Do what You can for us

Your Obeadent Servant
John Balls

TEXTUAL ALTERATIONS 5: meet] *after del illeg.* 7: Earn] 'n' *over illeg.*

372   From George Watson in London to [William] Chisolm in St Botolph, Colchester, 22 April 1828

London April 22nd 1828

Mr Chisolam

Sir

You may be supriz^d at my writing to you before the Useual time but I
5 beg Leave to Give my Reason. *Sir* about 7 or 8 months agoe you was
Kind Enough to send my Daughter Hannah Watson a few Shillings to
Gett a Trifle or 2 for herself & Child she made the best use of that few
shillings for that Purpose and Return.d her thanks to you *Sir* for the same.
Sir altho it is my wish not to Trouble you yet *Sir* when I look at her and
10 Child at this time I can not do any other wise than Inform you that they
are both at this time destitute they have not got a Second thing to put on
she has only one old Patch.d Gown and scarcely abit of flannell the Childs
Dress is what I bought him 2 Years agoe and is now Quite worne out - I
Put a New P^r of Shoes on is feet Last Week stood me in 4^s but it is not in
15 My Power to do more I do say that both Mother and Child has half their
Support from me - think Sir what is 2.4./- Per Week for a Woman &
Child 6 year old - wich that is all when I have Gave the Man 6^s for his

Trouble - this *Sir* is the Reason I wrot to you at this Time humbly begging the favour of you Sir to send a Little for her and Child to gett a few Nessasaris as no one wants them more than they. I have no other way *sir* than humbly Solliciting you for them as they Cannot Present themselfs before you *Sir* Mr Russell will Call on you about the 8th of May wich will be the Regular Time. I humbly hope no offence my Daughter has been begging of me to send her & Child home sooner than be both so Naked as they are but I thought I had best Write to you Sir she & myself humbly thanks you and Gent^n for all favours & Remain
   with the Greatest Respect
            Geo. Watson

TEXTUAL ALTERATIONS 11: they] *interl with caret.* 19: send] *interl with caret.*
RELATED CORRESPONDENCE Elizabeth Watson had been admitted as an in-patient to the Essex & Colchester Hospital on 10 April 1827 and was released on 8 May 1827 (notes from Essex & Colchester Hospital).

373 From George Watson [in London, April 1828]

Sir

I Recv^d of Mr Russell 10^s due March 23 I humbly beg the favour if you Please to Give him this month when he Calls with this wich will be due the 20th of this month
  I am Sir humbly thanking
  you for all favours
  Geo Watson

CIRCUMTEXT Note from other hand below text: '1828/ Rec^d 10.0 Ap[ril] 12 Paid Joseph Russell'.
PLACE and DATE Inferred from circumtext.

374 From R. Springet in Romford [Essex] to [William] Chisolm in St Botolph, Colchester, 7 May 1828

          Romford May 7 - 1828
Mr Chislom Sir/
 I will thank you to Send Me 3 Pounds by Saturday the 10th as my Landlord is Going to Call for the Rent I am Sorey to truble you for So much but I cannot Doe Without it with so Large fameily an a flicted Whife But

if you Can Get me a Situvation Near hom I Shold Like it much Better as I think Provishen & Rent is Not So Dear as thay are hear Pleas do not fail on Sending as my Lanlord Dont Like to be Disapointed and I owe afew shilings beside

10   I Remain your
          omble Survent
          R Springet
Pleas to Send by the wellington Coach for R Springet at M^r P Collins Mill Romford

TEXTUAL ALTERATIONS 3: the 10th] *interl.* 10: I] *after del* 'Your'.
CIRCUMTEXT Note from other hand on outside: £2 10s sent per Wellington Coach.

375   From Elizabeth Hines in St Anne, Soho, London, to the overseers of St Botolph, Colchester [18 June 1828]

To the Overseers of the Parish St Botoloph Cholchester
Gentlemen
     I am sorry to be under the necessity of making application to you for Parish Releif for my Daughter Eliza Hines but she is at present afflicted
5 with Fits which renders her incapable of getting her Bread in Servitude she has been attacked with a violent Fit in the Street & she has been picked up 3 times lately last Sunday night she was picked up and carried to the workhouse in St Giles the Doctor blid her in the neck and temple if I have not some relief I must send her home. Please to write to me as soon
10 as you can as she lies very ill as present

                              I am Gentlemen
                         Your most Ob^t Ser^t
                              Eliz^t Hines

   Gentlemen Pleas to
15 Direct to
   Mrs Marshall
   47 Old Compton st Soho
   for Mrs *Hines*

TEXTUAL ALTERATIONS 17: Soho] *interl below.*
     CIRCUMTEXT Confirmation from a surgeon of St Giles Infirmary at bottom of page (hand A), followed by confirmation from a further witness in Soho on next page (hand B, name illeg). Note from parish officer of St Botolph, Colchester, below signature (hand C): 'Sent 1 £ by Post', 19 June 1828.
     DATE Date of postmark.

376   From George Watson [in London] to [William] Chisolm in St Botolph, Colchester, 1 July 1828

M[r] Chisolam

Sir Permitt me to beg the favour of you to Send my Daughter a Months Money up this Week by M[r] Russell and I will Go to him Next Tuesday for it the Month will not be due untill the 11th of this Month. but I ask it *Sir* as a favour as I am at this Time a Cripple with my Right Arm in a   5 Sling having Fractur.[d] My Shoulder 3 Weeks Last Friday and at this Time I cannot do for myself much More assist my Chilldren Sir I hope you will Grant me this small favour and *Sir*

I am with all due Respect
Geo Watson   10

Tuesd Morn[g]
July 1st 1828

PLACE Inferred from text.

377*   From [Benjamin] Brooker [in Ipswich, 10 July 1828]

sur plese to send mises Brooker Boyes muney Buy rouse for hi am in grate wants of it plese not to fal senden it

WRITING This slip of paper is from the same hand as the letters from Benjamin Brooker of December 1825 and April 1826 from Ipswich to St Peter, Colchester (**510, 521**).
SPELLING 1: Buy rouse] *read* 'by Rouse' (*surname*).
CIRCUMTEXT Note from other hand below text: 'July 10th 1828 £1..6 James Mills'.
PLACE The reference to the bearer of the requested money (and the letter?) is to the same person as in Benjamin Brooker's letters from Ipswich to St Peter, Colchester, which suggests that the present letter was also sent from Ipswich.
DATE Inferred from circumtext.

378   From George Watson [in London] to [William] Chisolm in St Botolph, Colchester, 22 July [1828]

Sir

I Recv[d] from M[r] Russell 10[s] wich Pay[s] My Daughter up to the 11th day of this month I Return you my thanks. *Sir* M[r] Russell Inform.d me that

you told him that when the Gent[n] holds their Monthly Meeting you would
5 try and Gett a few Shillings for her *Sir* I humbly thank you for y[r] Kindness Sir 6 Weeks agoe Last Friday I Mett with a Very Serous Accedent
by a fall I Fractur.d or Broke my Shoulder my arm is at Present Useless
altho thank God I hope to do well but at Present I can do no work *Sir*
under those Curcumstances I take the Liberty of begging a favour of you
10 wich as you have been so Kind as to signify you would Oblidge me in any
Kind of way you could I do think you will not Refuse me next Friday Sir
my daughter will have 2 Week[s] money due the favour I beg *Sir* is if you
will have the Goodness to Give M[r] Russell 10[s] when he Leaves this Note
wich Will be Advanceing 2 Week forward wich 10[s] will Pay her up to
15 Agust 22nd Sir I humbly thank you for all favour and I am Sir with all due
Respect

> Y[r] Most Obeident
> & HB Serv[t]
> Geo Watson

20 Tuesday
July 22nd

TEXTUAL ALTERATIONS 11: way] *after del illeg.* 12: daughter] 'ter' *interl at end of line.* 12:
Week[s]] *after del* 'B'.
CIRCUMTEXT Note from other hand below: payment of 10s ordered on 24 July.
DATE Year from filing note on outside.
PLACE Inferred from text.

379 From Robert Ray [in Setchey, Norfolk] to William Chisolm, assistant overseer of St Botolph, Colchester, 26 August 1828

August 26th 1828
Sir in Answer to yours of the 23 Ins[t] I have to State that certain Pecuniary
Matters which I do not fell Called upon to State to you Prevent me doing
that for My Parents which my Inclinations me to I have three Children to
5 Look to and Support many Debts to discharge and heavy Expences now
Bearing upon me - when these are over if I have it in my Power and my
Father should Survive *I shall fell it a Duty* to do what is in my Power for
him but Certainly not thro a threat of Being Compelled By your *Select
Vestry You or any Other* Person or Persons my Father Paid Rates and
10 Taxes to the Parish of St Botolfs a Great number of Years to help Support
others and he is now entitled to that which he receives by a more Recent

Act than that of the 43 of Eliz any Letters Sent to me after the Date of this
will Returned unopened
    I am Sir Your
    Obe^t Servant   15
    Robert Ray
To Mr Wm Chisolm
Ass^t Overseer of
the Parish of St Botolps Colchester

TEXTUAL ALTERATIONS 4: Inclinations] 'i' *over* 'e'.
CIRCUMTEXT This letter was written on the inside of the letter referred to at the beginning,
that is from William Chisolm, assistant overseer of St Botolph, Colchester, to Robert
Ray, excise officer, in Setchey, 23 August 1828: 'I am directed by the Select Vestry [...]
to apply to you for the maintainance of your Aged Father Richd Ray in pursuance of the
43 of Eliz. Whereby the Parents and Children are bound to support each other - I hope
you will immediately attend to this application and prevent further Expences. I think you
only need to be r[eminded] [*paper torn*] of you Duty and not to be compelled.'

380   [From Elizabeth Baker in St Botolph, Colchester, 15 September 1828]

Sir

I come here to relate a case between myself and my husband Baker
which I am very sorry to trouble you Gentlemen upon such an occasion
we have been married upwards of 33 years and I have had a family and
brought them all up in a decent manner and living in this Town sorry to   5
make my affairs known to the public at large stating the case for the last
4 years that he has used me very ill, that he has not given me more than 7
or 8^s per week for the 2 months together for instead of bring^g his money
home to support his Family he have spent it in all manner of bad Company there is for the last 3 years he has given me the bad disorder which   10
has almost cost me my life and the 1st time he gave it me he concealed the
matter till I was almost dead but I forgave him if he did not do the like
again, and about 4 months ago I found that he had brought me in the same
situation and when I told him the state that I was in he left me and has
been gone 14 weeks and I have not had 1^d from him, I have sent to him   15
several times but he never will send me any money therefore it is not in
my power to support myself + two Children and my desire is Gentlemen
that you will make him allow me 4 or 5^s per week which is in his power to
allow if you please to force him for he has said he will not allow me 1^s

20 and he *[wo^d rather]* spend all his money with all the bad women in Halstead
    than give me any Therefore Gentlemen I hope you will take it into Con-
    sideration that I can by no means live with a man of this description - and
    Gentlemen I hope that if you come to any agreement with my husband as
    to his paying me somuch per week that you will let the money be paid
25 into the hands of the overseers of the parish of St Botolph for me to receive it
    from them

TEXTUAL ALTERATIONS 6: known] *interl above del illeg.* 8-9: his money home to support]
interl with caret above del 'it to'. 12: if] *after del* 'and'. 15: not] *after del* 'had'. 18: him]
after del 'h' *and* 'make'. 19: you please to force him] *above del* 'he please to'. 21: take]
after del 'th'. 21-22: Consideration] 'er' *over illeg.*
  WRITING The letter was written by James Barker, surgeon in Colchester.
  CIRCUMTEXT The letter is preceded by a statement from James Barker, surgeon in Colchester, 15 September 1828, which is in the same hand: 'I certify that Eliz^th Baker has been
under my care twice on account of the Venereal Disease which she states to me she
contracted from her Husband - that on the former occasion he called at my Surgery +
admitted the fact [...] Eliz^th Baker wishes for this certificate to prevent public exposure of
the circumstances in open Court.'

**381 From Ann Bacon in Sudbury [Suffolk] to [William] Chisolm
       in St Botolph, Colchester, 19 September 1828**

                                                    Sudbury Sepr 19 1828
Mr Chisolm
    Sir I am under the painful Nessessity of Applying to you as overseer of
the Parish to which My Dr Children belong for a further supply in conse-
5 quence of the rise of the flower Sir you are awere that two Stone of Bread
is scarcly sufficient for them without a single article beside which cost at
the presant price seven Shillings and I am allow.d for them only eight
which I find to be quite insufficiant My State of Health is such that I
cannot make up the deficiancy and My husband does not feel disposed I
10 have none to look to for them but you therefore I hope and Trust you will
be so kind as to send me some extry relief My Husband has done all he
can for them and cannot do more at presant there is no employ to be had
My Boy was taken as Apprentice to learn the silk trade but there was no
written agreement therefor when the Trade faild he was turnd off and has
15 been destitute eversince July Sir I acknowledge your former kindness to
me and feel greatfull for it and trust you will not desert My Children in
the presant defiently a speedy remittance will Much Oblidge Your

Hum^l Servant An Bacon
formerly Lester

I will meet the Carrier on tuesday 20

TEXTUAL ALTERATIONS 4: which] *over illeg.* 12: cannot do more at presant] 'cannot' *interl above del* 'will', 'more' *after del* 'no'; 'at presant' *interl with caret.* 13: Boy] *interl.*

382 From Susan Pitt in [St Giles] Colchester to [William] Chisolm, overseer of St Botolph, Colchester, 6 October 1828

Colchester Octr 6th 1828

Sir/

I beg leave to acquaint you for the information of the Parishioners of the parish of Saint Botolph, that Mrs Pitt, widow now residing in the parish of St Giles is going to break up House keeping she being unable to 5 maintain the expences any longer, by which my Daughter Sarah Baxter a Girl at the Age of 15 Years will be entirely destitude of any person to look after her conduct. You are well aware that young Girls of her Age are liable to form many an illicit connextion which I am fearful she will shortly do, she being in a manner acquainted with some young seafaring 10 Boys, who I am confident that there intentions cannot be honorable. I have seen my Daughter this morning and told her my intentions of addressing you, requesting that you will be pleased to order her an asslum in the poor house of the parish of St Botolph to which parish she belongs, and being well assured that you are the Gentleman who will always be 15 ready to render assistance to the needy. I most humbly solicit that you will cause the same to be done immediately or as soon as you conveniently can. She has constant employ at the Silk factory at the Weekly Wages of 5^s/. per week which she is agreeable that you should receive, by which she will not be of any burthen to the parish, further than her lodg- 20 ings, and Sir you are confident that a young Girl like her left to herself will soon be ruined. I therefore implore your Aid and assistance for her by which you will greatly relieve the distressed mind of her mother and infinitely oblige

Your most obed^t   25
hble Servt
Susan Pitt

383   From George Little in Thundersley [Essex] to the overseer of St Botolph, Colchester, 8 October 1828

Thundersley 8 Octb^r 1828

G Little to the Genteelmen of the Parish of Saint Botolopths Colslchester
Genteelmen in consequence of the great rice upon flower I am obleidged
to make an appeal to your benevolonce for more allownce for me my
5 wife and three children or else I am afraid I shall be obleidged to come
home to the parish for I am not able to maintain them I hope Genteelme
you will consider my request from your obedient and humble servent

George Little

plese to direct for me to Mr Bishops Shopkeeper Rayleigh

TEXTUAL ALTERATIONS 2: Colslchester] first 'l' *over illeg.* 5: obleidged] first 'd' *over* 'g'.
CIRCUMTEXT Note from other hand on outside: 'Mr Little not Granted Octr 1828'.
RELATED CORRESPONDENCE Six months before this letter, Thomas Bishop in Rayleigh
(about a mile from Thundersley) had informed the overseers of St Botolph, Colchester,
that George Little had married again and that there were now three children in his family,
but that he was 'not more than ½ a man or in fact do not earn more than a Lad of Sixteen
years of age' (letter of March 1828). Four years later, Bishop reported that Little, 'being
out of Employ has applied to me for something more weekly during the time that he
should if out of Employ apply to me rather than go to you' (letter of 10 December 1832).

384   From George John Tye to Mr Bugg in St Botolph, Colchester, 3 April [1829]

to Mr Bugg

Sir - I was not aware of your being Overseer when I made application
to Mr Inman for relieff this morning - the enclosd I beg to present If you
Can Send me a triffle to Subsist with till Monday you will do me a favour
5 as I am without most of the Common neccessaries of Life and am anxious
to git my Cloaths or rather rags wash^d to depart with on monday - and
have no means only by your kind assistance the Bearer will bring what
you will be Kind Enoug<h> to bestow upon me

I am Sir

10   very respectfully
                            your poor Humble Servant
                                         George John Tye

april 3rd

TEXTUAL ALTERATIONS 4: with] *interl with caret.*

WRITING and DATE Year inferred from the close scriptual similarity to the following letter from George John Tye (385). In both letters, which are in the same hand as all other letters from him, the size of the writing as well as the space between the lines are slightly bigger than in the previous letters, and the pen is somewhat coarser.

385 From George John Tye to Mr Theobald in St Botolph, Colchester, 4 April 1829

To/ Mr Theobald

Sir - Mr Bugg - have furneshed me with a pair of Shoes that fit me well - and I am very Sorry he informe me he Cannot Do any thing about my Cloathes &c that are pledg^d what I am to do I do not know - what I have on my back are in rags - my trowsers the Seat is out and gone and my 5 Coat in pieces - I wish to God I knew ware to beg a few Shillings for the purpose of geting them - I know well my Sisters family are all smart and ambicious - and and am afraid in my present situation my Brother in Law Should say to my Sister give that brother of yours afew Shillings till the time he is only a *begar* being deacently Cloathe^d - might make him the 10 more favonrable towards me - and he might be Enduced to take me amongst his conection & friends that might be of use to me - as I to well know the man - this Curcumstance haezard me up Exceedingly this I humbley beg to Submit to your own feelings and if you Can Say any thing to m^r Bugg for me or do any thing for my behalf - you will add to 15 the very great obligation I owe you I trust for whom I shall prove myself greatfull

I am Sir with great Respect
Your unfertunate Humble Ser^t
Geo John Tye 20

april 4th *1829*

TEXTUAL ALTERATIONS 9: to] *after del* 'your'. 10: being] 'g' *over* 'd'.

386 From Francis Fowler in [Bermondsey] London, October 1829

London October 1829

Honoured Sir

I take the Earlest oppertunity of writing to you concerning my dear Children, I have got alittle worKe but at present It is quite out of my

5　power to have the children with me which Is very *[---------]* to my mind
nor do I know how to act In my trying situvation as how long my worke
may Last I know not now I have afriend here who Is willing to assist me
In the Care of one of the Children the boy, but cannot have both nor can
they send for the Child as that is out of their power as well as my own
10　now Sir I hope you will pardon the Liberty I am about to take In requesting your Kind assistance and advice how to act, would you recive my
littel girle into the house for atime and send me the boy, I will do all In
my power to reclaim the girle as soon as possabl but as I have seen nothing of my wife sence I left Colchester, so that my case Is as you mast
15　suppose very trying for Strangers will not do for me without being well
paid and my Earnings will be but small I hope I have not been thought
neglecful that I did not write before for I do assure you Sir that my mind
has been much hurt not Knowing how to act and now Sir I must beg
Leave to Say again that It is wholy out of my power to support both the
20　Children, I humbly hope you will comply with my request and take my
littel girle and If you could In any way Send the boy I should gladly as
afather recive him, and If so will be thankful If you will take the troubel
to write to me and send word by what means the Child will come So that
theire may be no msitake In meeting him, and by so doing you will much
25　oblidge and relieve the mind of your

　　　　　　　　　　　　　　　　　Humbel Servant
　　　　　　　　　　　　　　　　　Francis Fowler

　　Please to direct
　　for me at Mr Pikes
30　near the Wite Bare
　　Long walk Bermondsy Square
　　Southwark
　　London

TEXTUAL ALTERATIONS 7: I know not] *interl with stroke*. 10-11: requesting] *after del* 'request'.

RELATED CORRESPONDENCE Six years later, Francis Fowler, cooper, residing in
Bermondsey, London, bound his son, William Fowler, apprentice to Samuel Evans, shoemaker in Bermondsey, London, for seven years. It is unclear whether the parish of St
Botolph, Colchester, contributed to the premium of £10, though there seem to have been
negotiations to that effect (letter from Robert Cooke to the overseers of St Botolph, Colchester, 13 July 1835; copy of apprenticeship indenture of 17 July 1835).

387 From James Anderson in Whitechapel, London, to the over-seer of St Botolph, Colchester, 8 December 1829

London Decr 8th 1829

Gentlemen

as I have not received an answer from the letter I sent you last week concerning the young man named William Hall who still continues in the same state as I before told you I am obliged to send you a second letter as 5 it is high time something was done I have been obliged to make application to the parish of Mile end Old Town wherein I live and he now lies and is not able to be removed they have relieved him and must continue so to do till I hear from you as his affliction is so heavy that he cannott be left night nor day at present there is no hopes of his recovery I have 10 inclosed a note given to me by the Overseer of the parish of Mile End Old Town who is much surprised that you have neglected the above danger-ous case after having informed you that I was and am inable to continue bearing the expence myself having a young family of my own and very scanty wages to do withall his father I suppose is still with you if he is he 15 must have a very stony heart never to send an answer to the letter I wrote to him I hope you will not gentlemen fail to attend to the above case immidiately

I Remain Gentlemen Your

most obedient humble servant 20

James Anderson

No 6 Thomas^s Street

near the turnpike

Commercial Road

Whitechapel 25

London

TEXTUAL ALTERATIONS 12: have] *interl at beginning of line.*

FURTHER EVIDENCE James Anderson was married to Elizabeth née Hall, the daughter of John Hall of Chelmsford. William Hall was his brother-in-law (born 1801) who had moved to London in 1823. For further details, see Sharpe, 'Bowels of compation', p. 90. See also **389** and **390**.

**388   From John Harvey in [Shoreditch] London to Mr Bugg, over-
seer of St Botolph, Colchester, 18 August 1830**

London 18th August 1830

Sir

I am extremly sorry to be so Nessessiated as to make an appeal to yourself and the other Gentlemen of the Parish - I was some time in London
5 out of a Situation consequently was obliged to part with some of my
things to subsist on - I at length obtain a Situation but was obliged to
leave it on account of my not being able to appear Respectable enough -
I have got another situation but am fearfull unless I do appear more
respectable than I am at present able to do - shall Ultemately be compell^d
10 to return to Colchester - as you was good enough to hold out - to me some
hopes of Assistance previous to my coming to London - I now pray you
will now do all in Your power to assist me - in my endeavours to keep
after this time from the parish - if I had £1..10..0 I could furnish myself
with everything I want - and faithfully trust shall not have occasion to
15 give you further trouble - if you would write to me and appoint any body
in London to pay me the Money you would confer a lasting obligation on
Your very
Humble Servant
John Harvey

20 No 12 Pitfield Street
Hoxton
London
PS. If I am Sucessfull I will endeavour to remit you the Money again

**389   From James Anderson in Whitechapel, London, to the over-
seer of St Botolph, Colchester, 1 December 1830**

London December 1st 1830

Gentleman

I am under the painfull necessity of writing to you conserning a young
man named William Hall son of John Hall whom I wrote a letter to last
5 week but have received no answer the above named William Hall is son
of the above John Hall and now lies in a very dangerous state <of> illness
which is inflamation on the chest & Rheumatic Gout the case is so far
dangerous that no hopes are entertained of his recovery I have the best of

advise for him he has been lying at my house 9 days in this condition I
have a wife and 3 Children to support out of 15^S per week so that I am 10
incapable of bearing so heavy a burden as the above I am very much
surprised that his Father who knows his complaint so well should neglect
coming or sending to me as it is almost a week since I wrote to him about
him as his father is known to you Gentlemen he being under your care as
an inmate or pensioner I fully expected that he would either have come or 15
sent to me but something must be done immediately as the young man is
as bad as he can well be and all expences are developed one me at present
so Gentlemen I hope you will take this case into your immediate consideration and inform his father of what I have here stated and please to
return me some satisfactory answer by return of post otherwise I must 20
throw the above case on the parish where he now lies

> I am Gentlemen your most obed^t
> humble servant James Anderson
> brother in law to the above W Hall
> No. 6. Thomas Street near Gloucester St 25
> Commercial Road Whitechapel

NB he cannot claim any parish but yours as he has not been an apprentice
nor a yearly servant in London

TEXTUAL ALTERATIONS 25: near Gloucester] *interl.*

**390 From Elizabeth Anderson in [Whitechapel] London to John
Hall in the poorhouse of St Botolph, Colchester, 15 December
1830**

> N° 6 Thomas Str^t Commercial Road
> Decr 15th *1830*

Dear Father/

Being doubtfull of your recieveing the letter that we sent to you about a
fortnight ago; we have sent you another, & we hope it will find you in 5
good health, but we are sorry to inform you that it leaves us in this greatest of trouble, as W^m has been lying at our house these three weeks as bad
as he can be to be alive, & not able to be removed since the hour he was
taken & we have wrote two letters to the Parish overseers & they have
sent us one letter in answer to say that they do not know any thing of him 10
but we shall make them know something of him for we have applyd to

this parish & they will make them know something of him, for it is impossible for us to bear the trouble & expence out of my husbands wages only
15/- Per week, & my being so ill, I am not able to do for him, therefore we
15 are obligated to have People to be with him night & day, As this is the
worst Illness he ever had, & as it is not my husbands brother, it is so much
the worst for me, & I must say that both W^m & me take it very hard that
you nor mary have not wrote, if you have recieved our first letter; But I
hope you will not fail in answering this by return of post, provideing you
20 can not come to see him, but I hope you will come if you possibly can if
you wish to see him alive for he so bad that his speech & his sencess have
left at times & when he has come to himself all his talk has been about
you, He has lately enterd into a benefit club Clubb & had he have been
free of it we should not have troubled the Parish, & it is of no use there
25 saying to put him in the hospital, for the Doctor of this Parish says he will
not be able to be removed for a long time if he ever gets over it, Dear
father, I hope you will come if you possibly can, if not I shall expect an
answer from you on Friday next that is by return of post, so no more at
present from your loveing Son & Daughter Wm Hall & Elizabeth Anderson
30 Please to direct to Mr Anderso<n>
No 6 Thomas Str Commercial <Road>
London

TEXTUAL ALTERATIONS 1: Road] *interl below with bow.* 4: your] *interl with caret.* 5: sent]
's' *over illeg.* 8: be] *interl with caret in left-hand margin.* 10: in answer] *interl with caret
above del* 'back'. 12: them] 'th' *over illeg.* 18: nor mary] *interl with caret.* 29: & Elizabeth Anderson] *interl at end of line;* 'Elizabeth' *above del* 'Sarah'.

FURTHER EVIDENCE Elizabeth Anderson (née Hall) was John Hall's daughter (see also
387). William and Mary were her brother and sister, born in 1801 and 1803. It is somewhat unclear why the writer first put down 'Sarah Anderson' as the last name. John Hall
did have a daughter Sarah, but her surname was Hall, as was that of his daughter-in-law
Sarah (née Gowlett) who was married to his son Thomas Hall who also lived in London.
See Sharpe, 'Bowels of compation'.

391   From Mary Balls in [St Mary] Maldon [Essex] to Mr Bugg in St Botolph, Colchester, 16 April [1833]

Sir/

I am sorry to Inform you that I stand in great need of what I wrote for
befor which is thirty shillings - as I ow 2^s8^d for rent and 6^s rates and I
expect to be summoned next week - but I have begg^d so hard untill I had

wrote to you to know wether you would be so kind to send It me as I have 5
not been troublesome to you before for ten years only for one pound
untill I come over this time twelve month - I should have come now but I
am so very poorly and could not borrow the money as I am so much in
debt now and my Husband earnes so very little now these 3 weeks he
earned one week 4^{s}9^d next 7^s next 6^{s}7^d I write this myself therefore would 10
be glad of an answer by the return of wain but my Husband wish^d me to
apply to the Overseer of maldon for reliefe that wee may be brought
home but as wee had been brought home once befor the gentlemen then
blamed us for not letting them know -

Sir I hope you do not think we wish to Impose - for as soone as found 15
before that I could do without It I come over on purpose to give It up - but
I hope and trust If you will be so kind a to Sport me now we shall be able
to do this summer - but after having my things sold off and the money
you where so kind to let me have was not sufficient to get what I wanted
I had a friend to let me have a few trifle so that I have been oblige to work 20
the money out which keep us so behind -

and now If I must have them sold off againe I must come home and
then what would be consequence - and I have a Daughter at home which
I am oblige to maintaine she has been in service but nobody wont keep
her as she has a complaint on her the St antonies fire she is 16 years of 25
age -

Mr Bugg - Sir I have taking the liberty of writing to you as I hope you
will be my friend as I have write to you before - and sinc that to M^r
Chisolm and we have recv^d no answer -

your Humble Servent 30
Mary Balls -

Maldon April 16

TEXTUAL ALTERATIONS 3: 2^{s}8^d] '8' *after del illeg.* 6: you] *interl with caret.*

DATE Year inferred from related correspondence.

RELATED CORRESPONDENCE On 2 September 1833, D. Pitcairn in Maldon wrote to the overseers of St Botolph, Colchester, that John Balls 'is now lying I doubt not on his Death Bed [...] He has reduced himself to entire poverty by his reluctance to make an application to you and 'has worked frequently when he ought to have been in bed'. Benjamin White in St Mary, Maldon, informed them on 9 September 1833 that Balls received 3s per week under a suspended removal order. On 25 September 1833, White wrote: 'John Balls has departed this world, he was buried last week, his Widow thinks she can do better staying with her friends here, if your parish will allow her something weekly, if 'tis agreeable to your Gent^n if not she must come home, the Relief for Family & the Funeral exp^s amount to 3.8.9 which will thank you for a remittance of, if you consent to her staying at Maldon.'

392   From Marian Nevill in Mersea [Essex] to Mr Pretty in St Botolph, Colchester, 15 November 1834

Mersea November 15th 1834

Sir according to your request I have taking the liberty of writing to you to let you know how I am and am happy to say i am better than i was wen i see you i see the doctor on tuesday and and he told me he thought he
5   should soon gain my speech so i should like to stay a little longer if you please as i am very comfortabl sir i should be very much obliged to you if you could send me a gown and a shawl for mine are so old and thin that they will not keep me warm c i remain
      your humble servant
10   Maryan Nevill

TEXTUAL ALTERATIONS 2: according] first 'c' *over illeg.* 3: am] *interl with stroke.*
WRITING Written on ruled lines in pencil.

393   From James Bottom in [St Saviour] London to Mr Pretty, overseer of St Botolph, Colchester, 5 August 1835

London Augst 5 1835

Mr Pritty I wish to Inform you I have made triall to work and was not able and the Docter ses I must not for I am not fit for he ses one weak wit make me so bad as not be Ever to work and it is not to be wondered at for my
5   suport is not Suffiont for me to gain Sthernk I Can have a house at 18 Pounds <a> year so I Could open some way of Buisness if you will be so Kind as to Adwance me a boute five Pounds to begin with and Pay the Rent I will Never trouble you for any thing a gain Neither for Death nor Docters
10   Mr Pritty Sir Plese to Comunicate as you Purposed to the Gentelman of the Parish or ho it may Concern
      Sir I Remain yours Dutifulle
      Ja^s Bottom

Since I saw you I have Removed to N° 4 Litell Gilford St Union Street
15 Borough my Land Lord at the other House said I could Never be able to work and I was forst to Leve it

SPELLING 5: Sthernk] *read* 'strength'.
RELATED CORRESPONDENCE Three months later, Nathan Smith, assistant overseer of the London parish of St Saviour's (Southwalk) wrote to Mr Pretty in St Botolph, Colchester,

that James Bottom 'still Continues Ill and I think cannot do without Your assistance at present I have given you Credit for £5 for whic[h] the Overseers are much obliged' (letter of 2 November 1835).

394   From Sarah Finch in Chatham [Kent], 1 January [1836]

Chatham Jany 1, 3/6

Mr Sworied

Haveing met with a friend liveeng at listed I Could not let the oppertunity pass without Notice and feel a pleasure in so doing I hope That this lines will meet you and all your family In good health but as it regard myself I 5
am But very poorly and have been much tried in Circumstances /during/ the p/as/t year - I hope my little henry is Quite well I am quite anxcous to hear of his Welfare and hope he is a good boy I should esteem A favour if you would oblige my with a few lines and be so kind as to enquire of m^r truns How W is getting on and inclose it in your letter As soon as 10
Convienant you will Please likewise to let the young female who will deleiver this see henry if In the way I rest feale sattisfid as it regard him if Place and your Care send me all particklars my daughter Is married since i saw you to A worthy Butcher A native of Essex you will Please presnt our Joint respects at all your family and self I have sent henry two neekchf 15
and 6^d for a new years Gift Wich is all i can spare this time as i am much tried to live this winter the times and work Being so bad

I remain Sir in Best
Bonds of freindship
Sarah Finch   20

Please to direct for
Sarah Finch at Georg Tylers
Butcher High Street Chatham

TEXTUAL ALTERATIONS 6: Circumstances] 'stances' *interl at end of line.* 7: anxcous] 'x' *over illeg.* 10: in] *interl.* 11: Please] *interl.* 14: you] *over del illeg.* 15: Joint] *over del illeg.* 16: Gift]'G' *over illeg.* 23: High] 'H' *over illeg.*

WRITING Probably the same hand as the letters from Sarah Finch from St George, London to St James, Colchester, of 13 and 24 January 1814 (**402, 403**). It is not clear on what grounds she was able to apply to both parishes.

395   From Isaac Bugg to the overseer of St Botolph, Colchester

Sir

I feel confident that the views taken of my disposition & Character have been mistaken by many Gentlemen who are concern'd in the management of the affairs of the Parish & I am ready to admit that I may have
5 strengthen'd those views in the moments of irratation when my afflictions & disappointments have press'd heavy upon my mind if that is the case I am sorry for it & beg most fully to be understood that whilst my affliction prevents my following my business as it at present does yet I am anxious to turn my mind to any thing that I am capable of under my
10 present state of debility whether it were any appointment within your reach or any thing I might be able to do by your assistance so as gradually to cease being burdensome to the parish which is very far from my wishes - I have thought I might succeed in travelling the country with a Pony & Cart having tried it for a short time some few years since in a line of
15 business that I well enough understand to give me great reason to believe I might do something considerable if not a sufficiency for the maintenance of my Familly thereby - I beg to leave it for the consideration of this meeting

& remain yours
20   most respectfully
Isaac Bugg

TEXTUAL ALTERATIONS 3: Gentlemen] 'le' *over* 'el'. 5: irratation] *first* 'a' *over* 'i'. 9: to turn] 'to' *over illeg.* 10: appointment] 'ment' *interl at end of line.* 16: sufficiency] 'ency' *interl at end of line.* 17: Familly] *second* 'l' *over* 'y'. 17: consideration] 'tion' *interl at end of line.*

RELATED CORRESPONDENCE Isaac Bugg was admitted as an out-patient to the Essex and Colchester Hospital, on the recommendation of the overseers of St Botolph, Colchester, on 4 December 1828 (letter from Essex and Colchester Hospital).

FURTHER EVIDENCE Isaac Bugg received £4 18s 6d for illness from 5 January till 23 March 1827. From October 1827 till April 1828, he received a regular weekly allowance of 9s and from January till June 1829 a weekly allowance of 8s on average. Early in 1828, he was reported as being 28 years old, his wife 27, and their four children between 1 and 7 (one child died in the summer of 1828) (ERO, D/P 203/12/45, St Botolph, Colchester, overseers' accounts).

396   From Mary Taylor in Hadleigh [Suffolk] to [William] Chisolm, overseer of St Botolph, Colchester, 17 August

hadleigh august 17

M^r chislem sir i hope you will not take it amiss with my trubleing you a boute my pay sir i am in great destress for it sir i owe 16 shilings for rent last quarter and the baker 1 - 15 and sir please to have the goodness to send my pay and i have one very ill and i canot get him aney thing to take   5
sir i am half staved if i dont pay every mounth thay dont like to let me have aney thing more and sir it is six Weaks since you payed me up to jluy the 7 this day sir i think i have a riath to my pay i can stop no longer without it

Mary taylor   10

TEXTUAL ALTERATIONS 2: sir] *interl.* 3: i am] 'i' *after del illeg.* 6: i am] 'i' *after del* 'a'. 7: Weaks] 'a' *over illeg.* 7: you] *after del illeg.* 8: jluy] 'u' *over* 'y'. 8: this] *after del illeg.* 8: have] *after del illeg.*

WRITING Clumsy hand, different from that of Mary Taylor's letter of 9 May 1821.

FURTHER EVIDENCE On 27 June 1826, the select vestry of St Botolph, Colchester, dealt with an application by Widow Taylor of Hadleigh 'for the arrear of allowance due to her from May 26th - upon investigating the case it appeared that Mr Heath had made the allowance up to Midsummer last - and Mr Shepherd was requested to call on the Family, & make his Report on the case - as the Son attended the meeting, it was determined that one week's allowance should be sent by him amounting to 6s' (ERO, D/P 203/8/2, St Botolph, Colchester, select vestry minutes). Heath and Shepherd were members of the select vestry, but the report commisioned from the latter has not been found.

St James, Colchester, pauper letters

397 From Rachel Shoreg in [Bethnal Green] London, 15 October 1810

London oct^r 15th 1810

Sir

I am very sorry to be under the nessesety of trobleing you at this time
but I have been a long time in a very weak state of health and still Con-
5 tinue so that I am not able to support myself my Children are all married
and got familys which thease dear times thay have as much as thay can
do to support and tharefore are not able to assist me I should be very
much oblidged to you if you will have the goodness to solicit at the gentleman of the Parish to grant me some weekly allowance or I must be under
10 the nessesety of comeing down in to the Country to be supported there I
beg your Pardon for trobleing you but I have no other Friend that I could
write to and if you will have the goodness it will be a Peace of true Charity
from your much oblidged

very Humble serv^t

15 N° 1 George gardens
Bethnel Green Road

Rachel Shoreg

398 From Mary Mayden [in St Leonard, Colchester], 30 September 1811

Gentlemen

I humbly beg leave to call your attention to my Case, of great affliction,
in consequence of which I am put to such Expense that I can barely provide the common necessaries of life, & when the cold weather sets in it
5 will not be in my power to purchase a sufficient quantity of Firing, I
therefore sincerely hope you will have the goodness to give me afew
Bushels of Coals to supply my want of that necessary article. I remain,
Gentlemen

your most humble Servant

10 Hythe Sept 30.1811.

Mary Mayden

WRITING Letter from skilled hand, signature from other, less-educated hand.
PLACE The Hythe was in St Leonard, Colchester.

399 From J. and C. Wire in Stratford, Essex, to Mr Brett, over-seer [of St James] Colchester, 9 December 1811

Honourd Parents

I feel myself under a Great Constricture to write as it Occasions Some very important questions first concerning Myself and your dear daughter which I will Mention briefly and I hope before I relate the Circumstance You as an Affectionate Parent will Consider it nothing more than an 5 absolute Nessity of My troubling you with a Letter in so Short time Your dear daughter has been Long Afflicted in fact ever Since we have Been in London and as Such I Consider Myself in duty Bound to Apply to those which I Consider of More Superior Judgement than Myself, which Occasions me so quickly to Apply to You, Since I wrote to You Last My dear 10 wife has Layd Confind to her Bed which as a Husband I had Medical Advice but to No purpose I Applyd to the Second which Information was Given Me that Her health Could Not Be restord Untill a Living Child Could Be producd which nothing Else would produce it but her Own Country air and as discharging the duties of a Husband I Consider it and 15 Important Subject therefore I Could Wish for Her to reside in Colchester as I informd you that Nothing Else would procure her Health but Change of Air Be Assurd Honourd Parent that It has been a very heavey Expence to <me> for Medical Advice and Refreshing articles to su<pport> her weakely Constitution and as such My Bussiness Been very dull for Some 20 time past has Not Inabld Me to let Myself have Sufficient Nesseseries, I hope You will Consider of My Circumstance for I have gone far as My Comming In would admit and In fact further therefore I am Under The Nessity Looking for Something for My dear wifes Benefit for I find Unless her health is restord it is imposible for Me to Support Such an Afflic- 25 tion, that I have been Attended with ever since we have been Married and as I have had every advice that Is proper I hope you will Consider if the Country will produce her health it would Be an Enastable pleasure to Me and Heavy expence Savd I hope as a parent you will Consider how I am Situated and that My dea<r> Wife Comes near to you as an Affectionate 30 parent But More Closer to Me as a Husband and partner And as My intention is not for My wife to Lay Upon you at Colchester I could wish as I See No Remedy any Other way for to Settle Myself with Her in the Country you will Consider it as brief as possible and Let Me know the Result of Your Mind as My wife is a Little Better and <----> She 35 Remains So I Could wish her to take <t>he Journey I Should have Sent

her Before But My Circumstance would Not admit as My Expences have
been very heavy I hope You will Not Consider that any thing has Occurd
through My Neglect for I Can Certify that I have Workd Night and day to
40 Support things So Long and as I Informd You before it is Absolute Nessity
requires Me to write to you at this present time I Shall expect a Letter
from you very quickly as what I write tis important

We Remain your Affectionate
Children J & C Wire

45 Decr 9th 1811

Direct at Mrs Lewis Stationer
Opposite Blue Boar
Stratford Essex

400   From J. and C. Wire in Stratford, Essex, 17 December [1811]

Honord Parents

My dear Wife with Myself feels Ourselves very much Uneasd On
account of not receiving any answer to the Letter which I sent you on
Monday Last which gives me great Suspicion that Something has Occurd
5 as I Must Own that We never found any disrespect from you yet as a
parent Nor We hope that No Offence is been given as Children I Related
in the Letter the particulars of My dear Wifes Health which I Should have
thought as a parent that it would have touchd the feelings to the *[--]<-->*
quick I Can Only repeat what I Mentioned in the Last letter that had I Not
10 been Wound Up with Affliction I Certainly would have Sent her down
before but It was not in My power as buisness is Very dull I hope dear
parent You are Not Unaquanted with the distest I have in been Intruding
to One which I hope to bear on My Memory who has display So kind
Attention to My dear Wife I hope to Say If this Letter Meets with Your
15 approbation you will Not delay in sending by return of post as My Wife
Could wish to come down on Saturday and as My Brother Chignell had
the Goodness to Say He would Bare her Expence down I Shall fully
expect him to Stand to promise as it really is not on my power to furnesh
My dear wife with Money to pay the Expence I hope dear farther you will
20 not delay in sending by return of post I have took the trouble to Go to
London and pay the post of this Letter because I was feerful My troubling
you so frequent with Letter would Be Offencive when you write you will
inform Me wither any of Her Brothers and Sisters will think it worth Loosing

a Little time to Meet her at the Coach as I am sure there as been no atten-
tion payd as respect to So near relations   25
J & C Wire 17 Dec^r
[*Postscript across left-hand margin of first page:*] Being fearful you did
not receive the Letter wh<ich> I sent on Monday Last that No Mistake
May be Made I Repeat the direction at Mrs Lewis Stationer Opposite
Blue boar Stratford Essex   30

TEXTUAL ALTERATIONS 16: Saturday] *interl above del* 'Friday'.
DATE Year inferred from reference to presumed senders' previous letter (**399**).

**401   From J. Harden in St Marylebone, London, to Mr Wetherley
        in St James, Colchester, 2 July 1813**

                                                               July 2 1813
Sir
   According to your wish I have been to the Church Warden and overseer
of the Parrish <an>d they told me they nevr do no such thing or they
would have to keep Clarks on purpose if they did the <------------> you   5
will send me sume Relevef for I have nevr made my settlement on this
parish If not I must fling smyslef upon this Parish and they must bring me
home
                                                       from your humble
                                                       servant J harden 10
please to Drict
No 32 Brown Street
Brinstow Square Marylebone

TEXTUAL ALTERATIONS 3: wish] *interl.* 5: would] 'o' *over illeg.* 6: sume] 'm' *over illeg.* 12:
32] *after del* '2'.
DESTRUCTION OF TEXT Three big mouse-eaten holes on left and right-hand edge.

402   From Sarah Finch in [St George] London, 13 January 1814

Sir
   I am under great Distress or I would not troubled <y>ou my Poor Husband Lies ill most of his time <he ca>nnot follow his employment and if
you will be so <kind> as to help us to atrifell to pay our rent I dont <wish>
makeing a practice of asking you But haveing m<y man> most all his   5

time ill and 3 children and the have been <all> ill on a fevour whitch as
distress us to a great agree and I cannot pay my rent without your kind
help I had 3 or 4 places <of wor>k but oblidg now to lose on account of
stoping <---------> to atend on my Poor sicke famley and our <--->
10 <lan>dlord means to put a broker in if I dont pay it and I am not able to
without your help if you will have the goodness to help us to one pound
I.ll thank <y>ou
                    from your most distress hum^l
                    Ser^t
15   Sarah Finch
        no 6 Princes St London road Surry
        London   Jen^y 13 1814

TEXTUAL ALTERATIONS 7: distress] 'd' *over* 'g'. 7: without] 'out' *interl with stroke.* 8: oblidg]
'd' *over* 'g'.
    WRITING This and the following letter (**403**) are from the same hand which in turn is
probably the same as that of the letter from Sarah Finch from Chatham, Kent, to St Botolph,
Colchester, of 1 January 1836 (**394**).
    DESTRUCTION OF TEXT Four big mouse-eaten holes on both edges.

**403   From Sarah Finch in [St George, London] to Mr Beat in St
James, Colchester [24 January 1814]**

Sir
    I am sorry to truble you But I am in great distress by my Husband being
under the Docters hands and all my Children have had the favour my poor
Husband is never well and I have had a few good Houses to work at and
5 now <a>m obliged to stay at home to attend on my <po>or Distressing
famely and we are so distressed <w>e Cannot pay the rent without a little
of your <ki>nd help as Coals and every thing is so dear <it> is imposable to
live as we are I have strove as long as I am able to maintain them But my
Landlord says he must have his rent and I Cannot pay it without selling my
10 goods and I am sory to do thoug theare But little the serve me If you will
send me what you think proper and if you send non I must bring them to
you But I am sorry to do it if you will be so kind on think on my distress
famley and send me a little now from your Distress^d hum^l Ser^t
    if you send nothing pleas to   Sarah Finch N° 6
15 send as soon as posable to tell   Princes St London
    me what is best to do   road near the Elphant
                                              & Castle Surry

DATE Date of postmark.

404   From William and Mary Mann in [Bethnal Green] London to Mr Wetherley in St James, Colchester, 21 March [1814]

March 21

Sir I hope that you will Excues my taking the Libity of wirting to you But My Being in So Much Distress ocaisions me to Doe it the Money that you was So kind to Relive me with I Layd outt to the Best Advantage But Every thing in London is So very Dear that theire is no Such a thing as   5
Living at all the Couls are 3 Shillings a Bushell And very thing is Dear in perpeotin and I have Gott so Litel work to Doe that wee Are almost Lost out stand at 3 Shillings a week therefore Dear Gentlemen I Hope that You will be So Good as to take it into Considreation to Be So kind as to Send ues Some thing to help use in our Disteres and wee Shall Be for 10 Ever Bound to pray for your Goodness William and Mary Mann

pleas to Dyrect to me William Mann No 51 Mrs Salmons Rents Coopers Gardens

Hackney Road near Shoreditch Church London

TEXTUAL ALTERATIONS 7: Lost] 'st' *over* 'ts'. 8: out] *interl below with stroke.*
SPELLING 7: perpeotin] *read* 'proportion'.
DATE Year from postmark.

405   From John Enos in Sheerness, Kent, to William Harden in Colchester, 17 January 1817

Sheerness Jainary. 17. 1817

Dear wife I take the opportuny of writing the few Line to you Hopping to find you well as Leve Me at preasint But veary unhappy in my mind to think we parted So uncarton But if you had been Hear you mit have gone with me and I ham with my master again and ham going out with him and   5 we march on Surtedy the 18 of Jumary and my Dear wife I have Left you my prise M tickket and I Exspect to git It to Day to Send to you and I wish you to goe to my friends if it is your pleashure and if you Goe you must inquire for parson Drove Near wisbridge the Iland of Ely the the County of Combridge Shire for my mother wood wish to See you Sarah marshall 10 and i hope we Saent be Long out not a Bove 4 or 5 years and I ham veary

Sorrow to Leave you That we have Been Such a Short time to geather and I ham veary Sorrow that you Did not Come Back and I hope as you have the morrage Lines you will take great Care of them and I Desired to
15 Be Remember to your forther and mother and Sisters and all Requirin frinds So no more at preasent from you affectionate Husbond
    answer this by Return of post
Dirict to John Enos privet 2 Division
68 Depot Sheerness Kent Elseware

TEXTUAL ALTERATIONS 3: unhappy] 'y' *interl at end of line.* 7: Exspect] 'ec' *interl above at end of line,* 't' *interl above* 'ce'. 7: I wish] 'I' *over* 'to'. 8: my] 'm' *over* 'y'. 8: friends] 'ds' *interl at end of line, in reversed order* 'sd' *interl left-handed of* 'd'. 11: or] 'r' *over* 'u'.

406 From James Russell in [Newington] London to the parochial authorities of St James, Colchester, 6 April 1833

London 6th April 1833
To the Parochial Authorities of the Parish of saint James in the town of Colcester In the County of Essex -
    Gentlemen/
    The Humble Applicant in case Is James Russel formerly a resident &c
5 in the Parish of St James and in the Same gained a Settlement by renting the Canteen in 1809 and conforming to the rules so laid down,
    I therefore do most Humbly beg leave to call your attention to my present situation who is after long affliction both me and my wife with many other Adverse Circumstances am under painful necessity of Calling on
10 you for some little support In the time of need haveing been out of Imploy for this last six months, am thereby deprived of every Comfort that is necessary for the support of Human nature and suffering every privation; I do therefore most Humbly beg your Immediate attention to an Individual so suffering
15   Gentlmen it is with the most Hertfelt pain that I thus address you, but being Compeld to do so I hope will plead my excuse and shield me from Your anger and so sincerely hope I shall be favoured with a speedy answer in hope of your kind Assistance -
            Am Gent Your Most Obd Servt
20   James Rusell
                    No 7 Trinity St Boro Southwork

WRITING Professional hand.

407 From Charlotte Game in Mendlesham, Suffolk, to Mr Jackson, overseer of St James, Colchester, 8 April 1833

Mr Jackson
  Sir/
As you Gentlemen did not Answer my last letter I thought you could not have received, it but I hope by return of Post that you will Answer this and send me Widwow Game my Girls pay as the Quarter day is past and 5 I am very poorly and in great need of it and by so doing you will much oblige Your
Humble Servt

Mendlesham   Charlotte Game Widow
Near Thwaite   10
Suffolk
April 8th 1833

408 From James Russell in [Newington] London to the parochial authorities of St James, Colchester, 13 May 1833

London 13 May 1833

To the Parochial Authorities &c of the Parish of Saint James
Colchester Essex

  Gentlemen/
I having having Applied to the Parish in which I now reside which 5 Parish have Afforded me all the relief thay are in duty bound to do thay also have Informed you the same in writing, You Genⁿ have not Attended to thire Application in My Behalf thearefore I am under the painful necessity of Begging most Humbly Your Attention to my situation who are suffering every privation for which nature Calls aloud for some relief 10 from You Gen^{tn} on whom I have the Right of calling in to my assistance I shall Gen^{tm} be under the Painfull Necessity of writing to You till I receve some reply which I hope will be speadely Done
Am Gen^{tn} Your Most Obe^d Humbl
Servent James Russell   15
N° 7 Trinity St Boro

WRITING Professional hand, same as that of previous letter from James Russell (**406**).

RELATED CORRESPONDENCE On 30 April 1833, J. & S. Invelle of Walworth (in Newington) had written to the overseer of St James, Colchester, on behalf of James Russell, saying that he was 61 years old and belonged 'to yr Parish by renting the Canteen in 1809 - after which he went to India'. They had further said that 'he wishes you to allow him weekly relief for a short time until he can obtain employ', and that 'he wrote to you some time since but has not rec^d an answer as it is not his wish to be permanently burthensome on his Parish he has requested us to write to you before his removal'.

409   From Mary Cooper in Chelmsford, 16 June 1833

Chelmsford June 16 1833

Sir

   I Write a few Lines to Say that I have got a dockter to atand apon my Sisster and if the gentelman will alow me 2.6 p^r week I will keep her here
5 at Presant if not I Must Sand her home dyrect Pleas to Answer this as Soon as it Sute you by So dooind you
        will must ablige your humble
            Survent
                 Mary Cooper
10 Opesite the alms
house Moulsham

TEXTUAL ALTERATIONS 1: 1833] *interl at end of line*. 3: got] *after del* 'to'. 3: atand] 'd' *over* 'g'. 6: it] *after del* 'Opertew'.

410*   From Lucy Baley [in St James, Colchester]

Sir

   pleas to take it into Consideration as I never will live with him any more and pray keep him from me if there is a possibility or I must go into the House
5   Your Humble Servant
             Lucy Baley

PLACE This obscure note, written on a small piece of paper (size 92 x 181 mm), bears no further information. The back is blank. It might therefore be assumed that Lucy Baley lived in St James, Colchester, and delivered it in person.

411 From Mary Sumner to Mr Breets

Sir

I hope you will not be offended at my asking a Small Favour from you
as I am in greate Distress at this time as I am Confined and my Poor Child
wants more till I am able at this Preasant time to get and I do not wish to
give you any Troble if I can get a Few days over therefore if you would   5
have the goodness to let me have two weekes Pay this day I will take it as
a Perticular Favour and you will greatly Ablige
your Humble Sarvant
Mary Sumner

Sir please to excuse   10
my writing as I have got
another one a Family

TEXTUAL ALTERATIONS 6: two] *over* 'one'. 11: as] *interl.*

St Peter, Colchester, pauper letters

412 From George Rowe in Bocking [Essex] to Mr Cod, over-seer of St Peter, Colchester, 21 November 181[7]

Bocking   Nov^b 21:181

Sir

I have Sent you a fue Lines wich I hope you will Not take it a miss about My Son as you Said that your it wold be in about 3 Weeks and that
5 you wold Let me know what the Gentleman agreed to do about it and as that is about 9 Weeks a goe and as I heard not fron you I Con Clued that you wold assist me Mr Frost agreed to take the Lad upon triall and he have been thear better then 5 Weeks and he Likes the Lad Quite woll and If you will Come forward to put the Lad to him he will take him for the
10 Money that I told you when I was over as he will take him till he is 21 years Old as he was 16 Last August wich I hope the Gentleman will Do what they Can for me as it will Corst me a Grat Deel to find him of things the time that he is thare and if I Gett him not thear I Cant Get aney thing for him to Do but to walk a bout the Streets and I Cant keep him So and If
15 you wold wish to Speake to Mr Frost I will ask him to Call upon you when he Come over as hee often Come over but to he Coming to Live thear he Say that he never had the thought of Coming Nor Nither Shall he Come I hope that you Send me an Ansner as Soon as you Can for I must Conclude one way or the other you way Send to me by John Redgreft the
20 Carrer wich Comes every Mondey Wedensday and Saterday he Sit up at the Bull Mary Parrish pleas to Derict for Me at Mr Durrants Saddler and Coller Maker Coggeshall

                                George Rowe

TEXTUAL ALTERATIONS 1: Nov^b] *over del* 'Dec^b'. 3: take] 'a' *over* 'h'. 4: it] *interl.* 7: wold] *interl.* 7: M^r] *after del* 'that'. 8: Lad] *inserted in left-hand margin.* 13: not] *interl.* 15: to Speake] 'to' *inserted in left-hand margin.* 17: thought of] *interl above del* 'of'.

    DATE Year from filing note on back.

413 From James Blatch to Mr Banister [1817]

Sir I hope you will not be angry in my Sending you this note as I am only home on the sunday So that I Cannot Come myself to you to State my

Case to you my self but my wife is very ill and Cannot Come up herself
and is in grate disstress and shall feel myself much Oblidge to you to send
me a Littel Money   5
I am in the Country at work for 13 shillings a week an have to maintain
myself

TEXTUAL ALTERATIONS 2: my] 'm' *over* 'y'. 6: week] 'k' *interl at end of line.*
DATE From filing note on back.

414   From George Rowe in [Great] Coggeshall [Essex] to Mr Banister, overseer of St Peter, Colchester, 15 February 1818

Coggeshall   Feby 15 1818
     Sir
I hope you will not take it a mist of Sending to you Conserning My Son
but Mr Frost wich me to Wright to you as he have Not heard from you as
you was Saying that you thorgh that thear wold be a Parrish Meeting the   5
Next Week wich is a fortnight a go as Mr Frost wold wich to know your
mind upon it as he have been So Long with him th<a>t it a hindrance to
him and the Lad for if he to be bound to him it is time that he Should be
Geting forward in the Beseness as he wold wich to have an Answer from
you as Soon as you Can   10
     from Me George Rowe

TEXTUAL ALTERATIONS 3: mist] *after del illeg.* 6: Next] *interl.* 8: time] *after del* 'that'.

415   From James Howell in Ely to the churchwardens and overseers of St Peter, Colchester, 16 February 1818

Sirs or Gentlemen
     I am sorry to inform You that my family is grievously afflicted with the
small pox which is prevalent all over Ely many of whom die in a Day *the*
Vaccination not preventing the same in many cases two of mine fell first
of which we have had occasion to sit up night and Day the others are   5
sickening and a dreadful time it is I therefore humbly hope You will have
the goodness to remit me some Money or give an Order to Mr Garratt for
the same otherwise I must get an Order of Removal and have the same
suspended while the family is removable which I am unwiling to do as it

10 will run You to heavy expences - relying on Your Goodness I will wait
Your answer as You have behaved genteel towards me I know the burthen
of Parishes I would not willingly extort from You 1 s/ but at present
Gentlemen mine is a case of the most extreme difficulty which I hope
and trust You will answer on sight herey otherwise I must action very
15 different circumstances which I apprehend from Your candour and generosity -

I am Y^r Ob^t Humble
Servt

Ja^s Howell

20 Ely the Isle
Cambrid^{re}
Feby 16th 1818
NB Pray dear Gentlemen answer me immediately -

TEXTUAL ALTERATIONS 7: give] *after del* 'give'.

RELATED CORRESPONDENCE On 28 January 1817, Mr Garratt in Ely had written to the overseer of St Peter, Colchester, that Mrs Howell had 'beged of me to write to you - beging that you will send her some releif - I can certify that the Family is at this time very much distress^d as three of their Children are very bad with the small Pox' (with note of answer at bottom that Mr Garratt was ordered to pay £2).

416 From Widow Shepperd in Romford, Essex, to the overseer of St Peter, Colchester, 8 May 1818

Romford May 8 1818

Honerd Sir

It is with great regrett that I am Obdleged to Petition to you again fer
Some Little relife from you as I am in Very great destress at this time for
5 I have been Confined to my Bed fer this Last three weeks with a Bad
fever wich hast reduced me to the Brink of the grave that I am so Very
weak and low that I am not able to due any thing to help my Self and I am
not in way off getting my Strengh up again as I have not a Penney to get
any thing to help me out off the trouble that I am in I thearfore though it
10 better to lett you now the destress that I am in then to trouble the Parish
that I am in hear thear fore Sir I hope you will take my requst into Consideration Your most

humble Servent
widow Shepperd near the
15   Lome Pond Romford essex

TEXTUAL ALTERATIONS 9: thearfore] *first* 'e' *over* 'a'. 10: that] *first* 't' *over illeg.* 13: humble] 'hu' *over illeg.*

417 From J. Berry in London to Elizabeth Berry in Colchester, 19 July 1818

London July 19th 1818

Dear Wife

This comes with my Love to you, and the Children I Rec^d your Letter on Saturday too Late to send you a answer by return of Post. as I was not where it was Directed. I am Very much Surprized at the Contents of your   5
Letter. Likewise at the usage you have receiv'd. you must go to the Overseers and acquaint them that I was not employ'd by Mr Woodcock but a very few Days. for Mr Woockcock told me himself. I had Been in the trade too Long. meaning that I was not young enough to satisfy him with Respect to work which is the case with every Master where I apply. for   10
work. as they will not Employ a Old Hand. while they can get Plenty of young ones. the fact is I find such Difficulty in getting Employment that I am greatly affraid I shall be under the nesessity of returning to Colchester myself shortly. I hope the Gentlemen will take it into Consideration and Reinstate you in your former situation but if not. if they will advance you a   15
few Pounds to buy a few Nesesarys with you must come to me and we must do the best we can as Long as we can Direct for me at the Raven & sun

     Your

         Affectionate Husband   20

           J.. Berry

TEXTUAL ALTERATIONS 5: Surprized] 'z' *over illeg.* 7: acquaint] 't' *interl at end of line.* 13: greatly] 'ly' *interl at end of line.*

418 From William James in Chelmsford to S. P. Carr in St Peter, Colchester, 20 July 1818

Chelmsford July 20 - 1818

Sir;

   You will I trust pardon my writeing to you, it is with great reluctance, but I know not to whom more properly to address myself, through necessity, I

5 am compeled, to make application to you, & the Gentlemen of the Parish,
humbly trusting you will afford to me some relief =
    My Case is, I am under difficulties, & distress, not having it in my power,
to bring in a sufficiency for the support of myself = my Wife, & Afflicted
Daugther, you well know, the Ill state of health my Daughter possesses,
10 for these ten Years past; she is now, & have been for many weeks past,
entirely laid aside, Incapable of doing any thing, or helping herself, & is
now under the Doctors hands = my Wife also have been very Ill, several
times, so as to be laid aside, since we have been at Chelmsford; & since
the first three weeks of our being here, she have been in an Afflicted state
15 = indeed both of them, have been confined to a bed of Affliction, together,
several times, so as to be totally unable, to support, or assist each other,
my Wife thanks be to God, is at this time better in health, but through
Infirmity, & Age, is so Enfeeble as to be incapable of doing but very little,
nor can I ever expect her to be much better, for she is now in her 70th Year
20 of Age = & myself 65 = had it not been for a kind Neighbour, or two, I
know not what we should have done, we have been, & now are, much
distressed, & indeed, Sir, my Earnings are not sufficient to procure the
common necessaries of Life, we have often known, & felt the want of
them = & I now feel the decays of Nature, advancing fast upon me, but
25 thanks be to God I can do as, I do, I am not worthy the least of his Mercies
Having thus, in some mesure stated my Case, I am come to the painful
task, of stating the Embarassment, I now am distressed under, it have not
been in my power, to keep myself, out of debt, the Principal, is the Rent of
the Tenement in which we live, having not been Able, to pay any part of it,
30 which have been going on from Michaelmass last, my Landlady is now
become very Impressive, & will not wait any longer, & Yesterday told me
she will proceed againt me, & make me pay her, by distressing me, & that
Immediately, the things we have, are only our Bed, & a few things bought
in for us, by a friend or two, when my things were sold of, which I trust
35 you well know, so that none of them are mine, & in this Situation we are in
great distress; & Humbly, Pray your Sir, to take our case into Consideration, & Afford us some Relief, the Rent I owe from Michaelmass last, to
Midsummer, at Seven Guineas a Year (not quite 3 Schill^{gs}. a week) amount
to [£]5 = ^s10 = ^d3 : another Quarter is now going on, & indeed Sir, tis not in
40 my Power, under present circumstances, to Extricate myself, from the
distress that must come on us, we Humbly Pray you to Assist us, & to
Instruct us what we must do, for it will be Extreemly distressing, to have

the few things taken from us; my Daughter at this time also, nearly confined totally to her Bed = will you Sir, have the goodness, to write to me, to Inform me, what I may Expect to be done for me, & what I must do, I 45 trust your goodness will do for us what you can = Several = Respectable Persons here, can affirm, what I have stated =

    Direct for me = Near the Windmill Inn, Clarkes Yard
              Moulsham = Chelmsford

[*Continued on next page:*] Indeed, Sir, I do to the Utmost of my Power, & 50 have done all I can, I have been very Ill myself = & have it not been for Illness = I think it probable, I could have done; = for myself & Wife, I certainly could do, very well but my Daughter, makeing the third, & that in such an Afflicted state constantly, caused me to drag very heavily on, & make it totally Impossible, for me to support it = nor do I know what to 55 do = I once more say, I Humbly Pray you, to take my Case into Consideration, trusting your goodness will lead you to Yield me Assistance, & Advise = indeed almost every week, at the latter part, I have not a Shilling, to help ourselves with, our little income, of <m>y Earnings, being always Exhausted = 60

    I must here rest my case with you, trusti<ng> you will condesend, shortly to relieve me, as I know not, how I shall Pacify my Landlady till I hear from you = I am Sir = & Gentlemen
        Your Humble Ser^{vt}
             W James Senr 65

TEXTUAL ALTERATIONS 15: together] *after del* 'a'. 21: we should] 'w' *over illeg.* 21: much] 'm' *over illeg.* 30: Michaelmass] *after del* 'Mi'. 36-37: Consideration] 's' *over* 'd'. 45: I may] 'I' *over illeg.*
CIRCUMTEXT Note in pencil from other hand at bottom of page: 'Send 4£'.

419 From William James in Chelmsford to [James] Allen, overseer of St Peter, Colchester, 7 August 1818

                          Chelmsford Aug^{st} 7 - 1818
Sir,
    Your goodness I Hope, will Excuse my writeing to you, I am Sorry to trouble you, or to be under the Necessity, to make any Application for Relief, I know you are not in Office, but if you can Consistantly speak for 5 me, it will proberbly be of some service to me, & my family, your past kindness, I thank you for, and as my friend, I am induced to write to you,

I wrote to Mr Carr, some short time back, stateing to him, my Uncomfortable situation, the Ill state of health of my Wife, since the first three
10 weeks, of coming to Chelmsford, and the continued Ill state of my Daughter, every thing taken together, now I have made tryal, I find I am totally
unable to support, and what to do I know not, I certainly cannot procure
the common necessaries of Life, we often know what hunger is I could
support myself & Wife, but I find I cannot support the three, nor can I pay
15 my rent, I asked Mr Carr, and through him, the Assistance and Advise of
the Gentlemen, what they would advise me to do, for my Landlady, declares she will enter an Action into my house for a forceable payment of
the rent, which from Michaelmass last to Midsummer, Amount to $^£$5 =
^{s}10 = ^{d}3 = which I am Utterly unable to pay, but Sir I beg you to refer to
20 Mr Carr = if you have not seen the Letter I hope not to Affend, I humbly
interceded for a Letter to Instruct me, what I must, do, I sometimes think
M^r C - had it not, as I have not heard from him, nor from any other
Quarter, I have no claim to make, but humbly rely, on the goodness &
generosity of the Gentlemen, for Assistance, and Advise, in respect of
25 myself, I humbly own, I am not worthy of the smallest notice, but my
Wife, and Daughter, is the Grief of my heart = let me Intreat with all
humbleness if Possible, something to be done for us, that the distress we
dread may not come upon us, for sure we are, our Landlady will wait but
few days longer =
30 Forgive me the Liberty, Sir, I have taken of writeing I humbly pray for
some advise to be given, to releave our minds = we are under great distress
          Sir, Your Humble Servt W James
          Clarkes Yard - Near the Windmill Inn
35   Moulsham, Chelmsford
I am aware I should pay the Postage, you will Excuse it, as I really have
not six pence to pay it with
[*Added at bottom of next page:*] The little Job, Ann had to do for M^{rs}
Allen is done & will send it the first Opportunity kind respects to Mrs Allen
40 &c

420 From James Howell in Ely to the overseers of St Peter, Colchester, 13 September 1818

Gentlemen,

I hope You will excuse my troubling You again but necessity compels me as I dare not travel without a License As a common inspector lives in this place I really am in a great strait for wants of them As the Gentleman who credits me with Goods will not suffer me to have them without one 5 for fear of a seizure. Since I enclosed my Old Licence to You I have been a Gleaning for the family but that resource is exhausted I therefore humbly hope and trust You will allow me some part of the License and I must sell something out of the House to make up the remainder.

The Gentleman in Ely who advanced me Money last Year by Your 10 Orders will have no Objection to advance any Sum You shall think proper towards purchasing my License as he well knows my Distress and in case You doubt my Word You may refer to him on the subject Relying on Your Goodness I humbly hope and trust You will do something for me for which as in Duty bound I shall be humbly thankful -   15

> I am Y^r Obed^t H Servt
> James Howell
> Ely in the Isle
> Cambridge^{re}

sep^r 13th 1818   20

PS. without Assistance I must hazard to find bread and if detected I know not what will become of the family as I must go to prison for my small quantity of Goods will not pay the fine if You oblidge me this time I will endeavour to do without any further Assistance for a Year if Possible

TEXTUAL ALTERATIONS 9: out of the House] *interl with caret.*

421 From William James in Chelmsford to Mr Banister in St Peter, Colchester, 19 September 1818

Chelmsford Sepr 19 = 1818

Sir,

I Received Your Letter with the three pound, you favoured me with, for which I thank you, and paid it towards my rent = I would not be Burdensome to you, Sir, could I avoid it, and having, fully stated my Case before, 5

I need not be tiresome, in doing it again, and if I were not necessiated, far
should it be from me to make any application, but as I before said, tis
wholly out of my power to make good my Rent, my Landlady gave me
Notice on Yesterday, Friday, to pay her by next Tuesday Sennight, in
10 failure of which, she will take Legal means and pay herself = I cannot
avoid applying to you, and the Gentlemen of the Parish, for Assistance in
paying my Rent for me, for in the Afflicted state of my Family, and using
every Exertion in my power, I cannot do it, and I do hope, and trust, if
you will so far condescend, as to allow me the Amount of the Rent, at this
15 time, and in future, which I trust you will, I will use every endeavor to
keep from being more burdensome to you, for as I before said, I can
provide for myself, and Wife, but the Afflicted state of my Daughter is
such, that I cannot support it, without some assistance, were it not so, I
would ask for nothing; Sir, as I said before, at Michaelmass day, I owe a
20 Years Rent, which Rent is seven Guineas deducting, the 3 Pounds you
sent me there Remain due, four pound, Seven Shillings = I humbly trust
you will do it for me, for if she is permited to take our few things from us,
as I before said are not mine, I know not what I shall do, I commit my
case to you, humbly trusting you will take it into consideration and grant
25 me Relief = I hope not to be under the Necessity, of comeing home to my
Parish, Indeed Sir, as I said before, I have done, & will do, all that is in
my Power,

I am Sir, with due Submission,
Your Hum^le Ser^vt, Wm James
30   Clarkes Passage, Near the Windmill Inn
Moulsham Chelmsford

TEXTUAL ALTERATIONS 8: gave] 'g' *and* 'v' *over illeg.* 11: Parish] *over del illeg.* 16: burden-
some] *final* 'e' *interl at end of line.* 20: deducting] *over del illeg.*

422   From William James in Chelmsford to James Allen in St Peter, Colchester, 18 March 1819

Chelmsford March 18 = 1819
Sir,
I have to beg your Excuse, for again troubling you, with a few Lines;
You will remember the request I made, to the Gentlemen of the parish,
5 when I was at Colchester, for something of an Allowance, considering

the Afflicted state of my Daughter, and was incourag^d to hope, from the
kindness shown me, and whatever that was to be, you had the goodness,
to Offer to send it to me =

Mr Banister told me I should hear from him, in a few weeks, what it
should be, but I have not heard from him at present; If, Sir, tis not intrud- 10
ing too much, on your kind, Friendship, I will thank you, to befriend me
again, in sending, what the Gentlemen may think proper, and giving me a
line of Information, I need not say any more on the subject, as I stated all
I could when, I was with you, I will only say, my Daughter have been,
and is very Ill, indeed, my Wife have, also been very bad, and is very 15
poorly now, Indeed, Sir, I have had a hard time of it, and very trying,
since I was with you, for 5 weeks, I had scarcely any Employment, but
thank God I have a little at this time, but Mr Merrit, have had nothing
since for me to do, = My Wife & Daugher, give their Duty to You & M^{rs}
Allen = to Betsy & others;   20

Trusting, Sir, You will Pardon, this Application
I most Humbly & Obediently = Subscribe mysel = your
dutiful Ser^{vt} W James
I have by this post sent a line to Mr Banister

**423   From William James in Chelmsford to Mr Banister in St Peter,
Colchester, 18 March 1819**

Chelmsford March 18 = 1819
Sir,

You will Excuse me in writeing to you, you are not a Stranger to my
Application, nor need I say, but little on the subject, as I stated it to you,
when I was at Colchester, you gave me Incouragement to hope, for some 5
allowance, for my Daughter, considering her afflicted state, and said I
should hear from you in a few weeks, but I have not at present, which
induced me to write to you, Mr Allen, offered at that time, to send to me,
whatever you and the Gentlemen, might deem Necessary = for which we
will thank you, my Daughter have been been, & is very Ill indeed = as 10
have also my Wife, & now is = and since I was with you, for 5 weeks I
had scarecly any thing to do; at this time I have a little = but Mr Merritt,
have not had any, Employment for me since that time, I thank you, and
the Gentlemen for favors past, trusting you will send what you think proper
for her relief =   15

As I said to you, I can, while health is continud to me, Provide for myself,
& wife, but tis too much for me, in my Advanced Age = to make provision
for us all, I should be happy to do it if I could = Pray Sir, lett me hear from
you, in a few days,

20   I am Sir, Your Hum^le Ser^vt

Wm James

TEXTUAL ALTERATIONS 8: offered] *second* 'f' *over illeg.* 13: Employment] 'nt' *interl at end
of line.*
CIRCUMTEXT Note in pencil from other hand at bottom: '2s 6[d] p[er] week'.

424   From Benjamin Hewitt in Whitton [Suffolk] to the overseer of St Peter, Colchester, 31 March 1819

1819 Whitton March 31

Sur i have a plied to our overser for releif and he will not relive me a
cording to mr banister order when i was over at his and so i should be a
blidge to you sur if you would send me sum money if you please for i
5 have not got any work yet or other wise i must come home for i have sold
all most every thing i have pleas to give me an answer by return of post or
other wise i must come home directley

Benjamin Hewitt

Whitton

TEXTUAL ALTERATIONS 3: mr] *after del illeg.* 6: of] *after del illeg.*
CIRCUMTEXT Note from other hand at bottom: 'I have requested the overseer of Whitten
to give alittle at atime and transmit the acc[oun]t here JB'.
RELATED CORRESPONDENCE On 9 March 1819, John Goldsmith, overseer of Whitton, had
written to the overseer of St Peter, Colchester, that Benjamin Hewitt 'have Had very
Little to Do Ever Since He was with you, to my Knowledge he was Down to Ipswich
three Days Last week and Had the Promise of work, but the Answer was they Could not
Get their money in, and he have walkes the Town Over Since that time and Some Say
they Can Give him work in a fortnight and Some in a month'. On 9 April 1819, Mr
Banister, overseer of St Peter, Colchester, wrote to Whitton: 'If you will have the goodness to relieve Hewett a little and let me know when you wish me to remit you the amount
you shall have it again as I before told you as it is troublesome and improper to send him
cash'. An account for April till July 1819 on same paper reveals that Hewitt received a
regular allowance of 5s. On 25 July 1819, Goldsmith wrote to Banister: 'Hewett have
Been in a Poor state ever Since I was at Yours for the want of work I have Employ^d Him
Upon the Parishes Account to Get a Little towards rent but He allways wanted the money
to Get Victuals with, but now he Have Got a Harvest with one of our Largest Occupiers so
now I am In hopes if he is Able to go through with His Harvest I shall Have my Rent at
Michalmas I was forst to advance this Last 5^s for Him to Get a Sithe & Sickle.' Apparently, that letter went back to Whitton and was then returned to Colchester, for it bears a

note of receipt for £2 from Mr Child, the overseer of St Peter, Colchester, dated 20 June 1819, signed by John Robinson, coachman, and countersigned by Goldsmith.

425   From William James in Chelmsford to Mr Banister in St Peter, Colchester, 11 August 1819

Chelmsford Augst 11th = 1819

Sir,

The letter you had the goodness to Convey to me, by Miss Merritt, in April last, Informing me of the Agreement of the Parish, to allow me two & Six pence a week for my Daughter, from the 25 of March as long as 5 she was with me, I Received with thankfulness -

a while after, I wrote to you by Favor of a friend, thanking you, & the Gentlemen, for the kindness, but not hearing from you since that time, Induces me to suppose you did not receive it, & to write to you again & will be thankfull to you, to remit it to me, as you please, Indeed Sir, my 10 Daughter have been, & now is, very bad indeed, have not Able to be out since last May twelve Month, she is very weak & low, Confined to her room, & frequently to her bed, it is the Astonishment of all who know, or see her, that she is alive, my Wife have been very bad indeed, but is somewhat better, I have a trying time, but as yet, I ask not for Assistance, 15 but for my Daughter, nor hope I shall not, I hope Sir, you will be so kind, to send to me in a few days, as your promised Assistance have been, & now is much wanted = without which I know not what to do, Mr Allen would if you please, send it to me =

I hope not to Offend, but not receiving any thing from you, thought best 20 to write again, relying on your kindness

I am yours, & the Gentlemens Hum^{le} Servt

W James

If applying to you, I make wrong Application = I will be glad to be sett right =   25

TEXTUAL ALTERATIONS 3: Miss] *inserted in left-hand margin.* 5: from the 25 of March] *interl with caret.* 11: Able] 'A' *over illeg.* 13: Astonishment] 'nt' *interl at end of line.* 24: Application] 'Appli' *over illeg.*

CIRCUMTEXT Note from other hand at bottom of letter: 'Sent the 26 Aug^t [£] 3.5.0 being up to Michs 1819' (hand A). Note in pencil from other hand on back: 'has Mr Allen a convenient opportunity of forwarding [£] 1.12.6 to Mr James at Chelmsford'. Further note in pencil, crossed out, on following page: 'from what time is James to receive 2/6 p^r week' (hand B).

426 From Benjamin Hewitt in Whitton, Suffolk, to the overseer in St Peter, Colchester, 23 September 1819

1819   September 23
   Sur i send you thease few lines to in form you that i am out of work and
have been ever since harvest and i have three quarters rent to pay and if i
do not pay it the 29 of september my land lord say he will take my things
5 and so i should be wary much a blidge to you gentlemen to a sist me if
you please or otherwaies i must come home for i have stopt a way till i
am all most naked but i have work at the 11 of octber till christmas if you
will a sist me till then or els i must come home the 29 of september but i
hope you will send me something please to give me an answer in a day or
10 two weather i should come or not
             please to direct to me
             benjamin Hewitt whitton near ipswich
                 Suffolk

TEXTUAL ALTERATIONS 2: you] *after del illeg.* 7: work] 'r' *over del illeg.* 7: the] *over del
illeg.*
   CIRCUMTEXT Note from other hand at bottom: 'remitted to Mʳ Jnᵒ Goldsmith (his Landlord) A one Pound Note by Mʳ childs Coachman', 27 September 1819.

427 From T[homas] Mills to Mr Robinson [6 October 1819]

Sir
   I ham very sorry but Obligation forces me to call on you fer releif as my
Children have not bread anuff in the house for the Day and I ham now
going to Buers with asmall Bill of five shillings to supply thayer wants so
5 I Remein
                                          your Hmble Saᵗ
                                              T Mills
6 Oclock

WRITING Same hand as letter from Thomas Mills in Wethersfield of 19 October 1820 (**433**).
   DATE Date of filing note on back.

428 From Benjamin Hewitt in Whitton [Suffolk] to the overseer in St Peter, Colchester, 12 April [1820]

April 12

Sur i should be much a blidge to you sur if you would give mister gold-smith an order to give me a few shillings when i am realey destred for it is a great way to come over there every time i want a few shillings for i have but a little work at present but i am in hopes i shall have more by and 5 by but i can not make out with out a little help at pressent benjamin hewitt whitton

TEXTUAL ALTERATIONS 3: shillings] 'n' *over illeg.* 5: more] 'e' *over illeg.* 6: out] *after del illeg.* 6: help] *after del illeg.*

CIRCUMTEXT Note from John Goldsmith, overseer at Whitton, at bottom of page: 'Hewett is a tenent of Mine and the above I believe is Correct but I want some of Your advice to Know How I am to order about my Rent that is £1..s4..d9'.

DATE Year inferred from the location of the letter within the broad chronological order of the archive.

RELATED CORRESPONDENCE On 2 May 1820, John Goldsmith, overseer of Whitton, wrote to the overseer of St Peter, Colchester, about Benjamin Hewitt: 'I Believe the Man would worke now if He could Git it to Do for He Has Been Very Seady Ever Since a good wile Before Christmas, so you Have it to Consider wether to Have Him Home or Relieve Him Here.' On 20 June 1820, Goldsmith wrote again. 'Hewett inform[d] me after He was at Colchester Last month that You Had Sent some money for me by the Post.' But the money never did arrive, and meanwhile Hewitt was in arrears with rent of £2 9s 6d.

429 From William Harvey at Gosport Barracks [Hampshire] to the Revd William Marsh in St Peter, Colchester, 23 June 1820

Gosport 23th June 1820

Honoured Sir{ I Sergeant Harvey am now under the nessesity to Inform your Honour of My Destress with Such a Large Fammily of A Wife and 4 Children to Maintain out of my Bear Pay Wife an two of My Children So ill that i am drove to Such Destress that I cannot tell what to do Which 5 i have thought Proper to aquaint your Honnour of My Sad destress hop-ing that Your Honour Will be So good as to Consider my Case and to Beg of the Gentelman of this Parish for a Smal Relief at this time of My Wife and to dear Beabes So ill an have Bee So for this 2 Months Pas Sir I William Haven am very Sorry to be trubelin[g] the Gentelman but am 10 now Drove to that destress that i am oblged to do So for I cannot tell what to do

Sir I Hope you will be So good as to Show this to
the Gentelman I am your Humbel and obedent
15   Servant William Harvey

William Harvey Sergeant
in the 2 Royal Veteran Batt[n]
Gosport Barracks

TEXTUAL ALTERATIONS 4: Wife] *interl.*

430   From William James in Chelmsford to Mr Swinborne, 29 June 1820

Chelmsford June 29 = 1820

Sir,

I trust, I am not wrong in my adress to you; being Informed, you are
Overseer, of the Parish of S[t] Peter

5   I conclude you well know, the Allowance made by the Gentlemen, to
me of two Shill[gs] & six pence P[r] week, for the support of my Daughter,
while she continued with me, in her Afflicted state, which from that time,
up to Lady day last, have been regular, remited to me, for which I return,
my humble thanks; she is yet with me and in the same Afflicted state, you
10   will do a kindness, in sending me the Amount for the last Quarter, up to
Midsummer, indeed Sir, it is much wanted for her support = M[r] Allen,
who sent me the last, and which was received safe, can give you Information, on the Subject; will you Sir, be so Kind, to send it as a small parcle
(as he did) by M[r] Clarry the Coachman = directed for me, to the care of
15   M[r] French, at the Ship Inn, Chelmsford I shall receive it safe = as it is
there Clarry stops = and for which I will thank you = Excuse my Mentioning time, but will be thankfull, for it, as soon as you can, being much
in want

I am Sir Your Hum[le] Serv[t]
20   Will[m] James

TEXTUAL ALTERATIONS 15: Chelmsford] 'ford' *interl at end of line.*

431 From William Harvey at Gosport Barracks [Hampshire] to the Revd William Marsh in St Peter, Colchester, 6 July 1820

Gosport Barracks 6th July 1820

Sir/

I beg leave to trouble you again as I have not received any Answer to my Letter sent you about 10 Days since, applying for some relief as my Family are very Poorly and my Pay not sufficient to support Six - and we 5 are in expectation of soon leaving this place, that if I have no relief from the Parish, I shall be under the disagreeable Necessity of sending them as it is imposible for me to support them, I most humbly beg that you will take my case in to consideration and be pleased to give me an Answer, we are expecting to go to Irland or Jersey,   10

Your most obedient
& very Humble
Servant
William Harvey Sergeant
2nd Royal Veteran Batt[n] 15

432 From William James in Chelmsford to Mr Swinborne, 10 September 1820

Chelmsford Sep[r] 10 = 1820

Sir,

My daughter continues with me, in the same afflicted state = I will be much Obliged to you, to do me the favor, of sending the Allowance, granted by you, and the Gentlemen, on her Account, of $^{s}2=^{d}6$ P[r] week, as 5 you sent me by Clarry the Coachman, at Midsumer last = it being now Michaelmass = directed for me to the Care of M[r] French, at the Ship Inn Chelmsford =

You Sir I trust will excuse my troubling you, as I would not, could I avoid it   10

Your Humble Ser[vt]
W[m] James

You will do me a kindness, in sending to me, this week, or begining of next = for wich I will thank you =

TEXTUAL ALTERATIONS 14: wich] 'c' *over* 'h'.

433   From Thomas Mills in Wethersfield [Essex] to Mr Swinborne, 19 October 1820

Gentelmen

I Received a letter from my Wife and she inform's me that you have stopt har pay I ham sorry to inform you I have only 1^s..6^d a day and I ham sorry to say that will not maintain my famley if I could git any thing
5 better to do I should be happy to imbrace it as fer the three Children that go to the nationale Schole thay have not a dress fit to go to Church in and God knowes I cannot Provide them with one therefor I must Lay at your Goodnes<s>
so I Remain Yours
10   Humble Sar^t
                        Th^s Mills
Weathersfield Octr 19..1820
PS if you will have the goodness to inquire of Mr John Fenton he will steat to you that my pay is only 1^s..6^d aday

TEXTUAL ALTERATIONS 6: Schole] *after del* 'thay'. 14: steat] 'e' *over* 'l'. 14: is] *below del* 'sir'.

434   From William James in Chelmsford to Mr Swinborne, 30 December 1820

Chelmsford Decr 30th = 1820

Sir,

You will, I trust Excuse my Application - but as Another Quarter is past, since I Received your last favor and for which I thank you - I esteem
5 it my duty to Inform you, my Daughter is still with me, and continue in the same Afflicted state, and have been much worse - you will do a great kindness in having the goodness, to send the Allowd amount, for the last Quarter, up to Xtss, - be so good to direct, as before
For me, to the care of Mr French = Ship Inn Chelmsford = - If you will
10 send it me in two, or three days, you will do me a furthur kindness for which I will thank you,
            Subscribing our Joint Duty to you, and
            the Gentlemen
                    I am Your Hum^{le} Ser^{vt}
15   W- James

435 From William James in Chelmsford to Mr Swinborne, 11 January 1821

Chelmsford Jan^ry 11 = 1821

Sir,

Pardon my writeing to you again; having wrote to you, on the 30th of Decr last, and not Receiving any thing from you, fearing it may have Escaped your memory, as you said it did, the last Michaelmass, (when 5 you had the goodness of sending to me) I hope not to Offend, in takeing the Liberty, of thus reminding you -

You Sir will do me a great kindness, in sending to me, the Allowance, granted for my Daughter, for the Past Quarter, up to X^tmass, we are in great need of it, and for which, will thank you humbly - 10

Mr Clarry the Coachman (by whom you sent it before) comes up from Colchester, on Saturday Morning, Pray Sir, will you have the Goodness, to send by him, directed for me, to the Care of Mr French, Ship Inn, Chelmsford -

I would not have wrote, nor mentioned time, If it were not a time of 15 Necessity

I am Sir Your Hum^le Ser^vt

Wm James

PS My Daughter is yet in the same Afflicted state

CIRCUMTEXT Note in pencil from other hand at bottom: '[£] 1.12.6'.

436 From J[ames] Tracey in Chelmsford, 25 February 1821

Chelmsford Feby 25 1821

Sir/

I am sorry that I am under nessety of trouble you for sum further assistence for I am Still out of imploy at present their fore Sir I hope you Will have the goodness to Consider me somthing by the bearer Wich I 5 hope it Will be the Last time I Shall have to trouble you for I Expect to go to Work Soon if not my famly must Come home soon and I Cannot Safe them from it

Sir/ Your humble Servent

J trasey 10

TEXTUAL ALTERATIONS 3: trouble] 'r' *over* 'h'.

RELATED CORRESPONDENCE On 28 January 1823, George Wray wrote from Chelmsford
that James Tracey had hardly had any work for seven weeks and needed assistance.

437   From William James in Chelmsford to Mr Swinborne, 29 March 1821

Chelmsford March 29 = 1821

Sir,

Your goodness will I trust excuse my Application.

My Daughter is yet with me in the same Afflicted state, not in the least
5 better, I will thank you Sir, if you will be so kind, to send the Quarterly
Allowance up to Lady day last, as you sent to me at the last Xt,mass
Quarter, by Mr Clarry the Coachman, by whom I send this, I have asked
him to call on you, as I think it the least trouble to you -

be so good, to direct it for me, to the Care of Mr French, Ship Inn -
10 Chelmsford

I am Sir your Hum^{le} Ser^{vt}

Wm James

438   From William James in Chelmsford to Mr Swinborne, 5 April 1821

Chelmsford April 5 = 1821

Sir,

Pardon my writeing again, having wrote by Mr Clarry on Thursday last,
but not having Rec^d any thing from you, I feard it have escaped, your
5 memory, Excuse me thus remindg you; indeed Sir, you will do me a great
kindness, in sending the Allowance, for the last Quarter, granted me for
my Daughter, as we are in great want of it, and for which I will humbly
thank you, work having been so very Slack with me for some weeks, that
we really, have not been able to procure common Necessaries, which
10 make us somewhat distressed, but trust it will again revive -

Pray Sir have the goodness, to send it by Clarry, (or I know not what I
shall do,) whom I will ask to call on you - Friday Afternoon - or Saturday
Morn^g - as he come up on Saturday - I would not trouble you, with this
Application if not compell'd by Necessity - will you direct for me to the
15 care of Mr French, as before, - but I will endeavor to see Clarry, on Satur^y,
when he comes up -

Pray excuse me, my Daughter is unable to help herself, my Wife nearly the same,

I am Sir, Your Hum^{le} Ser^{vt}

Wm James 20

439 From William James in Chelmsford to James Allen, 31 May 1821

Chelmsford May 31 = 1821

Sir,

I trust you will Excuse my writeing to you, but tis to Ask of you a favor, which I trust you will grant me, which is, to be so kind, to Advance to me; the Amount of the Money, for this Quarter, up to Midsummer next, 5 Allowed by the Parish, (for which I owe you my thanks,) and then take it, to repay yourself, the Advance; as by the last I Received, I conceive Mr Bryant is Overseer, you will do me a great kindness, as I am in need of it, to pay my Landlady, as Part of Rent, for which I am Indebted up to Last Quarter, (she being very Clamorous, & a strange Woman), in doing which, 10 I shall be Able to Satisfy her, if I pay her now, work having been very dead, & Slack, have been the Occasion of my being behind with her - and having Experienced your Friendship, in many Instances, Induces me to make this Application - trusting you will favor me; having no claim on your kindness, I ask it of you, as of one, who have extended Friendship, 15 undeserved, in many times of need, for which I retain a gratefull remembrance, I hope, & trust, not to Offend = & hope you will favor me, in sending it for me - to the care of Mr French - Ship Inn Chelmsford -

My Daughter continues in the same State, some times better, then again worse = Wife much the same, gets weaker, & more feeble, Able to do 20 very little, I am well as can Expect, for which, Sir, I am thankful, much lies upon me, as Age advances, weakness Increase's, I often think shall have to give up, with Gods Bless^g, I will hold on, as long as I can, but Indeed, Often, I cannot procure necessaries for Natures support = hope you Sir - M^{rs} A -& family are well 25

as in duty bound, we Join, Respectfully, & thankfully, your Gratefull, Obedient Ser^{vts}

W = A & A James

TEXTUAL ALTERATIONS 7: I conceive] *interl with caret.* 26: your] *after del* 'your'.

440   From George Rowe in [Great] Coggeshall [Essex] to the overseer of St Peter, Colchester, 19 June 1821

June 19:1821   Coggeshall

   Sir I am Sorry to have to truble you but In the Parrish wear I Live wich is Bocking thay have Rated all that Do not Belong to the Parrish and the Overcear Call for the Rate Last Monday and we wass Not able to pay it
5 and he Gave Uss till Next Satterday Week to hear What the Gentlemen wold Do for he Say that thear is a Great meaney whear thay are Not able to pay the Parrishs pay it for them to Keep them in Work So as Not to have them Home the Rate for Uss to pay for this Quarter is ^{s}4. So the Overcear wold wish to hear from you in time or Elce he will Sell Somthing
10 for the Money Quarters Day is Near and I have Got to pay a Quarters Rent and my Wife is So afflicted with her head and Eys that she Cant See but Left to Gide her Sulf Not able to Do what we have to Do in the house Not so much as to thred a Needle and if the Gentelmen think Not of Complying with this Request I see no other Sincs but we Must Come
15 home as We have but ^{s}8 a Week for Every thing wich I hop the Gentle-men will take in to Considerration and Send either to me at Mr Durrants Coller Maker Coggeshall or to Mr Golding Overcear Bocking
               from Me George Rowe

441   From James Howell in Ely, 31 July 1821

Ely   July   31   1821

   Gentlman i rite to inform you that my old licences that you Gentlman was two pound towards larst year is run out and the new ones take place the first of august and I dare not go one Day without them if I Do I Shall
5 be taking up and put to prison away from my five por Children Gentlman it is not in my power to Get four pound my self I have hard work to Get them a half a living as itis but Gentlman as you are Good as to help alittle I will Do all that I Can to keep away from trubling you Gentlman for one year Gentlman if you will be So Good as to arsk the Larst overseers you
10 will find that 2 pound is the reaguler alounce thay Give me in a year for this Larst five years pray Gentlman rite as soon as you Can as I dar not Goe one Day with out them
plese to deract for James Howell
Broad Street Ely Cambridge Shire

I Ham your humbel   15
Servant Ja^s Howell

TEXTUAL ALTERATIONS 9: overseers] *after del* 'the L'. 11: Gentlman] *last* 'n' *interl at end of line.*

RELATED CORRESPONDENCE On 29 March 1819, Mr Garratt in Ely had written to Mr Banister, overseer of St Peter, Colchester, requesting to let him know 'what money you sent last week as Howell has taken the Letter from the post office and has taken the money and is destroyed part of the letter he is now in the House of Correction I have taken from him £2 - he is a very Drunken bad Ch[a]racter - his Wife could maintain herself and children Well if he would Keep away.' Banister had ordered him to 'pay the 2£'(note of answer), and further payments of £2 to Howell had been sent on 18 February and 21 March 1820.

442   From George Rowe, 6 August 1821

August 6 : 1821
Sir I hope you will Not take it a Miss of my Sending you of a fue Lines as you Requested in your Letter that I wold Send the Pertickelery how I Gaind my Settlemant wich was by been an Apprentise to Mr James Herbert on North Hill and I have Never Lived eany whear No other then as a   5
Weekly Servent and I Count that I have Left Colchester full 30 Years but if you Enquir of Mr Banister he will Gave you an account of Me I was wich to Send to You a gain that through the affliction of my Wife and Other things Lay So heavey appon me that I am Not able to pay the Rates wich the Gentleman have been So Good as to wait to See if you will Do 10
eaney thing for Me as thear will Soon be 2 Quarters to pay wich I hope you will take in to Considerretion a Geve me an Answer to Mr Burrants Coggeshall or Near the Horse and Groon Bocking End
                                                        from Me George Rowe

TEXTUAL ALTERATIONS 4: James] 'J' *over illeg.* 13: Near] *after del* 'the'.

443   From William James in Chelmsford to [Josias] Bryant, 30 August 1821

Chelmsford Augst 30 = 1821
Sir,
    I am sorry, to be under the necessity of makeing application to you (as Overseer) I have refraind from it as long as I can; your kindness, I trust

5　will meet my case, while I state it to you - We have suffer'd much, both
　　myself & Wife, for the want of the Necessaries of life, work being so very
　　slack, that often I have little Employment for weeks together, but then it
　　have revived again, and I have press'd on, though with dificulty, and now
　　work have been so long slack, that we have many times been without
10　food, no, not a sufficiency of bread only not a Shilling, nor a penny to
　　procure any, by which means our healths are much impair'd, and at this
　　time, and for some time past, my Wife laid aside, not Able to do any thing
　　my daughter also, continues in the same state, I have been very Ill, (& am
　　not recoverd,) some weeks = I am Advised to make this Application = I
15　humbly ask you Sir, to be so good, if possible, to send me something for
　　present relief, health I hope will return, & work revive, had I not Obtaind
　　some Credid, & friends, I must have made Application, sometime back, I
　　must not be tedious, but we fell our health decling day after day, I hope
　　you will grant us, some Immediate relief, at this time, we have no bread,
20　nor money, to procure any, nor any Visible means so to do, not having a
　　Job to do; now Sir I must leave my case with you; you will make it known
　　to Mr Allen -
　　　　Our dutifull respects to M^r & Mrs Allen, to you & Mrs Bryant & should
　　be glad of Advise
25　　　　　　　　　I am Obediently, Your Hum^{le} Ser^{vt}
　　　　　　　　　　　　　　Wm James

Textual alterations 21: leave] *interl with caret.*

444　From William James in Chelmsford to [Josias] Bryant, 5 September 1821

Chelmsford Sepr 5 = 1821

Sir,

　　I trust you will excuse this second Application, hopeing not to Offend;
　　I write with due submission -
5　　Having stated my case to you on Thursday last, I trust you have taken it
　　into Consideration, and are disposed to afford us relief, under such Impression, I have asked Mr Clarry, to call on you again, by whom, on his
　　return, I humbly ask the Favor of you, to be so good, to send to us; I am
　　sorry to Apply, but not hearing from you, what am I to do, since I wrote
10　to you, I have earned 18 pence only, in every respect, our case remain the

same as then, I do not deceive you, we are really, in a half starving situation, it have not been in my power, to purchase any meat, these 6 weeks
past, we have now a piece of Bread only, we are in want of every Necessary, for the support of Nature, and cannot procure any without your kind
assistance, in several Cases I have obtain Credit, but I cannot ask for 15
more, therefore must remain as we are, till you are pleased, to send us
relief, at our advanced Age, these things are hard, and surely call for
Commiseration; if it cannot be done otherwise, will you do me the Favor,
as you did last Quarter, to advance the Allowance made to me, on
Account of my Daughter, up to Michaelss Quarter next, & then retain it to 20
pay yourself, I should be glad to have avoided that, but indeed, Sir, we
cannot Exist, at this perishable rate, If work was to be had, I could do
comfortable; I should be glad of Advise, from Mr Allen, & you, I know
not who else to apply to = M^r A - have ever been my Freind, in Applying
to you, I conceive myself, Applying to him also,   25
    Pray let me hear from you on Clarry's return -
        I am Sir Yours Obediently
                Wm James

445* From William James in Chelmsford to James Allen, 25 September 1821

             Chelmsford Sepr 25 = 1821
Sir,
    I trust you will Excuse me writeing to you, but as you told me, when I
was last time with you, if any thing occured in which I wanted, Advise or
Relief, to let you know, and not suffer myself to be in distress, nor put 5
myself to the trouble, or Expence of coming to Colchester, but to write to
you, as that would do as well, and that you would do, what was in your
power for me, provided I did all I could on my part, to procure a
Livelyhood, indeed Sir, this I have done, but as I stated to Mr Bryant, that
work from time to time having been so very slack, & Illness together, 10
have put it out of my power, to go on as I could wish, and work have
continued in the same dead state, as when I wrote last to M^r B -, I have
Earned, but 15 Shillings, since that time, five of which I Expended, for
Materials, to do the work with - and the most part of what M^r B - had the
goodness, to send me, I paid where I had been Credited, and what remained, 15
was Expended, for Immediate, necessaries of Life - it will be Vain to

repete over again what I wrote to M^r B - on our distressed case, I would
refer you, Sir, to those Letters, I can only say, things are with us, as they
then were, and we Live very spareingly indeed, and I can now say, we
20 have not, so much, as one Shilling, to help ourselves with, nor a Job in
view, at present, (in this I am not worse of than my Neighbours,) -
    I must say, my Rent is behind, the Allowance made for my Daughter,
which I Applied to that purpose, I have now been under the Necessity of
useing, for to provide the necessaries of Life, and am now in Expectation
25 every day, of the few things we have, to be seised on, and taken from us,
indeed Sir, we are truly Miserable -
    I do find that without some Assitance, tis Impossible for me, to recover
myself - to stand my ground, or support ourselves, had I Regular Employ
I could do it, but in this dead state of Employment, I find it Impossible =
30 what to do I know not, nor how to apply for relief, your past friendship,
and what you said to me, Induces me to ask your Advise, what is the best
for me to do, I know not, to whom to Apply but yourself - and I hope to
receive your Advise, I much wish, and would do all in my power, to
Avoid coming home to my Parish, as I do think, I can do much better
35 here, than to do that, but I cannot Procure, common necessaries, without
some furthur Aid, for which I make no pretence of Claim, but ask as a
favor - I am thankfull for the Allowance given us, it is a help, but not
Competent, in our present state of things - will you, Sir, be so kind, to do
what you can for us - to write to me, what step to take, what you would
40 have me do - If you wish me to Apply in any other way, or to any other
person, I will follow your Instruction - I hope Sir - something will be
done for me, to stop the threatining proceedings of my Landlady, to take
away the Comfort, of our few goods from us in which case I see no
remedy, to keep us from utter ruin = I am Indebted to her $^£4=^s10=^d6$, up to
45 Michaelmass; and more Expence, will follow such a step,- I must Leave
my case with you, trusting you will be my friend, as you have ever been
- I humbly ask pardon, for troubling you, and as humbly Intreat your
advise, and Answer =
    I have Interceded with my Landlady, to give her an Answer, on Mon-
50 day or Tuesday next, You will do me a great favor, if you will condesend,
to write to me, by that time, then I can give her an Answer, - Pray Sir
Excuse me,
                My Wife and Daughters Duty to M^r & Mrs Allen, &^{c}
                        I am Sir Your Obed^t, Hum^{le} Ser^{vt}
                                Wm James

If by post   55
Wm James - Bell - hanger
Near the Windmill Inn
Moulsham
Chelmsford Essex
If by Clarry - as Usual -   60

[*Postscript at bottom of page:*] Sir I would have p^d the postage of this, but really, have not six pence to do it

TEXTUAL ALTERATIONS 19: and we Live] *interl with caret.* 44: Indebted] 'n' *over* 'd'.

446   From James Howell in Ely to the overseers and churchwardens in St Peter, Colchester, 13 October 1821

Ely Octr 13 1821

Gentlman I rote Sumtime to you Consaning the Reguler a lowance Wich is alowed me per year and you Gentlman never sant it but Never faild untell this time I have been alowed two pound per year with 5 Children and that Is all I trubel you Gentlman for in one year <a>nd that is to healp   5
towards a four pound Licences Wich I ham oblidged to have Every year Gentlman I Carry a few Goods in the Contrey to Sell and that Is the Way I Get bread for my faimly as I know Nothing Elce to Get a leving but Dear not Carry nothing out without thay are inshured and that is not in my power to Do it my sulf and the Gentlman That Credit me the Goods is not   10
willing to Let me have any untell thay are made Saft as the pennalty Is 10 pound or Go to Prison 6 mounths and Gentlman that wold be My Lot and then my wife and family wold have to Leve Ely wer all my bread lays Gentlman the Larst time I was at Colchester for it the overseears told me that it was much better for to rite for it than to Come So many a miles   15
afterit

I Ham your Humbel Servant
Ja^s Howell Broad Street
Ely Cambridge Shire

447   From William James in Chelmsford to [Josias] Bryant, 18 October 1821

Chelmsford Octr 18 = 1821

Sir =

I Embrace the Opportunity, to send a few Lines by our Friend, Mr Green, who called on us this Morning,

5   I Received your favor safe, for which I am much Obliged to you, but it would not have overcome, the demand of my Landlady; but a kind Lady, in Chelmsford, who will know our case, made for us a Contribution, by which I was enabled, to pay her my Rent, and so overcome that difficulty - I was charged Eighteen pence, for the postage, for the Letter, and its

10   Contents, and was Obliged to pay it - My Wife, & Daughter, are no better, nor can I say, that I expect it; - I believe I may say, that on Saturday last, my daughter was worse, than she have been since we left Colchester, but is somewhat better, -

Employment continues very slack indeed, at present I have very little

15   to do, & at this time Nothing, I hope work will revive, there is no prospect of it at this time, which consequently, is attended with scantiness; of the necessaires of provision, which Dispirit me, & mine very much - I hope it will revive - I conceived it my duty, to embrace this Opportunity, to Acknowledge your favor, & return you our thanks -

20   My Wife, Daughter, & myself, Join in respectfull
                duty; to M^r, & Mrs Allen - to you &
                Mrs Bryant = &^{c}
                    I am Sir, yours Obediently
                    W- James

TEXTUAL ALTERATIONS 8: and] 'n' *over illeg*, 'd' *interl with caret*. 10: it] *interl with caret at end of line*.

448   From William James in Chelmsford to [Josias] Bryant, 1 January 1822

Chelmsford Jan^{ry} 1st, = 1822

Sir, you wished me, that unless Clarry would call, and leave my letters with you, to send by the Post, as it would be Cheapest, which in now doing I trust not to offend, nor in makeing Application, for the favor, of

the Quarter allowance up to X^{tss}, and Sir, if you can add to it, a small 5
donation, it will be a favor, for which we shall be thankfull, we humbly
thank you for the last, it was a great blessing, in supplying our wants, and
relieveing our distress, since that time, I have had some Jobs to do, and at
this time have, but not sufficient, for the support our Nature requires, but
for what we have, we desire to be thankfull, I experience the decays of 10
Nature so much, that I cannot work as I have done, nor as I wish to do, my
Wife more so than myself, she have been very Ill, and confined to Bed,
her weakness is so, she is Able to do but little, nor can we Expect, her
strength to recover; my daughter have been rather better, but is now
relaps'd again, and not able to hold up, I think it my duty to give this 15
statement I thank God for the Degree of health I enjoy, tis a great blessing, at my age, and while it continues, I will endeavor to do the best I can
- we all Join in gratefull Duty, to M^r, & Mrs Allen, to yourself & M^{rs} B -,
sincerely wish^g you all, a happy New Year, & many a one - Clarry, this
week comes up, on Wednesday & Friday if you will have the goodness, 20
to send to me by him on Friday I will ask him to call on you - and will
endeavor to see him when the Coach comes in, but will you direct for me
to the Care of Mr French- Ship Inn = I am Sir your dutifull Hum^{le} Ser^{vt}

W James

**449 From George Rowe to the overseer of St Peter, Colchester, 13
March 1822**

March 13 : 1822

Sir

I hope you will Not take it a miss of My trubling you but as I have Not
heard from you from the Last Letter I have Sent to Let you Know that the
Overseer Calld Last Week to Say that he must have the 2 Quarters Rats 5
that Is Due up to the 25 of this Month for all Must be Settld Next Week
wich I hope you Send me and Answer to thes fue Lines wich My Wife is
So Bad that I am forst to Get one to Do what we have to Do for See Cant
See to Do Littel or Notthing So that I Cannot pay the Rats

from me Geroge Rowe 10

TEXTUAL ALTERATIONS 4: the] *interl.* 7: Wife] *interl.* 8: to Get] *interl.* 8: for] *after del* 'for'.
9: So] *after del illeg.*

450   From William James in Chelmsford to Josias Bryant, 27 March 1822

Chelmsford March 27 = 1822

Sir,

Since your last sending to me, my daughter have been very bad; and for several weeks worse than since we have been at Chelmsford, is at this
5 time somewhat better - my Wife also continues much the same, only gradually her weekness increases, - as for myself am often very unwell, and find the decays of Nature Increasing on me day after day, but I am thankfull, I continue as I do - work is slack & meanly paid for - and I am not Able to do a days work as I have done, I do not wish to be always
10 makeing complaint, but to be thankfull, for what have been done for us, - but indeed Sir, we live very scantily & hard, not having sufficient for Natures support, & we feel it very much - I thought it my duty, to make to you this statement & I trust not to Offend - Will thank you, Sir, if you please, to send to me, the Quarters Allowance, by Clarry, as you have
15 usually done, he comes up, on next Friday, Sunday, & Tuesday, I will ask him, to call on you in that time as soon as I receive it, I have to pay it away, you will do me kindness; if you can send me a trifle more with it, we shall be glad & thankfull - I have not now a Shilling to help ourselves with, & work very slack - we humbly thank you for every favor, - direct
20 for me as Usual to the Care of Mr French

  my Wife - Daughter & myself - respectfuly
  present our Duty to M^r - Mrs Allen - to you Sir
  & your spouse - should be glad to hear of your wellfare
    Your dutifull Ser^{vt}
25   W James

CIRCUMTEXT Note of answer from other hand at bottom: '28 March 32/6 inclosed'.

451   From William James in Chelmsford to John Cooper, 20 May 1822

Chelmsford May 20 = 1822

Sir,

I trust you will Excuse, my writeing to you, but, as Overseer, I have a request to make to you, as I have afore done, to your Predecessor, &
5 which, I trust, you will also grant me

With submission, Sir, it is this, I am Peremptorily call'd on, to make good
a demand on me, by Saturday Evening next, and if not done, I shall be
troubled for it on the Monday Morning next, you will do me a great kindness,
by Advancing for me, the present Quarters Allowance, up to Midsummer
day next, in lieu of sending it to me at that time, in doing which, I hope to be   10
Able to satisfy the demand, which will prevent me much Unpleasantness,
& Expence; Relying on your kindness, for the favor I ask, I have made the
Promise so to do, & without which, I cannot Accomplish the demand,
trusting you will favor me within this week; you can if you please, send it
to me, by Clarry the Coachman, to the Care of Mr French, Ship Inn, Chelms-   15
ford, I shall have it safely -
My daughter, & Wife, continues in much the same state
Indeed Sir, I wish not to be always makeing Complaint, but work with
me, is very slack indeed, & scantily paid for, & in every respect, it is with
us, as I have generally stated to your Predecessors; Provision is not so   20
cheap here as in Colchester, we too often Experience, the sad want, of
Common necessaries, sufficient to sustain Nature, we Acknowledge, with
thankfulness, every kindness we have Received, & hope to be grateful -
I am Sir, your Hum^{le} Ser^{vt}
Wm James   25

TEXTUAL ALTERATIONS 11: will] *interl with caret.* 12: Unpleasantness] *after del* 'Unpla'.
18: makeing] *after del illeg.*

452   From William James in Chelmsford to John Cooper, 25 May 1822

Chelmsford
Sir,
Trusting you will do me the favor, I have wrote to you for - I have asked
Mr Clarry, to call on you, for a small parcle for me -
You will Excuse me so doing, but will you do me the kindness, to lett   5
me have it by him, on to Morrow Sunday - for which I shall be thankfull
Your Obed^t Hum^{le} Ser^{vt}
Wm James
Saturday May 25
1822   10

453   From William James in Chelmsford to James Allen, 28 May 1822

Chelmsford May 28 - 1822

Mr Allen,

    Sir,

    I pray your Excuse in thus troubling you, for I am under the Necessity,
5 of again Applying to you, as my Friend, - being indebted to my Landlady,
who peremptorelly, insist on having it at furthest this week, or she will
enter a distress into the House (she had spoke to one to do it last week,
but she have prolonged it this week also) and will not wait longer, and as
I cannot make a sufficiency of my self, to satisfy her; I wrote last week to
10 Mr Cooper as Overseer, stateing my Case, and Asking the favor, to advance for me, at this time, the Quarters allowance up to Midsum^r in Lieu
of it, at that time, by which means, I shall be Able at this time, to satisfy
her, & without it, I must sink, for I cannot otherwise get through it, I see
Mr Clarry this Day, he see Mr Cooper, who told him, it was not due till
15 Midsum^r & he could not pay it -

    Now Sir, I, intreat you as my Friend, take my Case into your Conside-
raton, & have the goodness, to advance for me the Quarters Money, & at
Midsumer, Receive it yourself as Repayment, it will be doing me a great
kindness - & without wich, I see no means of Avoiding Distress - I am
20 Encouraged to write to you, (though very Reluctantly,) because you told
me, if at any time I was in trouble, so to do, & what was in your power you
would do for me - and as Midsum^r is so near at hand, this I trust you will
do, If so, will you sent it, by Mr Clarry, who will be up, on Thurs^y, & Satur^y
I know you do not like much Intreating, but I do not know a Friend, who
25 would be so ready, to do this for me, as yourself, I forbear to say more,
and I could not say less =

    my Wife & daughter continues much the same & Work is very Slack
indeed

    I will see Clarry on Thursday, & if I do not hear from you then, will see
30 him again on Saturday / I hope no Offence

              Our Joint Duty to you Sir&
              M^{rs} A - M^r & Mrs Bryant
              Yours Obediently W James

T EXTUAL ALTERATIONS 10-11: advance] 'ce' *interl at end of line.* 15: Midsum^r] '^{r}' *interl at end of line.*

454   From William James in Chelmsford to [James] Allen, 29 July 1822

Chelmsford July 29 - 1822

Sir

I am sorry, and it is painfull to me, to trouble you again, you will pardon me for so doing - it is pressing Necessity, Compels me to state, that I have made every possible Effort, in my power, to procure a maintainance, and support, while I have been in Chelmsford, and have held out to this   5
time, aided by the Generous assistance, obtained for me, by your kind inteference, in my behalf, which have not been in vain, but admidst all Privation, and Exertion, that I can use, I find I cannot, with any Effect, proceed furthur, work being so Slack, that as I before mentioned, I have not half employ, and im many weeks I have had nothing to do - I do not 10
mean successive weeks - I have been Living in hope, that work would have revived, but tis not so, but gets worse; much are we Obliged, to some kind Friends in Chelmsford, for Yielding us a generous support, or we could not have borne up so long as we have, for many weeks past, sometimes work, & sometimes none, my Earnings have been but small, 15
not more on Avarage, than six Shillings, or six, and six pence, a week, as near as I can tell - (I may say for some Months this have been my case) with which we cannot procure Necessaries, to support health nor Nature, for the want of which, I find health and strength decaying fast, so that when I have a little work to do, I find myself, through Age, and fatigue, 20
incapable to perform it, Walking into the Country five or six Miles in a morning, working the Day, and returning home at Night, is a task that I cannot, but without great dificulty perform, several times I have thought, I could not gett home, and it have been the Occasion, of my being Ill, for two or three days, this I attribute, in a great degree, to the want, of con- 25
stant Nourishment, to keep up my strength, and of Age aded there too, being now within one Year of Seventy - at this time I am Unwell, and have been several days -

My Wife, have for a long time, been very week, and feeble, as I have formerly stated, but now I am sorry to say, have been very Ill indeed for 30
some weeks, and I believe, chiefly owing to the want of proper nourishment, to support her Nature, which we cannot procure, she have, since last Thursday sennight, been wholly laid aside, and not Able to keep up, nor walk across the room till Saturday last, being so faint and week, at her stomach, and Inside, and so full of pain, she is somewhat better, but I 35
cannot suppose, she will regain her strength, nor do I think her time to be

long in this world, Age is without doubt one cause, being now in her 74
Year

My Daughter continues much in the same state, sometimes better, and
40 then worse again, she have on the whole, for some little time been better,
but is now worse again

In makeing this statement, Sir, I hope not to Offend, I know not to whom,
I can so freely Communicate my Condition, as to you, who have been my
friend, and I hope for its continuance, I thank you and the Gentlemen for
45 every favor received, I wish not to be troublesome Necessity compels me,
to ask for assistance, for aded to the above statement, we are literally in a
perishable state, I have not now one Job to do nor one Shilling, to help
ourselves with, could I have walked, I would have to Colchester, to have
stated my Case, but I cannot - nor can I pay for Rideing - Permit me, Sir,
50 to Ask for some Immediate, Temporary Assistance to be afforded to us,
we are much in want, and stand in great need at this time, it have been
suggested to me, to ask for some regular Allowance, in Addition to that
Allowed for my Daughter, on Consideration, of so much lying on my
hands, and not being Able to support it, not even with the Assistance, of
55 Friends here, which have been generous indeed, but that we cannot always
expect -

After this statement, in which I could have been more brief, I must leave
our cause in your hands, and Consideration, trusting you will procure, and
send something for our present relief -
60 We humbly pray, that you and the Gentlemen, will take it into Consideration, and Yeild us some furthur Aid, for our support, we must leave it to
your own feelings, and kindness, without which, sure I am, we cannot
Exist much longer, should it be wished for us to come home to our own
Parish, I know not how it can be Accomplished, and indeed Sir, provided
65 it can be ordered so, as for us to continue here, we shall be thankfull, and
that on many Considerations, which would be tiresome to state, I fear I
am too much so, as it is -

I hope nothing I have said, will be Misconstrued, I know that writeing
is too apt so to be -
70 I asked the Revd Mr Wards advise, stated my case to him, he Offerd to
write for me, which have done, and I have here Inclosed it, to you, he
have been very kind on many Occasions -

It will be a great kindness to let us hear from you as soon as convenient -
My Wife, and Daughter with myself
75   Present, Dutifull Respects

I am Sir your Hum^{le} Ser^{vt}

Wm James

If - Sir, this Application does not meet your Approbation, I will thank you, for Information, what course is best for me persue -

TEXTUAL ALTERATIONS 14: have borne] *interl with caret.* 18: which] *interl with caret.* 61: to] *interl with caret.* 66: tiresome] *final* 'e' *interl at end of line.*

RELATED CORRESPONDENCE Possibly knowing this letter itself, but certainly knowing of it, J.G. Ward, rector of Chelmsford, wrote to James Allen, overseer of St Peter, Colchester, on the same day: 'I have undertaken to second W. James's application to you by stating what I know concerning him. The family maintains here a very exellent character by the whole of their conduct. He seems most industrious, & anxious for work. But the scarcity of work, & his own growing infirmities make it impossible for him to support his family. They want, one & all of them, more nourishment than they can get. The wife is quite weighed down with age & weakness. The daughter's lengthened affliction renders her an object of the greatest compassion. On the whole, I can conscientiosly recommend them to your notice for such assistance as the Parish may think fit.'

455 From James Howell in Ely to the overseers and churchwardens in St Peter, Colchester, July 1822

Ely   July   1822

Gentlman now if you Please I Should be Glad if you will be So Good as to Sand that Small trifel of money wich is a lowed me per year two pound Gentlman is all that i Get but Gentlman be So Good as to add a small trifel to that for my Wife now lays in and that maks hus Six Children and   5
five of them is under a elven years of age and I find it wary hard to Get on Gentlman be So Good as to rite as soon as You Can as you now I Cannot travel one Day after the mounth is out if i do I Shall be taken up and Put to prison as I Cannot Pay the Penalty of ten Pounds

I ham your Humbl   10

Servant James Howell

Broad Street Ely

Cambridge Shire

TEXTUAL ALTERATIONS 2: Should] *after del* 'r'. 8: Put] 'P' *over illeg.*

456   From James Howell in Ely to the overseers and church-wardens in St Peter, Colchester, 5 August 1822

Ely 5th August 1822

Gentlman I rote about a fortnight a goe Consarning the money wicth is alowed me per year but never reseved any but never failed sanding before the Larst time that I was in Colchester the Gentlman tould me that
5 I had better rite for it then to Come So many miles for it Gentlman I have six Children and the way I Get them bread is by Carring a fue things to sell about the Country I have Lived in the town a long wile and by been nowen I have the Goods in Creadett but Gentlman i ham oblidged to have a licences to Carry them and it is not in my power to get them my Sulf
10 Gentlman my Licences was due the first of auguest and I Dear not go one Day with out them if I do I Shall be taking up and put to prison and then my Children will whant for bread Gentlman if you look in the book you will find that two pounds is what I have per year towards the four that is what I hav to pay for the Licences Gentleman pray rite by return of post
15 as i dear not Go one Day out and i donot now any thing else to Get a liven
by
sir
I Ham your Humble Servant
James Howell broad Street
20 Ely Cambridge shire

TEXTUAL ALTERATIONS 2: goe] 'g' *over* 'G'. 2: wicth] 'c' *over illeg.* 4: the] 't' *over illeg.* 8: nowen] *last* 'n' *interl at end of line.* 8: Gentlman] *last* 'n' *interl at end of line.* 11: up] *after del illeg.* 11: prison] 's' *over illeg.*

457   From William James in Chelmsford to John Cooper in Colchester, 30 September 1822

Chelmsford Sepr 30 = 1822

Sir,

I thank you for the last favor, of one Pound you sent to me, it was a great relief; I stated my Case to you at that time; I have had some Employment,
5 since then, though not more than I than stated; could I help it, I would not ask for a single Shilling - I use every endeavor in my power; but Sir, with sorrow I say it, with a Debilitated Wife, & an Afflicted Daughter, I cannot

provide common Necessaries; I know what you wrote to me last, but I know not what I shall do -

I have asked Clarry to call on you, by whom I humbly trust, you will send 10 the Quarter Allowance, for my Daughter, I reserve that as a part for my Rent, but not being half sufficient, for the half Year that I owe; I hope you will consider me, and let me have something more, by way of assistance, to inable me to do it, indeed Sir, I cannot of myself = Pray Sir, do not be angry with me, I so much feel the Infirmities of Age, that I cannot do, as 15 I should be glad to do -

I must again leave my Case with you -

          I am Sir Yours Obediently

              Wm James

direct for me   20
to the Care of
Mr French
Ship Inn
    Chelmsford
If you Sir, will favor me, by Clarry on Thursday on which day he comes 25 up I will thank you, as I will then endeavor to see him

TEXTUAL ALTERATIONS 26: up] *interl with caret.*
    CIRCUMTEXT Note from John Cooper on outside: 'Quarters allowance due at Mich^s [£]1-12-6'.

458   From Mary Martin in Ipswich [13 December 1822]

Sir/

I hope you will excuse my sending these few Lines to inform you I have not receiv'd the Money due to me for Henry Martin. as I am inform'd Mrs Disney has left the House, would be much Oblig'd to you if you would inform me who I am to receive it from - the 10 weeks pay was due 5 last friday 13th which is 1 £ and you will much oblige your Hum Servt M. *Martin*

Please to direct to Mary
Martin at Mr Greens
    Angel Lane St Clements   10
        Ipswich

DATE Date of note of receipt on back.

RELATED CORRESPONDENCE Mary Martin's son Henry Martin was an illegitimate child for whom she received a regular allowance from the parish of St Peter, Colchester, which in turn received payments of 1s 6d per week from his father Henry Bloomfield. There is a long series of letters from him concerning his payments which he often requested to postpone (letters from Henry Bloomfield in Ipswich of 3 November 1819, 11 February 1820, 16 May 1820, 24 July 1820, 30 January 1821, 8 March 1821, 1 May 1821, 30 July 1821, 29 August 1821, 20 March 1823, 15 April 1823, 21 October 1823, 10 January 1824, 22 January 1824, and four undated letters).

459 From George Rowe in Bocking [Essex] to the overseer of St Peter, Colchester, 10 January 1823

Jen^y 10 1823

Sir

I have Sent you fue Lines to State the Setewation that I am in at this time for the Last tine that I was over I tated to you the afflction that my
5 Wife Labord Under but a 18 Weeks agoe on Sunday in a fue howrs was quite Deprived of her Pressus Site wich I am forst to have one to Do for her and wich makes it heavey for Me that I Do Not know What to Do the Last time I Revesed ^{s}4 for the Rats wich 1 Quarter I paid and to Last Quarter Day thear is 2 Quarters Due and in the State that I am in I Cannot
10 pay it for Week Day and Night was a Continull Expence to yours the Meens but to No Effect for She will Never See to No more in this World I have Stated my afflicion and I must Leve it to your Considerration the 2 Quarters Due is ^{s}7.^{d}6

From Me George Rowe
15   Bocking

TEXTUAL ALTERATIONS 8: for] *after del illeg.*
CIRCUMTEXT Note from Samuel Golding, overseer of Bocking, on next page, confirming George Rowe's account.

460 From Benjamin Hewitt in Whitton, Suffolk, to the overseer of St Peter, Colchester, 20 January 1823

1823 Janr 20

Sur i have sent you thease few lines to in form you that i can not make out any longer with out i have some releif for my whife have been ill so long and the weather have been so bad that i have not had any thing to do

for this last month only now and then a little mending and that fourteen 5
shillings that you gave me when i was over thear did not go fer towards
the midwhife and nurce for i have had a nurce for this last month and the
last three months i have had a woaman to wash and to do for my famly
and i am be hind of my rent one pound up to last mickelmas and if you
send me one pound i will try and make out the winter for my land lord 10
come and told me that if i ded not give him some money this week he
would destress me for he say he want some money and some he would
have and i hope you will send me one pound if not send me word and i
will come over direct to me if you pease
                Benjamin Hewitt whitton   15
                Near ipswich suffolk

TEXTUAL ALTERATIONS 2: form] 'fo' *over illeg.*
  CIRCUMTEXT Note from other hand at bottom of page: 'Paid by H H Hayward'.
  RELATED CORRESPONDENCE On 23 April 1822 John Goldsmith, overseer of Whitton, had
written to the overseer of St Peter, Colchester, about Benjamin Hewitt: 'i believe He is for
His worke Ly so much a monge the workeing Hand that we have Done His Work there is
no money for it. I Belief He Has a Good Deale of Trouble after a few shilling wen he Has
Earnt it.'

461   From William James in Chelmsford to James Allen, 25 February 1823

Chelmsford Feb^{ry} 25 = 1823
Sir,
    I trust when you read my statement, you will Excuse me, in writeing to
you -
    on Wednesday last I wrote to   5
Mr Cooper stateing my case, praying him to lay the Address, I sent to
him; Addressed to the Minister, ChurchWardens, Overseers, and Gentle-
men, of the Parish, before them, humbly Intreating to take my Case into
Consideration not supposing, it could be done immediately, but if Possible to
Afford me some Immediate relief, as I had not Money, nor a Job to do, 10
and my Wife, in a very Infirm state, I was in Expectation of hearing from
Mr Cooper to day by Clarry, but did not - pray Sir will, you enquire of M^r
Cooper he can shew you my statement -
    Sir, I ask pardon for troubling you, as since I wrote to Mr Cooper, I have
to Inform you of a great change in my Wife, who is much worse, and have 15
been Obliged to take to her Bed, ever since Friday, and we do think cannot

recover, Doct^r Miller, have been to see her Yesterday, and to day, he is of
Opinion she cannot, we are much distress'd, for I have not six pence to
procure any thing with, tis a heart rending Case to us, will you, Sir, have
20 the goodness, to speak to Mr Cooper, or any thing you think proper, and if
possible, to procure some tempory relief, to be convey'd to us, by Clarry,
as he returns up on Wednesday Morning; I will ask him to call on M^r
Cooper for it, as I know not any step, I can take but this - I would not have
wrote, but through the greatest distress - I thought it best to send by the
25 Post, and would have paid the Postage, but had not six pence to pay it with
I find myself Ill to day, having had no rest, these three Nights,
              Our duty to you Sir, Mrs Allen - &
              Family
                  I am Your Hum^{le} Ser^{vt}
30   Wm James

TEXTUAL ALTERATIONS 9: Consideration] *final* 'on' *interl at end of line.* 17: Doct^r] 'o' *over
superscript* 'r'.

462   From William James in Chelmsford to [James] Allen, 26 February 1823

Sir   Chelmsford Feb^{ry} 26 = 1823
    This is with mine, and Daughters Duty to you, and Mrs Allen, thanks
for every favor -
    My dear Wife is now no more, she departed this Life, Yesterday,
5 Wednesday, about half past, two O'Clock in the Afternoon, I Received a
Letter, with a one Pound Note, from Mr Hayward, for which, we were
thankfull, not having, one penny, to help ourselves with, - I did not expect,
her to have gone so soon, but had no hopes of her recovery - she is now
gone to rest, I hope you will Excuse, my again writeing to you, but looking,
10 to you as a Friend, I am encouraged, being now, by her Death, surrounded
with difficulties respecting her funeral, the Expences of which, I am
unable to defray, I hope it will be considered, and something furthur, granted
to Assist me in it, to inable me to bury my dead, I am sorry to make this
Application, but Sir may I ask you to Apply for me = this one application,
15 after another, I know is great, and Unpleasant = I hope any Inconsistance,
will be passed by my Grief and Confusion is very great more than half of

the one pound, was gone before I Received, it, having been Obliged to be
Credited, before I Received it,

Our thankfull Duty to

you & Mrs Allen

W & A James

20

TEXTUAL ALTERATIONS 16: will] *after del* 'I hope'. 17: the] *interl with caret.* 18: be] *after
del* 'having'.

463 From George Rowe in Bocking [Essex] to the overseer of St Peter, Colchester, 21 March 1823

March 21.1823

Sir

I have Sent you a Line wich I hope you will Not take it a miss to inform
you that the Overcear Call for a Quaters Rate wich is ˢ3 Due up to the 25
of this Mounth wich I hope the Gentelemen will Send it for the Overcear 5
Say it Must be Paid Next Week as the year is out and then if you Pleas
thay will taket ½ yearly and that will make It Come Rite with the year
and Less Truble for you for the State that my Wife is in of Blindness I am
forst to have me to Do for Uss wich I am Not Able to pay it wich I wold
wich to Do all I Can for her and Not to Truble you No more then I Can 10
help but it is a heavey afflition for She and me

from me

George Rowe Bocking

TEXTUAL ALTERATIONS 4: Overcear] 'O' *over illeg.*

464 From William James in Chelmsford to Mr Hayward, 25 March 1823

Chelmsford March 25th = 1823

Sir,

You will do me a kindness, to have the goodness, in sending me the
Quarterly Allowance, by Mr Clarry, whom I have asked to call on you, -
I here express my thanks, for the favor, done me, in that you sent me to 5
Assist, in the Expences, for the Burial of my Wife, I could not clear my

way, and am somewhat in debt, on that account, and had nothing left to
subsist upon -
       I have at this time a fery little Jobs to do, but I really think, Nay, I may
10 safely say, that unless, you make me, some Allowance, more than I have,
I must come home, I am willing to do all I can,
       My daughter continues much in the same Afflicted state, - at present I
am very Indiferent, but hope to gett better - my Expences, certainly will
not be so much as they were, but my Earnings, will not be equal to my
15 Necessary wants -
       I am thankfull Sir, for every favor, and with Gratitude make my
Acknowledgments - and hope not to offend -
                    I am Sir, & Gentlemen,
                    Your Hum^{le} Ser^{vt}
20   Wm James

CIRCUMTEXT Note at bottom of outside, from same hand as letter: 'by Mr Clarry'.

465   From Joseph Thoroughgood in London to Robert Alden in St Peter, Colchester, 5 May 1823

London May 5th 1823

Sur{
       Having Bean Informed by my Parish that you have bean Pleased to take
one Shilling out of Few of the allowence that you ware Pleased to allow
5   me when I Left hom with my famley you made not that I Should Steate
the vagens I Receve for you know Long ago and I ham Sorry at this tim to
Inform you that Since Christmes my master is Dead and the young Gentleman are Going to Give up Bisness and in that account I Should be
oblidge to Seek a fresh master and ware to find one at this time I dont
10 know for ther are meny out of work at this tim and I ham Sure I Cannot
Surport my famly unless I ham in work But the matter is this if I Cannot
Get a Living hear I Can do as meny man do I must Com home for the
Provisons are Rising Every Day and Instead of taking any thing [of] I
was Going to ask for Sumthing to Pay the Docters Bill with for I have had
15 my youngest Child under the Docters hands for the Last munth But I hop
that you will Conceeder my famly and But that Shilling on again as I dont
Ask for no more at this tim for I Can ashur you that I dont enjoye a Good

State of health mysulf for I have Lost a Deal of tim this winter thrugh
Being Ill
 I Should be oblidge to you to Let me know the Answer as Soon as you 20
Can my mother will Rite Next week
So I Remain yours
   Joseph Thoroughgood

TEXTUAL ALTERATIONS 4: allowence] 'ce' *interl at end of line.* 6: for] *interl.* 9: master] 'ter'
*interl at end of line.*12: as] *after del illeg.* 18: mysulf] *after del illeg.*

**466 From Benjamin Hewitt in Whitton, Suffolk, to the overseer of
   St Peter, Colchester, 6 June [1823]**

June 6
 Sur i hav sent you a few lines to in form you that i have but a little work
now and they come to me for the poors rate from last mickelmas and i
cannot pay it and they sommods me on the hall this week and i must pay
it with in a few days or els they will destress me for it so i hope you will 5
send me a little money and if not i must come over for i have no work
now not at this time for things being so deer that make it a grate deal
wons for me for the poor cannot spare any money for shoes now
     Benjamin Hewitt
     Whitton near ipswich   10
     Suffolk

TEXTUAL ALTERATIONS 3: they] 't' *over illeg.* 7: not] *after del illeg.* 8: cannot] *after del
illeg.*
DATE Year from filing note on outside.

**467 From Benjamin Hewitt in Whitton, Suffolk, to the overseers of
   St Peter, Colchester, 17 June 1823**

1823 June 17
 Sur i have sent you thoes few lines to in form you that if you do not send
me One pound betwen this and munday i must come home with my famly
for i have no work nor no money and the rate must be paid before next
teusday and i cannot pay it if you do not send me it and if you do not send 5
it me i must come home for work on monday or els for releife and if you

send it me i will try and ceep a way till mickelmas and then i expect i must
come home for i cannot pay rent and rates to

Benjamin Hewitt

10   Whitton Near ipswich

Suffolk

TEXTUAL ALTERATIONS 5: cannot] *after del illeg.*

468   From William James in Chelmsford, 25 June 1823

Chelmsford June 25 = 1823

Sir=

I beg your Excuse, for my writeing to you again, I know not to whom
else I can write, as who are Overseers I know not, and I am sorry to
5 trouble you, Sir, in makeing Application, for the Quartyly Allowance
granted me, it will be a kindness done me, could I have it on Saturday, by
Mr Clarry, as he Comes up, on that Morning, I will ask him to call on you,
for that purpose - I have had a little work to do, and now have at this time,
but have been in Embarrasment, ever since the death of my Wife, and
10 cannot overcome it, if Sir, something could be done for me, at this time,
by way of assistance, it would be of great use to me, as I am behind, in
both Rent, and poor rates; I made Application to excuse me the rates,
which in past was granted me but not to the full; and I have paid one; and
I now am Indebted two, and the Overseers have been with me, and say, I
15 must go on paying, or they must bring me home, I am willing to do all I
can, but I cannot pay them, my strength, and all my faculties, fail me very
fast and I have been, and am very Unwell, my daughter continues much
the same, we are thankfull for every favor,

Duty to You, Mrs Allen - &

20   Your Hum^le Ser^vt

W- James

Please to direct for me
to the care of Mr French

TEXTUAL ALTERATIONS 7: as] *after del* 'on Saturday'. 13: which in past was granted me]
interl with caret.

469   From Benjamin Hewitt in Whitton, Suffolk, 30 June [1823]

June 30

Gentelman i have sent you word that if you do not send me some money
by return of post that i must come home with my famley directly for i
have not had any thing to do this last six weeks not a bove 2 or 3 shillings
a week and i have pauned till i cannot paun any longer and i have not got   5
any Whittels <n>or yet any money i will swar<--> <----> do not know
what i shall for whittels till you send me some
     Benjamin Hewitt Whitton
     Near Ipswich Suffolk

DATE Year from filing note on outside.

**470   From George Craddock in Westminster, London, to Robert
Alden in St Peter, Colchester, 16 July 1823**

Mr Alden
    Sir

I wrote to you last week Stating that I was in Great distress owing to the
want of Employment And that I expected to have Asituation Verry Shortly
But as I have not had Any Answer I now make this Aplication to you   5
when I left Colchester you promised that in Case of Real Distress you
would Send me Some Relief I have Got aplace to go to on the 28th of this
month But without asistance from you I shall be Oblidged to leave London before that time as I have not at this time ashilling to Buy Victuals
for my Self and family I hope you will Lay this my aplication Before the   10
Gentlemen of the parrish that they may Consider And Send me Some
Relief as Soon as posable and as you promised to Send me atrifle to Buy
afew Goods with as Soon as I was Settled I am In hopes I shall be Settled
for agood while and I will not troble you any farther pleas God I have my
health while I remain in London or if I can posably help it for years But if   15
I should be Oblidged to leave London under my preasent Circumstances
I shall be forced to part with what few things I have I hope therefore the
Gentlemen will Consider this my aplication and Send me Such Relief as
they think proper I stated in my former aplication that the Gentlemen of
this place told me if I aplied at all to them they Should Send me home   20
     I remain Sir you Verry Humble And Most
     Obedent Servant George Craddock

To Mr Robt Alden Colchester
                              London July 16 - 1823
25 p<lease to> Direct To
    <George C>raddock
    N° 99 Chapter Street
    Regent Street Horseferry
    Road Westminster

TEXTUAL ALTERATIONS 14: and] 'n' *over* 's'.

471   From James Howell in Ely to the overseers and churchwardens of St Peter, Colchester, 4 August 1823

Ely august 4 1823
   Gentlman i right to informe that my old licences is out and i dear not
travel one day without anew one from the first of august and you Gentlman
alow me two Pound per year towards Gettinge anewone my famely is Six
5 but the oldes Child at fifteen is out at Servis So i have but five at home
and the oldes of thum is but twelve years so i find it wer hard to Get them
all foode Gentlman Plese to rite by return of Post as i dear not star one
day without my Licences if i do i Shall be taken up and but to Prison as i
Cannot Pay the Pantley of 10 Pounds Gentlman Plese to help me all you
10 Can for it wold be Wery hard if i was Put into Prison a way from my
family Gentlman iwll not trubel you but once ayear
Sir
I ham Your Humbel Servant
James Howell broad Street
15   Ely Cambridge Shire

TEXTUAL ALTERATIONS 8: i Shall] 'i' *interl.* 11: iwll] 'll' *interl.*

472   From William James in Chelmsford to [James] Allen, 28 September 1823

                              Chelmsford Sepr 28 = 1823
  Sir,
   I trust you will Excuse, my writeing to you, not knowing who are the
Overseers at this time,

I will thank you, Sir, to do me the kindness, to obtain the Quarters Allow-   5
ance for me, If you permit it, to be Left with you for me, I will ask Clarry
to call at your Shop for it, he will come up again, on Tuesday, at which
time, I will see him; by this means no Expence will attach to it, -

My Daughter is at this time, much worse than she have been for some
time past, not able to be about, these last three weeks; a Surcession <of>   10
Blissters, have been Applied to her side, for the las<t> fortnight past, up
to this day, which is still open, she is a great suferer, she requests her
dutifull Respects, to Mrs Allen, your self, and friends, to which I add
mine also,

Under the Gratefullest Obligation   15
I am Sir, and Gentlemen, Your
Hum^{ble} Ser^{vt} W- James

TEXTUAL ALTERATIONS 15: Gratefullest] 'r' *over* 'a'.

473   Fom George Rowe in [Great] Coggeshall [Essex], 8 November 1823

Nov^b 8 1823

Sir

I have Sent you a Line to Say that the Oversear Call for the Rats this
Week and he Say that he Chant Waite No Longer then Monday for he
will Strain for them I Shold have Been over Last Friday but the Weather   5
was So bad and my Wife Continews Blind that out of 6 Shilling a Week
I Cannot pay them I am forst to have my Daughter at home to Do for her
and my Rent is Gest 5£ a year thear for I hope the Gentelman will think of
it and Send me Word by Redgrift to Night for if thay Do Not I Canott
Continnew wear I am   10

George Rowe

Coggeshall

the Rates Due up to Last Mickelmas is a ½ Year wich is ^s6.^d6

474   From George Rowe in [Great] Coggeshall [Essex] to the over-seer of St Peter, Colchester, 16 November [1823]

Nov^b 16

Sir

I have Sent you a Line wich I am Sorrey to Truble you for the Rates but
I forst to it wich Sent Last Saterday but Did Not Receve No answer so
5 that the Gentealman Gave me a Nother Week to See what you wold Do
wich hope the Gentealman will take it into Considerration and Send me
and answer by Return of Van wich Sets out at 3 oclock wich will Spear
me the time to Come over George Rowe Coggeshall

TEXTUAL ALTERATIONS 4: so] 's' *over* 'S'. 8: the] *interl.*
DATE Year from filing note on outside.
RELATED CORRESPONDENCE On 19 March 1824 Samuel Golding, overseer of Braintree,
wrote to the overseer of St Peter, Colchester, concerning George Rowe: 'The Destresses of
the Poor man threw the offliction of the wife Compells the man to Call on you for Sum
Pecuniary assistance - and in Consideration of the steady and indusrious Character which
they have in the Noughbourhood In Duceness me to write for them The man works at
Coggeshall and has To Pay his Logeing there and his wife been quite Blind with the
Kings Evell in her fase that She Can do the Poor man no Good as to Labour . and he is in
arer of one Half years Rate - and I believe has no means of Paying it without your assistance'.

475   From William James in Chelmsford to Robert Alden, overseer of St Peter, Colchester, 14 December 1823

Chelmsford Decr 14 = 1823

Mr Alden,

Sir,

In Conformity to your instruction to me, when I see you in Chelmsford,
5 I apply to you, and the Gentlemen of the parish - I have to state, that my
Daughter have been very bad, for many weeks past, and under the Doct^rs
hands, but is now better than she have been you will be doing me a kindness, to send me the Quarterly allowance, up to X^tss day next, and for
which I will thank you; I ask it as a favor; by Mr Clarry the Coachmen,
10 who comes up this week, Wednesday, Friday, & Sunday If you please to
convay it to him; as I cannot ask him, to come down to you, as you do not
live in his path, direct for me as Usual -
To the care of Mr French - Ship Inn = Chelmsford
I am your Hum^le Ser^vt
15   Wm James

TEXTUAL ALTERATIONS 7: be] *after del* 'being'. 8: allowance] 'a' *over illeg.*

476 From George Craddock in Westminster, London, to Robert Alden, 19 January 1824

London Jany 19th 1824

Mr Aldon

you Sent me word that if I could not make out to Get alivelyhood without trobling the parrish for releif I was to Come again to Colchester I hope therefore you will send me word if I am to Come or Send me atrifle 5 of money as I have not Been able to follow my imployment for these three weeks and I cannot Suport my Self and family without your assistance I should rather Remain if you will help me when in distress as my employer will not take another man in my place if I am not able to go to work for amonth longer I should not have trobled you now nor any other 10 time if please God I might have my health Neither Should I have trobled you so Soon now if my own sickness had Been all but my wife have been Verry ill for Six weeks and not able to go out of doors and Both my Children have had the small pox Verry Bad Indeed and not hardly recoverd yet which altogether have Brought me Verry low I hope therefore you will 15 have the goodness to Send me an answer as Soon as posable and I must act as you Directs me and Remain you Verry

Humble and obedient Servant

Georg Craddock

= Please to Derict =   20

To George Craddock

99 Chapter Street

Regent Street

Westminster London

I received the pound you Sent me in July Last for which I Send you and 25 the Gentlemen of the parish my Sincere thanks.

**477   From William James in Chelmsford to Robert Alden, over-
seer of St Peter, Colchester, 24 January 1824**

Chelmsford Jan^(ry) 24 = 1824

Mr Alden,

   Through necessity I am compeled, to make application, to you, and the
Gentlemen of the Parish
5   For three weeks past, I have had a Violent pain in my Right Arm, and
the last fortnight, have been unable to do any work, it being so weak and
painfull, as not to be Able to raise it up, but hope it will soon be better, I
have not been Able to earn, one Shill^g, this last fortnight, and at this time
without the means of subsistance, I ask the favor for some temporary
10 relief, which I hope will be granted to me, of your goodness, for which, I
shall be thankfull I leave my case to your consideration, and trust something will be done for me, for the present =
                                  I am Gentlemen
                                     Yours Obediently
15   Wm James

   Please to send to me by
   Clarry y^e Coachman -
   to the care of Mr French
   Ship Inn - Chelmsford -

TEXTUAL ALTERATIONS 11: and] 'a' *over illeg.*

**478   From William James in Chelmsford to [James] Allen in Col-
chester, 7 February 1824**

Chelmsford Feb^(ry) 7 = 1824

Sir

   With much reluctance I write to you again, not wis<hin>g to trouble
you, and did not Necessity comple me, I would not do it, I trust you will
5 Excuse me -
   When Mr Alden was at Chelmsford I see him, and when he last wrote to
me, he said if I had Ocasion to write, to send to him, as Overseer -
   I wrote to Mr Alden on Thursday Sennight last stating the Necessity, I
was then under, of makeing Application, for some present relief, which I
10 hoped, by the goodness of the Gentemen, would be granted to me, as at

that time, I for three weeks past, had so Violent a pain in my Right Arm, and weakness, as disabled me from doing my work, (since that time, a blisster, have been Applied, but at present, I am not Able to work, nor raise it upwards) I asked the favor, for some tempory relief, as I was then without means of subsistance, and must have been, all this last week, had 15 it not been, for a friend, and this day I came to my last six pence, I hope something will be done for me, for the present, but as Mr Alden have not sent, nor wrote to me, I am under the necessity of writeing to you, not knowing who else to apply to - I hope I shall in time get better, and if Sir, any thing can be done for me, by communicating my case, I shall be 20 thankfull, as I am on all Occasions -

I am Sir & Gentlemen

Your Hum^le Ser^vt W James

479 From William James in Chelmsford to Robert Alden, overseer of St Peter, Colchester, 1 March 1824

Mr Alden,   Chelmsford March 1 = 1824
  Sir,

I am Sorry, to be under the same necessity of writeing, as I was, when I wrote to you in Jan^ry last, & to Mr Allen, on the 7th of Feb^ry, I therein stated, my Condition, & Necessity, the reason of my Incapacity for work, 5 Ocasioned by a strain, in the Nerves of my Arm, and Rheumatism falling into it, which still continues; on Saturday, I was reduced to the same straight as then, having expended my little all - and have nothing more to subsist on, I am under the necissity of makeing (which I hope will be granted), some further Application, till I get better, which I hope will not be long, I 10 return my thanks, to the Gentlemen, for what was done for me which I received safe, I am not willing to make application only by you, as you told me so to do, n<or> would I make any, at no time, did not necessity co<mpel> me, I have done the best I can do, I hope you will not delay, to use such means, as you deem proper, I trust the Gentlemen will afford some furthur 15 relief, as I know not what to do, nor what step more proper for me to take, if there be, I will be thankfull for Information, as I would not do any thing to give Offence, If I must come home, to my Parrish, I must, I must do - something, all the last week, I had not, nor now have, half sufficient to support Nature,   20

I am with duty, & Gratitude
Your Hum^{le} Ser^{vt}
W James

TEXTUAL ALTERATIONS 18: must,] 's' *over* 't'.

480   From Benjamin Hewitt in Whitton, Suffolk, to the overseer of St Peter, Colchester, 23 March 1824

1824

Gentelmen i hope you will send me one pound towards my rent for if
you do i will Make a friend and borrow some to make it All right up to the
25 of march for if You do i will not ask you for any more All the summer
5 and if not i shal be Forst to leave my house for my landlord Say if i do not
pay all up at the 25 i Shall leave it Directly for i cannot Make it up with
out you send me one pound & gentelmen i hope you will try it Once more
and i will try all i can to Ceepe of you for now the sumer is a Comen an i
hope i shall have more work please to let me have it on the 25 if You do
10 send it

please to Derect to Benjamin
Hewitt Whitton Suffolk
March the 23

481   From William James in Chelmsford to Robert Alden, overseer of St Peter, Colchester, 30 March 1824

Chelmsford March 30 = 1824

Mr Alden,
    Sir

With great reluctance, and contrary to my own feelings, I am under the
5 Necessity, of writeing to you again, Impressed with gratitude for every
favor Received - Having stated my Case fully in preceding Letters, you,
with myself, will deem it Unnecessary and tiresom, to go over the same
ground again, I well know, what you said in your last Letter, and Indeed
Sir, I would not now, nor at any time, make Application, if urgent neces-
10 sity did not compel me, but what am I to do, when in distress; I can only
say, that my Inability for work still continues, yet my Arm is getting

better, so as I have, a little more use in my hand, but not so as to be Able
to do work of any consequence, had it not been for a friend or two, I could
not, subsisted as I have, at this time, I have not six pence, to help myself,
and I cannot at present work for any, but hope I shall in a short time I will 15
thank you, to have the kindness, to send the Quarterly Allowance, this
week, which is Allowed for my Daughter she have been, for the most
part, of the last week totally laid aside, and is but little better now, shall
be thankfull for the advance, of a few shillings more for present support,
without which I know not, what I shall do, as I always make a reserve of 20
the Quarterly money, for rent so that I cannot, take from that, a single
shilling, If you will have the goodness, at this time, to make it up two
Pound, it will be a kindness done me, were I Able to Provide for myself,
I would not be burdensom on you - Indeed, at my Age, Too much feel the
decays of Nature I am thankfull, I am Able to do at my work, as I do, & 25
gladly will I do what I can -

I hope and trust, the Gentlemen will condesend, to give me some furthur
assistance, in my present necessitous, Situation

I am with bounden Gratitude

Gentlemen = Your Hum^{le} Ser^{vt}   30

Wm James

Sir
Please to send to me
as before, by Mr Clarry
Coachman = to the Care   35
of Mr French = Ship Inn
      Chelmsford

TEXTUAL ALTERATIONS 7: Unnecessary] 'ry' *interl at end of line*. 15: time] 'e' *interl at end of line*.

482 From James Howell in Ely to the parish officers of St Peter, Colchester, 16 April 1824

Gentlemen I hope your goodness - will pardon my Liberty in Sending this
Letter as you will find it is upon a particular Occasion - I know Our a
greement where not to trouble you only once a year yet upon this present
Business I flatter my Self that you will do the favour that I must beg of
you to Comply with - my Eldest Son have been in a School where they 5

put poor Boys Out to a Trade - but it depends upon great Intrest when they dont belong to the Town the Gentlemen at Ely are So kind as to take it in Consideration - Our great family 6 Children - which is a Large Concern to Support - yet not in Our power to do So well by them as we Could
10 wish - now Gentlemen the matter Lays with you to assist in a few necessary Cloathing for our poor Boy as it really is not in our power to get any for him - Sutable to aplace Our Ely Gentlemen will do us that Kindness to put him Out apprentice to a Trade and give the Sum of Twenty pound with him but his master expects to have him Cloath'd in a decent manner
15 and then he will provide necessarys dureing his apprenticeship - how Can we posibley miss such an Opportunity - for the Benifit of our poor Boy and as I have Stated to you Gentlemen Our Situation - upon this Subject hope the Lord will Send us a friend to help us through Our Business - for we Esteem it a Very great favour in doing such a kindness, I would have
20 Come Over my Self but my wife being in the family way I Could not So Conveniently Leave Home I have two more Boys in the Same School <an>d we are in great hopes with their good behaviour to get the Chance a gain - pray Gentlemen, grant this great favour to make our poor Boy decent to go Into a respectable family Mr Garret Grocer is One of the
25 Feffoes to the Charity - and you may Send an Order to him if you please to do the kindness - as Our Ely Gentlemen is willing to do So great a favour we dont like to Intrude in asking for apparal, and without he have necessarys provided he will not be able to go to the place hope your goodness will Imediately Send an answer, which if you please may - direct
30 Your Letter to Mr Garret and Inclose what you think proper beging you will not delay writeing - as Quick as posible - as the - Gentlemen wishes to know how to have the Business Settled - with the person that they wish him to Engage with - from your Humble Servant
James Howell
35 Ely April 16th 1824

TEXTUAL ALTERATIONS 3: only] *interl with caret.* 11: our] *interl above del* 'your'. 11: Boy] *interl with caret.* 30: Your] 'Y' *over illeg.* 32: Settled] *after del* 'St'.

CIRCUMTEXT Note of answer of 26 April 1824 to James Howell from other hand at bottom: parish officers 'are of opinion you do not belong to them and under such circumstances decline of course rendering you any more assistance'.

483   From Joseph Thoroughgood in Bermondsey, London, to [Robert] Alden, 19 April 1824

London April 19ᵗʰ 1824

{Sir{

I Write to you and to the Rest of the Gentlemen of the Parrish Informing you of my Situvation at this time witch I hop you will take into
Concidration it is in vain for me to Inform you of my Leving Colchester   5
the Case of wich you whill Know when I Left home and Ever Since I
have Receved 2ˢ Pʳ week and I have done my Endever not to Truble you
for no more wich I have had many Trubles to Incountor with Ever Since
Last Easter I have had Affliction in the family I have had a Laing In and
Two Burrels within this 5 mounth with this Little Boy that Lays dead at 10
this tim in the house - the Reason of my Sending to you at this time is
Becaus I ham in a deal of Truble at this time on Account of my not being
Able to Pay the Expence that Attended the Last funiral and now it is
Pleased God to take form us another witch Involve us so much that I
Cannot Git out of it without Aplying to you and I hop you will not denigh 15
Gents the Request that I whould make at this time is this that if you will
oblidge me with the favour as to defray the Expences that this f[-/unirel
will Come to and to Cleare the other Bill witch ther is 15ˢ 6ᵈ Remaining
So with this I Expect it will not be not very Little Short 2ᶠ-0ˢ-0ᵈ - and
Gent if you will do that for me I will Indever to do without that Two 20
Shilling Pʳ week witch you Allow me at this time if you Should wish to
Inquire into my Curcumstances you are at Liberty to Send Any Purson
you think Proper and they will find me at Nº 24 Pages walk
Grange Road Burmondsey

Gentⁿ you will be Pleased to favou[r] me with a few Lines as Soon as 25
Posble you Can witch I hop will be on Tuesday the 27 and by doing So
you will Grately oblidge me and I hop that I Should not have to Truble
you no more [un]til I will do my Endevor so to do withe the help of God
Joseph Thoroughgood

TEXTUAL ALTERATIONS 5: vain] 'n' *over illeg*.8: Ever] *inserted at beginning of line*. 9:
Affliction] 'ion' *over illeg*. 9: had a] 'had' *interl*. 10: Burrels] 'e' *inserted*. 10: within this
5 mounth] *interl*. 14: witch] *over del illeg*. 15: Git] *over del illeg*. 17: favour] 'ur' *over
illeg*. 21: time] *interl at end of line*. 25: Pleased] *after del illeg*.26: the] *interl*. 29: Joseph]
after del illeg.

CIRCUMTEXT Note from other hand on next page: at a vestry meeting on 23 April 1824 it
was agreed to allow Joseph Thorougood £2 'on Consideration of Deducting the 2/- pʳ
Week'.

**484   From William James in Chelmsford to Robert Alden, over-
seer of St Peter, Colchester, April 1824**

To the Minister Church Wardens - Overseers and Gentlemen, of the Parish
of St Peter = Colchester

Chelmsford April = 1824

Gentlemen,

5   Having in former Letters, endeavour'd to state with accuracy, my present
situation, I am convinced, tis not needfull, to make it again; in my last to
Mr Alden, I stated my Necessities, & wants, with truth, & humility, &
thankfull for the sixteen Shillings, already sent to me, as also for every
favor; I acknowledge, with thankfulness, and Gratitude, your Benevo-
10 lence, for the ^{s}2 = ^{d}6 p^r week, for my Daughter, who continues much the
same - I Received the Quarters money from Mr Alden - I did in my last
supplicate for something more, as I had not any money to help myself
with, and did not wish to take, one Shilling from that, as it was a reserve
for Rent - but M^r A - said the Gentlemen would not allow more, and that
15 I must do as well as I could - Gentlemen, what was I now to do in my
situation? I had then stated, the Disabled state of my Arm, nothing to
procure, any thing with, and through weakness, and pain, could not work,
to bring any thing in, so it is now, but it is better than it was, yet not so, as
to do but very little, with it and mends very slow indeed, I cannot raise it
20 up at present,

And now Gentlemen, look at the time, I have been in this state for 15 or
16 weeks, & but very little, have I been Able to do - both myself and
Daughter, have Experienced, the want, of the common necessaries of
Life, and had it not been, for some Friends, we could not have subsisted -
25 that friendship cannot continue - and have been Obliged to make use of
the Quarters money for subsistance, & paying for some necessarys I was
trusted for - Gentlemen, I would not be troublesome, I wish to Submit, I
wish not to come home, but in my present situation, I know not what to
do; If you cannot grant some furthur Relief - we cannot subsist -
30 I should wish to spend, the remainder of my Days, where I am, it cannot be long, E'r my head, must be laid in the dust - and I do not suppose
it possible for me to be more suitable employed, at home, than I am here,
where I am As by the decay of Nature, Strength, & Faculties, which which
Increases, as Age advances, I can do only light work, but I am willing,
35 with Pleasure, & thankfulness, to do what I can - I have said in a former

Letter, I wish not Intentionally to give you any Offence, so say I again and, I have asked your Advise what to do -

When I was last at Colchester, (which is 4 or 5 Years back) to make personal Application, the Gentlemen told me, when I had any to make, to do it by Letter, and spare Trouble, and Expence in coming, I walked then, 40 but now, I could not for want of strength - nor could I pay the expence to ride,

Gentlemen; I hope and trust, you will in some way, most Agreable, to yourselves, take my Case into your Consideration, and grant me, Relief -

Otherwise, I can see no Alternitive, but our coming home, which if 45 possible, we hope to Avoid -

Thus have I stated my Case, and could say more, but having done it in former Applications, and now fearfull, of being tiresome, to you, having wrote more than I, intended, I leave to you; Praying for your Candid consideration, and the Communication, of the result, to me - 50

Knowing, Easter, to be the most Public Season, for the Discussion of Parish business, I embrace this Opportunity

Gentlemen, I am Your Hum^{le} Obed^t
Ser^{vt} Wm James

PS, Mr Alden, I will thank you to lay this, before the Gentlemen, at the 55 Easter Meeting, and I thank you for your kindness

TEXTUAL ALTERATIONS 14: Gentlemen] *final 'n' interl at end of line.* 49: more] *interl with caret.* 51: for] *after del* 'for'.

485 From Richard Player in Chatham, Kent, to the overseers of St Peter, Colchester, 11 May 1824

Chatham 11 May 1824

Sir

I should wish to have my Sister to live with me if you will have the goodness to alow her something a Week she as rote to me for a Trifle of money wich is not in my power to give if this meets your Aprebation give 5 her some Cloths and pay all nesery expences for her comming & i hope i Shall never be under the nesesity of sending her Back by sending Answer you

will Olblige Your &c
10 Richd Player
Chest Arms Tap
Chatham
Kent

TEXTUAL ALTERATIONS 6: &] *interl.*

SENDER Despite the close temporal and geographical proximity with the letter from Mr Player from Rochester of 6 December 1824 (**490**) it remains unclear whether there is a personal link. The two letters are from different hands.

486   From William James in Chelmsford to Robert Alden in Colchester, 25 June 1824

Chelmsford June 25 = 1824

Mr Alden,

I have to communicate my thanks, by you, to the Gentlemen, for every favor, I have Received, from them, and assure you, I would never make
5 any Application, but on the most pressing Occasions, my Arm, is better than it was, but far from being well, and I fear it never will be, I cannot raise it up, and pain continues to attend it, = I am thankfull, I am Able to do a little work, yet with much dificulty, and Scanty provision = I am as yet, under Embarresments; My daughter, continues, in much the same state,
10 sometimes better, & then again worse; it will be a favor done me, if with the Quarterly Allowance for her, a few Shillings more, could be granted, at this time, as I really much, need it, you will excuse me in this =

I thought it my duty, to write, and as Mr Clarry, comes up on Tuesday, & Thursday I will thank you to send on one of those days, Please to direct
15 as usual, for me to the Care of Mr French

I am as in duty bound = Gentlemen
Your Hum^{le} Servt W= James

TEXTUAL ALTERATIONS 6: will] *interl with caret.* 7: do] *interl with caret.* 12: will] *interl with caret.*

487   From James Howell in Ely to the overseers and churchwardens of St Peter, Colchester, 24 July 1824

Ely   July   24   1824

Gentlman i rite once more to inform you that i expecet ever day loosen
of my wife for the wants of Substies she is now in har trubl expecten
every minnute to be delivered and it is not in my power to get needfull
things for har for i have Strained my sulf in bying Cloathes for one of my   5
boys the Gantlman of the fefeess in Ely left in thre hands to binde all boys
prantice that is born in Ely and twenty pound each boye Gentlman perhaps You may think by the favour that i belong to ely but i donot i ham
rady Gentlman any time to swear to your parrish and na other Gentlman
i Should like for You to insure of any Gentlman in ely if i tell you the   10
truth Gentellman i have at this time five Children and four of them is
under nine years of eage and i have nothing to trust to for trade but hawk
the Cuntry afew Goods as i have in Credite and so i have been on for
sixteen years but Gentlman at this time i ham drove at my witsens So i
hop Gentlman You will Sand me atrifel to help me in this distress Gentlman   15
pray do what you Can for me donot let us be past Home) Sir I ham yours
Ja^s Howell broad Street Ely Cambridgeshire

TEXTUAL ALTERATIONS 4: delivered] 'ed' *interl at end of line*. 6: hands] 'ds' *interl at end of*
line. 7: pound] 'd' *interl at end of line*. 11: Gentellman] *first* 'l' *over illeg*.
SPELLING 14: witsens] *read* 'wits' ends'.

**488   From William James in Chelmsford to Robert Alden, over-
seer of St Peter, Colchester, 27 September 1824**

Chelmsford Sepr 27 = 1824

Mr Alden,

I conceive it my Duty, to state to you, that my Daughter, continues in
her usual afflicted state; as for myself, I am as well in health, as I can
expect to be; my Arm is better, but not recover'd its strength, but contin-   5
ues week, & painfull, I have had some Jobs to do, which have enabled
me, not to be burthensone to you this Quarter only for the Usual Quarterly allowance, which I trust, you will have the goodness, to send by M^r
Clarry, this week, as it will be doing me a kindness = I think he comes
u<p> on Thursday, & Saturday,   10

I am, as in Gratitude boun\<d\>
to the Gentlemen, = & you =
their Hum^{le} Ser^{vt}
Wm James

15 Please to direct
for me, to the
Care of Mr French
Ship Inn,
Chelmsford

TEXTUAL ALTERATIONS 7: this Quarter] *interl with caret.*

489   From George Craddock in Westminster, London, to Robert Alden in St Peter, Colchester, 6 October 1824

London Octr 6th 1824

Mr Alden

I am Sorry to troble you and the Gentlemen of the parish for asistance
but Necessity oblidges me to do it for I have no Shoes to my feet nor yet
5 my wife and Children I have only two Blanketts asheet and the Coverlid
I brought from Colchester with me my wages is not Suffcient to provide
me with necessaries without Some asistance I hope therefore you and the
Gentlemen will Consider and Send me Some money to Get me afew Necessaries with as the winter is Coming on and our Children ar Grown to
10 Big altogether to Sleep in the Same bed with us we want to Make up
another place for them to Sleep in and Cannot do it without Alittle help
from you the last time I wrote to you I was Ill for Seven weeks - I did not
like to write again if posable I could do without it But at that time I was run
behind agood deal And part of the Doctors bill is not paid yet. I hope
15 therefore you will have the Goodness to Answer this as Soon as you
Convineintly Can
and you will Verry much oblidge Sir your

Verry Humble and most Obident
Servant George Craddock

20 Please Direct
George Craddock
99 Chapter Street
Vauxhall Road
Westminster

TEXTUAL ALTERATIONS 10: to Make] *over del illeg.* 16: Convineintly] *second* 'n' *over illeg.*

490 From Mr Player in Rochester [Kent] to Mr Halkin in St Peter, Colchester, 6 December 1824

Rochester Dis 6.1824

Sir I Should be much ablige to you if you would Send Me Sarah players money to we am agoing to move Some Distence off if you Will be So good as to Send it Next week as we leave be Leave be fore the quarter

    Mr Player   5

    Delf lane Near

    Rochester

TEXTUAL ALTERATIONS 2: Sarah] 'h' *over illeg.*

SENDER Despite the close temporal and geographical proximity with the letter from Richard Player from Chatham of 11 May 1824 (**485**), it remains unclear whether there is a personal link. The two letters are from different hands.

RELATED CORRESPONDENCE In June 1820, Mr Harward, vestry clerk of Rochester, had written to the overseer of St Peter, Colchester, that his parish had advanced £6 2s to Eleanor Player and requested the money to be remitted. On 18 July 1820, he had sent a reminder, and added: 'We have so many Paupers of this description [not settled] hanging upon us that we shall be under the necessity of suspending Payment of their allowances unless we have more regular remittances.' On 12 July 1821, he requested the remittance of £2 12s which had been advanced to Sarah Player.

In his letter of 22 March 1824 to Mr Stuart, overseer of St Peter, Colchester, Mr Barnard of Rochester had taken the case of Player as the point of departure for a more general observation on the advantage of inter-parochial cooperation in dealing with paupers residing in places in which they were not settled. In such cases, the parishes should try to avoid litigation, as that was often 'to the detriment of both parties; giving the Lawyers only the advantage [...] our maxim is to act candidly with all Parishes with which we have any connection, in order to save the useless expenditure which too often follows a difference of opinion. And it is only in very doubtful cases that we think it right to appeal to the Courts.'

491 From William James in Chelmsford to Robert Alden in St Peter, Colchester, 28 December 1824

Chelmsford Decr 28 = 1824

Mr Alden, Sir,

With due submission, I think it my duty to acquaint you, for the Information, of the Gentlemen, that my Daughter, continues in her Usual Afflicted state; - myself as well in health, as I can Expect, at the Age of 71 Years   5

the Infirmities, of which, attend me, my Arm is much the same as when I
wrote last, and my situation, & Employment also, so that I have not been
for this Quarter, burthensome to you, for which I am thankfull; I trust you
will have the goodness, to send the Usual allowance for my Daughter, by
10 Mr Clarry this week, as it be a kindness,

      I am Yours Obediently
       Wm James

direct for me as Usual, to the Care
of Mr French
15 for which I will be thankfull

TEXTUAL ALTERATIONS 6: much] 'm' *over illeg.*

**492 From George Rowe in [Great] Coggeshall [Essex] to the over-
seer of St Peter, Colchester, 5 January 1825**

Jeneary 5:1825
 Sir
 I have Sent you a fue Lines wich I hope you will Not take it a miss to
Say that Oversear Call at my House for 2 Quarters Rates Due up to
5 Cristmas wich 7^s and 6^d wich I hope you will have the Goodness to Send
me for thay thay must have it Directley for the time is up as poor Wife
Continews in the Same State of Blindness quite Unable to Do for Sulf
that I am Not able to pay it from me
      George Rowe
10   Coggeshall

493 From Mary Martin in Ipswich, 21 January 1825

          Jenuary 21st 1825
 Sir/
 Please to send the Boys Money By the bearrer, & My Son was six years
old Ninth of November Last 1824 & the Last time I saw H. Bloomfiled at
5 Ip^s he had Left his place & was going home to his mothers at Melton I
Cannot Say ware he is But I heard he was as gardiner that way, direction,
Mary Martin, at Mr Green^s Angel Lane St Clements Ipswich

TEXTUAL ALTERATIONS 7: Lane] 'a' *over illeg.*
CIRCUMTEXT Note in pencil from hand on back, referring to relief payments of 12s 6d for a coffin and 14s 6d for a nurse for three weeks .

494 From George Craddock in Westminster, London, to Robert Alden in St Peter, Colchester, 23 February 1825

London February 23^d - 1825

Mr Alden

    I am under the Necessity of Trobling you once more for asistance you Sent me word in your last that by the request of the Gentlemen of the parish I was not to write any more I hope they dont Consider me an   5 Imposter or them wages they Say is better in Town than the Country that is true but work is Verry dull now in London Sometimes I have earned from 6 to 7 Shillings p^r week and hardly ever exceeded 12= I pay 3^s/6^d p^r week for aroom this must be paid work or play or turn out I have no freind to Give me not So much as the worth of ashilling at any time and now at   10 this moment I have but one Shilling in my possion to Subsist on till Saturday Next and then if the weather is fine I shall have four Shillings after my rent is paid to Keep us fair the ensuing week I hope therefore the Gentlemen will take it into Consideration And Send me apound and I will ashure you and them this shall be my Last aplication I will ever make for I can-   15 not Get on without I will Come home altogether and there Stop I would have Come now but my Cloaths are all Sold and pawned to Keep my family Sooner than I could Troble you oftner except what I now have on my back So if I was to Come I should be in astate I should not like to See my Self in in Colchester   20

    But if the Gentlemen would rather I would Come home have the Goodness to Send me word And I will obey their Commands - I hope you will have the Goodness to Answer this as Soon as posable you Can In So doing you will

Verry much oblidge Sir your Verry humble and most   25
        Obedient Servant
               George Craddock

please Direct
Geo Craddock
99 Chapter Street   30
Vauxhall Road
Westminster

495   From Benjamin Hewitt in Whitton, Suffolk, to the overseer of St Peter, Colchester, 13 May 1825

1825   May 13

Sur i have sent you a few lines to in form you that my whife have been
wary ill for six Weakes and she was put to bed last monday three Weeks
and now the Child is dead so i want something Towards the expences for
5 they are a grate deal For my whife cannot do any thine for her famly not
Yet i should not have sent to you if my whife Had not been ill and the
child beeing Dead the expences are so much that i cannot pay it with out
you send me something towardes Them i should come over this morning
only it Was so Wet so i hope you will send me something <b>y return of
10 post

                          Benjamin Hewitt Whitton
                          Near ipswich suffolk

TEXTUAL ALTERATIONS 5: her] *interl.* 6: and] *after del* 'and the'.7: child] *after del illeg.* 7:
with] 't' *after del illeg.*

CIRCUMTEXT At bottom of page, note from Robert Alden, overseer of St Peter, Colchester,
to Mr Barber, presumed overseer of Whitton: 'This man had on March 12 Last a Pound
note I will thank you to inform me What to do in this Case I Whould have Call^d on you
But I am so Lame with my foot that I cannot stand on it' (hand A). Facing that note, in
left-hand corner of page, answer from other hand: 'Suppose you was to send 20/. Note I
think *[one]* had better under these Circumstances' (hand B).

496   From William James in Chelmsford to Robert Alden in Colchester, 22 June 1825

                          Chelmsford June 22 = 1825

Mr Alden,
    Sir,
    I conceive it my duty to state to you, that my daughter, still continues in
5 an Afflicted state, as Usual - for my own part, I am as well as I can expect
to be, weekness, & Infirmities, creep fast on me, but with the little work,
I have had, though with great difficulty, I have passed another Quarter,
without appliying for Extra relief for which I am thankfull, - If you can
have the goodness, to send me the Quarers Allowance, on Saturday by,
10 Clarry, it will be doing me a favor for which, I will thank you, and the
Gentlemen

Your Hum^le Ser^vt
Wm James

Please to direct
for me as Usual   15

Textual alterations 9: the] *interl with caret.*

---

497   From George Craddock in Westminster, London, to Robert Alden in St Peter, Colchester, 13 July 1825

London July 13th 1825

Mr Aldon

I am Extremely Sorry to be under the Necessity of Trobling the Gentle-men of St Peters parish at this Season of the year for Relief but to Inform you that I am Verry Ill So as Not to do anything whatever Nor able to go   5
out of doors is the preasent Ocation of my writing I was taken Verry Ill 3 weeks ago with the Bowell Complaint Ocasioned through Catching agreat Cold And it has brought the piles on me So Bad that I am not able hardly to walk about at all I am under Amedical Gentleman's Instructions at preasent and if you would wish to make any Reference to him I will Send   10
you word where to write to him a<t> the Same time I hope you will Send me Some money for my preasant <sup>port and that of my familys

In So doing you will Verry much Oblidge
Gentlemen your Verry Humble and
Most Obedeint Servant   15
George Craddock

Please to Direct
George Craddock
96 Chapter Street
Vauxhall Road   20
Westminster
NB Sir/ if you think you Can Send me any advice in my preasent Condi-tion I would be Verry hapy to Try anything that might be Subscribed for me

Textual alterations 7: Ocasioned] 'O' *over illeg.*

498   From James Tracey in Bishop's Stortford, Hertfordshire, to Robert Alden in St Peter, Colchester, 22 July 1825

July 22 1825

Sir

Your Petitioner Ja^s Tracey is sorry to inform he is under the necessity of Applying to you for some Assistance, as his Wife was confined with a
5 boy about Eleven weeks since and has been ill ever since till within this last week, and he himself has been confined to his room with an inflamation in his Eyes for this month and still continues in G^t Excruciating Pains getting no rest night or day nor cannot see to guide himself, he considers it to be Occasioned by some Grit flying in his Eyes, he therefore most
10 earnestly prays for your kind Assistance as he is at this time in great need of it having Eight in family to support, and not likely to get about at present, if the the Gentlemen will have the goodness to send him two pounds or what they think proper under those circumstances he will not trouble nor intrude on there goodness any further should he be able to get
15 to work again in a week or twos time

James Tracey

X

his mark

[*From other hand:*]
20 Plees to Drect to
me James Tracey
Stone Mason Near
the Castle New Town
Bishop Stortford
25 Harts

TEXTUAL ALTERATIONS 5: weeks] over illeg, *del* 'ths' *interl*. 5: been] *over illeg*. 5: ever] *interl with caret*. 6: last] *interl with caret*. 6: week] *over illeg*. 6: has] *after del illeg*. 7: G^t] *interl with caret, above del* 'the'. 11: and] *over del illeg*.

WRITING The sender's address at the end of the letter is probably from the same hand as the letter from James Tracey in Chelmsford of 25 February 1821 (**436**).

RELATED CORRESPONDENCE During the year following this letter, Mr Ashby, overseer of Bishop's Stortford, sent four letters to the overseers of St Peter, Colchester, regarding James Tracey, who was a stonemason, and his family of a wife and six children. On 11 August 1825, he wrote that his wife was ill and requested relief. On 24 August 1825, he reported Tracey himself, his wife, and three of their children were ill and needed relief, advising Colchester against any consideration of having him removed, 'as he is well situated for work and can (provide he has his health) support his family without any assistance'. On 16 June 1826, Ashby wrote that Tracey's wife had died recently and that he was left with 5 children, and on 20 July 1826, that two of his children were ill.

499 **From George Craddock in Westminster, London, to Robert Alden in St Peter, Colchester, 1 August 1825**

London aug^t 1st 1825

Mr Alden

I am Verry Sorry to be under the Necessity of Trobling you again I am
at this time in averry bad State of health worse than when I wrote to you
last my Complaint is become Verry Serious So that I must go to the hos-   5
pital for I am Not able to pay adoctor I have no money to buy Victuals for
my family I have been Ill Now Six weeks Come friday And I hope you
will Show this to the Gentlemen of the Parish And they will have the
Goodness to Send me word withir they will A low my family Amaintai-
nence if I go to the hospital as they Cannot Subsist without or wither they   10
would rather I should Come home And be under medical asistance at
Colchester And take my family under their own Care if I go to hospital In
London the Surgeon that has Atended me Says without dought I might be
brought about in three or four weeks but Something must be done without
delay or afistile Might be the Consequence of that delay My Employer has   15
promised me let the time be long or Short of my Illness there will be work
for me whenever I am able to go to it And Indeed he has been Verry Kind
to me during that time I hope Gentlemen you will take my Case into your
Sireous Consideration and Send me your Commands as Soon as you Can
& I will Comply acording But I hope you will Send me Some money for   20
my present Subsistance - I remain Gentlemen
your Verry humble and most Obedient Servant at Command

Geo Craddock

Gentlemen if you would rather I should go to Any Medical Gentleman in
London and Show my Case to him before I go to hospital as you might   25
Know many in Town I shall be Verry Glad to do it as it will give me
Satisfaction So far that you will be then fully Satisfied Concerning me
And if it is your wish for me to do So Send me word when And to whom
I shall go if you please your Humbel

Servant   30

Geo Craddock

NB Please Direct George Craddock 96 Chapter
Street Vauxhall Road Westminster

TEXTUAL ALTERATIONS 6: buy] 'u' *over* 'y'. 20: &] *interl with caret.* 28: you] *after del*
'you'.

500   From George Craddock in Westminster [London] to Robert Alden in St Peter, Colchester [17 August 1825]

Mr Alden I hope the Gentlemen will Send me Some more assistance as I have Not Got one Shilling in the world to by Bread without pawning my things which I must do untill you write I am Verry Sorry to Troble you So often but Necessity Oblidges to do it But I am hapy to Say I feel my Self
5   better Since I have been under Surgeon White And if I am Able to go to work if afortnight I will not Troble you any more But if I am Not I will Not Troble you again for this three weeks if you will have the Goodness to Send me apound this time I have not Earned one peny for these Nine weeks Come friday Noon nor have I been hardly able to go out from
10 home at all I could not get Into Hospital So many have been Taken Ill through the heat that there is no room I hope you will have the goodness to Answer this as Soon as posable you Can and you will
Much Oblidge your Verry Humble and Obedient Servt
                                                                Geo Craddock
15 Please to Direct to George Craddock
96 Chapter Street
Vauxhall Road
Westminster

CIRCUMTEXT Note from same hand at top of page: 'I certify Geroge Craddock who is an out patient of the Westminster Hospital is unable to follow his Employment for the Suport of himself and family.' Signed from other hand: 'Anthony White Westminster Hospital Augt 17th 1825'.

501   From George Craddock in Westminster [London] to Robert Alden in St Peter, Colchester [5 September 1825]

Mr Alden I am Sorry to Troble you again I was in Great hopes when I wrote last that I should have been able to go to work before now But I Keepe Bleeding So Much Internaly that I am hardly able to crawl about at all Mr White desires me to live as well as I can as he Says my Com-
5   plaint will be long time Getting well without it as it is as much owing to aweakinside as any thing that Keeps me back I have now been Ill twelve weeks any I have Received from you three pounds and the letters I pay 1^s..6^d Each you might easily Imagine how I am forced to live I hope you will Send as Soon as posable and if you would wish me to Come home I

am Verry Desirious to fulfull your request for I am Verry much afraid I 10
shall Never be well again

I remain Gentlemen your
Most Obedient and aflicted
Servant George Craddock

Please Direct 15
99 Chapter Street
Vauxhall Road
Westminster

TEXTUAL ALTERATIONS 1: Alden] *after del* 'Ad'.
CIRCUMTEXT Note from same hand at top of page: 'I certify that George Craddock who is
an out Patient of the Westminster Hospital is unable to follow Any Employment for the
Support of himself and family.' Signed from other hand: 'Anthony White Surgeon to the
Westminster Hospital Parliament Street September 5th 1825.'

502 From William James in Chelmsford to Robert Alden in Colchester, 26 September 1825

Chelmsford Sepr 26 = 1825

Mr Alden,

S<ir,> with due submission, I wri<te to> Inform you, my Daughter continues in the same Afflicted Changeable state - my own health, is as well
as I can expect, for which, I am thankfull, my employment have been 5
such, this Quarter, as to keep me (but with great dificulty) from asking
relief for myself, which I will not, unless necessity Compels I am slack at
this time - I hope not to Offend, but, you will do me a favor, in sending the
Quarterly Money this week- Mr Clarry, comes up on Thursday, & Saturday, could you send by him, on Thursday, it will afford me much relief, for 10
which I will thank you

Your Hum^{le} Ser^{vt}
Wm James

Please to Direct for me by him as Usual

503 From George Craddock in Westminster [London] to Robert Alden in St Peter, Colchester [5 October 1825]

Mr Alden I am Sorry to be under the Necessity of Trobling the parish
again Mr Surgeon White advised me to go into the Country for alittle

time which I acordingly did after receiving your last letter and I am Sorry
to say I returned again on tuesday last but Nothing betterd by my Jorney I
5 should have wrote this yesterday but after Coming from the hospital I was
forced to go to bed Imeadeately Mr White has givin me into the physicians
hands as my Case is I am Sorry to Say Verry bad and without Relief
Shortly I fear will end with my life for I am Verry Ill Indeed -

I hope the parish Gentlemen will have the goodness to Send me Atrifle
10 more than apound this time for I am in Great wants of it as you might
Supose or else I must write again Sooner I will endeavor to make as little
do as I can

In Answering this by return of post you will Verry much Oblidge your
Verry Humble Obedient and aflicted
15   Servant
                                George Craddock
99 Chapter Street
Vauxhall Road
          Westminster

CIRCUMTEXT Note from same hand at top of page: 'I certify that George Craddock who is an
out Patient of the Westminster Hospital is not able to follow any Employment for the
Suport of Himself and family.' Signed from other hand: 'Anthony White Westminster
Hospital Octr 5th 1825.'

**504   From George Craddock in Westminster [London] to Robert
          Alden in St Peter, Colchester [22 October 1825]**

Mr Alden

I am verry Sorry that I am under the necesity of trobling the Gentlemen
of the parish again for relief but I am hapy to Say I think my Self alittle
better than when I wrote to you last time I hope please God Ishall be once
5 more Restored to my health though I am at this time Very Ill and weak I
hope the Gentlemen will take my Case into Consideration and alow you
to Send me two pounds this time for I am in Dept for rent thirty Shillings
And the landlord Says plainly if he is Not paid within afew days he will
Seize what few things I have to pay himself my wife and myself have
10 pawned all our Cloaths for Victuals at diferent times hoping week after
week I should be able to go to work I hope therefore the Gentlemen will
Grant what I request this time I am Sorry I have been So expensive to
them And hopes with the Blessing of God for the Sake of my own family

and the parish likewise that I shall be once more able to work for their and
my own Suport But at this moment I have not aloaf of Bread Nor one 15
peny of any Kind of money whatever Nor do I Know where to Get any of
either till I hear from you for the Credit Door is Shut against me But God
I hope will provide for

me And mine till that time I trust

I remain Gentlemen your Aflicted　　　　　20

Verry Humble and most Obedient Servant

Geo Craddock

99 Chapter Street

Vauxhall Road

Westminster　　　　　25

CIRCUMTEXT Note from same hand at top of page: 'I certify that George Craddock who is an
out patient of the Westminster Hospital is unable to follow Any employment for the
Suport of Himself and family.' Signed from other hand: 'Octr 22nd 1825 Henry Bond
Apothecary.'

**505　From William James in Chelmsford to Robert Alden in Col-
chester, 2 November 1825**

Chelmsford Novr 2 = 1825

Mr Alden

Sir,

If necessity did not compel, I would not trouble you, in asking for any
Relief, my work have fallen of, ever since you sent to me last, and indeed 5
before that time, in so much, that I now experience the want of common
necessaries, having not, at this time any more to subsist on, or to look to,
for support, If Sir, you could sent me only a few Shillings, for present
support, I shall be thankfull; work will again return, I doubt not, I only
state facts, I write with grief, for tis hard for me at my Advanced Age, I 10
rely on your goodness, & that of the Gentlemen,

I am yours, Obediently

Wm James

I will thank, to send by Clarry, or I know not what I shall do, I ask it as a
favor -　　　　　15

506   From Benjamin Brooker in Ipswich to Robert Alden, overseer of St Peter, Colchester, 7 November 1825

Ipswich Nov^{br} 7 1825

Mr Aldan Sir

I Take this Oppurtunity of Riting to you to Inform you that I have no Employment and are not Likely to have Any at this time of the Year and
5 also my Wife and Child Continue Very Sadly and None of us Can Earn Anything. And you May if you Please Send the ten Shillings Pr week as We Greatly Want it if you Do not think propper to Send it We Will Come home Pray Sir Send Me a Positive Answer By Mr Rouse on Wednesday Next

10   Benjamin
            Broker

TEXTUAL ALTERATIONS 3: Oppurtunity] *first* 't' *over illeg.*

WRITING Hand different from that of the letters from Benjamin Brooker of 2 December 1825 (**510**) and April 1826 (**521**).

RELATED CORRESPONDENCE On 20 October 1825, Edward Chapman, overseer of St Nicholas, Ipswich, had written to the overseer of St Peter, Colchester, that Benjamin Brooker, a fellmonger, who had gained his settlement through service with Mr Smith of St Peter, Colchester, was 'in great Distress', with his wife and two children 'one of whome is Very bad with the Small Pox and his wife Very Ill', and that he had been out of work for some time. Chapman asked Colchester to say 'what you would have me Do for them.'

507   From Robert Gosling in Portsmouth to Robert Alden, overseer of St Peter, Colchester, 13 November 1825

Portsmouth Novr 13th 1825 HM Ship Rainbow

Kind Sir

In reply to yours received this day i am sorry to acquaint you that i have not had this opperttunity of Complng with my whifes request i have twice
5 been on shore since her leveing me at Chatham but it so unfortuneately happenad that i could not git aney bisness done as the Magistrates whare all gone out each time and ower ship being ordered for sea dyrectly after i could not git any live to come on shore thare has not been any neglect on my part as i think it my duty to contribute all that lyes in my power to hir
10 happyness and comfort i think that their cannot be aney difficality in her claimeng of my Parrish Wich is Witham as i never have been any whare else to Claim any Settle ment since leveing that place wich was when i

was quite yong and i have been in his Majistys service with the Exception
of a few months ever sense i should be very happy if it was so that it could
be Settled for i am not in any likely hoods of being on shore for some 15
time as we do not now the day we may leve England but if any posebality
of doing it hear i can asure you that it shall be done plse to tell my Whife
that i am quitte will we only this day arived hear we have had a very bad
passage round for it has blown a gale of wind since leving Chatham So
Remain your   20

Humble Sarvant
Robert Gosling

I am kindly thankfull to you for your trouble in Writing

TEXTUAL ALTERATIONS 1: Rainbow] *interl below at end of line.* 12: to] 't' *over* 's'. 14:
should] 's' *over illeg.* 14: could] 'o' *after del illeg.* 19: Chatham] *interl with caret.*

RELATED CORRESPONDENCE Robert Gosling's wife lived in St Peter, Colchester. From
early December 1825, she received a weekly allowance of 2s which was reimbursed by
the parish of Witham, her place of settlement, by means of quarterly payments. In July
1827, the allowance was raised to 3s (letters from Mr Philbrick, overseer of Witham, to
Robert Alden, overseer of St Peter, Colchester, 6 December 1825 and 4 July 1827). On 13
February 1826, Philbrick wrote to Alden that he had received two letters from her in which
she had not given her precise address (only 'Colchester', without parish), and asked him
'to inform the woman when she has to write again to get some person to write for her, for
there is no such thing as making her Letters out' (further letters from Philbrick to Alden
concerning payments, 20 June, 5 and 29 December 1826).

**508   From George Craddock in Westminster, London, to Robert
Alden in St Peter, Colchester, 29 November 1825**

London Novr 29th 1825

Mr Aldon

I am Verry Sory to Inform you and the Gentlemen of the Parish that I
am not able to work at Preasent And that I am Greatley Obliged to them
for what they have done for me In my afliction which has been Long and 5
Severe it was 24 weeks last Saturday that I have not earned one penny
And I hope you will have the Goodness to Send me An Answer to this as
Soon as you Can And if you would wish me to Come home Send me
word for I do not know what to do for every Article of apariel belonging
to me & my wife is either pawned or Sold except what is on our Backs 10
But if please God I should be able to go I expect asituation in the Contry
in the Spring as my Brother in Law has promised to Get it for me if the
Gentlemen think proper to Relieve me I will Not Troble them oftner than

Real Necessity Oblidges me But if they would rather I would Come to
15 Colchester I must Come Imeadiately for I cannot do longer without Asistance
I have left the Hospital three weeks ago as uncurable the Gentlemen there
advised me to live as well as I could And told me posably I might Get
better in the Spring But Medecines was of no more use to me & that they
Could do no more for me
20 I remain your unfortunate And afflicted
Most Humble And Obedient Servant
George Craddock
99 Chapter St
Vauxhall Road
25   Westminster

**509   From William James in Chelmsford to Robert Alden, over-
seer of St Peter, Colchester, 30 November 1825**

Chelmsford Novr 30 = 1825

Mr Alden
a few weeks back, I wrote to you, stateing my case, and humbly asking
some temporary relief, which I much stood in need of, and have so done,
5 since that time, Necessity, only, comples me, again to write, which I hope
will not give affence, I have no need to trouble you, with again stating my
case, as it is similar to my last Application, for as then, work is such, as I
cannot procure, sufficient support to sustain Nature, indeed for Instance,
Yesterday I walked four Miles only = and through fatigue, and lack of
10 strength, in the dark of the Evening, I was forced to sitt down, on a stop in
a Vilage, fainting, and with much dificulty got home, this was Ocasioned,
through want of Necessary Nourishment = and this day, I am very Unwell =
now Sir, I think I need not say more, only humbly Solicit which I trust will
be granted, some temporary relief, thus I submit my case, and ask the
15 favor, at your hands = I cannot, at present subsist as I am = by & by, I shall
have some work to do at a house, but that will be some time, as the house
is not in reading nor will it be done in the Winter = Pray let me hear from
you = I am Gentlemen, Your Hum^{le} Ser^{vt}
Wm James

Textual alterations 8: cannot] 't' *interl at end of line*. 12: want] 't' *interl with caret*. 13:
Solicit] *followed by del* 'id'.

510* [From Benjamin Brooker in Ipswich, *before* 2 December 1825]

ihave sent to you mister holden that i have no wark to doe and you must
send me sum muney i have Bean hout of wark a 11 weaks have not arnt
But 1 pound i was at wark wen vou sent me that muny at muster pues it
was But afue days i have arnt But 2 shilens for three weaks i have pond
all my things and i have got my furest and if you doe not send me sume 5
muney i shall came home ass possiBle my wife expcts to Be put to Beed
every day and thear is a procts for me in a few weaks But when i git in to
warke prars i may never truBle you no more But if you wil not help me
thrw one kurtor you must surport my wife and famely all ther lifestme
when theare is a nesety i nevery will try to make my self a setelmenet 10
aney more
you sent ward that my wife arnt a greate deal of muney sureny she
youst to arnt a goudeal But she have arnt nothing latly and she is not
likeley to arn aney more for sumtime you sed i might have Bean at mister
Clopper At this time But your pertner node nothing a But my Busens 15
you may tel mester rouse to Cole at mester pues then e wil tl you all
aBut my Busens
ples to send me sum muney Buy rouse on fridy to pay sum of my deats
of if not i shall cume over next munday and git ahuse in my houn parshes

TEXTUAL ALTERATIONS 1: must] *after del* 'mst'. 3: wark] *over illeg.* 4: was] *after del illeg.* 10:
theare] *after illeg.* 13: have] 'v' *over illeg.* 13: and] *after del illeg.* 15: But] *after del* 'I'. 15:
nothing] *after del* 'noh'. 16: tl] 'l' *interl.* 18: to] *after del illeg.*
WRITING Same hand as letter from Benjamin Brooker of April 1826 (**521**).
PLACE Inferred from other letters from Benjamin Brooker.
DATE Date of note of receipt on back.
CIRCUMTEXT Note from other hand on back: 'Decr 2nd 1825 Sent by *Rouse* to B Brooker
10/-'.

**511 From William James in Chelmsford to Robert Alden in Col-
chester, 16 December 1825**

Friday C<helmsfo>rd Decr 16 = 1825
Mr Alden: & Gentlemen with humble submission
I am very Unpleasantly, and totally contrary to my Inclination, under the
necessity, of writeing again, I have been so very Ill, as not to be out of my
house, but 3 times, since last Sunday, sennight, and indeed but for the 5
kindness of friends, I must have been without provision of any kind, for

days past = Gentlemen, indeed this was my Case this Morning without
bread, or provision of any kind, nor any money to procure any, not a morsel
for dinner had not, a Neighbour brought a piece in, I will not multiply
10 Complaint = I Related my Case to a Gentleman this day, who did not
Relieve, but directed me to write to my Parish again, at present I am not
Able to earn any thing, I am greatly in need, of Immediate = tempory
relief, or Perish I must, if you cannot otherwise relieve me, be so good to
send the Quarterly Allowance to me, for my Daughter, up to Xt^{ss} day next,
15 but that will be breaking into that, which is reserved for another use, I here
state not half my case, but pray you to take it into your Candid Consideration, and grant me such Assistance as my Case requires
                    with due Submission I am Gentlemen
                         Your Hum^{le} Servt
20   Wm James
I Recd 5 Shill^{gs} you sent for wch I thank you
[*Added on outside, written crosswise*:] I must Just say I have had no
Casual relief since my Arm was bad, wich is nearly 2 Years only my
daughters Allowance

TEXTUAL ALTERATIONS 5: indeed] *final* 'd' *interl at end of line*. 11: Relieve] *after del* 'not'. 11:
write] 'te' *interl at end of line*. 15: another] 'er' *interl at end of line*.

512   From George Craddock in Westminster, London, to Robert Alden in St Peter, Colchester, 20 December 1825

London Decr 20th 1825

Mr Alden
   I am Sorry to Inform you that I still Continues Verry Ill And I am
greatly afraid I shall Never be any better for I can hardly get Breath to
5 move about And I think I am in adecline for Iwent to aphysician last
week - And Iasked him to tell me plainly if he could withir there was any
hopes of my recovery And he Said I might but there was no great
likelyhoods at preasent best if I could live over the Spring I might get
better I have no posable means of Suport for myself and family wee have
10 had nothing more than bread for Several days past And on Sunday last I
can Call God to witness wee had no more than about apound of bread
between us four till Six in the evening afreind Called and gave us ashilling
I hope the Gentlemen of the parish will Send me Something for preasent

Suport And Send me word to Come home as I had much rather as my
Distress Cannot be augmented But will by that means I hope be Lightned 15
except there was any hopes of my being able to follow Employment for
our Suport - I remain - Sir/

your most Humble Obedient and afflicted
Servant George Craddock
99 Chapter Street Vauxhall   20
Road Westminster

I have had apromise of Agentleman In Westminster of aletter to go to the
principal Physician of St Bartholomews hospital in the Coarse of this
week And I hope he will do me some good

TEXTUAL ALTERATIONS 16: Employment] 'ent' *interl at end of line.*

513 From George Craddock in Westminster, London, to Robert Alden in St Peter, Colchester, 11 January 1826

Mr Aldon   London Jany 11st 1826

I am Sorry to Inform you that I remain Still very Ill I have Been to
adoctor to day and he gives me but little hopes of Recovery But tells me
the Spring of the year will dry me he has given me Some medicene and
Desired me to Send the prescriptions to you And to Inform you that if you 5
will write to him post paid he will give you afull Information Respecting
my health his Name is Doctor McDonold Near the Elephant and Castle
Kent Road London as he Says he never made apractise of Signing letters
Any other way you may See by his papers that I am In avery Ill State of
health which I hope you will have the Goodness to Send back to me again 10
I hope I shall receive benefit from this medecine I am always So full of
Bodily pain every Minute without Any Intermission of ease that I am
Quite Meloncolly Not for my own fate alone Because I hope God will
have mercy my Soul as I pray to him day and night I hope my prayers will
be answered - But it is my wife And Children that Lays heaviest on my 15
mind But I hope God will provide afreind for them if he Should think
proper to take me from them -

I hope you will have the Goodness to Send me an Answer And Some
Subsistance as Soon as posable -

20 I remain your Very humble and most
Obedient Afflicted Servant
George Craddock
99 Chapter Street
Vauxhall Road
25 Westminster

TEXTUAL ALTERATIONS 12: Minute] 'te' *interl at end of line.*

514 From George Craddock in Westminster, London, to Robert Alden in St Peter, Colchester, 31 January 1826

London Jany 31st 1826

Mr Alden

Sir) I am Sorry Still to Say I am no better But Rather worse Neither do I expect that I ever Shall be any better in this world for I can hardly Get
5 Breath enough to walk about even alittle I am In the Greatest of pain in my Chest and Continualy Bleeding inside And all Medical assistance Seems to do no good But Rather harm I am greatly oblidg^d to the Gentlemen of the parish for what they have done for me in the Same time I shall if ilive afew weeks longer be Oblidged to Come home to you unless the Spring
10 Should make any Change in me for the Better which I am much afraid it will Not although the Doctor tells me it will But I think he means I shall be out of this world and if that it Should please God to take me out of this world I hope I shall be better of than being here - I hope you will have the goodnness to Send me some Subsistance in Return as Soon as you Can
15 and you will much Oblidge your Verry Humble Obedient and
aflicted Servant George Craddock 99 Chapter Street
Vauxhall Road Westminster

TEXTUAL ALTERATIONS 12: and] *interl with stroke.* 12: it] *inserted in left-hand margin.*

515 From William Wilsher in Norwich to the minister of St Peter, Colchester, 16 February 1826

Norwich Feby 16 1826

Sir

I hope you will excuse my writing to you I have wrote to the Overseer of the Parish twice before but can obtain no answer from him I have been

out of employment for these last 22 weeks and cannot get any worke to 5
do I was an apprentice to Mary Everett of the Parish of St Peter Colchester
Baker and Mr Francis Mayor of Norwich have examined me & have
made me swear my Settlement to the said Parish and I would thank you to
inform the Overseer if he will not send me some allowance as parochial
Relief I and my family must be past home for through acomplaint I am 10
afflicted with I cannot follow the Bakers trade nor has not for these 8
year's for I have been Weaveing but no worke of that kind is going in
Norwich at this time Numbers agoing to their towns every day for want
of work

                If you would be kind 15
                enough to Answer this by
                return of Post you'll
                much Oblige your's &c
                    Wm Wilsher

PS/ Direct 20
for Wm Wilsher N°5
near the Whale Bone's
St Clements
     Norwich

TEXTUAL ALTERATIONS 21: W^m] *after del* 'of'.

516 From George Craddock in Westminster, London, to Robert Alden in St Peter, Colchester, 21 February 1826

Mr Alden   London Feby 21st 1826
  I am Sorry to Troble you but Necessity Oblidges me for I am Still in
averry Bad State of health But I think my Self Something Stronger than I
was when I wrote to you last time as I have not lost So Much Blood
Inwardly as before my Brother and my wifes freinds have Requested me 5
to Come into the Country And promised to Suport both myself and family
untill May Next if I should live so long and in that time I shall either Get
Better or worse they have wrote twice to me to Come Renewing their
promises And I should like to Go if you will be So Good as to Send me
Some money to bear my expences there I think it will ease me of you as 10
I should now would not Troble you while I remained there and if it should
please God to take me from my family while there my wife and Children

would be Among their freinds when I would rather have them I have Not
the least thoughts that I shall ever be able to do Any work though I am
15 Something better for I believe myself to be in Aconsumtion And nothing
Else If the Gentlemen of the parish will have the Goodness to Send me
two pounds I will go down into the Country And I should like to go on
monday Next as I can Get half way down that day And the Next day I
could wark home I cannot travel by Night In awagon as that would make
20 me worse Instead of Better And to go from London all the way by the
Coach would be 48 Shillings for us all so that you I hope are Convinced
that less money would Not Bear my Expences there I hope you will have
the Goodness to Answer this so I may be ready to go or Stop <I> remain
your Verry Humble Obedient
25   A<nd> afflicted Servant Geo Craddock
                  99 Chapter Street
                  Westminster

TEXTUAL ALTERATIONS 13: them] *after del* 'have'. 23: be] *after del* 'be'.

517　From William Wilsher in Norwich, 12 March 1826

                                Norwich Mar 12..1826
Honored Sir/
    I have taken the liberty of writing to you onve more hopeing you will
excuse my troubleing you as it is far from my wishes I sent a copy of my
5 examination to the Overseer of your parish signed by the Overseer of the
Parish I now live in in Norwich about afortnight ago last tuesday and
have not rec^d any answer from him and he promise'd to answer me with
relief &c as soon as I remited my examination & signed by the Overseer
of the Parish but he has given me no answer which make's me trouble
10 you with the examination as you will find enclosed & I hope you will
forward it & Mr Alden with relief for me as soon as possible or otherwise
I must be were I am which will be more expense to the Parish & that is
not my wishe's by so doing
        Sir you will much Oblige your
15   Humble Servant
                        Wm Wilsher

Direct for
me N° 5 St Clements
near the Wales Bones
            Norwich   20

CIRCUMTEXT Copy of answer from Robert Alden, overseer of St Peter, Colchester, 14
March 1826, on back: 'Wm Willshire I Re[ceive]d you Letter you Wrote to Mr Marsh and
that you Wrote to me and I find you do not Belong to the Parish of St Peter and as Such I
cannot Relieve you.'

**518   From George Rowe in [Great] Coggeshall [Essex], 13 March
        1826**

                            March 13 1826
Sir
    I have Sent you Line according to your Request wich I hope you will
Not take it a miss to Say that the Overcear Calld for the Rates the Other
Day and Sayd that he wold be Glad if I wold Send to you for them for the   5
time was Geting Near when thay Setteld Accounts wch I hope you will be
So Good as to Send me the Money by Mr Redgrift and if you Can Do a
Littele Triffell for me I shall be Glad for I am in a Sad Settewation at this
Time from
me George Rowe   10
                            Coggeshall

TEXTUAL ALTERATIONS 8: me] *inserted in left-hand margin.* 8: I shall] *after del* 'if well'.

**519   From William James in Chelmsford to Robert Alden in Col-
        chester, 14 March 1826**

                            Chelmsford March 14 = 1826
Mr Alden,
    Sir,
    With due submission, I have a favor to ask of you, & trust you can, &
will do it for me -   5
    This have been a trying Quarter to me, having had but little to do, but at
this time, I will not trouble you, with my dificulties, I thankfully Acknowledge your last kindness, and you will do me another, if by any means you

will send me this Quarters allowance, so that I can have it, any time this
10 week, or at furthest, by Monday next, as I have a demand on me, which I
must pay on that Day, the Neglect of my not doing, will bring on me distress, & Trouble = which I wish to avoid, & having no other means of
doing it but by making this Application to you, I hope, & trust, your goodness, will excuse this request, & do it for me as Quarters day is so near;
15 Clarry come up on Saturday & Monday, by whom if you send - direct for
me as Usual =

I am respectfully yours & ^e

Wm James

I ask as a favor = & trust I shall not be disappointed

TEXTUAL ALTERATIONS 15: Saturday & Monday] *interl with caret, above del* 'Friday, &
Saturday'.

520   From Ann Craddock in Westminster, London, to Robert Alden in St Peter, Colchester, 17 April 1826

Mr aldon   London april 17th 1826
   I am under the necessity of trobling you for My husband is gone into
the Contry and is going to Stop with his brother this Summer for he was
not able to go to take that Situation that he was promised he was verry Ill
5 at the time wee had your last letter I expected he was going to die for
several days he wrote to his brother and he sent for him to Come down to
him he has been gone near amonth he sent me word he was got better and
able to do a little work and that he Should Stop in the Contry all this
Sumer and Said imight Come to him as Soon as I could bat he had no
10 money to Send me So that if I come I must get thare how I could for he
had no power whatever to asist me but told me to write to you if Ichused
and I hope you will Send me apound to Convey me down to him or I
might Come to you for he told me he would never write to you again But
I thought I had Better write to you and I will do as you pleas though I
15 Should rather go to him and I hope we shll not trouble you any more
though we have Been very troublesom But we never Sent till we was in
grat destress your answer will much oblidge your verry humble and most
obedeint Servant

ann Craddock

20 No 7 fredrick St Regent St

vauxhall Road westminster

[*On left-hand side of page, facing valedictions:*]
I should like to go on Saturday next as i shall not have So good aconveyence till the Saturday following

TEXTUAL ALTERATIONS 8: Contry] *after del illeg.* 14: and] *after del illeg.* 20: Regent] 'nt' *interl above del illeg.*
CIRCUMTEXT Filing note on outside: 'G[eorge] Craddock'.

521 From Benjamin Brooker [in Ipswich] to [Robert] Alden, overseer of St Peter, Colchester [April 1826]

Mister holdon i have not Bean in Consent wark all this Koiter i have lost more then a mointh for trade have Bean so bad that my master voild not sol nothing my wife have Bean very Bad for some weaks and i have Bean forst to have a porsson to se after har she have not arnt nothing this Koitr the oversers have rated me this Koter 13 6 it was not in my pour to pay it   5
and thay came and toke my things for the rats. thay doe not like of making my self a setelment in nekeles paresh gentlmen if you will a sest me threw this kouter ishal have But one more and then i shal Be nonore troBle to you But if you doe not plese to send me sume muney i shal leve the house when she have Bean a Bead er munth my wife was put to Bed last saday   10
and she is very Bad at this time if you do not send me sum muney i shal have to cole a pon nekels pares for a realefe for my case is veray ard at this time my landlrd came after his rent last weake But i have not a shilen towards it i shold like to make my self a setelment whar i ham But it vould not Be in my pour to doe it without your help the oversers came and told   15
me that i had noe Bisens to hire that house thay told me if i had a cape war i was thay vold not a troBlme But thay har a tring to git me hut plese to send me ward By rouse as sone as poseBle
Benjaman Brooker

TEXTUAL ALTERATIONS 1: not] *after del* 'lot'. 6: thay] *after del* 'tay'. 8: kouter] *after del illeg.* 9: send] *after del* 'plese'. 10: when] *after del* 'next weake'. 13: after] *after del* 'after'. 13: rent] *after del illeg.* 14: shold] *after del illeg.* 15: my] *after del* 'in'. 15: doe] *over del illeg.* 16: told] *over del illeg.*
DATE Date from filing note on outside.
WRITING Same hand as letters from Benjamin Brooker of 2 December 1825 to St Peter, Colchester, and of 10 July 1828 to St Botolph, Colchester (**510, 377**).

522   From George Craddock in Westminster, London, to Robert Alden in St Peter, Colchester, 19 July 1826

London July 19th 1826

Mr Aldon

I am Verry Sorry to be under the Necessity of Trobling you And I am Still more Sorry to inform you that my health is very bad that I am not
5 able to do any laborous work at all the only thing I have done Since I returned from the Country is to Sell alittle fruit or go Sometimes on an erant or any light Employment I can Get to do and there is at this time so many thousands of Strong hearty men out of work in london that it is Almost Imposable to get any thing to do at all And If I had Not returned
10 to this Quarter where I was Known I must have aplied to you long ago or come home But if you think you Can help me into Any thing whereby I can live without being Troblesome to you at Colchester I shall be Verry thankfull to Come for I could testify on oath if required that I have not eat apeny worth aday of Anything Except Bread these Six weeks put one day
15 against another I hope you will have the goodness to Send me an Answer And Some Subsistance as Soon as you Can and you will much Oblidge

Please Direct to   your Verry Humble And most
94 Chapter Street   Obedient Servant at Command
Vauxhall road Westminster   Geo Craddock
20 George Craddock

[*Continued on back, written crosswise:*] Mr Alden, I have not lately been to any Surgeon or Medical Gentleman at all I have Been And Still Continues to take Something for Strengthening my Inside - But Mr White tells me good living would be the Best thing for me But if you think
25 proper or the Gentlemen of the parish Should think so I will Continue to Come to Colchester So that you might have me Examined by any medical Gentleman you might Chuse to take me before

523   From George Craddock in Westminster, London, to Robert Alden in St Peter, Colchester, 21 August 1826

<Lo>ndon August 21st 1826

Mr Alden

I am Verry sorry to be under the necessity of trobling you again for Relief And I am likewise Verry Sorry the Gentlemen of the parrish are

disatisfied at my not being able to work for the Suport of myself and 5
family I was eight weeks with my friends in the Country And during that
time I was not able to work one day they where not able to Suport us any
longer which Ocasioned me as Summer was aproaching to return to London And try if I could gain alittle Suport by Selling fruit which I did as
much as my health would permit me to do - And Contrary to my own 10
wish I aplied to you last time my wife being desirous to try every honest
means wee posably could to Keep out of the workhouse only for her
perswasions I should have come home then and now I must Inform you
as near as posable the State of my Complaint every time I go to a place of
easement my fundament Comes down and be it what time of day it will I 15
am forced to go to bed Imeadiately for two or three hours in the most
Excruciating pains posable And at all times I wear abandage to that part
to Keep it in Its place - And I am So Short Breathed that I can hardly get
about at any time the - Gentlemen of the parish will have the goodness to
deal with me as they think proper And I shall be perfectly Satisfied with 20
their desicion but if they Should think proper not to Send me any more
relief I hope you will have the goodness to Send me apost paid letter as
Soon as you posably can - for literrealy Speaking we have lived ahalf
Starved life these Sixteen months past - so that it matters not to me where
I spend the remainder of my miserable Existance hoping that god will 25
have mercy on my Soul I remain the
      Gentlemens and your Obedient And Verry Humble
          Servant Geo Craddock
94 Chapter Street Vauxhall
road Westminster 30

524 From George Craddock in Westminster, London, to Robert Alden in St Peter, Colchester, 30 August 1826

                    London Aug[t] 30th 1826

Mr Alden
  I made Aplication by litter to you for releif the 22nd or if the Gentlemen
of the parish thought proper not to Send Any I hoped you would have
post paid aletter to me I hope you will have the Goodness to answer this 5
So as I might have it on friday or if I do Not hear from you that day I must
leave London on Saturday to Come to Colchester for Realey I do not
Know how I can Subsist till that time I am Gentlemen your

Verry Humble and Most Obedient
10   Afflicted Servant
                                      George Craddock
Please to direct
to 94 Chapter Street
Vauxhall Road
15   Westminster

525   From George Rowe to Robert Alden in St Peter, Colchester, 24 September 1826

Sept 24 1826
Sir
   I have taken the Liberty to Send to you to inform you that a ½ year
Rates is Due to the Parrish Next fryday wich is Micklmes Day wich is ^{s}7
5 wich if you will have the Goodness to send it by Mr Ridgrift in the Corse
of the Week I Should be Oblidge to you as the time is up by So Doing I will
thank you
George Rowe

TEXTUAL ALTERATIONS 3: a] *interl.* 4: is ^{s}7] 'is' *interl.*

526   From George Craddock in Westminster, London, to Robert Alden in St Peter, Colchester, 3 October 1826

London Octr 3^{d} 1826
Mr Alden
   Sir) I am once more oblidged to troble you for Asistance And I hope
please God it will be the last time for agreat while And Indeed I sincerly
5 hope it may be the last time altogether as I have got alight Situation as
doore or Gate Keeper by day time at alarge Building A small distance
from Town procured for me by a Gentlemen who is Clerk of the works as
he has Known me ever Since I have been in London he thinks I shall be
able to perform that duty Ill as my health is as I have nothing to do but
10 admit the workmen in and out and no Strangers I shall have abox to Sit in
but I have no Cloaths except what is at the pawnbrokers Not so much as
would fetch Seven Shillings if iwas to Strip myself Naked I have no Shoes

that I can go out of doors with my wife and Children I am Sorry to Say are
Quite as bad of I want to Get my Cloaths out And Indeed must before I
can Got to my place which is to be Next Monday Shoes I must have as I 15
must apear Clean And tightdy or I cannot go there I hope the Gentlemen
of the parish will have the Goodness to Send me two pounds It will be
Sufficient to Cloath my Self and I hope God almighty will enable me to
provide for my family without Trobling them any more but anyways I
will not Troble you any more for 3 months if I could have your Answer 20
on friday I shall be Verry much Oblidged to you as I have to Give aposative
Answer on Saturday morning <whether> I can Come or not -
    I remain your Verry Humble
          And Obedient Servant
              George Craddock   25
Sir)
please Direct
To Geo Craddock
92 Chapter Road
Vauxhall Road   30
Westminster
[*Postscipt on right-hand side at bottom of page, facing address of
sender:*] I did not received your letter with the pound note till the next
tuesday I went twice to the post office about it

TEXTUAL ALTERATIONS 17: be] *after del illeg.*

527 From William James in Chelmsford to Robert Alden in Colchester, 13 November 1826

                      Chelmsford Novr 13 = 1826
To the Minister, Church Wardens, Overseers, & Gentlemen of the Parish
of St Peter Colchester
    I trust you will excuse my Application, it is Necessity compel me to
make it, I humbly ask for some present Casual relief, for I am at my Last 5
Extremity, not having any thing to subsist on, nor not knowing where,
nor how, to procure any, I did hope not to have been under this Necessity
any more, but work is so fallen of, I have for the last 5 weeks not Earned
more than $^s4=^d6$, nor can I find any revival of work at present, yet, I trust
it will return; I have been hard put to it, several times, since my last 10

Application, of this kind, but now I am really without any subsistance, I
humbly pray the Gentlemen to afford me some Immediate relief, tis a truth
I know not of any subsistance for the Morrow; the last past week I have
living on a scantiness of Bread only, I beg of your Clemency, some Casual
15 Assistance for the Present, relying on your Compassion for relief, I, intreat
you to Consider my case, & I will wait on Mr Clarry when he next come
up, which I think is on Wednesday to know the result; any Expression
here, which is Conceiv'd to be Amis, I beg to be forviven thankfull for all
past favors, anticipating future ones
20   I am Gentlemen, your most
                       Obed^t Hum^le Servt,
                              Wm James

T EXTUAL ALTERATIONS 2: Minister] *interl with bow, above* 'Church'. 5: I humbly] *after del*
'I humbly'. 9: ^s4] *over del illeg.*

**528   From George Craddock in [Westminster] London to Robert
        Alden in St Peter, Colchester, 12 December 1826**

                                              London Decr 12th 1826
Mr Aldon
     I am Verry Sorry to be under the Necessity of Trobling you but the
Suituation which I told you in my last I was going into I am Deprived of
5   Since the 16th of Novr last the work is Shut up till march Next owing to its
being so late in the Season before it was begun the Surveyor Said the
foundation would Not Stand there has been so much Rain And Verry
heavy - And I am greatly afraid I shall not be able to get Another Situation till that is opened again for the Streets of London is now full of Men
10 all Decriptions in astate of Starvation for want of work I hope the Gentlemen will have the Goodness to Alow you to Send me two pounds this
time as I am by <----> Next 18 Shillings behind in Rent which must <be
pa>id before the 25 which is Q^r Day or I shall loose what little things I
have if they will be So Kind as to Send that much I shall be Verry much
15 Oblidged to them And promise you that I will Not Troble you again for
two months or more if I can posably Subsist for with only one pound I shall
not have Enough to by aloaf of bread and pay my rent I am shure that no
person Can Guess at the Distress I have felt at times and am likely to feel
this winter But if the Gentlemen would rather I should Come home than

Send me any more releif have the Goodness to Answer this as Soon as 20
posable and you will Verry
    much /Obli/dge your Verry Humble and
      <Afflic>ted Servant Geo Craddock
please Direct
Geo Craddock   25
N°7 Fredrick S^t
Vauxhall road London

529 From William James in Chelmsford to Robert Alden in Colchester, 12 December 1826

          Chelmsford Decr 12 = 1826
Mr Alden
 Sir - With thankfulness I Receivd the favor of ten Shillings sent to me
by Mr Clarry which was a relief to us - I must beg your Excuse, which I
hope will be granted, for now again, I know not what to do, as I have had 5
but very little work to do, I am at a great Strait, and reduced to my last, and
now nothing to do, nor do I expect it at present, as work is very slack
indeed, I must cast myself, on Parish benevolence, for relief, if consistant
to afford it to me, if not, I ask the favor, to send me the Quarters Allowance, up to Xtmass, which is near at hand = Mr Clarry will be up on 10
Friday next, at which time I will see him and I entreat you to lett me have
something by him, but how I shall subsist till that time, I know not, as I
have nothing to do, thankfull for all past favors, I rely on your goodness
for future ones, trusting the best will be done for me that can I am sorry to
trouble you, If Necessity did not comple me, I would not do it, I ask it a 15
favor,
Pray send to me if Possible
on Friday by Clarry
you may direct as Usual
      I am Sir   20
        your Hum^{le} Ser^{vt}
          W James
Excuse me, I would pay the Postage but have not ^{d}6

TEXTUAL ALTERATIONS 7: at] *interl with caret.*

530   From George Craddock in [Westminster] London to Robert Alden in St Peter, Colchester, 20 December 1826

London Decr 20th 1826

Mr Alden

I am Verry Sorry the Gentlemen Should think it has ever been in my power to Save mony to Suport my Self from the few days work I have
5 been able to do Since last June twelvemonths And even that little if it had been like Labour I could not have performed it would to God I was able to Labour hard as I formely have done and that it was as easily procured as then - then I should not have Trobled them for assistance but those good days are gone for ever from me I firmly believe But I Know Gods
10 Tender mercies are over all his works And apart is I hope decreed for me - in my last request I told you I had 18^s/0 to pay for rent I paid it and 1^s/6^d for the Letter So I had 16^d left. Knowing this is abad time to be thurst out of doors And it is Verry likely to be with me And mine averry Dull Crismass Such a One as wee have Never before Seen for when the
15 Greater part of the Inhabitants of this land are Enjoying Good Crismas Cheer wee must Learn to be Content with almost or I might Say hungry bellies as Indeed I have not any other prospect but if the Gentlemen had been So Kind as to have Sent me the Sum I so much wanted and Realy Stood so much in need of it would have Released my mind from that
20 Troble and anxiety I have long labourd under and on the other hand I would not have Trobled them again if it had been posable for me to Suport nature till I had been Called to my Employment again And I leave it to the Gentlemen to Determine wither they will be plea<s>ed to fulfull my former request or not as I shall Readily Comply to their Decesion wishing them
25 and you health peace and plenty A mery Crismas and ahapy new year I remain with Due Respect your Verry
Humble Obedient And unfortunate unhealthy
                    Servant George Craddock
                    N°7 Fredrick Street
30   Vauxhall Road
[Postscipt on back of first page, written crosswise:] Mr Alden if the Gentlemen Should think proper to permit you to write have the Goodness to write Soon enough for me to receive your letter on Saturday as there will be no post to Town either Sunday or monday And you will much
35   oblidge your Humble Servant Geo Craddock

531   From Benjamin Hewitt in Whitton, Suffolk, 8 January 1827

1827

Sur i have sent to in form you that i Have but a wary littel work now at
this time And so genteelmen i hope you will Send me something for wok
will be Wary dull this quarter and their is a years rates you have not to me
and The overseer will not wait any longer And i am behind of my rent   5
and so Gentellmen i hope you will send me Two pounds and then iwill
not troubel you any more this winter if i can help it and so i hope you will
send by return of post if not i must come over but i thought it would be
best to send for it would be less expence i have four small children that
Cannot earn any thing   10

> Benjamin Hewitt Whitton
> Near ipswich Suffolk
> January 8

TEXTUAL ALTERATIONS 3: time] *interl at end of line.* 9: i] *after del illeg.*
WRITING Capital letters at beginning of several lines.

**532   From George Craddock in [Westminster] London to Robert
Alden in St Peter, Colchester, 7 February 1827**

Mr Alden   London Feby 7th 1827

I am this time Obligated through real Distress to Aply to you for relief
for I have Neither Money Victuals Nor Credit Nor I do not Know what or
which way to Get one Loaf of Bread untill I have your Answer which I
hope and earnestly pray you will have the Goodness to Send as Soon as   5
posable for I am More harder put to this time than I ever was In all my life
I never Intend writing to the parish Any more for I canot do without your
asistance I will Come home And should have been with you aweek ago
only that place I was last in will we think be opened again as soon as the
weather Brakes then i hope to be all right without trobling you Again -   10

> I am Sir your Very Humble
> and Most Obedient Servent
> Geo Craddock

N° 7 Fredrick St
Regent St Vauxhall   15
Road London

533   From Benjamin Hewitt in Whitton, Suffolk, 16 February [1827]

Feb 16

Sur i have sent to you a gain for something for what you sent me was
only a nuf for the rates and i would not a sent to you any more but i cannot
make out any longer with out something for the weather have been so
5   shap that i could not do much if i had it to do so genteelmen i hope you
will think a bout my famley they cannot earn any thing and i should not a
rent but i am in great destress at this time and if i do not heare from you
sur i must come home with my famley next week for i cannot make out
any longer without some releife
10   Benjamin Hewitt whitton
Near ipswich Suffolk

DATE Year from filing note on outside.
RELATED CORRESPONDENCE On 10 April 1827, John Goldsmith, overseer of Whitton, wrote
to the overseer of Colchester St Botolph, requesting relief for Benjamin Hewitt. He had
four children, and his wife was said to be 'all most worn out Being up with Her Husband'.
The reason for that was that Hewitt lay 'very dangerously ill of typhus fever', as attested
by W. Hamilton, surgeon in Ipswich, in the same letter. On 2 May 1827, Goldsmith wrote
to Robert Alden, overseer of St Peter, Colchester, that Hewitt was 'getting to His Shop
again but He is Very Weake and the Docter Say He must take Red wine and Bark for Some
time'; that he had been given £2 6d and that the doctor's bill amounted to £2 7s 6d. On 13
May 1827, Goldsmith told Alden that Hewitt was better since he had been well attended
by Hamilton. He said 'the Fever Has Been Very Bad in our Parish for this Last two Years'
and that Hamilton had 'thought it would be Necessary to Let Him [Hewitt] Have a Little
more wine for the Wheather was Cold for fear the Complaint Shold Return'. For that
reason, they had spent 'Eighteen Pence more than You Ordered', and the total amount due
to Mr Hamilton was £4 17s 6d. A little later, Goldsmith acknowledged the receipt of that
sum, and added: 'I Call,ᵈ upon Hewett & found Him at Worke He is Quite finely & Very
Thankful to think the Docter is Paid' (letter of May 1827).

534   From William James in Chelmsford to James Allen, 17 March 1827

Chelmsford March 17 = 1827

Sir,

I beg of you to pardon me, in the Liberty I take, of writeing to you, not
knowing to whom else to write, necessity compels me - Work have been
5   very slack for a long time I have had very little to do for the last six
months, not sufficient to purchase the scanty Necessaries for Subsistance,
I wrote to Mʳ Alden between Michaelˢˢ & Christˢˢ stating my Case, &

Recd from him 10 Shill^{gs} at one time & ^{s}2=^{d}6 at another, Exclusive of
Quarterly allowance, this was about a fortnight before Xt^{ss}, since that, I
have not made any application, yet have been much in want, both my self 10
& daughter, are much reduced to a state of Extreme weakness, haveing
chiefly fed on a scanty provision of bread & Potatoes, I will not dwell on
hardships; I must of Necessity Apply for Relief = I am now full Pounds
in debt for Rent, Landlady declares she will distress for it I have it not in
my Power to Pay, & have no Alternative left, but by thus stating my 15
Case, applying with humble Submission to the Benevolence of you Sir,
& the Gentlemen, to Consider, and Commiserate, my Case, and to bestow on
us at this time, something Casual, beside the Quarterly Allowance, to enable
us to make satisfaction, so that we may Escape the distress we so much
dread, at this time I am destitate of work, but trust it will Revive, I have no 20
means of procuring, I have put of Application to the last Extremity, I Beg
& hope something will be done for us, & sent to us, the latter end of the
week, if Possible by Quarter day, as we dread, that Day coming, If nothing
more can be sent by that time I beg the Quarters Allowance, may be sent,
& if more time is wanting for Consideration of our Case, I beg for some- 25
thing to be done for us as soon as possible, If tis Consistant to make you
my Friend in stateing my Case, I most humbly thank you, relying on your
kindness, I must wait the Event, & beg it may be made known to me as
soon as Possible, for I can truly say, we we are in great distress of mind
                    Sir I am Obediently Your   30
                    Hum^{le} Ser^{vt} W- James
[*Added on back of first page, written crosswise:*]
Sir I will write to Mr Alden as Usual, for the favor for the Quarterly
Allowance to be sent to me by Mr Clarry, who comes up on Friday, &
Sunday = & state to him that I have made an Application to you, (as I 40
suppose you will Communicate something of it to him)

TEXTUAL ALTERATIONS 8: time] 'e' *interl at end of line*. 12: Potatoes] *after del illeg*. 28:
known] *final* 'n' *interl at end of line*.

535   From William James in Chelmsford to Robert Alden in Colchester, 20 March 1827

Chelmsford March 20 = 1827

Mr Alden

I am very unwell, work having been very dead, tis but little I have had
to do, the last 6 months, & am brought very low in boddy, & much
5 distress'd in mind, my Daughter also, I have made application to Mr Allen,
I beg for something more than the Quarterly Allowance, & hope it will be
granted, being in debt, which I could not avoid, I ask the favor if it can be
done, to send with <t>he Quarter Allowance, so as I can have it by Quarter
day, & if my Case cannot be Considerd by that time, pray do lett me have
10 the Usual Allowance, on Friday or Sunday, by Clarry, he comes up on
those days, or I shall be put to Trouble, I trust Mr Allen will state my case,
& the Gentlemen give the Assistance, I so much need, I humbly beg, &
hope not to Offend

your Hum^le Ser^vt
15   W James

536   From George Rowe in [Great] Coggeshall [Essex], 28 March [1827]

March 28

Sir

To Sent you a fue Lines wish I hope you will Not take a Miss to Say that
my Due up to Saday Day and I for Got to Send as I was thinking of Easter
5 and will be Glad if you wold Send them by Mr Redgrift to Night for thay
Call for them the 2 Quarters is ^s7^d6 by So Doing I Chould Abledge to you

G Rowe

Coggeshall

DATE Year from filing note on back.

537 From Ann Craddock in Westminster [London] to Robert Alden in St Peter, Colchester [24 April 1827]

Mr Alden

I aplied to you last week for some money to take me into the Contry to my husband and I most humbly request you will have the goodniss to Send me an answer by saturday or else not at all as I cannot go there without your asistance but I can get to you without by being pased home   5 which I must do on Saturday if I do not here from you but if I could get back to hampshire I should Strive much against Coming nar you ever any more

     I remain your verry humble and most
     obedient Servant ann Craddock   10

I should not have wrote this only I expected you had Sent and youer answer was delaind or overlooked in the post office I means to perswaide my husband never to write any more to you but Come home if wee Cannot do without assistance

no 7 fredrek Street Regent Street   15
vauxhall road westminster

TEXTUAL ALTERATIONS 6: but if] *over del illeg.* 6: I could] *after del* 'cold'.
  CIRCUMTEXT Filing note on outside: 'G[eorge] Craddock'.
  DATE Date of filing note on outside.

538 From William James in Chelmsford to Robert Alden in Colchester, 20 June 1827

Chelmsford <J>une 20 = 1827

Mr Alden,

you will Excuse me, writeing to Inform you, that I am no better of, than when you see me, for since then, standing on the top of a pair of steps, & the string breaking, they fell, & myself with them on a pair of Stairs   5 which Injured me, so much in my side & Arm, that I could not stir, nor speak for some minutes, this was 6 weeks last Monday, I am getting better, but not recoverd, I have been bad Indeed; My Daughter continues much the same, and if, Sir, you could, with the Quarterly Allowance do me the favor, of a few Shillings, in Addition, it will be a great relief, M^r   10 Clarry comes up on Saturday, & Monday, If you can send to me on the

Saturday, I shall be thankfull, as I am for every favor; will thank you to
direct as Usual = but I will see Clarry, if I can on that day,
With Gratitude, Your Hum^{le} Ser^{vt}

15 W James

TEXTUAL ALTERATIONS 9: Quarterly] 'ly' *interl at end of line.* 11: you] *interl with caret.*

539   From Mary Death in Hacheston, Suffolk, to Robert Alden, over-seer of St Peter, Colchester [4 September 1827]

Hacherston <------> 4

Sir
   I am sorry to troubell you but as I have rote to My Daughter two Letters
and have had no answer I am quite surprised and very unhapy To think
5 that I can not hear wether She be Dead or not I should be very much
oblidge to you if you will be so kind as To favour me with a few Lines yes
to let Me know of her wether Dead or a Live
I am Sir your umble servent
Mary Death
10 The unhappy mother
of Maryann Cudbord

TEXTUAL ALTERATIONS 7: to] *after illeg.* 7: or] *after del illeg.* 11: Cudbord] 'u' *over illeg.*
DATE Date of filing note on outside.
RELATED CORRESPONDENCE On 30 November 1827, James Mason in Hacheston wrote to
Robert Alden, overseer of St Peter, Colchester, that Mary Cuthbeart's husband had run
away and that her mother, a poor widow, was unable to support her.

540   From William James in Chelmsford to Robert Alden in Colchester, 7 September 1827

Chelmsford Sepr 7 = 1827

Mr Alden,
   Sir,
   I am Sorry to be under the Necessity, of again makeing Application, for
5 some Casual relief, for since my last Application, work have been very
slack indeed, I have had but little to do, and for the last three weeks, have
Earned only 5 Shill^{gs}, would be thankfull, for some tempory relief, I will

not be tiresom in much writeing, nor would I apply <if> necessity did not
Compel me, I will only beg your referance, to my last Application, when
you saw me at Chelmsford, I am at this time, much the same as I was 10
then, I, really have expended my last, have nothing to subsist on, nor
Nothing to do; I hope, & pray, you will Relieve me, by Mr Clarry, he
comes up on S<u>nday & Tuesday; I cast myself, on the Clemency,
thankfull for past favors, trusting your Excuse for any thing amiss,
Your Hum^{le} Ser^{vt}   15
W James

TEXTUAL ALTERATIONS 10: much] *after del* 'I am at'.

541   From William James in Chelmsford to Robert Alden in Colchester, 13 September 1827

Chelmsford Sepr 13=1827

Mr Alden = &
   Gentlemen,
   Very Reluctantly, do I write now again, and sorry to trouble you, or the
Gentlemen, nor do I ever do it, only when reduced to a state of want, & 5
distress, nor even then always, but when I wrote last week, I had
expended my all, since that time have not had a single Job to do, but have
been Living, or half Living on borrowing - my strength is worn out, by
the Infirmity of Age, & the want of Necessaries to support it - I could
inlarge on this point, but this must suffice - Excuse me - Urgent necessity 10
Compels me, Friends Advise me, & would write for me, if it would do
me any good, by so doing - I hoped to hear from you to day by Mr Clarry
- I humbly hope, & ask, Relief from you by him on Saturday - I do not
dictate how, or in what way, but rely on your goodness, or I know not what
I shall do, nor how I shall get a piece of bread, - I hope not to Offend - I 15
want Instruction - I do not want to Apply to the Parish where I am - but
have been advised so to do, for Casual relief - but I think this would be
wrong - my Daughter is very bad at this time, & have been for several
days, & under the Doct^{rs} hands - Myself not half well - Neither of us,
according to the Course of Nature, are not likely to Live long -   20
   I know the Quarterly Allowance is near, I would not willingly break
into that, but I must leave all with you, to do by me as you please
   Only, Pray, send to me on Saturday, by Clarry, or as you think proper -

I commit myself to you - &
25   am your Hum^le Ser^vt
W- James
I would have paid this Letter,
but cannot

TEXTUAL ALTERATIONS 4: now] 'w' *over illeg.*

542   From George Craddock in Bishop's Waltham, Hampshire, to Robert Alden in St Peter, Colchester, 3 November 1827

Curdidge Lane Novr 3^d 1827

Mr Alden

Necessity Oblidges me to troble you for your asistance And to Inform you that I have been Verry Ill Along time Since I have been in the Country
5 and for these last three months my wife has been Verry Ill the greatest part of that time Confined to her bed which has Reduced us to poverty and misery beyond what you might Conceive for as I am now alive and writing this to you we have Neither bed nor back Cloaths to Call our own Neither ashirt I have nor Stocking to Change with Myself my wife nor
10 Children And our Brothers and Sisters have not got it in their power to Relieve us with those Necessaries Although they have treated us with all the Kindness in their power But as you Sent my wife word you Should Not Answer Any more letters when you Sent her the pound to bring her to the Country to me I should Not have trobled you with this if my wife
15 had been able to take the Jorney to Colchester I have to much love and feeling for her to be myself the Ocation of her death of further Illness But if I had known the twentyeth part of what would have befallen me Since I left you I would Not have left you in Any acount let my fate have been as it would But please God I live I will Never Spend another winter as I
20 have the two last pinched with Cold hunger and Sickness And no friend near to Soothe or Relieve or do ahand turn without Reward my Humble Request now is that the Gentlemen will Grant you liberty to Send me two pounds to by each of us Shoes and a change apiece and Some bed Cloaths and it will be the last time iwill write untill you See me if I am able to
25 Come but if please God I have my health I shall not troble you again this winter as I have work althrough hardly Enough to buy provisions Still I

will make out Somehow or other without trobling you again if I can but
have Some Cloaths to wear to work in and to Cover me at Night

with Humility and Duty

I remain your Obedient Servent 30

at Command Geo Craddock

I expect this letter will be in the London post office on tuesday as I had
afriend Brought it there on monday But if you do not Answer this by the
13th of this month I hall expect you will not write But if the Gentlemen
will not alow you to Send me Any mony I hope you will have the Good- 35
ness to post pay an Answer to me as that expence will not be much to you
and you will Mr Alden Oblidge

your Humble Servant

Geo Craddock

Sir Please Direct 40
To Geo Craddock
at Mr Leamings Curdidge Lane
Near Bishops waltham

Hants

RELATED CORRESPONDENCE On 3 December 1827, Thomas Laming in Bishop's Waltham
wrote to Robert Alden, overseer of St Peter, Colchester, that George Craddock and his
family were ill but could not be removed. He pointed out that 'if you Refuse them assistance
we will Continue to get the woman taken Care of for the Present and send the husband
home though it will be much against our will'.

543 From William James in Chelmsford to Robert Alden in Colchester, 8 November 1827

Chelsmford Novr 8 = 1827

Mr Alden=

& Gentlemen of St Peters Colchester -

I Humbly pray your Excuse, my Writeing, but Necessity & Distress
Compels me, or I would not do it, I mean not to Trouble you with writeing 5
much, as my Case is the same Over & again the same, as you will per-
ceive, by refering to former Letters - Indeed I know not what to do, for
several weeks had nothing to do, & when I have tis only a few small Jobs,
& that in a long time, my Spirits & strength are Quite worn down - Eye
sight fail me so much, that I cannot see to do any thing by Candle light & 10
work so little to do - & Strength failing me, that I cannot Earn enough to

get bread - I have been Striving & going on, as well as I can, that really I
cannot do it any Longer - In my Last I asked for Relief, & Instruction; I
Received Relief, (thankfully), but not Instruction - I humbly ask it again
15 - as I declare I have nothing to do at this time, nor nothing to Subsist on -
& for Instruction, for what I am to do in future - I have been told, if I had
any Application to make, to do it by writeing, & not to come to Colchester,
but if I must come I must, to hear what can be done for me, but how I
know not, as I cannot walk, nor can I pay for Carriage to ride, I, intreat
20 something may be done, without my coming,
   If the Gentlemen will Condesend to allow me something a week to
enable me for a Maintainance, I would be thankfull; I cannot do more
than I do, & that is but little my Necessaries for the support of Nature are
so scanty, that I really am in so debilitated a state, that I am frequently
25 fainting through weakness - I Humbly Pray for some Immediate Casual
relief, or, (tis speaking plainly) I must faint, & die - Indeed I thought I
should last Night, I have gone to the last Extremity - I am in debt, Rent
behind, Poor Rates behind - have Borrowed 5 Shill^{gs} of Mr Clarry - Pray
lett me know what I must do, & how I must proceed, whether or not I
30 must throw myself entirely on the Parish - I may obtain Relief here, but
then they will call on you for it - the Overseer call'd on me Yesterday for
the Rates, & say something must be done in them this week - I Expect the
Landlady to be Impatient also - Indeed I say again I know not what to do;
I am in a deplorable state - I cannot sufficiently explain myself
35 I thankfully Acknowledge your favors Receivd from you - I Beg not to
Offend, & trust not; & must leave my Self, & Case with the Gentlemen,
& you -
   For the present Urgency lett me hear from you by Clarry = he comes up
on Sunday
40 & the Gentlemen Answer as soon & you can - I have gone on to the last
Minute = Excuse me hopeing some work might come in; but tis not so &
my last money expended
         I am Gentlmen, with Gratitude
             your Hum^{le} Ser^{vt}
45   W James
Mr Baker on North Hill, have a Brother in Chelmsford, a Chymist, he is
Church Warden, he told me he would do any thing for me he could,
&would sign his name to my Letter, or write if it would do me any good
= & so said the Minister

I am far from being well - & my Daughter, This Evening, <i>s taken 50
worse than Usual

TEXTUAL ALTERATIONS 6: same] 'e' *interl at end of line.* 13: cannot] 't' *interl at end of line.*
40: to] *interl with caret.* 50: far] *interl with caret.*

544   From Benjamin Hewitt in Whitton, Suffolk, 11 December 1827

December 11 1827
Sur i have sent you a few lines to in Fome you that work is wary dead at
this time and i cannot make out with out Some a louence and their is a
years rates if you please to pay work is more Dull At this time then i have
known it For some years and my rent is rose up to six guines a year   5
Please to Derect to
Benjamin Hewitt Whitton
Near ipswich Suffolk

**545   From Benjamin Hewitt in Whitton, Suffolk, to the overseer of
St Peter, Colchester, 18 February 1828**

Feb 18 - 1828
Gentelmen i troubel you a gain for i Will a sure you that work is wary dull
at this Time and my fameley cannot eann any thing And what you sent
me was not a grate deal more Then my rates and that you agreed to pay
for me And i do not say but you be haved well to me in my a flicken but i   5
took between two and three pounds that i had oun me at that time for i
was wary sadley for a long time so genteelmen i hope you will send me
some thing for i am in grate Destress at this time and you may depend i
will not troubell you only when i am forced to do it so sur i hope you will
send me something then i think i can make out the summer   10
Benjamin Hewitt Whitton Near
Ipswich Suffolk

546 From Elizabeth Norman in St George in the East, London, to Robert Alden, overseer of St Peter, Colchester, 19 February 1828

London Feb^r 19th 1828

Mr Alden

Sir

Having Received a Letter from You Dated the 12 of Feb^r Which I Did
5 not Receive till the 18 Instant the Cause of that Delay I Cannot Account
for My Having a Claim on the Parish of St Peters in Colchester, Can be
Explained In a few Words, My Husband When Living in London Never
Hired a house Nor Never Paid 1 Quarters Rent, Unless by Way as a Lodger,
he Did not Live but in two Small Houses & those two Belonged to My
10 Son Isaac Norman of Which, We Paid him no Rent I have been Lodgin in
the Same House I am Now Living in for Upwards of three Years, If When
this is Laid before You Gentleman & they Whant any further Particulars
my Son Isaac Norman is Ready to Explain, also If an Affidavit Should be
Required he Will take Upon himself to Prove the Contents of this Letter
15 Since the Death of My Husband my Health is very much Impaired at My
time of Life often Impaing of the Benefits of Providence Smiling on me
but Now the Reverse, I am Obliged to Solicit aid for my Support of Which
I feel myself Intitled for Such Aid from You therefore I must once more
Remind You that Unless You Assist I Must be Under the Painful Neces-
20 sity of throwing myself Upon the Parish for Work in London has Been
Very Bad So Much So that My Children Cannot Assist me as they Would
for most of them have Large famlys my Age is 63 Years last September
Begging an Answer as Early as Possible as Such I Will much Oblige
Your &c -
25   Elizabeth Norman
N° 4 Salter Street Cannon S^t
Road St Georges in the East
PS Would thank You to Adress as Above
Accep my kind Respects to Yourself Wife & family & all Inqui/ri/ng
30 frie/n/ds Not forgetting my Mother

TEXTUAL ALTERATIONS 19: Under] 'Un' *over illeg.*

**547   From Elizabeth Norman in [St George in the East] London to
        Robert Alden, overseer of St Peter, Colchester, 14 March 1828**

London March 14 1828

Mr Aldon
    Sir
I Reciv^d Your Letter and am Glad to find You are all gread about my
Settlement my telling You what I Could Do With for Week is out of my
Power for I must Leave it to You to Settle Weakley apon me You must be   5
aware thall all I have to Live upon is Cheifly upon my Earnings as my
Sons Can Do but Little for me I<f> Sir You Will allow me Such money
Will be Sifficent to half Maintain me Would also Request Some Advance as
Early as possible as I am much in Whant of the Same
        Wishing You & Yours all Well &   10
        Remain Sir Your Ob^t Servant
        Elizabeth Norman

PLACE Inferred from previous and following letters from Elizabeth Norman (**546, 548**).

**548   From Elizabeth Norman in [St George in the East] London to
        Robert Alden, overseer of St Peter, Colchester, 23 April 1828**

London April 23 1828

Mr Alden
    Sir
feel Somewhat Surprised in Not Receiving an Answer to the Letter
Sent to you Six Weeks ago You must be aware of my Suitivation according   5
to the Letter I Sent you Would therfore Beg to hear from You as Quick as
possible If Not Necessity Will Compel me to Come Down to Colchester
& throw myself Upon Your Bounty Let me Beg of You to Use no Delay
better Send me Some Relief or Word When I Can Receive Some hope
that You & Your family are all Well But Myself am Very Unwell Accep   10
my Respect to You all and
                        Remain Sir
                            Your Ob^t Servant
                            Elizabeth Norman
                            20 Salter Street   15
                            Cannon St R^d

549   From George Rowe in Braintree, 18 September 1828

Sept 18 1828

Sir

I hope you will Not take it a Miss of my Sending to you for the Rates as thay have Call for them and the time is Nearly Up wich the 2 Quarters is
5   ˢ6.ᵈ6 wich if you will have the Goodness to Make a passell of it and Send it by Mʳ Brooks the Braintree Coach as I am Removed from Coggeshall to Braintree and he will Bring it for me and by So Doing I Shall be Ablidge to You

George Rowe
10   Braintree

TEXTUAL ALTERATIONS 3: will] *interl.*

550* From William James in Chelmsford to Robert Alden in Colchester, 28 September 1828

Chelmsford Sepʳ 28ᵗʰ 1828

Mʳ Alden,

when I was with you at Colchester, the allowance then made to me, you said was final & any furthur Application mad by me, would not be
5   attended to, & that you should not give me any Answer, but that I must come home, I am thankfull, for what was then granted to me, & for the regular manner it have been, & is, paid to me, by Mʳ Baker, I have used every Exertion, in my power, & work so little to do, & my health, & strength, & Eye sight so much impair'd, that I am arived to my last extremity, &
10   can do no more, my Landlady have seised on my all, & desired me to quit on Tuesday, but now she says on the Monday, michaelmassday, & she will take away our goods &ᶜ, & we be turned into the street, my daughter have been very bad indeed & in one Evening, did Void not less than two Quarts of Congealed blood, our Case is truly distressing & we must come home,
15   how that is to be done I know not I can truly say we have been living a half starving Life, & now have very little to subsist on, only the 4 Shillᵍˢ you allow us, for if I had a Job come in, I could not do it, & now, Sir, tis come to that, I must do something, shall I apply to the Parrish Chelmsford, for Relief & bring me home, or will you send me Relief to gett ourselves
20   home, or send to Mʳ Baker, & impower him to do it for you, which I

believe he would do, on your writeing to him, I wish not nor do I presum to
dictate, I cast myself entirely on you, will you have the goodness to write
to me directly, what I must do, home I must come, but I have not the
means of doing it, in myself, I hope not to Offend, far be frome me, so to
do, Necessity (real Necessity) Compel me to write, & with the deepest 25
Humility, & Thankfulness, I have done,

        I am your Obed^t Hum^{le}

Servt Wm James

If you write to me by the Post, you may direct for me = To be Left at

Mr Farnes Stories = Bricklayer   30

near the Windmill Inn Moulsham Chelmsford

        or If to Mr Baker =

Mr Willm Baker Chymist

        Chelmsford

        If by Mr Clarry   35

Direct as Usual = to th Care

        at Mr French

TEXTUAL ALTERATIONS 4: final] 'l' *interl at end of line*. 15: we] *interl with caret*. 18: to that]
'to' *interl with caret*. 32: near the Windmill Inn] *inserted towards left-hand edge of page*.
   WRITING This is the last letter surviving from William James. As in the previous one
(543), his handwriting is larger than in his other letters and tends to get somewhat clumsy.
   RELATED CORRESPONDENCE On 4 October 1828, Mr Baker wrote from Chelmsford to the
overseers of St Peter, Colchester: 'Mr James your Pauper here, has been to me several
times in a great deal of trouble, his landlady has taken his goods for Rent, in which he
seems to be much behind, he says he has written to you for advise what to do, I expected
you would write to him or me advising him, would you wish me to advance a sum sufficient to convey him home, or shall be conveyed through the officers of this Parish, he will
not proceed either way until he hears from you.'

551 From George Rowe in Braintree, 8 October 1828

                Oct 8 1828

Sir

   To hope you will Not take it a miss of my Sending to you for the Money
for the Rates wich is ^{s}6 and ^{d}6 for the half year wich thay applid Severell
times for it and I Sent a Note to you by the <Coa>ch Near 3 Weeks Back
but Not hearing Nothing from you I have Sent by the Braintree Cart wich 5
Sets up at horse and Groom Mary Parrish as I Live at Braintree at this
Time If you will have the Goodness to Send it By the Post Cart Man I

Shall have if Saft as I think you had Not the Last Letter I Sent to you by
10 So Doing I Should Be Abidge to you Pleas to Make a Passill of it
                                    George Rowe
                                        Braintree

552   From Elizabeth Brigg in Brightlingsea [Essex] to Robert Alden, overseer of St Peter, Colchester, 18 December 1828

Brightlingsea December 18 - 1828
    Mr Aldam Sir I have to Begg The favour of you To Shew these few
lines To the Gentelmen To Aquaint them that I have Been A flected Sum
litel Time back And hope thay Will Consider my Case for I Am Onable To
5 Do It my Sulf I would have Come but Am Unable
        I Am yours Umble
        Sirvent Elizabeth Bragg

NAME Filing note on outside: 'Brigg'.
CIRCUMTEXT Note from Walter Holliday, overseer of South Weald, on back, saying that £5
8s were due for allowance to Mrs Brigg from 21 January to 20 September 1828 at 3s per
week. Note of answer from St Peter, Colchester,: 'I Sent 6 Pounds and that paid 4 weeks
forward from the date hereof'.
RELATED CORRESPONDENCE In a letter of 22 January 1828 to the overseer of St Peter,
Colchester, Walter Holliday had informed him that Mrs Griggs (mistaken for Brigg) 'Continues Very ill at Preasant for she Cannot be Left alown therefore I dont think She will
Continued Long'. That letter is from the same hand as the above letter from Elizabeth
Brigg, but Walter Holliday's signature is in another hand (which is the same as that of his
circumtext to the latter).

553   From James and Margret Howell in Ely to the overseers and churchwardens of St Peter, Colchester, 20 January 1829

Ely January 20 1829
    Gentlman I rite to in form you of My distress that i ham Now in I have
6 Children under 13 years of age and at this time Gentlman I Cannot Get
them bread for at this time i have Made a hand Most of My Goods for My
5 Children and I have no one to Help Me but God Gentlman My Husborn
Cannot help me but very little for he Have Got avery bad Lege and it
disscharde a Grte deel from the bone braking two year ago so Gentlman I
hop you will send Me a trifle to Get Me a few Goods for Me to work for

My Children the remanir Part of the winter Gentlman you have been wery
Good in Lowing Me 2/6 per week But what is that among so many for out 10
of that I have 1/6 to pay for Reant and one Shilling to pay for shoes So
Gentlman I have Nothing to Give My babs and by My industry and the
bread flwer is so dear that My small stock of Goods will not Get My babs
food so Gentlman pray do Send Me a Small trifel to help Me throw the
winter you all Gentlman now that this parrish is behaved well to hus in 15
bandgen one of My Children to a trade and no doubt But what My others
will be the same wen thay are 14 years old if we Could but Stop in the
town but we Cannot Stop but wery few days to be peerished we went to
Mr Garratt and he Cannot do any thing for hus Without a order
Sir   20
I Ham your Humbel Servant
Ja^s and Margret Howell

TEXTUAL ALTERATIONS 4: time] *inserted in left-hand margin.* 6: me] *interl.* 7: disscharde] 'de'
interl at end of line. 7: year] 'r' *interl at end of line.* 9: remanir] 'a' *interl.* 12: and by] *after*
del 'and by'. 13: the] *after del illeg.* 15: Gentlman] *after del illeg.*

554   From Benjamin Hewitt in Whitton, Suffolk [January 1829]

Sur i have sent to inform you that i have no work At this time nor have not
had but wary little For some time so i cannot make out any longer With out
some releife i am sorrow i cannot make out With out troblen you but
flower being so dear and Work so dull that i am forst so gentlemen i hope
you Will a low me something for a few weeks now and then I hope work
will come in but i am realy in great destress At this time so gentlemen i 5
hope you send me something Derectly for my famly are realy in want at
this time
              Benjamin Hewitt Whitton near ipswich
                            Suffolk

                                                                                               10
DATE Date from filing note on back.
   WRITING Capital letters at the beginning of each line.
   RELATED CORRESPONDENCE In his letter of 19 December 1828 to the overseer of St Peter,
Colchester, W. Hamilton, a surgeon in Ipswich, claimed £2 5s for attending Benjamin
Hewitt and family when they had typhus fever.

555   From George Craddock in Westminster, London, to Robert Alden in St Peter, Colchester, 9 February 1829

Mr Aldon   London Feby 9th 1829
    I was in great hopes I should not have been under the Necessity of Trobling you for any asistance But the late hard frost throwed me out of work And I have no likelyhoods of getting in again at preasent I have
5 now been out four weeks and I realy do Not Know how to get Any provisions Not So much as one loaf of Bread this week Except I can fall in somewhere to Earn ashilling or two which is Verry uncertain there are so many men out of Employment Not Hundreds but thousands in London at this time I hope that you And the Gentlemen of the parish will Send me
10 Some money for my preasent Suport and if posable I can Get work I will Not Troble you again - I am Sir/ your Verry Humble
and most Obedient Servant
Geo Craddock
no 7 Frederick Street
15   Regent St- Horsferry Road
Westminster
London
[*In left-hand bottom corner of page, facing valedictions:*] My wife has not been able to earn was at Colchester last year And is now in avery bad
20 State of health

TEXTUAL ALTERATIONS 7: ashilling] *after del illeg.*

556   From George Craddock in Westminster, London, to Robert Alden in St Peter, Colchester, 17 February 1829

Mr Aldon - Sir)   London Febu^y - 17th - 1829
    I aplyed to you the begining of last week for Some asistance And I feel Verry much hurt that you did not Send me either money or aletter to Say the Reason you Refused me any asistance I informed you that I had been
5 out of work for Amonth which is now going on Near Six weeks if I had been at home I could have made aplication Imeadiately for Releif but being unwilling to Troble you if posable I staid as long as I could before - I wrote to you I hope you will have the goodness - to answer this as Soon as posable for I can not Remain as I am but afew days longer And I

further hope you will have the goodness to post pay the letter for I shall 10
have no money Not one penny - without Something Verry unexpeted I
should put it my way - I remain your Verry Humble and
        most Obedient Servant Geo Craddock
          no 7 Fredrick Street Regent Street
          Vauxhall Road westminster

557   From George Rowe in Braintree to Robert Alden in St Peter, Colchester, 7 March 1829

                                  March 7 1829
Sir
    I hope you will Not take it a miss of my trubling you with a fue Lines as
I Expected To heave heard from you with Respect of the Money for the
Rates as thay Doant Like to waite So Long for the Monny as the first Rate 5
was Due Last Cristmas with if you will have the Goddness to Remitt the
Money by M^r /T/anbrody Carrier by So Doing
I shall be Abidge to you
        George Rowe
        Braintree   10

TEXTUAL ALTERATIONS 3: you with] 'you' *inserted in left-hand margin.*

558   From George Rowe in Braintree to Robert Alden in St Peter, Colchester, 11 May 1829

                                March 11 1829
Sir
    I Revecerd the Answer you Sent and I was Sorry to hear it as you told
me when I was over that You wold pay the Rates wich you Say as the
Reson for paying them is Becorce I am at home but if Eaney thing it the 5
Worse for Me Only I am handay to see to her for She have Not Seen me
to know me for this years and what I Request of you is No help to me but
I wold wish to Do as Long and as Sir as I Can and that is Rule of the
Parrish that you know for the Overcer told me that he Paid a Deel of
Monny that Way as it Cost me all I Can Get to pay my Way this Quarter 10
for Rent is £1.^s5 and the Rates for the ^1/2 year is ^s7.^d6 and what with

haveing me to Do what I have to Do at the Worst adwantage I Can Not
pay the Monney and to Leve the place will Not be No adwantage to you
as I am Between 60 and 70 years of Age and I find I am Not fitt to Do
15 Good Worke that if I Leve this place I Cant Get a Nother as my time of
Life that If you will Consider on it and Give me an Answer Next Satterday
By the Bearer of this Not as he will know the Settewation that I am in as
it is No Bennefett to me Only to keep me hear

George Rowe
20 Braintree

TEXTUAL ALTERATIONS 16: Give] *interl.*

559   From Edward Mills in Brisley, Norfolk, February 1832

Brisley Norfolk Feby 1832

Sir) I received Yours which requested my examination to be taken, and
sent by the Parish Officer of Brisley, but as I did not apply to them for
relief, it have not been taken but I can assure you that my examination.
5 when taken at Colchester by Thomas Hedge Esqr and again taken at Bures
St Marys, By, the Revd James Dear. and the Revd Leroux. Two of the
Magistrates for that Hundred it was clear in both cases that I made a
Settlement in St Peters by living with Mrs Emma Gonner. and was by an
order from the last mentioned Magistrates. brought to your Parish and
10 relieved untill I got the better of my lameness. which was from the effects
of Rheumatic Gout or Fever. I have not since made a Settlement in any
way. but if the Parish is not satisfied. I must come to Colchester. but I am
at this time very unwell I have not been able to do my Business for the
last Month. I am so unhappy about my Bills that are unpaid at Brandon
15 and the threats that I receive every Week. from the Persons to whom
they are due, some by Lawers Letters, and Others that seem to be
deturmined to inform the Board, if they are not paid in a short time, I
received a Letter from a Mr Issacon an attorney at Mildenhall, by the
order of one of my Creditors werein he say that if the Amount is not paid
20 to him on or before the 12th March. that he himself shall be Obliged to
inform the Board. as several of my Creditors have appli^d to him to get
their Bills from me. Therefore I humbly beg of the Gentlemen to consider
the matter without delay and do that which seems to themselves most Just
and wise. I can say of a Truth it is apainful task for me to be obliged to ask

for their assistance. but if I had submitted to my unfortunate fate without 25
makeing it Known to them possible they mite have blamed me in that
case. but I have laid the case before them actually as it is. Therefore they
are at liberty to do that which they think proper. nothing but an advance
of Thirty Pounds will enable me to meet the immediate demant of my
Creditors. and to continue in the Imployment. without being Called upon 30
by the Board to pay my Debts or leave the Imployment. which if that
should be the end, it will bring home to St Peters Parish Thirteen of us, and
only one out of that number are able to get ist own living you mention in
yours to me that the Gentlemen said a 100 £ ayear, was apretty income
and that it is were there are not half the number in family it has cost me for 35
the last seven Years at the rate of 32 £ ayear fro. House. Rent & Rates.
the remainder of a 100 was but a scanty. sum to supply the different
callings of a Family like mine with a Sickly Wife always under Medical
attendance and for the Most part of five years obliged to have a Woman in
the House.   40
    [*Written crosswise on last page:*] The amount of my Debts as Collected
from the Bills. amounts to between 40 & 50 Pounds. and if the Parish will
advance me 30 £ iwill Indeavour to settle the rest with my Creditors, and
return 10 £ out of the 30 to then by two payments. within Eighteen Months
from the Date of their - advance, if so, - and if not so. both the Parish and 45
my self must
                       submit to the Fate
Please to let me have an Answer by the 3^d of March next
                I am Yours & Respectfilly
                    Edward Mills   50
                         Excise Officer
                        Brisley Norfolk
{NB I think I have some recolection of you being in the Garden seed
way, at the time I was at Gonners.}
{I have no doubts but you have <s>ome knowledge of me   55

TEXTUAL ALTERATIONS 8: Settlement] *after del illeg.* 25: fate] *interl with caret.* 44: out]
after del 'to'. 55: have] *over illeg.*
    WRITING Written on ruled lines.

560 From Margaret Howell in Ely to the overseer of St Peter, Colchester, 16 April 1832

Ely April 16th 1832

Gentlemen/

My Husband is very ill with the Cholera Morbus, and cant get out of Bed. and I have been Ill with the same Complaint and the Oldest & Young-
5 est of our Sons are also ill. and the Trade is all stoped so that when a Hawker goes to call the Vilagers from Ely the People refuse them admitance and I return You My sincere thanks for the 10^s/ You sent us but what is that for 7 of us for a month and unless You send us Relief we must have it from this Parrish And then when we get better they will send
10 us home for We are in great distress I am

Gentlemen Your Humble

Servt Margaret Howell

April 16 1832

CIRCUMTEXT Note from other hand underneath, 16 April 1832: 'This woman's statement is correct John Muriel Surgeon Robt Stevens M:D: Ja^s Garratt.'

561 From William Wilsher in Norwich to the overseer of St Peter, Colchester, 18 September 1832

Norwich Septr 18.. 1832

To the Overseer's of St Peters

Gentlemen

I am truely sorroy to be obligated to send to you under the present
5 circumstances but necessity drives me to it, for I have not any regular employment and my Wife's affliction for nearly these last three year's and I have got friends for her assistance for medicene at the dispensary but they would not keep her on as patient only 2 weeks they then said they could do nothing for her and told me she must have all the nourish-
10 ment I could get her but for want of employ it is not in my power, and I am reduced to the same straits that I were in when I made the application to you last year I therefor trust as it is not a cause of my own seeking but the hand of providence that has appointed this affliction you will endeav-our to relieve me with a trifle for to enable me to get through as you were
15 so good as to relieve me last year I trust you will do the same this and by

so doing it will be avery great act of charity as it is not in my power to get
what is necessaryly wanted your answer will oblige

> your's Respt^y
> Wm Wilsher

opposite of Mr High's   20
St Clements
Norwich

TEXTUAL ALTERATIONS 17: what] *over illeg.*
CIRCUMTEXT Anonymous undated draft of answer to overseers of Norwich on back of
first page: 'Wishire has again made Application to the parish for relief Stating that his Wife
is in a dreadful State of Health (He has changed his residence and Say Direct for WW -
opposite In Highs St Clements) will you have the Kindness to Step in and hear & See if
his Report be Correct and if you think he realy want it they have it in Contemplation to
give him a Sovereign but not more.'

562   From Edward Mills in Brisley, Norfolk, to Robert Alden in St Peter, Colchester, 23 September 1832

> 1832 Brisley Norfolk Sept 23^d

Sir/ I have to inform you that I am not allowed to take to my Business untill
I am provided with a Horse to perform my Duty with. therefore if the
Parish will not advance me the Sum of Eight or ten Pounds. I shall be at
Colchester with my Family. with in the space of a week or Ten Days. as   5
I am out of Pay and have not one Shilling to help myself Therefore I hope
The Gentlemen will be so kind as to Answer this per return of Post.

> I am Yours &c &c
> Respectfully
> Edwd Mills   10

TEXTUAL ALTERATIONS 3: the] *inserted with caret.* 7: this] *after del* 'as'.

563   From Margret Howell in Ely to the overseers and church-wardens of St Peter, Colchester, 3 October 1832

Ely octber 3 1832
   Gentlman I rite to inform You of the trubel i ham now Left in my husband is taken away from me and put to prison for a dad of two pounds
seven shillin wich we run for bread for the Children in the Cholery sickners

5 Gentlman my Husbon and Sulf and two Children was bad five weeks and
Could not arn one Shilling and now Gentlman i ham an as Bad a trubel my
husband is Got to remain in prison for six weeks for the Cort Date and
Gentlman It is not in my power to maintain all my Children myself So
ihope Gentlman you will healp me in the Time Mr Garratt wished me to
10 Rite he nowes my trubel Gentlman you tould me the larst time that i was
at Colchester that you wold healp me wen in Grat need for it wold be
much beter then to troll the Children So many miles
     Sir
     I Ham your Humbel Servent
15   Margret Howell

TEXTUAL ALTERATIONS 3: dad] 'd' *over* 't'. 4: shillin] 'in' *interl at end of line*. 5: weeks] 's' *interl at end of line*. 6: Could] 'u' *inserted*. 11: wold healp] 'wold' *interl*.

564   From William Wilsher in Norwich to the overseers of St Peter, Colchester, 8 November 1832

Gentlmen
    I am sorroy to say that I have no employment nor do I know when I
shall I truely thankful to you for the sovereign you sent me and made up
the remainder for one Quarters Rent <lef>t of the half year's that was due
5 but haveing no employment I am in avery bad situation and under the
necessity of troubleing you again which I am truely sorroy for but if you
will be so kind as to let me have a trifle more I will do my endeavours to
remain here if not I must sell my things & pay my debts as far as I can &
come home to you as I cannot live here without your assistance
10   I am Your's Resp^y
                   Willm Wilsher

Norwich Novr 8
1832 St Clements
near the Walebones
15 New Catton

TEXTUAL ALTERATIONS 3: the] 'h' *over illeg*.
    RELATED CORRESPONDENCE On 20 December 1832 Mr Howe jun. wrote from Norwich to his father Mr Howe sen. in Colchester, St Peter: 'I am troubled and troubling you about Wiltshire again, when you authorized me to advance Wiltshire a Sovereign he had just obtained one peice of work which he finished last Monday week and has obtained now since and will certainly not be able to obtain any more till after Christmas [...] I have

given him four shillings out of the Sovereign, they must pay one Quarters rent this Xmas or have their sticks taken for it that is 1$^£$7^{s}6^d. I have 16^s/- in hand and think if the Parish will send him down another Pound or the Quarters Rent I could give him the remainder of the first Pound for three or four weeks, he might then obtain work, and not trouble them any more this Winter. if they will not do that for him he must come home, and be much more expensive, as he is troubled with Hernia they cannot compel him to work - William Newton comes to Norwich on Saturday, I wish you would let me know what they intend to do with him he wanted me to Write before, but I put it off from time to time in hopes he might obtain something to do - do not forget it.'

565   From James Howell in Ely to the overseers of St Peter, Colchester, 16 January 1833

Ely Jany 16th 1833

Gentlemen/

I am sorry I am under the necessity To inform You that My Daughter Sarah is with Child by a young Man whose Name is George Murray and this Parrish is about passing her home and George Murray Immediately   5
He and his Friends know when that is to take place he will leave Ely for London where is elder Brother has been working as a Rope Maker those last fourteen Years. and now he has Established himself as Master man in a firm with his Second Brother and George Murray is at Present working for them as Journeyman now Gentlemen the Question I have to ask you   10
whether it will be better to have her passed home To her parrish - so that it gives George Murray an opportunity of going away where perhaps You may never find him or whether You think well to come to Ely to take him whereby he may Marry My Daughter or otherwise indemnify Your Parrish from all expences. Gentlemen having stated My Daughter case and the   15
Young Man's as plain as my poor abilities will allow Me I will thank You to write me in which Way You would wish Me to proceed Please to Direct to James Howell

     Potters Lane Ely

     I am Y^r most Oba^t Humble Servt 20

     J. Howell

[Postscriptum on top of the next page:]
We are Creditably informed He is going to leave on Thursday 23 January instant and if You come to Ely send for Me in as private Way as You can

     I am Gentlemen Y^{rs} 25

     &c Ja^s Howell

TEXTUAL ALTERATIONS 5: her] *interl with caret*. 7: Brother] *interl with caret*. 7: been] *after del* 'Bro'. 8: himself] *interl with caret*. 9: and] *after interl and del* 'at Ely'. 12: perhaps] *after del* 'perh'.

566 From William Watson in [St Marylebone] London to Robert Alden, overseer of St Peter, Colchester, 29 January 1833

London Ja^n 29 *1833*

Sir i am under the necessity of applying to you for releaf as my health is bad that i am not able to doe Sufficent work to support my self and Wife through my Long afflition thare is a Letter at my Mothers that i ad from
5 the Doctor in August to certify that i was to come into my natif air for the benifit of my health but i ad not the means to com with and i shall be glad if you would alow me a trifle a weake till i get better if not i am a fraid that i shall be forst to through my self on the parish that i Liv in

i Remane Your Humble Servent
10 William Watson
25 Marelebone Lane Oxford street

TEXTUAL ALTERATIONS 1: London] *after del* 'Lon'. 4: Mothers] *after del* 'the'. 4: that] *after del illeg*. 5: for] *after del* 'f'. 7: you] 'u' *over illeg*. 11: 25] *after del illeg*.

567 From Edward Mills in Brisley, Norfolk, to the overseer of St Peter, Colchester, 9 May 1833

Norfolk Brisley May 9th 1833

Gentlemen & Parishoners. I beg to lay before you the present state of my Situation. which you will se by the Enclosed Letter, that I am called upon by the Board to give my reasons for not being provided with a Horse
5 having been once before called upon, the consequence will be unless I am provided with a Horse within a fortnight from the date of my Letter which I have Transmitted to the Board, I shall be discharged. without any remuneration for my past services. and Ultimately must come home with Twelve in Family to your Parish for subsistance; should it seeme to be
10 expedient. to transmit any sum you may think fit Toward the purchase of a - Horse of the price of Ten Pounds. it will be Graciously received by me & Family - as I have not the smalest means of procureing this. for my continuing in the Excise. having no one of my Family relations able to

assist me with one Shilling. therefore Gentlemen hope you will answer this
as soon as possible. that I my fate may Know, what ever you have to 15
Transmit on this Business please to do it to Mr Francis - Frohawk Overceer
of this Parish if you do not think proper to correspond to me, as that is the
Gentleman that will have the trouble of bringing us to Colchester. Immediately I am - Discharged,

I am   20
Gentlemen
Your Obedient Servt
Edwd Mills Excise Officer

WRITING Written on ruled lines.

**568   From James Howell in Ely to the overseers of St Peter, Col-
chester, 14 October 1833**

Ely 14th Octr 1833

Gentlemen;
   I beg to solicit pardon for the trouble herein given, and trust the
reasonabless of my request will do away all Offence.
   Some time since myself, wife, and one of our Children were attacked 5
by Cholera most seriously, the effect of which I have not yet entirely
recovered from -
   Mr Robert Stevens of this place attended us in his Profession as a medical
Gentleman. His Charge for attendance I believe you are in the Possession
of - He has again applied for Payment of his account; and as I am 10
circumstanced (advanced in Age and Poverty, and having three Children
under 12 Years of Age), it is utterly out of my power to make him any
remuneration for the services he Kindly exercised towards us in our
affliction: indeed we cannot feel too grateful towards him; and therefore
we most earnestly implore our petition that you will discharge the Bill 15
may be Granted.

I am,
Gentlemen,
Your obed^t Humble Servant,
James Howell.   20

P.S. In consequance of a complaint I have upon me I am frequently obliged
to have Mr Stevens's aid, or it would be fatal

TEXTUAL ALTERATIONS 5: since] *interl with caret*. 5: were] *interl with caret*. 12: 12] *after del* '3 Ye'. 13: services] *after del* 'kind'. 14: we] *after del* 'if'.

RELATED CORRESPONDENCE Some time after this letter, James Howell went to Isleham in Suffolk. On 15 October 1825, J. Woods and G. Fletcher, overseers of that place, wrote to the overseer of St Peter, Colchester, that James Howell, who had a wife and four children, had broken his leg. They reckoned with expenses of about £10, and asked what St Peter, Colchester, was prepared to remit; 'otherwise we shall be under the necessity of obtaining an order of removal and getting it suspended which will caus you a much greater expence than complying with our request'. St Peter, Colchester, seem to have agreed, for on 11 January 1826 Woods and Fletcher sent an account of payments made to Howell amounting to £9 14s 6d.

569 From Edward Mills in Brisley [Norfolk] to the overseers of St Peter, Colchester, 28 October 1833

Gentlemen/

The bearer of this Letter is my Wife who is come to inform you of the near arrival of me and Family to your Parish House, which nothing shall prevent, but your compliance to the request, which is if you do not think
5 expedient so to do. you shall see me, and Ten or Eleven Children as soon as possible after the Recept of a Letter from my Wife, - Informing me of your ansser =

If I am not provided with about Ten Pounds to Purchas a Horse by the thursday the 6th Nov 1833
10   Gentlemen
                                         I am your humble Servt
                                         Edward Mills
Brisley Octr 28th 1833

TEXTUAL ALTERATIONS 13: 1833] *interl below*.

570 From William Wilsher in Norwich to the overseers of St Peter, Colchester [1 January 1834]

To the Overseer's of the Parish of St Peter in Colchester in Essex, Gentlemen/

I am truely sorroy to say I am under the necessity of makeing an application to you for relief but my case is a very hard one my Wife being so much
5 afflicted & not haveing any worke by the two & three weeks together and being also afflicted myself with a very bad rupture and am myself in wants

of a double trusse for it and at the same time thretned by my Landlady to distress for a Quarter & ahalf's Rent and also in debted for medicine's for my wife which for want of employ I am not able to pay them & I trust under these distressing cercumstances you will take it into consideration & allow me a Trifle towards my Rent &c your answer will much Oblige

Your's Resp^{y}
Willi^{m} Wilsher

near the Wale Bone's St Clements, Norwich

DATE Date of postmark.

RELATED CORRESPONDENCE On 7 January 1834 Mr Howe jun. wrote from Norwich to Mr Howe sen. in Colchester, St Peter: 'Agreable to your request I look'd in upon Wiltshire last night. there is misery and wretchedness, with poverty plainly apparent in their house but I found he had that day obtained a peice of work, but the manufatoring is so slow that those who have constant work are [ob]liged to play three or four days betw[een] [*paper torn*] every peice, upon enquiring I find he is indebted a half years rent all but 13 shillings, which is 2 guineas, and a few shillings to their doctors, - Perhaps they might save a few shillings in the Summertime, but that is a thing which does not enter their heads as they (situated as they both are in respect to health) are sure you must releive them, your officers of course must do what they please but I think if they were to send three pounds, out of which the rent to be paid and the remainder to be given to them as appears necessary, they would not be again troublesome till about this time twelve month.'

On 18 January 1834 he wrote again. He had advanced 15s to Wilsher who had called on him and produced a certificate from Lancelot Dashwood, surgeon, saying that Wilsher was 'labouring under a double scrofal hernia' and that he required 'a good double truss which will cost 25^{s}/-^{d}'. Howe suggested 'the Overseers had better send the money Down and let the truss be bought here as it is much better he should be fitted; as they cannot be so certain of the size by measure'.

571 From Benjamin Hewitt in Whitton, Suffolk, to the overseer of St Peter, Colchester [2 January 1834]

sur i am sorrow that i have to trouble you a gain but i have been ill for six weakes so that i have not been abel to do but awary littel work i had a docter and he bled me and i had a box of pills to take and i was getting better then the rumath*[e]*ck sesed me in the hands and arlms so that i could do but a wary littel work and i have got five shilings to pay the rate and our overseer say that he must have it betwen this and monday next because that is his pay and if you do not beleive this gentelmen our overseer told me he would send you a letter to satesfie you that it is true and i am in grate destres for i have got no money at all now Benjamin Hewitt
Whitton
Near ipswich suffolk

TEXTUAL ALTERATIONS 5: wary] 'y' *over illeg.* 5: shilings] 'l' *over illeg.* 9: Benjamin] *after del* 'i'.
DATE Date of postmark.

572   From Benjamin Hewitt in Whitton [Suffolk] to the overseer of St Peter, Colchester, 6 January 1834

Janr 6
Gentelmen i am sorrow that i have to trouble you but i have been ill for more then six weeks so that i have not been abel to do but a wary littel work in that time and i had the docter to pay and i owe the last quarters
5 rate and that should be paid before to day for this is the town meeting to day and so gentelmen i cannot make out with out a littel of your a sistens any longer
                    Benjamin Hewitt Whitton

TEXTUAL ALTERATIONS 4: owe] 'w' *over illeg.*
CIRCUMTEXT Note from John Goldsmith, overseer of Whitton, 6 January 1834, underneath: 'I Do Certifie the above Statement to be true'.

573   From Ellen Broker in Leicester to Robert Alden in St Peter, Colchester, 20 January 1834

                              Leicester Janurary 20 1834
Sir/ Please to send me word weither James Broker his at your Workehouse or wheither he has been there for he has Left Leicester for three weeks Please to send for I Intend to throw myself on this Parish and be
5 sent with orders for the Overseer his a going to write to Goverment for the half of his Pension for I Cannot maintain myself for I have tried for this last three weeks has trade is verry Bad Please to Direct to William Homes Brok Street Leicester
Sir/ this Comes from Ellen Broker the Wife of James Broker -

574 From James Howell in Ely to Robert Alden, overseer of St Peter, Colchester, 30 January 1834

Ely Jenry 30 1834

Sir I reseved yours but have Not heared any thing of George Murry Sir if at Ely he is Cept up Close his frinds are all at home and wery still about it Sir i Cannot inform you any furder at this time as Soon as i Can i will rite without Deley Sir plese to tell my wife to Come home for i ham wery bad   5 and but a lettle Stay to my family

Sir I ham

Your Humble Servent Ja^s Howel

TEXTUAL ALTERATIONS 3: are] *after del illeg.* 5: my] *over del illeg.*

RELATED CORRESPONDENCE On 21 August 1832, Robert Stevens, a surgeon in Ely, had written to the overseer of St Peter, Colchester, saying that £4 were due to him for attending James Howell. Stevens had claimed the same sum on 11 July 1833, saying that Howell was 'at this time seariously ill again' and that 'unless you send an order for the amount I shall as soon as he is able to be removed have him & family passed home'. Apparently Colchester had complied with it, for on 19 November 1833 he had written again and informed them that Howell was 'very ill with disease at the neck of the bladder & unable to do any kind of work, I have been obliged to draw off his water for many days'.

575 From Benjamin Hewitt in Whitton [Suffolk] to the overseer of St Peter, Colchester, 13 February [1834]

Feb 13

Gentelmen i am sorrow to troubel you a gain but i have but a wary littel work at this time and my being ill so long that iam wary much in destress at this time and my boys being out of work for they will not employ only them that belong to the parish so gentelmen i hope you will take that in to   5 consideration and send me somthing if you send me a pound gentelmen i will try my best endaver to keep from you all the summer i would not a troubled you but i am reley fost for i am in grate destress i have pauned my things till i have got no more so i must beg a littel of your a sistens if you please   10

Benjamin Hewitt Whitton

TEXTUAL ALTERATIONS 6: pound] *after del* 'po'.

DATE Year from postmark.

576   From William Green in Ipswich to Robert Alden, overseer of St Peter, Colchester, 20 February 1834

Ipswich Feb. 20 1834

Sir/

I take the Liberty of writing these few lines to you concerning the Boy I
have exerted myself to the utmost endeavouring to get him out as an
5 apprentice to some Trade & to find him a Master. but in Vain. but I have
a Brother a Master Bricklayer living in the same parish where the boy is
and he says he will learn the Boy the Business if he is provided with
Clothes which Sir is entirely out of my Power to find him with as I am
afflicted & not able to do but little work & cannot find but little to do &
10 my wife but Just up after her confinement. therefore Sir I must leave It to
yourselves hoping you will be so kind as to provide him with what you
think proper for him as it is entirely out of my Power to do it and if I lose
this opportunity it may be some time before i could meet with any thing
Else for him -

15   from your Humble Servt
                                                       Wm Green

TEXTUAL ALTERATIONS 3: concerning] *second* 'n' *interl with caret.* 10: confinement] 'm'
over del illeg.

577   From James Ludbrook to the overseer of St Peter, Colchester, 23 April 1834

April 23 - 1834

Gentleman i humbly beg pardon for taking this liberty of writing these few
lines to you but i have not the conveniency of coming to state it to you by
word of mouth i sincerely return you many thanks for what i have received
5 from you which was more than i deserved but still there is one favour
more which i hope and trust will be the last and i hope you will not think
that i write this with a flattering tongue for i do assure you that i shall use
my best endeavours to oblige my Master and likewise to Redeem my
Carracter again i would not have troubled you but i have not earnt any
10 money over my wages at present but i expect to do so before long therefore
if you will grant me the sum of ten Shillings to Pay for a Coat and a pair of
Trowsers which i have got offerd to me very cheap and which i am very

much in wants of for Sundays as my Jacket gets soon dirty in the Stable
and my Trowsers are torn i have but one Shirt but i will try and get if you
will be so kind as to grant me this favour   15
    I wish to explain to you Gentleman that i do not wish you to give me
this mony but i wish to return it again as soon as it lays in my powers so
to do i wish to state to you likewise that if you think that i want this
money to put to a bad use your extremely welcome to see the things that
i have mentiond the reason i ask this favour is becase i am very much in   20
wants of them and i shall not have the oportunity of having of them again
so cheap at what they are offered to me now Gentleman i hope that i shall
be enabled now to make up for my past Conduct which has been very
much to my disgrace and to gain esteem by those of whom i have been
lookt upon with disrespect and i wish to Abandon the Alehouse which   25
has been the cause of all my trouble and disgrace -
    Gentleman i can answer to this if called upon so to do I hope you will
keep this Letter to prove what i what i have stated to prove true
James Ludbrook -
[*On back of outside, facing first page of text:*]   30
From or unworthy and and undeserving
Servant James Ludbrook -
Gentleman i hope you will forgive me for my Past Conduct and i shall
endeavour to my Study to Amend

TEXTUAL ALTERATIONS 2: this] *after del* 'taking'. 3: lines] *interl below*. 14: will] 'w' *over
del illeg*. 16: to explain] 't' *after del illeg*. 16: you to] *after del* 'wish'. 21: not] *interl
below*.

**578   From James Howell in Ely to Robert Alden in St Peter, Col-
        chester, 1 May [1834]**

Ely May the 1 182*[-]*
    Gentlman i rite to inform you that Gorge Murry is Come to Ely and been
thre for 2 days Geting drunk but How Long is Going to Be thre i Cannot
tell no one knowes that i have Rote to you but my Sulf So Gentlman you
Can pleage your sulf about Comun Gentlman if you Come set up at the   5
wite Lion in the Lettle parrish and then sand for me saying that there is a
Lace man whant to sell me sum Gentlman if you Com Let it be in the
evening then i shall be at home but Gentlman if you think it wold be

better to stop to see wether he Sattles thre pray send me a latter by return
10 of post as i shall be Looking
Sir
        I Ham yours Ja^s Howel
        potters Lane Ely

TEXTUAL ALTERATIONS 3: Be] *after del* 'be brout'. 6: saying] 'y' *interl*. 7: sell] 'e' *interl above
del illeg*.
    DATE Filing note on outside: '1834'.

**579   From James Ludbrook to the overseers of St Peter, Col-
        chester, 12 July 1834**

Sir i should be obliged to you if you would be so kind as to let me have 6
shilligs to get some shoes as i have not Got any to wear i should not have
troubled if i had the means of Getting any myself but i have not earnt
anything over my wages for some time past i wish i had not to trouble you
5 at all for tis against my indination so to do therefore if you will be so kind
as to let me have it i shall not trouble you no more for sometime what i can
Buy for myself i will when i can I am obliged to you for past favours -
                                        James Ludbrook -
                                        July 12th 1834

TEXTUAL ALTERATIONS 1: so] *after del* 'as to let'. 3: not] *interl*. 7: i can] *after del* 'i the'.

**580   From William Wilsher in Norwich to the overseers of St Peter,
        Colchester, 22 December 1834**

Gentlemen
    I am truely sorroy to be obligated to write to you again but under the
present distressing cercumstances I am forced I haveing had but very
little worke for the last nine Months and my Wife being so afflicted I am
5 <obli>ged to make this application being so <dist>ressed for want of
employ I am back of my Rent for the last six Month's which is £1..16s..-
and hveing no means of paying haveing no worke nor any likelyhoods at
present & my Wifes affliction I cannot get subsistance and am very much
in need of your assistance in my present distressed situation, your answer
10 will much oblige your distressed applicant

Wm Wilsher

Norwich
Decr 22 1834

near the Whale Bones
New Catton St Clements 15
Norwich

TEXTUAL ALTERATIONS 6: £1] *over* '2'.

581   From William Wilsher in Norwich to the overseer of St Peter, Colchester, 2 January 1835

Gentlemen

I am sorroy to trouble you a second time but not haveing any answer from you I am obliged to write again for haveing no employ of any kind for the last month nor any likelyhoods at present, makes my <c>ase truely pityable and under the afflictions of my Wife & myself for if I could get a   5
Job of portering I could not do it on account of my ruptured state I should feel greatly obliged to you if you could send me a truss and return me an answer as I do not trouble you till I am drove to the greatest distress I wish it was in my power to do without it but it is not and I now hope you will give me an answer in a few days or I must make a further application 10
were I am

I remain yours truely W Wilsher

1835 Norwich
Jany 2}
PS/ the Particulars I give you in my last letter I hope you will give me an 15
answer to this Direct for me W. Wilsher near the Whale Bones new Catton
St Clements, Norwich

TEXTUAL ALTERATIONS 2: not] *interl with caret.* 3: of any] *over illeg.*
RELATED CORRESPONDENCE On 22 January 1835 Mr Howe jun. wrote from Norwich to his father Mr Howe sen. in St Peter, Colchester, reporting that Wilsher needed a truss of the size of 36 1/2 inches 'according to his own statement', and that 'he wants it very much and hopes you will send Down as soon as possible'. Apparently the truss which was sent was not appropriate. On 27 January 1835, Howe received a letter from Lancelot Dashwood, surgeon, who said that the truss Wilsher had shown him was 'quite unfit for his case. if he attempts to wear it it will ruin him [...] He is very badly ruptured and requires a Truss of a peculiar construction.' This is the last piece of evidence relating to William Wilsher, so we do not know whether he ever got the truss he wanted.

**582   From Benjamin [Hewitt] in Whitton [Suffolk] to the over-
seer of St Peter, Colchester, 19 January 1835**

1835 Janr 19

Gentelmen i am sorrow that i have to trouble you but trade is so bad at
this time that i cannot make out any longer without your a sistance for i
have no work for my famley at this time and i am be hinde of my rates
5 and rent so gentelmen i hope you will be so kind as to send me some thing
in stid of my coming over to see you for it is a good way to come but if
you do not send me something gentelmen i must come and see you but
gentelmen if you will send me a pound i will try and make out without
troubleing of you any more this winter if posebel i can
10   Benjamin Whitton Near
Ipswich Suffolk

TEXTUAL ALTERATIONS 2: you] *interl.* 7: gentelmen] *after del illeg.* 9: troubleing] 'l' *over* 'e',
'ing' *interl.* 11: Suffolk] 'S' *over* 's'.
WRITING From same hand as all other letters from Benjamin Hewitt.

**583   From George Webb Baynell in Romford [Essex] to Robert
Alden, overseer of St Peter, Colchester, 2 March [1835]**

Sir having recived a few lines informing me of the situation that you have
placed my Wife in i i should be much a blicht to you if you wold give her
a few Shilling to pay her expences up to me for that is not in my pour to
pay them as i have not got full impliment till the trade begin to revive but
5 i have had a dad eye for a weak since i have bean hear so that i have not
bean able to work through a pin getting in to it, For my master promist
me a ful seat of work as soon as the trade begin to revive if you do not
imust come back to Colchester and share the same as them for i ham
shure i cannot get work ther but if you will get me som work i will come
10 home, all i request of you is a few shillings if you will give her five
Shilling and my few thing that you taken when you paid the rent i will
not trouble you for any thing els
Romford March 2 1825
George Webb Baynall

TEXTUAL ALTERATIONS 2: i should] 'i' *after del illeg.* 5: hear] *interl at end of line.* 6: For]
after del 'so'. 7: ful] *after del illeg.* 9: shure] 'u' *over del* 'i'. 10: all] *after del* 'if'. 10: of]
'o' *over* 'i'. 10: shillings] *after del* 'shilling i will'. 10: give] 'v' *over illeg.*
DATE Postmark: 2 March 1835. '1825' is obviously a slip of the pen.

584 From James and M[argaret] Howell in Ely to the overseers of St Peter, Colchester, 1 April 1835

April 1 1835

Gentlemen

I am sorry to Wright to you on this Account Of so Great a dresstress as I am now in for my husban is taken ill with his Old Complant that he Cannot earn One Farthin for the famley nor yet Get Out of the house so Gentmen I shall 5 be oblig to Come home for when I hope you will Considr me and not take me Of my pay that you allowe me for it all I can do to Get Bread now but Getnmen you will take me Of I must Come and all my Famly Cardgebele for I can asure you that thers is no thing to do at Ely For I have Four that do not Earn me One halpenny so Gentmen you must Consider me As I am will to do As 10 Far as I can but with out your assitans i mu must yeald and Come home

James Owell
& M Owell

TEXTUAL ALTERATIONS 4: Complant] 'lant' *interl at end of line.*
CIRCUMTEXT Note from Robert Stevens, MD, Ely, 1 April 1835, on next page: 'Robert Howell is now ill under my care with diseased Kidney & Bladder & requires to have his water drawn off daily'.

585 From George Rowe in Bocking [Essex] to [Robert] Alden in St Peter, Colchester, 3 April 1835

April 3 1835

Sir

I hope you will Not take it rd of my Sending to you about the Rates but thay applide to me for them and Can assure you that I Cannot pay them you Will know the Settewtion that I am in that my Wife is Not able to See 5 to Do for Uss and I am forst to Get me to Do for Uss and pay for it and my Rent and Club wich Do Nott amount to Less then $^s3^d6$ a Week wich I have but $^s6$ a Week besides your $^s2$ for What I Do and the Gentlemen Said that thay wold pay the Rates as Long as Could Gat Employment and if thay Dont I must Come Home and I hope you will Send wich way I am to 10 Do by Mr Hodges as I must Give them an Answer to it

George Rowe
Bocking

TEXTUAL ALTERATIONS 4: me] *interl.* 4: pay] *after del illeg.* 5: Wife] *interl.* 10: Send] *interl.*

586   From Mary Braig in Brightlingsea [Essex] to the overseer of St Peter, Colchester

Sur

   Mrs braig wold be glad if you wold send har afue shillings more then
har commin pay as she is vary bad and has bin for this foortnight sothat
she is quit in nead and the gentelmen told har that thay wold send har som
5 if she was ill as har allowence is so vary lettil shuld be glad of auarnce as
sune as you can

i am yours

Mary Braig

Brightlingsea

10 September 12

TEXTUAL ALTERATIONS 10: 12] *interl.*

Great Dunmow pauper letters

587 From Hannah Hoy [in Deptford, Surrey] to Mr Fuller Esq., 13 October 1818

October 13th 1818

Gentlemen I very sary I ham under the nescesting to beg the small of favoure of Releife as my husband his met with exedent and un Capeble of wark and being in no Club and having a small famely or I shoulld not trouble you 5

so I ham your humble servant
harner Hoy

TEXTUAL ALTERATIONS 4: having] *interl.*
CIRCUMTEXT Note of same date from Abraham Ager, surgeon, below: 'James Hoy of New Cross is unable to follow any kind of employment, having bruised his arm from a fall, he is using the means necessary to his recovery, but will not be able to work in less than three weeks or a month.'
PLACE Inferred from circumtext. New Cross belonged to Deptford.

588 From Isaac Milbourn in Great Wakering [Essex] to the overseer of Great Dunmow, 31 December 1818

To the Gentlemen of the Parish of Gt Dunmow

Gentlemen I hope that you Will be So Good as to do Something for Me for I am very Poorly at this time and Cannot do but very Little Work and have had two Girls to Maintain Which i am not Able to do Which Makes Me to Ask you for Some Releif I have Got One of My Girls a place and i 5 Cannot buy her no Clothes and i hope that you Will be So Good as to Send Me Something to buy Some for her, if She has no Clothes her Misstress Say She Must Come away for She Cannot do without Cloths and i am not Able to buy any for her

Gentlemen i am very Sorry that i have to Trouble you But i Cannot help 10 it, And i hope that you Will Grant Me My Request

From your Hum^{le} Servt
Isaac Milbourn Senior

Gt Wakering
Decr 31 1818 15

TEXTUAL ALTERATIONS 7-8: Misstress] *first* 's' *interl.* 9: buy] *interl with caret.*

Little Dunmow pauper letters

**589   From Jemima Wetherly in Whitestable [Kent], to John Allen
in Little Dunmow, 10 November [1817]**

Whitestable (Nov^e 10
Dear brother we recied your letter and we was very soorry to hear you
have had two Such bad mishfortchin my Dear brother Mr Knott has Sent
you a Great Sum a one pound note wich I think it will not be much Sarvis
5   to you by your letters my Dear brother if I was in place I wold not Stay
there tow Starve I wold com home and let them Keep you a lietle wile
and then make them a lowe you So much a weeak and then you could go
back again for thay willnot Send you a nough to due you any good there
is so many poor to relife every day we or verry near all poor a like we all
10   goind in love With you I remain your lovin Sister Jemima Wetherly
your brother James is at hom

TEXTUAL ALTERATIONS 2: very] *interl.* 2: soorry] 'ry' *over illeg.* 5: Stay] 'a' *over* 'y'. 7:
much] *after del* 'mch'. 9: poor] *interl.* 10: Wetherly] 'ly' *interl below at end of line.*
CIRCUMTEXT '1817' interlined from other hand below 'Nov^e 10'.

590*   From Anonymous

pray Gentlemin will you be so kind as to grant me 6 yards of Calico and 5
yards and a half of sheeting and 6 yards of dyed Cotten

TEXTUAL ALTERATIONS 2: 6] *interl above del* '5'.
WRITING This note is written on a small slip of paper (size: 201 x 48mm).

Halstead pauper letters

591 From E. Harland in Ipswich, 2 August 1835

Ipswich August 2th 1835

Sir/

I hope you will excuse the liberty I have taken in sending you these few
lines but feeling myself very uncomfortable at haveing my pay stopt I
could not refrain from sending as I am not able to come I hope Gentle-   5
man you will consider my distress Mr Goodwin say he should be obliged
to you to write to him as it would be most Satisfaction to them to know
wither you would wish to have them continue paying my money if not
Gentleman you may expect me as I cannot do without some support as I
am getting into years I am getting very bare of clothes and I hope Gentle- 10
man you will advance a trifle more as I have not a Friend in Ipswich able
to do any thing for me

allow me to subscribe myself
your most humble servant
E Harland 15

TEXTUAL ALTERATIONS 4: at] *after del* 'to'.

592 From William Gale to the overseers and churchwardens of Halstead, 26 August 1835

1835 augst 26 - from William Gale

Sir in 1822 I was then Near 17 years old = and Maried to Elizbeth
pearce at Mary le Bone London Ware the Maried regester is to be had or
seean and prooved as it hes alredey Bean - this is the Copy in part - page
197 - W Lambert Backelor to Elizebeth Parse Spinster. by Bands augest   5
14th wedersday 1822 by R.St. Chapman Curate - witiness Thos Olbive ad
Sophia Haward - No 591 Curch Clark Wm Geopall - *and my I had* althow
a diferant Name it is identified I am the same person - Not Knowing
wether at that time my Name was Gale or Lambert under some defectely
& my Mothers Married Elisebeth Pearse died in 1828 May th 9 under the 10
Name of Martha Hill at Saint Gileses No 2015 *London* after I Maried har
she emedetely turned out to be a Comen woman upon th town of london
untill her deth by that Means she Changed har Name either from Married

Name or Maiden name to Martha Hill I surpose becorse it is Custom to do
15 so by that Kind of *[wimin]* - Now in 1823 Desember 25 I Maried to Mary
Ann South the first lived 5 years and a half after I was Maried to South in
Corse South was no wife at all Lawfull but was at any time at liberty to
Marry to any one else had she Knoing it - and when Elis pence died that
did not estabelish the Marige to South without we had bean Married over
20 again but left me a widener emidetely th first died - Now all the time I was
Maried to South I was liveing in adultey and hoardem = but being young I
did not think any thing of that untill this Larst 6 years it hes bean a berring
to Concience and a Biling seekret in my boosem - severall times in that
time I have tried to Git Clear of south but always a fraid to spout about th
25 first fear as it shold be a hard Case with me in Law as I had always Kept
it to my self from th first ever from my own Mother - but thear is ways
and Means tht every thing is to be discovered at Larst and I am Glad it is
out if pleas god it end well with me in it - for it is better th*[an]* to die in it at
Larist Now as South and I lived unhapy and Cold not be other ways
30 exspected under such a Case of adultey - South was in Corse No wife at
all by law - so I in Corse had No wife living but Cold by the first dying
Maring to any one Lawfuly - Knowing such to be th Case I did so
On the 18 of Jenyar 1835 I Married to Mary Ann Hart at Halstead -
wich Marige is Lawfull and hes bean so prooved by diferent Lawyears -
35 she is my Lawfull wife Child Born in widlock - Now har farther withholds
har from me and wold do any thing to fling the Marrig so as she is har sick
and ill state and aflicted Child shold belong to Halstead to be an exspence
to th parish prehaps at some time and prehaps a heavey one to - he will not
take one step to be satifyed by siviletey that his daughter is my wife - but
40 wold rather use such means as to bring up the South to apear a gainst me
in some Coart to prosecute me if posibell - Now South only want to Know
tht she is Clear and she is satifyed and have no wish to hurt me but Marig
to some other Man - Now I have spent th Larst shiling in Law going up to
London to git the Marige lines to git the deth regesty of th first to satify
45 him that Mary Ann was my Lawful wife I toke a lawyer over to halstead
to state to him that she was the Lawfull one-of-Law ofered to do eny
thing I Cold to sgit him satifyed but all of No use at all I Can do no more
untill I Can git more Mony = becorse th Lover of South is open a gaint me
if Mr Hart forse the Case yet South wold be satifyed and Glad to git Clear
50 wold Hart take Moderate steps to see the Case Clear = without Brings
me to a Cort of trial after taking every step I have and spent evy shilg and
turned my self into det also I take it hard -

Now Gentelmen I do not surpose you wont a Bargin to Maintain that
you have No right to = and I will thank you one and all to wisit Mr Hart
and talk and reason with him upon his being so absent and so set a gainst 55
me and will not beleave th truth althow I onse was an angell with him -

Now do not tell him I have note to you stating evry pertikelar of the
Case - but tell him tht you shall not indulge or incurage him to try to
feling a Beridon upon the parish that you have no right to at all *and* I
think it will have a good efect upon him Now he perpose to Cary his 60
daughter to my parish to see if they will exsept har - and in Corse tht will
be the way for me to be taking and sufer th Law and they will object to
har and you will object to har so the thear my be a exspence flung upon
you to deside the Case between th 2 parishes - when if Hart wold but be
perswaded with South with a lawyer to take such stepes to proove it by 65
formiliar terms = wich goes to /Lon/don at ease and any party satifeyed
and me have my lawfull wife - and th other set at libertey - and No exspence
to eith parish or partiey - I love Mary Ann as my life - and I beg of you to
impress the Case upon his and har minds tht he may Come round and
proove the Case by dockements and tht like without forsing of Law for 70
that is of No good when things Can Lawfuly be other ways setteled -

if you wont to drop a line to me upon th subject direct to Mee at M^{rs}
Layers Cappend Hall Near Colchester I shall be there at some time or
other but at prey I Keepe at a Long distance for Now -
your Most Humbell servint William /L/ Gale   75

TEXTUAL ALTERATIONS 15: 25] *interl above* 'Desember'. 71: good] *one* 'o' *interl.* 73: Near
Colchester] *interl.*

Havering-atte-Bower pauper letters

593 From Ann Garner [in Attleborough, Norfolk] to Mr Cook in Havering-atte-Bower [16 April 1795]

Mr Cook

Ann Garner the wife of James Garner Could wish to be hapy to Live with my husban again but I am very uneasy & unhapy that he have Left mee a Gain for I have been Lawfull maried to him 27 years and have had
5 thirteen Chilldren by him now I think It tis a unjust thing for you Gentle-man & officers to harber maried men thear from thear wife and familys now I understand the Letter wich m^r Cook sent to the Attlburg officer that he have a wife and family in your place and if he be thear I meen to be thear my self and beg of you to send me a Answer weather he be thear or
10 near for I think tis not proper for a nother woman to in joy my Right his Daught wich Laid in when he was thear have Laid il so to hart that thea think she out Live

From your humble servent
Ann Garner

TEXTUAL ALTERATIONS 3: husban] 'an' *interl at end of line.* 10: Right] 'h' *over* 'd'.
DATE Day of postmark (year illegible), year inferred from related correspondence.
PLACE From postmark.
RELATED CORRESPONDENCE On 13 April 1795, the overseer of Attleborough had informed the overseer of Havering that 'James Garner hes a wife and Three Children in this Town - he was here about Two or three week's Since'. This was an answer to a letter from Haver-ing, possibly that of Mr Cook referred to by Ann Garner in her letter, and apparently inquiring about James Garner's familial situation in Attleborough. If Ann Garner's refer-ence to Mr Cook's letter is correct, then James Garner had a second wife and family in Havering and hence was a bigamist.

594 From R[achel] Robson [in Gateshead, Durham] to Mr Waltom in Havering-atte-Bower, 18 October 1803

Oct 18 1803

Sir

have received my money & return You many thanks for the same I sertainly rote to Mr Exell last time my Sister tells me that the Gentlemen
5 are a going to take some of my money of I do not know which way theay can think I can do with less five of us to live out of it Clothing to find

<h>ouse rent to pay & I have not been able to get to do anything out of
doors all this summer as I have a young Child & no one to take care of it
I find many hardships now which I should not have done had we staid at
havering & then it would have been more expence to you all I hope Sir 10
that you will be so good as to speak for me as I am freindless & I hope
God will bless You for doing good for the fatherless & Widow from

Your Humble Ser R Robson

TEXTUAL ALTERATIONS 7: not] *after del* 'been'. 11: freindless] 'l' *over* 's'.
  PLACE From postmark.

**595 From Rachel Robson in [Durham] to Mr Waltom in Havering-
atte-Bower, 3 February 1804**

Feb 3 1804

Sir
   I have just received Your Letter which gives me a great deal of trouble
by reason of your saying you are a going to take away part of my money
I know not wich way you think that times are mended with me they are 5
mended to be sure but it is a great deal for the worse I have one more in
family than <I ha>d when my Dear Husband was Working for me <it>
takes up my time that I am not able <to ea>rn any thing as I have none of
my Children old enough to keep him it Costett me five <s>hillings every
week for bread than I have all things else to find out of the other House 10
rent & Clothing for us all for we cannot go quite naked so I hope that You
will be so good as to send my money as usal for I can by no means do
without it or else I must apply to the parrish I am in for my poor family
cannot starve for Six Shillings will not do nothing for them You wish to
know my Cristian name & age it is Rachel & I am 40 Years of age my 15
Chilldren Willm & Ann & James & Robert all under nine years of age
none of them neither able to Work nor want I heartly wish I had never left
Havering & then I should have had my Dear Husband alive & if You take
any of my money away You must send for <u>s again & that will not
Cost a little as I never will venture on the sea again I suffered so much the 20
last time s I must once more beg of You to be my Friend & speak a good
word for me & by so doing God will bless You for being good to the
Fatherless & Widow so no more at preasent from

Your Most Obedient
& Hum^le Ser^nt R Robson 25

TEXTUAL ALTERATIONS 3: deal] *interl with caret*. 7: was] *interl with caret*. 9: enough] *after del*
'en'. 16: Ann] *after del* 'he'.
   DESTRUCTION OF TEXT Left-hand edge of both pages damaged.
   PLACE From postmark.

Kirby-le-Soken pauper letters

596   From John Snell in Bristol to Sarah Mayhew in Great Yarmouth, Suffolk, 14 November 1818

Bristol Infermary Ward N° 5 November 14 1818

Honoured Mother unknown it was that i should ever Be able to write to you or my wife again, i write to you Because i have had no answer from my wife she Should have wrote, it would have Been no Consequence if it had Pleased god to Removed me, i hope you and my Wife & Babes are 5 well with heart felt sorrow is all that i can say or do for them, my suffring has Been great for this ten weeks Past i was so Bad that i Could not Be Removed But once in 48 Hours for some Considerable time i Remained six weeks in Bed Before i was able to sit up an hour or two in a day, But thanks Be to the Almighty god i can sit up 6 or 7 hours now and walk a 10 Little But the season of the year is very unfavourable to me and a nother thing is our Liveing is very Low and i Have not one peney to Assist my self with, a few Necessarys to make me strong But i must Be content & thank god i am in such a Blessed place Could i have Been taken in to this place when i was first taken i should have had a Little money But it was 15 ten Days Before i Could get Addmitance, in Consequence of Painting the wards, when first taken so Bad i had about one Pound six Shillings, But it soon went and glad to keep In the Lodgings that i was in till i could Be taken in to the above Place they Behave much Better to me than i Could have Expected they wash my Linen for me But god only knows when i 20 shall Be able to satisfy them, I have only Been master of one pound in Ireland & one in England since i sent you that two Pounds from Liverpool, in Ireland it Cost me seven Shillings out of that Pound for Doctering in Liverpool i had only nineteen Shillings Left to encounter a Sicknes & i never Could Recover above seven or eight Shillings after that some- 25 times two or three Days Pretty week then as soon i took a Little Cold so Bad not able to do a Day work and afraid to take to the sea, although i did not let our Countrymen know that, But it was not to Be wondered at for my Blood was in a most dreadful state, But i Belive the Docter have taken a good part of it away, had i the spring of the year to Rise in i might 30 enjoy Better health than i Have for years, I understand they only keep [Us] in 3 months a few days Before Christmas my time will Be up, if i do not Effect a Cure god only knows what i shall Do, at that time my whole

Concern was to send my wife the one pound note i had when i Arrived
35 there But i was taken the same evening with a Cold Chill, & so Continued
to get worse till i Could stand nor move, pray Mother do send me an
answer and a full Account of my wife and Babes if you can, pay the
Postage if you are able But dont Negelect give my love to my wife &
Babes I Remain your Afft^te son John Snell
40 [*Postscript across margin:*] You will know how to Direct By the ferstine

TEXTUAL ALTERATIONS 1: 1818] *interl at end of line.* 2: it was] *interl.* 4: Consequence] 'ce'
interl at end of line. 6: well] *interl with caret.* 7: not] *interl.* 10: walk] 'l' *over* 'a'. 17: so]
after del 'i had'. 19: Could] 'd' *interl at end of line.* 24: Sicknes] 's' *interl at end of line.*
25: Shillings] 'gs' *interl at end of line.* 30: spring] 'g' *interl at end of line.* 34: when] *after
del* 'at'. 35: evening] *first* 'n' *interl.*

FURTHER EVIDENCE John Snell lived in Great Yarmouth, where he worked as a mariner,
but had his settlement in Kirby-le-Soken. In 1814, he had married Mary Fitch, with whom
he had a daughter Mary (born 17 August 1817) and three further children (dates of birth
not given). (ERO, D/P 169/13/4, Kirby-le-Soken settlement examination: examination of
Mary Hill [formerly Snell] concerning the settlement of her daughter Mary Snell, 13 June
1835). John Snell's mother (or his wife) presumably passed his letter on to the overseers
of Kirby-le-Soken when she applied to them for assistance for his young family.

597   From Mary Snell in [Great] Yarmouth [Suffolk], 6 July 1827

Yarmouth July 6 1827
   Sir/
   I have taking the libbert of wrighting to request the favour of a remittence
of my money as I am much distress^d for the whant of it
5   Should have writing before but waited tell after the first monday in the
month as I though M^rs <---> would have giving you my dir<ection> I
have receivd from Mr Preston 8 Shilling - an one penny, I would thank
the Gentlemen if thay would lett me have my money a week before the
Quarter as I have to pay my rent at the Quarter, the last quarters rent I
10 have not paid I was oblg to brak into that to come over with please to
dirrect to me Ferrey Boat Row North Quay Yarmouth
                          I remain Your Obn Savn^t
                                                    Mary Snell
[*Postscript across margin:*] NB the Woman that was at my^n have left me
15 10 or 11 weeks Back

FURTHER EVIDENCE Mary Snell was the widow of John Snell (see **596**) who had died on the
14 June 1823. She later married William Hill (date not given), but still received an allowance from Kirby-le-Soken for the children from her first marriage (ERO, D/P 169/13/4,
Kirby-le-Soken settlement examination).

598 From Jane Pooley in Needham Market, Suffolk, to [William] Daniels in Kirby-le-Soken, 10 July 1827

Needham market Suffolk july the 10 1827

Kind Sir I take the Liberty to trobel you with theese few Lines hopen it will find you all in Good Health Bless God my Child is Getten about again but is a very poor Creature and I Get her all the nursments as I Can kind Sir this with my Duty to you and beg the favour of you to Send me a 5 trifel when you Can make it Conveant Give my Duty to all the <k>ind Gentelmen which always was So kind to <m>y Dear Children my Littel Girl is now of the Doctors hands Some weeks She have had a Blister opon her Stomach and kept o/pen 20 week I Expect I Shall have a Great Bill to pay the Doctor I have heard from my Daughter in London and She 10 is quite well and Doen well my 2 Littel Girls att home Send thar Duty to all the kind Gentleman from your
Humbel Sarvent jane pooley

TEXTUAL ALTERATIONS 11: Doen] 'D' *over illeg.* 12: from] *interl.*

599 From Mary Hill in [Great] Yarmouth [Suffolk] to Thomas Stone in Kirby-le-Soken, 30 July 1828

Yarmouth July 30 1828

Hon^d Sir

The Cause of my troubling you with my last Letter, was the last Letter I recived from Mr Danile was not directed right, that was sent back to the dead Office it was five Weeks before I had It, its being so long, I had 5 determined to come over, but Fortunately went to Yarmouth Office to Inquire after it, Mrs Seaman said there had been One, but not the name of the Row, therefore they could not find me she wrote to the Office at London, and it was sent down, and in a few days I had It

Sir I hope the Gentlemen will take it into Consideration and allow me for 10 the four Children as they did before, and not take the Shilling a week off - my Husband have been by the Month but is Now Discharged at Liverpool to git home as he can, in the Seafareing Trade every thing very dead at this time he is very kind to the Children and wish to do every thing for them that is in his Power, but Trade being so dull it is not in his Power it 15 was through his kindness that the Eldest is in so good birth so that he never

will be any more Expence to the Perish - Sir the Gentlemen will find there
will be fourteen weeks up to the second of August, Now if the Gentlemen
will think Proper to send me up to Michlemes it will make the Quarters
20 come right again as the Letters become Expence
                    I am Sir Your Hum^{bl} Servent
                            Mary Hill
            Please to direct
                            Mary Hill
25   Ferry Boat Row
                        Great Yarmouth
                To be left at the Post Office
                        till call^d for

CIRCUMTEXT Notes from Thomas Nunn, presumed overseer of Kirby-le-Soken, at bottom
of first and third page, dated 14 August 1828, ordering the payment of £5 (for 20 weeks at
5s from 4 May to 21 September 1828) from his account at Manningtree Bank.
    FURTHER EVIDENCE Mary Hill had formerly been married to John Snell (see **596**, **597**)
who had died in 1823. After the marriage to William Hill she still received an allowance
from Kirby-le-Soken for the children from her first marriage following their father's settlement in that place (ERO, D/P 169/13/4, Kirby-le-Soken settlement examination).

**600   From Mary Hill in [Great] Yarmouth [Suffolk] to Thomas
Stone Esq. in Kirby-le-Soken, 26 May 1829**

                                Yarmouth May 26th 1829
Sir I am Soray to put you to thes truble but I reseved a letter from the
Jantlmen and the told me that the could not alou me anay thing for my
boay until the Sen his indinters I Cannot sand tham for the boay is bound
5 and gon to Sea and I was forsed to destris my silfe to Cloth him the niver
had anay rasan to dout my uord I uold not have trobled the Jantleman if I
culd have dun uathout he is bound to Thomas blar of sundarland and I
think he have Got aviray good master and I hop Jantlmin you uill not be
so hard uith me as you uas uith me uhan you tuk 4 Shilins a uek for the
10 other boay and my silf for if you dont alou me 4 Shilins a uek for the thre
Gerals I must sind tham home the oldast boay have ben hom to london
from the Est indes and he is viray hapay on burd the Fame Captn Robert
Boulleng and I hope Jantlman you will tak it into a Considarashon for I
was forsed to plag my thengs to Cloth this uan I uas forsed to embres the
15 oppertunety for burth for boas ar viray Sars and I was Glid to Get him of
my hand as soun as posable if you ples Jantlman to Sind me a anser as sun

as posable and if you uill be so Good as sind me anay thing ples Sind the
Childrens munnay uith it if you ples to Derect to be lift at the post offec
til Cald for

I raman yoar abadent   20

humble Sarvint Maray Hill

TEXTUAL ALTERATIONS 12: Boulleng] *after del illeg.* 14: this] *over del illeg.* 15: him] *after del illeg.*

601   From Mary Harris in Boyle [Roscommon, Ireland] to William Daniels, overseer of Kirby-le-Soken, 22 February 1832

Boyle 22 Feby 1832

Sir/
   I humbly Beg you will be so good as to forward to me the money due to
the children of Thom^s Harris / late Sergeant in the 10th Regiment of Foot
/ Namely Rosanna and Thomas Harris. on the parish of Kerby in the   5
County of Essex the sum is two pounds - due on the 2nd of March next and
Postage from thence to Boyle will be Three shillings - and beg so doing
you will oblige Your humble and Most obed^t Servt

Mary Harris

Widow of   10

Serg^t Harris

late 10 Reg^t

To -
The Overseer of the Parish of Kirby
C^o Essex   15

22 Feby 1832

Sir -
   You will be pleased to Send a Certificate of the Amount due to the
Children Quarterly as I am intended to Get - Married to a Soldier of the 20
10th Regiment Named Wm Shar^p a Native of Lincolnshire in you failing to
Send the Certificate in Question I shall be under the Necessity of Going
back to the Parish in a very short time. The amount due at present You
will be pleased to Send as Soon as possible. in the Event of the Dept
geting <on> Route and that I should Remain after the <-----> for the want 25
of Anything to bear the Expences of M<yself> and Children. The Mayor

Commanding directs to me that he is to See the letter forwarded from you
I hope You will be good Enough to let me Know how Mr Foaker & Family is and likewise the Captain as the Adjutant of the 10 Depot would be
30   very Glad to hear from the Captain, I Endeavoured to Get this letter franked
but the Mayor Refused doing it until Such time as I get Married and from
thence all Communication from him to You wil be free from Expences -

I remain Yours Truly
Mary Harris

TEXTUAL ALTERATIONS 26: bear] *interl.* 27: directs] *after del* 'this'.
WRITING Professional hand.
CIRCUMTEXT Note from other hand to certify that William Sharp (name not clearly
decipherable) was currently with the 10th regiment at Boyle.

**602   From Mary Harris in Boyle [Roscommon, Ireland] to William
Daniels, overseer of Kirby-le-Soken, 18 May 1832**

Boyle 18th May 1832

Sir /
        I have the Pleasure of letting You Know that I have Received Your
letter of the 13^d March last with Two Soverings Enclosed in it which
5   became due to me from the Parish of Kirby C^o of Essex for the children
of Serg^t Thomas Harris late of the 10th Regiment of Foot Viz Rosanna
&Thos Harris on the 2^d of March I hope You will have the Goodness of
Forwarding to me with as little delay as Possible the Same Amount which
will become due on the 25" of May Ins^t and by So doing You will oblige
10   Your

Humble & most obed^t
Servant
Mary Harris

Mr Wm Daniels
15   Overseer of the
Parish of Kirby
C^o *Essex*
P.S. Direct to me in the Care of the Post Master Boyle - I paid 4/4 Postage
for the last letter M. Harris

TEXTUAL ALTERATIONS 6-7: Viz Rosanna &Thos Harris] *interl with caret.*
WRITING Professional hand.

CIRCUMTEXT Note from other hand at bottom: 'I certify that the two children of the late Serg^t Thos Harris are present with their Mother with the 10 Regiment at Boyle' (signature indecipherable).

603 From James Davey in Colchester to [Robert] Mumford, overseer of Kirby-le-Soken, 12 July 1832

James Davey ColChester July 23 1832

Genteel men I am very sory to think that I Can not help of senden to you & troblinG of youe But I have Been Bad For 4 weeks so that I Could not Git out But thanks Be to God I am Got quit puely so that I Can walk a Bout & 6 Shilings workinG pay From the Club Be sids the 3s & 9   5 penCe that that I have at mr porters therfor Genteel men I BaG the favour of youe as to send me a trifel per week By mr GoorG low for two or three weeks and By that time with the Blesens of God I shal Be a Ble to Go to work But Genteel men I Reseved the 6 shilinGs that youe sent me Last tusday week & I thank youe for it I am very week and Low ther for   10 Genteel meen ConCider this that I Canot Git But Litl to take to my selfe therfor I Canot Git well without a Litel to tak to

> Genteel men I BaG that
> You will think of me on
> saturday next   15

TEXTUAL ALTERATIONS 1: 1832] *interl at end of line.* 2: senden] 'en' *interl at end of line.* 7: two] *after del* '2'.

604 From Mary Harris in Strokestow [Roscommon, Ireland] to William Daniels in Kirby-le-Soken, 14 September 1832

Stokestown September 14th 1832

Dear Sir

I hope to be excused for my last letter, if there was any thing offensive in my last letter it was meant to give offense but this I Confess that a person in want of money may from a present necessity Say Some words   5 which will in time of Consideration be Regretted. Please to Send the money due for the Children as we are in want at present and the reason is we removed from Boyle being the head quarters We Came to this town as the Cholera was at head quarters and is Still we were very much afraid to

10 Continue there and if it Comes to this town we will be at a loss for money
by removing from this town. you will pleased to observe that by putting
one pound nineteen Shillings and Sixpence and give Sixpence for the
order to the post master there it will Save me Six pence on acc^t of the
order and alov the postage will come to a couple Shillings less to me, as
15 I enquired at the post office in this town and they informed me that the
order will acc^t but to Sixpence per pound and for the One pound nineteen
Shillings and Sixpence it will am^t but to sixpence by deducting Sixpence
from the 2£ and give that give Sixpence to the post master for the order
        Direct your order to the Stokestown Post office and the letter to me the
20 children are well and attend School every day No mor at present but
Remains Your
                        Humble & obedient
                        Servant & &-
                        Mary Harrass
25 The reason I put Wm Sharps name on outside is to free the expence as I
will get it franked for the future.

TEXTUAL ALTERATIONS 13: to the post master there] *interl with caret.* 15: acc^t] *after del* 'that'.
        WRITING As the contents of the letter shows, it came from Mary Harris. But the hand-writing is different from that of her other letters.
        CIRCUMTEXT Note from other hand on next page: 'I Certify that the Children of the late Serg^t Harras are living & present with the Detachment at Strokestow' (signature undecipherable).

605   From Mary Harris in Clonmel [Tipperary, Ireland] to Willliam Daniels in Kirby-le-Soken, 12 December 1832

                                        Clonmel 12th Decem^r 1832
        Sir
        I have to request you will have the Goodness to forward to me the
Amount due to the Two Children of Thomas Harris late a Sergeant in the
5 10th Regiment of Foot, Namely Rosanna & Thomas Harris on the Parish
of Kirby in the County of Essex which becomes due on the 20th of this
month I have also to State to you that I am after a very long March of
Eleven days and that the girl look very ill and little hopes of her recovery
therefore I hope you will be pleased to forward it with as little delay as
10 possible the Boy took ill likewise Since I arrivd here they are both on
their Sick bed with the Mazles this Quarter is very dear and impossible for

a Family to live without money I never was in need of help more than I am
at present and hopes you will take it into Consideration and relieve me as
Soon as possible - You will drict as usual to Clannel County Tipperera
Irland -

15

Iam Sir Your most
obed^t Servant
Mary *Harris*

To the Overseer
of the Parish of Kirby
   County Essex

20

TEXTUAL ALTERATIONS 9: delay] *interl with caret.*
   CIRCUMTEXT Certificate by Captain Mun below: 'that the two Children of the late
Sergiant Harris are living and present with their Mother'.

606   From Elizabeth Davey in Colchester, 19 February 1833

Choalchester Febury 19 1833

Gentlemen
   I beg pardon for the Libberty I have takin In wrighten to you but As my
moaney Is stopt this Last Week I feale very much hurt as my Famileay Is
very Large and my husbands Irnasings are so small that I find It hard to 5
git my children brad a lone Put It to yours selvs gentlman what Seven
shillings Per week to seport 8 Six children my husband and my self And
some times my husband Is fortey Miles from me and I have than to git
Threw with my famleay as I can In Wich gentlemen I concider a very
hard task for a women to Incounter with I hoap Gntleman as my moaney 10
Is In the hands of the Parish I hoop you will consider my Famleay and Let
me have It It Is But a small some but I find It Wery yousfull to me I trust
you will Bee so cind as to concider me and let Me have It If not my
husband must Come as I ashure you gentlmen I stand in need a nuff of It
as I have scase got a bead for my dear babes to Lay down on and whare I 15
Loock at than and think I fale that very clocelay to my self I trust thar are
some of the gentlmen that Will have a Parrents fealing as I shall feale
very thankfull to you

So no more from your
humble Servent Elizabeth
Davey

20

TEXTUAL ALTERATIONS 5: Irnasings] 'a' *over* 'e'. 8: Is] *after del* 'and'. 9: task] *over illeg.* 14: Come] *after del* 'Must'.

607 From Mary Hill [in Great Yarmouth, Suffolk], 3 June 1833

June 3rd 1833

I Mary Hill have received my pay due to my children belonging to the Parish of Kirby amounting to seven Pounds five shillings - this day & up to May 31st 1833 last past and do agree to take the sum of two shillings
5 and sixpence weekly for the term of three years from Friday May 31st to May 31st 1836 and then all my pay to cease - witness my hand this third day of June 1833

Mary Hill
X
10   her mark

TEXTUAL ALTERATION 3-4: & up to May 31st 1833 last past] *interl with caret.* 6: third] *interl above* 'first'.
PLACE Inferred from Mary Hill's previous and following letters (**600**, **610**).

608 From Mary Harris in Fermoy [Cork, Ireland] to William Daniels in Kirby-le-Soken, 20 June 1833

Fermoy 20th June 1833
Sir/
be pleased to Send the Money that became due on the 20th Instant to me for the Children of the late Sergent Harris Be So Good as to Send it as
5 Soon Possible as we do Not Know the moment we leave this place

No more at present
from Your Humble
Servt Mary Harris

609 From Mary Harris in Devonport [Devon] to William Daniels, overseer of Kirby-le-Soken, 18 September 1833

Devonport 18th September 183-

Sir/

I have to Inform you that we left Fanney where I had written to you before from and Came to devonport on the 2nd of August and the whole of the women were left behind to pay their own expences it Cost me one 5 pound from Cork to Come to devonport in the Packet which leaves me Very Much in need of Some Money to Support Me and My little Children I had to leave My little Cloths pawned to pay for My Passage, Sir I hope you will be So Good as to Send Me Some Relief as Soon as you Possibly you Can for there is None of the women allowed into the Bar- 10 racks on any Instance whatever in Consequence of Some of them dying Since the Came over and the Said it was with the Colrea Morbus the died
Sir
I would wish to let you Know that it falls due on the 20th September Ins^t
No more at present from your 15
Humble Servt
Mary Harris
Direct the answer to this letter to Mary Harris Devonport or Elsewhere -
to be left untill Called for -

TEXTUAL ALTERATION 10: you] *interl with caret.*

610 From Mary Hill in Great Yarmouth [Suffolk] to Robert Mumford, overseer of Kirby-le-Soken, 5 February 1834

Sir

I shall be humbly obliged by your goodness of remitting me £5. as mentioned in your note of 3^d June 1833. I would not now have addressed you on such a subject had not pressing circumstances compelled me - therefore solicit your kindness of remitting me the money, altho' not at 5 present due, by return of Post.

I beg to state that I have happened with a situation for my Daughter Mary my Eldest Child, and being unable to provide her with Clothes and other necessaries, I shall be obliged by your kindness of remitting me a Sum of money to assist in the purchasing of such, it really would be a 10

hard thing for her to lose this Situation for want of Apparel, and I therefore beg your kind assistance for her.

My husband having so little employment to do, he cannot render her the
assisting of with Clothes to go to Service, and we have now the youngest
15 Son come home, and he cannot obtain employment.

I beg your early Answer and compliance

I am Sir

Your obed¹ Serv¹

Mary Hill

20 Great Yarmouth
Martin the Shoemaker's
7 no - Goal Street
5ᵗʰ Febʳʸ 1834

P.T.O.

25 If you was so kind as to give me the balance of the £5. not at present due
to me, for my Daughter to buy Clothes to go to Service with, I shall be
humbly obliged.

Textual alterations 8: my] *interl above del* 'the'. 14: with] *after del* 'her'.
    FURTHER EVIDENCE In August 1833, Mary Hill had arranged for her daughter, Mary
Snell, from her first marriage (see **597**, **599**) to be taken by Mary Howlett, a tailoress at
Great Yarmouth, for a year. Mary Howlett was to teach her tailoring, Mary Snell to pro-
vide herself with all necessaries. The premium was a sovereign. As it turned out, Mary
Snell did work for Mary Howlett for a year, but she was boarded and lodged by her
mother, and the sovereign was not paid, so that she did not earn a new settlement (ERO,
D/P 169/13/4 Kirby-le-Soken settlement examination).

611   From Mary Hill in [Great] Yarmouth [Suffolk] to Robert Mumford, overseer of Kirby-le-Soken, 3 March 1834

Yarmouth 3ʳᵈ March 34

Sir

I hope you will excuse my writing to you again. I would not have troubled
you if that my Rant had not been due which I have got a half years Rant
5 to pay and my husband have not made only one Voyage since Christmas
and is now likely to remain at home for three Weeks longer I forgot to
Mention in my last Letter that I could not happen with any Gentleman to
pay me the Money my youngest Girl out of the town is but just /run a bad/
ill from the Long yourney that we took to come over and would not have
10 been so well as she is but from taking Nourishment twice a week from a

Lady who was so good to her and I have you to gudge what I had to spare
out of my but half years pay of being nine days on the road from Kirby
with the Children being so very ill from the featiege on the road and I hope
Sir that you will have the Goodness for to bestow on my Eldest Girl a few
Shillings to help to git a few things for cloathing as she is quite bare and 15
she have not brought me in a farthing for these tow years as I have to say
that even at this place they allow the Girls when they are out of work or
out of place a Shilling a week I knew the Money was not due when I sent
but I hope you will Sir have the Goodness to write by the return of post
hoping you will comply with my request as I shall be humbly obliged to you 20
I remain Sir your

most humble Servant

Mary Hill

612   From James Davey in Colchester, 10 June 1834

James Davey colChester June the 10 1834

   Genteel men I humley BaG that youe will not Be anGray of me of taken
Librty of writen to youe for a trifel mor money this week if youe will Be
So Good For to Send only 6 ShilinGs it will Git me somethnG to ware for
I am nearly naked my Self for I have not Get any Sharts nor stoCkens nor 5
trouses to war hardly to Cover my nakedness and I Canot Git a nuff to
fishroat with out A CothinG thearefor Genteel men perhaps youe will Be
so Good as to send me a few yards of Clorth wiCh will do as well as the
money for I rely am nearly naked and I Cante Git non to ware for my wife
is no Beter then she was wenn youe was hear nor Likly ever GitinG over 10
it But Genteel men your expenCes is Been very heavey that I Cant not
deny But I Consider that my Case must Bee the hardest therefor I humley
BaG that youe will Be so kind as to Grant me this favour By the Carer

TEXTUAL ALTERATIONS 5: nearly] 'ly' *interl.*

613 From James Davey in Colchester to Willliam Daniels in Kirby-le-Soken, 23 June 1834

James Davey Colchester June 23 1834

Genteel men I hope that youe will not take it a miss of my senden to youe for a small trifel to Git me a Little nurshment with for I am obliGht to Let my wife have my Club mony to Git food for the famly ther for Genteel
5 men I Canot Git any nurshment for my Self unless youe will Be so kind as to send mee som small trifle By GeorGe Low on saturday only to Git me a Little nurshment with For my self For two or three weeks if youe ples Genteel men I should Be thankful of it

TEXTUAL ALTERATIONS 1: 1834] *interl with caret.* 3: nurshment] 'nt' *interl at end of line.*

614 From J[ames] Davey in Colchester to Mr Robert in Kirby-le-Soken, 23 November 1835

Colchester Nov^m the 23 1835

Sir / I have here taking the Libetey of trasspassing on your time. - & Sir. I here Steate the Destress my familey are now In for the Want of a little Relive from the Parish. for I have Been destresse^dly Ill for a month
5 and What little I have from the Club Gentlemen is no more then a nuff then to fined the rent and fireing and myself and then there is none for the familey nor the doctor and as I hope I am a getting a little better I Want a great deal more then I Can Get for Wee have no more then 6^s Pr week to find Every thing with and therefore Wee do most humbley Bag of you
10 Gentlemen to be So Kind as to Send us Small Relive for a month or five Weeks untell I can gett my Strenth up to go to Work againe, and by So doing you Will for Ever obledg your humble and obdent Servant

    J - Davey More lane

    No 18 Colchester
15 NB Pray be So Kind as to Return answeer

TEXTUAL ALTERATIONS 4: from] *after del* 'for'. 5: from] 'rom' *interl above del illeg.* 7: better] *first* 't' *interl with caret.*

RELATED CORRESPONDENCE On 25 June 1834, Mr Pretty, overseer of St Botolph, Colchester, had written to the overseer of Kirby-le-Soken that Davey had applied for relief. His wife was ill, they had five children; 'he works some Miles from home', earning 8s per week.

There are also three undated letters in which J.B. Harrison, a blacksmith in Peldon, approached Robert Mumford, overseer of Kirby-le-Soken, about a certain Davy. It is not altogether clear whether that man was the same as James Davey, but the references, in Davey's earlier letters and that of his wife, to their family and to their want of clothes (**603, 606, 612, 613**) are clearly echoed: 'Davy says that he must come home he tells me he has nothing to were his things are in pawn he has no shoe worth twopence there fore he must come home so i shall have to git another I think youd better give him something to help him forward he tells me that he has got 5 Children & wife to live of 8^s per weeks weer is there Any thing for Cloathes gentellman & I hop you will Consider him.' The relationship between Harrison and Davey is similarly unclear. Peldon is about 5 miles south of Colchester, and it looks as though Harrison was his master, possibly with the some assistance from Kirby-le-Soken. In another letter he said that Davey 'has Being not gitten to Work this week Allthow hee has keep At it Lost on Time yet hee seemes on Satisfied About something as iff Leaving me'. Davey does indeed seem to have left him, though again the background, and the extent to which the overseers of Kirby-le-Soken were involved in arrangements with Harrison and with Davey's landlord, remain obscure. Harrison wrote 'that Davy Gave me notice to leave mee the 26 Ins & fortnite the Landlord will not Stop no longer For his rent he says he Cannot pay it he has no Shoes to wear good for any thing he means', and said Davey had announced that 'He shall come home he says he Cannot pay His rent'. It is obvious that Harrison knew Mumford personally, and that Dayey felt suspicious about their arrangements. Harrison went on: 'm^r mumford you told me to rite to you If any thing accured so Answere it If you please Sr Directely Dont Let him know irite to you As you did bee fore you told mee At the rose peldon you would No say you see mee he was angry With mee idid not say isee you.'

Lexden pauper letter

615 From Richard Kimberley in Torpoint, Cornwall, to the overseers of Lexden, 27 February 1834

Torpoint Feby 27 1834

Hon^d Gentlmen

I have once more taken the Liberty of Addressing you Respecting sending me some Relief, five weeks have now elapsed since I wrote to you on
5 the same subject, but receiving no answer I have Wrote now, in my former letter I informd you who to refer to, respecting my need of some small Relief during winter, which you may be assured I greatly stand in need of at this time, since I was discharged up to this time I have not earned ten shillings and now it will be five weeks before I can get employ for the
10 Summer, So Gentlemen I must inform you if you may not think proper to grant my request, I must and will come home my wife at this time is not able to wash her own Cloths

I Remain your humble Servant

Richd Kimberley Torpoint Cornwall

Textual alterations 9: can] *after del* 'am'.

St Mary, Maldon, pauper letters

**616 From Jonathan Sewell in Portsmouth to Mr Francis, over-
seer of St Mary, Maldon, 22 August 1811**

Mr Francis

    I would be much oblige to you in Sending the Steipend Due to me in
Alowance from the Parraish as I am Serving for I am Sorry I have to
mention But Indeed I am at this time very much in Wants of it Being
Eight Weeks Due On Friday and by Sending it you will very much Oblige   5
me You Can Send it by Post Office Order and then I Can Draw it at the
Post Office Portsmouth

In So Doving You Will Wery much

Oblige me your Humble

Servant Jonathan   10

Sewell

E Essex militia Portsmouth

Portsmouth 22nd August
    1811

**617 From Jonathan Sewell in Hilsea [Hampshire] to Mr Francis in
St Mary, Maldon, 9 December 1811**

Sir

    I Would be much Oblige to you to Send me the Money Due to My Wife
and Children For at this time I am Very Much in Wants I Would Not
Trouble you So Often But I am Drove to Great Necessity by Which I am
Oblige to have Recourse to Send So Very often for Every thing is So   5
Very Dear and Rent I have <to> pay makes it So with me that I Can
Ha<rd>ly Shift With What I Can Get and in Sending as Soon as Possible
You Will Very Much Oblige me your Humble Servant

Jonathan Sewell

East Essex Militia   10

Hilsea 9th Dec^r *1811*

618   From Jonathan Sewell in Portchester [Hampshire] to Mr Francis, overseer of St Mary, Maldon, 16 November 1812

Portchester Castle 16th Nov^{er} *1812*

Mr Francis
    Sir
    I would be much oblige to You to have the Goodness to Send up the
5 Money Due to me as the time alloted Expires Next Friday and shall be
much oblige to you to forward the Same to me as Quick as Possible as
things been So very dear Drives me to Every Avenue and can barely Gett
Bread with my Family In forwarding to me as Soon as Possible You will
very much oblige me
10   Your Humble and
                            obedient Servant
                            Jonathan Sewell
                            East Essex
                                Militia

15 Mr Francis Overseer
    Maldon

619   From Ann Doubty in Wivenhoe [Essex] to Mr Baker in St Mary, Maldon, 2 July 1813

July 2^d 1813

S^r
    Mr Baker it is about Six weeks a go since my Husband was with you,
when you promised to come over to Wivenhoe to see me, but you have
5 not been yet, my illness and Lameness is so bad that I am Oblig'd to have
a Woman to do for me as I cannot help my self to bring in a living I Hope
Sir, you will emidiately send me reliefe for I cannot do without Subsistance
I fully expected you to Settled something weekly to keep me from perish-
ing, Sir plese to answer this by comeing Directly as I cannot possibly do
10 without Assistance, as it is argent nesesity that I am forsed to Troble you,
Sir from your poor afflicted Perrishner in Disstress
                        Ann Doubty
    Wivenhoe

620   From Jonathan Sewell in Portchester [Hampshire] to Mr Francis, overseer of St Mary, Maldon, 20 August 1813

Portchester 20th August 1813

Sir/

I have to request the favor of you to send me the Eight Weeks pay due
to me on the 27th Ins^t I write before the time by we are under immediate
Orders for embarkation and shall be glad if you will send it me Without   5
any delay and you will greatly

Oblige your Humble Servant

Jonathan Sewell
East Essex Milit

Mr Francis   10
        Overseer Maldon

TEXTUAL ALTERATIONS 6: delayc 'a' *over* 'y'.

Mayland pauper letter

621 **From Isaiah Duce in St Bartholomew's Hospital [City of London] to William Duce, carpenter in Mayland, 29 March 1822**

London 29th March 1822

Mr Sharp

Sir I take the liberty of writeing to you hopeing this will find you in
good Health I wrote to you on the 18th March for a little Sum of Money
5 which not having receivd makes me rather Uneasy thinking it might have
miscarried if you have not send it I should be Exceedingly Obliged to you
if you would please to forword it by the next post for I am in great Want
of it at this time to pay for Washing &c Dr Sir when I am discharged from
this Hospital I should be glad if you would let me know in what Manner
10 you intend for my Conveyance down as I am much better and Expect to
be Discharged soon, I am Sir

with due respect Your Hble Servt

Isaiah Duce

Matthews Ward St Bartholomews
15   Hospital

FURTHER EVIDENCE Two months later, Isaiah Duce was dead. On 11 April 1822, St
Bartholomew's Hospital made out a bill for his treatment from 14 February till that day,
amounting to £2 2s plus 10s 6d 'to Convey him home'. On 9 June 1822, the overseer of
Mayland paid 13s for the burial fees for Isaiah Douse (D/P 382/12, Mayland overseers'
accounts and bills).

Mundon pauper letters

622 From James Taitt in Chelsea, London, to John Bourne in Mundon, 1 March 1816

Lower Sloane Street Chelsea March 1st 1816

Sir/ I avail my self of this opportuny to inform you of my presant situation that I am placed in .. should be very glad of your advise and mor so of your personall Assistance along with me I have ben with Mr Western two and three times every week since I cume to London .. Last Monday 5 week was the first time that he was eable to say there were no settlers to be sent out by Goverment this year .. I before that had ben Making all enquirece on the Bussnes that lay in my pour Amongst the Brockers and the shipping in hops of receaving the best information that could be obtained which I beleave I am passed of on Monday I want to the City 10 canall whare this Shipp lies I was abord a great part of the Day in hopes of seeing the Capⁿ but did not Nex Morning I sit out Early and was long wating for him then I could not bring him so low as I expected .. I had A freand at work I had a freand at work at the same time that greatly assisted me in the bussnes to Day I have brought him doun as low as £30 15 and we to find all sorts of provisions and Bedding in the boye and to carrie us to Quebeck .. I told him if Agreable to My freands I would except of the tearms but would let him kn[ow] sume time in Next weeks .. I wish very much to know your mind whither you would heave me endeavour to get A Place Next week at Lord Summervells Show or to 20 accept of the other I should be very glad to see you up on Monday or Tusday the last Day of the show on Tuesday .. if you could not cume for for Mr Lee to cume or if he could not for Mr Simpson .. there heave ben much time lost and I think it best brought to a conclusion .. be so good to writ to Me by Sundays post and inform me of sume of your comming 25 pleas to direct to C.C. Western over Cover to me his Direction is Chapple Street East

N° 18 Curzen Street

From your most Humble and obedient

Servant J. Taitt 30

P.S. Sir I think you might be of great advantage to me in eather Going a broad or in geeting a place at him .. you very well know My living in Mundon is impossable to support my large famely .. it is equaly distressing to me as

to your selves I shall call at Mr Westerns on Mond<ay> Morning expecting
35 your Answer
  Pleas to see Mr Lee and one of you cume I shall be grately dissapointed
if you do not
  The Name of this Ship is the Diana of Quebeck Carries 620 Tuns
                    From yours James Taitt

TEXTUAL ALTERATIONS 1: 1816] *interl at end of line.* 4: me] *interl at end of line.* 13: then]
after del 'and I'.

**623 From Ann Burder [in St Andrew Holborn, London] to John
       Bourne in Mundon, 9 April 1820**

                                              9. April Sunday 1820
To the Overseer of the Parish of Mundon
  Gentlemen/
  I beg leave to inform you of the Death of my Dear Husband which took
5 place this Morning about twenty minutes before Six as such humbly hope
you will allow what you may think necessary for his funeral at the same
time beg you will continue your allowance to me that I may be enabled to
support my Children as I have been under trying circumstances to get
him necessaries your early attention to this will be gratefully acknowl-
10 edged by your Ob^t Ser^t
                                                    Ann Burder
  NB. I beg to state that I have been oblidged to borrow the fortnights
money due last Saturday from Ladyday last - should esteem it a favour
that the Gentlemen would inform his Son Joseph Burder of the Decease
15 of his Father

TEXTUAL ALTERATIONS 1: 1820] *after del* '9'.
  CIRCUMTEXT Note in pencil from other hand below: 'Send £2 for Funeral Exp^s'. Copy of
answer from Richard Solly, overseer of Mundon, 13 April 1820, on back referring to
enclosed 'three Pounds for the Weekly pay due, and Funeral Expences; The sum always
allowed for that purpose is 2£: for the coffin £1/5^s. Stroud 4^s/6, Fees 7^s/6 4 Men 4^s/0'; and
requesting Ann Burder to state 'where you wish to receive your future allowance; which
I am authorized to state will be altered, but cannot name the Sum until the next Commitee
Meeting'.
  PLACE From postmark.
  RELATED CORRESPONDENCE In an undated letter from Mr Fetchham in London it is said
that Mrs Burder 'will be much oblidge to the Overseers of Mundon to send her quarters
money'.
  FURTHER EVIDENCE 'Ann Burder applied by Letter for a Weekly Allowance [...] granted
[...] 4^s pr Week' (ERO, D/P 238/8/1 Mundon vestry minutes, entry of 4 May 1820).

624 From Ann Burder [in St Andrew Holborn, London] to [John] Bourne in Mundon, 3 February 1821

febuary the *[3ᵈ]* 1821

Sir

am Sorry I that am Under the Necessaty to trouble you so Repeatedly but the Sum you sent me was not Sufficient for me to pay my Rent as it was Run so much Back owen to my not being able to get any Employmant 5 for my self or Children my poor girl is not able at present therefor my good Sir I trust you will Lay my destressed Case before the gentlamen and beg of them to send me a trifle to help me out of my present difficults as I never was so much in debt before in my Life I made a Request in my Last that you would have the goodness to send me a trifle in advance but 10 I Recived only one pound and that I Looked on as no due to me I have Recived only two pound since I saw you and now Sir I have one more Request to make and that is if you will have the goodness to send me the advance of my pay up to Lady day I should feel so much oblige to you for so doing as I trust as spring get up I shall be able get something to do for 15 my Self and poor girl but she is very Ill and I fear I shall Loose her I Recived yours of the 17 Inst but I did not get it tell the wednesday but hope you will have the goodness to send to me on Sunday as I shall go to the Cach for it by Complying with my Request you will

for Ever oblige 20
your humble servant
Ann Burder

CIRCUMTEXT Monthly account of cash payments made to Mrs Burder from May 1820 to February 1821, from other hand, on following page (probably from Richard Solly, overseer of Mundon).
PLACE Inferred from Ann Burder's previous and further letters (**623, 631-2, 637**).

625 From John Thurtell in Romford, Essex, to the overseer of Mundon, 1 February 1823

romfd esex febuary the 1 1823

to the overcear sir i am under the necesty of trobling you as mister wood wished me to wright to you as the children are very bare of Clothing and it dos knot Lay in my Power at Present to By them any and the wether is cold if you Could send me one Pound to By them few nesreyes and mister 5

wood would be very glad if you would send the order to him as there is
Clothing comes in the markett far Better then the clofs and cheper So
hope you will have the goodness to send the order to mister wood and sir
i have Plenty of work as soon as the wether Permits and i hope i shall be
10 able to mentain my family wthough any more alouance then what i have
so i hope you will answer this Letter by the 3 and sir
i am your humble servant
John turtle
sir i hope you will have the goodnes to send the quarters rent to mister
15 wood as he stoped from me and i onley gett 5 shilling wek the landlord is
but lad and would be thankfull for it

TEXTUAL ALTERATIONS 5: Could] 'C' *over* 'w'.

**626   From John Thurtell in Romford [Essex] to the overseer of
         Mundon, 13 May 1831**

Sir/
As the manner in which I receive the weekly allowance granted to me
by the parish as paid to me by Mr Talbot, is calculated to do me very little
service, (he paying me only a few shillings at a time, sometimes 1, 2, or
5 3) I should be very much obliged if you would allow me the sum of five
pounds, to last me from the present time until Michaelmas next, which
would enable me to have at once leather enough to be of essential service
to me, and do me much more good than the present plan of paying me a
few shillings at a time. - I should also esteem it a favor if you would send
10 my Rent direct to my landlord instead of paying it through Mr Talbot, as
he deducts two Shillings per Quarter from my landlord for his trouble, to
which my landlord objects. - A line or two by way of reply to this will be
very thankfully received by
Sir, Y^r humble Servt
15   John Thurtell,
Shoemaker.
Romford
May 13, 1831

TEXTUAL ALTERATIONS 3: to me] 'to' *after del* 'to be'. 9: send] *after del* 'also'.
RELATED CORRESPONDENCE On the same day, Mr Talbot, presumed overseer of Romford,
wrote to Mr Blakely, overseer of Mundon, presenting a distressing account of 'your worth-
less Pauper Thurtell'. His wife was 'wreched, destitute of every comfort, [...] very ill, and

can scarcly walk - and I do think almost starved - so much so, that I think it probable she will die in the Street [...] the fellow beats his wife tremendously - drives her out in a most brutal way'. He enclosed an extract from Mundon's overseers' accounts, referring to £36 expended for Thurtell's family from Lady Day 1830 till Lady Day 1831, and gave details of his family. His daughter Elizabeth (20) was in service in Dartford, while all others were at home: Harriet (15), William (13), Sophia (11), Charlotte (9), James (7), and John (2).

The case of Thurtell had occupied the parish officers of Romford and Mundon for some time and led to an extensive correspondence. On 22 December 1830, Talbot had written to John Bourne that they had had trouble with Thurtell, and that his wife had come 'crying bitterly, he had been beating her'. His family had had smallpox, and Talbot asked Bourne whether he was to continue to allow him 8s per week for another quarter. At Mundon, this had apparently been understood as suggesting that it might be better to send him home, an idea of which Richard Solly, overseer of Mundon, had expressed disapproval rather eloquently when he had written back to Romford on 31 December 1830: 'we beg to express our thanks for the trouble you have taken in behalf of the parish with our wishes that you will be so good as to continue the weekly advances to him & such other temporary means of relief as circumstances may render necessary, either in money, provisions, or Leather, as it may appear to you most judicious. - It is extremely difficult to decide what measures should be adopted with this man this family - We are fully aware that if Thurtell were a man of different habits he could not require the assistance he receives from us, but if we have him home, we do not think it probable it would improve him, or lessen our expenses, indeed we are of opinion that however little he may work in his present situation, he is quite as much employed, if not more, than he could be here, unless he was set to Husbandry Work, of which it is hardly to be expected he could or would do much.'

Thurtell had stayed in Romford and Mundon, his home parish, seems to have repaid whatever was advanced to him. On 3 February 1831, Talbot had written to Bourne that they had allowed him '50ˢ worth of Leather' and additional relief 'when they had the small pox - and with all these helps the Woman declares before Mʳ Wood and myself that at times she is almost starved. The Man is such a desperate fellow with his ugly Bull Dogs - that I am afraid to go to the house.' On 1 March 1831, he had reported that Talbot's wife had called on him. He thought she was in danger that if not given more help 'she will drop in the street, and amidst it all they keep dogs, rabbits and birds, and if the woman was to touch any of them, the man would I doubt not, knock her down, by all means take the family home'. On 18 March 1831, two months before the above letter from Thurtell himself, Talbot had written again: 'their wretched state of destitution for this last month, is frightful after such a handsome allowance as your parish makes to them, however I have done the best I could - many times have I seen the woman who has walked miles - came home at night - half naked - scarcly a shoe for her foot wet through - and not had - (if she tells truth) one bit of food all day except a few potatoes.'

627   From John Thurtell in Romford, Essex, to Richard Solly in Mundon, 12 August 1831

romford esexs august the 12 1831

mister solly sir i am under the nesety of righting to you as i have had the £2 pounds worth of lether acording to your orders as i receved on the 2 of

june but the 8 weeks is expired on sunday next but mister wood object
5 letting me have it he did knot under stand your order but i should be much
oblige to you if you would send mister wood pu*[---]* puntal order as i
want the lether to work on and should be much obliged to you to send the
order betwen this and sunday as it will throw me be hind as he dont let to
lik to lett me have id untill the qareter send the order so as i am to have it
10 every 8 weeks and
          you will much oblig your
          john hurtell

TEXTUAL ALTERATIONS 1: 12 1831] *interl at end of line.* 2: had] 'd' *over illeg.* 3: as i receved
on the 2 of june] *interl above* 'according ... but'.
      RELATED CORRESPONDENCE On 4 June 1831, Mr Talbot in Romford had written to the
overseer of Mundon, expressing bitter complaints about Thurtell's conduct and asking
him to 'send positive answer that I can show to him, touching his request for leather, as he
imputes all the blame to me that he does not have a quarters leather in advance'. On 9 June
1831, Talbot had sent another letter, saying that Thurtell had again asked for leather: His
wife, he went on, had called on him and Mr Wood 'and declared to us that she dared not
go to bed, the Children was then crying for food'.

628   From John Thurtell in Romford, Essex, to [Richard] Solly in Mundon, 2 December 1831

                    romford esexs December the 2 18013
to mister soley sir i am under the nesety of righting to you on the count of
this hevy complaint and i am quiat Destute of comman neserys to keep
my famey Clain and Decent and as every parish is giving those things
5 that is nesery to keep there one poor clane and Decent so i think it my
Deuty to aply to you for to send me som reliefe to help me as i have
plenty to keep me and my famely decend but through hevy afflictians i
have been obliged to pleg them and if you do knot send me som reliefe
the family must com home and i hope you will answer this with speed as
10 my wife is very Lame and is knot churched yet and in so doing your
humble servent
John turtle
you will be so good
as to answer this
15 by monday as i my give
the parrish answre

TEXTUAL ALTERATIONS 5: think] 'thi' *over illeg.*

RELATED CORRESPONDENCE On 12 September 1831, William Wood, presumed overseer of Romford, had written to Richard Solly, overseer of Mundon, that a friend of his was prepared to take one of Thurtell's daughters into service. But she was 'Destitute of Clothes', and he had wanted to know 'if you will give me an order to purchase a few things that are necessary'. On 11 December 1831, a week after the above letter from John Thurtell, Wood wrote to Solly and acknowledged the receipt of £2. He said that the doctor had gone to see Thurtell's family and 'found them very filthy'. His landlord expected six months' rent which he claimed Mundon had promised to him. 'I read the letter to Thurtle - says he shall write again to you'. The next letter Solly received from Romford, dated 2 January 1832, came from Mr Talbot who said Thurtell needed some extra relief (with note of answer from Mundon to advance 12s). A week later, Talbot addressed Solly again. He said that Thurtell's wife 'has so upset me and my family that I must shut the door against her - she cried aloud and took on most bitterly - and declared that she and the Children were starving - her husband ill at bed - Mr Wood would not give her a penny - I went to Mr Wood - and after she told tale of woes' (letter of 9 January 1832; similar letter from Talbot to Solly, 13 January 1832).

629* From Mary Keeling in Maldon [Essex] to [John] Sewell in Mundon, 28 October 1832

Maldon Oct 28 1832

Si^r I would be much a bliged to you if you will send my monny By *the Bearer*

8 weeks   0 - 16 - 0

mary Keeling 5

WRITING Skilled hand. Possibly this note, written on a small piece of paper (size: 160 x 40mm), was issued by the overseer of Maldon and then handed out to Mary Keeling to be produced at Mundon as her place of settlement. Mundon is 3 miles south of Maldon.

630 From J[ohn] Thurtell in Romford [Essex] to the overseers of Mundon, 8 November 1832

Romford Novr 8 1832

Sir

I take the libberty of Riting these few lines to you and I am Sorry to troble you on this occasion as Mr Wood refuses to let me have lether only by the month as I dont wish to have it by the month as it dont do me no 5 good I batter have it by the two months as it wont make no difference to you and it will do me a good deal more good for I sent to Mr Wood to let me have one pair high soes left three times one a day and he would not

and my lether is dew on the 12 of this month if you please Sir I would
10 thank you if you will send the answer by this and monday next to Mr Wood
to let me have the lether every eight weeks
     Sir

                         your humble Servant
                                J Thurtell

TEXTUAL ALTERATIONS 5: have it] 'it' *interl with caret.*

631 From Ann Burder [in St Andrew Holborn, London] to the churchwardens and overseers of Mundon, [21 December 1832]

To the Churchwardens and Overseers of the Parish of Mundon
    Gentlemen
    I most respectfully trust you will pardon the liberty I thus take in applying
to you for a small addition to my present allowance under the following
5 circumstances. Being now Sixty Four Years of Age and nearly Blind I am
thereby prevented from doing any thing towards my own Support the Sum
you are kind enough to allow me being barely sufficient to pay my rent and
was it not for a little assisstance I occasionally receive from my daughters
I must have starved. Thus situated I sincerely hope that during this
10 inclement Season you will comply with my request
    I further beg leave to add that you will very greatly oblige me by sending
my Money the Sunday before Christmas Day as I am obliged to pay my
Rent on the following Monday

                                   I remain
15   Gentlemen
                    Your most obed Humb^e Servt
                              Ann Burder

Gentlemen
20   I hope you will Excuse My Sending a Post Letter but My being very ill I
was not able go from Ely Court Holborn to M^[r] Yeldoms in the Commercial Road
    I Return Many Thanks for the 2 shill^s you was so kind send me by M^r
Ye<ldoms> last quarter

TEXTUAL ALTERATIONS 20: My] *interl.* 21: Ely Court] *interl.* 23: so] *interl.*
    DATE Date of postmark.

632 From Ann Burder in [St Andrew] Holborn [London] to the overseer of Mundon, 25 September 1833

To/ The Overseers of Munden Parish Essex
   Gentlemen
   I shall take it as a very great favor if you will oblige me by sending my
Quarters Money by Mr Yeldom the Maldon Coachman on Sunday Next
having my Rent to pay on the Monday   5
                 I am
                 Gentlemen
                 Your most Obed^t Hum^{ble} Servt
                 Ann Burder
                                  10
25 Septr 1833
10 Ely Court
Holbron

WRITING Skilled hand, possibly that of Benjamin Armstrong, churchwarden of St Andrew
Holborn.
   RELATED CORRESPONDENCE In a letter of 10 December 1833, the minister and the two
churchwardens of St Andrew Holborn, London, Gilbert Beresford, Benjamin Armstrong
and James Edmund Weedon, certified that Ann Burder lived at 10 Ely Court, Holborn.
There is a further certificate to the same effect, dated 18 March 1834, and signed by Gilbert
Beresford.

633 From John Thurtell in Romford, Essex, to the overseer of Mundon, 22 October 1833

                     romford esexs october the 22 1833
to the overcer sir i am under the nesety of righting to you as it Dos knot
Lay in my Power to suply the wants of my famely as the are in wants of
Linning and i want to gett Som beding and i should be obliged to you to
send one Pound and that would help me to Cloth the children against the   5
winter and if you dont Lett me have it i must send the famely home but
mister wood wished me to right as he will advance the money if you will
be so good as to send the order sir i have Plenty of work but mony is so
carce that i cant gett the redey money allways
   i hope you will have the goodnes to answer this by return of Post   10
                          i am sir your humble
                             servent John turtle

TEXTUAL ALTERATIONS 1: 1833] *interl at end of line.*

CIRCUMTEXT Note from John Linsell to Richard Solly, overseer of Mundon, below text: 'I am of Opinion it is Nessary to comply with Turtles request notwithstanding his threat to send his familey home shall be Obligd if you will let me have your Sentiments upon it return it by Bearer'. Below that, note from Richard Solly: 'By all means do what you think best.'

RELATED CORRESPONDENCE Richard Solly's frustrated response needs to be seen against the background of the rather dramatic course of Thurtell's case over the previous calendar year, which is witnessed in an extensive correspondence between Romford and Mundon. On 18 February 1832, Mr Talbot had written to Solly that he had given Thurtell leather worth 5s and 'kept back for rent' the remaining 3s of his allowance, after Thurtell's landlord had called on him. Solly had answered on 23 February1832 that Mundon was prepared to allow him some extra money for his rent, but only till Christmas (copy of answer, written crosswise over the text). On 7 March 1832, Mr Bourne had informed Solly that Thurtell's wife 'came to me crying to ask the favor to write to you, to send Mr Wood an order for Leather'. Answering a further letter from Romford (not found) Solly had discussed the question of Thurtell's arrears in rent and the threatened seizure of his goods (letter of 24 April 1832 to William Wood).

Then, in a letter of 12 July 1832, Solly had been informed by Talbot that Thurtell had been ill for the last three weeks. On 17 July 1832, Talbot had written again, this time to John Sewell. Thurtell's neighbours had reported that his wife and two children were ill, and 'that such a picture of distress and misery is rarely to be seen - the whole of them sleeping on a something called a bed - living in the greatest possible filth and dirt - the vermin crawling about them in a way that they may be scraped of in bunches'. The overseers had sent a doctor to see them, who had said 'that the man will die - he is so deaf that it is with difficulty he can hear anything said to him', and that it was 'absolutely necessary that a woman should be in the house as a nurse and some clean things got for them directly'. Shortly afterwards, the family had been found to suffer from a bad fever. James Parker, assistant overseer in Romford, wrote on 20 July 1832: 'I have been under the necessity of having their house completely cleaned out it being swarmed of everything Filthy buying him new sheets Blankets and wearing Linen'. He had asked whether Mundon was prepared to pay for medical attendance, 'if not I shall be necessitated to take out Suspend[ed] orders'. In July 1832, William Wood had told Solly that Thurtell's wife and children had become worse, and on 26 July 1832 James Parker, assistant overseer in Romford, had written that the wife was dead 'and three of her children are not likely to live, I am obliged to have two women constantly with them'.

Wood, Sewell and Solly had then tried to arrange a meeting at Chelmsford market, but failed to find a date which suited all of them. Meanwhile, Thurtell's eldest daughter had been found to be (back?) home. Wood had tried to get a place for her, 'but as the mother is no more' he thought 'it is probable Thurtell will want to retain her to keep House. I think as to the future arrangements respectg. Thurtell & family much must depend upon his chances of getting a living where he is [...] Thurtell always puts the best face on his prospects. I think he is likely to do quite as well, if not better without his wife, than he did with' (letter from Wood of 8 August 1832, with notes between Sewell and Solly). Later on, there had been some disagreement as to what allowance Thurtell ought to receive. But in the event, Mundon had repaid what Romford had advanced (letter from Bowers to Sewell, 13 August 1832; letter from Wood to Sewell, 17 August 1832).

634 From John Thurtell in Romford, Essex, to the overseer of Mundon, 22 December [1833]

romford esexs December the 22 183*[3]*
to the overcer sir i am under the nesety of trobling you as i am destute of
the Different sorts of Lether that i want as i have grate deale of Light
work bespok and i should be much oblige to you if you would send order
to mister wood to Lett me have thirty shilling worth of Lether such as i   5
want as i cannot do th<e> work i have to Do and it will be out of the next
2£ Pounds that is Deu as i have knot had knothing more then my alowance
is i havePlenty of work and Cannot Do it untill i have the Lether and it is
great hindrance to me s<o> i hope you will have the Goodnes to answer
this by return of Post you will much oblige   10
Jon turtle

635 From John Thurtell in Romford [Essex] to the overseer of Mundon, 12 February 1834

rom<ford> febury the 12 1834
to the overcer <sir I am> under the nesety of righting to you as i have
Plenty of good work and my costomes are getting out to work i am at
stand for the want of Lether and mister wood objects Letting me have any
wethought fresh order wich never Draw to the amount i allways Lave 10   5
shillings in hand but i would be much oblige to you Lett me have thirty
silling and be so cind as to send the order by return of Post and mister
wood would wish to have standing order when there three weeks to re-
new it gane as these stopegs hurts me i hope you will have the goodness
to right by return of Post   10
i am yours John turtle

TEXTUAL ALTERATIONS 8: wish] 'h' *over* 't'.

RELATED CORRESPONDENCE On 10 January 1834, William Wood in Romford had written
to John Sewell, overseer of Mundon, that Thurtell had received the 30s sent to him. He
had now six children at home: Harriet (19), William (10), Charlotte (8), Sophia (7), James
(6), and John (5). It should be noted that these ages do not quite match those reported
from Rochford in 1831 (see RELATED CORRESPONDENCE, **626**).

636   From Mrs Brown to John Sewell in Mundon

Sir i mrs Brown should be glad if you would give me few Shillings as we
have got eight Shillings to pay the nurse and with our five small Children
we cannot pay it

637   From A[nn] Burder in [St Andrew Holborn] London to Mr
Bowen in Mundon, 11 January

London January 11

Sir

    I hope you will Excuse the Liberty I take in troubleing you once more
but Necessity oblige me to Request the favour of you to advance me a
5 few weeks pay as the Long affliction of my poor Child have Run me so
much Back with my Rent and Likewise I have got a Bill of fourteen
shilling to pay to a Docter which I greatly fear will never be in my power
to do UnLess you Sir will have the goodness to spake to the Gentlemen
and thay kindly send me a few shillings towards it I should Essteem it a
10 great favour in you to mention it to them and trust they will kindly Consider the very great trials that I now Labour Under tell I get my poor
Children fixed in something for there future good I have just got my Boy
out again I hope he will keep it I have got no place for my girl now nor
have she Regained her strength Enough to allow her to take one at present
15 I Should not have Called in a Doctor but her Disorder was of so dangereous
a Nature which obliged me to it and now Sir allow me to apologize for
the Last Letter I sent I Called at the Inn and it was denied me tell I
Expected an Answer to the Last and then it was given me so I must plead
your forgiveness for the mistake I hope you will have the goodness to
20 sent to me on Sunday as I will meet the Coach at the Inn I trust to your
goodness to Excuse the Liberty

I now take and I Remain
your Ever much obliged
and greatfull Servnt
25   A Burder

Eleay Cort 11

TEXTUAL ALTERATIONS 9: Essteem it] 'it' *interl.* 15: Disorder] 'D' *over illeg.* 16: apologize]
after del 'apop'. 26: 11] *after del* 'December'.

638 From A[nn] Burder in [St Andrew Holborn] London to [John] Bourne in Mundon, 21 April

Sir

I Recived your favour of the 17 Inst and the money Safe and feel Extreemly obliged to you and the Gentlemen for there Goddness but as I have had my two Children at home this winter I must once more intrude on your goodness and beg the favour to advance me two pounds in 5 advance as I am in very great destress and this I trust will be the Last time that I shall be obliged to make such a Request as I have some hopes that my Boy will be intirely from me as I have an offer made me by a gentleman to take him as an Apprentice tell he is 21 if the Gentleman will have the goodness to assist with a Littel money to Buy him a few Clothes and pay 10 for his Indenture as its quite out of my power to do it without your kind assistance therefore I hope the gentlemen will kindly Consider that by advanceing a trifle now may Spare them many pounds afterwards as he will be interely of your parrish and as its a very good Business I Could wish very much to have him Learn it and if you think proper to write to 15 the Gentleman his Name is Page No 9 Warweck St golden Square St James London

and now Sir once more Let me beg of you to advance me two pounds and and at the Same time Let me know what the Gentlemen will allow me towards the Boys Expences I trust all to you Goodness haveing Recived 20 so many proofs of it I shall Expect to hear from you on sunday and shall meet the Coach so no more from your

Much obliged and gratfull
Servent
A Burder 25

London April
the 21

PLACE Parish inferred from previous letters from Ann Burder (**623**, **631**, **632**, **637**).

Navestock pauper letter

639   From Ann Pepper in Rochford [Essex] to the overseers of Nave-stock, 8 September 1829

Rochford Sept 8th 1829

Gent^m/

This is to Inform you that I am under the Necessity of writing to you for some Assistance, as I am almost unable to do for Myself, and am nearly
5 75 years of Age, I would thank you to take it into Consideration and write to the Overseers of Rochford to allow me something weekly, so as I can draw it at Rochford, It is through Necessity that I am Compell'd to trouble you, By Affliction, and Old age, and Nobody to assist me would thank you for an Answer as soon as you Possibly Can, by so Doing you will greatly
10 Oblige Your Humble Servant

Ann Pepper

CIRCUMTEXT Note from other hand below to 'Certify the above to be true', signed by churchwarden and overseer of Rochford.

White Notley pauper letters

640 From Mrs Wilkinson in Rickmansworth, Hertfordshire, 6 May 1831

May 6 1831 Rickmanswarth

honord Sir

think it not to great a libty that I hav taken in troublean you it is With Selican your goodness Respetian Elz King my neas as I hav gat a place to put her to far 2 years But I must find her in cloths and Washing which is 5
a great undertaking far me as I am onely a Sarvnt I hap that you will be so good as to git the gentman af the parich to pay her Expanceas dawn to me as it Quit out af my power far I hav beean ill far 4 manths past and I hav all my own Expanars to pay and the famely thath Beean very Expancif to me I must have her daun in a fortnit from this day it will cost an paund I 10
would Nat a beean so trublsam but I am not able to pay the manay and it takean her of the parich which I hap that the gentman will be so good as I hav dane so much fore tham and by so doean withe your goodness you will oblige youre humbel Savent
  Mrs Wilkinsam at Mrs Salthews   15
  Rickman warth harefard Shear
N B Be so good as send me an answere as soon as poseabale as I can do mothing till I hear from this

TEXTUAL ALTERATIONS 1: 6] *over illeg.* 6: undertaking] 'a' *inserted.* 6: onely] *after del illeg.* 7: to pay] 'to' *interl.* 8: power] 'r' *over illeg.*
WRITING 4: Selican] *read* 'soliciting'.
FURTHER EVIDENCE Eliz[abeth] King seems to have been the daughter of Widow King in White Notley. The latter was on regular relief (1s 6d per week). On 25 May 1831, she received 18s 'for Coachhire of her girl to Rickensworth' (ERO, D/P 39/12/1, White Notley overseers' accounts, 1830-1870).

641 From Mrs Wilkinson in Rickmansworth [Hertfordshire], 18 May 1831

May 18 1831 Rickmanswarth

Sir

I am oblidge to you and to the parishans far your Kindness you nead not be undar anay aprunsians that Eliz will be anay mar troube to you aftar

5 you will be so good as to send her an munday 23 the Rickmanswarth coch
that she camby By Liveas the Bull inn holborn By at *[12]* 3 in the afternoon but I will be obige to you if you will send me a few Lines to say
whear the coch cames to in tawn as I must send sum ane to meat her thear
By Return of post
10   Sir I Reman your humbal
          Sarvent Mrs Wilkinsan

TEXTUAL ALTERATIONS 5: the] *after del* 'R'. 6: camby By] 'By' *inserted in left-hand margin*
6: holborn By] 'By' *interl above* 'holborn'. 8: as] *after del* 'I'.

Peldon pauper letter

642   From James Wells in Stratford, Essex, to Mr Artkey in Peldon

Gentlemen

I was in hops before this time to have had Sum assistance Towards Clothing my poore Helpless Chieldren wich if posable I would endaver to provide for but i find it Imposable without your help Towards theare Cloothing thearefor I hop your goodness will take it into Considration   5 and as soone as posable i hope you to <be> so kind as to send me a trifull to Cover my poore lettel all most Naked babes in Number 6 of them wich fells my hands And heart full I Remaine in Indefrent helth thanks be to god for it as i hop those Loynes To find you my good friends All

From me James   10

Wells Stratford

Essex

TEXTUAL ALTERATIONS 5: thearefor] 'for' *interl at end of line.*
  PLACE Stratford belonged to the parish of West Ham.

Purleigh pauper letters

643 From William Thurtell in South Benfleet, Essex, to Mr Sanders, churchwarden of Purleigh, 1 February 1822

South Bemflett Feby 1st *1822*

Sir I Am Under Anesety of Riten to you For Sum A Sestent as my Fameley Is So large that I Cannot Seport them Without Sum help I have tried to Doe Without help as long as I Can For I have been Wary Ill my Self and
5 All my Famely for Sum time but I Am and My Cheld^{rn} <--> Got the better of It I I hant yarnt but Wery <lit>tel Money for this tow Month Not Half A Nuf <t>o Seport my Famely and My Wife Was Confind on Munday last Jenery the 28 With the Sixth Child Wich I Cannot Seport them Without Sum help At this time therefore I hope Gentlmen I hope you Will Consder
10 me and Doe Sumthing for me At this time I Would not A trubled you but I am Under Anesety of It At this time I Would A Come my Self but the distents Is So far and the loss of time All to Getherel and I hope you Will doe Sumthing for me by Riten

Plese to Drect to me as this

15   For Willm Thurtell
                                                                                            Carpenter South Bemflett
                                                                                            Near Rayleigh
                                                                                            Essex

   I Am Yours
20   Wm Thurtell

TEXTUAL ALTERATIONS 6: yarnt] 'y' *over del* 'G'. 9: Gentlmen] 'l' *interl.*
CIRCUMTEXT Note from other hand at top of page: 'by direction of the Vestry sent him £1 note'.

644 From William Thurtell in South Benfleet [Essex] to the overseer of Purleigh, 3 January 1825

Sir I Rite to Informe you that I have paid A Wery havey Expence Indeed At this time and I Am Under Anoblator of Riten to you for Sum Asistent At this time My Wife Is latley been Confind With the 7 Child Wich I have them All Now liven and my Wife have Been Wery Bade In deed for
5 A fortnight So that All Veseters thought that She Must Die But Bless be

to God She Is A Geten the Better of It But my Fameley Is So large and my Expence So Grate that I Cant doe Without Some More A Sistent then I have Sir I hope that you Will Conside me In this hevey Expence and help me In A Part of It and Consider A trifel More Par week for I Cannot Seport them With out Sumthing More then I have 10

Willm *Thurtell*

South Bemfleet
Jenery 3th 1825

TEXTUAL ALTERATIONS 5: All] *interl.* 8: hope] *after del illeg.*
    CIRCUMTEXT Note from other hand at top of page: 'agreed to send him One pound'.
    FURTHER EVIDENCE 'Wm Thrutell rel^d by Meet^g' £1 7s January 1825 (ERO, D/P 197/12/
3, Purleigh overseers' accounts).

Rainham pauper letters

645 From Mary Pavett in Rainham to Henry Pavett in Stratford [Essex], [2] March 1748

March th *[2]* 1748

Raynham

Loving Brother This Coms to Let you Now that My husban Died Yesterday and Desier to Now if you Will Com Down and See him Beried for he
5 Life in asad Conditon I desier to Now if you and your Brother Will Be at
the Expence of Bearing him if Not to goe to the parish and aquaint them of
it pray Send apuntal anser By the Barer of Whot is to be Don in the afaire
for Ihave Not got Whare With to Defray the Expence of Bering him for if
the parish Berries him I must be forst to Com Com to ham parish and With
10 What things I hav got I can Mak Shift Just to Live and if ham parish Will
is to be at the Charge Desier them to Send a note from thare hands but I
shall be glad if you Will Com Down for thare is Somthings that Will be of
Servis to you in your Way of Business he Came hom of the Satturday
Night and Died amonday Noon he Not got acoffin Nor I have got No
15 Money Soe pray Send Me Word by the Barer from your Loveing
Sister Mary Pavett

TEXTUAL ALTERATIONS 3: Now] *after del* 'R'. 5: Now] *interl.* 12: Down] 'n' *interl at end of line.* 14: No] *after del* 'to'.

CIRCUMTEXT Answer from Henry Pavett on back of page, dated 2 March [1748]: 'Sister I Recved your Leater I am Sory to her my Brother is dead I heave Ben with the Chorchworden and thay well not Bary him without Ranom Can find a setefiteket from there hands Rainom Praish must Beary him my Brother John and I Cant a ford to Beary him And the Parish must Wheare he did I Cant no Wais Come Down to See him Beared So my Love to you Henry Pavett'. This also explains how the letter came into the hands of the overseers of Rainham. Mary Pavett's brother (or brother-in-law) returned her original letter with his answer, with which she then proceeded to prove that she had found no assistance towards the burial of her husband from within the family.

PLACE Stratford belonged to the parish of West Ham, about 10 miles from Rainham.

646 From Amy Hill in Deptford, Surrey, to Mr Saunders, school-master in Rainham [19 March 1801]

Hond gentelmen

    & only frinds) It grives Me as food is Dear we canot get cloths to shift our selvs In my husband has only one old pach^d shirt To put on as well as the rest of the famly and shall be humbly thankfull for one piec Wich your goodness be pleased to grant I will Take care with th Blessing of   5 God almighty Not to ask for any moor then 4 yd^s of flanell and a few yd^s of stuf or any thing to make the child^{ren} gowns and skirt^s my husband as Well as the rest of us lies so hard I sometime think to Die as John Cook who doctor smith says Was starved he was at work with my husband a fortnight befor he died & has left a wife & Three Child^{ren} to the parish   10

    I thank god & thank your bountyfull Goodness to my eld^{ist} child^{ren} who is likd by Master & misstress^{is} as it is th first time I have asked any thing for my self so I hop it will be th last & hope you will not be angry) when my child^m grow out of th way or food cheeper I am shur I beleiv I shall not Trouble any mor any frind^s 15

                  Amy Hill

    New Cross North Turnpik

    Deptford surry

TEXTUAL ALTERATIONS 3: only] *after del* 'not'. 7: and] *interl with caret.* 9: who] *after del illeg.*
DATE Date of postmark.

647 From [Mrs] Wall to Mr Surig, churchwarden of Rainham, 23 June 1804

                            June 23th 1804

Mr Surig

  Sir

    I have taken the Libberty to writ to you to Let you know that my husband his a Cummin haut Of <the> Hospital nex tuday th<e> Docters have   5 <giv>en him hover If you think proper to fetch us home wee Shall Be glad if y<o>u have got a place for hus you may think Si<r> Becau<s>e <---->
the hospitall that wee wont nothing of yo<u> But I am a Woman that is not able to to get my Bred I which I wose I have got avery Bad Leg in Deed Else I wod not <b>efraid to get my Bread with Out the helpe Of a Parish   10

I have had nothen from you this Week Mr Surig never Cauled a for me I
seen him Rid by an a nother gentleman with him I hav a Seven Weeks
Rent a Munday Nex at 1.8 Per week the Peple wonts thair munny to Pay
thair Rent a Quarter Day if you Pleas to Send it
15 So I Remain Y^r St Wall

TEXTUAL ALTERATIONS 9: wose] 'o' *interl.*

648   From Hannah Wall in Mile End [Colchester] to Mr Masters in Rainham, 21 June 1805

Gentlemen I am sorry to trouble you By sending a Letter by Post, but
Nesessity obliges me to it, my youngest Child Died this Morning, I should
be oblight to you to send me my tree weeks Money, as Soon as you can
make it Convenient, as I am greatley Distrest for it, the Child has been
5 Poorly this month Back, and has run me to a deal of Expence with Doctor
& Medecins, I hope you will send me what Money you Think will Bury
him, as to my Other Child, he is almost Naked for want of Cloths, and
what to do I dont know, I am So much Distrested as to myself, my Cloths
are all in the Pawn Brokers I hope you will send me Relief as Soon as
10 Possible as I am greatley Distrest,
                              I am Gentlemen with
                              the greatest Respect y^r
                              Distresed widow
                              Hanagh Wall
15 Mile End
    June 21st 1805

TEXTUAL ALTERATIONS 2: youngest] 'yo' *interl with stroke.*

649   From Amy Hill [in Deptford, Surrey] to Charles Leeds in Rainham [12 December 1805]

Dear Sister & Brother
    I am Very Sory to tel you my husband Very Ill in a pleursy fever & has
not been abel to get out of bed without help for moor then a week past &
as I hav no moor then four shillings p week for four of us to liv on besid^s

my Husband is being ill I cannot earn a shilling as he is not fit to be left I 5
am sorry to be so Troublesom but will be Very thankfull for you to report
it to the gentlemen as I believe he Will not trouble any body long I wish I
could get him som wine to make a litel way for him but it is so very dear &
he must die without nurrishment Bless & thank the gentelmen Was it not
for my Husband lying so Ill I should not think of Troubling their good^{ne}ss 10
but if thay can spare me something til my husband if pleas god is betta I
should be Humbly thankfull
    My Child^{ren} Join with me in lov to You & Cousins & hops thes will find
you all in better helth then it leavs us
From your aflected Sister Amy Hill 15
                New Cross
If not two troublesom pray send a letter as soon as posibel & let me know
how you all are & I hav been grately Disapointd but this world is full of
Nothing else

TEXTUAL ALTERATIONS 3: not] *after del illeg.* 4: for] *interl with caret.* 5: Husband is] 'i' *interl above del illeg character.* 9: gentelmen] 'men' *interl at end of line.* 10: Ill] *after del* 'heavey on my hands'. 18: I] *after del* 'it yours is [showing well]'.
    DATE Date of postmark.
    PLACE New Cross belonged to Deptford.

650   From Thomas Briggs in London Hospital [Whitechapel] London to Mr Hayser in Rainham, 27 January [1806]

                        London Hospitall janry 27
Sir this with My Dutty to you and Should Esteem it a Great favour if you
would Send Me a triffel of Money to pay for My washing and to Gett Me
Some Littel nourishment More than what the House allows Me as i am a
Getting a Littell Better and in so doing you will releife and Much Oblige 5
your Humbell
                  Servant
                            thomas Briggs
please to Diret
for Me in johns 10
ward London Hospital
white Chappell road
        London

DATE Year from postmark.

651 From Thomas Briggs in London Hospital [Whitechapel, London] to Mr Hayser in Rainham, 24 March 1806

Mr Hayser/

It is now some since I received any Thing from you and I am very much in wants of a Trifle as I have no Prospect of coming out soon I expected my leg comeing off a Fortnights ago but, Sr Wm Blizards alterd his mind
5 and would not take it off.

I remain

Sir

your obliged and ob^d Ser^t

Thomas Briggs

10 London Hospital

March 24th 1806

TEXTUAL ALTERATIONS 4: leg] 'e' *over illeg.*

652 From Amy Hill to Mr Heathroat [27 March 1815]

S^r

I am grately Obligd to th gentelmen for their kind Charity & humbly Beg their favour to guive me as I never moor shall trouble them but this one time I asking for Change of linining as I never was In such want of in all
5 my life & should be gratefuly thankefull for 2 Shifts pecs of flanel 1 gown hankerchief & apron be pleasd to grant me these & I never will ask you for any moor Cloths a long a I live & it is the first time I hav askd for myself & am in grate hopes I shall meet with your Charitable Blessing pray Gentelmen Consider me & if I offend for guive me pray
10 Amy Hill

DATE Date of postmark.

653 From Ann Gossling to Mr Lee in Rainham

Mr Lee

My Duty to him and the Coales is Not Com Yet that the Gentlemen Orderd me When I Was Over there Whhen I Was Over there that thay Wood Send the Order Over by Mr Lee and he has Bean up tvice and there

and there now Com I Am in Grate Distress and I have had A Sack A 5
Coales From the Overseres of Luseane for I have Now Work and I Am
A More Starveing for Fire & Vittle too I have Run My Self Almost 5
pound in Deat and if theay Consider Me that I Dray More Money and Pay
What I how and Git to Servese and if they Send Me Som Money to pay
the Sack of Coales and Send Me Some Coales Ile do the Best I Can the 10
Sack of Coale Comes to 4 Shillings So to Conclud

Your Humble

Survant Ann

Gossling

TEXTUAL ALTERATIONS 12: Your] *after del illeg.*

Rayleigh pauper letters

654 From Thomas Sagger in Springfield [Essex] to Mr Spinks in Rayleigh, 1 October 1809

Octr 1 - 1809

Sir/

I have sent you thease few lines to let you know we stand in great nead of a months pay as every thing is so excesssive dear and especially Flowr
5 that we Cannot provide for our Family without a little more assistance our Children all eat so very harty that it Costs me 15 shillings a weak for flowr and what is there more for every other Necessary that is wanting in a Family like ours where there is none able to bring in a shilling that we are sadly put to it this dear time my Children have not got a bit of shoe to
10 their feet nor myself neither and I have not a shilling to spare to by none it is more than I Cand do to fill their bellys I hope the Gentlemen will Consider me and send me a months pay and send it by Mr Ardly on Friday next if he will have te goodness to bring it for us I made free to rite to you as you was in office last so I hope M^r spinks you will do me the Favour to
15 speak to the fresh Overseer and the Gentlemen to let me have it as I stand in such great nead of it at this time when my Wife Came over before she got very wet and got a great Cold that she has not been well Since that it is all against us at this time my Wife receivd a fortnight pay of you and the time is up next Tuesday -

20
I hope this Will find you and
Mrs Spinks and Family all well
from Your Humble servant
Thos Sagger
Springfield

FURTHER EVIDENCE Thomas Sagger in Springfield received regular payments in 1815 through Mrs Audles (ERO, D/P 332/12/5, Rayleigh overseer's accounts).

655 From Ann Prigg in Southminster [Essex] to the overseer of Rayleigh, 2 November 1809

Southminster Essex November 2^d 1809

Gentlemen I am very sorry to be under the disagreeable necessity of troubling You with this Letter. But every necessary of Life has now become so extremely dear that I find it impossible to support myself with my present allowance. I hope and trust I shall give no offence, which I should 5 be sorry to do. But I must beg Your Assistance in some way. And leave it to Your Goodness either to increase my weekly Allowance or to send me what You think proper to enable me to get some Firing for the Winter for it is totally out of my power to get it without Your Assistance. I really stand in Need of support. And find great difficulty to get a piece of Bread 10 otherwise I would not have troubled You. I hope You will favour Me with an Answer immediately or Direct to Mr Patrick as is most Agreeable to You. And whatever You are so kind as to send will be thankfully received

by Your Humble Petitioner

Ann Prigg 15

TEXTUAL ALTERATIONS 1: 1809] *interl at end of line.*

656 From Ann Benson in Rochford [Essex], 26 February 1825

Rochford Feby 26 1825

Sir

I have received 10/ of Mr Mayfield for my Son John should be obliged if you will write whether it is to be continued weekly till he is able to work Wich am fearfull will be a long time before he is again able to 5 Maintain his family as he continues in a very weak State -

Yrs Humble Servt

Ann Benson

TEXTUAL ALTERATIONS 6: his] *after del* 'his'.

WRITING This letter survives only in a copy made by the overseer of Rayleigh.

CIRCUMTEXT Note of answer from Joseph Markwell, overseer of Rayleigh, dated 26 February 1825 in same hand as the letter, 'that if Benson could not do without relief, he must be brought home in the regular way'.

657   From Richard Porter in Ashby-de-la-Zouch [Leicestershire] to the overseer of Rayleigh, 10 March 1826

To the Overseers of the Poor of Rayleigh County of Essex
Gentlemen/
I your Parishioner Richard Porter of Ashby de la Zouch County of Leicester in the most pitiable distress implore your kind assistance. I have
5 as the Doctor states suffer'd a severe loss in the death of my poor wife & what still heightens the distress is that my money has departed too a seven weeks illness of my own by a Rheumatic fever (from which I had just recover'd) My Father in law's illness and death who lived with us & was buried three weeks ago and lastly the illness and death of my poor wife
10 from the same complaint have reduced me to the lowest Ebb She has left me with a Family of four children the youngest quite an infant and I am only indebted to the exertions of my poor but kindhearted neighbours for the little comfort that is left me. You will be pleased to take pity on my circumstances and administer some relief to me as soon as you can I trust
15 you can have no doubt of who I am. I have a Sister in Rayleigh whose name is charlotte and who married a Person of the name of Henry White. hoping you will not forget me I beg to subscribe myself
                              Your very humble Servant
                              Richard Porter
20 Ashby de la Zouch March 10. 1826
PS. I must leave it to you to direct as you think proper be it to me or to the overseer of Ashby I shall be sure of it reaching me

TEXTUAL ALTERATIONS 17: me] *interl with caret.*

CIRCUMTEXT Statement from William Ingle, surgeon, on next page: Richard Porter's wife died on 9 March 1826 after an illness of three weeks and the 'inconvenience & expence unvoidable attendant on this event is felt severly by him & has it is to be feared & regretted reduced him in his circumstances seriously'. Signed also by W. M. Donall, vicar of Ashby-de-le-Zouch.

WRITING Judged from the last signature in the circumtext, it seems likely that the letter was written by the vicar of Ashby-de-la-Zouch, as indeed the following letter (**658**) also suggests.

658 From Richard Porter in Ashby-de-la-Zouch [Leicestershire] to Joseph Markwell, vestry clerk of Rayleigh, 24 March 1826

Ashby de la zouch 24 March 1826

To Mr Markwell

Sir/

I rec^d your letter of the 21st of March and in reply to it can only say that I am assurebly a parishioner of the Parish of Rayleigh my circumstances 5 Sir I have truly laid before you and in addition can only observe that if you do not choose to send me something for relief I must be obliged to bring myself and family to the parish in which I was born It is my wish Sir to follow my occupation here and to be as little burdensome to you as is consistent with my circumstances and I should certainly feel much 10 obliged to you if you would transmit me something by the hands of our overseers (as I am sometimes absent from Ashby a week or two) to assist me in my distress hoping Sir you will consider my case as a pitiable one and that what I write to you is perfectly true. I beg Sir to subscribe myself

your obedient Servant 15
Richard Porter

TEXTUAL ALTERATIONS 1: 24] *interl with caret.* 9: Sir] *interl with caret.*

659 From Thomas Brown in Romford [Essex] to the churchwardens and overseers of Rayleigh, 14 August 1826

Gent^n

I am sorry of being under the necessity of troubling you with this, to inform you that I have been at a great Expence in maintaining my Mother who is Rachael Stebbings, the Widow of the late Robert Stebbings, who was Killed by a fall of a Tree on the Farm called the White House, near 5 the Mills in your Parish about three years since, and now She is very much Afflicted so that it is beyond my power to do any thing further for Her, I have applyed to the Parish Officers of Romford where She now is, and they wish me to Write to inform you of the Subject, wither you will receive her without an Order from this Parish to prevint Expences, if you 10 will do that, I have no Objection in bringing her Home myself any Day, that you will please to Appoint to Receive her, You will please to send me an Answer soon as Possible, what you think best to be done without

troubling this Parish, as She very much wish to be removed Home to
15 Rayleigh, And by so doing you will greatly Oblige Gent[n]

Your Ob[t] Serv[t]
Tho[s] Brown

Swan Inn Romford
14 Aug[t] 1826

TEXTUAL ALTERATIONS 7: do] *interl with caret.* 8: Her] *after del* 'for'. 10: without] 't' *interl at end of line.* 12: Appoint] 't' *interl at end of line.* 13: without] 'out' *interl with caret.*

660   From Richard Porter in Ashby-de-la-Zouch [Leicestershire] to the overseer of Rayleigh, 18 September 1826

Ashby de la zouch
Sep[t] 18[ht] 1826

Sir/

I have taken the liberty of again applying to you having never received
5 any answer from my letter to you about six months ago - In that letter my
Case was stated to you by the vicar And the doctor that attended my
family, but should that letter have miscarried I here also beg leave to say
that my wife died in March last of a fever that was very prevalent here,
And I myself have been Ill of a Rheumatic fever for three months And
10 Am now left a widower with four small children and not any of them
capable of doing any thing, I have Endeavoured all in my power to not
trouble you, but am now obliged to apply to you having no other recourse
left, and most humbly hope that you Consider my situation otherwise I
shall be obliged to be brought with an order to you not having it in my
15 power to provide for them any longer without some assistance from you
- you nead not doubt of me being a parishioner to you my father and
mother were both and I have not gained a settlement Else where - I hope
you will send me an answer by return and direct for me or to the overseer
of this parish -

20   I Rem[n] your most
humble Servant
Richard Porter.

661 From Lucy Shuttleworth in Nottingham to the overseer of Rayleigh, 28 January 1828

Nottingham January 28th 1828

Gent[n]

I am under the necesstiy of writing to you for relief. in consequence of the death of my husband. which was on Friday last. as the Overseers of the parish of S[t] Mary has been so kind as to find him a coffin & ground to   5 bury him, it is by their request. I write to you. as I am left with 3 small Children, & myself Lame of one hand, & unable to do very little for our Subsistance & as I shall not be able to maintain myself & fa<mily> & pay my rent, by what little work <I am> able to do. my Landlord will distrain upon my Goods for rent. & I shall be obliged to fling myself   10 wholly upon the parish. when I am destitute of a Home which it will be impossible for me to keep together. without some relief, as the same few lines is signed by the Overseer & Doctor of the parish. I hope you will be so kind. as to attend to this & allow me something for my support

   I am   15
         Gent[n]
               Your Humble Servant
                     Lucy Shuttleworth
Signed by
P.S. M[rs] Shuttleworth
            Sheridan Street   20
            Old Elass House Lane
            Nottingham

CIRCUMTEXT 'turn over' at bottom of first page (after 'support', l. 14) has been omitted as falling outside the text. Note from overseer of St Mary's parish and J.R. Tatham, surgeon, below text: 'The Statement of facts in this Letter is correct'.

662 From Mrs E. Reilley in Westminster, London, to the church-wardens and overseers of Rayleigh, 25 March 1828

London March 25th 1828

Sir

I beg leave to inform you that my Mother the Widow of the Late John Smith who was Drownd ten Years ago this month She is living with me and has done for sevn Years I have ben much Afflected and through that   5 so many expenses which renders me incapable of keeping her any longer

without Sum Allowance from her parish I hope Sir you will be kind anough
to speak to the Gentlemen of the parish respecting her being allowed
Something per week towards her surport She is now Eighty Years of age
10 and very lame through one of her Legs being very bad which is the Cause
of her Suffering much pain I Should be much obliged Sir by your writing
me an answer to this as Soon as posable and let me know what you
Gentlemen will allow her or I must be under the painful necessity of sending
her home to her Parish I shall therefore wait your early reply I must beg of
15 you sir to pardon me for not adressing this letter by your Nam as I had not
the pleasure of knowing it I remain Sir your Most Obedent Servant
        E Reilley
PS
Please to derect to
20   Mrs Reilley
No 35 Charles Street
        Westminster
        London

TEXTUAL ALTERATIONS 6: incapable] 'b' *over* 'p'.

**663   From Elizabeth Goodman [in Shoreditch, London] to Mr Clay-
ton Esq. in Rayleigh, 25 June 1831**

        1831   Elder St Spital Square
                    Norton Falgate, June 25th
D^r S^r
    Like all troublesome indigent persons I begin my Letter, by beging you
5 to excuse the trouble I am about to give you, but recollecting your long
standing friendship (& particular for My d^r Husband)/ I summons resolu-
tion to Lay before you my case, you know S^r I have been receiving my
poor 2^{s}6^d p^r week of Mrs Nelson, & on Monday last she sent me word she
wanted to see me, & then told me she should not advance me the money
10 any longer, for when she sent her account to Mr Markwell the last time
but one she omited in her bill one month, which she sent word (soon as
she look'd over her book & found the case) but that it did not signify until
the next time of sending, that she had just rec'd the last remitance with
out the left month, & she would therefore decline paying unless the money
15 was sent first, now my D^r S^r as the suspension of payment trifling as it is,

would be vital to me, as it is always used for rent, I must beg of you to intercede for me & let me know where I am to receive it, & I hope at the *proper usual* time, I last receiv'd it on the 11th June on the 9th of July is the time for me to have again 10^s pray assist me in it & write me the effect

I am very sorry Mrs Nelson should loose any thing on my acc^t for, as 20 she says, she derives no benefit from it, she is also very kind to me in answering for me to the amount of the needle work in my hands, (that is the value I mean) which is a great thing for me, no one can tell how we work for our bread, I am up every Morn^g at 4 oclock, some times for ware houses, (when we can get no better) at 2^d p^r shirt - - 25

I should not having taken the liberty of troubling you, but some how or other we have unwittingly offended my old, much valued, & *once kind* Friend Mrs Ruffle, God only knows how, some months gone my unfortunate Daughter wrote her word she had some thoughts of coming into Essex (as she had an Invitation), for a week, longer she could not stay 30 from home, & said if agreeable she would call on Mrs Ruffle & spend a day or two, but from that time we have never heard from her, some reason there must be, what we know not, it has made us both un happy, as no one knows but those who have experienced it, the misery of being slighted when down in the World, but God is all sufficient, he does & will support 35 us, Of course I could not ask a favour of Mrs Ruffle, fearing it might be deemed an intrusion My d^r Marian lokks very bad as must be supposed, from her great anxiety for her Fatherless Children, & perseverance to maintain them, her fatigue is great some days she walks from 15 - to 20 Miles to deliver her Tea, & at her return is quite exhausted who could 40 have thought she would have been able to get through what she has She joines me in respectful Comp^t to Mrs Clayton, M^r & Mrs Walker & y^r Daughter, & self should you S^r have any spare time when in London I cannot express how glad we should be to see you, or how kind we should take it to think all the World had not for gotten there were such people 50 still in being - I hope you will have the charity & feeling to write as s<o>on as possible, as I shall be anxious ti<ll> I hear how it is settled

with best wishes for your self & Family I am

D^r S^r Y^{rs} truly

Eliz^l Goodman 55

TEXTUAL ALTERATIONS 8: word] *over del illeg.* 34: those] 'th' *over del* 'wh'. 54: truly:] 'ly' *over del illeg.*

RELATED CORRESPONDENCE On 28 June 1831 Joseph Markwell, presumed overseer of Rayleigh, answered: 'I write to inform you that I shall be in Town on Friday next and will see Mrs Nelson as to your weekly pay there is a mistake which no doubt when I see Mrs Nelson she will be satisfied If Mrs Nelson should not continue to pay you the 2/6 a week I will appoint another person for that purpose equally as convenient to you and will apprise you of such alteration /if any/'.

664   From Elizabeth Goodman [in Shoreditch, London] to Joseph Markwell in Rayleigh, 3 September 1831

Sep^tr 3rd 1831

D^r S^r

I as usual, sent to Mrs Nelsons to day expecting to receive my trifling pittance you cannot immagin my surprise & disappoindme/nt/ when,
5 instead of money, the answer was Mr Markwell had been there, but had left none, nor said any thing about it, & that Mrs Nelson since the Dispute of her word had declined paying any un til paid first in to her hands, but S^r altho it is to you, as it once was to me a trifle, it is now of great consequence, I cannot look my Landlord in the face as my rent is always paid
10 by that money - I am certain it must have slip'd y^r memory, or you would not subject me to so much misery, I am *ready & willing* to take my oath that I receave it regular once a month, with this alteration only I beleive at first I had it on the Sunday (for I was then living at Newington, & had occasion to come every Sunday to Aldgate) & dated my receipts forward
15 on the Monday Mrs Nelson on my applying to her kind^s indulged me by paying me on the Saturday it being my rent day since I have removed I have every date regular, as I received it, in a book I keep on purpose - I hope my d^r S^r you will have the goodness to send it up directly as I have nothing I can put in pledge, to satisfy my Landlord, for indeed I am much
20 in wants of many comforts & necessaries I am certain you will be Sorry for me when you recollect how I have once been, & how I am now driven to<-->distress God knows I have hard work to get even bread with the greatest industry, pray excuse my troubling you, but poverty drives me to it Your complying with my request of Sending it to Mrs Nelson on Monday
25 will greatly Oblige Y^r Hum^b S^t

Eliz^e Goodman

For your Satisfaction I have sent you a list of my time of receiving the money for one Year
1830

30	Sep^t 4th	Recd of Mrs Nelson 10^s -
	Octr 2nd	d -	d -	10 -
	Oct 30	d -	d -	10 -

Nov 26th	d -	d -	10 -		
Dec 26th	d -	d -	10 -		
1831 Jany 22nd	d -	d -	10 -	35	
Feby 19	d -	d -	10 -		
March 19	d -	d -	10 -		
Apr^l 14	d -	d -	10 -		
<May> 14	d -	d -	10 -		
<June> 11	d -	d -	10 -	40	
July 9	d -	d -	10 -		
Augs 6th	d -	d -	10 -		

which make due to me on the 3rd of Sep^r - 10^s -I hope you will assist me
all you can, & beg the Gentlemen to consider me a trifle for Clothes
against Winter - For I am in want of many necessaries   45

TEXTUAL ALTERATIONS 7: S^r] 'r' *over illeg.* 12: alteration] 'e' *over* 'a'.
PLACE Inferred from Elizabeth Goodman's previous and following letters (**663, 665**).

**665   From Elizabeth Goodman [in Shoreditch, London] to Joseph
Markwell in Rayleigh, 26 January 1832**

1832
Jany 26th
No 10 Elder Street
Spital Sq^r
Norton Falgate 5

D^r S^r/

I beg pardon for troubling you with this, but the omission of my poor
pittance at the regular time (which was last Saturday) has much
inconvenienc'd me, as my rent was due for a month & the Landlord who
is very kind to me, to take it so, has ask'd for it several times I am quite 10
uncomfortable about it, for having to call & ask Mrs Nelson many different
time I fear she may think me troublesome, let me beg you will in pitty to
my feelings remit it directly & ease my mind, if you S^r will turn to y^r Books
you will find me correct as to the time for God sake do not neglect sending
of it as I shall call upon Mrs Nelson for it on Saturday, with all due Submis- 15
sion

I am S^r y^rs
Truly Eliz^h Goodman
The last time I rec'd it was Decr 23rd on which day it was due

TEXTUAL ALTERATIONS 7: with] 'h' *over del illeg.* 10: ask'd] *over del illeg.* 12: you] *after del* 'you'. 14: do not] *interl with caret.*

666   From Elizabeth Goodman [in London] to Joseph Markwell, overseer of Rayleigh, 26 December 1832

1832   Dec^b 26th

D^r S^r/

I cannot omit writing you a Letter of thanks for so kindly, & promptly attending to my request, & affording me the releif I ask'd of a pound
5 which was (& is) indeed a great comfort to me, It is not in my power to express half what I feel of the Subject, but suffice it, there never was anything more wanted, or more charitably applied, sincerely wishing you & yours all the blessings of the ensueing year, without any of its miseries & may they never know the reverse I have done
10   Concludes me yours most
                Sincerely Oblig'd
                    Eliz^a Goodman

CIRCUMTEXT Note from same hand on left-hand side of outside, facing the address: 'politely favor'd by Mrs Nelson'.
PLACE Inferred from Elizabeth Goodman's other letters.

667   From E. Smith in Finsbury [Shoreditch], London, to Mrs Menesfield in Rayleigh, 26 March 1833

London March 26 1833
4 Queen Street
Finsbury

My dear Freind
5   I am very Sorray to be so troublesum to you but I beg leve to inform you that I wrote to you a Fortnight ago and beged of you to Speak to Mr Beshop and to beg of him to Send my monay up and as I have not heard from him nor you I fear that Mr Bishop has Sent it and it is lost but I <hop>e that is not the Case there was four Months due on the Eleventh of
10 this month dear Friend I am very much destressed for it I Should be so much obliged to you to tell Mrs Beshop that I have never received it and Should feel so much obliged to him if he will be kind anough to get it for me and send this week I hope you and Famly are all Well my leg is very

bad I get much lamer then I was Mrs Riellys love to you and she is very
poorly my love to Mrs Sawall I hope She is well dear Friend I hope I shall 15
have the money on Friday or Saturday as I am so much in want of it
I remain your Sincer well wisher
   E Smith

TEXTUAL ALTERATIONS 9: four] *after del illeg.*
 CIRCUMTEXT Note from other hand on back: 'paid to Mrs Bishop [£]2.5[s].0[d] to Lady
day to send it to London'.

**668 From Elizabeth Goodman [in Mile End Old Town, London] to
Joseph Markwell, overseer of Rayleigh, 1 October [1833]**

          no 1 Assembly Row
          Mile End Road
Mr Markwell
 S^r/
Necessity will I hope plead sufficiently for my troubling you with this 5
as I think you would not neglect the time to send my poor pittance had it
not escaped yr memory begging you will have the goodness to remit it
directly you can as I am in great wants of it
    I am S^r with Due respect
    Y^{rs} truly Eliz^h Goodman   10
Oc^{tber} 1st

CIRCUMTEXT Note from other hand below signature: '10^s Mrs Goodman'.
 DATE Year from postmark.

**669 From Elizabeth Goodman [in Mile End Old Town, London] to
Joseph Markwell, overseer of Rayleigh, 23 December 1833**

      1833   Monday Dec^b 23^d
Dr Sir/
I was much disappointed on Saturday when I went to Mrs Nelsons to
hear my money was not come also, Sunday & Monday, I hope, & beg
you will have the goodness to send it as soon as you can, I have at the 5
same time to intreat you to assist me as you humanely did last Year, for
indeed I am much in wants of common necessaries amongst them a

decent Stuff Gown for as I now go out to work at my needle at Several
Gentlemens houses I must go respectable or not at all, & to make it worse
10 for me I have had several attacks of the Spasms this Year which brought
on the Jaundice at the time, which left me very weak, without the means
of having comforts which I at my time of life *particulary* require in such
a case My dear Childs health also is very bad, so that it is not in her power
to do for me all she would wish *her* young daughter has been out patient
15 of the London Hospital 3 months with some alarming appearance of a
Cancer in her breast, indeed S^r our troubles have *been*, & are still very
heavy praying God may hear my *prayer* & that you may render me help
in my trouble concludes me
    yr oblig'd
20   Servant
                    Eliz^h Goodman

TEXTUAL ALTERATIONS 9: respectable] 'able' *over del illeg.* 12: having] *over del illeg.*
PLACE Inferred from Elizabeth Goodman's previous and later letters (**668, 671**).

**670   From Elizabeth Goodman [in Mile End Old Town, London] to
Joseph Markwell, overseer of Rayleigh, 19 May 1834**

                                    May 19th 1834
Mr Markwell
    S^r/
    I have been anxiously waiting since Saturday May 10th for my money,
5 as that was the time when due, & must acknowledge very much disappointed *not* receiving it as my Landlord regulary looks for his rent & it
always goes towards it, he has asked more then once for it, *pray d^r S^r* do
not neglect sending it by return of coach, & if not unpleasen[t] to you,
you wou'd add another obligation to the many already confer'd on me, if
10 you send me a month in advance, as the time is going on towards it, &
you know not how much you would assist me in complying with this
request, with best wishes for you & y^s I am d^r S^r
            Y^{rs} truly
                    Eliz^e Goodman

TEXTUAL ALTERATIONS 10: complying] 'ing' *interl with caret at end of line.* 12: Y^{rs}] 'Y'
over illeg.
PLACE Inferred from Elizabeth Goodman's previous and following letters (**669, 671**).

671 From Elizabeth Goodman [in Mile End Old Town, London] to Joseph Markwell, overseer of Rayleigh, 28 August 1834

Sir/

Excuse my troubling you but as you have before obliged me I hope you will have the kindness to advance me one Month to that due on Saturday next making one Pound as we have had one of my Grand children ill and the little extras have put me out of the way paying my rent as I before told 5 you I use it for that purpose and with best thanks for all favors I beg to subscribe myself

Y^r Oblig^d hum^{ble} Ser^t

Eliz^a Goodman

No 1 Assembly Row 10

Augst 28^h *1834*

WRITING Hand different from other letters from Elizabeth Goodman.

672 From Mrs Smith in Chatham [Kent] to Joseph Markwell, overseer of Rayleigh, 13 December 1834

December 13th 1834

Gentlemen

I am sorry to be so much trouble to write but I was was forst to write as I ant received no money for to weeks Gentlemen I have been down to the House twice before I wrote to see whether the money was sent haveing to 5 pay 8 pence for the letter in awnser to the one I sent and when I asked Mr Marsh if their was any money sent for me and Mr Marsh made Awnser to say the be<st> way it would be for me to go home to my town parsh to live and Mr Marsh thinks it a great Deal of trouble to pay me as if he ad to pay out of his own pockett 10

So I am your Humble Servant

Mrs Smith Chatham

TEXTUAL ALTERATIONS 8-9: parsh to live] 's' *over* 'r' *in* 'parsh'; 'to' *interl.*

RELATED CORRESPONDENCE On 20 July 1834, Joseph Markwell, overseer of Rayleigh, had written to the Marine Office in London, inquiring whether any part of William Smith's wages was 'allotted to his wife and family, belonging to this Parish; and who were Conveyed here from Chatham, on her husband being called out into actual service'.

673   From Elizabeth Goodman [in Mile End Old Town, London] to Joseph Markwell in Rayleigh, 18 December [1834]

1 assembly Row Mile End
Road
Dec^ber 18th -

My D^r S^r

5   Permit me once more to throw myself on y^r mercy, & feeling as you
well Know how I have been situated, & how great my deprivations have
been situated, & how great my deprivations have been, & God Knows
how hard it is to feel & bear - *but to the point* I hope you will beleive me
when I say how *much*, very *much* I am distress'd for under linnen, stock-
10 ings (of which I have but one pair, & those mended all over) & indeed
wearing apparel of all sorts, & that since that time (which I am sure was
a mistake) that the two Shillings came short I was oblig'd to put my only
decent Gown in pledge to make up the money & have not had it in my
power to redeem it since, & by that means have not been able to go out of
15 doors to or even to a place of worship, hard work at my time of life, in the
course of human nature I shall not trouble you many times more, I have
often experienc'd y^r kindness at this time of the year, & *hope beg* &
entreat you will assist me as you have before done prehaps I never may
have another year to want it) with a pound in addition to my poor ten
20 shillings which is due on Saturday next, pray d^r S^r do not fail sending it
on that day as our landlord has been asking for it I wish I might beg for
the two Shilling left to get my Gown with, from pledge by doing this I
shall be on duty bound & pray for you & yours &
am D^r S^r
25   Truly Y^rs Eliz^h Goodman

Textual alterations 14: out] 'o' *over illeg.* 18: prehaps] *over del illeg.*
    Writing The text after 'prehaps' (l. 18) has been written crosswise over the foregoing
text, running along the left-hand edge of the page.
    Date Year from postmark.

674 From Elizabeth Goodman [in Mile End Old Town, London] to Joseph Markwell, overseer of Rayleigh, 23 December 1834

Dec^{ber} 23rd 1834

Mr Markwell

S^r/

In pitty to the feelings of a poor unfortunate Woman forgive my troubling you with another Letter, but indeed I am almost driven to dispair by 5
extream necessity which must plead the excuse, I am so much distress'd
for common necessaries in cloathing, besides the rent being over due -
For Godsake d^r S^r do not be angry with me & depend on it nothing but
distress direful could make me do as I do in so troublesome a manner -
beging you not to fail (in mercy) sending the Money directly, I pray 10
sincerely you nor Y^{rs} may never know the heavy trouble I have, hopeing
you will do all you can for me Concludes

    Me Y^{rs} truly Eliz^a Goodman

TEXTUAL ALTERATIONS 5: almost] 'm' *over illeg.*
Place Inferred from previous letters from Elizabeth Goodman (**668-71**, **673**).

675 From Maria Hurrell, 2 March 1835

March 2nd *1835*

Sir/

I am requested by my Mother to say agreeable to your directions by
letter last Monday, she has coll^d upon Mrs Nelson at the Bull every day
this Week and can hear no tidings of the Money she also wrote you a 5
Note one day in the Week and sent it to you by the Coachman, she would
be much obliged by your enquiring and setting it right I trust she may not
be charged with the postage of this as the seven pence for your last letter
I was Obliged to pay and I can indeed my ill afford it, she would not have
sent this but was fearful the Money might be last and I am 10

    Sir
    Y^r hum^{bl} Ser^t
    Maria Hurrell

Rochford pauper letters

676 From Dinah Martin in Hayes [Middlesex] to Thomas White in Rochford, 11 February 1803

Hayes Febury the 11 1803

Dear Cousin

ihave just taken the opertuneity of riteing those few Lines to you in hopes it will find you and your Littel family in good health as this Leaves
5 me and my Child thanks be to god for it and ihave once more taken the Liberty to ask you the favour to go to Mr Wise and ask him the favour to send me atrifle for the Child as the Weather is so Cold ihave not things to keep her warm and ihave had no work this nine Weeks and it is out of my power to get her any thing at present and she has made shift as Long as
10 she Can and the Genteleman will send me something for her iwill not truble them no more this year if please god ihave my health and Limbes and Mr White iam Sorry to give you the trouble but ihave no firend but you pray send me answer ware they will or no my husband is at plymouth Dock and will be very glad to hear from you but ihave never seen him
15 since isee you and ihope god will make you amends for your kindness to me fo<r> you and your Wife allwayes show the greatest kindness to me and my Child give my kind Love to your Mother and all firends and Except the same your self from your unfortunate Cousin Dinah Martin Direct for mrs martin near the White hart
20 hayes

RELATED CORRESPONDENCE On 4 July 1803 William Dawson in Hayes wrote to William Lawson, presumed overseer of Rochford, acknowledging the receipt of the money for Dinah Martin and reporting that she and her child were 'in good health'. On 11 June 1804, he wrote to him to the same effect.

FURTHER EVIDENCE Dinah Martin had received an allowance from Rochford of 3s per week in April 1802. It is not clear whether and to what extent she was supported after that date (ERO, D/P 129/12/3, Rochford overseers' accounts).

677 From Joseph Skewer in Great Wakering [Essex], 1 May 1803

May 1st 1803

Josepth Skewer of the parish of great wakering not being able to Find Sufficent Cloaths For his Children he Humbly asks the Officers and Gen-

tlemen of the parish of Rochford to Supply him with a few articles For three Children as a pear of Shoeas Some Cloth For Shirts Some Flannel 5
for Coats For the three oldest theay being in wont of them at this time

RELATED CORRESPONDENCE On 1 October 1803, Daniel Rivers in Great Wakering wrote to Mr Bright, overseer of Rochford, acknowledging the remittance of the money ('collection') he had advanced to Joseph Skewer.
    FURTHER EVIDENCE On 2 May 1803, the vestry of Rochford allowed Joseph Skewer at Great Wakering three pairs of shoes and 'cloth for 3 shirts' (ERO, D/P 129/8, Rochford vestry papers).

678   From Joseph Skewer in Great Wakering [Essex] to the overseer of Rochford, 6 November 1803

Nov^br 6 1803
    Joseph Skuer of the parish of G^t wakering being left with 4 Children and paid 5 pounds Rent & rates he therefore is not able to by Cloathing For his Children he Humbly bags of the Gentlemen of the parish of Rochford to Releave him with Some Cloth for 4, Children a pair of Shoaes 5
for 4 Some Flannel for 4 Children a peace of Something For Froks for 2 girles as thay are now in greaat want & he being wolly unable to Support them himself

679   From John Maseon in Crays Hill [Essex], 12 August 1804

    Crays Hill Aug^st 12: 1804
Sir this is to Inform you that young Cole that is with me is in Wants of Shoes and a Hatt his Shoes I have had mended as Long as <they> can be mended Please to Send me an answer where I am to gett them for him at
m^r Sarett or Elsewere   5
                    Y^rs John Maseon

680   From Mr W. Gepp in London to the Revd [Joseph] Wise in Rochford, 8 November 1804

London 8th Novr 1804

Sir

I understand want has been made after me for the Expences of Main-taining Mrs Gepp and Child by the Parish officers the Gentlemen might
5 have spared themselves that trouble for its not long since I wrote to her Father since her, stating my situation of being wholly out of an way of getting a livelihood but that nevertheless I was willing for them to Chuse one Freind and me another to Stipulate what was a fair allowance under my Circumstances to which I have never received any Ans^{er} I am now
10 willing to come to Terms with the Parish and give security for such allowance as I can afford - Therefore if you will have the goodness to address a Letter to *Mr Fenchetts* N° 2 Great Prescot Streat or to Mr *Isaac Gepp* Stratford when Inturn to Town I shall have the Letter and will imediately attend to -
15   I am yrs hbl Servt
             W Gepp

681   From S. Gepp in Heathrow, Middlesex, to John Bright in Rochford, 13 December 1804

Heathrow

Sir/

It is now more than a Fortnight since I wrote to Mr Wise respecting the settlement of my Child, & am much surprised at my not receiving any
5 answer, particularly as I inform'd him I had a situation in View, which I feard to lose, and which has really been the Case as I am now destitude of a Situation, having my Child with me, I shall therefore esteem it a Favor if you will speak to Mr W. for me to know if he will permit me to place my my Child in the Workhouse till some Settlement is made for him as it
10 is impossible for me to do anything for him myself - If you will have the Goodness to answer this as soon as possible it will greatly oblige yours Respectfully

S Gepp

13 Decr 1804 }
15 Mr East's Heathrow near Cranford Bridge
             Middlesex

682   From Ann Rayner in Little Wakering [Essex] to the church-wardens and overseers of Rochford, 2 November 1806

Lt Wakering

Nov 2 1806

Gentlemen

I Am wery much Aflicted and wery ill At this time and am Quite uncapable of keeping those two poor helpless Orphans Without the A   5
sistants of you gentlenen Which I hope will take In to considerration And Allowe me some small trifle with them Both As the Eldest is Not A ble for go to service Nor to do for her self

from your Hamble
Petitioner Ann Rayner   10

TEXTUAL ALTERATIONS 6: gentlenen] *last* 'en' *interl with caret at end of line.*

683   From Mary Craske in Thurston [Suffolk] to the Revd [Joseph] Wise in Rochford, 11 May 1807

Revd Sir/

I hope you will have the goodness to excuse the liberty I take in sending these few line

In the first place I beg leave to return my Sincere thanks to the Revd Mr Wise, & to all who have assisted me with my discarded Children which   5
assistance if I cou'd have shifted without; no once surely wou'd have been more ready - The thoughts of being an incumbrance to me, is a daily Persecution & more so as I find it impossible at present to do without the allowance

Death makes strange alterations in families, which occations me to have   10
my three children with me the eldest will go from me at Mick^s she was twelve last Nov^r; but has not been well, in short we have all been very poorly; but (thank God) are getting bet^r - I hear Southampton harbours the Author of Our destiny, his eldest Son wrote to him & had an Ans^r he enquired how many there were a live in both families - is in a Regiment   15
as a Pay Master - I shou'd like to know what attonement he has made to (Almighty God) from his great crimes & think one step towards forgiveness wou'd to remit all he could possibly spare to his Inquir'd Parish

Altho I have not Wrote to Rochford lately the obligation I am under is
20 seldom from my mind & have requested Hailstone to make my best
acknowledgments for what I have been oblige*[d]* to receive - This Easter
I have began to keep a little school which I hope my Ans^r in time M^{rs}
Pyrrell very much approved of it & say its very much wanted in the place
so *hope* I shall have success in time - I hope to do the best in my power
25 for the future welfare of my poor Children - as I am sure I have nothing so
truely at heart as to see them capable of providing for themselves & never
after that to be troublesome to a Parish. I am glad to say the children are
very well esteem'd for their conduct which I hope will be lasting. -
I humbly request the Revd Mr Wise will please to order the payment of
30 what is due to this Parish to be sent as the Overseer will not pay any more
without it - I beg leave to subscribe myself
Revd Sir

Your truly Thankful

Servt
35
Mary Craske
Thurston May 11th 1807

TEXTUAL ALTERATIONS 7: incumbrance] 'brance' *interl at end of line*. 25: nothing] 'hing' *interl
at end of line*.

RELATED CORRESPONDENCE On 21 December 1803, William Ranson in Thurston had
written to the overseer of Rochford about Mrs Crake (mistaken for Craske) and her three
children 'which by her Industry and Your allowance she support very decently for she is
a very Industrious and respectable Woman'. Over the following five years, John Hailstone, overseer in Thurston, sent six further letters in which he either gave his half-yearly
accounts for the allowance paid to Mary Craske (between 6s and 7s per week) or
acknowledged the receipt of the reimbursements from Rochford, and in most of which he
reported that she and her three children were all well (letters of 12 December 1804, 28
March 1805, 16 December 1805, 2 June 1807, 16 November 1807, 21 November 1808).
Occasionally, he added that she 'is a very Industrious Woman and takes great Care of her
family, and is willing to shift with as little as possible she Can', or that 'She work very hard
and is a Woman that take great pains for a Living' (16 December 1805, 21 November
1808).

684   From S. Beckwith in [Clerkenwell] London to J. Round, over-
seer of Rochford, 27 May [1807]

London May 27th
Gentelmen
It is with the greatest reluctance that I am forced to apply to you for
relief for my Daughter as I am totaley unabel to pervide for her and my

Self without some assistance If you will allow her a few Shillings per 5
week I Should then be enabled to provide for us both if you do not the
consequence will be that I must thorw myselfe uppon the parrish witch I
should be very unwilling to do as it can be so easily avoided my mother
will recive whatever you may think proper to allow the child she beaing
not quite six years old of coarse is not able to do aney thing for her living 10
- an answer to this will will gratly oblidge your humble Servt S Beckwith

> No 9 Baynes Row
> Cold Bath fields
> London

TEXTUAL ALTERATIONS 4: am] *interl with caret.* 6: enabled] *after del* 'abel'. 6: do] *after del*
'do'.
DATE Year from postmark.

685 From Mary Craske in Rushbrooke [Suffolk] to Joseph Wise in Rochford, 26 February 1809

Revd Sir/

I hope you will excuse the freedom of this Let^r & trust you may when
the case is represented by me - The only requests I have to make to you &
the rest of Rochford Gentlemen is to Write to Thurston & give them
authority to pay to me this Quarters allowance as I find sufficient reason 5
to request it; to help to bear expences which can not be avoided in respect
to my Children - I beg leave to return my own & childrens unsted thanks
for the very kind support which unfortunately we where obliged to ask of
Rochford - I was determined to lessen their expence as soon as it was
possible therefore sent my Son forty miles away last Easter, but a child of 10
10 years can not do much towards support therefore I have found him a
great expence tho' away , but I thought it was for the best & I still think
the same; But poor fellow I hear he has lately had the scarlit Fever; I can
not help thinking it is very hard to be separated so young from a Mother
who is concious she has done every thing in her power for the Good of all 15
her children & given them the best advise - I cou'd find no other meens of
taking the collection off at Easter, but taking myself into a Farmhouse &
doing the Work of an uper Ser^t; but it was upon the following condition
that I might take my Daughter with me to learn her how to work & to give
her an Idea how to get her living, her age is 12 & she's very desirous of 20

improving, as thank God they all are Thurston Officers paid the 3^s/ per Week up to the Feb^y - previous to that my child was ask'd out for a short time & they stopt Three Weeks pay, which was thought by some very unnecessary as I have always conducted myself I have paid pounds to the
25 Doctor & have it to Show by Bill & many people say they Wonder how I have done & got through as I have, but am sure I have done no more then my Duty nor that so well as I coud wish - To speak minutely what I cou'd wish wou'd be tiresome to a Gentleman Therefore I refrain beging the request I have made may be complied with as I cou'd wish to make ends
30 meet before I take a further charge upon me - If any Rochford Friend comes this way I beg leave to say I live at Mr Hustley near Rushbrook Hall two miles off Bury - I shall be at Thurston shortly & shall hope to meet a favourable reply in consideration of what I have mentioned - I hope my Dutiful respects may prove acceptable to all those whom I &
35 mine have been troublesome to -
   I am Revd Sir
    Y^r very much oblig'd Ser^t
    Mary Craske
Rushbrook 26th Feby 1809
40 PS this Summer I had the satisfaction to hear from the youth Mr Swain was so great a friend to, & he wish'd me to send his best Remembrance to all Friends. He was on Board his M.S. Belliquire at Madrass & Sind - A more dutiful Let^r never was wrote & more accurate ac^t [gave] allow^d by a Gentleman who saw it that had been to the same Places He sent two
45 Sheets But never mention'd his fathers name tho' he has left us but little reason My advice to his Sons have even been to acknowledge him in the best manner they can —

TEXTUAL ALTERATIONS 2: the] *interl with caret.* 24: myself] 'self' *interl at end of line.*
RELATED CORRESPONDENCE On 7 June 1809, John Hailstone, overseer of Thurston, sent a reminder to Rochford to settle their account with him for the allowence of Mary Craske, saying that she 'have had nothing of me since my last account'. He reported that she worked as a housekeeper to Mr Hustler, and that her daughter worked for himself.
 Two years later, Charles Tyrell in Thurston wrote to Mr Bright in Rochford that Mary Craske had found an apprenticeship for her son with a baker and requested £10 towards the cost. Thurston, he said, supported her plan (letter of 22 May 1811). Romford agreed, as is evident from his letter of 19 July 1811 in which Tyrell reported that the apprenticeship indentures for her son had been signed properly and that he had 'paid her ye Ten Pounds according to [your] Order'.

**686   From Lucy Humphreys in Shipley [Sussex] to the overseers
of Rochford, 18 April 1809**

Gentlemen

Compeled by the pressing hand of Necesity I have taken my Pen in
order to acquaint you that I am the Wife of Thomas Humphreys that
belongs to the Parish of Rochford and that he is now serving in the 82^d
Reigment of the Line and is in expectation of going abroad in Conse- 5
quence of which myself being now Pregnant and two Children shall be
under the Cruel Necessity of being brought home to Rochford by the
Overseers of Horsham as I am no longer entitled to the County Pay which
I receiv'd at Horsham for myself and Children while he was in the Sussex
Militia which in an unguarded moment he left to Volunteer into a regular 10
reigment of which Conduct he I belive sincerely repents. and there is no
way to get out of it unless he could get the sum of forty pounds. and if you
Gentlemen would be so kind and condesanding to let him have about
twenty Pounds he will try evry Posible means to get the other Part and
then he would come to Rochford with a thankful heart and enlist into the 15
Esex Militia as a Substitude and gladly Pay you back evry Shilling and be
the means of keeping us his unhappy wife and Children from the distress
that hangs over our heads and from being perhaps a burden to you for
many years Gentlemen if you will be so kind as to listen to my petition as
I sincerely hope you will for the sake of my Poor helpless Children and 20
may you that are Parents of Children never feel the anxeity of mind which
I now feel. and may that humanity which becomes the Character of a
Christian and a Gentleman be displayd by you in my behalf. if not I must
though with great reluctance be brought home. I hope you will be so kind
as to send a few lines as soon as Posible to let me know whether you will 25
grant this favour or not for this business requiers Speed and I am confident my husband will pay you again with a thankfull heart and will keep
his family from troubling you any further.

Please to direct for Lucy Humphreys Shipley near Horsham Sussex to
be left at the Burells Arms   30

I remain your
humble Servant
L Humphreys
Shipley April
18th 1809 35

TEXTUAL ALTERATIONS 12: way] *after del* 'other'. 19: years] *before del* 'for which'.

687   From Dinah Martin [in Hayes, Middlesex] to the overseer of Rochford, 24 August 1809

August the 24 1809

   Gentellmen ihope you will parden the Liberty ihave taken to send to
you but distress obliges me and ihope you will take it into Consideration
and grant me the favour iam going to ask you as my Child is not yet
5 Eleven yars old and you have not alowed me any thing for her this five
years and it is not in my power to maintian her and Cloth her as Every
thing is so very dear and iwas very Lame all Last winter and not able to
do for my self for four months and run in debt with my baker and now he
has terubled me for the money and distressed me of Every thing and iam
10 not able to pay it and now at this time my husband sister peggey would
take the Child and get her place if you would have the goodness to send
me the vallue of one pound to get her some Clothes if not imean to Come
home with her and you must take the whole Expence but irote to you first
to ask the favour of that small sum if you will grant it ihope ishall not
15 truble you any more with the blessing of god if she has her health pleas to
have the goodness to send me answer ware you will do any thing for her
by the van and iwill meet it at White Chapel and if you dont send me the
mony imust Come home next jurney as ihad as Live be at rochford as any
ware iremain your most humble servant and in duty bound will Ever pray
20   Dinah Martin
ihave not heard any thing of my husband for some years

TEXTUAL ALTERATIONS 20: Dinah Martin] *after del* 'Dinah Martin'.
PLACE Inferred from the previous and following letters from Dinah Martin (**676, 691**).

688   From Thomas Sadler in Great Wakering [Essex] to J. Bright in Rochford, 30 September 1809

1809 Mr Bright Rochford Septr 30

   Sir missis Belchir his Sent my Wifes Sister To us She was Sent Last
Sataday Septr 24 To me at great weakring The Little girl Schorlott day
She Is Sister To my Wife and She dos knott like To See missis Belchir
5 Turn her a way Thot She Is put in To The work is that She Dos nott know
nothing how To goe To Sarvis nor To know how To do any Thing that a
yong girl ought To know Fitt for Sarvis Sir If you Will give me Three

Shilings by week and Things wich She Wants for nesreirs wich Is a pair of
Shoos and cloth for Shifts a frock Two pinafors and Stockins and Sir if So
please To Latt her have The Things at gt weakring wher we Live and if 10
you please To give me Three Shilings By wek and find her Things Suffisint
for a Year I will Take her and Bring her up fit for Sarvis Being Sister To us
But pervisings is So deer That I no ways Can do it Under Sir I am Your
ombl Servind Thos

Sadler gt weakring 15

689 From Mary Brooks in Danbury [Essex] to the overseer of Rochford, 17 November 1809

Danbury 17th Nov^{ber} 1809

Sir

This is to acquaint you that I am no better of my lameness; I should
have wrote to you before but waited to see whether I should be better of
my lameness.) -   5
I hope you will have the goodness to pay the Woman that looks after
my legs, as I am not able to pay her myself out of my pay. I am sorry that
I have to inform you that I am not any better and that I am not able nor not
fit to be removed yet, I should wish to stay where I am a few weeks
longer perhaps there may be an alteration for the better.) I am sorry that I 10
am oblig'd to be so troublesome to you, but I do assure you, that I do with
as little from you as possible I can for I have to pay 9^d per week for my
Room where I am at, and as I cannot help myself to any thing I am oblig'd
to ask the people in the House where I am at to do every thing for me in
respect to waiting of me, and for that reason I am oblig'd to give them a 15
trifle per week for their civility to me although I cannot afford it out of
my pay I should be much oblig'd to you to send me an answer whether
you will be so good as to pay the Woman for looking after my leg as I am
not able to pay her out of my weekly pay -

From Mary Brooks 20
Of Danbury

TEXTUAL ALTERATIONS 19: her] *interl with caret.*
WRITING This letter was probably written by John Brett, overseer of Danbury. It is from
the same hand as his letter to the overseer of Rochford of 4 March 1810, though that letter
is from another hand than his earlier letter to Rochford (see related correspondence).

RELATED CORRESPONDENCE It may be assumed that Mary Brooks had received a regular allowance from Rochford for years. On 21 March 1803, Daniel Balls in Danbury had sent Rochford a reminder for £2 14s (27 weeks at 2s for October 1802 to April 1803), though it is not clear what she had received before or afterwards. Some years later, John Brett, overseer of Danbury, wrote to Rochford that Mary Brooks 'is in Avary bad Estate For she has been Confined to her bed for Some time Not Able to do for herself that She Varied all her Neibours out In Doing for her that I am Abliged to have Awoman with her Constant to do for her I ast our Potacry to go and see her which he did And he Said that one of her feet is Puterfide but he thinks shes Not unmovable for its Posable She may by Some time' (letter of 22 December [year not given, probably 1808]). On 29 September 1809, Isaac Belcher, overseer of Danbury, reminded the overseer of Rochford of the weekly payments made to Mary Brooks from Easter till Michaelmass 1809. He requested to pay the money to Samuel Brooks 'who will call on You on Rochford Fair - And I have to inform You that the Poor Woman is at this time in great distress she is veary Ill and Lame confined to her Bed & have been for some time, she bags the favour of You, to send her a few Shillings as her Weekly allowance is not sufficient for her in her present Situation - which I can assure You she does not ask for without the greatest need of or if You please to order what is necessary to be done for her, our next overseer Mr Brett will attend to her and do no more then is realy necessary'. We do not know what Brett did for her. His last letter is of 3 March 1810: 'This is to inform you that Mary Brooks was removed by Death last Night. She died about nine o'Clock which was a very happy releave as pleased the Almighty to take her out of this World as she has underwent a long and very heave affliction'.

690 From Mary Brooks in Danbury [Essex] to the overseer of Rochford [*before* 4 March 1810]

Gentlemen

I hope you will not be offended at my troubleing you with these few lines but Nesesity Drove me to Send to you for the weather has been so Could and I have been So veary ill for Some weeks or I Should not have troubled

5   you I hope Gentleman you will be So good as to Consider me a trifel till I Get better as I hope I Shall when the weather Gets warm

from me
Mary Brooks

Deansbury

DATE Inferred from the fact that Mary Brooks died on 3 March 1810 (see **689**, at end of RELATED CORRESPONDENCE).

691   From Dinah Martin in Hayes, Middlesex, to the overseer of Rochford, 1 July 1810

Hayes, Middx July 1st 1810

Gentlemen

This is to inform you that I Dinah Martin have been very Ill & am at this time under the Doctor's Hands & am entirely unable to procure any subsistence if you will be so good as to allow me some trifle till I am able   5
to work you will greatly add to the Comforts of

Your most Obliged Humble Servant

Dinah Martin

Send an answer by return of post

WRITING This letter was written by William Dawson, presumed overseer of Hayes, as it is from the same hand as his letters of 4 July 1803 and 14 July 1804 (see **676**). Dinah Martin's other two letters are from a different hand (**676, 687**).

CIRCUMTEXT Statement from other hand, signed by the vicar and churchwarden of Hayes, on second page, above final line of text: 'Hannah [*sic*] Martin is in a state which requires some relief immediately'.

692   From Sarah Ateradge in Canewdon [Essex] to Mr Bright in Rochford, 8 July [1810]

Gentleman i must beg the favour of you to be So Good as to Let me have the Doctor to put me to bed for i am wery Bad and have for this fortnight i have Such bad time that i am afraid to trust to awoman i have not been able to Do any thing for my Self for a fortnight my Husband has been to try to work but he is So weak that i am afraid he will not hold it if you will   5
be So Good as to Grant me the favour i have asked you i Should be much obliged to you

i am your Humble
Servant

Sarah Ateradge   10

Canewdon
July 8

TEXTUAL ALTERATIONS 2: to put me to bed] *interl*. 4: for a fortnight] *interl with caret*.

DATE Year inferred from related correspondence.

RELATED CORRESPONDENCE On 16 June 1810, Mr Page in Canewdon had written to the overseer of Rochford that James Attridge 'is ill of a Fever, and desired me to write to you for relief, him & wife being in want of your assistance', and that the doctor, a certain Marsh, had seen him.

693 From Robert Hoy in Sheereness, Kent, to Mr Bright in Rochford, 25 August 1811

1811 Augst 25

Shareness Robert Hoy
To Mr Bright

Sir I am sory to trouble the gentlemen But I am under the nessity of
5 informing them if I am not Aloud sothing thay must Come home to them
againg for thay cannot Do without some necessarys of witch I am Not
able to git without some assitance And Mr Townsen will not have any
more To do with it for he told my Wife he Could not git his money in
again so she Has not resived any pay for a month So I have been obliged
10 to git a few things at Trust for them so I hope the gentlemen Will not
Object Omiting to my Wife as theare is ten shillings deu that is parst if
thay please to send her a pound and then she can pay the Debt that she has
contracted and pass on again for a wile till it comes de<u> again please to
forward it to the gentlemen as soon oppotunity suites you I shall wait for
15 an answer what thay pleas to do before I send them home please to direct
to Robert Hoy Royal marin on board of HMS Raisonarble Shareness
Kent
I am Sir your obident Humble Servant
Robert Hoy

TEXTUAL ALTERATIONS 4: gentlemen] *final 'n' interl at end of line.* 5: informing] *after del*
'l', 'ing' *interl at end of line.* 6: for] 'r' *over del illeg.* 6: cannot] *second 'n' over del illeg.*
6: necessarys] 'ece' *over del illeg.* 7: will] 'ill' *over del illeg.* 11: theare] *last 'e' interl at*
end of line. 11: please] *interl at beginning of line.* 14: gentlemen] *final 'n' interl at end of*
line. 14: soon] *interl.* 15: thay] *over del illeg.* 18: Servant] 'nt' *interl at end of line.*

CIRCUMTEXT Sender's address on outside (from same hand as letter) countersigned by
commanding officer.

694 From Daniel and Mary Gray in [Clerkenwell] London to Isaac Harvey, overseer of Rochford, 8 September 1823

N° 37 Pare Tree Court Clarkenwell Close
Sepr the 8 - 1823

Gentlemen

I suppose You have heard of my great Misfortune by my Husband
5 Accidend which I thank God he is at preasant a live but it may be by what
I am Informed a great while before he is Able for Imployment if please

God Should Spare him and as myself and Child with my Lodgins to gett
thro I am not able to do myself which I Humbly beg you will Consider
my Calamitious Case to help me In such a way As is most a greable to
your Sentiments And Send me a few lines by what way you pur pose to 10
Convey it to me by the direction above

So Gentlemen I beg to leave every
thing further for this Time with
Due Respect Your[s]
Danill & Mary Gray 15

695   From Elizabeth Ann Manning in Islington [London] to the overseer of Rochford [12 November 1829]

N° 6 Liverpoll Road Islington

Sir

   I ame sorry I ame under the necesity of Troubling you with a Letter
respecting the allowence we Receive from Rochford M[r] Evans have Stoped
paying me as he have wrote twice to Rochford and have Recved no   5
answer he Recivd a Letter from M[r] Harvy dated 18th July to say the 42
week should be payd and we ware to recive 4[s] pr week from that time and
he would be in London in a short time and would call and pay him M[r]
Evans think it is verry unhensom to keep him out of his mony as long M[r]
Evans wished me to write as his might be sent to the wrong person not   10
knowing who is Overseer now - I ame verry sorry to say that the most of
my ernings the year round have not been more then 4[s] pr week a pon an
average and 3[s] goes for Rent the Boy have been Arent Boy for this Last
15 Months but I have to Lodge and Wash and Mend and keep him on the
Sunday for the trifle whitche he get will no more then find him in Shoo   15
Leather as he is allways on the foot so I will leave you to judge how I ame
situated I have not been able to get any woork only what M[r] Evans have
been so good as to let me have for in the sumer when the work was rather
slack I went from one shop to the other to try for wrork but they had more
hands then they had work for as the Trade is very Bad we are oblidge to   20
set a great many hours for a little mony I know my Constitution feel the ill
effects of Low Living and confinement if I I was not of a contented mind
I must have sunk before now but I know there is a good God whitch have

allways helped me throu my troubles as I have had my share tho not of my
25 own seeking

I remain your Humble Servent
Elizth Ann Manning

TEXTUAL ALTERATIONS 3: Troubling] 'u' *over del illeg.* 12: pon] 'n' *over del* 'm'. 19: shop]
'p' *over* 'm'. 20: hands] *interl.* 21: a great] 'a' *over del* 'g'.
DATE Date of postmark.
WRITING Written on ruled lines.

696   From Elizabeth Ann Manning in Islington [London] to Mr Camport in Rochford, 4 January 1830

N° 6 Liverpole Road Islington Jan 4th 1830

Sir

I have taken the liberty of troubling you with a few lines respecting the
4ˢ Pr Week that I ame allowed from the Parish of Rochford Mr Evens the
5 Gentlman that I work for was the person that was so kind as too pay me
the Money by the desire of the Overseer the first payments where payd at
the time but it have been standing a Great length of time and Mr Evens
cannot think of Advancein me any more excepting he is Paid the Money
he have Advanced as his money is Laying dead I have wrote twice too the
10 Overseer but cannot recive an Answer Sir if you will have the goodness
too speak too the Overseer in my behalf I shall be verry thankfull if the
payment is stopt I must be sent home for it is imposible for me too subsist
upon my ernings which upon an Average is no more then 4ˢ Pr week if it
was not for the too youngest it would be immatereall where I Live Sir if
15 it will not be too much trouble to answer this you will greatly oblige your
humble Servent

Elizth Ann Manning

TEXTUAL ALTERATIONS 3: troubling] 'o' *over del illeg.*
WRITING Written on ruled lines.

697 From John Sams in Chelmsford to Mr Harvey, overseer of Rochford, 13 January 1830

Chelmsford 13 Jany 1830

Mr Hearvy i have Rotee theas few Lines to you to Say that Mr Johns the
over Seare of Chelmsford Rote to you on Last Monday week to Inform
you i have Not had any Implyment Scarse Sense i Left Rochford i have
arnt onley 3 Shillings and 6 Pence Sence i came home again and i Should 5
think it is Much better for the Perisioners to a Low *Me a* trife hear till i
can get inployment as Soon as i can get work i Shall not be any troble to
the Parish and if i have Not Some thing i Must come home again directly
John Sams

WRITING Name written across left and right hand margins.

698 From Elizabeth Ann Manning in Islington [London] to the overseer of Rochford, 25 February 1830

No 6 Back Road Islington Feb 25 1830

Sir

Mr Evens have stoped paying me the Money that I ame Alowed from
the Parish of Rochford so would thank you to let me know where I ame to
apply too for it hope Sir you will not faile too answer this Letter by Saturday 5
or Sunday for I can asure you this have been I verry trieng Winter for me
as fireing have been verry dear and that I could not do without but I can
asure you I have not had hardly anuf to support nature with if I do not
recive an answer to this I must come to Rochford next week but hope you
will not request that as it would be througing be backwarden then what i 10
am as it would be a lose of time as I have not got any Friends to do the lest
trifle for me and it is not in the Power of my Children too assist me yet
but hope when they get a few more years over ther Wagers are verry low
at Present but thank God they are verry Steady which is a great blessing
I Remain your humble Servent E A Manning 15

TEXTUAL ALTERATIONS 6: or Sunday] *interl*. 11: Friends] 'i' *interl*. 13: low] *interl at end of line*.

699   From Ann Benson

Gentlemen

I hope you will be so kind as to Grant me a nurse and m^{rs} Creek as it is not in my Power to pay them myself

Ann Benson

FURTHER EVIDENCE In 1829 there are occasional references to 'widow Benson' or 'Mrs Benson', as in the 'list of Clothing Granted at the Michaelmas Meeting' of the vestry of Rochford (ERO, D/P 129/8, Rochford vestry minutes). It is not clear whether the sender is the same Ann Benson as the one writing from Rochford to Rayleigh, 26 February 1825 (**656**).

700   From J. Borcham, 12 November

Nove^r 12 Sir I will thank you to give my Father my Alowance will spair my Coming over

J Borcham

701   From John and Elizabeth Maseon in Crays Hill, Essex, 30 April

Crays Hill April 30th

Sir this is to Inform you that my Daughter is dead and was Buried yesterday & this is a Bill of Expences from the overseer of this Parish the form that the Poor is Buired Some times there is Six to Carry and Some times there
5   is Eight to Carry and the Custom is to give Each man one Shilling a Peace Sir I Should be much oblidg^d to you if you would Send me an answer weather I am to Receive the money of Mr Laritt or which way I am to Come at it

from Y^{rs} John Maseon
10   & Elizabeth maseon
PS
Please to Direct to me
for John Maseon
to be
15   left at The Shepherd
and Dog Crays Hill
Essex

TEXTUAL ALTERATIONS 2: Daughter] 'ter' *interl at end of line*. 3: overseer] *final* 'r' *interl at end of line*. 4: the] *inserted above del* 'a'. 6: would] *interl*. 14: to be] *after del* 'Crays Hill'.

702   From S. Stearns

Honred Gentle men as it is inconvent for me to come to the meeting I have sent these Lines to aquaint you of my disstress which I hope will give no offence the Collection that you have sent me this last two weeks I can not do with atall which I trust you know if you take in considderation and if you will not allow me more I must give my familey up to you which I am 5 sorry to do I desire to do all that lay in my power for them but without more assistance i cannot keep them

S Stearns

Stanford Rivers pauper letter

703 From Jane Hogg in Ingatestone [Essex] to Mr Andrews in Stanford Rivers, 12 January 1824

1824   Ingatestone J^{eny} 12th
  Sir should be oblige to you to pay my Husband my littell Boy pay as I
Cannot Come my self up to febbery 1th you will oblige me

Jane Hogg

5 as I have not Resevd any sence Nov^{e} 1 1823

TEXTUAL ALTERATIONS 5: not] *interl.* 5: any] *over del illeg.*

Stansted Mountfitchet pauper letter

704 From Elizabeth Shepphard [in Leyton, Essex], 19 September [1813]

September 19

Sir i take this oportunety of writeing to you and send to let you Know that
i ham vary poorly hand if you plese to send me my months money i should
be vary glad by Return of post No Mor at Prsent from your humble Servent
Elesebeth Shepphard Plese to send to me to Be left hat the thached house   5
for the widdow

Pettit Hollowaydown Essex

TEXTUAL ALTERATIONS 1: 19] *interl at end of line.* 5: to Be] *after del* 'ha'.
  DATE Year from postmark.
  PLACE Holloway Down belonged to Leyton Parish.

Theydon Garnon pauper letters

705   From Mary Howe to Mr Ranking in Coopersale [Theydon Garnon], 13 January 1731

Jenaw 13 day 1731

Mr ranking this is to let you know that the doxtor have done what he can
for me but my iees are never the better but rather wors i ame to be dis-
charge^d next wandsday i hope you will be so kind as to send me word
5 how i must come home by next wandsday morning so with humble sarvis
to you and your good wife

sir I hope you will exquese me in wrighting of a letter but i did not
know no other way So i rest your humble sarvant

mary how patient in

10 [*continued crosswise in left-hand margin*] peter ward

TEXTUAL ALTERATIONS 3: iees] *after del* 'ey'.
PLACE Coopersale belonged to Theydon Garnon.

706   From Mary Marshall to the churchwardens and overseers of Theydon Garnon, 1 September 1736

Gentlemen

I am very sorry I am forst to be so troublesome you were so good as to
give me one Guine which I was forst to lay out I have sent word of every
penrey at the Botto<m> I must beg your Godnesses to send me one half
5 Guinea more and I hope that God will bless me and in able me to geet my
bread without being troublesome any more I was forst to geet a small
malter for bread of my Landlady for without I cant geet my bread I beg
you will please to send it me as I may goe to work from your poor parishner

Mary	expence a Sunday	
10 Marshall	and monday	... 0=1=0
Sep^t y^e 1st	Coach hire	... 0=3=0
1736	Shoes & p<->ting for me	: 0=3=0
	my Childs shoes	... 0=1=6
	my Baker	... 0=1=6

one apron that was pledg	: 0=1=0 15
my rent	. . . 0=10=1
	: 1=0=0

they are very urgent for a Certificate

707 From Sarah Stone in London, 5 November 1736

Sir

My Dau[gt] now lyes ill of the Small pox, and I am now reduced to the utmost Extremity, If Your Charity will Etend so far as to relieve me in this my present necessity, I Shall as in duty bound ever pray

I am Your Distressed Serv[t] 5
Sarah Stone

Nov[r] 5th 1736
P.S. I lodge at M[rs] Bells in Leicester Street near Grays Inn Lane.

WRITING Professional hand.

708 From Widow Camp in Widford [Essex] to Mr Humerson in Coopersale [Theydon Garnon], 12 July 1759

M[r] Humerson

Iam very Sorry that Iam Oblidged to write to you for Some Releife but Can no way[s] help it I have been very Ill a Long time and Oblidged to have a Doctor to attend me which hath brought me to Great Nescesity which Ihope you will Consider me Something for it is very Hard with me at 5 present and by doing this I Shall Ever be bound to pray for you Ishould not have sent to you only being too Hard Drove

From your Disttresed
Humble Ser[t] to Command
widdow Camp 10

widford July
y[e] 12th 1759
The <bottom of page torn off>

TEXTUAL ALTERATIONS 8: Disttresed] 'r' interl below.
PLACE Coopersale belonged to Theydon Garnon.

FURTHER EVIDENCE Widow Camp received a regular weekly allowance of 2s. The payments were not given in May, but again from June 1759. On 27 July 1759, she received 8s 'for a nirse three weeks' and further 7s 'for Extrordiny Charges' (ERO, D/P 152/12/4, Theydon Garnon overseers' accounts).

709 From Ann Wood in Bethnal Green, London, to Mr Peggrim, churchwarden in Coopersale [Theydon Garnon], 1 April [1802]

Mʳ Peggrim
    Sir
    I hope you will excuse my freedom in addressing you with these lines wich his to request you to be so kind as to make me a remittance, as I
5 have not receiv'd any, for twenty weeks therefore Sir I hope you will not forget me now, as I have a strong healthy growing Girl to maintain & being of a weak habit of body myself it his not in my power to live with What independence, wich I Should otherwise be glad to do, I should have come down but my health as been very indifferent and I have not the
10 means of discharging expence of this nature -
                                    remain Sir yours with Grattitude
                                                    - Ann Wood -
                        London April 1 - north Place bethnal Green

DATE Year from postmark.
PLACE Coopersale belonged to Theydon Garnon.
FURTHER EVIDENCE On 17 April 1802 the overseer paid £2 6s for 23 weeks to Ann Wood in Bethnal Green. She received a regular allowance of 2s.

710 From Elizabeth Mines in [Bermondsey] London to William Archer in Epping [1808]

Gentlemen i am verry sorry to think that as i am under the Necessity of troubleing you owin to my Distressed state for i cant Get my money untill that you send me Certificate to identifi me a gainst this to go to Greenwich College and to be signed by the minster & Churchwarden of the
5 said parish and to send me an Answer by the Return of post and to direct it for Elizabeth mines a the Royal Oak Kent street borough of south works

TEXTUAL ALTERATIONS 2: i] *interl.* 3: you] *interl.* 3-4: to Greenwich] *after del* 'g'. 4: the minster] 'the' *interl.* 4: &] *over del* 'war'. 6: it] *interl above* 'for'.
DATE Year from postmark.
PLACE Epping was 2 miles north of Theydon Garnon.

711   From Hannah Collesson in Rye [Sussex] to the overseers of Theydon Garnon, 18 October 1819

Rye 18th October 1819

Gentelmen

Ihave not Trobled you for Sum years and now Gentelmen I am in Great Distres and Ihope you will Relieve me for Iam Widow this 14 years and Ihave not Trobeled you Ihope now Gentelmen you will Send me Sum   5
Relive for Iam in Grate want Iam now at Rye in Sussex and Iam in Grate want Ihope you will Send me a Trifull of money to Relieve me to help me on Ihave got all my Famerly all of but 3 Children with me and Iam Growing old and Cant do so much as Ihave don and the Times now are very Bad. Gentelmen if you dont Send me Sum Relieve Imust Com Home to you my 10 Name Hannah Collesson Living Garnesh Hall with John Bishop
   Direct your Letter Isaac Doust Living in Rye in the County of Sussex -
So Iremain your Hum^{ble} Servant
Hannah Collesson

TEXTUAL ALTERATIONS 10-11: my Name] *interl with caret.*

Theydon Mount pauper letters

712 From Elizabeth Brown in St Bartholomew's Hospital [City of London] to the churchwarden of Theydon Mount, 30 December 1769

Sir

I have not had aney thing dune to me Sence i ham bein hear i hame to come out of the houes one Tuesday next i hope you will be so good as to Send for me doun i not havun aneye ware to goe from your houmbell
5 Sarvt

Eliz Brown

Desember 30 1769
Aldud Warde Barthlow hospotal

TEXTUAL ALTERATIONS 7: 1769] '6' *over* '9'.
FURTHER EVIDENCE Elizabeth Brown had received a regular weekly allowance of 1s before she went into hospital. In St Bartholomew's Hospital, she was visited by the overseer of Theydon Mount, as is evident from the recordings in his account book: 'paid with Elizabeth Brown in the Aspitle' 3s 6d, and 'My Jurney and Expences & gave her' 14s; journey to London 4s, and 'gave Elizabeth Brown' 2s; 'A jurney to London' 4s, and 'Stopt for Elizabeth Brown In the a Spitle' 5s (ERO, D/P 142/12/1, Theydon Mount overseers' accounts, entries of 22 December 1769, 1 January 1770, and 24 January 1770).

713 From Harriet Baker in Plaistow [Essex] to the overseers of Theydon Mount, 21 March 1831

1831 March 21ᵗʰ Plaistow

Sʳ by the desire of Harriet Baker which she thought it her duty to dew to have me to write to you that is to Let you now that the young man that she is with Child by is asely to be taken for he is home from sea and is come
5 to the parish where he belong and if you wish to get her a Husband you must be quick about it for she and I both saw yesterday and he Talked with Harret and me and she Expects her time Every Day

so no more from
your Harret Baker

714 From Thomas Kellnby in Springfield Gaol [Chelmsford] to the overseer Theydon Mount, 20 April [1831]

Spingfeild Convict
Gaole
April 20th 18/31/

Sir/

    I Thearefore address you with thise letter to inform you that I have very   5
ill and thanks be to god I now gitting Better of my illness I shall Estiem it
as a pertuculare favoure if you wold inform me when Hariett was Confined that I my be inable to gudg how long that I am to be Confined heare
plase to give my love to her and I think long till the time comes that will
releise me from thise as the place is all to gather wheary unhealfull   10

        I conclude with
        my kind love to all
        that ask after me
           Your &c
           Thomas Kellnby   15
NB plase to send me Answer By the return of post and pay the postage of
the letter if you plase

West Thurrock pauper letters

715 From George Oliver to Mr Long, overseer of West Thurrock [1770]

Mr Long Overseer Sir I hope the gentleman will take it in consideration to allow me something a week for my family the gentleman you have got a family and you must now than a little how to keep a family I have been ill fourteen weeks and I aint had only ten shillings of you and haw do you
5 thing I must keep my family so I have three shillings a week to pay house rent I never trouble you for any think when I am weell It aint my wish now If i could help it there is six of us in family there is nare a one of them able to bring any thing in I cant set here and see my family want when I am close to my own parish I hope in a little while I shall be able to
10 come out again and then I shant want to trouble you gentleman no more I thank you sir to send me an answer

George Oliver

TEXTUAL ALTERATIONS 2: my] 'm' *over illeg.* 4: had] 'd' *over illeg.* 5: three] 'h' *over* 'r'. 6: trouble] 'r' *over* 's'.
DATE Year from note from other hand at top of page.

716 From Eliza Farrant in Bromley, Middlesex, to the overseer of West Thurrock, 10 February [1809]

Eliza Farrant widow willan farrant feb 10 809
To
the Gentlemen westthoughrack parish Ian Gentleman my Husband bean Ded afteer a Sicknes of Ten weeks he Died the 29 October Left me a
5 helpless widow and wery mach afflicted and aged with all as bean in my 64 yare of my age and not abel to do any longer without your assistance as things is so wery Dear and Rents wery Dear sing Rowe 26 per week as I am not git my Liven and pay my Rent I have too <child>ren that is not out of my care nor fit <to be> left to themselves as the youngis is but 2
10 yares old Gentlemen if you will taket on Conciderateon and a Low me the Sum of 36 week I hope I shall I shall not Trobell you for any thing <e>lce and if not I must Come home as This is my wish as the Ofecers of westham parish sore my Husband before Justis Qarell at berking <->ro

by sending to westham you will know <th>e truth of it and not bean abel to
Come for the <re>nt money I beg you will answer this Letter your 15
Determanaicon from your hu^m servient <if> you pleas to Derect for me
widow Farrant <i>n farmer man Sq/ae/r no 16
<i>n Brambley Near Bow midsex

TEXTUAL ALTERATIONS 1: farrant] 't' *interl.* 4: Sicknes] 'es' *interl at end of line.* 6: do]
interl. 6: your] 'r' *interl at end of line.* 11: not] *interl.* 14: abel] *interl.* 15: <re>nt] *interl at
beginning of line.* 16: servient] 't' *interl at end of line.* 18: Near] *after del* 'S'.

Tolleshunt D'Arcy pauper letter

717　From Edward Abbott in London [Hospital], Whitechapel, London, 27 April 1801

London Infirmary

Sir/

Misfortune alone could have induced me to trouble you with these unwellcome lines, which I hope will not fail of their purpose.

5　Which is humbly to request some relief of the Parish such a way as you may think proper, from my unhappy case, which is as follows.

As I was working at a Building on the 21st of April Ins^t one of the walls gave way and fell upon me, & Bruised me very much so that I was taken to the London Hospital, where I fear it will be some considerable time

10　before I shall be able to get out, as I am not able to get out of Bed; but I had no Bones broke. My Family is 5 in Number, 3 small children, none able to do any thing for a living, therefore I hope the Gentlemen will consider my Family, and allow us something for a little while, as I hope in afew weeks to get about again, & go to work

15　　　　　　　　I am Sir your unfortunate
　　　　　　　　　　Humble Servant
　　　　　　　　　　　Edwd Abbott .*

White Chapel
Apr 27 1801

20　　　　　　　　　　　　　* formerly Apprentice to
　　　　　　　　　　　　　　　Mr Ja^s Ray

TEXTUAL ALTERATIONS 7: one] *after del* 'when'. 13: while] 'h' *after del* 'i'.
WRITING The letter was written by W. Manning, minister.
CIRCUMTEXT Confirmation by attending surgeon of London Hospital on next page (from other hand), with additional signature of W. Manning, minister (same hand as letter).

Upminster pauper letters

718 From Ann Sinclair in Northfleet, Kent, to [Thomas] Talbot in Upminster, 11 April [1802]

Northfleet kent
April th 11 18<02>
Sir I have taken the liberty to trouble you once more, for the Money for
Mr Kings Children if you Please the Bigest girl has been Very bad with
the Ague for a long Time, And the Father has had A misfortune to Skold 5
his Foot And has not been able to do any thing for a long Time, Sir if you
Please to be so kind as to send me the Money I Shall be very much Obleiged
to you, Sir there is 16 weeks due
From your humble Servant
Ann Sinclair 10
[*Written crosswise across left-hand margin*] Pleas to Direct as before

CIRCUMTEXT Year from postmark.

719 From Ann Sinclair in Northfleet [Kent] to [Thomas] Talbot in Upminster, 5 September 1802

Northfleet Sepr 5th 1802
Sir/
I Received the 2$^£$ Note very Safe, & am Extremley Sorry I have
Neglected Sending You an answer According to your desire, but I hope
Your Goodness will Excuse it, as Illness was the reason. I have been 5
Very bad for Some time & could not get an Opportunity to write before
Now, Sir to the best of my knowledge there is 17 weeks due on Saturday
Next, be so kind to send it as Soon as Possible if not to much trouble. I
would be greatly Obliged for 3$^£$ Instead of two, as my Illness has been
very heavy & am Sir your 10
Very Humble S^t ann Sinclair

WRITING This letter is from the same skilled hand as those from Ann and Richard King in Gravesend (except **729, 734, 736**). Gravesend and Northfleet were about a mile apart.

720   From Ann Sinclair in Gravesend [Kent] to [Thomas] Talbot in Upminster, 25 September 1802

Gravesend Sepr 25th 1802

Sir/

I have wrote this to Let You know I Received the two Letters Very Safe, & return you many thanks for the Same & Likewise for Your Trouble,
5 I would wish to know the reason I am Charged 10^d for Every Letter I receive from you whereas I used only to Pay 5, but Sir when you Send Again will be Sufficient time to Let me know. I do not wish to Trouble you to write on Purposes, & am Sir Your Very

Humble S^t
10   Ann Sinclair

TEXTUAL ALTERATION 4: Likewise] *interl above del* 'you'.
WRITING This letter is from the same skilled hand as those from Ann and Richard King in Gravesend (except **729**, **734**, **736**).

721   From John Hicks in Cheshunt [Hertfordshire] to [Thomas] Talbot in Upminster, 29 December 1802

Cheshunt 29 Decr 1802

Sir

I must again Beg you to intersed for me to procure me some Assistance
- I am a great deal in arrear with my Rent & Not able to *work* but very
5 little Nor can I get any to do *at* this time of the Year - I am quite *distress^d*,
therefore hope I shall find favor with the *Gentlemen* and get some releif
I am thankful for former favours particultary to you - & remain Sir your

Most Ob^t Hbl Servt
John Hicks

TEXTUAL ALTERATIONS 3: intersed] 'd' *over illeg.* 5: at] *interl with caret.* 6: releif] 'f' *over illeg.*

722 From Richard King in Gravesend [Kent] to [Thomas] Talbot in Upminster, 28 April 1803

Gravesend April 28th 1803

Sir/

Yesterday I received Yours with the Inclosed 2[£] Note Very Safe & return You many thanks for the trouble you have, Sir I Should Esteem it as a great favor if You will be So kind To Let me have the money for the 5 children cloathing as Soon as is Convenient to you, for my Eldest Girl has had the Ague all winter, She is rather on the mend now but destitude of cloaths as well as the Other, & times being So hard that it is not in my Power to get for them & now the Impress Breaking out makes it Still worse I Hope Sir you'll Excuse my troubleing You so Much & 10

Am Sir Your Dutiful
St Richard King

WRITING Extremely skilled hand, same as that of Ann Sinclair's letters from Northfleet (**719, 720**).

723 From Richard King in Gravesend [Kent] to [Thomas] Talbot in Upminster, 14 August 1803

Gravesend Augt 14th 1803

Sir/

I received Yours with the Inclosed One Pound note, & return You many thanks for the Same

& am Sir Your very 5
Humble S^t R King

724 From Richard King [in Gravesend, Kent] to [Thomas] Talbot in Upminster, 9 October 1803

Sir/

I received Yours with the one £ Inclosed & retrun You many thanks for the Same & am

Sir Yours Humble S^t
Richard King 5

October 9th 1803

CIRCUMTEXT Place from postmark.

725   From Richard King in Gravesend [Kent] to [Thomas] Talbot in Upminster, 13 November 1803

Gravesend Nov[r] 13th 1803

Sir/

I received Yours with the £1 note very safe, & thank You kindly for the Same, Sir I am sorry to trouble you, but I have a forther favor to beg of
5 You, which is Concerning My Eldest Dau[r] she is grown ungovernable, & will not Stay out in Service, & it is not in my Power to keep her allways at home, if you would be so kind to Speak to the Gentlemen Next Meeting Night, for them to take the Same in Consideration, as She is very willing to be Put out apprentice & it will be the better for her, to be a Distance from
10 Me, & if you will be So kind to accept her home & Put her Appremtice to a farm or any thing Else you Please, I will be Ever bound to Pray for You, for I am Certain it will save her from Destruction, I hope Sir you'll not think me to troublesome, I am sir Your very Humble S[t]

Richard King

TEXTUAL ALTERATIONS 3: for] 'f' *over illeg.*

726   From John Hicks in Cheshunt [Hertfordshire] to [Thomas] Talbot in Upminster, 2 March 1804

I am again under the Necessity of Applying to my Parish for Relief - and thro your Interest I hope to be releieved from Approaching distress - I have contracted Debts which I am not, nor am I *likely* to be able to pay - besides, as I get older find it more difficult to get imploy, and can Ear<n>
5 but little - However I will endeavour to Shift <in> the Summer if I can Obtain some relief for <the> Present, which I Humbly the gentlemen will <not> think unreasonable

I S[r] your <mo>st ob[<t>]
Hbl Servant
10   John Hicks
Cheshunt 2 March 1804

TEXTUAL ALTERATIONS 2: Approaching] 'o' *interl with caret.*

727   From Richard King in Gravesend [Kent] to [Thomas] Talbot in Upminster, 18 March 1804

Gravesend March 18th 1804

Sir/

I received Yours with the 1[£] note Inclosed, Very Safe, & return you many thanks for the Same & am

Sir Your Hum   5
=ble S[t] Rich[d] King

728   From John Hicks in Cheshunt [Hertfordshire], 20 March 1804

Cheshunt 20 March 1804

I took the liberty (last Friday week) to write to you to Ask releif, not receiving any, nor an Answer, makes me fear it has *miscarried*,

I must beg you to intercede for me and get me something for I am distress - My Wife is bad <and> has not been able to earn a penny for   5
Months, <------> likely to recover a *great* while, - I have but little imploy I hope I shall receive some relief soon or I must go Entirely upon my Parish, if I <am relie>v[d] here I shall have some little light Jobbs <------->
Gentlemen where we are known

I am S[r] our Ob[t] Hbl   10
Serv[t]

John Hicks

TEXTUAL ALTERATIONS 5: to] *interl.*
DESTRUCTION OF TEXT Left-hand edge of paper heavily damaged.

729   From Richard King in Gravesend [Kent] to [Thomas] Talbot in Upminster, 22 April 1804

Gravesend April 22nd 1804

Dear Sir

I hope you will not take it amiss in my troubling you with a line or two Concerning taking my Girl for she is inlinked with a very bad set of Company and i do not know what to do with her for i think if she was   5
away from here it might be the means of saving her from Coming to ruin

as i should be very unhappy her Coming upon the town if i could prevent
<it> I should have been extremely Oblige to you if you <would> have
call,d upon me but if it meets with your Approbation that i should bring
10 her over the First Monday in next Month i hope Sir i shall not Offend in
so doing i shall be thankful for an answer if it is not troubling you to
much

From Your

Humble Servant

15 Richd King

730 From Richard King in Gravesend [Kent] to [Thomas] Talbot, 1 July 1804

Gravesend July 1st 1804

Sir

I hope You'll not be offended at my writing to You, for I am very
uneasy Concerning My Daughter, as I have heard a very odd Account
5 About her, which makes me unhappy, I would be Extremly obliged to
you if You will favor me with a few Lines I ask to Let me know where
she is & if she is well & am Sir

Your Humble S^t

Richard King

731 From John Hicks in Cheshunt [Hertfordshire] to [Thomas] Talbot in Upminster, 29 August 1804

<Si>r

I must again beg the Assitance of my Parish thro, your Interest, for I am
much distress^d with my Wife & my own Infirmities - she has an Abcess
in her side which renders her incapable of Earning any thing -
5 I do all in my power but cannot get Necessarys Suffcient to support
Nature Every Neigbouring Gentleman will testefy of my telling you the
truth respecting our Case &c four of whom have sign^d their Names to this

I am your Hble Servt

John Hicks

10 <Ch>eshunt 29 Aug^t

1804

TEXTUAL ALTERATIONS 5: my] *after del illeg.* 6: testefy] *after del interl* 'of'. 6: of] *after del illeg.*
CIRCUMTEXT The text is followed by four signatures: Ann Perrand, Jos[ep]h Blundy, R[ichar]d Profsen, and Samuel Reed. Judged from the handwriting, it is possible that John Hicks's letter was written by Ann Perrand.

732   From Richard King in Gravesend [Kent] to [Thomas] Talbot in Upminster, 16 December 1804

Gravesend Decr 16th 1804

Sir/

on friday Last the 14th I received Yours with the 1 £ note Inclosed very Safe & return You many thanks for the Same - Sir I am very Sorry to hear my dau^r cannot a Place, I am very uneasy in my mind, As I have been   5
Informed She has Spoke very disrespectful of me, & my wife, in Saying were are not married Such an Aspersion from my own child has given me great uneasiness, & what could Induce her to Say So Surprises me very much, as my wife allways behaved to her Like a Mother, I beg Sir if it is not to much trouble to send me a few Lines if such a thing is true & my   10
wife will Come & Produce our Certificate to satisfy you & the Gentlemen & we are Lawfully married, my wife has been unhappy So since She heard of it She would have come over but we had it not on pur Power to undertake the Journey, Sir I hope I am not troublesome I beg an answer & Am Sir Your   15

Humble Ser^t Richd King

TEXTUAL ALTERATIONS 13: over] *interl with caret.*

733   From John Hicks in Cheshunt [Hertfordshire] to [Thomas] Talbot in Upminster, 2 January 1805

Sir

I must again take the liberty to trouble you on my behalf - I need not enumerate my distresses to you I Am sure you can judge and feel for me; as I grow older I got more Infirm, my Wife *quite* helpless -

I hope my Parish will give an Order upon *this* Parish to pay me some-   5
thing *weekly* during the winter - I cannot earn enough to support nature

I leave all to *you*, hopeing you
will get something done to make
me *tollerable* comfortable
10   I am S^r your very Ob^t Hble
Servt in distress,
John Hicks

Cheshunt 2 Jan^y
1805

TEXTUAL ALTERATIONS 2: need] *interl with caret.* 3: older] *interl with caret at end of line.*
RELATED CORRESPONDENCE Samuel Reed, overseer of Cheshunt, wrote to the overseer of
Upminster on 6 March 1805. 'I find John Hicks has been with you am very glad to find
you will give him relief, his Wife & him being both worn out by hard labour, a more
Industrous couple of Honest Labourers are not be found'. The answer he received from
the vestry clerk of Upminster said it had been agreed that he should 'pay him 5^s per week
towards his support until further Orders - His wife's situation, his age, character, & his
family partly placed around him from whom he may have trifling helps - all incline us to
afford them relief where they are rather than remove them home' (copy of letter of 18
May1805). In the following year, the overseer of Upminster received three letters from
Francis Penny, vestry clerk in Cheshunt, in which they were requested to pay their outstanding bills for the allowance to Hicks (letters of 22 May 1805, 23 May 1806, and 26
June 1806).

734   From Richard King in Gravesend [Kent] to [Thomas] Talbot in Upminster, 9 April 1805

April 9 1805 Gravsend
Sir i have Received your Letter with A 1 pound Note inclosed and Return
you Many thanks for the Same Sir plese to Give our Kind Love to Maria
I am your Humble
5   Serveant R King

TEXTUAL ALTERATIONS 3: Kind] *interl below at end of line.*

735   From Joseph Rogers in London to [Thomas] Talbot in Upminster, 10 June 1805

London Juⁿ 10 1805
Honred genteelemen I Bag the faver of Whrighting these fue Lines to
in form you that I Ham Hurt My Hand & I Ham in Capeebel of Warking

& if you Will Be So Kind as to send Me a trifell to Help Me I shall take it
as a faver af you for I Had the Misforting to Have a Peeace of Hot Iron   5
Stuck in to the Back of My Hand & if it Was Not for that I should Not a
trubeld the genteelemen a tall I Joseph Rogers
Please to Deract to M^r skilton
No 9 New Rode Neear Whell
Squeeare for Joseph Rogers   10

CIRCUMTEXT Signature from other hand (but apparently with the same pen) at bottom:
'Thos Skilton'.

736   From Richard King in Gravesend [Kent] to [Thomas] Talbot in Upminster, 14 October 1805

Gravesend oct 14 1805
   Sir we Received your Letter very Safe and am very much oblige to you
for the Same i Still Remain
your Humbel
         Servent Ritchard   5
             King

TEXTUAL ALTERATIONS 2: Received] 'ved' over 'v'.

737   From Ann King in Gravesend [Kent] to [Thomas] Talbot in Upminster, 19 November 1805

                                          Gravesend Novr 19th 1805
Sir/
   I hope you will Excuse me Writing to you, but it is to Inform You my
husband Richard King has been Dangerous Ill & I am fearful he will
Never recover again he is rather better at the writing this but the docter   5
thinks he cannot get over it, Sir if you will have the Goodness to speak to
the Gentlemen for him for Assistance, I shall be Ever bound to Pray for
you, as he being Ill we are deprived of Every means of support, & the
Last Money you was so good to send went Intirely to Pay our Rent, I am
in great distress to get nourishing things for him, Sir you have allways   10
been a great friend to us, & God will Ever bless you & am Sir Your
Humble Ser^t
                                          Ann King

WRITING This letter is from the same skilled hand as those from Richard King in Gravesend (except **729, 734, 736**).

738   From Ann King in Gravesend [Kent] to [Thomas] Talbot in Upminster, 29 November 1805

Gravesend Novr 29th 1805

Sir/

I received Yours with the 1$^£$ Note Inclosed Very Safe & return You many thanks as it came Very Acceptable Indeed, for my husband
5 remains very Ill, & is as low as he Possibly can be, I hope the Gentlemen will take our case into consideration but Good Sir I need not remind You, as your Goodness is So Great, I hope Sir you'll not be angry my not Answering yours before, but I could not get an opportunity

I am Sir Your Humble St Ann King

WRITING This letter is from the same skilled hand as those from Richard King in Gravesend (except **729, 734, 736**).

739   From Richard King in Gravesend [Kent] to [Thomas] Talbot in Upminster, 9 February 1806

Gravesend Feby 9th 1806

Sir/

I received Yours with the £1 Note Inclosed very Safe, & return You thanks for the Same Sir About 2 months Ago, I wrote to you Informing
5 you I was very Ill & requesting you to have the goodness to speak to the Gentlemen in my behalf to allow me Something More for my own Support, but I do not think you received it, I am very Sorry to Inform You I am now very Ill & Obliged to keep my bed. there has been but very little to do this winter & what there has been, I have not been able to attend,
10 which has been a Sad denial to me, I am now reduced to a very low ebb, & am fearfull I Shall never get my health again, Sir I hope you will have the goodness to do what you can for me You have Ever been kind, have Pity on my distressed Situation, my wife was comeing to bring my family home not hearing from you, but She is very Ill herself & not Able to
15 do Any thing I hope Please God, she will get better for my familys Sake,

Sir I hope you will not be angry at my troubling You with Such a long letter I

remain Sir your very
Humble St Richd King

TEXTUAL ALTERATIONS 12: for] *over illeg.* 14: but] *interl with caret.*

740 From John Hicks in Cheshunt [Hertfordshire] to [Thomas] Talbot in Upminster, 4 July 1806

Sir

I am very unwilling to Trouble you again with my distresses, having to thank you and the rest of the Gentlemen for their kindness But my wife has been a long time so very bad that she is not able to do anything for herself, is oblig^d to have a Person *continually* with her - the Expence of which I *cannot* maintain without the Assistance of my Parish which I humbly pray they will give I do all the labour I *possibly* can but the expence of a Woman is too great for me to bear 5

I am Sir your very
oblig^d Hbl Servt 10
John Hicks

Cheshunt
3 July 1806

TEXTUAL ALTERATIONS 3: rest] 'st' *over illeg.* 3: for] 'r' *over illeg.* 4: she] *interl.* 8: great] 't' *over* 'd'.

741 From Mary-Ann Smith in [St Giles without Cripplegate, City of] London, to Mr Banks in Upminster, 2 March 1807

London March 2th 1807
Gentlman I have Petitioned for my son Charls if you please to send him to Morrow moring March 3th by theer coach I sent last month but did not received any Answer if you please to send 2 pounds besides his cloaths and paying is Expences I will take Charge on him myself to see him pro- 5 vided for youll excuse me coming the Expences is so much - my daughter mary is well

I shall meet the stage to morrow in white Chapple I hope you will not
disappoint me

10   so no more from your humble servant
                                     Maryann Smith formerly Adams

TEXTUAL ALTERATIONS 1: March] 'ar' *over* 'ra'. 3: Morrow] *after del* 'morrow'. 5: and]
interl. 6: much] *after del* 'mu'. 10: servant] 'ant' *interl at end of line*. 11: Adams] *interl
below del* 'adams'.
    FURTHER EVIDENCE On 7 June 1806, the vestry of Upminster had dealt with a letter from
the parish of St Giles without Cripplegate, saying that Mary-Ann Smith (late M.A. Adams)
had been delivered of a male illegitimate child. The answer agreed upon had informed St
Giles without Cripplegate 'that we are willing to receive and provide for the said Child
when ever they will send it home' (ERO, D/P 117/8/8, Upminster vestry minutes).

**742   From Francis Freeman in Middlesex Hospital [St Marylebone],
London, 5 March 1813**

London March the 5 1813
    dear Sur I wrot theis few layns to you and I hop it will find you all well I
hop you ould parden my rud nes for riten to you but I am quit destres hir for
money wee have so litel in the hospitel to live on wee have but 3 hopith of
5 bread a diay it is not a nof for even <m>eal wee have no tee no suger no but
buter no chis and onley met 3 days and Broth and Gruel and that is all that
wee ar all most starved for wont I thank god I am geten beter but I can not
stop hire onles you can send mee a letel money for to help mee I can not
stop If you dont send as sun as posabel you can by the retorn of post I am
10 ver sorey to trobel you so I most conclud with my dutey to you fransed
                                                                    friman

ples to dereack to
mee franses freeman
Birds ward Middelsex
15   hospital London

TEXTUAL ALTERATIONS 7: wont] *after del* 'wat'.

**743   From Mary[-Ann] Smith in Clerkenwell [London] to the over-
seer of Upminster, 5 January 1814**

To the Gentlemen of the Vestry of Upminster Essex. Mary Smith formerly Mary Adams humbly Solicits your Assistance for Fredrick Adams

her Son. whom she had before she Married Smith & the Child was Passed
to Upminster from Cripple - Gate and in a short time I fetched him away.
I beg leave to request the favor of two Pounds for to relieve me in my 5
present distressed Circumstance. have had my Goods Seized for Rent.
and am at 34 Turnmill Street Clerkenwell. in Ready Furnished Lodgings
having two more Children & having nothing but what I work for & my
Husband through distress has diserted from home & if you'll send me the
small sum I request it will enable me to buy a Bed &c. so that I shall have 10
no occasion to trouble you any more if you do not grant me this favor I
shall be under the necessity to pass the Child immediately frorom
Clerkenwell Parrish to you. will thank you for an Answer by the Rumford
Choach next Wednesday will wait a the Inn for it my Son Charles is
bound Apprentice and do very well. 15

Gentlemen Y^r H^{ble} Servant

Mary Smith

Jany 5th 1814

TEXTUAL ALTERATIONS 3: Married] *after del* 'before she'.
WRITING This letter is from the same hand as that from Mary-Ann Smith in London
(**741**).

744 From Mary[-Ann] Smith in [Clerkenwell, London] to Mr Banks in Upminster, 10 February 1814

Gentlemen/
I wrote to you last Week concerning my Child who belongs to your
Parrish shall be glad to know if you will send me up the small sum I sent
for if not I must send him Home immediately I particularly wish to know
if I am to send him by the Coach or regularly passed by Clerkenwell 5
Parrish. I hope you'll not fail to grant me to the favor I request as I am loft
to part with him & have not troubled you for the last seven or eight Years
for neither of them you always found me punctual in my word.

I am Y^r H^{ble} Servant

Mary Smith 10

Feb 10th 1814
NB. beg the favor of an answer by the Coch to morrow

TEXTUAL ALTERATIONS 4: must] 't' *interl below at end of line*. 5: not] *after del* 't'.
WRITING This letter is from the same hand as that from Mary-Ann Smith in London
(**741**).

745   From J.B. Crowest [in Upminster] to the overseer of Upminster, 13 March 1819

Gentlemen

Impelled by necessity I again appeal to your Benevolence for that assistance which my present peculiar circumstances absolutly need. -

About 3 Years since I stated the particulars of my Case to you, to which
5 you promptly & kindly attended, by placing my second Son on a situation, which, I doubt not will ultimately prove advantageous to him you &*[c]*; & which act of generosity I would thro'd his medium gratefully acknowledge.

But what I have more particularly to request on the present occasion, is that you would be pleased to take into consideration, the late long, &
10 serious affliction, with which in the order of Providence Myself & family have been visited nearly 12 months, almost without intermission; during which time my expences have been so great, that notwithstanding every affort I have made to defray them I find myself yet much insolved, from which, under the present Circumstances of my family, it will be impossible
15 for me to extricate myself. The Doctor's Bill (which is only in part) amounts to more than £12 I should have solicited an order for Medical attendance but was unwilling to trouble you, not being at all aware of such a long affliction as it has proved to be - And as an additional trouble & expence, I am charged in the sum of £9..7..6 for a Tax upon my Horse & Cart, to
20 which I appealed upon the ground of entire ignorance of being at all liable to pay for any Carriage, or Horse kept exclusively for the purpose of attending divine Worship, as mine evidently were, having neither let or lent them on any occasion, during the term stated in the assessment, but I attained no further redress than the pity of the Commisioners who
25 observed „It was a hard case + that no blame attached to me" Thus that Gentlemen you see at least in part what are my present circumstances, which I leave for your consideration, not dowbting but that you will exercise your wanted liberality toward me whereby you will encourage industry, evince your regard to the principles of benevolence and Confer a lasting
30 obligation Upon

Gentlemen

Your most obed humble Servant
J B Crowest

Saturday night March 13 1819

TEXTUAL ALTERATIONS 6: will] *after del* 'will'. 6: you &*[c]*] *interl.*

746 From Thomas and Mary Lutterell in Burnham Westgate [Norfolk] to the overseers of Upminster, 19 August 1834

Burnham Westgate Aug^st 19th 1834

Gentlemen

Having wrote 2 or 3 Letters before to you beging the favour of you to have the goodness to remitt to me a Sum of Money to enable me to pay my Rent which is now due being the sum of 5^£ for a Cottage I now live in 5 & hire in the Parish aforesaid but not having received any Answer from you Gentlemen I have been Obliged to swear my Settlement, & I am advised by the Magistrate Clerk to inclose you my Examination whereby if you will give yourselves the trouble of peruseing of it over you will find that I belong to your Parish, therefore it is from extream necessity 10 that I am forced to write to you hopeing you will send me trifle of money to enable me to pay my Rent as Michaelmas is drawing near & unless the Rent is paid my few Articles will be seized and Sold of to pay the same & I shall then be Obliged to be relieved by the Parish of Burnham Westgate aforesaid & the parish will then get an Order out against me and bring me 15 home, which can be avoided if you will have the goodness to remitt me a sum of money to enable me to pay my Rent & if I am brought home to your Parish it will be attended with a still further Expence, as it is extream necessity that has obliged me to make the aforesaid application to you as I do not wish to incur any further Expence on your than can possibly be 20 avoided, as my wife & myself are 2 narly helpless Creaturs and not able to bring scarcely anything in towards obtaining a livelihood, So I beg and pray of you Gentlemen to take my deplorable & miserable situation into your humane consideration & return me an answer by return of Post or as soon as possible and remitt me some towards paying my Rent or to let me 25 know your Gentlemans determination whether you will remitt me a sum of money for the above purpose or whether I must come home, as there is no time to loose as I expect to have my Goods seized and sold almost every Day if the Rent is not paid So waiting an answer from you Gentlemen,

I am your most obedient and 30
Humble Servants
Thomas & Mary Lutterell

Little Waltham pauper letter

747 From Ann Clark in [Bermondsey, London] to the Revd Dr Chambers in Little Waltham, 9 October 1768

octeber ye 9 1768

    To the woshabel gestes of the paresh the Humble Purtision of ann clark seting forth my grat destress Showing I pade five pound at the indey house to git Him of he after words indever[d] to woork at abrookous But

5 got ahurt in his leg which was histeth and left me and my famaley in the gratest destress ef your Goodness will bee pleesd to send me sum relefe so That with industry imay bee able to git my bread or Else must bee oblidg to com don and my famaly upon The paresh I beeg your goodness will take it in to considerasion and send me som reelefe as soon as you

10 Reeceive this my husband beeing deed and weeakes Ans his sickness and burel has drove me to the Gratest destrees in complying tith this your Poor purtisinor will bee in duty ever bound To pray for you ihad a letter from scotland

And informs me that

15   All my frends thare is

Ded which mad me not

Go on my iorney so made

no youse of my pas

Ps

20 plees to Derect

For me to bee

Left at the son

in wite street

near sant gorges

25 church in the Boorow -

Sourthwork

Pray send an answar

By the next post

TEXTUAL ALTERATIONS 3: five] 'i' *over* 'o'.

Wanstead pauper letter

748   From Timothy Woodward to Mr Drake in Wanstead, 1766

\<I\> make bold to trouble you to let you \<kn\>ow that Mr Mold who is the
master \<of the\> house where I am Denies me the liberty of a person
going with me to Doctor Taylor twice a week he has told me Downright
that I shall go no more I humbly beg of you to be so kind as to think of
some way or other to help me at this time for I find myself much better   5
then when I came & it will be a great pity for me to lose this oportunity
that you have been so kind as to give me under the blessing of God whereby
I may have my sight restored \<-----\>th

sir in so doing you will
oblige your Humble servant   10
Timothy Woodward

\<----\> 2 1766

TEXTUAL ALTERATIONS 11: Woodward] 'd' *interl at end of line.*

South Weald pauper letters

749 From Rebecca Robinson in Woolwich, Kent, to Mr Pollis in South Weald, 28 May 1818

Woolwich 28 May 1818

Sir/

I am sory that I cannot yet acquaint You with the Christain Name of M[r] Wallis late of Your Parish but I expect in a few Days to be able to give the
5 information. I am likewise extremely sory to trouble you again for some subsistence for the support of my family. but if it can not be remitted without inconvenience I must ultimately become troublesome to this Parish I hope Sir you will excuse the liberty I have taken but real necessity compells me to take such steps
10 I remain

Sir

Your very humble servant

Rebecca Robinson

Please address Rebecca Robinson
15 Red Lion Street

Woolwich Kent

750 From Mrs Robinson, 17 October 1818

Gentlemen & Ladies

I take the liberty to inform You of my Mothers calamities that the will of the Almity as been pleased enough take away her Eyesight which I am now under the nessity of Keeping a Girl on purpose to attend on her their
5 fore have been for some time past at a great expence Hope Gentlemen You will take it into considerration and make me some allowance at Easter -

You will Oblidge

M[rs] Robinson

formerly M[rs] Pluckrose
10 Oct[r] 17 1818

CIRCUMTEXT On back: copy of entry in marriage register of Woolwich, concerning the marriage of William Pishlow and Anne Willow (no date). Whether this means that the writer of the letter used a piece of waste paper from the parish chest of Woolwich, we do not know. Neither is there any clue as to whether Mrs Robinson was related to of Rebecca Robinson (see **749**).

751 From Mary Lee in Dunton [Essex] to the overseer of South Weald [4 January 1819]

to the prisheners of weal jentellmen i have took harrit Bigs She came to me on 24 of december 1818 and if the gentellmen will give me one Shiling per week i will take hir untill next mickelms 1819 But i cant think to keep hir if you dont Give hir some cloths for she wants cloths very Bad and i should like to see hir go desent 5

  I am your most obedent
  Mary lee at Dunton

TEXTUAL ALTERATIONS 2: 1818] interl *at end of line*.
 CIRCUMTEXT Date (of receipt?) at bottom, from other hand.

752 From James Randall in St Thomas's Hospital [St Thomas, London] to the overseer of South Weald, 4 May 1825

  Williams Ward St Thomas Hospital
4 May 1825
 To the overseer of South weald
 Sir
 This comes to inform you that i am geting better and i expect to be 5
discharged from the Hospital on thursday week but i am in a very weak state i cannot walk only with two sticks the Doctor i am under seems to think that the country air would be of great service to me now but i am very bad off for clothes my shirts and shoes are very good but the rest of my clothes are all to rags my trowsers are very bad and so is my coat i 10
hope you will have the goodness to send me a trifle to get me some cloaths and pay my expences home for i am quite destitute of any means of geting home without your assitance and i hope you will send me some clothes as i have not had any since i become chargeable to the parish but shirts and shoes and i am in great want of them you will have the goodness to send 15
an answer before tomorrow week

     From your humble Servant
     James Randall

TEXTUAL ALTERATIONS 13: tomorrow] *after del* 'by'.

RELATED CORRESPONDENCE In a letter 5 January 1824, J.H. Allenson, surgeon in Woolwich, had informed the overseer of South Weald that James Randall, a bricklayer's labourer, had been in his care since August 1824, suffering from rheumatism and ophthalmia; that Randall had been supported by his mother, who was no longer able to do it; and that he would appreciate some help from the parish.

Woodford pauper letters

753 From William Rolf in Sudbury [Suffolk] to Mr Darwood in Woodford, 14 November 1836

sudbury Nov^{ber} 14 1836

Dear sir i have then the troble of wrighting to you by Mr Seyers ordes
stateing that he cannot think of paying me any more Money untill the Bill
is paid for Mr Seyer says there is allmost a yeare Due to him ever since
you come Doun to sudbury that you settle on me at four shilings a weeke   5
M^r sadinton sent word the Bill should be paid at is Bank in London and it is
not paid and he is eving on easy a bout it and he hav sent a letter since a
bout it and a bout me and my wife and famly sir my wife haveinge been
confind of a nother child three weekes a go last thusday and i have been
fost to have a woman in the house ever since and for a month be for she   10
was confinde she was so every ill she could do nothing for har famely and
i have seven Children and trade is so bade and flower giting so Dear that
i should be fost to come home if the Gentleman do not a lowe me somthing
more and i hope you will be so good as to speeke to thee gentleman a
boute me and to ask the gentlman weether thay will be so kinde as to give   15
me a small trifull to pay the nuss and i have beene fost to run into Deet and
i shul never be able to pay my rent and my club wich if i was ill i should not
have aney thing if i do not pay the money in the club and my Children is
half naked onely one my bigest boy earn one shiling and sixpenc and my
anther earn nothing a tall and there is no work in sudbury only velveds and   20
i now nothing a bout them my Master have gave me one to learn on and i
cannot earn nothing not yet and he sayes the parish must do somthing for
me untill i can [e]arn and i should be fost to come hom if the Gentleman do
not send me somthing as soon as my wife is able to come and i hop you
will spake to the Gentleman for me and show these few Lines to them and   25
i hope you will not be offened of me ind wright to you for i was orded to
wright to you

so i remain your

trobbsom servent

Wm Rolf   30

T EXTUAL ALTERATIONS 14: so] *after del illeg.* 15: thay] 'a' *after del illeg.* 17: i shul] *after del*
'and'. 17: my] *interl.*

FURTHER EVIDENCE Two days later, the guardian of the poor at Woodford paid the postage of 10d for this letter ('postage for letter received from Wolf [mistaken for Rolf] in Sudbury', recorded on 16 November 1836). And on 26 November 1836, he paid 2s 6d for 'Provision & Lodging for Wm Rolfe of Sudbury from Thursday night the 24th till Saturday for him to go before the Board' (ERO, D/P 167/12/18, Woodford overseers' accounts). Within the vestry records of Woodford, there is also an earlier reference of 6 February 1827: 'Rolf W^m of Sudbury applied for Relief Ordered 6[s] 6[d]' (ERO, D/P 167/8/6, Woodford vestry minutes).

754   From William Boreham in Kilby [Leicestershire] to Mr Darwood, 1 December 1836

Kilby Decr 1 1836
  Sir
  I Should be much obliged to you to lay this before the Gentlemen at the Vestry meeting
5 Gentlemen
  I Should be much obliged to you if you could assist me with a trifle per week through the winter months for I have little or no work to do Mr Kelble has hired a boy this winter so what the Boy cannot Do I do But Mr Kebble obliges me to work 7 clear hours for 1^s per Day and this is not
10 constant only as work fallsout I did not troble you last winter for I had work nor would I have done it this if I could possible done any how without I have had great expences this year for doctrine and I have not done with it yet 3 of my Children was ill with the Scarlet fever for 2 months one died and only Mr Kebbl to assit me with a few Trifles I have been in Leicester-
15 shire 12 years But this is by far the worst winter I have seen and rather than see such another I will return to my parish
                        from your Humble and obedient
                             Servent Wm Boreham

TEXTUAL ALTERATIONS 12: expences] *second* 'e' *interl with caret.* 12: and] *after del* 'this year'. 13: with the scarlet fever] *interl with caret.* 15: rather] *after del illeg.*

CIRCUMTEXT Note from other hand at bottom of page: 'The writer is son of Wm Boreham now on the permanent list of out door poor in this parish of Woodford'.

FURTHER EVIDENCE In the vestry books of Woodford, William Boreham is recorded on three earlier occasions. On 5 July 1824, he was granted a 'Pr Shoes for Mary aged 14'; on 5 February 1828, he 'Applied for a Pair Shoes & Calico for two Children Ordered the Calico'; and on 10 April 1833, he was allowed £2, 'to be paid by Mr Kelbel in such a way as he thinks proper' (ERO, D/P 167/8/6, Woodford vestry minutes).

Wormingford pauper letters

755 From Ellen Humm, Isle of Wight, to Thomas Hallum in Wormingford, 30 April 1824

Isle white April 30 1824

Sir I take Liborty in writing afew Lines to hoping that yow and the gentlemen will grant me one Request it is my wish to go to Ireland and take the Child with me as there is aship going from the Isle white I wish to go if the gentlemen will allow me there for the Child as I think it makes no differ- 5
ence to them where I am if the will I never shall trouble them for Any allowence for meself soo I will be greatly abliged to you and the gentlemen if you Plase to advance me six mounths Pay going also Let me know how Long is the Parrish to allow my Child as I should wish to know if you doent wish to allow me in Ireland yow will send it to Sarget Edward Palmmer 54 10
Redgt he will send it to me Every 4 mounths I Cant stay much Longer hear Every thing is so very dear on account of all the soldiers Everything is so Cheap in Ireland I Could Leave the Child with my mother and go to servace as I Certainly must do somthing for meself as 26 aweek is very Little to maintain this Great boy and Cloth him Plase to determain what is 15
to be done as the ship will be going in afew days if you allow me in Ireland you will derect to Cathrin Cassidy Ballina County Ireland that is my mothers mame Perhaps I may be at servace some destance when the Child Pay will Come due that she may write for it as I wish to Let you Every thing Sir I hope yow will send answer derectly as I Cant go untill I am 20
settled one way or other if you be Plased to advance me six mounth Pay derct to Edward Palmmer sare^t 54 pedg^t Allenny Barricks Isle white new Port I receved two Pound from M^r martin Harvey he mentioned to me that you were to be overseeer the next tine sir by so doing you obblige me very much 25

Sir I remain your
Humble servant
Ellen Humm

TEXTUAL ALTERATIONS 2: writing] *after del* 'addre'. 3: Request] 't' *interl at end of line*. 10: to allow] *after del* 'to send the'. 10: send] *after del illeg*. 12: soldiers] *after del* 'Armmy'. 13: with] *after del* 'whi'.

756   From Ellen Humm, Isle of Wight, to Mr Stannard in Wormingford, 10 May 1824

Isle of Wight
10 May 1824

Sir

I have to inform you that i am now preparing to go to Ireland, I therefore
5 beg you will be Pleased to make me an advance of 6 Months Pay to
ennable me to go on my Pessage the Ship is now in Cowes Harbour your
reply is very urgent as She will sail in a fu days,

If My request cannot be complied with you will be pleased to remit the
Pay as useal to Serjiant Edward Palmer 54th Regiment whom I Can Depend
10 upon to send it to me, he Knowing my Place of residence in Ireland -

I have ritten to Mr Allum and got no answer *I will give you my reasons
to Leaving this Place*:

the Child is becoming very expencive in clothing and will soon require
schooling and other necessaries which I Can Purchis much chapper in
15 that Country than I Can here

I remain your Humble servant
Ellen Humme

in Preconce
of Sergeant Palmer
20   54 Rgt

TEXTUAL ALTERATIONS 19: of] *interl after del* 'from'.

RELATED CORRESPONDENCE and FURTHER EVIDENCE Thomas Hallum, overseer of
Wormingford, wrote to Edward Palmer in Newport, Isle of Wight, on 13 May 1824: 'in
consequence of a Letter sent to him by Ellen Humm dated April 30th - - 1824. have
Inclosed three One pound Notes for herself and child in the letter and directed it to Sergjant
Edward Palmer 54th Regiment and put the letter into the Colchester post office' (copy).
This is also in evidence in the overseers' accounts of Wormingford, where it says that
Ellen Humm was sent £3 'With a Letter' on 13 May 1824 (ERO, D/P 185/12/3, Worming-
ford overseers' accounts).

757 From Thomas Rush [in Bocking, Essex] to the overseers of Wormingford, 12 June 1825

June 12 1825

Hon^d Sir

I Thos Rush am sorry That I have to trouble you but Necessity Obliges me to write As you have been Kind in putting me to learn to be a Shoe-maker which I thank you for you Sir know the perticulers of the indenture 5 therefore I need not relate it but One thing I mention my Fathers word In promising to maintain Me but I believe he would not have promis^d So if he had Considered the expence Attending it yet I know not his Wages but as I have seen nor herd any thing of him sence I have been bound which was a month last Thirsday therefore I Conclude that his intention is aultred 10 And If so a plan must be adopted My Master thinks it Consistent to Relese Me from the bond which subsists between Me and him on account of my having little Support for Reasons well founded as I shall grow week and unfit for doing him but little Service and likewise grow naked for want of Clothing as Sir the Money that I received after the busness was setled 15 which was 1 pound Bought but little as I was oblig^d to pay the expences to Coggeshall which Cost 4 shillings 2 shillings for an apron 6 shillings for a Shoe for the longest leg and a consider Able Sum for tools to work with yet I am destuted of an high Shoe which I want Sir I hope you will send word by next Saterday By my Father if he Comes if not I hope by 20 post as my Mother Is not able to Come you promis^{/d/} her 16 Shillings for the last quarter Rent to put her foward and then to Allow her 5 shillings per month therefore she would be glad to know where she is to receive it for she is omitd taking the pay at Mr Sodleys I hope you will forgive Me in writting to you but Unless Something is done I shall be oblig^d to give it 25 intirly up

As I remain your

Humble Servant Thos Rush

NB I forgot to mention what my Mother received at Coggeshall at my Father which was 4 Shillings and not any Sence and being not well she is 30 unfit for work but she hopes no offence if she takes the pay at Mr Polleys for he h<as> recieved no answer to give it up

TEXTUAL ALTERATIONS 7: he] 'h' *over* 'D'. 12: subsists] 'ts' *interl at end of line*. 12: on] *after del illeg*.

RELATED CORRESPONDENCE On 24 March 1825, Ralph Polley in Bocking wrote to the overseer of Wormingford, 'Your Parishioner Thos Rush, has requested me to persuade you to bind him to some trade, by which he might ultimately be enabled to obtain a livelihood without troubling you for that purpose - He has made choice at Shoe making has found a person who has given him terms, to which if you are inclined to aceede, the master is ready to engage him, and to fulfil on his part - the man who has offered to take him is not a man of an unexceptionable character, I however know but little of him, he having been at Bocking in business for himself but a short time - It is certainly desirable, under the existing circumstances of the Lad - (he being very industrious steady and desposed to work for himself) to place him at some trade, by working at which, he might obtain an honest & [...]stable livelihood - I dont think the mans terms are extravagant, in proportion to the demands I have accasionally heard made by Masters, for Lads whom we as Guardians have been desirous of apprenticing the Lad as he is now situated, has no means of living but upon your bounty, and being in health - he of course requires more support than he is likely to derive from a Parish According to the terms proposed by the Shoemaker, he will be a considerable expence to you for two years to come - It remains however for your serious consideration to dispose of him as you think proper - he is deserving your attention - for he possesses what in the present day among laboureres is rare - a desinclination to apply for Parish relief & a desire to live by his own work & industry - I believe he has tried shoe making a little, & has no doubt of being able to do it. He tried Silk weaving but did not succeed - Should you feel disposed to assist him, and are inclined to do it - through my hands, I than be most happy to execute any commands you may please to give.'

758 From Thomas Rush [in Braintree] to Mr Hicks in Wormingford, 18 July 1830

July 18 1830

Hon^d Sir

By necessity I am Oblidged to write to you the Affliction which my mother has Is a trying and expensive one And as I have not wherewith to
5 support it I must apply by the wise of those who well knows of my trouble to the gentlmen of her Parish I have received 6^s 6^d of my father for one month for a person thats confin^d to her bed with A Cancer in the womb And is oblidged to be stript almost every hour of the day and night I need not tell you Sir of the expence Which you can give an give an Idea of
10 yourself it is such an expence that I have gone in debt so far that the people will not let me have Any thing else and as Sir She Is one of your poor and never was much trouble to you I hope you will do something for her and if you cannot Or I might say will not I must comit this affair into the hands of the gentlemen of this parish I have not seen my farther for
15 this fortnight It must be done now for nobody will not come to assist her unless I can support them I hope you will commit it to Mr Polley for he knows how I am or any gentlemen of this parish So I can receive it or if my Father can bring it by whendsey or tuesday but if Not I hope no offence but I must have something of somebody

Excuse the writing 20
I remain your humble
Servant Tho[s] Rush

TEXTUAL ALTERATIONS 9: expence] 'ce' *interl at end of line.* 17: or if] *after del* 'by'.

PLACE From postmark.

FURTHER EVIDENCE Thomas Rush was allowed £1 'towards his wifes affliction' on 22 July 1830, and the same sum 'towards the Burial of his Wife' on 25 July 1830. Further entries referring to Thomas Rush (like 5s 'lost one week lame', 13 August 1830) suggest that he was the letter writer's father who lived in Wormingford (ERO, D/P 185/8/3, Wormingford vestry minutes).

APPENDIX

List A.1: Essex Pauper Letters, 1731-1837, by place of sender

No.	Sender	Place of receipt	No.	Sender	Place of receipt

Ashby-de-la-Zouch, Leicestershire
657	Richard Porter	Rayleigh
658	Richard Porter	Rayleigh
660	Richard Porter	Rayleigh

Attleborough, Norfolk
| 593 | Ann Garner | Havering AB |

Little Baddow, Essex
| 20 | John Gibson | Braintree |

South Benfleet, Essex
| 643 | William Thurtell | Purleigh |
| 644 | William Thurtell | Purleigh |

Billericay, Essex
| 17 | John Barnes | Braintree |

Bishop's Stortford, Hertfordshire
| 498 | James Tracey | Colchester SP |

Bishop's Waltham, Hampshire
| 542 | George Craddock | Colchester SP |

Bocking, Essex
412	George Rowe	Colchester SP
459	George Rowe	Colchester SP
463	George Rowe	Colchester SP
585	George Rowe	Colchester SP
757	Thomas Rush	Wormingford

Boyle, Roscommon, Ireland
| 601 | Mary Harris | Kirby LS |
| 602 | Mary Harris | Kirby LS |

Braintree, Essex
16	Thomas Cleare	Braintree
79	Thomas Cleare	Braintree
30	Maria Cousins	Braintree
549	George Rowe	Colchester SP
551	George Rowe	Colchester SP
557	George Rowe	Colchester SP
558	George Rowe	Colchester SP
758	Thomas Rush	Wormingford
80	Robert Sewell	Braintree
81	Joseph Wright	S Bumpstead

Brentwood, Essex
| 43 | Joseph Brand | Braintree |
| 49 | Joseph Brand | Braintree |

Brightlingsea, Essex
| 586 | Mary Braig | Colchester SP |
| 552 | Elizabeth Brigg | Colchester SP |

Brighton, Sussex
| 88 | Joseph Derham | S Bumpstead |

Brisley, Norfolk
559	Edward Mills	Colchester SP
562	Edward Mills	Colchester SP
567	Edward Mills	Colchester SP
569	Edward Mills	Colchester SP

Bristol, Gloucestershire
| 596 | John Snell | Kirby LS |

Bromley, Middlesex
| 716 | Eliza Farrant | W Thurrock |

Burnham Westgate, Norfolk
| 746 | T./M. Lutterell | Upminster |

Cambridge, Cambridgeshire
89	Thomas Albion	S Bumpstead
93	Thomas Albion	S Bumpstead
253	Thomas Carritt	Chelmsford
254	Thomas Carritt	Chelmsford
45	George Whitaker	Braintree

Canewdon, Essex
| 692 | Sarah Ateradge | Rochford |

Canterbury, Kent
| 281 | Jane Cross | Colchester SB |

Chatham, Kent
394	Sarah Finch	Colchester SB
485	Richard Player	Colchester SP
672	Mrs Smith	Rayleigh

Chelmondiston, Suffolk
| 39 | Adam Turthing | Braintree |

Chelmsford
326	Sarah Challis	Colchester SB
409	Mary Cooper	Colchester SJ
283	John Hall	Colchester SB
290	John Hall	Colchester SB
291	Sarah Hall	Colchester SB
292	John Hall	Colchester SB

No.	Sender	Place of receipt	No.	Sender	Place of receipt
293	Sarah Hall	Colchester SB	491	William James	Colchester SP
294	Sarah Hall	Colchester SB	496	William James	Colchester SP
295	Sarah Hall	Colchester SB	502	William James	Colchester SP
296	John Hall	Colchester SB	505	William James	Colchester SP
297	John Hall	Colchester SB	509	William James	Colchester SP
298	John Hall	Colchester SB	511	William James	Colchester SP
299	John Hall	Colchester SB	519	William James	Colchester SP
302	John Hall	Colchester SB	527	William James	Colchester SP
303	John Hall	Colchester SB	529	William James	Colchester SP
309	John Hall	Colchester SB	534	William James	Colchester SP
310	John Hall	Colchester SB	535	William James	Colchester SP
313	Sarah Hall	Colchester SB	538	William James	Colchester SP
315	Sarah Hall	Colchester SB	540	William James	Colchester SP
318	John Hall	Colchester SB	541	William James	Colchester SP
319	John Hall	Colchester SB	543	William James	Colchester SP
321	Sarah Hall	Colchester SB	550	William James	Colchester SP
330	John Hall	Colchester SB	714	Thomas Kellnby	Theydon M
341	John Hall	Colchester SB	29	Hannah Porter	Stebbing
418	William James	Colchester SP	697	John Sams	Rochford
419	William James	Colchester SP	350	Thomas Strutt	Colchester SB
421	William James	Colchester SP	436	James Tracey	Colchester SP
422	William James	Colchester SP	94	James Willson	Gt Burstead
423	William James	Colchester SP			
425	William James	Colchester SP	*Cheshunt, Hertfordshire*		
430	William James	Colchester SP	721	John Hicks	Upminster
432	William James	Colchester SP	726	John Hicks	Upminster
434	William James	Colchester SP	728	John Hicks	Upminster
435	William James	Colchester SP	731	John Hicks	Upminster
437	William James	Colchester SP	733	John Hicks	Upminster
438	William James	Colchester SP	740	John Hicks	Upminster
439	William James	Colchester SP	40	Stephen Linzell	Braintree
443	William James	Colchester SP	44	Stephen Linzell	Braintree
444	William James	Colchester SP	50	Stephen Linzell	Braintree
445	William James	Colchester SP			
447	William James	Colchester SP	*Chester-le-Street, Durham*		
448	William James	Colchester SP	36	Elizabeth Watty	Braintree
450	William James	Colchester SP			
451	William James	Colchester SP	*Clonmel, Tipperary, Ireland*		
452	William James	Colchester SP	605	Mary Harris	Kirby LS
453	William James	Colchester SP			
454	William James	Colchester SP	*Great Coggeshall, Essex*		
457	William James	Colchester SP	280	Thomas Morse	Hereford
461	William James	Colchester SP	414	George Rowe	Colchester SP
462	William James	Colchester SP	440	George Rowe	Colchester SP
464	William James	Colchester SP	473	George Rowe	Colchester SP
468	William James	Colchester SP	474	George Rowe	Colchester SP
472	William James	Colchester SP	492	George Rowe	Colchester SP
475	William James	Colchester SP	518	George Rowe	Colchester SP
477	William James	Colchester SP	536	George Rowe	Colchester SP
478	William James	Colchester SP			
479	William James	Colchester SP	*Colchester, Essex*		
481	William James	Colchester SP	380	Elizabeth Baker	Colchester SB
484	William James	Colchester SP	410	Lucy Baley	Colchester SJ
486	William James	Colchester SP	603	James Davey	Kirby LS
488	William James	Colchester SP	606	Elizabeth Davey	Kirby LS

No.	Sender	Place of receipt	No.	Sender	Place of receipt
612	James Davey	Kirby LS	441	James Howell	Colchester SP
613	James Davey	Kirby LS	446	James Howell	Colchester SP
614	James Davey	Kirby LS	455	James Howell	Colchester SP
363	Thomas Goody	Colchester SB	456	James Howell	Colchester SP
301	James Haxell	Colchester SB	471	James Howell	Colchester SP
398	Mary Mayden	Colchester SJ	482	James Howell	Colchester SP
122	Lucy Nevill	Chelmsford	487	James Howell	Colchester SP
140	Lucy Nevill	Chelmsford	553	Margaret Howell	Colchester SP
227	Mr Noon	Chelmsford	560	Margaret Howell	Colchester SP
382	Susan Pitt	Colchester SB	563	Margaret Howell	Colchester SP
41	Sarah Smee	Braintree	565	James Howell	Colchester SP
266	Harriet Twin	Chelmsford	568	James Howell	Colchester SP
273	Harriet Twin	Chelmsford	574	James Howell	Colchester SP
364	George Tye	Colchester SB	578	James Howell	Colchester SP
648	Hannah Wall	Rainham	584	J.M. Howell	Colchester SP

Crays Hill, Essex
| 679 | John Maseon | Rochford |
| 701 | J./E. Maseon | |

Danbury, Essex
| 689 | Mary Brooks | Rochford |
| 690 | Mary Brooks | Rochford |

Debden, Essex
| 11 | John Dennison | Gt Bardfield |

Dedham, Essex
| 222 | Robert Griffith | Chelmsford |

Deptford, Surrey
646	Amy Hill	Rainham
649	Amy Hill	Rainham
587	Hannah Hoy	Gt Dunmow
1	Sarah Taylor	Aveley

Devonport, Devon
| 609 | Mary Harris | Kirby LS |
| 68 | William Marsh | Braintree |

Great Dunmow, Essex
| 78 | John Cardinal | Braintree |

Dunton, Essex
| 751 | Mary Lee | |

Durham, Durham
| 595 | Rachel Robson | Havering AB |

Edmonton, Middlesex
| 279 | Thomas Bray | Gt Chishall |

Ely
| 415 | James Howell | Colchester SP |
| 420 | James Howell | Colchester SP |

Farningham, Kent
| 27 | James Tidman | Braintree |

Feering, Essex
| 13 | Ann Hitchcock | Braintree |

Fermoy, Cork, Ireland
| 608 | Mary Harris | Kirby LS |

Gateshead, Durham
| 594 | Rachel Robson | Havering AB |

Gibraltar
| 95 | George Pateman | Gt Burstead |

Glemsford, Suffolk
| 261 | Harriet Twin | Chelmsford |

Gosport, Hampshire
| 429 | William Harvey | Colchester SP |
| 431 | William Harvey | Colchester SP |

Gravesend, Kent
722	Richard King	Upminster
723	Richard King	Upminster
724	Richard King	Upminster
725	Richard King	Upminster
727	Richard King	Upminster
729	Richard King	Upminster
730	Richard King	Upminster
732	Richard King	Upminster
734	Richard King	Upminster
736	Richard King	Upminster
737	Ann King	Upminster
738	Ann King	Upminster
739	Richard King	Upminster
720	Ann Sinclair	Upminster

Hacheston, Suffolk
| 539 | Mary Death | Colchester SP |

No.	Sender	Place of receipt	No.	Sender	Place of receipt

Hadleigh, Suffolk

362	Hannah Steward	Colchester SB
322	Mary Taylor	Colchester SB
396	Mary Taylor	Colchester SB

Halstead, Essex

233	Hugh Constable	Chelmsford
235	Hugh Constable	Chelmsford
108	Davey Rising	Chelmsford
112	D./S. Rising	Chelmsford
129	D./S. Rising	Chelmsford
131	Susannah Rising	Chelmsford
142	S./D. Rising	Chelmsford
153	S./D. Rising	Chelmsford
169	S./D. Rising	Chelmsford
185	Susannah Rising	Chelmsford
202	S./D. Rising	Chelmsford
208	D./S. Rising	Chelmsford
164	Samuel White	Chelmsford
180	Samuel White	Chelmsford
182	Samuel White	Chelmsford
184	Samuel White	Chelmsford
193	Samuel White	Chelmsford
197	Samuel White	Chelmsford
207	Samuel White	Chelmsford
241	Samuel White	Chelmsford
242	Samuel White	Chelmsford
252	Samuel White	Chelmsford
264	Samuel White	Chelmsford

Hampstead, Middlesex

| 101 | William Holden | Chelmsford |
| 103 | William Holden | Chelmsford |

Hayes, Middlesex

676	Dinah Martin	Rochford
687	Dinah Martin	Rochford
691	Dinah Martin	Rochford

Heathrow, Middlesex

| 681 | S. Gepp | Rochford |

Hertford, Hertfordshire

121	Rody Jolliff	Chelmsford
178	Rody Jolliff	Chelmsford
198	Rody Jolliff	Chelmsford
210	Rody Jolliff	Chelmsford
90	Mary Pannel	S Bumpstead

Hilsea, Hampshire

| 617 | Jonathan Sewell | Maldon SM |

Horringer, Suffolk

| 98 | Sarah Arbon | Canewdon |

Hull, Yorkshire

| 288 | Samuel Balls | Colchester SB |

Ingatestone, Essex

703	Jane Hogg	Stanford R
132	Phebea Joice	Chelmsford
83	William Trudget	S Bumpstead

Ipswich, Suffolk

174	Susan Alexander	Chelmsford
377	Benjamin Brooker	Colchester SB
506	Benjamin Brooker	Colchester SP
510	Benjamin Brooker	Colchester SP
521	Benjamin Brooker	Colchester SP
576	William Green	Colchester SP
109	Susannah Halls	Chelmsford
111	Susannah Halls	
123	Susannah Halls	Chelmsford
134	Susannah Halls	Chelmsford
135	Susannah Halls	Chelmsford
156	Susannah Halls	Chelmsford
172	Susannah Halls	Chelmsford
591	E. Harland	Halstead
353	Elizabeth Hines	Colchester SB
356	Elizabeth Hines	Colchester SB
458	Mary Martin	Colchester SP
493	Mary Martin	Colchester SP
300	Mary Mitchel	Colchester SB
304	Sarah Mitchel	Colchester SB
307	Sarah Mitchel	Colchester SB
311	Sarah Mitchel	Colchester SB
314	Sarah Mitchel	Colchester SB
237	Robert Tapple	Chelmsford
21	Phillis Webb	Braintree
22	Phillis Webb	Braintree
31	Phillis Webb	Braintree
33	William Webb	Braintree

Isle of Wight

| 755 | Ellen Humm | Wormingford |
| 756 | Ellen Humm | Wormingford |

Kelvedon, Essex

| 99 | William Ardley | Chelmsford |

Kilby, Leicestershire

| 754 | William Boreham | |

Laindon, Essex

| 12 | Jacob Brown | Gt Bardfield |

Leeds, Yorkshire

| 58 | Edward Orwell | Braintree |

Leicester, Leistershire

| 573 | Ellen Broker | Colchester SP |

No.	Sender	Place of receipt	No.	Sender	Place of receipt
	Leyton, Essex		344	Thomas Hall	Colchester SB
704	E. Shephard	Stanstead MF	345	Thomas Hall	Colchester SB
			346	Thomas Hall	Colchester SB
	London, unspecified		347	Thomas Hall	Colchester SB
84	G. Allam	S Bumpstead	162	Ann Herbert	Chelmsford
417	J. Berry	Colchester	710	Elizabeth Mines	Epping
250	Thomas Carritt	Chelmsford	483	J. Thoroughgood	Colchester SP
327	Rachel Clark	Colchester SB			
332	Rachel Clark	Colchester SB		*London, Bethnal Green*	
333	Rachel Clark	Colchester SB	114	John Argent	Chelmsford
343	Edmund Cross	Colchester SB	26	William King	Braintree
349	Edmund Cross	Colchester SB	32	William King	Braintree
680	Mr W. Gepp	Rochford	62	William King	Braintree
666	E. Goodman	Rayleigh	404	W./M. Mann	Colchester SJ
152	Mary Hearsom	Chelmsford	397	Rachel Shoreg	Colchester SJ
125	Jane Hills	Chelmsford	284	Sarah Withnell	Colchester SB
165	Jane Hills	Chelmsford	286	Sarah Withnell	Colchester SB
168	Jane Hills	Chelmsford	287	Sarah Withnell	Colchester SB
170	Jane Hills	Chelmsford	709	Ann Wood	Coopersale
215	Jane Hills	Chelmsford			
35	William King	Braintree		*London, Chelsea*	
37	William King	Braintree	622	James Taitt	Mundon
38	William King	Braintree			
42	William King	Braintree		*London, Christchurch*	
51	William King	Braintree	157	Arthur Tabrum	Chelmsford
53	William King	Braintree	171	Arthur Tabrum	Chelmsford
54	William King	Braintree	173	Arthur Tabrum	Chelmsford
67	William King	Braintree	179	Arthur Tabrum	Chelmsford
72	William King	Braintree	189	Arthur Tabrum	Chelmsford
74	William King	Braintree	204	Arthur Tabrum	Chelmsford
75	William King	Braintree	200	Arthur Tabrum	Chelmsford
76	William King	Braintree	212	Arthur Tabrum	Chelmsford
128	Ann Marsh		216	Arthur Tabrum	Chelmsford
217	Mercy Pool	Chelmsford	223	Arthur Tabrum	Chelmsford
220	Mercy Pool	Chelmsford	229	Arthur Tabrum	Chelmsford
735	Joseph Rogers	Upminster	234	Arthur Tabrum	Chelmsford
64	John Spearman	Braintree	238	Arthur Tabrum	Chelmsford
71	John Spearman	Braintree	245	Arthur Tabrum	Chelmsford
707	Sarah Stone		260	Arthur Tabrum	Chelmsford
465	J. Thoroughgood	Colchester SP	272	Arthur Tabrum	Chelmsford
352	George Watson	Colchester SB			
359	George Watson	Colchester SB		*London, City*	
360	G./H. Watson	Colchester SB	712	Elizabeth Brown	Theydon M
368	George Watson	Colchester SB	274	Thomas Carritt	Chelmsford
372	George Watson	Colchester SB	278	Henrietta Carritt	Chelmsford
373	George Watson	Colchester SB	621	Isaiah Duce	Mayland
376	George Watson	Colchester SB	167	Jane Hills	Chelmsford
378	George Watson	Colchester SB	285	John Seowen	Colchester SB
			741	Mary-Ann Smith	Upminster
	London, Bermondsey		77	Henry Spearman	Braintree
747	Ann Clark		224	Isaac Wright	Chelmsford
386	Francis Fowler	Colchester SB	236	Isaac Wright	Chelmsford
339	Thomas Hall	Colchester SB			
340	Thomas Hall	Colchester SB		*London, Clerkenwell*	
342	Thomas Hall	Colchester SB	684	S. Beckwith	Rochford

No.	Sender	Place of receipt	No.	Sender	Place of receipt
127	Rachel Brown	Chelmsford		*London, St Anne Soho*	
151	Rachel Brown	Chelmsford	305	Elizabeth Hines	Colchester SB
176	Rachel Brown	Chelmsford	306	Elizabeth Hines	Colchester SB
206	Rachel Brown	Chelmsford	312	Elizabeth Hines	Colchester SB
694	Daniel/Mary Gray	Rochford	361	Elizabeth Hines	Colchester SB
116	David Rivenall	Chelmsford	375	Elizabeth Hines	Colchester SB
225	David Rivenall	Chelmsford	328	George Tye	Colchester SB
743	Mary-Ann Smith	Upminster	334	George Tye	Colchester SB
744	Mary-Ann Smith	Upminster	335	George Tye	Colchester SB
	London, Islington			*London, St George*	
695	Elizabeth Manning	Rochford	402	Sarah Finch	Colchester SJ
696	Elizabeth Manning	Rochford	403	Sarah Finch	Colchester SJ
698	Elizabeth Manning	Rochford	113	Mary Hearsom	Chelmsford
	London, Kensington			*London, St George, Hanover Square*	
199	Eliza Jackson	Chelmsford	211	Mercy Pool	Chelmsford
	London, Lambeth			*London, St George in the East*	
118	Isaac Harridge	Chelmsford	316	James Clark	Colchester SB
102	Mary Munrow	Chelmsford	546	Elizabeth Norman	Colchester SP
106	Mary Munrow	Chelmsford	547	Elizabeth Norman	Colchester SP
107	Mary Munrow	Chelmsford	548	Elizabeth Norman	Colchester SP
117	Mary Munrow	Chelmsford	104	David Rivenall	Chelmsford
7	Elizabeth Sheepard	Aveley	115	David Rivenall	Chelmsford
247	John Wybrow	Chelmsford	130	David Rivenall	Chelmsford
			139	David Rivenall	Chelmsford
	London, Mile End New Town		146	David Rivenall	Chelmsford
6	Mary Wood	Aveley	175	D./S. Rivenall	Chelmsford
			181	D./S. Rivenall	Chelmsford
	London, Mile End Old Town		183	D./S. Rivenall	Chelmsford
668	Eliz. Goodman	Rayleigh	186	David Rivenall	Chelmsford
669	Eliz. Goodman	Rayleigh	188	S./D. Rivenall	Chelmsford
670	Eliz. Goodman	Rayleigh	190	D./S. Rivenall	Chelmsford
671	Eliz. Goodman	Rayleigh	191	D./S. Rivenall	Chelmsford
673	Eliz. Goodman	Rayleigh	192	David Rivenall	Chelmsford
674	Eliz. Goodman	Rayleigh	194	David Rivenall	Chelmsford
267	Jane Wall	Chelmsford	196	David Rivenall	Chelmsford
			201	David Rivenall	Chelmsford
			203	David Rivenall	Chelmsford
	London, Newington		205	David Rivenall	Chelmsford
137	Thomas Carritt	Chelmsford	209	David Rivenall	Chelmsford
154	Thomas Carritt	Chelmsford	218	David Rivenall	Chelmsford
214	Isaac Harridge	Chelmsford	221	David Rivenall	Chelmsford
406	James Russell	Colchester SJ	231	David Rivenall	Chelmsford
408	James Russell	Colchester SJ	232	David Rivenall	Chelmsford
			239	David Rivenall	Chelmsford
	London, St Andrew Holborn		244	Sarah Rivenall	Chelmsford
270	Sarah Albra	Chelmsford	249	David Rivenall	Chelmsford
623	Ann Burder	Mundon	257	David Rivenall	Chelmsford
624	Ann Burder	Mundon	262	David Rivenall	Chelmsford
631	Ann Burder	Mundon	265	Sarah Rivenall	Chelmsford
632	Ann Burder	Mundon	275	David Rivenall	Chelmsford
637	Ann Burder	Mundon	277	Sarah Rivenall	Chelmsford
638	Ann Burder	Mundon	248	Isabella Weeden	Chelmsford

No.	Sender	Place of receipt
London, St Giles-in-the-Fields		
85	Mary Ann Page	S Bumpstead
London, St Luke Old Street		
338	Elizabeth Lane	Colchester SB
348	Elizabeth Lane	Colchester SB
354	Elizabeth Lane	Colchester SB
355	Elizabeth Lane	Colchester SB
London, St Martin-in-the-Fields		
324	S./J. Moore	Colchester SB
329	S./J. Moore	Colchester SB
331	S./J. Moore	Colchester SB
336	S./J. Moore	Colchester SB
337	S./J. Moore	Colchester SB
London, St Marylebone		
742	Francis Freeman	Upminster
401	J. Harden	Colchester SJ
110	Samuel Hearsum	Chelmsford
246	Samuel Hearsum	Chelmsford
228	William Holden	Chelmsford
230	William Holden	Chelmsford
243	William Holden	Chelmsford
263	William Holden	Chelmsford
87	Ann Trudgett	S Bumpstead
566	William Watson	Colchester SP
London, St Pancras		
271	W./S. Duke	Chelmsford
55	Maria Godfry	Braintree
65	Maria Godfry	Braintree
69	Maria Godfry	Braintree
70	Maria Godfry	Braintree
73	Maria Godfry	Braintree
28	James Smith	Braintree
34	Mary Smith	Braintree
London, St Saviour		
393	James Bottom	Colchester SB
120	Arthur Tabrum	Chelmsford
London, St Thomas		
752	James Randall	S Weald
London, Shoreditch		
663	E. Goodman	Rayleigh
664	E. Goodman	Rayleigh
665	E. Goodman	Rayleigh
46	James Gray	Braintree
48	James Gray	Braintree
388	John Harvey	Colchester SB
133	Ann Marsh	Chelmsford
667	E. Smith	Rayleigh

No.	Sender	Place of receipt
282	George Watson	Colchester SB
320	George Watson	Colchester SB
London, Spitalfields		
97	William Pryor	Gt Burstead
London, Stepney		
256	Mary Mason	Chelmsford
258	W./M. Mason	Chelmsford
London, Westminster		
470	George Craddock	Colchester SP
476	George Craddock	Colchester SP
489	George Craddock	Colchester SP
494	George Craddock	Colchester SP
497	George Craddock	Colchester SP
499	George Craddock	Colchester SP
500	George Craddock	Colchester SP
501	George Craddock	Colchester SP
503	George Craddock	Colchester SP
504	George Craddock	Colchester SP
508	George Craddock	Colchester SP
512	George Craddock	Colchester SP
513	George Craddock	Colchester SP
514	George Craddock	Colchester SP
516	George Craddock	Colchester SP
520	Ann Craddock	Colchester SP
522	George Craddock	Colchester SP
523	George Craddock	Colchester SP
524	George Craddock	Colchester SP
526	George Craddock	Colchester SP
528	George Craddock	Colchester SP
530	George Craddock	Colchester SP
532	George Craddock	Colchester SP
537	Ann Craddock	Colchester SP
555	George Craddock	Colchester SP
556	George Craddock	Colchester SP
124	Jane Hills	Chelmsford
177	Jane Hills	Chelmsford
187	Jane Hills	Chelmsford
289	Mary Rabey	Colchester SB
662	Mrs. Reilley	Rayleigh
London, Whitechapel		
717	Edward Abbott	Tolleshunt DA
387	James Anderson	Colchester SB
389	James Anderson	Colchester SB
390	Eliz. Anderson	Colchester SB
650	Thomas Briggs	Rainham
651	Thomas Briggs	Rainham
308	Sarah Davis	Colchester SB
126	Mrs Death	Chelmsford
251	David Rivenall	Chelmsford
57	John Spearman	Braintree

No.	Sender	Place of receipt
59	John Spearman	Braintree
60	John Spearman	Braintree
61	John Spearman	Braintree

Maldon, Essex

369	John Balls	Colchester SB
371	John Balls	Colchester SB
391	Mary Balls	Colchester SB
629	Mary Keeling	Mundon

Mendlesham, Suffolk

407	Charlotte Game	Colchester SJ

Mersea, Essex

392	Marian Nevill	Colchester SB

Mildenhall, Suffolk

158	Susan Bright	Chelmsford
161	Susan Bright	Chelmsford

Mitcham, Surrey

219	Isaac Betts	Chelmsford

Needham Market, Suffolk

598	Jane Pooley	Kirby LS

Newmarket, Suffolk

82	Thomas Turner	S Bumpstead

Northfleet, Kent

718	Ann Sinclair	Upminster
719	Ann Sinclair	Upminster

Norwich, Norfolk

15	Thomas Elsegood	Braintree
47	William Goodwin	Braintree
14	George Smee	Braintree
19	George Smee	Braintree
52	James Smee	Braintree
18	Samuel Spooner	Braintree
23	Samuel Spooner	Braintree
24	Samuel Spooner	Braintree
66	Susan Spooner	Braintree
515	William Wilsher	Colchester SP
517	William Wilsher	Colchester SP
561	William Wilsher	Colchester SP
564	William Wilsher	Colchester SP
570	William Wilsher	Colchester SP
580	William Wilsher	Colchester SP
581	William Wilsher	Colchester SP

Nottingham, Nottinghamshire

661	Lucy Shuttleworth	Rayleigh

No.	Sender	Place of receipt

Plaistow, Essex

713	Harriet Baker	Theydon M

Portchester, Hampshire

618	Jonathan Sewell	Maldon SM
620	Jonathan Sewell	Maldon SM

Portsmouth, Hampshire

507	Robert Gosling	Colchester SP
616	Jonathan Sewell	Maldon SM

Rainham, Essex

645	Mary Pavett	Stratford

Rayleigh, Essex

325	George Little	Colchester SB

Rickmansworth, Hertfordshire

640	Mrs Wilkinson	W Notley
641	Mrs Wilkinson	W Notley

Rochester, Kent

490	Mr Player	Colchester SP

Rochford, Essex

656	Ann Benson	Rayleigh
639	Ann Pepper	Navestock

Romford, Essex

100	William Ardley	Chelmsford
583	George Baynall	Colchester SP
659	Thomas Brown	Rayleigh
416	Widow Sheperd	Colchester SP
351	Mrs D. Springet	Colchester SB
357	R. Springet	Colchester SB
365	R. Springet	Colchester SB
374	R. Springet	Colchester SB
625	John Thurtell	Mundon
626	John Thurtell	Mundon
627	John Thurtell	Mundon
628	John Thurtell	Mundon
630	J. Thurtell	Mundon
633	John Thurtell	Mundon
634	John Thurtell	Mundon
635	John Thurtell	Mundon

Rushbrooke, Suffolk

685	Mary Craske	Rochford

Rye, Sussex

711	Hannah Collesson	Theydon G.

Setchey, Norfolk

379	Robert Ray	Colchester SB

No.	Sender	Place of receipt

Sheerness, Kent
| 405 | John Enos | Colchester |
| 693 | Robert Hoy | Rochford |

Sheffield, Yorkshire
| 91 | Edward Roads | S Bumpstead |
| 92 | Edward Roads | S Bumpstead |

Shipley, Sussex
| 686 | Lucy Humphreys | Rochford |

Southminster, Essex
| 655 | Ann Prigg | Rayleigh |

Springfield, Essex
| 654 | Thomas Sagger | Rayleigh |

Stratford, Essex
119	Sarah Manning	Chelmsford
160	Sarah Manning	Chelmsford
195	Sarah Manning	Chelmsford
213	Sarah Manning	Chelmsford
226	Sarah Manning	Chelmsford
240	Mr Manning	Chelmsford
255	Sarah Manning	Chelmsford
259	Sarah Manning	Chelmsford
268	Sarah Manning	Chelmsford
276	Sarah Manning	Chelmsford
642	James Wells	Peldon
399	J./C. Wire	Colchester SJ
400	J./C. Wire	Colchester SJ

Strokestow, Roscommon, Ireland
| 604 | Mary Harris | Kirby LS |

Sudbury, Suffolk
381	Ann Bacon	Colchester SB
317	William/Ann Lester	Colchester SB
358	Ann Lester	Colchester SB
370	Ann Lester	Colchester SB
753	William Rolf	Woodford

Sutton, Surrey
| 10 | John Smith | |

Thaxted, Essex
| 136 | Sarah Baynes | Chelmsford |
| 144 | Sarah Baynes | Chelmsford |

Theydon Garnon, Essex
| 705 | Mary Howe | Theydon G |

Thorpe-le-Soken, Essex
| 105 | William Day | Chelmsford |

No.	Sender	Place of receipt

Thundersley, Essex
| 383 | George Little | Colchester SB |

Thurston, Suffolk
| 683 | Mary Craske | Rochford |

Torpoint, Cornwall
| 615 | Richard Kimberley | Lexden |

Upminster, Essex
| 745 | B. Crowest | Upminster |
| 56 | Abraham Stuck | Braintree |

Great Wakering, Essex
588	Isaac Milbourn	Gt Dunmow
688	Thomas Sadler	Rochford
677	Joseph Skewer	Rochford
678	Joseph Skewer	Rochford

Little Wakering, Essex
| 682 | Ann Rayner | Rochford |

Wethersfield, Essex
| 433 | Thomas Mills | Colchester SP |
| 63 | John Smoothy | Braintree |

Whitestable, Kent
| 589 | Jemima Wetherly | Lt Dunmow |

Whitton, Suffolk
424	Benjamin Hewitt	Colchester SP
426	Benjamin Hewitt	Colchester SP
428	Benjamin Hewitt	Colchester SP
460	Benjamin Hewitt	Colchester SP
466	Benjamin Hewitt	Colchester SP
467	Benjamin Hewitt	Colchester SP
469	Benjamin Hewitt	Colchester SP
480	Benjamin Hewitt	Colchester SP
495	Benjamin Hewitt	Colchester SP
531	Benjamin Hewitt	Colchester SP
533	Benjamin Hewitt	Colchester SP
544	Benjamin Hewitt	Colchester SP
545	Benjamin Hewitt	Colchester SP
554	Benjamin Hewitt	Colchester SP
571	Benjamin Hewitt	Colchester SP
572	Benjamin Hewitt	Colchester SP
575	Benjamin Hewitt	Colchester SP
582	Benjamin Hewitt	Colchester SP

Wickham St Pauls, Essex
| 86 | Mrs Mansfield | S Bumpstead |

Widford, Essex
| 708 | Widow Camp | Coopersale |

No.	Sender	Place of receipt	No.	Sender	Place of receipt

Wivenhoe, Essex

No.	Sender	Place of receipt
619	Ann Doubty	Maldon SM
269	Elizabeth Philbrick	Chelmsford

Woolwich, Kent

No.	Sender	Place of receipt
323	Anonymous	Colchester SB
138	Thomas Cooper	Chelmsford
141	Ann Cooper	Chelmsford
143	T./A. Cooper	Chelmsford
145	Ann Cooper	Chelmsford
147	Ann Cooper	Chelmsford
148	Ann Cooper	Chelmsford
149	Ann Cooper	Chelmsford
150	Ann Cooper	Chelmsford
163	T./A. Cooper	Chelmsford
166	Ann Cooper	Chelmsford
749	Rebecca Robinson	S Weald
2	James Smith	Aveley
3	James Smith	Aveley
4	James Smith	Aveley
5	James Smith	Aveley
8	James Smith	Aveley

Great Yarmouth, Norfolk

No.	Sender	Place of receipt
599	Mary Hill	Kirby LS
600	Mary Hill	Kirby LS
607	Mary Hill	Kirby LS
610	Mary Hill	Kirby LS
611	Mary Hill	Kirby LS
597	Mary Snell	Kirby LS

Place not traced

No.	Sender	Place of receipt	No.	Sender	Place of receipt
590	Anonymous	Lt Dunmow	715	George Oliver	W Thurrock
699	Ann Benson	Rochford	750	Mrs Robinson	
413	James Blatch	Colchester SJ	442	George Rowe	Colchester SP
700	J. Borcham		449	George Rowe	Colchester SP
636	Mrs Brown	Mundon	525	George Rowe	Colchester SP
395	Isaac Bugg	Colchester SB	155	Daniel Rust	Chelmsford
96	William Catt	Gt Burstead	159	Daniel Rust	Chelmsford
9	E. Feild	Aveley	25	Samuel Spooner	Braintree
592	William Gale	Halstead	702	S. Stearns	
653	Ann Gossling	Rainham	411	Mary Sumner	Colchester SJ
652	Amy Hill	Rainham	366	George John Tye	Colchester SB
675	Maria Hurrell	Rayleigh	367	George John Tye	Colchester SB
577	James Ludbrook	Colchester SP	384	George John Tye	Colchester SB
579	James Ludbrook	Colchester SP	385	George John Tye	Colchester SB
706	Mary Marshall	Theydon G	647	Mrs Wall	Rainham
427	Thomas Mills	Colchester SP	748	T. Woodward	Wanstead

List A.2: Essex Pauper Letters, 1731-1837, by sender

No.	Sender	Date
717	Edward Abbott	27 Apr 1801
89	Thomas Albion	9 Nov 1833
93	Thomas Albion	26 Mar 1837
270	Sarah Albra	16 Apr 1829
84	G. Allam	28 Jul 1817
387	James Anderson	8 Dec 1829
389	James Anderson	1 Dec 1830
390	E. Anderson	15 Dec 1830
323	*Anonymous*	29 Mar 1826
590	*Anonymous*	
98	Sarah Arbon	21 Sep 1825
99	William Ardley	15 Oct 1820
100	William Ardley	17 Jan 1823
114	John Argent	28 Apr 1824
692	Sarah Ateradge	8 Jul 1810
380	Elizabeth Baker	15 Sep 1828
713	Harriet Baker	21 Mar 1831
410	Lucy Baley	
369	John Balls	25 Mar 1828
371	John Balls	7 Apr 1828
391	Mary Balls	16 Apr 1833
288	Samuel Balls	14 Jan 1816
17	John Barnes	24 Jul 1827
583	George Baynall	2 Mar 1835
136	Sarah Baynes	18 Dec 1824
144	Sarah Baynes	2 Feb 1825
684	S. Beckwith	27 May 1807
656	Ann Benson	26 Feb 1825
699	Ann Benson	
417	J. Berry	19 Jul 1818
219	Isaac Betts	17 May 1827

No.	Sender	Date
413	James Blatch	1817
700	J. Borcham	12 Nov
754	William Boreham	1 Dec 1836
393	James Bottom	5 Aug 1835
586	Mary Braig	12 Sep
43	Joseph Brand	15 Apr 1831
49	Joseph Brand	18 Jul 1831
279	Thomas Bray	12 Mar 1788
552	Elizabeth Brigg	18 Dec 1828
650	Thomas Briggs	27 Jan 1806
651	Thomas Briggs	24 Mar 1806
158	Susan Bright	19 May 1825
161	Susan Bright	29 May 1825
573	Ellen Broker	20 Jan 1834
377	Benjamin Brooker	10 Jul 1828
506	Benjamin Brooker	7 Nov 1825
510	Benjamin Brooker	
521	Benjamin Brooker	Apr 1826
689	Mary Brooks	17 Nov 1809
690	Mary Brooks	
712	Elizabeth Brown	30 Dec 1769
12	Jacob Brown	
636	Mrs Brown	
127	Rachel Brown	26 Jul 1824
151	Rachel Brown	18 Apr 1825
176	Rachel Brown	27 Dec 1825
206	Rachel Brown	15 Jan 1827
659	Thomas Brown	14 Aug 1826
395	Isaac Bugg	
623	Ann Burder	9 Apr 1820
624	Ann Burder	3 Feb 1821
631	Ann Burder	21 Dec 1832
632	Ann Burder	25 Sep 1833

No.	Sender	Date	No.	Sender	Date
637	Ann Burder	11 Jan	500	George Craddock	17 Aug 1825
638	Ann Burder	21 Apr	501	George Craddock	5 Sep 1825
			503	George Craddock	5 Oct 1825
708	Widow Camp	12 Jul 1759	504	George Craddock	22 Oct 1825
			508	George Craddock	29 Nov 1825
78	John Cardinal	29 Jun 1835	512	George Craddock	20 Dec 1825
			513	George Craddock	11 Jan 1826
137	Thomas Carritt	21 Dec 1824	514	George Craddock	31 Jan 1826
154	Thomas Carritt	7 May 1825	516	George Craddock	21 Feb 1826
250	Thomas Carritt	13 Sep 1828	520	Ann Craddock	17 Apr 1826
253	Thomas Carritt	14 Oct 1828	522	George Craddock	19 Jul 1826
254	Thomas Carritt	26 Oct 1828	523	George Craddock	21 Aug 1826
274	Thomas Carritt	18 May 1829	524	George Craddock	30 Aug 1826
278	Henrietta Carritt	10 Jun 1829	526	George Craddock	3 Oct 1826
			528	George Craddock	12 Dec 1826
96	William Catt		530	George Craddock	20 Dec 1826
			532	George Craddock	7 Feb 1827
326	Sarah Challis	1 Aug 1826	537	Ann Craddock	24 Apr 1827
			542	George Craddock	3 Nov 1827
747	Ann Clark	9 Oct 1768	555	George Craddock	9 Feb 1829
			556	George Craddock	17 Feb 1829
316	James Clark	9 Jul 1819			
327	Rachel Clark	7 Aug 1826	683	Mary Craske	11 May 1807
332	Rachel Clark	5 Sep 1826	685	Mary Craske	26 Feb 1809
333	Rachel Clark	5 Sep 1826			
			343	Edmund Cross	13 Jan 1827
16	Thomas Cleare	29 Jan 1827	349	Edmund Cross	20 Feb 1827
79	Thomas Cleare				
			281	Jane Cross	24 Apr 1755
711	Hannah Collesson	18 Oct 1819			
			745	J. B. Crowest	13 Mar 1819
233	Hugh Constable	23 Nov 1827			
235	Hugh Constable	2 Dec 1827	603	James Davey	12 Jul 1832
			606	Elizabeth Davey	19 Feb 1833
138	Thomas Cooper	10 Jan 1825	612	James Davey	10 Jun 1834
141	Ann Cooper	22 Jan 1825	613	James Davey	23 Jun 1834
143	T./A. Cooper	28 Jan 1825	614	James Davey	23 Nov 1835
145	Ann Cooper	11 Feb 1825			
147	Ann Cooper	25 Feb 1825	105	William Day	7 Dec 1823
148	Ann Cooper	3 Mar 1825			
149	Ann Cooper	12 Mar 1825	126	Hannah Death	8 Jul 1824
150	Ann Cooper	27 Mar 1825			
163	T./A. Cooper	20 Jun 1825	539	Mary Death	4 Sep 1827
166	Ann Cooper	1 Jul 1825			
			11	John Dennison	3 May 1836
409	Mary Cooper	16 Jun 1833			
			88	Joseph Derham	19 Mar 1833
30	Maria Cousins	16 Dec 1828			
			619	Ann Doubty	2 Jul 1813
470	George Craddock	16 Jul 1823			
476	George Craddock	19 Jan 1824	621	Isaiah Duce	29 Mar 1822
489	George Craddock	6 Oct 1824			
494	George Craddock	23 Feb 1825	271	William/S. Duke	20 Apr 1829
497	George Craddock	13 Jul 1825			
499	George Craddock	1 Aug 1825	15	Thomas Elsegood	22 May 1826

No.	Sender	Date	No.	Sender	Date
405	John Enos	17 Jan 1817	576	William Green	20 Feb 1834
716	Eliza Farrant	10 Feb 1809	222	Robert Griffith	25 May 1827
9	E. Feild		283	John Hall	8 Dec 1814
			290	John Hall	6 May 1816
394	Sarah Finch	1 Jan 1836	292	John Hall	19 Mar 1817
402	Sarah Finch	13 Jan 1814	296	John Hall	5 Jun 1817
403	Sarah Finch	24 Jan 1814	297	John Hall	26 Aug 1818
			298	John Hall	9 Sep 1818
386	Francis Fowler	Oct 1829	299	John Hall	24 Sep 1818
			302	John Hall	11 Dec 1818
742	Francis Freeman	5 Mar 1813	303	John Hall	21 Dec 1818
			309	John Hall	5 Feb 1819
592	William Gale	26 Aug 1835	310	John Hall	11 Feb 1819
			318	John Hall	6 Sep 1819
407	Charlotte Game	8 Apr 1833	319	John Hall	12 Nov 1819
			330	John Hall	3 Sep 1826
593	Ann Garner	16 Apr 1795	341	John Hall	11 Jan 1827
680	Mr W. Gepp	8 Nov 1804	291	Sarah Hall	4 Mar 1817
			293	Sarah Hall	31 Mar 1817
681	S. Gepp	13 Dec 1804	294	Sarah Hall	24 Apr 1817
			295	Sarah Hall	20 May 817
20	John Gibson	18 Jun 1828	131	Sarah Hall	21 Jun 1819
			315	Sarah Hall	2 Jul 1819
55	Maria Godfry	23 Oct 1832	321	Sarah Hall	15 Mar 1820
65	Maria Godfry	18 Jun 1833			
69	Maria Godfry	23 Sep 1833	339	Thomas Hall	20 Dec 1826
70	Maria Godfry	25 Sep 1833	340	Thomas Hall	4 Jan 1827
73	Maria Godfry	21 Apr 1834	342	Thomas Hall	11 Jan 1827
			344	Thomas Hall	18 Jan 1827
663	Eliz. Goodman	25 Jun 1831	345	Thomas Hall	25 Jan 1827
664	Eliz. Goodman	3 Sep 1831	346	Thomas Hall	28 Jan 1827
665	Eliz. Goodman	26 Jan 1832	347	Thomas Hall	5 Feb 1827
666	Eliz. Goodman	26 Dec 1832			
668	Eliz. Goodman	1 Oct 1833	109	Susannah Halls	1 Feb 1824
669	Eliz. Goodman	23 Dec 1833	111	Susannah Halls	5 Feb 1824
670	Eliz. Goodman	19 May 1834	123	Susannah Halls	21 Jun 1824
671	Eliz. Goodman	28 Aug 1834	134	Susannah Halls	4 Nov 1824
673	Eliz. Goodman	18 Dec 1834	135	Susannah Halls	Nov 1824
674	Eliz. Goodman	23 Dec 1834	156	Susannah Halls	15 May 1825
			172	Susannah Halls	
47	William Goodwin	1 Jul 1831	174	Susan Alexander	15 Nov 1825
				[*daughter of* Susannah Hall]	
363	Thomas Goody	9 Feb 1828			
			401	J. Harden	2 Jul 1813
507	Robert Gosling	13 Nov 1825			
			591	E. Harland	2 Aug 1835
653	Ann Gossling				
			118	Isaac Harridge	10 Jun 1824
694	Daniel/Mary Gray	8 Sep 1823	214	Isaac Harridge	19 Mar 1827
46	James Gray	11 Jun 1831	601	Mary Harris	22 Feb 1832
48	James Gray	2 Jul 1831	602	Mary Harris	18 May 1832

No.	Sender	Date	No.	Sender	Date
604	Mary Harris	14 Sep 1832	124	Jane Hills	29 Jun 1824
605	Mary Harris	12 Dec 1832	125	Jane Hills	7 Jul 1824
608	Mary Harris	20 Jun 1833	165	Jane Hills	27 Jun 1825
609	Mary Harris	18 Sep 1833	167	Jane Hills	14 Jul 1825
			168	Jane Hills	1 Oct 1825
388	John Harvey	18 Aug 1830	170	Jane Hills	5 Oct 1825
			177	Jane Hills	29 Dec 1825
429	William Harvey	23 Jun 1820	187	Jane Hills	28 Mar 1826
431	William Harvey	6 Jul 1820	215	Jane Hills	28 Mar 1827
301	James Haxell	10 Dec 1818	305	Elizabeth Hines	1818
			306	Elizabeth Hines	1818
113	Mary Hearsom	10 Mar 1824	312	Elizabeth Hines	9 May 1819
152	Mary Hearsom	18 Apr 1825	353	Elizabeth Hines	27 Jul 1827
			356	Elizabeth Hines	27 Sep 1827
110	Samuel Hearsum	5 Feb 1824	361	Elizabeth Hines	1 Jan 1828
246	Samuel Hearsum	11 Jul 1828	375	Elizabeth Hines	18 Jun 1828
162	Ann Herbert	1 Jun 1825	13	Ann Hitchcock	22 Dec 1823
424	Benjamin Hewitt	31 Mar 1819	703	Jane Hogg	12 Jan 1824
426	Benjamin Hewitt	23 Sep 1819			
428	Benjamin Hewitt	12 Apr 1820	101	William Holden	29 Jul 1823
460	Benjamin Hewitt	20 Jan 1823	103	William Holden	15 Nov 1823
466	Benjamin Hewitt	6 Jun 1823	228	William Holden	1 Oct 1827
467	Benjamin Hewitt	17 Jun 1823	230	William Holden	22 Oct 1827
469	Benjamin Hewitt	30 Jun 1823	243	William Holden	2 Jun 1828
480	Benjamin Hewitt	23 Mar 1824	263	William Holden	10 Feb 1829
495	Benjamin Hewitt	13 May 1825			
531	Benjamin Hewitt	8 Jan 1827	705	Mary Howe	13 Jan 1731
533	Benjamin Hewitt	16 Feb 1827			
544	Benjamin Hewitt	11 Dec 1827	415	James Howell	16 Feb 1818
545	Benjamin Hewitt	18 Feb 1828	420	James Howell	13 Sep 1818
554	Benjamin Hewitt	Jan 1829	441	James Howell	31 Jul 1821
571	Benjamin Hewitt	2 Jan 1834	446	James Howell	13 Oct 1821
572	Benjamin Hewitt	6 Jan 1834	455	James Howell	Jul 1822
575	Benjamin Hewitt	13 Feb 1834	456	James Howell	5 Aug 1822
582	Benjamin Hewitt	19 Jan 1835	471	James Howell	4 Aug 1823
			482	James Howell	16 Apr 1824
721	John Hicks	29 Dec 1802	487	James Howell	24 Jul 1824
726	John Hicks	2 Mar 1804	553	J./M. Howell	20 Jan 1829
728	John Hicks	20 Mar 1804	560	Margaret Howell	16 Apr 1832
731	John Hicks	29 Aug 1804	563	Margaret Howell	3 Oct 1832
733	John Hicks	2 Jan 1805	565	James Howell	16 Jan 1833
740	John Hicks	4 Jul 1806	568	James Howell	14 Oct 1833
			574	James Howell	30 Jan 1834
646	Amy Hill	19 Mar 1801	578	James Howell	1 May 1834
649	Amy Hill	12 Dec 1805	584	J./M. Howell	1 Apr 1835
652	Amy Hill	27 Mar 1815			
			587	Hannah Hoy	13 Oct 1818
599	Mary Hill	30 Jul 1828			
600	Mary Hill	26 May 1829	693	Robert Hoy	25 Aug 1811
607	Mary Hill	3 Jun 1833			
610	Mary Hill	5 Feb 1834	755	Ellen Humm	30 Apr 1824
611	Mary Hill	3 Mar 1834	756	Ellen Humm	10 May 1824

No.	Sender	Date
686	Lucy Humphreys	18 Apr 1809
675	Maria Hurrell	2 Mar 1835
199	Eliza Jackson	27 Aug 1826
418	William James	20 Jul 1818
419	William James	7 Aug 1818
421	William James	19 Sep 1818
422	William James	18 Mar 1819
423	William James	18 Mar 1819
425	William James	11 Aug 1819
430	William James	29 Jun 1820
432	William James	10 Sep 1820
434	William James	30 Dec 1820
435	William James	11 Jan 1821
437	William James	29 Mar 1821
438	William James	5 Apr 1821
439	William James	31 May 1821
443	William James	30 Aug 1821
444	William James	5 Sep 1821
445	William James	25 Sep 1821
447	William James	18 Oct 1821
448	William James	1 Jan 1822
450	William James	27 Mar 1822
451	William James	20 May 1822
452	William James	25 May 1822
453	William James	28 May 1822
454	William James	29 Jul 1822
457	William James	30 Sep 1822
461	William James	25 Feb 1823
462	William James	26 Feb 1823
464	William James	25 Mar 1823
468	William James	25 Jun 1823
472	William James	28 Sep 1823
475	William James	14 Dec 1823
477	William James	24 Jan 1824
478	William James	7 Feb 1824
479	William James	1 Mar 1824
481	William James	30 Mar 1824
484	William James	Apr 1824
486	William James	25 Jun 1824
488	William James	27 Sep 1824
491	William James	28 Dec 1824
496	William James	22 Jun 1825
502	William James	26 Sep 1825
505	William James	2 Nov 1825
509	William James	30 Nov 1825
511	William James	16 Dec 1825
519	William James	14 Mar 1826
527	William James	13 Nov 1826
529	William James	12 Dec 1826
534	William James	17 Mar 1827
535	William James	20 Mar 1827
538	William James	20 Jun 1827

No.	Sender	Date
540	William James	7 Sep 1827
541	William James	13 Sep 1827
543	William James	8 Nov 1827
550	William James	28 Sep 1828
132	Phebea Joice	11 Oct 1824
121	Rody Jolliff	12 Jun 1824
178	Rody Jolliff	2 Jan 1826
198	Rody Jolliff	15 Aug 1826
210	Rody Jolliff	2 Feb 1827
629	Mary Keeling	28 Oct 1832
714	Thomas Kellnby	20 Apr 1831
615	Richard Kimberley	27 Feb 1834
722	Richard King	28 Apr 1803
723	Richard King	14 Aug 1803
724	Richard King	9 Oct 1803
725	Richard King	13 Nov 1803
727	Richard King	18 Mar 1804
729	Richard King	22 Apr 1804
730	Richard King	1 Jul 1804
732	Richard King	16 Dec 1804
734	Richard King	9 Apr 1805
736	Richard King	14 Oct 1805
737	Ann King	19 Nov 1805
738	Ann King	29 Nov 1805
739	Richard King	9 Feb 1806
26	William King	20 Nov 1828
32	William King	30 Apr 1829
35	William King	5 Aug 1829
37	William King	25 Feb 1830
38	William King	12 Mar 1830
42	William King	9 Apr 1831
51	William King	16 Dec 1831
53	William King	18 Jul 1832
54	William King	18 Oct 1832
62	William King	11 May 1833
67	William King	17 Jul 1833
72	William King	4 Mar 1834
74	William King	31 Jul 1834
75	William King	Sep 1834
76	William King	2 Oct 1834
338	Elizabeth Lane	12 Dec 1826
348	Elizabeth Lane	7 Feb 1827
354	Elizabeth Lane	20 Aug 1827
355	Elizabeth Lane	23 Aug 1827
751	Mary Lee	4 Jan 1819

No.	Sender	Date	No.	Sender	Date
317	William/A. Lester	30 Aug 1819	256	Mary Mason	21 Nov 1828
358	Ann Lester	13 Nov 1827	258	W./M. Mason	30 Nov 1828
370	Ann Lester	1 Apr 1828			
381	Ann Bacon	19 Sep 1828	398	Mary Mayden	30 Sep 1811
	[*former* Ann Lester]				
			588	Isaac Milbourn	31 Dec 1818
40	Stephen Linzell	27 Sep 1830			
44	Stephen Linzell	18 Apr 1831	559	Edward Mills	Feb 1832
50	Stephen Linzell	24 Nov 1831	562	Edward Mills	23 Sep 1832
			567	Edward Mills	9 May 1833
325	George Little	26 Jul 1826	569	Edward Mills	28 Oct 1833
383	George Little	8 Oct 1828			
			427	Thomas Mills	6 Oct 1819
577	James Ludbrook	23 Apr 1834	433	Thomas Mills	19 Oct 1820
579	James Ludbrook	12 Jul 1834			
			710	Elizabeth Mines	1808
746	T./M. Lutterell	19 Aug 1834			
			300	Mary Mitchel	30 Sep 1818
404	William/M. Mann	21 Mar 1814			
			304	Sarah Mitchel	29 Dec 1818
695	Eliz. Manning	12 Nov 1829	307	Sarah Mitchel	4 Jan 1819
696	Eliz. Manning	4 Jan 1830	311	Sarah Mitchel	30 Mar 1819
698	Eliz. Manning	25 Feb 1830	314	Sarah Mitchel	29 Jun 1819
119	Sarah Manning	11 Jun 1824	324	S./J. Moore	7 Jun 1826
160	Sarah Manning	26 May 1825	329	S./J. Moore	24 Aug 1826
195	Sarah Manning	26 Jul 1826	331	S./J. Moore	4 Sep 1826
213	Sarah Manning	19 Feb 1827	336	S./J. Moore	12 Sep 1826
226	Sarah Manning	28 Aug 1827	337	S./J. Moore	19 Oct 1826
240	Mr Manning	14 May 1828			
255	Sarah Manning	27 Oct 1828	280	Thomas Morse	12 Mar 1750
259	Sarah Manning	4 Dec 1828			
268	Sarah Manning	13 Apr 1829	102	Mary Munrow	9 Nov 1823
276	Sarah Manning	21 May 1829	106	Mary Munrow	18 Dec 1823
			107	Mary Munrow	29 Jan 1824
86	Hannah Mansfield	5 Jan 1827	117	Mary Munrow	4 Jun 1824
128	Ann Marsh	26 Jul 1824	122	Lucy Nevill	16 Jun 1824
133	Ann Marsh	11 Oct 1824	140	Lucy Nevill	15 Jan 1825
68	William Marsh	22 Sep 1833	392	Marian Nevill	15 Nov 1834
706	Mary Marshall	1 Sep 1736	227	Philip Noon	24 Sep 1827
676	Dinah Martin	11 Feb 1803	546	Elizabeth Norman	19 Feb 1828
687	Dinah Martin	24 Aug 1809	547	Elizabeth Norman	14 Mar 1828
691	Dinah Martin	1 Jul 1810	548	Elizabeth Norman	23 Apr 1828
458	Mary Martin	13 Dec 1822	715	George Oliver	1770
493	Mary Martin	21 Jan 1825			
			58	Edward Orwell	3 Dec 1832
679	John Maseon	12 Aug 1804			
701	J./E. Maseon	30 Apr	85	Mary Ann Page	27 Sep 1825

No.	Sender	Date	No.	Sender	Date
90	Mary Pannel	22 Dec 1835	116	David Rivenall	29 May 1824
			130	David Rivenall	2 Aug 1824
95	G./M. Pateman	7 Jun 1834	139	David Rivenall	12 Jan 1825
			146	David Rivenall	22 Feb 1825
645	Mary Pavett	2 Mar 1748	175	D./S. Rivenall	15 Nov 1825
			181	D./S. Rivenall	30 Jan 1826
639	Ann Pepper	8 Sep 1829	183	D./S. Rivenall	27 Feb 1826
			186	David Rivenall	13 Mar 1826
269	Elizabeth Philbrick	14 Apr 1829	188	S./D. Rivenall	28 Mar 1826
			190	D./S. Rivenall	26 Apr 1826
382	Susan Pitt	6 Oct 1828	191	D./S. Rivenall	10 May 1826
			192	David Rivenall	May 1826
490	Mr Player	6 Dec 1824	194	David Rivenall	18 Jul 1826
			196	David Rivenall	29 Jul 1826
485	Richard Player	11 May 1824	201	David Rivenall	27 Sep 1826
			203	David Rivenall	12 Oct 1826
211	Mercy Poole	12 Feb 1827	205	David Rivenall	15 Dec 1826
217	Mercy Poole	30 Apr 1827	209	David Rivenall	25 Jan 1827
220	Mercy Poole	18 May 1827	218	David Rivenall	15 May 1827
			221	David Rivenall	18 May 1827
598	Jane Pooley	10 Jul 1827	225	David Rivenall	24 Aug 1827
			231	David Rivenall	25 Oct 1827
29	Hannah Porter	2 Dec 1828	232	David Rivenall	31 Oct 1827
			239	David Rivenall	4 Apr 1828
657	Richard Porter	10 Mar 1826	244	Sarah Rivenall	3 Jul 1828
658	Richard Porter	24 Mar 1826	249	David Rivenall	12 Sep 1828
660	Richard Porter	18 Sep 1826	251	David Rivenall	20 Sep 1828
			257	David Rivenall	22 Nov 1828
655	Ann Prigg	2 Nov 1809	262	David Rivenall	12 Jan 1829
			265	Sarah Rivenall	25 Feb 1829
97	William Pryor		275	David Rivenall	19 May 1829
			277	Sarah Rivenall	May 1829
289	Mary Rabey	16 Mar 1816			
			91	Edward Roads	1 Jan 1837
752	James Randall	4 May 1825	92	Edward Roads	12 Jan 1837
379	Robert Ray	26 Aug 1828	750	Mrs Robinson	17 Oct 1818
682	Ann Rayner	2 Nov 1806	749	Rebecca Robinson	28 May 1818
662	Mrs E. Reilley	25 Mar 1828	594	Rachel Robson	18 Oct 1803
			595	Rachel Robson	3 Feb 1804
108	Davey Rising	1 Feb 1824			
112	D./S. Rising	15 Feb 1824	735	Joseph Rogers	10 Jun 1805
129	D./S. Rising	1 Aug 1824			
131	Susannah Rising	27 Sep 1824	753	William Rolf	14 Nov 1836
142	S./D. Rising	27 Jan 1825			
153	S./D. Rising	24 Apr 1825	412	George Rowe	21 Nov 1817
169	S./D. Rising	4 Oct 1825	414	George Rowe	15 Feb 1818
185	Susannah Rising	1 Mar 1826	440	George Rowe	19 Jun 1821
202	S./D. Rising	4 Oct 1826	442	George Rowe	6 Aug 1821
208	D./S. Rising	24 Jan 1827	449	George Rowe	13 Mar 1822
			459	George Rowe	10 Jan 1823
104	David Rivenall	5 Dec 1823	463	George Rowe	21 Mar 1823
115	David Rivenall	4 May 1824	473	George Rowe	8 Nov 1823

No.	Sender	Date	No.	Sender	Date
474	George Rowe	16 Nov 1823	52	James Smee	22 May 1832
492	George Rowe	5 Jan 1825			
518	George Rowe	13 Mar 1826	41	Sarah Smee	12 Nov 1830
525	George Rowe	24 Sep 1826			
536	George Rowe	28 Mar 1827	667	E. Smith	26 Mar 1833
549	George Rowe	18 Sep 1828			
551	George Rowe	8 Oct 1828	2	James Smith	5 Sep 1831
557	George Rowe	7 Mar 1829	3	James Smith	8 Feb 1832
558	George Rowe	11 May 1829	4	James Smith	6 Sep 1832
585	George Rowe	3 Apr 1835	5	James Smith	25 Sep 1832
			8	James Smith	21 Mar 1833
757	Thomas Rush	12 Jun 1825			
758	Thomas Rush	18 Jul 1830	28	James Smith	30 Nov 1828
			34	Mary Smith	25 Jul 1829
406	James Russell	6 Apr 1833			
408	James Russell	13 May 1833	10	John Smith	26 Jan 1835
155	Daniel Rust	8 May 1825	741	Mary-Ann Smith	2 Mar 1807
159	Daniel Rust	25 May 1825	743	Mary-Ann Smith	5 Jan 1814
			744	Mary-Ann Smith	10 Feb 1814
688	Thomas Sadler	30 Sep 1809			
			672	Mrs Smith	13 Dec 1834
654	Thomas Sagger	1 Oct 1809			
			63	John Smoothy	19 May 1833
697	John Sams	13 Jan 1830			
			596	John Snell	14 Nov 1818
285	John Seowen	18 Oct 1815	597	Mary Snell	6 Jul 1827
616	Jonathan Sewell	22 Aug 1811	77	Henry Spearman	1834
617	Jonathan Sewell	9 Dec 1811			
618	Jonathan Sewell	16 Nov 1812	57	John Spearman	25 Nov 1832
620	Jonathan Sewell	20 Aug 1813	59	John Spearman	8 Dec 1832
			60	John Spearman	5 Apr 1833
80	Robert Sewell		61	John Spearman	8 May 1833
			64	John Spearman	8 Jun 1833
7	Elizabeth Sheepard	18 Feb 1833	71	John Spearman	8 Feb 1834
416	Widow Shepperd	8 May 1818	18	Samuel Spooner	16 Jan 1828
			23	Samuel Spooner	20 Sep 1828
704	E. Shepphard	19 Sep 1813	24	Samuel Spooner	Oct 1828
			25	Samuel Spooner	17 Nov 1828
397	Rachel Shoreg	15 Oct 1810			
			66	Susan Spooner	21 Jun 1833
661	Lucy Shuttleworth	28 Jan 1828			
			351	Mrs D. Springet	Mar 1827
718	Ann Sinclair	11 Apr 1802	357	R. Springet	12 Nov 1827
719	Ann Sinclair	5 Sep 1802	365	R. Springet	18 Feb 1828
720	Ann Sinclair	25 Sep 1802	374	R. Springet	7 May 1828
677	Joseph Skewer	1 May 1803	702	S. Stearns	
678	Joseph Skewer	6 Nov 1803			
			362	Hannah Steward	17 Jan 1828
14	George Smee	9 May 1826			
19	George Smee	26 Feb 1828	707	Sarah Stone	5 Nov 1736

No.	Sender	Date	No.	Sender	Date
350	Thomas Strutt	20 Feb 1827	87	Ann Trudgett	23 Oct 1831
56	Abraham Stuck	2 Nov 1832	82	Thomas Turner	11 Jan 1817
411	Mary Sumner		39	Adam Turthing	4 Jun 1830
120	Arthur Tabrum	11 Jun 1824	261	Harriet Twin	31 Dec 1828
157	Arthur Tabrum	17 May 1825	266	Harriet Twin	29 Mar 1829
171	Arthur Tabrum	16 Oct 1825	273	Harriet Twin	13 May 1829
173	Arthur Tabrum	13 Nov 1825			
179	Arthur Tabrum	5 Jan 1826	328	George Tye	19 Aug 1826
189	Arthur Tabrum	29 Mar 1826	334	George Tye	7 Sep 1826
200	Arthur Tabrum	3 Sep 1826	335	George Tye	11 Sep 1826
204	Arthur Tabrum	11 Dec 1826	364	George Tye	11 Feb 1828
212	Arthur Tabrum	18 Feb 1827	366	George Tye	18 Feb 1828
216	Arthur Tabrum	18 Apr 1827	367	George Tye	25 Feb 1828
223	Arthur Tabrum	26 May 1827	384	George Tye	3 Apr 1829
229	Arthur Tabrum	4 Oct 1827	385	George Tye	4 Apr 1829
234	Arthur Tabrum	28 Nov 1827			
238	Arthur Tabrum	31 Mar 1828	648	Hannah Wall	21 Jun 1805
245	Arthur Tabrum	10 Jul 1828			
260	Arthur Tabrum	23 Dec 1828	267	Jane Wall	29 Mar 1829
272	Arthur Tabrum	6 May 1829			
			647	Mrs Wall	23 Jun 1804
622	James Taitt	1 Mar 1816			
			282	George Watson	24 Apr 1813
237	Robert Tapple	30 Dec 1827	320	George Watson	21 Feb 1820
			352	George Watson	22 May 1827
322	Mary Taylor	9 May 1821	359	George Watson	20 Nov 1827
396	Mary Taylor	17 Aug	360	G./H. Watson	18 Dec 1827
			368	George Watson	10 Mar 1828
1	Sarah Taylor	31 May 1825	372	George Watson	22 Apr 1828
			373	George Watson	Apr 1828
465	J. Thoroughgood	5 May 1823	376	George Watson	1 Jul 1828
483	J. Thoroughgood	19 Apr 1824	378	George Watson	22 Jul 1828
625	John Thurtell	1 Feb 1823			
626	John Thurtell	13 May 1831	566	William Watson	29 Jan 1833
627	John Thurtell	12 Aug 1831			
628	John Thurtell	2 Dec 1831	36	Elizabeth Watty	11 Feb 1830
630	John Thurtell	8 Nov 1832			
633	John Thurtell	22 Oct 1833	21	Phillis Webb	14 Jul 1828
634	John Thurtell	22 Dec 1833	22	Phillis Webb	13 Sep 1828
635	John Thurtell	12 Feb 1834	31	Phillis Webb	18 Dec 1828
			33	William Webb	7 Jul 1829
643	William Thurtell	1 Feb 1822			
644	William Thurtell	3 Jan 1825	248	Isabella Weeden	3 Sep 1828
27	James Tidman	27 Nov 1828	642	James Wells	
436	James Tracey	25 Feb 1821	589	Jemima Wetherly	10 Nov 1817
498	James Tracey	22 Jul 1825			
83	William Trudget	24 Feb 1817	45	George Whitaker	3 Jun 1831

No.	Sender	Date	No.	Sender	Date
164	Samuel White	20 Jun 1825	399	J./C. Wire	9 Dec 1811
180	Samuel White	26 Jan 1826	400	J./C. Wire	17 Dec 1811
182	Samuel White	25 Feb 1826			
184	Samuel White	27 Feb 1826	284	Sarah Withnell	2 Oct 1815
193	Samuel White	16 Jun 1826	286	Sarah Withnell	11 Dec 1815
197	Samuel White	3 Aug 1826	287	Sarah Withnell	19 Dec 1815
207	Samuel White	22 Jan 1827	308	Sarah Davis	25 Jan 1819
241	Samuel White	21 May 1828		[*former* Sarah Withnell]	
242	Samuel White	30 May 1828			
252	Samuel White	3 Oct 1828	709	Ann Wood	1 Apr 1802
264	Samuel White	19 Feb 1829			
			6	Mary Wood	13 Dec 1832
640	Mrs Wilkinson	6 May 1831			
641	Mrs Wilkinson	18 May 1831	748	T. Woodward	1766
94	James Willson	31 Oct 1833	224	Isaac Wright	31 Jul 1827
			236	Isaac Wright	10 Dec 1827
515	William Wilsher	16 Feb 1826			
517	William Wilsher	12 Mar 1826	81	Joseph Wright	6 Dec 1816
561	William Wilsher	18 Sep 1832			
564	William Wilsher	8 Nov 1832	247	John Wybrow	18 Aug 1828
570	William Wilsher	1 Jan 1834			
580	William Wilsher	22 Dec 1834			
581	William Wilsher	2 Jan 1835			

List A.3: Essex Pauper Letters, 1731-1837, by date

705	13 Jan 1731	683	11 May 1807	589	10 Nov [1817]
706	1 Sep 1736	684	27 May [1807]	412	21 Nov 181[7]
707	5 Nov 1736	710	[1808]	413	[1817]
645	[2] Mar 1748	716	10 Feb 1809	414	15 Feb 1818
280	12 Mar 1750	685	26 Feb 1809	415	16 Feb 1818
281	24 Apr 1755	686	18 Apr 1809	416	8 May 1818
708	12 July 1759	687	24 Aug 1809	749	28 May 1818
748	1766	688	30 Sep 1809	417	19 July 1818
747	9 Oct 1768	654	1 Oct 1809	418	20 July 1818
712	30 Dec 1769	655	2 Nov 1809	419	7 Aug 1818
715	[1770]	689	17 Nov 1809	297	26 Aug 1818
279	12 Mar 1788	690	[4 Mar 1810]	298	9 Sep 1818
593	[16 Apr 1795]	691	1 July 1810	420	13 Sep 1818
646	[19 Mar 1801]	692	8 July [1810]	421	19 Sep 1818
717	27 Apr 1801	397	15 Oct 1810	299	24 Sep 1818
709	1 Apr [1802]	616	22 Aug 1811	300	30 Sep 1818
718	11 Apr [1802]	693	25 Aug 1811	587	13 Oct 1818
719	5 Sep 1802	398	30 Sep 1811	750	17 Oct 1818
720	25 Sep 1802	617	9 Dec 1811	596	14 Nov 1818
721	29 Dec 1802	399	9 Dec 1811	301	10 Dec 1818
676	11 Feb 1803	400	17 Dec [1811]	302	11 Dec 1818
722	28 Apr 1803	618	16 Nov 1812	303	21 Dec 1818
677	1 May 1803	742	5 Mar 1813	304	29 Dec 1818
723	14 Aug 1803	282	24 Apr 1813	588	31 Dec 1818
724	9 Oct 1803	619	2 July 1813	305	[1818]
594	18 Oct 1803	401	2 July 1813	306	[1818]
678	6 Nov 1803	620	20 Aug 1813	751	[4 Jan 1819]
725	13 Nov 1803	704	19 Sep [1813]	307	4 Jan 1819
595	3 Feb 1804	743	5 Jan 1814	308	25 Jan 1819
726	2 Mar 1804	402	13 Jan 1814	309	5 Feb [1819]
727	18 Mar 1804	403	[24 Jan 1814]	310	11 Feb 1819
728	20 Mar 1804	744	10 Feb 1814	745	13 Mar 1819
729	22 Apr 1804	404	21 Mar [1814]	422	18 Mar 1819
647	23 June 1804	283	[8 Dec] 1814	423	18 Mar 1819
730	1 July 1804	652	[27 Mar 1815]	311	30 Mar 1819
679	12 Aug 1804	284	2 Oct [1815]	424	31 Mar 1819
731	29 Aug 1804	285	18 Oct 1815	312	9 May 1819
680	8 Nov 1804	286	11 Dec [1815]	313	21 June [1819]
681	13 Dec 1804	287	19 Dec 1815	314	29 June 1819
732	16 Dec 1804	288	14 Jan 1816	315	2 July 1819
733	2 Jan 1805	622	1 Mar 1816	316	9 July 1819
734	9 Apr 1805	289	16 Mar 1816	425	11 Aug 1819
735	10 June 1805	290	6 May 1816	317	30 Aug 1819
648	21 June 1805	81	6 Dec 1816	318	6 Sep 1819
736	14 Oct 1805	82	11 Jan 1817	426	23 Sep 1819
737	19 Nov 1805	405	17 Jan 1817	427	[6 Oct 1819]
738	29 Nov 1805	83	24 Feb 1817	711	18 Oct 1819
649	[12 Dec 1805]	291	4 Mar 1817	319	12 Nov 1819
650	27 Jan [1806]	292	19 Mar 1817	320	21 Feb 1820
739	9 Feb 1806	293	31 Mar 1817	321	15 Mar 1820
651	24 Mar 1806	294	24 Apr 1817	623	9 Apr 1820
740	4 July 1806	295	20 May 1817	428	12 Apr [1820]
682	2 Nov 1806	296	5 June 1817	429	23 June 1820
741	2 Mar 1807	84	28 July 1817	430	29 June 1820

431	6 July 1820	**475**	14 Dec 1823	**140**	15 Jan 1825
432	10 Sep 1820	**106**	18 Dec 1823	**493**	21 Jan 1825
99	15 Oct [1820]	**13**	22 Dec 1823	**141**	22 Jan 1825
433	19 Oct 1820	**703**	12 Jan 1824	**142**	27 Jan 1825
434	30 Dec 1820	**476**	19 Jan 1824	**143**	28 Jan [1825]
435	11 Jan 1821	**477**	24 Jan 1824	**144**	2 Feb 1825
624	3 Feb 1821	**107**	29 Jan [1824]	**145**	11 Feb 1825
436	25 Feb 1821	**108**	1 Feb 1824	**146**	22 Feb 1825
437	29 Mar 1821	**109**	1 Feb 1824	**494**	23 Feb 1825
438	5 Apr 1821	**110**	5 Feb 1824	**147**	25 Feb 1825
322	May 9 [1821]	**111**	[5 Feb 1824]	**656**	26 Feb 1825
439	31 May 1821	**478**	7 Feb 1824	**148**	3 Mar 1825
440	19 June 1821	**112**	15 Feb 1824	**149**	[12 Mar 1825]
441	31 July 1821	**479**	1 Mar 1824	**150**	[27 Mar 1825]
442	6 Aug 1821	**113**	10 Mar 1824	**151**	18 Apr 1825
443	30 Aug 1821	**480**	23 Mar 1824	**152**	18 Apr 1825
444	5 Sep 1821	**481**	30 Mar 1824	**153**	24 Apr 1825
445	25 Sep 1821	**482**	16 Apr 1824	**752**	4 May 1825
446	13 Oct 1821	**483**	19 Apr 1824	**154**	7 May 1825
447	18 Oct 1821	**114**	[28 Apr 1824]	**155**	8 May [1825]
448	1 Jan 1822	**755**	30 Apr 1824	**495**	13 May 1825
643	1 Feb 1822	**484**	Apr 1824	**156**	[15 May 1825]
449	13 Mar 1822	**115**	4 May 1824	**157**	17 May 1825
450	27 Mar 1822	**756**	10 May 1824	**158**	19 May 1825
621	29 Mar 1822	**485**	11 May 1824	**159**	25 May [1825]
451	20 May 1822	**116**	29 May 1824	**160**	26 May 1825
452	25 May 1822	**117**	4 June 1824	**161**	29 May [1825]
453	28 May 1822	**118**	10 June 1824	**1**	31 May 1825
454	29 July 1822	**119**	11 June [1824]	**162**	1 June 1825
455	July 1822	**120**	11 June 1824	**757**	12 June 1825
456	5 Aug 1822	**121**	12 June 1824	**163**	20 June 1825
457	30 Sep 1822	**122**	16 June [1824]	**164**	20 June 1825
458	[13 Dec 1822]	**123**	21 June 1824	**496**	22 June 1825
459	10 Jan 1823	**486**	25 June 1824	**165**	[27 June 1825]
100	17 Jan [1823]	**124**	[29 June 1824]	**166**	1 July 1825
460	20 Jan 1823	**125**	[7 July 1824]	**497**	13 July 1825
625	1 Feb 1823	**126**	[8 July 1824]	**167**	[14 July 1825]
461	25 Feb 1823	**487**	24 July 1824	**498**	22 July 1825
462	26 Feb 1823	**127**	26 July 1824	**499**	1 Aug 1825
463	21 Mar 1823	**128**	26 July 1824	**500**	[17 Aug 1825]
464	25 Mar 1823	**129**	1 Aug 1824	**501**	[5 Sep 1825]
465	5 May 1823	**130**	2 Aug 1824	**98**	[21 Sep 1825]
466	June 6 [1823]	**488**	27 Sep 1824	**502**	26 Sep 1825
467	17 June 1823	**131**	27 Sep 1824	**85**	[27 Sep 1825]
468	25 June 1823	**489**	6 Oct 1824	**168**	1 Oct 1825
469	30 June [1823]	**132**	[11 Oct 1824]	**169**	4 Oct 1825
470	16 July 1823	**133**	[11 Oct 1824]	**503**	[5 Oct 1825]
101	29 July 1823	**134**	[4 Nov 1824]	**170**	5 Oct 1825
471	4 Aug 1823	**135**	[Nov 1824]	**171**	16 Oct 1825
694	8 Sep 1823	**490**	6 Dec 1824	**504**	[22 Oct 1825]
472	28 Sep 1823	**136**	18 Dec 1824	**505**	2 Nov 1825
473	8 Nov 1823	**137**	21 Dec 1824	**506**	7 Nov 1825
102	9 Nov 1823	**491**	28 Dec 1824	**172**	[8 Nov 1825]
103	15 Nov 1823	**644**	3 Jan 1825	**173**	13 Nov 1825
474	16 Nov [1823]	**492**	5 Jan 1825	**507**	13 Nov 1825
104	5 Dec 1823	**138**	10 Jan 1825	**174**	[15 Nov 1825]
105	7 Dec 1823	**139**	12 Jan 1825	**175**	15 Nov 1825

508	29 Nov 1825	**333**	[5 Sep 1826]	**222**	25 May 1827
509	30 Nov 1825	**334**	7 Sep 1826	**223**	26 May 1827
510	[2 Dec 1825]	**335**	11 Sep 1826	**538**	20 June 1827
511	16 Dec 1825	**336**	12 Sep 1826	**597**	6 July 1827
512	20 Dec 1825	**660**	18 Sep 1826	**598**	10 July 1827
176	27 Dec 1825	**525**	24 Sep 1826	**17**	24 July 1827
177	29 Dec 1825	**201**	27 Sep 1826	**353**	[27 July 1827]
178	[2] Jan 1826	**526**	3 Oct 1826	**224**	31 July 1827
179	5 Jan 1826	**202**	4 Oct 1826	**354**	20 Aug 1827
513	11 Jan 1826	**203**	[12 Oct 1826]	**355**	23 Aug 1827
180	26 Jan 1826	**337**	19 Oct 1826	**225**	24 Aug [18]27
181	30 Jan 1826	**527**	13 Nov 1826	**226**	28 Aug 1827
514	31 Jan 1826	**204**	11 Dec 1826	**539**	[4 Sep 1827]
515	16 Feb 1826	**528**	12 Dec 1826	**540**	7 Sep 1827
516	21 Feb 1826	**529**	12 Dec 1826	**541**	13 Sep 1827
182	25 Feb 1826	**338**	[12] Dec [1826]	**227**	24 Sep 1827
183	27 Feb 1826	**205**	[15 Dec 1826]	**356**	27 Sep 1827
184	27 Feb 1826	**530**	20 Dec 1826	**228**	1 Oct 1827
185	1 Mar 1826	**339**	20 Dec 1826	**229**	4 Oct 1827
657	10 Mar 1826	**340**	4 Jan 1827	**230**	22 Oct 1827
517	12 Mar 1826	**86**	5 Jan 1827	**231**	25 Oct 1827
186	13 Mar 1826	**531**	8 Jan 1827	**232**	31 Oct [1827]
518	13 Mar 1826	**341**	11 Jan 1827	**542**	3 Nov 1827
519	14 Mar 1826	**342**	11 Jan 1827	**543**	8 Nov 1827
658	24 Mar 1826	**343**	13 Jan 1827	**357**	12 Nov 1827
187	28 Mar 1826	**206**	15 Jan 1827	**358**	13 Nov 1827
188	28 Mar 1826	**344**	18 Jan 1827	**359**	20 Nov 1827
323	29 Mar 1826	**207**	22 Jan 1827	**233**	23 Nov 1827
189	29 Mar 1826	**208**	24 Jan 1827	**234**	28 Nov 1827
520	17 Apr 1826	**345**	[25 Jan 1827]	**235**	2 Dec 1827
190	26 Apr 1826	**209**	25 Jan [1827]	**236**	10 Dec 1827
521	[Apr 1826]	**346**	28 Jan 1827	**544**	11 Dec 1827
14	9 May 1826	**16**	29 Jan 1827	**360**	18 Dec 1827
191	10 May 1826	**210**	2 Feb 1827	**237**	[30 Dec 1827]
15	22 May 1826	**347**	[5] Feb 1827	**361**	1 Jan 1828
192	May 1826	**532**	7 Feb 1827	**18**	16 Jan 1828
324	7 June 1826	**348**	7 Feb 1827	**362**	17 Jan [1828]
193	16 June 1826	**211**	12 Feb 1827	**661**	28 Jan 1828
194	18 July 1826	**533**	16 Feb [1827]	**363**	[9 Feb 1828]
522	19 July 1826	**212**	18 Feb 1827	**364**	11 Feb 1828
325	[26] July 1826	**213**	19 Feb 1827	**545**	18 Feb 1828
195	26 July 1826	**349**	20 Feb [1827]	**365**	18 Feb 1828
196	29 July 1826	**350**	20 Feb 1827	**366**	18 Feb 1828
326	1 Aug 1826	**534**	17 Mar 1827	**546**	19 Feb 1828
197	3 Aug 1826	**214**	19 Mar 1827	**367**	25 Feb 1828
327	7 Aug 1826	**535**	20 Mar 1827	**19**	26 Feb 1828
659	14 Aug 1826	**215**	28 Mar 1827	**368**	10 Mar [1828]
198	15 Aug 1826	**536**	28 Mar [1827]	**547**	14 Mar 1828
328	19 Aug 1826	**351**	[Mar 1827]	**369**	25 Mar 1828
523	21 Aug 1826	**216**	18 Apr 1827	**662**	25 Mar 1828
329	24 Aug 1826	**537**	[24 Apr 1827]	**238**	31 Mar 1828
199	27 Aug 1826	**217**	30 Apr 1827	**370**	1 Apr 1828
524	30 Aug 1826	**218**	[15 May 1827]	**239**	4 Apr 1828
330	3 Sep 1826	**219**	17 May 1827	**371**	7 Apr 1828
200	3 Sep 1826	**220**	18 May 1827	**372**	22 Apr 1828
331	4 Sep 1826	**221**	[18 May 1827]	**548**	23 Apr 1828
332	[5 Sep 1826]	**352**	[22 May 1827]	**373**	[Apr 1828]

374	7 May 1828	557	7 Mar 1829	50	24 Nov 1831
240	14 May 1828	266	29 Mar 1829	628	2 Dec 1831
241	21 May 1828	267	29 Mar 1829	51	16 Dec 1831
242	30 May 1828	384	3 Apr [1829]	665	26 Jan 1832
243	2 June 1828	385	4 Apr 1829	3	8 Feb 1832
20	18 June 1828	268	[13 Apr 1829]	601	22 Feb 1832
375	[18 June 1828]	269	[14 Apr 1829]	559	Feb 1832
376	1 July 1828	270	16 Apr 1829	560	16 Apr 1832
244	3 July [1828]	271	20 Apr 1829	602	18 May 1832
377	[10 July 1828]	32	30 Apr 1829	52	[22 May 1832]
245	10 July 1828	272	6 May 1829	603	12 July 1832
246	[11] July 1828	558	11 May 1829	53	18 July 1832
21	14 July 1828	273	13 May 1829	4	6 Sep 1832
378	22 July [1828]	274	18 May 1829	604	14 Sep 1832
599	30 July 1828	275	19 May 1829	561	18 Sep 1832
247	18 Aug 1828	276	21 May [1829]	562	23 Sep 1832
379	26 Aug 1828	600	26 May 1829	5	[25 Sep 1832]
248	[3 Sep 1828]	277	[May 1829]	563	3 Oct 1832
249	12 Sep 1828	278	10 June 1829	54	18 Oct 1832
250	13 Sep 1828	33	7 July 1829	55	[23] Oct 1832
22	13 Sep 1828	34	25 July 1829	629	28 Oct 1832
380	[15 Sep 1828]	35	5 Aug 1829	56	2 Nov 1832
549	18 Sep 1828	639	8 Sep 1829	630	8 Nov 1832
381	19 Sep 1828	386	Oct 1829	564	8 Nov 1832
251	20 Sep [1828]	695	[12 Nov 1829]	57	25 Nov 1832
23	20 Sep 1828	387	8 Dec 1829	58	[3 Dec] 1832
550	28 Sep 1828	696	4 Jan 1830	59	8 Dec 1832
252	3 Oct 1828	697	13 Jan 1830	605	12 Dec 1832
382	6 Oct 1828	36	11 Feb 1830	6	13 Dec 1832
383	8 Oct 1828	37	25 Feb 1830	631	[21 Dec 1832]
551	8 Oct 1828	698	25 Feb 1830	666	26 Dec 1832
253	14 Oct 1828	38	12 Mar 1830	565	16 Jan 1833
254	26 Oct 1828	39	4 June [1830]	566	29 Jan 1833
255	27 Oct 1828	758	18 July 1830	7	18 Feb 1833
24	Oct [1828]	388	18 Aug 1830	606	19 Feb 1833
25	17 Nov 1828	40	[27 Sep 1830]	88	19 Mar 1833
26	20 Nov 1828	41	12 Nov 1830	8	21 Mar 1833
256	21 Nov 1828	389	1 Dec 1830	667	26 Mar 1833
257	22 Nov 1828	390	15 Dec 1830	60	5 Apr 1833
27	27 Nov 1828	713	21 Mar 1831	406	6 Apr 1833
258	30 Nov 1828	42	9 Apr 1831	407	8 Apr 1833
28	30 Nov [1828]	43	15 Apr 1831	391	16 Apr [1833]
29	2 Dec 1828	44	[18 Apr 1831]	61	8 May 1833
259	4 Dec 1828	714	20 Apr [1831]	567	9 May 1833
30	16 Dec 1828	640	6 May 1831	62	11 May 1833
552	18 Dec 1828	626	13 May 1831	408	13 May 1833
31	18 Dec 1828	641	18 May 1831	63	19 May 1833
260	23 Dec 1828	45	3 June 1831	607	3 June 1833
261	31 Dec 1828	46	11 June 1831	64	8 June 1833
262	12 Jan 1829	663	25 June 1831	409	16 June 1833
553	20 Jan 1829	47	1 July 1831	65	[18 June 1833]
554	[Jan 1829]	48	2 July 1831	608	20 June 1833
555	9 Feb 1829	49	18 July 1831	66	21 June 1833
263	[10 Feb 1829]	627	12 Aug 1831	67	17 July 1833
556	17 Feb 1829	664	3 Sep 1831	609	18 Sep 1833
264	19 Feb 1829	2	5 Sep [1831]	68	22 Sep 1833
265	25 Feb 1829	87	23 Oct 1831	69	[23 Sep 1833]

632	25 Sep 1833	**612**	10 June 1834	**11**	3 May 1836
70	25 Sep 1833	**613**	23 June 1834	**753**	14 Nov 1836
668	1 Oct [1833]	**579**	12 July 1834	**754**	1 Dec 1836
568	14 Oct 1833	**74**	31 July [1834]	**91**	1 Jan [1837]
633	22 Oct 1833	**746**	19 Aug 1834	**92**	12 Jan 1837
569	28 Oct 1833	**671**	28 Aug 1834	**93**	26 Mar 1837
94	31 Oct 1833	**75**	Sep 1834		
89	9 Nov 1833	**76**	2 Oct 1834	**9**	[*no date*]
634	22 Dec [1833]	**392**	15 Nov 1834	**12**	[*no date*]
669	23 Dec 1833	**672**	13 Dec 1834	**79**	[*no date*]
570	[1 Jan 1834]	**673**	18 Dec [1834]	**80**	[*no date*]
571	[2 Jan 1834]	**580**	22 Dec 1834	**96**	[*no date*]
572	6 Jan 1834	**674**	23 Dec 1834	**97**	[*no date*]
573	20 Jan 1834	**77**	[1834]	**395**	[*no date*]
574	30 Jan 1834	**581**	2 Jan 1835	**396**	17 Aug
610	5 Feb 1834	**582**	19 Jan 1835	**410**	[*no date*]
71	8 Feb 1834	**10**	26 Jan 1835	**411**	[*no date*]
635	12 Feb 1834	**675**	2 Mar 1835	**586**	12 Sep [*no year*]
575	13 Feb [1834]	**583**	2 Mar [1835]	**590**	[*no date*]
576	20 Feb 1834	**584**	1 Apr 1835	**636**	[*no date*]
615	27 Feb 1834	**585**	3 Apr 1835	**637**	11 Jan [*no year*]
611	3 Mar 1834	**78**	29 June 1835	**638**	21 Apr [*no year*]
72	4 Mar 1834	**591**	2 Aug 1835	**642**	[*no date*]
73	[21 Apr 1834]	**393**	5 Aug 1835	**653**	[*no date*]
577	23 Apr 1834	**592**	26 Aug 1835	**699**	[*no date*]
578	1 May [1834]	**614**	23 Nov 1835	**700**	[*no date*]
670	19 May 1834	**90**	22 Dec 1835	**701**	30 Apr [*no year*]
95	7 June 1834	**394**	1 Jan [1836]	**702**	[*no date*]

Sources

This section lists all Essex parish records which form the documentary basis of the present edition. These are, first, the files of overseers' correspondence from which the pauper letters have been selected, along with the related correspondence (ERO class marks in bold type); second, all other records referred to in the apparatus, most notably overseers' accounts, vestry minutes and pauper lists. In the attempt to trace people featuring in pauper letters in other parish records, numerous further sources were also consulted. But those in which no traces of paupers could be found are not listed here. All sources are held at the ERO.

Aveley
D/P 157/8/3	Vestry minutes 1800-1836
D/P 157/12/10	Overseers' accounts 1824-1831
D/P 157/12/11	Overseers' accounts 1831-1836
D/P 157/18/12	Overseers' correspondence, 1751-1838

Great Bardfield
| **D/P 67/18/4** | Overseers' correspondence, 1824-36 |

Braintee
D/P 264/8/10	Select vestry, book of memoranda, 1817-36
D/P 264/8/13	Vestry minutes, 1828-33
D/P 264/8/16	Select vestry minutes, 1811-41
D/P 264/12/31	Overseers' weekly disbursements, 1824-31
D/P 264/18/24	Overseers' correspondence, 1685-1835
D/P 264/18/34	List of outdoor poor, 1829-1830

Steeple Bumpstead
| D/P 21/16/4 | Overseers' settlement correspondence 1861 |
| **D/P 21/18/3** | Overseers' correspondence, 1817-57 |

Great Burstead
| D/P 139/8/8 | Vestry minutes 1823-1828 |
| **D/P 139/18/7** | Overseers' correspondence, 1814-23 |

Canewdon
D/P 219/12/45   Overseers' accounts 1816-1822
D/P 219/18/1   Overseers' correspondence, 1746-1824

Chelmsford
D/P 94/8/6   Select vestry minutes 1825-1826
D/P 94/12/17   Overseers' accounts: pauper ledger 1823-1826
D/P 94/12/36   Overseers' accounts.
D/P 94/18/42   Overseers' correspondence, 1800-34
D/P 94/18/53   List of outdoor poor, 1819-20.
D/P 94/18/55   List of out-door poor, 1822-3.
D/P 36/28/3   List of outdoor poor, 1828-9
                      (kept among Great Coggeshall overseers' papers).
D/P 264/18/31   List of the out-door poor, 1826-7
                      (kept among Braintree overseers' papers).
D/P 94/18/42   Report of John Sheppee on his journey to London,
                      13 December 1823
                      (within overseers' correspondence)

Great Chishall
D/P 210/18/1-3   Overseers' correspondence, 1776-89

Great Coggeshall
D/P 36/18/1   Overseers' correspondence, 1750-1829

St Botolph, Colchester
D/P 203/8/2   Select vestry minutes 1821-1827
D/P 203/8/3   Select vestry minutes 1826-1828
D/P 203/12/4   Overseers' accounts 1753-1756
D/P 203/12/41   Overseers' accounts 1816-1818
D/P 203/12/42   Overseers' accounts 1818
D/P 203/12/43   Overseers' accounts 1821-1825
D/P 203/12/44   Overseers' accounts 1826
D/P 203/12/45   Overseers' accounts 1826-1829
D/P 203/18/1   Overseers' correspondence, 1750-1850

St James, Colchester
D/P 138/18/1, 11 Overseers' correspondence, 1810-33

St Peter, Colchester
D/P 178/18/23   Overseers' correspondence, 1815-38

Great Dunmow
D/P 11/18/16   Overseers' correspondence, 1818-48

Little Dunmow
D/P 95/18/3   Overseers' correspondence, 1818-29

Halstead
D/P 96/18/1   Overseers' correspondence, 1835

Havering-atte-Bower
D/P 64/18/3   Overseers' correspondence, 1791-1828

Kirby-le-Soken
D/P 169/18/12 Overseers' correspondence, 1725-1855
D/P 169/13/4   Settlement examinations 1742-1843

Lexden
D/P 273/18/2   Overseers' correspondence, 1834

St Mary, Maldon
D/P 132/18/1-2 Overseers' correspondence, 1801-1813

Mayland
D/P 383/18   Overseers' correspondence, 1822-4

Mundon
D/P 238/8/1   Vestry minutes 1820-1832
D/P 238/18/1   Overseers' correspondence, 1807-43

Navestock
D/P 148/18   Overseers' correspondence, 1825-41

White Notley
D/P 39/12/1   Overseers' accounts, 1830-1870.
D/P 39/18/5   Overseers' correspondence, 1823-35

Peldon
D/P 287/18/1, 7, 10 Overseers' correspondence, 1748-1827

Purleigh
D/P 197/12/3   Overseers' accounts 1820-1830
D/P 197/18/5   Overseers' correspondence, 1786-1825

Rainham
D/P 202/18/13, 15 Overseers' correspondence, 1748-1846

Rayleigh
D/P 332/18/1 Overseers' correspondence, 1799-1830
D/P 332/12/5 Overseer's accounts 1794-1829

Rochford
D/P 129/8 Vestry minutes 1785-1824
D/P 129/12/3 Overseers' accounts 1801-1802
D/P 129/18/10 Overseers' correspondence, 1773-1830

Stanford Rivers
D/P 140/18/1 Overseers' correspondence, 1810-34

Stansted Mountfitchet
D/P 109/18/4 Overseers' correspondence, 1740-1813

Theydon Garnon
D/P 152/12/4 Overseers' accounts 1746-1772
D/P 152/18/14 Overseers' correspondence, 1731-1837

Theydon Mount
D/P 142/12/1 Overseers' accounts 1769-1799
D/P 142/18/3 Overseers' correspondence, 1769-1861

West Thurrock
D/P 374/28/1 Overseers' correspondence, 1770-1850

Tolleshunt D'Arcy
D/P 105/18/11 Overseers' correspondence, 1711-1801

Upminster
D/P 117/8/8 Vestry minutes 1803-1813
D/P 117/18/2A Overseers' correspondence, 1743-1834

Little Waltham
D/P 200/18/1 Overseers' correspondence, 1768

Wanstead
D/P 292/18/2 Overseers' correspondence, 1766-7

South Weald
D/P 128/18/9   Overseers' correspondence, 1807-56

Woodford
D/P 167/8/6   Vestry minutes 1818-1836
D/P 167/12/18   Overseers' accounts 1835-1836
D/P 167/18/19   Overseers' correspondence 1809-50

Wormingford
D/P 185/8/3   Vestry minutes 1828-1948
D/P 185/12/3   Overseers' accounts 1814-1828
D/P 185/18/6   Overseers' correspondence, 1803-33

Bibliography

Printed sources

The A to Z of Regency London introd. P. Laxton (London Topographical Society, 131; 1985).

Brown, G. *The English letter-writer; or, the whole art of general correspondence* (6th edn; London, 1800).

Burnett, J. *Destiny obscure: autobiographies of childhood, education and family from the 1820s to the 1920s* (Harmondsworth, 1982).

Burnett, J. *Useful toil: autobiographies of working people from the 1820s to the 1920s* (Harmondsworth, 1977).

Eden, F. M. *The state of the poor* (3 vols; London, 1797).

Essex people 1750-1900: from their diaries, memoirs and letters ed. A. F. J. Brown (ERO Publications, 59; Chelmsford, 1972).

Johnson, C. *The complete art of writing letters* (London, 1779).

Mather, W. *The young man's companion* (13th edn; London, 1727).

PP 1803-4 XIII *Abstract of answers and returns relative to the expense and maintenance of the poor.*

Secondary works

Anderson, H., and Ehrenpreis, I., 'The familiar letter in the eighteenth century: some generalizations', in *The familiar letter in the eighteenth century* ed. H. Anderson, P. D. Daghlian and I. Ehrenpreis (Lawrence, Kansas, and London, 1966) pp. 269-82.

Ashby, A. W., 'One hundred years of poor law administration in a Warwickshire village', in *Oxford Studies in Social and Legal History* ed. P. Vinogradoff (vol. 3 [no. 6]; Oxford, 1912) pp. 1-188.

Ashforth, D., 'Settlement and removal in urban areas: Bradford, 1834-71', in *The poor and the city: the English poor law in its urban context, 1834-1914* ed. M. E. Rose (New York, 1985) pp. 58-91.

Ashforth, D., 'The urban poor law', in *The new poor law in the nineteenth century* ed. D. Fraser (London, 1976) pp. 128-48.

Baasner, R., 'Briefkultur im 19. Jahrhundert. Kommunikation, Konvention, Postpraxis', in *Briefkultur im 19. Jahrhundert* ed. R. Baasner (Tübingen, 1999) pp. 1-36.

672

Baines, D., 'Population, migration and regional development' in *The economic history of Britain since 1700* ed. R. Floud and D. McCloskey (2nd edn, 3 vols; Cambridge, 1994) ii, pp. 29-61.

Baugh, D. A., 'The cost of poor relief in south-east England, 1790-1834', *Economic History Review* 28 (1975) pp. 50-68.

Blaug, M., 'The poor law report reexamined', *Journal of Economic History* 23 (1963) pp. 229-45.

Bourdieu, P. *The logic of practice* (Cambridge, 1990).

Bourdieu, P. *Outline of a theory of practice* (Cambridge, 1977).

Bowers, F., 'Transcription of manuscripts: the record of variants', *Studies in Bibliography* 29 (1976) pp. 212-64.

Boyer, G. R. *An economic history of the English poor law, 1750-1850* (Cambridge, 1990).

Burke, P., 'Introduction', in *The social history of language* ed. P. Burke and R. Porter (Cambridge, 1987) pp. 1-20.

Butt, J. *The mid-eighteenth century* ed. G. Carnall (The Oxford History of English Literature, 7; Oxford, 1979).

'The Centre for Scholarly Editions: an introductory statement', *Proceedings of the Modern Language Association* 92 (1977) pp. 583-97.

Chartier, R., 'Leisure and sociability: reading aloud in early modern Europe', in *Urban life in the renaissance* ed. S. Zimmermann and R. Weismann (London and Toronto, 1989) pp. 103-20.

Chartier, R., 'The practical impact of writing', in *The history of private life* ed. P. Ariès and G. Duby, vol. 3: *Renaissance to enlightenment* ed. R. Chartier (London, 1989) pp. 111-59 and 615-17.

Cipolla, C. M. *Literacy and development in the west* (Harmondsworth, 1969).

Clanchy, M. T. *From memory to written record: England 1066-1307* (2nd edn; London, 1993).

Clark, P., and Souden, D. (ed.) *Migration and society in early modern England* (London, 1987).

Clout, H., 'London in transition', in *London: problems of change* ed. H. Clout and P. Wood (London, 1986) pp. 23-32.

Cobb, R. *The police and the people* (Oxford, 1970).

Cobb, R. *A sense of place* (London, 1975).

Cole, W. A., 'Factors in demand 1700-80', in *The Economic history of Britain since 1700* ed. R. Floud and D. McCloskey (2 vols.; Cambridge, 1981) pp. 36-65.

Coleman, D. C., 'Growth and decay during the industrial revolution: the case of East Anglia', *Scandinavian Economic History Review* 10 (1962) pp. 115-27.

Coleman, D. C., 'An innovation and its diffusion: the "new draperies"', *Economic History Review*, 2nd ser. 22 (1969) pp. 417-29.

Constable, G. *Letters and letter collections* (Typologie des Sources du Moyen Âge Occidental, 17; Turnhaut, 1976).

Coulmas, F. *The writing systems of the world* (Oxford, 1989).

Daunton, M. J. *Progress and poverty: an economic and social history of Britain 1700-1850* (Oxford, 1995).

Davis, N. Z. *Fiction in the archives: pardon tales and their tellers in sixteenth-century France* (Stanford, 1987).

Digby, A. *Pauper palaces* (London, 1978).

Eastwood, D. *Governing rural England: tradition and transformation in local government 1780-1840* (Oxford, 1994).

Emmison, F. G., 'Relief of the poor at Eaton Socon', *Publications of the Bedfordshire Historical Record Society* 15 (1933) pp. 1-98.

Erith, E. J., 'Introduction', to *Catalogue of Essex parish records 1240-1894* ed. F. G. Emmison (ERO Publications, 7; 2nd edn, Chelmsford 1966) pp. 1-39.

Farge, A. *Fragile lives: violence, power and solidarity in eighteenth-century Paris* (Cambridge, Mass., 1993).

Fergus, J., 'Provincial servants' reading in the late eighteenth century', in *The practice and representation of reading in England* ed. J. Raven, H. Small and N. Tadmor (Cambridge, 1996) pp. 202-25.

Garside, P. L., 'London and the home counties', in *The Cambridge social history of Britain*, vol. 1: *Regions and communities* ed. F. M. L. Thompson (Cambridge, 1990) pp. 471-539.

Gaur, A. *A history of writing* (British Library; London, 1984).

George, M. D. *London life in the eighteenth century* (London, 1925; repr. Harmondsworth, 1976).

Ginzburg, C. *The cheese and the worms: the cosmos of a sixteenth-century miller* (London, 1980).

Gowing, L. *Domestic dangers: women, words and sex in early modern London* (Oxford, 1996).

Graff, H. J. *The legacies of literacy: continuities and contradictions in western culture and society* (Bloomington and Indianapolis, 1987).

Grieve, H. E. P. *Examples of English handwriting 1150-1750* (ERO Publications, 21; Chelmsford, 1954).

Hampson, E. M. *The treatment of poverty in Cambridgeshire* (Cambridge, 1934).

Hector, L. C. *The handwriting of English documents* (London, 1958).

Hobsbawm, E. J., 'The machine breakers' (1952), in his *Labouring men: studies in the history of labour* (London, 1964) pp. 5-22.

Hobsbawm, E. J., 'The nineteenth-century London labour market', in *London: aspects of change* ed. R. Glass (London, 1964) pp. 3-28.

Hobsbawm, E. J., and Rudé, G. *Captain Swing* (Harmondsworth, 1973).

Hornbeak, K. B., 'The complete letter-writer in English 1568-1800', *Smith College Studies in Modern Languages* 15: 3-4 (1934) pp. i-xii and 1-150.

Hornbeak, K. B., 'Richardson's "Familiar Letters" and the domestic conduct books', *Smith College Studies in Modern Languages* 19:2 (1938) pp. 1-29.

Hunecke, V., 'Überlegungen zur Geschichte der Armut im vorindustriellen Europa', *Geschichte und Gesellschaft* 9 (1983) pp. 488-512.

Hunt, E. H. *British labour history 1815-1914* (London, 1981).

Hutchings, A. P., 'The relief of the poor in Chelmsford 1821-1829: case histories and paupers' correspondence', *Essex Review* 65 (1956) pp. 42-56.

Ingram, M. *Church courts, sex and marriage in England, 1570-1640* (Cambridge, 1987).

Karweick, J., '"Tiefgebeugt von Nahrungssorgen und Gram". Schreiben an Behörden', in S. Grosse *et al. 'Denn das Schreiben gehört nicht zu meiner täglichen Beschäftigung'. Der Alltag Kleiner Leute in Bittschriften, Briefen und Berichten aus dem 19. Jahrhundert. Ein Lesebuch* (Bonn, 1989) pp. 17-87 and 188-89.

King, P., 'Crime, law and society in Essex, 1740-1820' (Univ. of Cambridge Ph. D. thesis, 1984).

Kuchenbuch, L., 'Ordnungsverhalten im grundherrlichen Schriftgut vom 9. zum 12. Jahrhundert', in *Dialektik und Rhetorik im früheren und hohen Mittelalter* ed. J. Fried (Schriften des Historischen Kollegs, Kolloquien 27; Munich, 1996) pp. 175-268.

Kuchenbuch, L., Sokoll, T., *et al. Einführungskurs Alteuropäische Schriftlichkeit* (FernUniversität Hagen, 1988).

Kussmaul, A. S., 'The ambiguous mobility of farm servants', *Economic History Review* 34 (1981) pp. 222-75.

Landau, N., 'The eighteenth-century context of the laws of settlement', *Continuity and Change* 6 (1991) pp. 417-39.

Landau, N., 'The laws of settlement and surveillance of immigration in eighteenth-century Kent', *Continuity and Change* 3 (1988) pp. 391-420.

Landau, N., 'The regulation of immigration, economic structures and definitions of the poor in eighteenth-century England', *Historical Journal* 33 (1990) pp. 541-72.

Laslett, P., 'Mean household size in England since the sixteenth century', in *Household and family in past time* ed. P. Laslett and R. Wall (Cambridge, 1972) pp. 125-58.

Laslett, P., 'Size and structure of the household in England over three centuries', *Population Studies* 23 (1969) pp. 199-223.

Le Roy Ladurie, E. *Montaillou: the promised land of error* (London, 1978).

Lees, L. H. *The solidarities of strangers: the English poor laws and the people 1700-1948* (Cambridge, 1998).

Leonard, E. M. *The early history of English poor relief* (Cambridge, 1900; repr. London, 1965).

Lindert, P. H., 'Unequal living standards', in *The Economic history of Britain since 1700* ed. R. Floud and D. McCloskey (2nd edn, 3 vols; Cambridge, 1994), i, pp. 357-86.

The London encyclopaedia ed. B. Weinreb and C. Hibbert (revised edn; London, 1993).

Malcolmson, R. W. *Life and labour in England 1700-1780* (London, 1981).

Mantoux, P. *The industrial revolution in the eighteenth century* (London, 1928; repr. 1964).

Marshall, D. *The English poor in the eighteenth century: a study in social and administrative history* (London, 1926; repr. 1963).

Mathias, P., 'Adam's burden: historical diagnoses of poverty', in his *The transformation of England: essays in the economic and social history of England in the eighteenth century* (London, 1979) pp. 131-47.

Morison, S., 'Calligraphy', in *Encyclopaedia Britannica* (14th edn; London, 1929) iv, pp. 614-18.

Morison, S., 'The development of hand-writing', in A. Heal *The English writing masters and their copy-books, 1570-1800: a biographical dictionary and a bibliography* (Cambridge, 1931; repr. Hildesheim, 1962) pp. xxxiii-xl.

Müller, W. G., 'Brief', in *Historisches Wörterbuch der Rhetorik* ed. G. Ueding (Tübingen, 1994- [*not completed*]) ii, cols. 60-76.

Neumann, M., 'Speenhamland in Berkshire', in *Comparative developments in social welfare* ed. E. W. Martin (London, 1972) pp. 85-127.

Neumann, M. *The Speenhamland county: poverty and the poor laws in Berkshire 1782-1834* (New York, 1982).

Nikisch, R. G. M. *Brief* (Sammlung Metzler, 260; Stuttgart, 1991).

Nikisch, R. G. M., 'Briefsteller', in *Historisches Wörterbuch der Rhetorik* ed. G. Ueding (Tübingen, 1994- [*not completed*]) ii, cols. 76-86.

Ong, W. J. *Orality and literacy: the technologizing of the word* (London, 1982).

Pollard, S., 'Labour in Great Britain', in *The Cambridge economic history of Europe*, vol. 7: *The industrial economies: capital, labour, and enterprise* ed. P. Mathias and M. M. Postan (Cambridge, 1978) pp. 97-179.

Pooley, C., and Turnbull, J., 'Migration and mobility in Britain from the eighteenth to the twentieth centuries', *Local Population Studies* 57 (1996) pp. 50-71.

676

Poynter, J. R. *Society and pauperism: English ideas on poor relief, 1795-1834* (London, 1969).

Reaney, P. H., *The place-names of Essex* (English Place-Name Society, 12; Cambridge, 1935).

Redford, A. *Labour migration in England, 1800-1850* (London, 1926; 2nd edn, Manchester, 1964).

Robertson, J. *The art of letter writing: an essay on the handbooks published in England during the sixteenth and seventeenth centuries* (London, 1943).

Robinson, H. *The British post office: a history* (Princeton, N. J., 1948).

Roper, L. *The holy household: women and morals in reformation Augsburg* (London, 1989).

Rose, M. E., 'The administration of the poor paw in the West Riding of Yorkshire (1820-1855)' (Univ. of Oxford D. Phil. thesis, 1965).

Rose, M. E., 'Settlement, removal and the new poor law', in *The new poor law in the nineteenth century* ed. D. Fraser (London, 1976) pp. 25-44.

Rublack, U. *The crimes of women in early modern Germany* (Oxford, 1999).

Rudé, G. *The crowd in history: a study of popular disturbances in France and England 1730-1848* (New York, 1964).

Rudé, G. *Hanoverian London 1714-1808* (History of London, 1; London, 1971).

Sabean, D. W. *Power in the blood: popular culture and village discourse in early modern Germany* (Cambridge, 1984).

Sabean, D. W. *Property, production, and family in Neckarhausen, 1700-1870* (Cambridge, 1990).

Schofield, R. S., 'Dimensions of illiteracy, 1750-1850', *Explorations in Economic History* 10 (1972-3) pp. 437-54.

Schulte, R. *The village in court: arson, infanticide and pouching in the court records of upper Bavaria 1848-1910* (Cambridge, 1994).

Schulz, H. C., 'The teaching of handwriting in Tudor and Stuart times', *Huntington Library Quarterly* 7 (1943) pp. 381-425.

Sharpe, P., '"The bowels of compation": a labouring family and the law c. 1790-1834', in *Chronicling poverty: the voices and strategies of the English poor, 1640-1840* ed. T. Hitchcock, P. King and P. Sharpe (London, 1997) pp. 87-108.

Sheppard, F. *London 1808-1870: the infernal wen* (History of London, 2; London, 1971).

Slack, P. *The English poor law, 1531-1782* (Cambridge, 1995).

Smith, G. C., '"The poor in blindness": letters from Mildenhall, Wiltshire, 1835-6', in *Chronicling poverty: the voices and strategies of the*

English poor, 1640-1840 ed. T. Hitchcock, P. King and P. Sharpe (London, 1997) pp. 211-38.

Snell, K. D. M. *Annals of the labouring poor: social change and agrarian England, 1660-1900* (Cambridge, 1985).

Snell, K. D. M., 'Pauper settlement and the right to poor relief in England and Wales', *Continuity and Change* 6 (1991) pp. 375-415.

Snell, K. D. M., 'Settlement, poor law and the rural historian: new approaches and opportunities', *Rural History* 3 (1992) pp. 145-72.

Sokoll, T. *Household and family among the poor: the case of two Essex communities in the late eighteenth and early nineteenth centuries* (Bochum, 1993).

Sokoll, T., 'Negotiating a living: Essex Pauper Letters from London, 1800-1834', in *Household strategies for survival, 1600-2000: fission, faction and cooperation* ed. J. Schlumbohm and L. Fontaine (*International Review of Social History*, Supplement 8; Cambridge, 2000), pp. 19-46.

Sokoll, T., 'Old age in poverty: the record of Essex pauper letters, 1780-1834', in *Chronicling poverty: the voices and strategies of the English poor, 1640-1840* ed. T. Hitchcock, P. King and P. Sharpe (London, 1997) pp. 127-54.

Sokoll, T., 'Selbstverständliche Armut. Armenbriefe in England, 1750-1834', in *Ego-Dokumente. Annäherungen an den Menschen in der Geschichte* ed. W. Schulze (Berlin, 1996) pp. 227-71.

Sokoll, T., 'Voices of the poor: pauper letters and poor law provision in Essex, 1780-1834', in *Poverty and relief in England from the sixteenth to the twentieth century* ed. A. Digby, J. Innes and R. M. Smith (Cambridge, forthcoming).

Solar, P. M., 'Poor relief and English economic development before the industrial revolution', *Economic History Review* 48 (1995) pp. 1-22.

Song, B. K., 'Agarian policies on pauper settlement and migration, Oxfordshire 1750-1834', *Continuity and Change* 13 (1998) pp. 363-89.

Song, B. K., 'Landed interest, local government, and the labour market in England, 1750-1850', *Economic History Review* 51 (1998) pp. 465-88.

Spate, O. H. K., 'The growth of London, 1600-1800', in *An historical geography of England before 1800: fourteen studies* ed. H. C. Darby (Cambridge, 1936) pp. 529-48.

Stedman Jones, G. *Outcast London: a study in the relationship between classes in Victorian society* (Oxford, 1971).

Stephens, W. B. *Education, literacy and society, 1830-1870: the geography of diversity in provincial England* (Manchester, 1987).

Stephens, W. B. *Sources for English local history* (Cambridge, 1981).

678

Tanselle, G. T., 'The editing of historical documents', *Studies in Bibliography* 31 (1978) pp. 212-64 (repr. in G. T. Tanselle *Selected studies in bibliography* [Charlottesville, Va., 1979] pp. 451-506).

Tate, W. E. *The parish chest: a study of the records of parochial administration in England* (3rd edn, Cambridge, 1969; repr. London, 1983).

Taylor, J. S. *Poverty, migration, and settlement in the industrial revolution: sojouners' narratives* (Palo Alto, Cal., 1989).

Taylor, J. S., 'A different kind of Speenhamland: nonresident relief in the industrial revolution', *Journal of British Studies* 30 (1991) pp. 183-208.

Taylor, J. S., 'The impact of pauper settlement 1691-1834', *Past and Present* 73 (1976) pp. 42-74.

Taylor, J. S., 'Voices in the crowd: the Kirkby Lonsdale township letters, 1809-36', in *Chronicling poverty: the voices and strategies of the English poor, 1640-1840* ed. T. Hitchcock, P. King and P. Sharpe (London, 1997) pp. 109-26.

Thompson, E. P., 'The crime of anonymity', in *Albion's fatal tree: crime and society in eighteenth-century England* ed. D. Hay *et al.* (Harmondsworth, 1977) pp. 255-344.

Thompson, E. P., 'The moral economy of the English crowd in the eighteenth century', *Past and Present* 50 (1971) pp. 76-136.

Thorpe, J. *Principles of textual criticism* (San Marino, Cal., 1972).

Tilly, R. H., 'Popular disorders in 19th century Germany', *Journal of Social History* 4 (1970) pp. 1-40.

Ulbrich, C., 'Zeuginnen und Bittstellerinnen. Überlegungen zur Bedeutung von Ego-Dokumenten für die Erforschung weiblicher Selbstwahrnehmung in der ländlichen Gesellschaft des 18. Jahrhunderts', in *Ego-Dokumente. Annäherungen an den Menschen in der Geschichte* ed. W. Schulze (Berlin, 1996) pp. 207-26.

Ulbricht, O., 'Supplicationen als Ego-Dokumente. Bittschriften von Leibeigenen aus der ersten Hälfte des 17. Jahrhunderts', in *Ego-Dokumente. Annäherungen an den Menschen in der Geschichte* ed. W. Schulze (Berlin, 1996) pp. 149-74.

Unwin, G., 'The history of the cloth industry in Suffolk', in *Studies in economic history: the collected papers of George Unwin* ed. R. H. Tawney (London, 1926) pp. 262-301.

Vincent, D. *Bread, knowledge and freedom: a study of nineteenth-century working class autobiography* (London, 1981).

Vincent, D. *Literacy and popular culture: England 1750-1914* (Cambridge, 1989).

Wales, T., 'Poverty, poor relief and the life-cycle: some evidence from seventeenth-century Norfolk', in *Land, kinship and life-cycle* ed. R. M. Smith (Cambridge, 1984) pp. 351-404.

Webb, S. and B. *English poor law history, I: the old poor law* (London, 1927; repr. 1963).

Webb, S. and B. *English poor law history, II: the last hundred years* (London, 1929; repr. 1963).

Wells, R., 'Migration, the law, and parochial policy in eighteenth and early nineteenth-century southern England', *Southern History* 15 (1993) pp. 86-139.

Williams, K. *From pauperism to poverty* (London, 1981).

Wrightson, K., and Levine, D. *Poverty and piety in an English village: Terling 1525-1700* (New York, 1979; 2nd edn, Oxford, 1995).

Zeller, H., 'A new approach to the critical constitution of literary texts', *Studies in Bibliography* 28 (1975) pp. 231-64.

Zeller, H., 'Struktur und Genese in der Editorik. Zur germanistischen und anglistischen Editionsforschung', *Zeitschrift für Literaturwissenschaft und Linguistik* 19/20 (1975) pp. 105-26.

Index of Persons

Richardson, Daniel, 165
Richardson, Mr, of Brentwood, doctor, 125
Richardson, Mr, of London, 129, 130
Rickson, John, overseer of Canterbury, 293
Riddel, James, of London, 222
Rippon, William, overseer of St Sepulchre, London, 217
Rising (Raison, Risen, Rison, Rizon), Davey (David), pauper of Chelmsford in Halstead, 34, 64, 226, 227, 228, 259; letters from, **108, 112, 129, 142, 153, 169, 202, 208**
  Susan (Susanah), daughter of, 177, 259
  Susannah (Sasan, Susan), wife of, 34, 64, 177, 227, 258, 259, 260; letters from, **112, 129, 131, 142, 153, 169, 185, 202, 208**
  Thomas, son of, 177, 206
Rivenall (Revenall, Revenel, Revenell, Revinall, Revinell, Rivarnell, Rivenell, Rivernall, Rivernell, Rivernill, Rivinall), David (Davy), pauper of Chelmsford in St George in the East, London, 39, 53, 55, 63, 64, 65, 174, 265, 266, 279, 287; letters from, **104, 115-6, 130, 139, 146, 175, 181, 183, 186, 188, 190-2, 194, 196, 201, 203, 205, 209, 218, 221, 225, 231-2, 239, 249, 251, 257, 262, 275**
  Alfred, son of, 174, 202, 229, 231, 232
  David, son of, 174, 202, 225, 229, 240
  Edward, son of, 174, 202, 229, 231, 232
  James, son of, 174, 202, 229, 240
  Mary, daughter of, 174, 229, 240
  Sarah, daughter of, 174, 229, 240
  Sarah, wife of, 39, 53, 63, 64, 65, 174, 182, 198, 202, 238, 239, 240, 253, 257, 266, 269, 273, 286; letters from, **175, 181, 183, 188, 190-1, 244, 265, 277**
  William, son of, 174, 202, 229, 240
Rivers, Daniel, of Great Wakering, 583
Roads, Edward, pauper of Steeple Bumpstead in Sheffield, 76; letters from, **91-2**
  wife of, 163
Robenson, Mr, of Haverhill, 163
Robert, Mr, of Kirby-Le-Soken; letter to, **614**
Robinson, John, coachman, 397
Robinson, Mr, of St Peter, Colchester; letter to, **427**
Robinson (*former* Pluckrose), Mrs, pauper of South Weald, 55; letter from, **750**
Robinson, Rebecca, pauper of South Weald in Woolwich, 629; letter from, **749**

Robson, Rachel, pauper of Havering-atte-Bower in Durham and Gattshead; letters from, **594-5**
  Ann, daughter of, 519
  husband of, 519
  James, son of, 519
  Robert, son of, 519
  William, son of, 519
Rogers, Joseph, pauper of Upminster in London; letter from, **735**
Rolf (Rolfe, Wolf), William, pauper of Woodford in Sudbury; letter from, **753**
  wife of, 631
Round, J., overseer of Rochford; letter to, **684**
Rouse, Mr, 359, 456, 459, 467
Rowe, George (Geroge), pauper of St Peter, Colchester, in Bocking, Braintree and Great Coggeshall, 53, 65; letters from, **412, 414, 440, 442, 449, 459, 463, 473-4, 492, 518, 525, 536, 549, 551, 557-8, 585**
  wife of, 406, 413, 422, 425, 431, 432, 511
Rudkin, John, of St Botolph, Colchester, 306; letters to, **295-7, 304, 307, 311**
Ruffle, Mrs, 573
Rush, Thomas, pauper of Wormingford in Bocking and Braintree; letters from, **757-8**
  wife of, 673
Russell (Rusel), James, pauper of St James, Colchester, in Newington, London; letters from, **406, 408**
  wife of, 382
Russell, Joseph, 348, 354, 357, 359, 360
Rust, Charles, of Chelmsford; letter to, **155**
Rust, Daniel, pauper of Chelmsford; letters from, **155, 159**
  Sarah, wife of, 207, 208; letter to, **159**

Sadinton, Mr, 631
Sadler, Thomas, pauper of Rochford in Great Wakering; letter from, **688**
  wife of, 590
Sagger, Thomas, pauper of Rayleigh in Springfield; letter from, **654**
  wife of, 566
Salthew, Mrs, of Rickmansworth, 555
Sams, John, pauper of Rochford in Chelmsford; letter from, **697**
Sanders, Mr, churchwarden of Purleigh; letter to, **643**
Sanders, Thomas junior, of Cheshunt, doctor, 123, 126
Sarett, Mr, 583
Saunders, Mr, of Rainham, schoolmaster; letter to, **646**

Index of places

Index of subjects

RECORDS OF SOCIAL AND ECONOMIC HISTORY
(New Series)

24. *The Register of Thetford Priory, Part 1: 1482–1517*. D. Dymond. 1995
25. *The Register of Thetford Priory, Part 2: 1518–1540*. D. Dymond. 1996
26. *The Diary of Robert Sharp of South Cave: Life in a Yorkshire Village, 1812–1837*. J. E. Crowther & P. A. Crowther. 1997
27. *The Poll Taxes of 1377, 1379 and 1381, Part 1: Bedfordshire–Leicestershire*. C. C. Fenwick. 1998
28. *Letterbook of Greg & Cunningham, 1756–1757: Merchants of New York and Belfast*. T. M. Truxes. 2001
29. *The Poll Taxes of 1377, 1379 and 1381, Part 2: Lincolnshire–Westmorland*. C. C. Fenwick. 2001